The Principles of Project Finance

The Principles of Project Finance

Edited by
ROD MORRISON

Routledge
Taylor & Francis Group

LONDON AND NEW YORK

First published 2012 by Gower Publishing

2 Park Square, Milton Park, Abingdon, Oxon OX14 4RN
711 Third Avenue, New York, NY 10017, USA

Routledge is an imprint of the Taylor & Francis Group, an informa business

First issued in paperback 2016

British Library Cataloguing in Publication Data

The principles of project finance.
   1. Capital investments. 2. Capital investments--Case
   studies. 3. Project management--Finance. 4. Project
   management--Finance--Case studies.
   I. Morrison, Rod.
   658.1'52-dc23

Library of Congress Cataloging-in-Publication Data
Morrison, Rod.
   The principles of project finance / by Rod Morrison.
       p. cm.
   Includes index.
   ISBN 978-1-4094-3982-0 (hardback)
   1. Project management--Finance. I. Title.
   HD69.P75M6747 2011
   338.90068'1--dc23

                                                          2012001152

ISBN 978-1-4094-3982-0 (hbk)
ISBN 978-1-138-24568-6 (pbk)

Contents

List of Figures

List of Tables

About the Contributors

Dr Atif Ansar is a Research Fellow at the BT Centre for Major Programme Management, Saïd Business School at the University of Oxford. He took his Bachelor's degree at the School of Foreign Service at Georgetown University and his Doctorate at the University of Oxford. Prior to joining the BT Centre, he extensively consulted on infrastructure and social development for the World Bank, and in the area of structured and project finance in Russia, Ukraine, and Africa for private sector clients.

Banu Aslan is a qualified Turkish lawyer and joined Bezen & Partners in 2008. After her first state examination in Osnabrück (Germany), she also completed her law studies at the Istanbul University. She advises clients mainly on banking, project finance, energy and infrastructure related issues.

Anne Baldock (abaldock@hotmail.co.uk) heads the Global Projects, Energy and Infrastructure Group at Allen & Overy LLP. During her 30 years in private practice, she has acted on projects in the power, energy and infrastructure sectors including the first ever UK PFI project to close, the first to be financed by a bond issue and the first to use LIFT techniques. She currently serves on the board of the Nuclear Liabilities Financial Assurance Board and is a trustee of Cancer Research UK. Ms Baldock is retiring from Allen & Overy shortly.

Katharine Baragona is a senior bank executive/US lawyer/UK solicitor with over 20 years of international project finance practice and experience. A member of The World Bank's Financial Solutions Group in the role of Senior Infrastructure Finance Specialist, Kate is currently leading the Bank's guarantee interventions in Nigeria, Ghana, Cote d'Ivoire, Mauritania and Democratic Republic of the Congo.

Yeşim Bezen is a qualified solicitor (England and Wales) and was previously employed by Clifford Chance LLP's London Office. She advises domestic and international clients on various law matters with a particular focus on banking, structured and project finance transactions as well as energy and infrastructure matters.

Stanley Boots (stanley.boots@hoganlovells.com) is a consultant of Hogan Lovells' Hanoi office with broad experience advising on PPP, infrastructure, energy (including power/renewable power) and natural resources projects in Vietnam and across the region. He is recognised as a leading voice in the development of PPP in Vietnam.

David Borthwick ACII joined the insurance industry in 1976 and joined Marsh Ltd in 1989. David is practice head of Marsh Limited's Structured Finance Practice (senior lenders' insurance adviser) and Project Risk Practice (Public sector and sponsor insurance adviser to public private partnership projects). Prior to Joining Marsh, David's principal activity was the servicing of major commercial clients in all classes of insurance together with broking and claims handling.

Jean-Pierre Boudrias is a Director in the Energy Group in New York where he is a senior member of Credit Suisse Project Finance practice. Prior to joining Credit Suisse in 2004, he was an Associate in the Leveraged Finance Group at CIBC World Markets. Since joining Credit Suisse, Jean-Pierre has worked on a number of financing and advisory assignments for power and utilities clients, including debt offerings for Plum Point (Project Finance North America Deal of the Year – 2006), Sandy Creek (Project Finance North America Deal of the Year – 2007), Alta Wind (North American Wind Deal of the Year - 2010). Prior to Credit Suisse, Jean-Pierre had also worked at Caisse de depot et Placement du Québec where he invested in infrastructure. Mr Boudrias received his MBA from the University of Western Ontario and his BBA from HEC - Montreal in Finance. He is also a Chartered Financial Analyst (CFA).

Marie Bouvet-Guiramand joined Gide Loyrette Nouel's Project Finance practice in 2002. She specializes in French and international projects (North Africa, Asia and Eastern Europe), acting mainly for sponsors and lenders, in social infrastructure, transport, water and power infrastructure projects. Marie negotiates project documentation as well as financing documents. She holds a diploma from HEC Business School in addition to her law degree and is a member of the Paris Bar.

Hugh Boylan is currently completing his postgraduate studies at the University of Oxford.

Matthew Brown is a partner in the London office of Latham & Watkins. His practice focuses on representing sponsors, lenders and governments in all aspects of project development and project finance, particularly in the energy sector. He has significant experience in structuring and documenting the commercial arrangements amongst the parties to major project transactions as well as structuring and documenting debt, equity and security arrangements for finance transactions.

Peter Brown works within the Corporate Finance department at PwC, a market leading infrastructure finance advisor. He has a wealth of experience in advising both public sector and private sector clients on major infrastructure projects, mainly related to the transport sector. His work has largely focused on PFI/PPPs transactions, with recent deals including the precedent-setting M25 Widening PFI project where he was an advisor to UK Highways Agency.

Edward Chan (edward.chan@linklaters.com) is a banking partner at Linklaters LLP. He specializes in complex structured financings, particular those driven by tax, capital adequacy or other regulatory requirements. He also follows changes to bank regulation and maintains a particular focus on Basel III and on transaction work arising from regulatory change.

Phillip Cornwell (Partner) is the Head of Allens' Project Finance Group and has advised on some of the largest and most significant power, infrastructure and resources projects in the Asia Pacific region. Phillip is rated as one of the world's top project finance and banking and finance lawyers.

Catriona Coulthurst works in the Corporate Finance Advisory team at PwC, specializing in advice to the Government and Infrastructure sectors. Catriona's experience in the sector focuses on the PFI/PPP market and specifically advice to infrastructure funds in secondary market transactions.

Stephen Crane is Senior Adviser to the UK Government's Green Investment team, having spent 25 years in three of the most successful project finance banks in recent times: NatWest 1987–91 and 1994–2000, Deutsche Bank 1994–97 and Bank of Tokyo-Mitsubishi UFJ 2000–2011. He has led a number of large transactions across the main sectors of Project Finance, but has been particularly prominent in the Power and Renewable Energy sectors.

Julien Brusau Cuello joined Gide Loyrette Nouel's Project Finance practice in 2007. He specializes in project finance, PPPs, banking transactions and privatizations, both in the developing and developed world. A dual UK and France-qualified lawyer, Julien is fluent in both English and French and has extensive experience working in both civil and common law jurisdictions. Julien is currently based in Moscow, after several years spent at Gide Loyrette Nouel's Paris and London offices.

Simon Currie is Global Head of the Energy practice at Norton Rose Group. Norton Rose has a team of over 250 renewable energy specialists worldwide with experience of closing hundreds of clean energy transactions. Simon advises developers, utilities, lenders and investors on the development, financing and acquisition of renewable energy assets. Chambers & Partners UK 2012 describes Simon as 'widely acknowledged as a leading expert in the energy industry, with a particularly strong reputation in renewable energy.'

Simon Dickens is a partner in the London office of Latham & Watkins practising principally in the Project Finance and Development practice group. He is also a member of the firm's Africa, India, Oil & Gas, Energy and Islamic Finance practice groups. Mr Dickens has represented developers, lenders and governmental entities in oil and gas, LNG, petrochemical, fertilizer, power generation, solar power and other commodity-based projects.

David Edwards works within the Corporate Finance department at PwC, a market-leading infrastructure finance advisor. He specializes in providing commercial and financial advice to public and private sector partners in infrastructure finance transactions, primarily in the education and transport sectors. His recent experience includes advising Tyne & Wear Integrated Transport Authority on the New Tyne Crossing Project and the UK Department for Transport on the Thameslink Rolling Stock Project.

José Virgílio Lopes Enei is a partner at the Brazilian law firm of Machado, Meyer, Sendacz e Opice Advogados, co-head of the infrastructure department. He is the author of the book *Project Finance: financiamento com foco em empreendimentos* and ranked as a leading lawyer in Brazil by IFLR 1000, Chambers & Partners and Revista Analise da Advocacia, in the areas of project finance, energy and infrastructure.

Ben Farnsworth has extensive experience acting on complex project finance transactions in Australia, Africa, the Middle East, Europe and North America. He has acted for sponsors and finance providers in a wide range of industries, including mining, power, telecommunications, water and infrastructure.

Jérôme Guillet is a founder and Managing Director of Green Giraffe Energy Bankers (GGEB – http://www.green-giraffe.eu), created in early 2010 and focused on renewable energy financial advisory services. He has 15 years in the energy project finance industry, including direct involvement in most non-recourse offshore wind construction financings closed to date, including the recent billion-euro financings for C-Power in Belgium and Meerwind in Germany. A graduate of Ecole Polytechnique, he holds a PhD in Economics from the EHESS in Paris.

Melville Haggard is a member of the Advisory Group on the UK Government's Green Investment Bank and a former Adviser to the UK Department of Environment Food and Rural Affairs on the financing of waste infrastructure. Melville has over 30 years' experience as a project financier including positions held with Bank of Tokyo-Mitsubishi, Lloyds Bank International and Arbuthnot Latham. In 2011 he established Quartermain Advisers Limited www.quartermainadvisers.com to advise private and public sector clients on the financing of energy and waste infrastructure.

Jennifer L. Hara is Vice-President, Marketing for Taylor-DeJongh, where she is part of the management teams for strategy, business development, marketing and training. She leads the proposals team, manages projects and supports the recruitment and research functions. She assists with client outreach and communication and with all corporate marketing activities, including conference management and sponsorship, branding and public relations. She is also a manager of the firm's government contracts.

James Harris (james.harris@hoganlovells.com) heads Hogan Lovells' Asia infrastructure and project finance practice. He is the managing partner of the Vietnam and Singapore offices with 24 years' experience advising on projects in various industry sectors across Asia, Middle East, UK and Australia. He also heads Hogan Lovells' Asia Infrastructure Group. Recognized as a leading PPP/project finance lawyer in industry publications, he is a regular presenter at conferences throughout Asia.

Mark Henderson has spent over 25 years in project finance. Beginning at Kleinwort Benson, later Dresdner Kleinwort, then Société Générale, Mark worked as a financial adviser and project finance lender on many 'first' projects in Europe, South America and South East Asia. In 2004 Mark established the Power & Renewable Energy team at Investec. Mark moved to the world of private equity in 2011, joining LDC's London team to lead their Cleantech & Environmental sector coverage.

Clare Rhodes James (clare.rhodes-james@mottmac.com) is a Divisional Director, Renewable Energy at Mott MacDonald. A Chartered Engineer with 20 years' experience, she advises governments, lenders, developers and utilities on power generation projects and transactions across a variety of technologies and in a wide range of countries across Asia, Africa, Latin America and Europe.

Andrew Kinloch set up Logie Group in 2003 to offer specialist advice on infrastructure finance in Asia. Advice covers i) government policy, e.g., the Indonesian MOF re its support for some $15 billion of capex in the power sector; ii) raising new funds for new projects; iii) acting in distressed situations, e.g., as an expert witness in the $425 million Manila airport Terminal 3 arbitration. He spent 2010 at the ADB as Head of PPP Advisory Services before returning to the private sector. His advice is based on 20+ years Lead Arranging and advising on project, export and structured financings in Sydney with Westpac; in London with IBJ/ Mizuho then UBS; and in Hong Kong where he ran Global Structured Finance, Asia Pacific for WestLB at a time when it was in the top five Lead Arrangers of project finance globally. For more details, please visit www.logiegroup.com.

Rebecca Kotkin is an analyst in the Debt Capital Markets Group within the Investment Banking division of Credit Suisse, based in New York. Rebecca is focused on the structuring, marketing and execution of energy, utility and project finance debt offerings. She has been concentrating on this sub-group since joining the firm in 2009. Rebecca holds Bachelor of Science degrees in Accounting and Finance from Georgetown University's McDonough School of Business.

Simon Lassman, CFA, Associate Director. Simon has extensive greenfield and brownfield project finance advisory, modelling and arranging experience in sub-Saharan Africa and the Middle East, principally in the infrastructure and petrochemical spheres and some acquisition finance experience. He has broad experience with the major development finance institutions, MIGA and export credit agencies in structuring African financings. Prior to SCB, Simon was with a niche research consultancy and KPMG advisory, working on cross-border transactions.

Suellen Lazarus (suellen@lambertlazarus.com) has over 28 years' experience in emerging markets, banking, international finance and managing sustainability issues in projects throughout the world. As an independent consultant based in Washington, DC, Ms Lazarus recently managed the Strategic Review for the Equator Principles Financial Institutions (EPFIs), which was undertaken by the EP Association to provide a strategic vision for the Equator Principles (EPs) prior to embarking on their update process. She worked for 23 years in the World Bank Group where she was Director of IFC's Syndications Department responsible for mobilizing funding from international banks for IFC projects. She has considerable hands-on experience in project finance and structured finance, having served as a principal investment officer on some of IFC's largest and most complex deals. Ms Lazarus was the Special Assistant to the Executive Vice-President of IFC for three years and also the Advisor to the US Executive Director to the World Bank. From 2006 to 2009, she was relationship manager for ABN AMRO in Washington, DC, developing funding products for the World Bank Group and establishing the bank's leadership role in emerging markets, sustainability and the environment, and microfinance.

David Ledesma is an independent gas and LNG consultant with over 20 years' LNG experience gained through the development of projects in Asia and the Middle East. David provides commercial, financing and strategic support to National and International energy companies globally. He regularly writes on gas and LNG and presents at conferences. David is a Fellow of the Oxford Institute for Energy Studies and co-authored its books *Gas in Asia* (June 2008) and *Gas in the Middle East* (March 2011). More details at www. south-court.com.

Robert Lewin is Director of Project & Infrastructure Finance at Investec Bank. Robert has led teams advising on public private partnerships in Europe, Asia, South America and the Middle East. His clients include both public sector sponsors and successful private bidders. Projects encompass transportation, water, oil & gas and power.

Robert has extensive experience in the rail sector including in particular urban rail such as Manchester Metrolink, South Hampshire LRT, Lagos, Tel Aviv, Tyne & Wear, Barcelona LRT, Bangkok MRTA and BTSC, São Paulo Metro, Jakarta MRT, Trenes de Buenos Aires and an LRT in Malaysia.

Paulo de Meira Lins is an Investment Officer with the International Finance Corporation – IFC, private sector arm of the World Bank Group, active in structuring public-private partnerships (PPPs) in infrastructure. Before joining the IFC, he worked for four years as Presidency Officer at the Brazilian Development Bank (BNDES), the main long-term infrastructure financer in South America, in charge of structuring PPPs in transportation and energy.

James Neal is the global head of Ernst & Young's Project Finance Group and head of the Infrastructure Advisory practice. He has been involved in project finance for over 25 years acting as an adviser, a funding arranger and a lender. He has advised on the financing of over US$30 billion worth of projects in the energy and infrastructure sectors including PPP projects in the defence, communications, transport, waste management and health sectors.

Jean-Louis Neves Mandelli is an associate in the Project Development and Finance Group of Shearman & Sterling LLP. He has experience in advising major Brazilian corporates in connection with the development and financing of projects outside of Brazil. He is a Brazilian national and is based in the firm's London office.

Terry A. Newendorp, founder of Taylor-DeJongh, has more than 35 years' experience in international and cross-border capital investments, project and structured financing, corporate financing and private placements of capital. He has negotiated and closed deals in 75 countries, aggregating more than $70 billion, in the energy, oil and gas, and infrastructure sectors. In addition, he has extensive experience with government and multilateral financing institutions, including ECAs.

Dennis Nordstrom is a partner in the London and Washington offices of Latham & Watkins. He specializes in the development and financing of energy sector and other infrastructure projects around the world. He has extensive experience in all phases and aspects of project development. Mr Nordstrom's particular expertise is in the energy sector, including oil and gas, power and water projects.

Keith O'Donnell ACIB, DipFS, MBA MCISI is an international banking specialist with over 20 years' experience covering asset and energy investment in Europe, Middle East and Africa. He advises clients in respect to structuring cross-border debt facilities. He has underwritten large scale investment loans and syndicated large cross-border financings to banks and other institutions primarily in Europe, Middle East and Africa. He established the upstream financing business at KBC Finance Ireland and currently heads its global energy business team.

Liam O'Keeffe, Managing Director, Head of Project Finance, Global Loan Syndication Group. Liam is responsible for the syndication of project finance transactions in the EMEA region at Crédit Agricole CIB and has more than 20 years' experience in the market. Before joining Crédit Agricole CIB, he worked at CIBC and KPMG. Liam has a BSc degree in Civil Engineering from Bristol University. He is also a Chartered Accountant and a Fellow of the Association of Corporate Treasurers.

Marc Partridge, as Co-head of Gazprombank's Project and Structured Finance Department leads the bank's work as arranger and financial advisor for major projects, notably in Energy and Infrastructure. Mr Partridge joined Gazprombank in 2006 after over 20 years with Crédit Lyonnais (now Crédit Agricole) and Arab Banking Corporation. For over 15 years, he has acted as arranger and financial advisor on Project Finance in Russia, Eastern Europe, Southern Africa, the Maghreb, South America, and the Gulf.

Eero Rautalahti (erautalahti@edwardswildman.com) is a partner at the international law firm Edwards Wildman in London. He has more than 20 years' experience of financing and corporate finance transactions. After several years in a senior in-house position in an international mining company, he ran the mining and metals practice of a leading global law firm. Recognized by Legal 500 as a leading mining lawyer, he lectures and writes extensively.

Charles Russell is an economist working in the transport sector. A director of leading consultancy Steer Davies Gleave for nearly 20 years, Charles has led the company's work in the area of private infrastructure finance-supporting government, investors and lenders in significant transport infrastructure (roads, rail, airports and ports) across the world. Across all his work Charles has fought to ensure that the traffic forecasts on which major projects are based are developed in response to the real world and are clearly understandable to those who seek to rely on them.

Christopher Ryan is a Washington DC-based partner in the International Arbitration Group of Shearman & Sterling LLP. He has extensive experience in international arbitration and litigation and has represented private and governmental clients before international arbitral institutions, international dispute resolution bodies, and US federal courts.

John M. Sachs is a Director in the Washington, DC office of Taylor-DeJongh, where he leads transaction teams representing private sector and government clients in the international energy and infrastructure sector. Mr Sachs has advised clients on privatization, project finance and M&A transactions. His experience also includes structuring and raising finance from different liquidity pools, including local and international bank debt, multilateral and bilateral agency financing.

John Sellers has 30 years and $30 billion of project financings to his credit starting with both JP Morgan and Chase before joining Salomon Brothers. He became Global Head of Project Finance for Paribas in Paris in 1991. In 2002, he was an advisor to the California Power Authority before serving six years of community service in California and Arizona. He is now a Principal in Yavapai Regional Capital (www.yavapairegionalcapital.com).

Bob Sheppard is an attorney and former investment banker who was previously co-head of the Global Project finance Group at Bank of America. He has worked extensively with multilateral agencies, both as a financial advisor to private sector clients and as a consultant to the agencies. He teaches international project finance in the MBA programme at the University of South Carolina and in 2010–2011 was a visiting scholar at Stanford University.

Howard Steinberg is a New York-based partner in the Project Development and Finance Group of Shearman & Sterling LLP. In the past 10 years, he has worked on the development and construction of over 100 energy and infrastructure projects across 100 countries worldwide, including in Brazil. Mr Steinberg is named a leading lawyer in project finance by IFLR 1000 and Chambers & Partners.

Kelann Stirling is an associate in the London office of Latham & Watkins, practising principally in the Project Development and Finance practice group. She has represented sponsors, lenders and governmental entities in connection with financings of oil and gas, LNG, wind energy, solar power, ethanol and infrastructure projects and has experience in all aspects of project development. In addition, she has significant experience in acquisition financings in the energy sector.

Ravi Suri is regional head of SCB's Project & Export Finance business with extensive experience in the power, water, oil and gas, infrastructure, petrochemicals, refining, LNG and renewable sectors. He has led large cross-border teams for projects in the Middle East, South Asia and Africa in Project Finance. Before joining SCB, Ravi was Senior Vice-President – Integrated Energy with ABN AMRO, with responsibilities for the Asia-Pacific region. He was responsible for setting up the Structured Finance Unit in India. Prior to ABN AMRO, he was with GE Capital. He has a MS in Chemical Engineering from North Western University USA and has attended executive education programmes at Harvard, MIT, Cambridge University and London School of Economics.

L. Viswanathan (l.viswanathan@amarchand.com) is a Partner in Amarchand & Mangaldas. He has worked on restructuring of US$3 billion Dabhol Power Project, financing of India's first LNG regasification terminal, privatization of Mumbai International Airport, US$2.5 billion financing of a 4000 MW Power Project, US$3 billion financing of a Pan-India mobile network and the recent acquisition of a large greenfield coal mines, rail and port infrastructure project in Australia.

Mathias von Bernuth is a São Paulo-based partner in the Capital Markets Group of Shearman & Sterling LLP. He focuses on New York law advice to US and Latin American, mainly Brazilian, companies in the areas of capital markets, mergers and acquisitions, financing and restructuring.

Rob Watt advises leading domestic and international banks, sponsors, contractors and governments on financing transactions. This includes project and structured financing, PPPs, leveraged acquisitions, property financing and capital markets, as well as general corporate finance. He has worked on transactions in Australia, Asia, the United States, the Middle East and Europe.

Matthew Worth (matthew.worth@linklaters.com) is a Solicitor and a Managing Associate with the Hong Kong office of Linklaters. His practice spans a broad range of debt finance related work, with a particular focus on leveraged and structured lending, portfolio M&A and prudential regulatory matters.

Introduction

Welcome to *The Principles of Project Finance*. This book has been put together to explain and illustrate the ideas behind an important concept in the global capital markets – project finance. This technique is used to fund large capital expenditure projects, usually in the energy or infrastructure arenas.

Project finance is positioned at a key point between the global capital markets and the energy and infrastructure industries. Unlike some other now notorious parts of the capital markets, it is used to fund real assets with long economic shelf lives.

To explain and illustrate the ideas behind project finance, the book is made of chapters written by a range of leading players in the market from around the world.

The book is split into four sections.

The first section reviews various themes and issues key to the project finance market – views from bankers, lawyers and advisers plus chapters on bank, bond and multilateral finance and a look at environmental, insurance and construction market issues.

The second sector looks at how project finance is used in various sectors of the energy and infrastructure market – renewable energy, oil and gas, mining, PPPs and roads and transportation.

The third section then takes an in-depth look at various projects finance markets from around the world – Australia, Vietnam, Indonesia, India, Turkey, Russia, Africa, France, USA and Brazil.

Finally, the fourth section presents a series of Top 10 deal case studies from the pages of Thomson Reuters Project Finance International (PFI), the leading source of global project finance information.

I started at PFI some time ago, more years than I care to remember, and was struck by the importance of the project finance technique on a global basis. Project finance is a highly specialised niche market, certainly, but in 2010 it topped the US$200bn mark according to PFI's tables.

The technique involves funding a large capital expenditure project via non or limited recourse financing. This means a project company is established to build and run the project which raises both debt and equity to fund the project. This project company solely depends on the performance of its asset to provide a return to its equity and debt investors.

The project sponsors behind the project company can, and do, provide various guarantees on the performance of the project and its project company. The level of support provided will determine just how non or limited recourse the project financing is. However to be a project financing, the equity and debt holders need to share in important aspects of the risk inherent in the project – construction risk, operationing risk, political risk and revenue risk.

Project finance has been around for some time. Some say it started when independent power projects (IPPs) were first financed in the USA in the late 1970s, others that it dates back to the development of the North Sea oil fields in the 1970s while others say it dates back to the reserve based lending (RBL) sector backing US oil independents after the Second World War.

Others take the concept much further back. In one article in PFI, Plutarch, ancient biographer of notables such as Alexander the Great and Cato, was revealed as no fan of project finance. In describing an early non-recourse ship-financing deal entered into by Cato, he damned the technique as "condemnable." Not sure what he would have made of subprime mortgage securitisations.

In the modern age, however, the concept really motored in the 1990s alongside the Asia markets boom, followed by the US power market boom and then the take-off of the public private partnership (PPP) concept to fund governmental infrastructure. All the while the oil and gas and mining industries were well served by the technique.

Looking into the future, large scale oil and gas projects and a host of renewable energy financings appear to offer the best deal prospects. But the project finance market has been adapting to the needs of its clients whatever they required, all the way back to Cato.

Rod Morrison
Editor
Thomson Reuters Project Finance International.

1 Themes

1 Project Finance – A Banker's Reflections

STEPHEN CRANE
Green Investment Team

Like most bankers in 2007/9 I thought that whilst the industry as a whole deserved the battering it received, I felt that the project finance sector could hold its head up with some justification as to its place in the industry and indeed society. There was many a dinner party where I was brave enough to explain I was a banker, not any old banker but a project financier.

I have worked in three of the most successful banks in the field of project finance over the last 24 years: NatWest, Deutsche and BTMU. From its natural resource origins, I have seen the great product growth spurt stemming from the UK privatisation of electricity in the early 1990s, the development of private finance initiative (PFI)/public private partnership (PPP) and the export of the contract based product into Europe and then globally. Yet there were times during this period, in the late 1980s and 1990s in particular, when the appropriateness of project finance as a banking product was questioned.

Sponsors have blown hot and cold over its effectiveness and deployment and banks themselves questioned the merits of project finance. I recall a previous boss commenting that strong views existed as its survivability as a product and it was regarded as 'too long, too complicated and too cheap'. In saying, too long he meant the tenor was too long as credit officers and financial controllers with balance sheet responsibility held a view that banks with an inherent short term funding base should not lend beyond their own funding cycle. It was also by its nature complicated and complex as the projects themselves needed great understanding. The combination of the exceptional need to lend over what was regarded as the long term with a documentation basis that, whilst undeniably thorough, was to some due-diligenced to death and hideously complex and thus demanded premium pricing. Of course, it rarely received the pricing so desired and thus the product was criticised as not commanding an appropriate premium over corporate pricing.

Reflecting on the original observation, my colleague could have also meant when he said long just how long in terms of time it took to close the deal. In my career, I have been more than conscious of this as a lead transactor and as a manager and I will draw on experiences as to how this additional criticism can be addressed.

In the course of this chapter, I will come back to these central comments (dare I say accusations) as the banker in whichever organization he/she has worked would have had to deal with similar themes in order to persuade their bank strategically and economically to develop a project finance business and compete for scarce capital.

The chapter will focus on the viewpoint of the banker although I cannot rule out the occasional foray across the table to my advisory experience to make a point or two when needed. It will focus predominantly on closing the original deal but with 'a weather eye open' to the demands and merits of project monitoring.

I will be seeking to draw out as to what makes a good project financing.

Let's start by saying that to make a good project financing, it needs to be first and foremost a good project. A good project also needs to work for all stakeholders and not just for the banks. There has been many a project that banks have congratulated themselves on a good deal's work only to find that they have made mortal enemies of the entire cast of sponsors and sometimes the contractual parties, although it would be rare to alienate the full suite of parties! A good project also needs to close in a reasonable time frame, pay sensibly according to the risk and should have limited risk of default. I do not think there is a deal that has closed where during the negotiation a banker (normally those with more experience) has remarked that all they seek is simple repayment of the money lent in the first instance at some reasonable return! The need to close is critical but not at all costs, for obvious reasons. When I started out in the late 1980s, it could genuinely be said that no project finance deal had lost money. The forest products industry, novel technology projects in the environmental sector and seemingly anything with the word 'Euro' in the project name put paid to that. And this was before the sovereign debt crisis!

Good project finance bankers rarely move outside of the industry so are proud of their career track record. Knowing when to close out a deal is a skill but the better skill is knowing when the position is becoming marginal and too risky.

I'd like to start by looking at the role of the sponsor. Sponsors have many motivations in using project finance and come in many guises and one of the fascinations of the industry is that one frequently encounters unique situations, the solving of which makes the job more interesting than say the corporate market. However, in my view one can distil the type of sponsor into three basic forms: those that wish to use project finance but have the option to deploy corporate funding sources should they wish, those who are persuaded by partners to use the product but would prefer not to and those that have no choice but to use the product to stay in the deal they may well have originated.

There are good, bad and indifferent sponsors in all categories.

The classical good sponsor and one that credit committees wish to see present are those in the first category, namely someone that has elected to use the product out of choice and in all probability has a wide ranging involvement in the project apart from being a financial sponsor. This sponsor is a natural supporter of project finance and understands and appreciates its idiosyncrasies and indeed may even be responsible for some. Their motivation is likely to be based around having a good track record of using project finance before and an intelligent understanding as to the merits of the product. These merits are likely to be one of the following, which is by no means comprehensive:

- The ability to achieve more leverage for the project than would otherwise be possible on a corporate basis;
- To diversify funding sources (banks will often lend more and not necessarily consolidate lending if undertaken on a project basis);
- To achieve a longer tenor than would otherwise be available corporately, and

- The value that comes from the disciplines of the due diligence process conducted by banks and their advisers.

To this list could be added, but rarely spoken about by banks especially in front of the credit committee, the desire to genuinely share risk of the project or the country in which the project is being undertaken.

I have always been pleasantly surprised by sponsors who have admitted that they value the due diligence effort as in nothing else from a motivational perspective, it seems (at least when the comment is made) that the effort is appreciated. I'm sure the oft-maligned lawyers feel the same. Sponsors in this category also appreciate that the monitoring rigour of a project financing is a virtue and not an inconvenience as they welcome the reporting needs as a means of adding discipline to their own internal controls.

This then (at least from a text book or credit perspective as they tick all the boxes) is the ideal sponsor, but such benevolence to the credit side of the bank comes at a cost: terms that might not be quite right and a price that might be too cheap. It will probably mean though that this type of sponsor is using the product for the right reason and is likely to be mindful of repeat business so they should in theory strike a fair position in the negotiation game. These deals are the staple of the market, have a high credit quality (usually) and when critical moments occur during a construction delay or a dispute they will work with banks to resolve the issue. It's not difficult to understand why credit functions like transactions, sponsored by this type of party.

Examples of good sponsors would be experienced Middle Eastern governmental-owned agencies that have a track record of using project finance for their infrastructure and energy needs. They will have a track record of successfully closing transactions and at times of stress will have provided considerable support in getting the deal closed. Such sponsors will understand the motivations of the banks but are not necessarily out to wring the best possible deal from the banks. It should be no surprise then such sponsored deals are fiercely competed for. Even if the economic return can be questioned, when the entire relationship is factored in, these are high-class deals.

The second category of sponsor has the same ability to proceed with project finance, but are either testing the water and trying out the project as some sort of corporate experiment, or are in the deal because the demands of the JV project structure are such that project finance is the only way to proceed. This is altogether more testing ground as pricing and terms can be just as challenging as the credit standing can be very good but the motivations are different. The reluctant sponsor will often lack the understanding of the core ingredients and will bemoan the due diligence, often hankering after the relative simplicities of corporate finance. Negotiation can be difficult as the last thing the PF banker wants is to alienate his corporate banking colleagues but sometimes this is unavoidable. I have lost count of the times this happened to me in my formative years! Some parties who may start off in the process as say a fuel supplier but become a sponsor, can be quite difficult and 'fail to grasp' the needs of the project – a good example being a seemingly complete lack of understanding (deliberate or otherwise) for direct agreements.[1]

---

1   Direct Agreements are agreements between the Lenders and contractual counterparties that give certain rights and protections to the lenders in the case of Borrower default.

This can all lead to a greater deal execution timeframe but in some strange way the sense of satisfaction on closing night can be more rewarding if the obstacles that have been overcome have met with a degree of acknowledgement that the banker has done a good job. In some cases, it is possible to convert a few non-believers en-route to the closing and sponsors can then be reclassified under the first category.

A difficulty with the experimental sponsor is the risk that they might change their mind throughout the process and simply proceed with a corporate solution, through either changed circumstances or changed strategy. Such situations can be quite rare but in more recent years I have witnessed a greater tendency for this to happen.

A clear example of where this can happen is in the political arena where the Sponsor is a governmental entity. There was the occasion of the cancellation of a major European road project due to failure of the deal to close before the election date. In this instance the new government cancelled the financing. Another example was a power project in Estonia which failed to proceed due to changing political circumstances. More frustrating for bankers is the project that goes ahead but without the much-hoped-for project financing. An example might be the hypothetical utility that elects to access the bond market as a result of the central treasury team (in this instance detached from the project team) assessing that an expensive project financing cannot be justified on simple mathematical comparisons. This may happen notwithstanding nine months' work from a banking syndicate. There is no easy answer to mitigate against these events except to be vigilant as to whom to work with, set a deadline to close so that reassessment is not feasible and work like hell to get corporate 'buy in' from more senior levels from such a Sponsor. Of course 'drop-dead fees' are what the text book would demand but, in practice, these are rarely available. The loss of several millions in fees/swap income and margin near to the end of the reporting year can be quite chilling on the team target.

The last type of sponsor is my personal favourite as they need the product to ensure the project proceeds. They can work with other category sponsors but to meet the test they need to have sufficient weight that they carry their partners with them. The obvious issue is that the Bank's credit function may not share the same view. The internal challenge of getting the deal approved is often more hazardous than the external negotiations.

This assertion is not the stuff of text books but as the job of the PF banker is also to be fairly paid and to close out the deal (preferably in a reasonable timeframe) then a sponsor who needs to use PF is preferred. The ideal sponsor will fight hard in negotiation but the deal can and should end up being sensibly balanced in the bank's favour but not to the point of unfairness. It should be priced a little higher reflecting the circumstances and all matters being equal the deal should close in a more efficient matter. This presupposes that the Sponsor is experienced of course, but even if they are working on their first deal, the cost and inefficiency of a learning experience on the first deal can be used with considerable effect on repeat business. If the banker has done his job properly then his chances of securing such repeat business are quite high. I've never liked one-off deals with no chance of repeat business. Project finance deals last a long time and the relationship should be continued not only on the project monitoring process but into future transactions. Of course, deals with all sponsors can be rewarding but sponsors who are similarly motivated and need the deal to close in the same manner as the banker but without the ethos that one can find with larger sponsors with options to threaten to 'not do the deal' are in my opinion better to deal with.

I'd now like to spend a little time on some key banker concerns before concluding with what makes the ideal project finance deal.

Motivation for the Project

One of the attractions for a banker of project finance is the tangibility of the product and the genuine sense that we are financing something real, clearly visible and hopefully good for society and wider economic growth. This is one of the reasons why so many bankers in the sector endure as they simply like the sector and what they are doing and the sense of satisfaction of being involved in building something long lasting. I know I have felt like this.

The key issue is that there must be a need for the project and not just the brainchild of some government or sponsor. Financing a project that is debatable economically that relies on subsidies can be fraught with risk. There are many exceptions: the renewables regime, social infrastructure etc, where there is widespread political and social acceptance of the need for a project. But the so-called white elephant risk can be real. Examples would be roads that nobody really wanted, encouraged by governments for some manifesto reason and financed by bankers who badly miscalculated or failed to understand the intricacies of traffic risk.

In other cases, the commercial nature of a project may be debatable even if the base need for its promotion is understood. This is a grey area, but a good example would be the alternative energy sector as it was called before the renewable energy sector became mainstream. There were many examples where the idealism and enthusiasm of sponsors were too much for naïive bankers and a number of projects were financed that lost money. I recall a tyre burning plant in the UK and the US had many more innovative projects where entrepreneurs were attracted by tax breaks and attractive subsidies – the point being that whilst bankers understood the motivation – it was not really the best of motivations. Better examples would be situations in say the UK where the local authority has a pressing need for the facility and the technical choice would be tailored to ensure risk was minimized.

There are two distinct risks for the project finance banker: a deal that goes bad involving a long-term chronic work-out and/or losing money and less concerning but still very real to the origination side of the business; a deal that does not close. The project motivation takes on a more subtler tone in this context as the deal might otherwise stack up from a risk perspective, but will it close out? Here the banker needs to look more deeply into the motivations of the sponsors but also at the individuals within the sponsoring entity. They also need to assess with increasing regularity the chances of the consortium winning a bidding competition or assess the reliability of the regulatory regime that will underpin the project. This assessment is vital and could be described as whether the project 'passes the smell test'. In other words, is the project for real and are the people also for real and if so do they stand a good chance in a competitive environment. I worked on a deal several years ago when looking back, I was clearly wasting my time, but I didn't have the experience to see the signs.

Bankers need to look out for people within organizations that are operating in a vacuum without support from the treasury function, for organizations that have a reputation for fickleness and dare I say an inclination to experiment and explore options but with a tendency not to follow through.

Backing bidders can be a lottery and it is little wonder that banks have very recently decided to support multiple bidders on large procurement projects. Before multiple bid strategies were widely practiced, it was more normal practice for a Bank to select a bidder to back. In some cases this involved bidding to back a bidder, the so-called commercial horror of 'bidding for a bid'. These situations are obviously much more difficult to predict and nobody has the true Midas touch, but an assessment of the motivations of the people within the organisation is essential.

The Importance of a Good Deal Team

This may be somewhat obvious and it can cross over with other observations but I cannot stress enough the need to have a motivated group of commonly minded people to close the deal, on both sides of the negotiation table. I have mentioned already the dangers of long drawn out processes and the risks that a corporate reappraisal may bring. One way to counteract this is to move fast so that momentum is not lost.

The deal team on the bankers' side includes advisers. Whether legal, insurance, technical, environmental market, tax or accounting, all parties need to be up to the task and preferably hand chosen and with a track record of performing well and to deadlines and most important of all be able to act commercially. There is no point in over-focussing on the negatives if a deal needs to close and be marketed. The key is to ensure that the showstoppers are highlighted early so they can be dealt with and 'paralysis through analysis' is avoided.

The deal team includes banks and this can be extensive if the deal is large and underwriting is not an option or is limited. Most banks have corporate ego, but not all can lead the deal. The lead banking negotiator is critical – he/she needs experience, attention to detail, be able to get into the mindset of his/her opposite number and carry the respect of the banking group. If this breaks down, deals normally close out but not without attendant stress, lost time and great inefficiency. Some banks have reputations of being difficult – this can be down to corporate ethos or associated with an individual. Sometimes these organisations/people are best avoided. Sometimes they can be useful to drive through some points of negotiation and sometimes they are foist upon the banking group as the sponsor has a reason to include them. The best way to respond to this is to make it a personal challenge to bring them along, although occasional outflanking manoeuvres where they find themselves isolated on certain points may be necessary to engineer. If in the position of leading a bank group, the best advice would be to never isolate yourself (as you can always be replaced) and always have one/two banks more than needed. This obviously applies from the Sponsor perspective as well.

It is vital to do whatever is necessary to use whatever influence you may have to ensure the Sponsor has the right balance and resources on his deal team, which includes advisers. This is easier said than done of course, but it is often necessary to make representations to key and senior sponsor contacts midway through a deal. This can only be undertaken with confidence if the banking side is performing well. A good strategy is to have the occasional 'fireside chat' and throwing in the conversation a few self-criticisms of your own side and how you intend dealing with them. This can help break the ice and allows a way to influence how the sponsor side is performing. A few critical issues can also be agreed in this informal way.

Legal representatives are vital. Banks need someone who knows the law (an obvious point but sometimes I've wondered whether they are frustrated principals and have forgotten the legal basics) and can offer constructive and commercial advice but without taking over the proceedings. I have worked with some tremendous lawyers and legal teams who dove-tail immaculately with the banking team. There is a great sense of satisfaction of an entire team performing as one to close out a deal. When in closing mode, a good legal team is an impressive sight.

Other Banking Hot Buttons

TANGIBLE SPONSOR COMMITMENT

This relates to not only the equity commitment but other contractual involvement and how long the sponsors intend to stay in the project as an owner or counterparty. Whereas bankers understand the Sponsors desire for flexibility in recycling capital, project finance is a long term business and banks get involved in the most part because they have relationships with Sponsors' and need to believe that part of the wider relationship is a shared commitment to remain in the project. I have always felt on weak ground in trying to explain to a credit committee just why banks should allow sponsors to sell out completely after say two years of a 20-year deal. Canny sponsors of course cite the transferability clause that bankers regard as boiler plate. My point is that project finance is a long-term business and in fairness to banks they need to be convinced that the parties present and future are motivated to stay the course. The new sponsor (who may not feature as a relationship sponsor) who bought at the top of the market will have a different motivation to the original sponsor. Banks will be more relaxed if the original sponsor has another involvement in the project or if they commit to maintain a reduced holding. This area of debate is often a critical area.

As a further aside there is a lot to be said for a bank to have a policy to avoid the refinancing of the original project. Some opportunities will be lost for sure and it will hurt the bottom line and not enhance relationships, but there are a greater proportion of refinanced projects that get into difficulty than original projects as a result of higher leverage. Even if they are sound projects, if the market is particularly competitive when the refinancing happens, then the chances of further recycling capital is probably quite remote.

REAL BUT SENSIBLE DOWNSIDE CASES

Bankers need to look with great care at the Base Case and the downsides. Cover ratios have become tighter in recent years, sometimes with perfectly good reason but in some cases, banks have put themselves at risk of the circumstances of what we call a combined downside. A few years back, contracted power deals had an unwritten industry standard of having a base case of 1.3:1. As the competitive environment intensified, this became 1.25:1 and quickly 1.2:1. With hindsight, these base case reductions were perfectly justified and the architect of these revisions to the standard did a good job in stressing that no matter the base case reduction, it was difficult to envisage a situation where the project would perform so poorly where the risk of repayment was seriously under threat. The obvious and biggest risk on these deals is off-taker failure and if this happened then 10 pips on the cover ratio would not have resulted in a substantially more protected deal.

In other cases, say in the natural resources sector with the risk of wildly fluctuating oil prices and genuine development risk, or the wind industry with wind variation, price risk and maintenance cost uncertainty it is in my view downright dangerous to lend at central prices and P50 wind and the same cover ratios. Killing a project in the testing ground of the modelling room is essential but it cannot be overdone. Years ago I was worried about a fuel efficiency break even before our technical adviser explained that it was practically impossible to build a plant so badly. An area that is however more difficult to predict relates to traffic volumes. There are too many deals where banks have got this badly wrong. It's a market for the brave and committed.

EARLY WARNING SIGNALS

These concern having the ability to influence the project if it is showing signs of distress. I have always favoured sensible triggers to force the borrower to engage in a cure programme. I prefer to do this through a covenant package as opposed to Event of Default (EoD) sledgehammer. Of course banks need EoDs but once these are triggered 'all hell can break loose' internally as deals that go into default have to be reported frequently and the regulatory requirements are time consuming. My preference to 'talk' earlier to Borrowers predates the recent overly zealous control arrangements banks have been compelled to put in place but it still stands the test of time.

EFFECTIVE MONITORING AND THE BENEFITS OF BEING AGENT

Linked to the above point, I cannot stress enough the need for effective monitoring. The choice of agent is a vital selection decision as a good Agent will develop an effective relationship with the borrower, provide advice to both the syndicate and borrower to ensure that inconsequential issues are minimized but be on the case when needed to protect the bank's interests. Being agent has genuine responsibilities but the job done well has its rewards. Hopefully the payment is fair, influence and information is greater and there should be a head start in the refinancing discussions. A poor agent, sometimes referred to as the post box agent is a disappointing development that the industry should guard against as it is not in anyone's long term interest.

The Perfect Deal

The perfect deal should have motivated parties at both corporate and individual level with an edge to the negotiations to keep people sharp and honest. It should have a genuine timetable that is real with no risk of a corporate alternative, i.e. the project can only happen with a project financing. It should have a closing schedule that is intense that people believe in and buy into (unlike so many deals that may still be great deals but have false dawns through initial dishonesty or naivety as to timescale). It needs to be economically attractive to all parties and banks are paid fairly to ensure timely financial close. If market conditions allow, it should be preferably unwritten either solely or with a small club of role banks. Some large club deals can still be highly rewarding as the satisfaction in bringing together a diverse bank group is very satisfying, but as a personal preference, a genuine underwriting has a sharper edge as not only has it got to close but it has also got to be sold later. The practice of pre-syndicating a deal is undeniably clever as it enables dual tracking and reduces risk but it can inspire what I would describe as 'back seat driving' where a would-be participant attempts to exert influence on the proceedings pre-close.

As regards structure, the only comment I'd like to make is that the perfect deal should have a natural refinancing incentive, either through a natural milestone (e.g., at the end of construction), pricing step up or an obvious re-leverage opportunity. This is to allow the banker to exit the deal should they so elect to recycle capital, or alternatively lead the refinancing. Banks will find that this often works well for Sponsors as they have similar incentives to refinance when the project has been de-risked.

Finally, to be perfect it needs to be a market-leading deal or what might be described as a pathfinder deal e.g. the first of its kind in a sector or country that is keenly followed by the market. There are many examples although if I'm honest, not all have met the timetable aspiration. Even if deals take too long (and most do) there is a tremendous sense of satisfaction in closing for instance, the UK's first IPP, Portugal's first PF and say Egypt's first export LNG project.

2 *Dos and Don'ts for Successful Projects*

ANNE BALDOCK
Partner, Allen & Overy

There are many ways to define a successful project but no matter how hard we try, we cannot get away from the fact that most people, when they speak of a project being a good project rather than a bad one, are referring to a project that has been built on time, to budget, had no teething troubles (either technically or revenue generation wise) during its early years of operation and continues to roll on into the sunset with little or no intervention from any party other than the operator and the ultimate customer/ purchaser of services. No matter that a project may have operated smoothly for the last 10 years and resulted in higher than expected returns for investors – if, during those crucial construction and commencement of operations months or years it has faltered in any manner then it will never, repeat never, get to bear the proud badge of a 'successful' project.

What then can one take from this 'definition' of a successful project that will assist in bringing only good projects to fruition? Well, maybe one lesson is that not all projects that falter in the early years are forever doomed to be problematic and loss making, but surely, the lesson that seems to be screaming at us the loudest is that there is no substitute in a projects context for good planning, common sense and a sensible, balanced and healthy aversion to excessive risk. Yes, maybe the true lesson to be learned is the one that has recently been taught so resoundingly to the banking community as a whole, namely, 'there is no such thing as a free lunch.'

Too often, even today, investors (both public and private) come to the project finance market with the aspiration of financing their dream project with, as they see it, large amounts of (other people's) funding, whilst spreading the unpalatable risks associated with their venture to others. Any investor coming to the table with this mindset must, and will, be disabused of their notions fairly swiftly but the lingering dregs of this mindset can and will make negotiating any project finance deal tortuous and lengthy and will certainly not assist in attempting to keep the project to a set timetable!

My advice to those that hold the above view of project financing as a tool is – do not even attempt to undertake your venture using project financing. Most assets that are to be project financed will be long term assets. Their viability will only become apparent over the long term. Equity investors in projects should not believe that they are going to get rich quickly. What they are undertaking is a long term investment that will bear fruit and reap rewards over the medium to long term.

Bank investors in project finance transactions are, on the other hand, not likely to ever get rich – albeit they will make a comfortable living! They are making a much smaller return over a much shorter period. They will seek to protect that small return by every means they can possibly think of – and then some – this is not unreasonable (or perhaps in some cases it is) but it is just a fact of project finance life. If a sponsor truly has faith in his project he should be looking to protect his investment and to retain his project, not to nickel and dime the lenders out of the protection they feel is necessary to protect their return. If a healthy respect for the differences in approach between equity and debt can be maintained at all times then many of the often tortuous negotiations can often be short circuited.

A reasonable stance at the negotiating table not only assists in keeping projects to time but also helps to forge a relationship with others around the table. A relationship that will continue for a long time and which will be invaluable if rocky times ensue. It is worth spending the time, up front, analysing your project, stress testing it and looking hard at all the little shocks that will come at it throughout its life (certainly its early life). To the extent that you are able to do this wearing multiple stakeholder hats and anticipating each particular stakeholder's requirements, then so much the better. You should then be prepared to share that knowledge (good and bad) with others and to seek a sensible way through the mire that is a Greenfield Project. Remember, if you won't take a particular risk then the chances are, nobody else will. However, if you haven't even thought about a particular risk and that risk is brought to the table by others, then it's a dead cert that nobody else will take it. In order to argue convincingly that others should share a risk then you have to be able, hand on heart, to say that you would be prepared to take that risk yourself.

What then can each of the parties to a project financing transaction do to put themselves in the space that is most likely to lead to a successful project? I set out below some of my thoughts (as an observer and 'legal putter together' of projects for over 20 years. I am sure that there are a number of other issues that I will have forgotten, I am sure that there will be many reading this who will say 'no, she's wrong, we can be much tougher than that and get away with it.' I am sure that there are circumstances where they will be right. However, what I offer here are some observations as an interested but non-partisan bystander who generally 'stands-by' right in the middle of the structuring and negotiating action.

The Public Sector

My first set of observations/advice is made in respect of the public sector. I start here mainly because many of those entering into project finance transactions from the public sector side are doing so for the first time. They feel uncomfortable in their PF shoes. They feel like the new boy starting in the fifth form of a rough comprehensive school with a whole posse of sixth form private sector bullies who know exactly where all the classrooms are and what the protocol for the school day is. Often, the project director is only undertaking the project using PF techniques because it is currently the politically chosen manner of doing things, a manner which may well change overnight, and he has nothing to gain by making decisions that are not strictly within the brief he has been handed. What then can public authorities do to try to assist in ensuring that they procure, let and manage successful projects?

NUMBER 1, RULE OF LAW

The absolute number one requirement for successful projects is that they are undertaken in a stable and sustainable environment where the contracts and the relevant governing laws 'do what they say on the tin.'

In this regard, it is not just the contractual framework that is important. Clearly, the rights and obligations of the parties should be set out unambiguously and it is important that difficult nettles are grasped at the outset and not fudged in an effort to reach some false deadline for signing of documentation. However, the best contracts in the world are worth nothing unless those rights are supported by robust, stable and equitable laws which are enforced in a consistent and non-partisan manner by the relevant courts.

Better one contract where the project sponsors earn a little too much than to send shockwaves through the entire market or stifle much-needed investment in a sector by retrospectively amending contracts or imposing later tax regimes or regulatory frameworks to try to counter such over-payment. Any ad-hoc attempts to adjust the rights of the parties can lead to severe market unrest and a loss of confidence by other project providers. If authorities are nervous of the private sector beginning to earn super-profits then far better to deal with this issue up-front by setting a limit on the amount capable of being earned, taking an equity stake in the venture to share in the 'up-side' or inserting a 're-balancing' clause of the type enshrined in statute in Spain than to try to 'fix' the issue ex-post-facto.

At a time when one of the most precious resources globally is financial investment, the need to retain the confidence of potential investors and the need to make the doing of business in one's home country simple and straightforward is paramount. Outrage in the Australian mining sector where additional taxation is being imposed by central government is being mirrored by oil and gas exploration companies operating in the North Sea. Such spats of anger should be listened to. At a time when the economic position of so many countries is making it harder and harder to decide to invest, governments (including those in established western democracies) will need to think long and hard and take steps to ensure that the market view of stability and rule of law are maintained.

NUMBER 2, GOOD ADVICE

Get Good Advice, not just from those firms that specialise in giving advice to public authorities or understand fully the finances and legal constraints placed upon public bodies but from firms (financial, legal and technical) that are expert in the wider projects and financial markets. These people are able to advise not just on what the outcome of the current project or a particular action may be on the project in hand but can take a wider view and advise on the consequences for other projects or the public body's business more generally. They can also act as 'minders' to the public sector, having knowledge of how similar projects have been undertaken elsewhere and whether the stance being taken by one of the protagonists on this particular project is a stance that is generally held in the market and/or what steps have been taken to mitigate or get around such a stance or any particular risk in other situations.

In this respect, taking soundings from the market and interacting with potentially interested bidders, financiers and financial investors ahead of time is a useful tip. The UK Government learned this in a rather painful manner when their original attempt to procure bids for the design, build, maintenance and financing of prisons within the UK as private prisons financed through the PFI programme had to be withdrawn when funders refused point blank to accept the risk of occupancy levels being used as the marker for setting payment regimes. One cannot help but feel that this reluctance should hardly have been a surprise to government. The banking market was grappling with new concepts (PFI) in a new sector (prisons) where prison occupancy and prison sentencing policy is clearly dictated and controlled by the government payer. Credit to the government that these projects were eventually successfully resurrected and completed as availability payment projects which went on to form the basis for all of the early PFI accommodation projects undertaken by the UK government and to form the bedrock of the hugely successful programme of PFI/PPP projects undertaken by the UK. A pity perhaps that the lessons learned have not been highlighted to others in an effort to avoid repeats in other countries.

Further examples of the advice received by government perhaps being a little too public sector focussed are the UK NHS Lift Projects. The scheme (which took some 18–24 months in gestation) was intended to ensure that a single procurement would suffice to select the service provider that would be responsible for multiple projects to provide local health care, doctors' surgeries, dispensaries, clinics, etc to a particular local area. The procurement strategy was faultless. However, the government had failed to anticipate the manner in which multiple projects by the same consortium would effectively be financed and the original structure required major surgery during procurement of the first projects to ensure that the required pipeline could be met.

NUMBER 3, LISTEN

Listen to your advisers and be prepared for push back – prepare in advance for meetings and manage your internal client as well as the external project provider.

Much of the time spent by public authorities in negotiating contracts with the private sector arises as a result of an unwillingness to even try to understand the hopes and aspirations of the private sector ahead of large-scale set piece all-party meetings. All too often, the response of the public sector to comments and suggestions made by the private sector are dismissed without any real consideration and, as a result, when explanations are given as to why any such suggestion has been made, time is lost whilst such 'new' concepts have to be run up the chain of command internally after lengthy meetings have already taken place. If public bodies approach the issues raised by the private sector more empathetically rather than assuming that every change requested is an effort to 'do down' or 'get one over on' the authority then far more constructive dialogues may be undertaken at meetings and internal approvals can be sought ahead of time. Knowledge of the authority's wider stance on any particular issues gleaned during these pre-meeting discussions can also, then, be used to good effect during negotiating meetings rather than slowing down the process outside.

Good advisers will be able to understand much of what is being asked for and should be listened to when reviewing commentaries/approaches being adopted. Indeed, to dispatch one's advisers to request clarification of issues ahead of full party meetings and to ask the question, 'why?' can save much time and heartache during the key procurement phase of any project.

This open approach will also assist in trying to decipher commentaries made by competing bidders for the same project who choose to adopt a different negotiating style to requests for responses to information. Many is the time when an authority has selected the bidder who adopts the stance of 'everything is broadly acceptable provided we can discuss a couple of issues with you after we are appointed' only to discover further down the line that those discussions are around exactly the same 105 issues which were the requested amendments or points in respect of the information raised by other (perhaps more straightforward) bidders. An understanding and open approach will assist in teasing out the required information early on, as will the setting of clear parameters around the type of answers and level of detail required by way of response.

By the same token, public authorities who have a set way of doing their transactions and who are not prepared to adapt them should not run a process where they state that they are going to be flexible and take account of bidder requirements where they are not. Instances of this approach have been rife in the transport sector in the UK and elsewhere and serve only to frustrate bidders who spend millions of pounds in bidding in earnest and sharing their concerns, only to have them completely ignored when final bids are requested.

NUMBER 4, TRAIN UP

Finally, the advice that I would give to public authorities embarking on project finance or PPP programmes for the first time is train your people.

In this context, I am not speaking of the project manager during procurement but rather the people who will have to manage the living, breathing project through to completion and beyond.

There is always much talk around the fact that good Project Managers in the public sector just get to the position where they are comfortable in their shoes when they then get moved on to other departments or promoted to other jobs and the knowledge of how to get a project completed is lost to the public authority. Whilst it is true that this is frustrating, this lack of expertise merely delays the project at the early stages whilst new people get up to speed or makes the process of procuring a project a longer and more tedious process than it perhaps should be. However, such difficulties pale to insignificance in comparison to the differences over the life of a project between a successfully managed and operated project and a dysfunctional one. The issue of lack of expertise at the outset can easily be managed by, if necessary, hiring competent project manager consultants whilst the mismanagement of a live project will have a far wider reaching effect than the one-off procurement.

The training that public sector employees require for successful project management is training as to the manner in which they should look to enforce the letter of the contract and the options that might be available to them within the framework of the project portfolio of the relevant public authority more widely. What matters is that the manager seeks to obtain best performance from the project provider over the lifetime of the project rather than just squeezing the contractual provisions available to them 'until the pips squeak.'

An operating contractor who is shown some give and take – rather than being stung with maximum penalties for minimum misdemeanours each time they occur will, in the long run, provide better value. Whilst the penalty regimes and contractual rights set out between the parties within the hard-fought contractual arrangements have their place in a well-run project, they should not be taken as holy writ, but should be exercised and enforced with discretion and sympathy and an eye on value rather than cost.

It should perhaps be remembered that all legally binding contracts ultimately give the parties a right to sue for breach. Of course, in only a very few cases do the protagonists end up suing their case in court. Compromises and settlements are by far the more prevalent outcome. The settlement of an issue that is not fundamental to the performance of the contract and that that suits both parties – even if not catered for by the strict letter of the contract – is surely far more use to an ongoing project than a small (and often small-minded) victory on each minor point. Many is the time that a small missed target on day-to-day maintenance, answered help desk call-outs, etc have been utilised not to deduct penalty points or deduct payments but to perhaps obtain a fresh lick of paint on tired woodwork at the same time as maintenance is being carried out nearby or to repair or redirect a sewer on another project run by the same service provider.

PPP and other project contracts should be viewed as contracts that drive performance and drive value out of the services provided. They should not be seen as a revenue generation scheme by the relevant receiving authority.

Joint Venturers and Consortia

NUMBER 1, KNOW YOUR PARTNERS

Unsurprisingly, the best operating consortia are those comprising groups of persons coming together in a situation where respect, co-operation and understanding of the needs of the other members is high and the bargaining position of the relevant parties is equal. Unsurprising, also, is the fact that the stars are very rarely aligned in this manner.

In order to put together a bid, or any project for that matter, in a cohesive and co-ordinated fashion, it is important that the JV partner's inequalities and expectations are discussed and agreed well ahead of time. Any attempt to hide or fudge the issue will, inevitably, show up at a later date, in a far more public forum and will potentially discredit a bid and undermine the confidence of the letting party/financiers to that project.

Issues to be resolved in advance include:

* joint and several or several liability;
* tax positions of the parties and tax structuring issues;
* creditworthiness issues and manner of dealing (upfront equity/bank LCs, etc.);
* desire of the parties to finance on or off balance sheet; and
* negotiation of/voting on contracts with associated third parties (e.g. construction/ O&M arrangements which are typically sourced out by the associates of the JV members).

A failure to address such issues and an unwillingness to 'grasp the nettle' but to leave it to others (e.g. financiers/the public authority/their advisers – or worst of all your co-venturers) to point up the weaknesses in a JV or contracting structure generally leads to protracted and unhappy negotiations and sets a project off on a wrong foot with a mountain of trust and honesty to climb – never a good beginning.

NUMBER 2, KNOW YOUR FINANCIERS

Recognize early in the process that the lenders will have specific needs – think ahead and do the preparation work for a project with a clear understanding of those needs to prevent the need to repeat simple exercises two or three times.

For example, each funder will need to undertake KYC procedures – when setting up the new company, ensure that relevant documents are placed on a web portal that each can access so that the exercise is only undertaken once by the company. If your project is looking to utilize funds from international development banks then ensure that environmental surveys and monitoring procedures that you set up are set up at the outset in a manner that will mean that they comply with the World-Bank requirements. A lesser standard will be a false economy in terms of cost and time at the end of the day.

Recognise that if equity is to be injected into the project pro rata with commercial lenders then credit rating of the equity provider will be a key factor. If a bank LC is required, start working on obtaining this early on in the project development. Do not wait until two days prior to financial close when you have finally read the CP schedule to the borrowing and discovered that you need to negotiate specific forms of LC to comply with lender requirements or will have to seek unnecessary and complicated waivers for non-compliant (in terms of strict wording) LCs.

Set up accounting systems and reporting systems on day one in a manner that should satisfy the lenders and then take the time to read the information sections of the credit documentation carefully. Far too often those negotiating credit documentation spend their time arguing over materiality qualifications for covenants and events of default and skim over the reporting requirements, many of which can be exceedingly onerous on-going requirements for a project company to fulfil with limited personnel available to them, and at the same time as trying to manage a construction programme or operational facility. Remember, the reporting requirements are an on-going cost to the business. Rarely should lenders need anything which the sponsors do not (or will not) find useful. If large amounts of excess information and reports are being requested, a frank and open dialogue should be had to ensure that the 'bank's standard form' has not overtaken 'common sense' on the project.

NUMBER 3, MAKE THE TOUGH DECISIONS EARLY

Tempting though it may be if contracting parties are associated companies, don't try to make the construction or operating contracts too onerous on the project company. A construction contract or operating contract that has not been properly negotiated and prepared (as if between two truly third parties) will not pass muster with financiers who will seek to renegotiate a clearly one-sided contract – often resulting in a far tougher contract than might otherwise have sufficed.

The washing of a sponsor group's dirty washing in public is never an edifying experience and again leads to wariness throughout the project which is not conducive to long-term successful projects.

Although each project is individual to the needs of the parties and the associated geographies/market needs, there is a clear risk allocation in projects within each relevant sector which is broadly accepted within that sector. Sometimes, the differences between sectors have no logical reason to exist beyond market precedent. However, it is important that parties know what the generally accepted allocation is and highlight to other participants in the project where the risk allocation in this particular case differs from that norm. If this is done, together with a clear explanation as to why such an approach has been adopted then such a stance will be far more likely to gain acceptance and speedy resolution than where such issues have been 'negotiated' behind closed doors and presented to others as a *fait accompli*.

Sponsors should also clarify up-front the type and amount of completion support is required. Too often, this all important element is fudged at heads of terms and term sheet stages only to become the make or break point at the eleventh hour of negotiation when all parties have expended too much time and effort into the process to be capable of either backing out or backing down. Issues such as amount, principal or interest only, default payment versus on-going payments, required completion tests (timing, parameters, etc.) should be worked out in detail up-front in order to prevent major hiccoughs at a later stage. I have just recently been working on a project that has been shelved after 18 months of work as a result of a fundamental misunderstanding of the nature and amount of completions support being offered.

NUMBER 4, THINK ABOUT THE FUTURE

When entering into a long-term financed position, parties should always have one eye on the future and on how the project itself and also the project economics can be improved.

In this regard, thought should be given to whether or not a differential margin should be required pre- and post- operations and/or whether the credit facility is easily re-financeable once the riskier (and therefore inherently more expensive) part of the project has passed.

In this regard, the hedging arrangements put in on place day one will potentially have a large impact on the economics of a refinancing case and the ability to negotiate flexible hedging arrangements with embedded break provisions may (although initially more expensive to procure) prove to be a better long-term economic investment.

This is an issue not just for the private sector sponsors of a project. The UK government has often lamented the fact in public that its PPP sector has not evolved into a conglomeration of companies holding many and various PPP assets and taking a corporate holistic view across its portfolio, but has rather retained the structure of many small single-purpose project vehicles undertaking their own small projects.

This seems an odd lament indeed when the documentation which has been fought over and defended to the hilt, often against all rational instincts of those actually carrying out the projects, provides such barriers to any other structure <u>ever</u> being adopted. The requirement for 100 per cent interest rate hedging, the requirement for all re-financings and change-of-control arrangements to obtain prior approval, the need for major contractor changes to be approved, etc. – all seem to lead inexorably to fossilization of the project and an inability, or at least a major disincentive, for the private sector to drive further values and structures out of the projects – what a pity that such innovation and creativity have been stifled at the altar of standardization.

All Parties

DON'T SAY NO, ASK WHY?

Too many parties to a transaction will argue for a position in negotiations because that is the way the original document presented to the parties was drafted. Such documents have often been drafted with no thought or only limited understanding as to the current project needs and with the desire to protect a particular position in a particular manner. What must be remembered is that the manner in which a particular issue is dealt with in any document is almost certainly not the only way in which a particular position can be protected or a particular outcome achieved.

There are, of course, times when a tough stance in documentation will need to be taken and maintained. We have all at some stage banged our heads against the stone wall that is the development bank's standard form or ingrained policy. However, in the main, a rigid position is not required and a party's desired aims and goals can often be achieved in a manner which is far more palatable to the other side and which, in the context of a long-term 'partnership' arrangement, is probably far better suited to the task in hand.

Taking the time to understand 'why' provisions have been presented in a certain manner will usually assist parties to take their eyes 'off the page' of negotiations and concentrate on the consequences of their actions and the desired outcomes for the parties and the project.

Conclusion

It is always difficult to predict at the outset which projects will be successful – or even what success will look like. To give a famous example, work on the Clifton Suspension Bridge (one of Brunel's best known civil engineering projects in the UK) was started in 1831, but then suspended due to riots which drove away investors, leaving no money for the project, and construction ceased. Work recommenced in 1862 (after a concerted fund-raising effort by colleagues of the, by then late Brunel, and admirers at the Institution of Civil Engineers who felt it would be a fitting memorial. The project was completed in 1864, five years after Brunel's death and 34 years after its commencement. The Clifton Suspension Bridge still stands today, and over 4m vehicles traverse it every year. Who is to say that this was not a successful project?

But by most people's reckoning a successful project still remains a project that is built in the time anticipated, that is completed at the cost which was anticipated, that operates smoothly to provide services to the end-user at an affordable price and which provides a sufficient return for the contractor, operator, supplier, sponsor and other project stakeholders. One can only hope that some of the words written above will assist those desiring to undertake successful projects to ensure that this highly improbable and illusive confluence of events occurs.

3 *Role of Financial Advisors in Project Finance*

DAVID EDWARDS, PETER BROWN
and CATRIONA COULTHURST
Corporate Finance, PwC

In the coming years, there is a massive need for investment in infrastructure throughout the world. It is needed to meet demand from growing and increasingly affluent populations, to harness new technologies and to drive future economic growth. Even looking at the UK alone, the 2010 National Infrastructure Plan identifies the need to invest £200bn over the next five years.

Many governments face a period of severe budgetary pressure following the credit crunch and sovereign debt crises. Therefore, the delivery of this infrastructure will require significant private sector investment. Since the 1990s, governments have recognized that the involvement of private sector investors allows risks related to the construction and operation of infrastructure projects to be transferred efficiently to the private sector. The UK's National Infrastructure Plan sets out the importance the Government places on unlocking private investment on an unprecedented scale to achieve the required investment.

Financial advisors will play an important role in helping governments achieve their investment targets for infrastructure by identifying opportunities to attract private sector investment, structuring transactions to achieve efficient risk transfer and helping governments procure and monitor effective private sector partners.

Financial advisors also provide valuable support to private sector investors. Advisors help investors identify opportunities, develop winning tenders, arrange finance and mitigate commercial and financial risks on infrastructure transactions.

This chapter provides an overview of the role of a financial advisor throughout the development and procurement cycle for a public private partnership (PPP) transaction. It identifies key players within the financial advisory market, why they add value and what activities they complete.

The Advisory Market

Table 3.1 sets out the most active advisors in the project finance market globally over the 10 years to 2010.

Table 3.1   Global deals by value and number of deals closed for the 10 years to 2010

Rank	Advisor	No. of deals	Value ($m)
1	PwC	346	95.083
2	Macquarie	185	77,741
3	SG	59	62,803
4	HSBC	67	62,333
5	Citigroup	71	55,508
6	Ernst and Young	237	47,599
7	KPMG	147	43,725
8	BNP Paribas	47	35,149
9	Royal Bank of Canada	45	22,271
10	Grant Thornton	109	10,932

Source: Project Finance International, January 2011

As illustrated by this table, the market is dominated by professional services firms and investment banks, although a number of small, boutique firms are also active in the market. Each type of advisor tends to have different strengths, as summarized in the following table:

Table 3.2   Types of advisor

Type of Advisor	Differentiating strengths	Potential weaknesses
Investment Bank	Investment banks can provide lending facilities and derivatives alongside financial advice to their clients. Proximity to internal credit departments can allow banks greater insight into their considerations.	Lack of independence both in terms of judging different funding sources and on securing most competitive financing price due to position as potential lender as well as advisor. Also more liable to changes in corporate strategy (e.g., exiting a particular market).

Professional Services	Professional Service firms offer financial advice which is independent of the source of finance, free of any inherent or perceived conflicts of interest. They also provide access to integrated specialist tax and accountancy advice, complimentary services as part of the wider project finance transaction.	Not able to directly provide lending and/or derivatives alongside advice.
Boutique	Boutique financial advisors are able to provide specialist advice and market knowledge, often advising on unusual projects in niche areas of the market.	Can be reliant on small number of employees. If these employee(s) leave, then standard of advice could be compromised. Do not have as strong a brand as other players.

Why do Sponsors Engage Financial Advisors?

Clients entering the project finance market require financial advisors for a number of reasons.

MARKET KNOWLEDGE

Advisors have detailed and up-to-date market knowledge. This insight helps clients structure and deliver projects efficiently by using best practice from precedent transactions. For example, advisors' knowledge of what risks private sector investors have been willing to bear allows governments to structure transactions that allocate risks efficiently. Advisors' knowledge of commercial and financing terms achieved on recent transactions strengthen clients' positions in negotiations with funders and contractors.

Large, multinational advisory firms add particular value across national borders, where they often have local advisors who provide international investors detailed knowledge of the marketplace. Transactions across different sectors also present their own idiosyncrasies, meaning that advisor experience of past transactions can be key to the success of a client that is inexperienced in the sector.

SPECIALIST KNOWLEDGE AND EXPERTISE

The development and execution of project finance transactions requires a range of specialist financing skills. Advisors provide a wide repertoire of these skills that clients may not possess in-house. For example, both public sector and private sector clients will typically rely on analysis that requires the development of complex spreadsheet models. Advisors have sophisticated templates and specialist staff that they use to develop robust and efficient models.

RESOURCING

It is inefficient for all project finance parties to maintain the skills and knowledge base of a financial advisor, particularly when these skills will be used on only a small number of transactions in which an individual client is directly involved. Resourcing requirements on a Project Finance transaction can vary unpredictably throughout the project. Financial advisors offer large and flexible teams with available capacity of skilled staff to ramp-up resource allocation as necessary. This allows the client to use their own resources with greater efficiency, concentrating their efforts on their day-to-day business activities and seeking out new investment opportunities.

INDEPENDENT INSIGHT

Experience and understanding of both private and public sectors is crucial to client success. For governments, project success is dependent upon being able to simultaneously attract private investment, and achieve the value for money and its wider economic and political objectives. These can, for example, include a reduction in spending while achieving political goals such as strong service levels or service availability. To aid this, financial advisors can provide insight to private sector expectations and assess the commercial viability of a project, but also have the understanding of government to help balance conflicting public sector objectives. For the private sector, advisors can assist in their interpretation of public sector motives or requests, which provides clarity on the incentives for each party in the transaction. Independent review of proposed solutions limits the avoidable risk exposure of both public and private sector clients.

INVESTOR CONFIDENCE

Independent financial advice brings the further benefit of investor confidence. A well-known independent advisor brings credibility to a project. A wider range of potential investors will be encouraged by independent assessment of a project, which will increase the competitive process and result in more competitive financing rates and commercial terms.

KNOWLEDGE SHARE

Financial advisors and clients should take a collaborative approach to their projects. As a result, there may be some scope for knowledge share between the client and the advisor. This will increase client familiarity with transactions of this particular type, an auxiliary benefit to the client, particularly if they intend to embark on similar transactions in the future.

When appointing a financial advisor, it is important to give consideration to the elements outlined in sections 2 and 3 in order to understand first your requirements and then how the strengths and weaknesses of the different potential advisors will have an impact. What are your key reasons for employing an advisor? What role do you want them to play? Which services are most important to you, and what benefit are you seeking from using them? You will then need to identify how each advisor matches up against these criteria.

The Role of the Financial Advisor

The core objective for every financial advisor is maximization of client value.

In meeting these client objectives the financial advisor provides two integrated streams of advice. The advisor provides commercial guidance at the outset and throughout the transaction, including efficient risk allocation and negotiation advice. In support of these commercial recommendations the advisor also provides financial advice, for example market testing, finance raising and the financial modelling of a project. These elements should be delivered simultaneously as part of the overall advisor package to ensure decisions are efficient while also commercially viable.

In the next section we discuss the possible tasks of the financial advisor at each stage of a transaction. The extent of the role of the advisor at each stage should be determined by the individual needs of each client. A client with greater in-house financial expertise may require less financial modelling support, for example. The role of the financial advisor is to identify options, assess value for the client and make recommendations, but the final decisions are those of the client. The value of advisors is maximized where sponsors work closely and collaboratively with advisors, maintaining the independence of decision making.

Tasks Undertaken by the Financial Advisor

The typical project finance transaction can be split into four broad stages:

1. Feasibility stage
2. Tender stage
3. Financing/Financial close
4. Contract management/Performance.

Financial advisors play an important role in each one of these stages. While the tasks vary between the stages, the basic principle of providing integrated commercial and financial advice to maximize client value remains the same across the transaction. Below is a brief guide to the role in each stage, with a case study of a real-world example. Appendix A also provides a table setting out in more detail the range of tasks that financial advisors typically undertake at each stage for both the public sector procurer and the private sector contractor.

FEASIBILITY STAGE

This stage is focused on determining the project that will be undertaken, and the procurement and financing methods that will be used. The bulk of this work will be carried out by the public sector procurer, and so this is where the greatest need for financial support will come.

Decisions that will need to be taken by the procurer include the project scope, the risk allocation that will be pursued between the public sector procurer and private sector contractor, how the need for finance will be met, and the intended timetable. This will need to consider a wide range of options both for the project scope and the approaches

Case Study 1 – M25 Road Widening PPP (UK)

In the early years of the new millennium, the UK Highways Agency had identified a number of potential major capital projects that would deliver significant economic benefit. Considerable work was undertaken to identify:

1. The procurement and financing method that would provide best value for money, taking into account the updated project appraisal guidance within the UK Treasury's 2003 Green Book.

2. The project that was most suitable to be undertaken.

The conclusion of this analysis was that the proposed widening of the M25 should be undertaken through a PPP structure. This offered strong economic benefits, while ensuring that the project specification offered the deliverability required.

These decisions were made through rigorous options appraisals that needed strong financial support from PwC. The work encompassed both financial analysis, including value for money and affordability, and testing the appetite of both contractors and funders for a number of alternative possibilities.

Further work was then undertaken on the structure of the procurement. Ultimately, it was decided to take the widening forward as one procurement rather than in batches, as it allowed for synergies and integration within the widening and maintenance of different sections. However, the widening itself should take place in two separate stages, mainly to avoid unacceptable disruption to the motorway. The funding for these two stages would be undertaken separately in order to improve the deliverability of the project. The transaction for the first of these stages, worth over £6bn and with over £1bn in finance, closed in May 2009.

taken, based on the value and costs of each one, and the extent to which they are deliverable.

Financial advice needs to have significant input at this stage. There is no point in deciding upon the scope of a project, only later to find that it is either unaffordable or undeliverable. Decisions taken at this early stage can have a dramatic effect on the success of a programme.

Financial advisors can assist the public sector in analysing the value for money and affordability of the various options, providing assumptions for financing costs, advising on the commercial structure that best suits the project, and they can help to identify the risks involved and the most efficient way of allocating them. They can also conduct market soundings to ensure that there is sufficient appetite both from potential contractors and funders to make the project deliverable and achieve a sufficient level of competition.

For the private sector contractor, the work is likely to be much more limited. However, possible roles include helping to identify and analyse potential investment opportunities, or testing the level of funder appetite for projects under consideration.

Case Study 2 – RailCorp Rolling Stock PPP (Australia)

Initially, there were only two potential local suppliers for a PPP worth over AUS$3.5bn to supply train rolling stock to the New South Wales Government. This raised potential issues around the contestability of tender, with the state needing to heighten competition at a time when there was some scepticism in the international market about receptiveness to innovative approaches.

After market sounding, it was decided that the tender would be opened to solutions with single deck as well as double deck trains, which allowed two more foreign contractors to enter the competition. This required clear and innovative tender appraisal processes for evaluating between the two different types of train, taking into consideration the benefits and risks of each.

A two-stage bid process was developed with an irrevocable decision on the procurement of single deck trains after the first stage. PwC played an integral part in developing the tender structure and evaluation, the innovative payment mechanism that had higher standards than previous deals, and conducted workshops with bidders to resolve any outstanding issues. Due diligence was undertaken on the full supply chain of each bidder, and a staggered asset delivery profile was introduced to ensure deliverability.

This approach ensured that value for money was achieved through greater competitive tension, with the deal closing to a tight schedule in December 2006.

TENDER STAGE

For the public sector, the tender stage involves inviting contractors to provide their proposed solutions, further refining and agreeing the terms of the transaction, and determining which contractor should be chosen to undertake the project. The structure of this process, and details of how it is conducted, should be designed to achieve the best value for money possible. Crucially, this means achieving the level of competition between bidders required for effective negotiation, and to put pressure on them to provide solutions that are the best possible value for money.

Private sector contractors will be focused on preparing and submitting their solutions, as well as negotiating the terms of the deal. They need to devise a bid that will give them the best chance of winning the tender, while maximizing the return for the risk that they are taking with their investment.

Financial advisors can play an important role on both sides of the deal. Tasks they do for either side include helping to inform tender strategy, conducting financial analysis to inform negotiations, building the appetite of funders/contractors and undertaking negotiations on financial matters.

There are also many tasks specific to one side. For the public sector procurer, tasks include input into the design of the payment mechanism to provide the right financial incentives to the contractor, drafting tender documents, analysing the financial position of the contractors, and evaluating the bids to ensure that the one that offers best value for money is chosen. This evaluation will, for example, need to take into consideration the different risk allocations that may exist for different bidders.

For the private sector contractor, tasks include building a financial model on which the pricing of the bid is based, conducting analysis using this model to determine the most efficient solution design, and drafting the financial sections of the bid documents.

Case Study 3 – Greater Manchester Waste PFI Project (UK)

This project for the Greater Manchester Waste Disposal Authority (GMWDA) is the largest waste PFI contract in Western Europe with a contract value over £4bn. The project structure includes twin Special Purpose Vehicles building and operating some 44 different facilities.

The preferred bidder at the final tender stage had a financing solution that included two debt underwriters. However, as the credit market difficulties reached their peak in 2009, these two original debt underwriters were not able to continue with the project. The funding solution had to be restructured, a task made much more complex by the wide range of non-standard issues arising from the twin SPV approach.

An innovative approach was required: the two transactions (one for each SPV) were 'stapled' together – meaning they were linked in such a way that each helped to support the finance of the other. A full range of possible finance mechanisms was investigated, with the result that the sources of funding were widened to include:

- European Investment Bank (EIB);
- a club of commercial banks;
- senior debt and capital contributions from GMWDA;
- a contingent layer of mezzanine debt from one of the sponsors to support part of the senior debt;
- the first ever investment by the new Treasury Infrastructure Finance Unit (TIFU), a government body set up to support investment during the credit crunch.

As financial advisor to the contractor, PwC led work that built the original structuring of the deal, the restructuring that took place to attract other sources of finance, and worked through the detailed relationships between each investment type. The deal, which included over £1bn of finance, reached financial close in April 2009.

FINANCING/FINANCIAL CLOSE

The objective of this stage is to structure and attract finance on the best terms possible. Financial advisors have a vital role to play, as they will have the specialist knowledge, experience and skills to analyse different potential finance structures, and deal with funders to achieve the best possible outcomes.

A wide range of finance types can be sought, including bonds, debt from commercial banks or multilateral finance institutions, mezzanine debt, third party equity or public sector capital contributions. Financial advisors should understand the appropriateness of each for the project under consideration, and which has proved attractive on recent similar deals. They will have the contacts and knowledge to investigate each potential source of finance, and be able to run the analysis required to help determine what balance offers best value.

They are also likely to have experience of running funding competitions and managing funder groups, as well as the knowledge of previous deals that puts them in a strong position to negotiate with funders. Finally on this stage, they can lead the process during financial close, including putting in place appropriate hedging arrangements for the project.

Case Study 4 – Operational School PFI Contract (UK)

This PPP project involved the new build of a secondary and primary school, as well as the extension and modernization of a number of other primary schools. During the operational phase of the contract, a review of performance was undertaken. As financial advisor, PwC undertook a review of the performance of the contract, including the application of the payment mechanism, implementation of key financial clauses within the project agreement and a review of variations to contract that had taken place.

The review highlighted that, although the overall performance of the contract was good, the Authority were not receiving the full value for money that it was paying for. PwC worked with the Authority to implement the payment mechanism, and understand the impact of deductions on the viability of the SPV. This initially led to greater payment deductions on the contractor, and ultimately led to a significant improvement in performance from the contract.

Further advice was provided through a value testing process, which included the provision of benchmark data, advice on the financial and commercial issues associated with introducing photovoltiacs at the schools, the further development of the Payment Mechanism model and reruns of the financial model to incorporate variations to date. The involvement of a financial advisor ensured that the Authority was receiving appropriate specialist commercial and financial advice during its negotiations and agreement with the contractor.

While most work at this stage is likely to be undertaken on the contractor's side, the exact split of tasks between the public sector procurer and the contractor will be determined by the structure of the tender process. For the public sector, it is important to retain at least some oversight to ensure that the terms and structure used represent good value to them as well as the contractor.

CONTRACT MANAGEMENT/PERFORMANCE

Once the deal has been agreed, financial advisors can play a role on a range of elements during the operation of the contract. In terms of day-to-day running, they can help ensure that the performance of the contract is monitored financially and kept to a high standard, for example by building a spreadsheet model that tracks performance or calculates payment deductions.

They can also advise on one-off issues, such as the structure and negotiation of any changes that may occur to the scope of the services provided, assist in refinancing of the deal, or provide financial support within any disputes that occur between the two sides. The support required will be specific to each project, and heavily dependent on the capabilities each side has to undertake these duties themselves. Where the public sector agency or private sector contractor undertakes only a small number of similar projects, it will often make sense to look for assistance from outside advisors.

Where Next for the Financial Advisors?

The FT's 'Future of Global Infrastructure 2010' sets out that more than £27 trillion needs to be spent on infrastructure over the next 25 years. Financial advisors will play a key role in helping governments deliver the value that the private sector can bring in bridging infrastructure gaps by attracting private sector investors to both new territories and new sectors.

NEW TERRITORIES

Large, international financial advisory firms often have a strong footprint in financial advisory and consulting services in emerging markets both in the developed and developing world. Combining thorough understanding of the requirements and constraints of the governments and contractors in new markets with extensive knowledge of best practice from established PPP markets, allows financial advisors to play a lead role in developing structures that allow governments entering the PPP market to unlock the opportunities offered by private investors in infrastructure. Their global reach also allows advisors to act as a guide to private sector investors looking for new opportunities in emerging markets, particularly in South America and Asia.

NEW SECTORS

Similarly, large professional services firms have the relationships and knowledge to find structures that allow governments and contractors to extend private sector finance into new and emerging sectors. This is particularly apparent in the renewable energy sector, where financial advisors have been at the heart of programmes such as the UK Government's Offshore Transmission and Carbon Capture and Storage Programme that harness private sector investment to help the UK meet its obligations to limit carbon emissions.

Appendix A   Table showing the possible detailed tasks for financial advisors

Stage in trans-action	Public sector/Procurer side	Private sector/Contractor side
Feasibility	Assist in clarifying objectives Assist in scoping options to meet objectives, incl. commercial structures Financial analysis/modelling of options appraisal Identification, costing and allocation of risk Review financial data available for completeness Indicative value for money analysis Market sounding to test appetite Affordability assessment Inform timetable Initial view on accounting treatment Draft relevant sections of outline business cases	Identify and evaluate potential opportunities Conduct market soundings to test funder appetite
Tender	Inform tendering strategy/structure Assist in building market appetite Design payment mechanism Determine evaluation criteria Draft relevant parts of tender documents Conduct financial discussions/negotiations with bidders, Assist in drafting financial elements within contract Build shadow financial model for use in analysis Establish accounting treatment Analysis of potential funding options Further analysis and determination of risk allocation Detailed risk-adjusted value for money analysis Conduct financial evaluation of bids, including review of financial models and calculating any required risk adjustments	Inform bid strategy Assist in building funder appetite Analyse and evaluate different funding structures Assist on financial discussions/negotiations with procuring authority incl. on payment mechanism Build financial model Provide financial analysis/results on cost profiles Run sensitivities to analyse risk profiles (i.e. how project performance is affected by cost overruns/changes in economic assumptions) Interact with accounting/tax advisors to determine correct treatment Draft financial sections of bid documents

Financing and Financial Close	Oversee funding competition (if used) and/or management of chosen funders on behalf of client Conduct remaining financial negotiations Input on financial detail of contracts Review and approve financial model Oversee financial close Final value for money analysis Draft relevant parts of final business case	Write information memorandum for potential funders Analyse different financing structures Inform strategy for funder management Conduct funding competition Detailed negotiation with funders Assist with financial negotiations with procuring authority Inform hedging arrangements Write financial close protocol Manage financial close process
Contract Management/ Performance	Assist with contract monitoring Evaluation of contract performance, and potential changes to the project Analyse areas of potential cost savings Conduct financial negotiation for any contract variations Oversee any refinancing on behalf of client Benchmarking and market testing as part of contract provisions Analysing and negotiating on any disagreements/disputes with contractor and assisting on contract terminations	Analyse financial performance of projects Build operating financial model to monitor project Test potential refinancing opportunities Conduct refinancing, including analysing potential structures, conducting funding competition, updating financial model Assist on financial negotiations for any contract variations Analysing and assisting negotiations on any disagreements/disputes and assisting on contract terminations

4 *Multisource Project Financing*

DENNIS NORDSTROM, partner,
SIMON DICKENS, partner,
MATTHEW BROWN, partner, and
KELANN STIRLING, associate
Latham & Watkins

Over the past two decades, the size of individual infrastructure and industrial development projects constructed globally has grown at a staggering rate. In years past, sponsors and developers interested in seeking limited recourse financing to fund the construction and development of such projects could turn to a single financial market (such as the commercial bank market or the capital markets) to meet all such funding requirements. Today, the sheer size of many large-scale developments coupled with recent changes in the global financial sector have made it economically inefficient for sponsors and developers of such projects to seek to meet their capital requirements by relying on a single source of financing. These changes have led to an increase in the number of multisource project financings. Multisource project financing is the financing of a project where the debt funding is raised from two or more sources and combined in the same capital structure, sharing the same source of debt repayment and the same security package. The most common sources of debt funding seen in multisource project financings include commercial banks, export credit agencies (ECAs) and multilateral agencies, the capital markets, the Islamic finance markets and sponsor senior debt. This chapter briefly describes the emergence of multisource project financing as a financing model, and includes a discussion of each of the frequently utilized sources of debt funding mentioned above, commenting on certain of the key advantages and disadvantages to incorporating each such source within the capital structure of a multisource project financing. In addition, this chapter discusses various ways that the intercreditor and other structural issues that may arise from combining different sources of debt in one capital structure may be addressed in a project's finance documents.

Background

Many large project financings closed over recent years have included at least two, and in some cases three or more, different sources of debt funding. Examples include:

Table 4.1   Examples of debt funding

Project Name and Country	Debt Raised and Sources of Debt	Financial Close
Papua New Guinea Liquefied Natural Gas ('LNG') ('PNG LNG') Project (Papua New Guinea)	Approximately US$14 billion total debt, including international commercial bank debt, ECA guarantees and direct loans and sponsor senior debt.	March 2010
Ras Laffan C Independent Power and Water Project (Qatar)	Approximately US$3.025 billion total debt, including international commercial bank debt, ECA guarantees and direct loans and an Islamic finance tranche.	August 2008
Nakilat Inc. LNG Vessel Programme Financing (Qatar)	Approximately US$6.8 billion total debt, including, senior and subordinated project bonds, international commercial bank debt and ECA guarantees and direct loans.	December 2006 (with further tranches raised in 2007 and 2009)

The increasing use of multisource project financing can be attributed to a number of factors. Firstly, the need for capital to fund energy, infrastructure and other projects around the world has continued to grow. Global debt raised through project financing transactions increased from US$131.7bn in 2000[1] to over US$227bn in 2010.[2] This general trend for increased overall amounts of project financing debt has led to a need for more and different sources of capital to support the implementation of global infrastructure and industrial development projects.

In addition to the overall increase in debt required to support a growing global project finance market, individual deal sizes also are on the rise. Of the Global Top 10 project finance deals as reported by Project Finance International for the full year 2010, all 10 had a total debt raised amount in excess of US$2bn and the largest had a total capital cost – debt and equity – of US$14bn.[3] In 2000, the largest project financing had a total capital cost of only approximately US$2.5bn.[4] The Jubail 2 export oil refinery project in Saudi Arabia, with a total capital cost in excess of US$14bn, was the largest deal by value in 2010.[5] That project was funded with 18 different tranches of debt financing, comprising a mixture of international and regional commercial bank debt, Islamic financial institutional debt, covered and direct ECA debt and sponsor loans, in an aggregate amount of approximately US$8.5bn and approximately US$5.5bn in equity contributed by the project sponsors.[6] The PNG LNG project financing, with a total capital cost of approximately US$18bn, was the largest deal by value in 2009. As indicated in the table above, the PNG LNG project

---

1   *2001 League Tables*, Project Finance International, 23 January 2002.

2   *2010 League Tables*, Project Finance International, 13 January 2011.

3   Project Finance International Yearbook 2011.

4   Project Finance International Yearbook 2001.

5   www.pfie.com.

6   www.pfie.com.

was financed with debt from a variety of sources. None of the commercial bank market, the capital markets, or any other individual source of financing, can provide sufficient debt to meet the capital requirements of a transaction of such magnitude. As deal sizes continue to grow, project sponsors increasingly will be required to consider multiple sources of funding in order to have a fully funded capital structure.

In addition to a generally growing market for project finance debt and growing individual deal sizes, other factors, such as the impacts of the global financial crisis, have contributed to the growing use of multisource project financing. The global financial crisis, and the implementation of new regulatory regimes (such as the Basel III reforms) that came in its wake, affected the lending capacity of many commercial banks. Such impacts have been reflected in a tightening of the availability of funds generally, a tightening of country limits with respect to debt that can be held on an institution's balance sheet, a shortening of the tenor of available debt, and an increase in overall pricing, in each case as compared to transactions that were financed prior to 2008. Moreover, lending decisions for commercial banks in some respects have become driven more by relationships with project sponsors than by a desire of the commercial banks to increase overall lending in the project finance sector. While the commercial bank market has recovered to a certain extent, the reduced lending capacity of the commercial bank market caused many sponsors to consider the inclusion of other sources of funding within their project financing plans.

In addition to some of the external factors noted above that have pushed sponsors towards multisource project financings, there also are other benefits associated with including multiple sources of funding in a single project financing that may lead sponsors towards consideration of such structures.[7] Such benefits include the efficiencies that can be gained by having a fully funded capital plan at the outset of project development and creating competition amongst the potential sources of funding in order to obtain better overall pricing, longer tenors and more flexible covenant packages.

However, structuring a project to accommodate multiple sources of funding can create a number of challenges. For example, complex intercreditor issues may arise when seeking to align the varying interests of multiple creditor groups. Project sponsors that wish to maximize potential sources of funding will need to consider the complexities inherent in multisource project financings as they formulate a finance plan and work with their legal and financial advisors to structure a transaction that will receive widespread market acceptance.

Sources of Funding

COMMERCIAL BANKS

General overview

Commercial banks remain the most common source of funding for project financings. A key benefit of loans from commercial banks is the flexibility that they offer to borrowers.

---

7   Equally, there can be benefits of initially pursuing, or structuring a project financing to include, multiple sources of debt, even if the project ultimately is not financed with multiple sources of funding.

The most common type of commercial bank loan used in project financing is a term loan, being a loan that has a specified duration and that is repayable in accordance with a pre-agreed repayment schedule. There is broad flexibility to agree a repayment schedule that best suits the needs of the relevant project. This includes flexibility as to when repayments will begin, whether the loan will be repaid in equal or variable payments over time and the frequency of interest payments (including the option to capitalize interest during construction of the project) in order to align the project's projected revenue streams and operating costs with the borrower's repayment obligations.

Commercial bank loans may be available from domestic commercial banks operating within the country in which the project is to be located as well as from international commercial banks that fund transactions in many different jurisdictions globally. Including domestic commercial banks in a capital structure may have advantages for the sponsors as local banks will have knowledge of local laws and customs as well as the ability to make loans in the local currency. It also may signal to the international commercial banks the importance of the transaction to the host country. However, in some developing countries, the domestic commercial bank market may not be sufficiently deep to meet the overall capital requirements for large-scale projects. Further, loans from domestic commercial banks in certain jurisdictions may be available only at higher pricing (i.e., the cost of borrowing, reflected in the interest rate and fees payable under the loan) and for shorter tenors than would be the case for loans provided by international commercial banks. The availability and attractiveness of domestic commercial bank finance will depend largely upon the location and nature of the project. Indeed, project financing in some sectors in certain countries, such as Brazil and India, tends to rely heavily on the participation of the domestic commercial bank market.[8] For example, the State Bank of India made aggregate project finance loans of approximately US$21.14bn in 2010 to fund 55 projects.[9]

Including commercial bank debt in a multisource project financing

Commercial bank loans may be included in a multisource project financing for a variety of reasons (in addition to those stated above), including:

- *Competitive pricing* – The pricing of commercial bank loans for projects traditionally has been very competitive compared to the pricing of project bonds.[10] However, as a result of the global financial crisis, the difference in pricing of these two sources has narrowed.[11]

---

8   *See* Guarav Sharma, *Global PF Debt Outlook 2011: No loosening – just pragmatic lending*, Infrastructure Journal, 21 March 2011, *available at* http://www.ijonline.com/GenV2/Secured/DisplayArticle.aspx?ArticleID=68370; *2010 League Tables*, Project Finance International, Issue 448, 13 January 2011 ('Indian loan volumes rose from US$29.9 billion in 2009 to US$54.8 billion in 2010. Indian banks are already starting to wonder if they can continue to fund their domestic market in this way').

9   Project Finance International league tables, PFI issue 448, January 13, 2011.

10   Joseph Tanega and Pawan Sharma, International Project Finance: A Legal and Financial Guide to Bankable Proposals 71 (Butterworths 2002).

11   *See* Deirdre Fretz, *Banks vs bonds*, Project Finance International, Issue 410, 3 June 2009; Matthew Martin, *The resurrection of the Gulf bond market*, MEED, 23 July 2009.

- *Flexible availability* – Commercial bank loans may permit multiple availability periods and draw downs. Projects often can benefit from the ability to draw down cash under a bank loan agreement over time as the project funds capital costs, rather than on a single date. This is particularly useful for greenfield or expansion projects where cash is required over an extended construction period (including to meet milestone payments under relevant construction contracts). Although borrowers will pay a commitment fee in exchange for lenders keeping funds available for drawing for an extended period, the commitment fee will be less than the interest that would be payable in respect of amounts drawn under the relevant finance documents. In contrast to a commercial bank loan, capital markets offerings typically are fully funded by bond purchasers on a single date. Although a bond financing may be structured to replicate the periodic draw down structures found in the commercial bank market[12] (for example, by requiring bond proceeds to be deposited with a bond security trustee who will release the funds to the issuer periodically upon satisfaction of certain conditions), interest in respect of the project bond would accrue on the total amount of the issuance from the outset.
- *Construction risk* – Commercial banks have the ability to analyse and price construction risk in a manner that other financing sources cannot. Amongst the most significant risks that a greenfield project faces are whether the project facilities will be completed on schedule and on budget, and whether the project facilities will operate in accordance with the project design so that the facilities are capable of generating the revenues required to repay the project debt when it becomes due and payable. Commercial banks are able to take an active role during the life of the loan to work closely with the sponsors to manage project risks (including construction risk). The ability to exercise such active deal management generally is provided for by way of information and monitoring covenants in the financing documents or, in some cases, by the inclusion of completion support by the project sponsors, which is available to repay the debt if the project does not reach construction completion by an agreed sunset date.
- *Lender relationships* – As noted above with respect to the management of construction risk, commercial bank lenders often take an active role in the administration of a project loan. Frequently, commercial banks participating in a project loan have long standing relationships with some or all of the project sponsors. By contrast, purchasers of capital markets debt have neither the ability nor the inclination to take active roles in managing such debt. Project sponsors may be able to leverage their personal relationships with commercial banks to obtain favourable loan terms.[13] This may include providing the commercial banks with the opportunity to augment their returns on the specific loans through the provision of ancillary business (for example, by placing interest rate or currency hedges with the commercial banks, or by maintaining accounts with certain institutions for general banking operations). Maintaining a more personal relationship with lenders also provides benefits to the project if a transaction does not proceed according to plan. While sponsors may

---

12   *See* Deirdre Fretz, *Banks vs bonds*, PROJECT FINANCE INTERNATIONAL, Issue 410, 3 June 2009 ('[T]he private placement market is becoming more open to draw-down financings, which ha[ve] long been a key advantage of bank loans over capital market deals').

13   *See* Matthew Martin, *The resurrection of the Gulf bond market*, MEED, 23 July 2009.

approach commercial bank lenders at any time during the life of the loan with requests to waive covenants, amend the terms of the finance documents or to forebear from calling a default, the providers of other sources of finance may not have such an ability to address the short term needs of the sponsors or the changing nature of a project following financial close.

Of course, commercial bank loans generally include a more extensive covenant package than may apply to other sources of finance. In order for commercial bank lenders to manage and monitor the loans actively, commercial bank loans frequently include requirements for the provision of information over the term of the debt. Covenant packages under commercial bank loans frequently include incurrence covenants (for example, restricting the incurrence of additional debt) that can be breached only through intentional actions on the part of the borrower or the sponsors, as well as maintenance covenants (for example, requiring the borrower or sponsors to maintain certain financial ratios, which may be required for certain actions, including for example, payment of dividends or distributions). By way of comparison, bond financings generally will include fewer covenants. This is because bondholders are not able or inclined to monitor a project closely or to manage changing risks over the term of the debt. While commercial bank loans tend to have fulsome covenant packages, the sponsors may be able to bring to bear their relationship with the lenders to effect modifications that are necessary to reflect the changing realities of the project over time.

The tenor of commercial bank debt often is an important consideration for project sponsors. Prior to the global financial crisis, the tenor of international commercial bank loans in certain transactions stretched to 20 years or longer. Although there have been indications that the tenor of commercial bank loans may be moving back towards pre-financial crisis norms (at least for certain greenfield projects[14]), international commercial banks often have not been able to provide loans with a sufficiently long tenor to suit certain types of infrastructure projects, such as those with long construction periods prior to generation of revenues. Similarly, in the past, domestic banks in many jurisdictions have not been willing to provide long-term loans,[15] being more comfortable providing debt with tenors in the range of five to seven years. Accordingly, sponsors often must look to other financial sources (such as the capital markets) to stretch the tenor of the overall finance package and to boost their returns from the project.

There also are other considerations relevant to certain commercial bank loan products. For example, a number of commercial banks (and other financial institutions) have committed to make loans available only to borrowers that comply with the environmental and social policies and procedures set forth in the Equator Principles. The Equator Principles were established by 10 private institutions on June 4, 2003,[16]

---

14   See *Global PF Debt Outlook 2011: No loosening – just pragmatic lending?*, INFRASTRUCTURE JOURNAL, 21 March 2011 ('Tenors have, in the main, returned to pre-crisis norms for greenfield projects as they are driven by what make best sense for the project and its sponsors, and most greenfield PF lenders prefer full amortization to refinancing risk especially in the EMEA region').

15   See E.R. YESCOMBE, PRINCIPLES OF PROJECT FINANCE 24 (Academic Press 2002) (noting that in some developing countries, project financing is not available from domestic banks as '[t]here may be no market for long-term loans in the domestic banking market').

16   See Andrew Hardenbrook, *The Equator Principles: The Private Financial Sector's Attempt at Environmental Responsibility*, VANDERBILT JOURNAL OF TRANSNATIONAL LAW, vol 40, 197–232, p. 199.

and there are now 70 equator principles financial institutions (EPFIs).[17] Under the Equator Principles, more stringent environmental and social standards are applied to projects located in countries that are not members of the Organization for Economic Co-operation and Development (the OECD), or in countries that are members of the OECD, but are not designated as high-income countries (as defined by the World Bank Indicators Database).[18] EPFIs generally will require (through loan covenants) any project in which they invest to comply with the applicable standards set forth in the Equator Principles. As such, sponsors should include an analysis of the project's likely categorization under the Equator Principles and the capital costs of compliance therewith in developing a project's finance plan.

EXPORT CREDIT AGENCIES (ECAs)

General overview

ECAs are private or governmental institutions established by nations with the objectives (amongst others) to provide financial support to (a) promote the export of goods and services from the ECA's home nation, and (b) support the development of projects that will produce desired imports (particularly natural resources) to the ECA's home nation. For example, in the context of an LNG project, an ECA may provide financing or other credit support (typically in the form of a guarantee or an insurance policy) where a contractor from its home country will construct the LNG facility utilizing a significant amount of goods manufactured in its home country, or where LNG produced by the project is to be sold to the home country of such ECA. ECAs may support a project in a number of ways, including through the provision of direct loans, political or commercial risk insurance or guarantee products, and interest rate support. In addition to their mandates to promote the export of goods and services or the import of natural resources, the mandate of ECAs often includes the development of projects of national importance in lesser developed jurisdictions where commercial banks may be unwilling to take political risk.

ECA support has become more prevalent in multisource project financings for the same reasons discussed in Part A of this chapter that have contributed to an increase in the use of multisource project financing generally. In fact, ECA and multilateral agency funding of projects in emerging markets increased from US$20.5bn in 2009 to US$27bn in 2010.[19] In the PNG LNG project, ECA direct loans and guaranteed facilities accounted for over half of the total project debt.

Including ECA debt in a multisource project financing

In addition to being an important source of liquidity in its own right, including ECA funding or support in a multisource financing structure may increase the attractiveness of

---

17   Website of the Equator Principles Association, http://www.equator-principles.com/index.php/members-reporting, viewed on 24 June 2011. Note that the Equator Principles are currently under review and are expected to be updated in the latter half of 2011.

18   Equator Principles, *available at* http://www.equator-principles.com/index.php/about-ep/the-eps.

19   *2010 League Tables*, PROJECT FINANCE INTERNATIONAL, Issue 448, 13 January 2011.

a proposed financing to commercial debt providers and may improve the terms available to commercial lenders. While commercial lenders may benefit from political risk insurance provided by an ECA, even where that is not the case, commercial lenders participating in a multisource project financing together with one or more ECAs also often feel that they benefit from the 'halo effect' of having such ECA participation in the capital structure. For example, where an ECA is providing credit support, the host government may be less likely to take action that would be objectionable to the government of the ECA's home country, such as expropriating assets or nationalizing industries. In addition, ECAs have stringent internal policies with respect to the environmental and social impact of the projects to which they provide financing. As such, they often require detailed diligence on such topics. Therefore, ECA participation in a multisource project financing can provide commercial banks with added comfort that another financier has conducted extensive diligence with respect to the project. Of course, the scope of each financier's diligence requirements, other internal processes and specific financing requirements must be considered by sponsors in contemplating a multisource project financing as the sponsors must coordinate closely such requirements and processes through advanced planning and preparation, including to determine whether or not financing terms should be agreed with potential ECA financiers before any other potential financing source is approached.

The ability or willingness of an ECA to support a project is driven by policy considerations (including those relating to support of home country exports and imports, and support of projects in developing countries). Therefore, availability of ECA support will depend on the location and type of project being financed. Where an ECA is providing funding that is tied to the value of the goods and services provided from the ECA's home country (known as 'tied funding'), the availability of, or amount of, ECA funding or support available for a project will be constrained by the actual level of procurement that the project is able to obtain from the relevant country.

Where an ECA is not providing a direct loan to a project, but is providing a guarantee or insurance policy for the benefit of commercial lenders providing direct loans (known as covered loans), ECAs typically will charge a guarantee fee or an insurance premium that will be in addition to the interest rate that is charged by the actual lenders. Although sponsors need to consider such fees or premia when assessing the overall cost of capital for a project, covered loans typically have lower interest rates than uncovered loans as the ECAs providing the guarantee or insurance take most, or all, of the political and/or commercial risks associated with repayment of project debt. As the entities providing covered loans know that, subject to the terms of cover, their debt will be repaid by the ECA or ECAs providing such cover in the event of a default by the borrower, the rate of interest required by such entities should not need to reflect any premium in respect of the risks covered by such ECA or ECAs.

Many ECAs are bound by the OECD Arrangement on Officially Supported Export Credits, which came into existence in 1978 and most recently was updated in March 2011 (the OECD Arrangement). Sponsors need to be aware of the limitations imposed by the OECD Arrangement when considering whether to include ECA loans or other credit support in a multisource project financing. The OECD Arrangement applies to all official support 'provided by or on behalf of a government for export of goods and/or services, including financial leases, which have a repayment term of two years or more.'[20] Thus, the limitations set forth in the OECD Arrangement apply only to tied funding arrangements. Notwithstanding that the scope of the OECD Arrangement is limited to tied funding support, the internal practices and policies of an ECA may require that some or all of the provisions of the OECD Arrangement be applied to untied loans or support provided by that ECA. The OECD Arrangement will impact the debt tenor, the repayment terms, and certain other terms, on which an OECD-compliant ECA will make debt available.[21]

While the above discussion is limited to ECAs, multilateral agencies, such as the International Finance Corporation (which is part of the World Bank group), the European Development Bank, the Asian Development Bank, the African Development Bank and the European Bank for Reconstruction and Development, also can be an important source of funding for a multisource project financing. Most of the considerations applicable to ECA support as discussed above apply equally (or similarly) to multilateral agency support.

CAPITAL MARKETS (PROJECT BONDS)

General overview

The capital markets have long been an alternative financing source for the large scale infrastructure and industrial development projects. For example, Ras Laffan Liquefied Natural Gas Company (3), a joint venture between Qatar Petroleum and ExxonMobil, successfully raised US$2.23bn in a three-tranche bond offering in 2009.

Although the capital markets may be the sole source of debt for a project, a multisource project financing may include a capital markets issuance to cover a portion of the project's total debt requirements. Additionally, even where a project does not seek capital markets debt at the initial financial closing, the project's finance documents often will be structured to accommodate future bond financings to fund further project capital requirements or to refinance some or all of the project's initial sources of funding.

While project bonds long have been used as a means to finance projects, they represent only a small portion of total global project financing.

---

20   Chapter I (*General Provisions*), paragraph 5 (*Scope of Application*), Arrangement on Officially Supported Export Credits, Organization for Economic Co-operation and Development, dated March 2011, *available at* http://www.oecd.org/officialdocuments/displaydocumentpdf?cote=tad/pg(2011)4&doclanguage=en.

21   The OECD Arrangement applies different standards for loans to projects located in 'High Income OECD countries,' as defined by the World Bank on an annual basis according to per capital GNI. See Chapter I (*General Provisions*), paragraph 11 (*Classification of Countries for Maximum Repayment Terms*), Arrangement on Officially Supported Export Credits, Organization for Economic Co-operation and Development, dated March 2011, *available at* http://www.oecd.org/officialdocuments/displaydocumentpdf?cote=tad/pg(2011)4&doclanguage=en (i.e., generally, project finance transactions are subject to a maximum repayment term of 14 years and a maximum weighted average life of the repayment period of seven-and-a-quarter years, but after 31 December 2011, a maximum repayment term of 10 years and a maximum weighted average life of the repayment period of five-and-a-quarter years will apply for project finance transactions where export credit support accounts for more than 35% of the project debt for a project in a High Income OECD country).

Table 4.2   Project bonds represent only a small portion of total global project financing

	Global Project Bonds	Global Project Loans
2000	US$20.8 billion	US$110.9 billion
2005	US$26 billion	US$140.3 billion
2010	US$19.7 billion	US$208.1 billion

Source: Project Finance International, League Tables for 2001, 2005 and 2010 (figures are approximate)

Since the global financial crisis, however, the industry outlook for project bonds as a source of financing for projects has improved steadily,[22] with project bond issuances in 2010 rebounding from just US$8.5bn in 2009.[23]

Including bond debt in a multisource project financing

Traditionally, the institutional investors that comprise the purchasers of project bonds have been attracted to investment grade transactions, typically with strong project sponsors and a steady, identifiable and predictable stream of revenues as the source of debt repayment. The most challenging risks for rating agencies to assess have been the risk that construction is completed on time and within budget, and the risk that the completed facilities will operate in accordance with design parameters. Therefore it is challenging for rating agencies to award investment grade ratings to greenfield development projects financed on a non-recourse or limited recourse basis. Accordingly, project bonds historically were considered to be an option only for refinancing term loan commercial bank debt once a project became operational.[24]

That trend began to change in 1996 when Ras Laffan Liquefied Natural Gas Company, a joint venture between Qatar Petroleum and ExxonMobil, successfully raised a US$1.2bn tranche of capital markets debt as part of a multisource project financing. The proceeds of that financing were used to fund the construction and development of a large LNG plant in the State of Qatar. As construction and performance risks are considered by the rating

---

22   *See* Danielle Myles, *Project bonds set to dominate*, INTERNATIONAL FINANCIAL LAW REVIEW, 23 March 2011 ('Project bonds are back. Banks facing new capital requirements have cut long-lending programmes – never their most profitable – and China's demand for resources has outstripped mulilaterals' funds. Project sponsors are now turning to the capital markets, and in many ways they've found their perfect fit. Bondholders can get their predictable annuity locked in, and developers their long-term funds.'); Deirdre Fretz, *Banks vs bonds*, PROJECT FINANCE INTERNATIONAL, Issue 410, 3 June 2009 ('Bond financings are becoming increasingly attractive as project sponsors find fewer banks able to participate in project financings.'); William H. Voge, Simon Dickens, Bryant B. Edwards, Jonathan R. Rod, Craig A. Stoehr, John N. Toufanian, of Latham & Watkins LLP, *Why Project Bonds Now?*, PRACTICAL LAW COMPANY, *available at* http://construction.practicallaw.com/9-500-5960?source=relatedcontent.

23   *2010 League Table*, PROJECT FINANCE INTERNATIONAL, Issue 448, 13 January 2011; *see also Global PF Debt Outlook 2011: No loosening – just pragmatic lending?*, INFRASTRUCTURE JOURNAL, 21 March 2011 (noting that notwithstanding the demise of the monoline insurers, '[i]nvestors such as insurers and pension funds, etc. are looking for long term, stable assets to match their long term liabilities. Hence there is a noticeable uptick in bond market activity, as we see from IJ's figures, albeit that uptick is from a low point 2009.').

24   *See* Matthew Martin, *The resurrection of the Gulf bond market*, MEED, 23 July 2009 ('When project sponsors are well-known names with good ratings, investors are interested and sponsors can get some benefits from the bond markets through refinancing.')

agencies and institutional investors to be physical risks with financial consequences, the risk mitigation factors employed by the project sponsors were financial in nature, importantly including firm completion guarantees offered by the creditworthy project sponsors. Since 1996, there have been several high-profile project bonds issued to finance the construction of projects in countries as diverse as Venezuela (the Cerro Negro oil project), Indonesia (the Paiton power project), Argentina/Chile (the InterAndes/Termo Andes power project), and United Arab Emirates (the Dolphin pipeline project), amongst others. Today, institutional investors may be prepared to take construction risk if they are comfortable that the project risks have been evaluated properly and that a suitable risk mitigation package has been put in place.

A recent example of a project that included both senior bonds and subordinated bonds as part of its initial capital plan is the Nakilat Inc. LNG vessel programme financing. The Nakilat Inc. LNG vessel program financing was put in place to finance the construction of a fleet of 25 LNG tankers that will transport Qatari LNG to markets globally. While the construction programme did not involve the development of any onshore facilities, the Nakilat Inc. transaction had many of the construction risks of a traditional greenfield project. Through the provision of a sensible risk mitigation package (including a pool of cross collateralized LNG vessels being constructed in three world class shipyards and long-term charter party agreements with Qatari LNG producers), Nakilat Inc. was able to raise a total of approximately US$6.8bn in three tranches between 2006 and 2009, which comprised US$1.15bn of capital markets debt that sits alongside senior and subordinated commercial bank debt, senior ECA direct loans and senior ECA covered commercial bank debt.

Including project bonds in a multisource project financing has a number of benefits. Unlike commercial bank debt that typically provides for floating rate interest, project bonds tend to be fixed rate instruments. Accordingly, including fixed rate project bonds in a capital structure can act as a natural hedge against the interest rate risk that may be inherent in other sources of finance.

Project bonds also may benefit the sponsors by providing longer tenor debt than might be available from commercial banks or ECAs. As institutional investors do not need to reserve capital when investing in bonds (as compared to regulated banks that are constrained by capital reserve requirements), in the early project bonds days, the capital markets were able to offer longer term financing than banks, which better matched the expected useful life of the projects. Over the late 1990s and early 2000s, however, banks responded by reducing loan pricing and by increasing loan maturities. Just before the credit crunch, banks were providing certain project loans with final repayment terms in excess of 20 years, durations that previously had been the sole domain of the capital markets. Since the global economic downturn, debt tenors available in both the commercial bank market and in the capital markets have shortened, but the likelihood of institutional investors returning to longer tenor debt seems greater than in the commercial bank market.

The institutional investors that purchase project bonds have different investment requirements than do commercial banks and ECAs. Institutional investors tend to be yield investors who match maturities of the bonds against their future capital requirements. Accordingly, institutional investors typically are not interested in being prepaid prior to maturity. This leads to the inclusion of make-whole provisions in bond transactions pursuant to which an issuer must pay a premium to prepay capital markets debt. While the institutional investors do not want to be prepaid, capital markets debt does allow for the creation of repayment terms that may benefit a capital structure. Historically, the principal amount of project bonds has been payable at final maturity only (that is, they have bullet maturities rather than having principal amortized over time).[25] Including a bullet maturity tranche of capital debt in a multisource project financing may ease pressure on the sponsors to repay debt in the early years of the project. Of course, including a tranche of debt that is not fully amortizing does introduce re-financing risk to the overall project.

Bond financing may be raised more readily when paired with commercial bank debt in a multisource project financing. This is because the inclusion of more loan-like covenants in a bond indenture, which an issuer is likely to be more willing to provide where it already has agreed to provide such covenants to commercial bank lenders, may improve the project bond's credit rating.[26]

As noted above, an advantage of including commercial bank debt in a capital structure is the flexibility such lenders have to respond to requests for waivers or amendments. Bondholders tend to comprise a large and disparate group of institutional investors. Accordingly, it is difficult (and sometimes impossible) for an issuer to obtain bondholder consent to amend the indenture or to obtain a waiver of certain rights or provisions. Where commercial bank debt is included in a capital structure alongside capital markets debt, the sponsors may be able to obtain greater flexibility under their finance documents than would be the case if capital markets debt were the sole source of financing. For example, where commercial bank loans and project bonds are pari passu obligations of a borrower/issuer and sit side-by-side at the same level of a project's capital structure, the project bonds often have the benefit of the more restrictive bank loan covenants through a common terms agreement, common security agreement or intercreditor agreement. Such agreements frequently contain mechanics that act as proxies for bondholder action so that an issuer will have the same flexibility to obtain waivers and consents for anything other than the most fundamental matters (such as releasing security or changing debt maturities or interest rates) as under the commercial bank tranche without having to approach the bondholders for approval.[27]

When considering whether to include capital markets debt in a multisource project financing, project sponsors frequently cite concerns about the (a) price of capital markets debt as compared to commercial bank debt and (b) timing of a capital markets issuance as a potential delay to achieving financial close. However, project sponsors may be willing to pay such marginally higher prices in order to have access to an additional source of capital that historically has provided longer term debt than was available in the commercial bank market. In the present post-financial crisis environment that has seen convergence in tenors as between the capital markets and commercial bank market, the difference in overall pricing of capital markets debt as compared to commercial bank debt

---

25   Not all project bonds have bullet maturities. For example, it has been reported that the US$1.25 billion project bond issued by Dolphin Energy Ltd. in 2009 was a 10-year amortizing bond.

26   *See, e.g., Abengoa forced to react*, INTERNATIONAL FINANCING REVIEW, Issue 1810, 27 May 2011 ('The upshot was that [Abengoa] was forced to react to investor feedback and include what was effectively a high-yield covenant package.').

27   *See* Danielle Myles, *Project bonds set to dominate*, INTERNATIONAL FINANCIAL LAW REVIEW, 24 March 2011 (discussing a proposal to address difficulties with respect to obtaining consents from bondholders and noting that in a multisource project financing that includes commercial bank debt and capital markets debt, 'if the bank debt accounts for a certain threshold then the bondholders' can be bound by the banks' decisions').

also has converged.[28] Indeed, it was reported that the pricing of the US$1.25bn project bond issued by Dolphin Energy Ltd in 2009 actually beat the pricing of the US$1.42bn commercial bank tranche raised by Dolphin Energy Ltd at the same time.[29]

The timing of a bond offering can have a significant impact on the success of such offering.[30] To obtain attractive pricing, it may be critical that the project is marketed to investors within a particular window of time, for example, during a period when the bond market has not been saturated by recent offerings of similar investments. This can prove challenging where project sponsors seek to close a capital markets offering simultaneously with other parts of a multisource project financing. As with coordinating a multisource project financing generally, this can be addressed through careful planning, coordination with advisors and management of the financing time line.

Finally, project bonds are securities that are capable of being traded in the capital markets. Transfer of commercial bank loans typically are subject to controls set forth in the relevant finance documents, including through the requirement of consent of the agent and sometimes the borrower. Governments have enacted securities laws intended to provide investors in securities with legal protection not provided to commercial lenders. Securities laws regulate who may buy securities, re-sales of securities and disclosure in offering documents. The securities laws that govern usually are those of the jurisdiction where the securities are offered and sold. Regardless of the applicable body of securities laws, the institutional investor market is focussed on one thing: adequate disclosure. Institutional investors typically require disclosure of all aspects of the project that may be considered 'material' to the investment. Disclosure is made through the preparation of a full offering memorandum, which is delivered to all potential investors several days before the management goes on a 'road show' to make in-person presentations to as many investors as it is able to meet. To avoid liability under certain securities laws, the offering memorandum must disclose all information material to an investor deciding whether to make an investment, as the potential investor does not have the ability (or inclination) to conduct an independent investigation into the project or its participants. In making their investment decisions, institutional investors are permitted to assume that all of the information disclosed to them in the offering memorandum and at road shows is correct and reflects complete information.[31] By contrast, reporting requirements for other key sources of debt addressed in this chapter generally are more limited as the commercial banks and ECAs supporting a project financing are able to conduct their own due diligence in assessing whether they will commit funds to a project. When including capital markets debt in a project's capital structure, it is essential that sponsors work

---

28   *See* Matthew Martin, *The resurrection of the Gulf bond market*, MEED, 23 July 2009 ('In the current market, bonds can also compete on price with traditional bank loans.').

29   When pricing is assessed over the respective base rates and the bank fees are included, the 'bond pricing was around 100 bps cheaper than the bank funding.' MEES, 3 August 2009.

30   *See* Danielle Myles, *Project bonds not limited to refinancings*, INTERNATIONAL FINANCIAL LAW REVIEW, 7 January 2011 ('Bond pricing is very volatile and bond markets can go away in a nanosecond....').

31   In the United States, Section 10(b) of the Securities Act of 1933 and Rule 10b-5 of the Securities Exchange Act of 1934 Rules provide a broad (and heavily litigated) basis for liability in securities transactions. Rule 10b-5 prohibits:
 • employing 'any device, scheme, or artifice to defraud';
 • making 'any untrue statement of material fact' or omitting 'to state a material fact necessary in order to make the statements made, in the light of the circumstances under which they were made, not misleading'; or
 • engaging in any 'act, practice, or course of business which operates or would operate as a fraud or deceit.' 17 C.F.R. § 240.10b5-1.

with experienced advisors to assist them to market a financing that is compliant with all relevant legal requirements.

ISLAMIC FINANCING INSTITUTIONS

General overview

Financing that is compliant with Islamic law, or Sharia, increasingly is being considered as a potential source of funds for a multisource project financing. Although Sharia-compliant financing has existed for centuries, only recently have Sharia-compliant structures been employed in the global banking sector.[32] Indeed, when credit markets tightened in response to the global economic downturn, sponsors of large infrastructure projects (especially in the Middle East) began to focus on Islamic finance as an alternative source of liquidity.[33] Given the resources of Islamic banks (which held an estimated US$250bn in assets in 2006)[34] and Muslim investors, Islamic finance can be an important funding source for sponsors to consider when structuring multisource project financings.[35]

Islamic finance products must comply with the following general principles:

1. Returns to financiers generally should be linked with the profits of an enterprise and derived from the commercial risk taken by the financier; Sharia views money as a means of exchange with no intrinsic value;
2. Sharia principles encourage financiers to become partners in the project and to share the profits and risk in the business instead of being pure creditors; profits should not be assured and therefore fixed returns on investment should not be guaranteed;
3. Transactions should be free from speculation or gambling (maisir); the prohibitions of Sharia usually do not extend to general commercial speculation as seen in most transactions, but aim to prevent speculation that may be considered gambling;
4. The existence of uncertainty (gharar) in a contract is prohibited; transactions where the price, time of delivery or the subject matter are not determined in advance may not be compliant with Sharia principles; and
5. Investments relating to alcohol, drugs, gambling or other activities prohibited (haraam) by Sharia are not permitted. [36]

As project financing is based on the revenues generated by a distinct project that generally are in industries that are not prohibited by Sharia law, both project sponsors and

---

32   See Christopher F. Richardson, *Islamic Finance Opportunities in the Oil and Gas Sector: An Introduction to an Emerging Field*, 42 TEXAS INTERNATIONAL LAW REVIEW, 119, 123 (2006–2007).

33   See Christopher G. Cross, Craig R. Nethercott, Harjaskaran Rai and Mohammed A. Al-Sheikh, *Islamic Project Finance*, PRACTICAL LAW COMPANY, *available at* http://finance.practicallaw.com/3-501-3312?q=islamic%20finance#a59612.

34   See Christopher F. Richardson, *Islamic Finance Opportunities in the Oil and Gas Sector: An Introduction to an Emerging Field*, 42 TEXAS INTERNATIONAL LAW REVIEW, 119, 123 (2006–2007).

35   See Heike Ruttgers, Mansur A. Noibi PhD, Jacques Bertran de Balanda and Foued Bourabiat, *Tifert: acid test for Islamic and conventionally-financed projects in North Africa*, INFRASTRUCTURE JOURNAL, 9 September 2009 ('The rapid growth of Islamic finance in [France, North Africa and Sub-Saharan Africa] and the huge estimated infrastructure investments anticipated in the MENA region will certainly see the rise of co-financings of the same or similar kind as the Tifert Project.'); Rahail Ali and Rustum Shah, *Square peg can fit a round hole*, PROJECT FINANCE MAGAZINE, 20 December 2004 ('In 2003 alone, Islamic financing accounted for 10% of the non or limited recourse infrastructure projects in the Middle East and North Africa.').

36   See Christopher G. Cross, Craig R. Nethercott, Harjaskaran Rai and Mohammed A. Al-Sheikh, *Islamic Project Finance*, PRACTICAL LAW COMPANY, *available at* http://finance.practicallaw.com/3-501-3312?q=islamic%20finance#a59612.

Sharia-compliant investors have recognized that project finance and Islamic finance are a good pairing.[37] There are various structures used for Islamic financings, some of which are analogous to capital markets offerings (Sukuk) and some of which employ financing terms consistent with conventional bank loans (Istisna'a and Ijara).[38] A key element of the most frequently used Sharia-compliant project financing structures is that the Islamic financiers generally are indirect owners of some of the underlying project assets, at least so long as the financing is in place.[39] Although the Islamic financiers may 'own' a portion of the assets in order to comply with Islamic finance principles, the financing structures employed in multisource project financings that have included a tranche of Sharia-compliant debt typically limit the returns payable to the Islamic financiers so that their return effectively mirrors the amounts paid to conventional lenders under the other tranches of debt. While the economics of Islamic finance and conventional finance may be managed easily, the ownership interest frequently required by Islamic financiers must be managed in the intercreditor and security arrangements when Islamic finance is combined with other conventional sources of debt to finance a single project.

Including Islamic financing in a multisource project financing

The obvious benefit of Islamic finance is that it allows sponsors to access a pool of capital that otherwise might be unavailable.[40] Islamic finance historically has been more expensive, and has had shorter tenors, than conventional debt. In recent years, however, Islamic financiers have become more cost competitive and have been able to offer Sharia-compliant products with tenors approaching those seen in the commercial bank market. As pricing and tenor available in the Islamic finance markets converges with the pricing and tenor available in the conventional financial market, Islamic finance may prove to be a competitive alternative for sponsors to consider.

One significant challenge faced by sponsors trying to structure a Sharia-compliant tranche of debt is that there is no settled Islamic jurisprudence. Accordingly, the interpretation as to what constitutes a Sharia-compliant structure varies from region to region, from country to country and even from bank to bank. Each Islamic financial institution has its own Sharia board or Sharia committee comprised of Sharia scholars. Each Sharia board sits independently and determines for itself whether a proposed structure is Sharia compliant. Therefore, sponsors may need to consult with multiple Islamic scholars when structuring a proposed Sharia-compliant financing before going to market with a

---

37   *See* Rahail Ali and Rustum Shah, *Square peg can fit a round hole*, PROJECT FINANCE MAGAZINE, 20 December 2004.

38   *See* Christopher G. Cross, Craig R. Nethercott, Harjaskaran Rai and Mohammed A. Al-Sheikh, *Islamic Project Finance*, PRACTICAL LAW COMPANY, *available at* http://finance.practicallaw.com/3-501-3312?q=islamic%20finance#a59612. Other Islamic project financing structures are the Murabaha and the Musharaka. *Id.* See Christopher G. Cross, Craig R. Nethercott, Harjaskaran Rai and Mohammed A. Al-Sheikh, *Islamic Project Finance*, PRACTICAL LAW COMPANY, *available at* http://finance.practicallaw.com/3-501-3312?q=islamic%20finance#a59612, for a description of common Islamic project-financing structures.

39   *See* Christopher G. Cross, Craig R. Nethercott, Harjaskaran Rai and Mohammed A. Al-Sheikh, *Islamic Project Finance*, PRACTICAL LAW COMPANY, *available at* http://finance.practicallaw.com/3-501-3312?q=islamic%20finance#a59612.

40   *See* Christopher F. Richardson, *Islamic Finance Opportunities in the Oil and Gas Sector: An Introduction to an Emerging Field*, 42 TEXAS INTERNATIONAL LAW REVIEW, 119, 122 (2006–2007).

transaction.[41] This is of particular importance as Islamic investors may require a fatwa (an opinion) issued by a Sharia board or committee confirming that the transaction is Sharia compliant prior to committing to make an investment in a particular project.[42]

The Istisna'a and Ijara structure that frequently has been used in project finance transactions is similar in structure to a conventional sale and leaseback arrangement pursuant to which the relevant assets are sold to the Islamic financiers and then leased back to project, with the project company often receiving an option to purchase the assets at the end of the term of the financing. While such structures are flexible and accommodate Sharia principles, the transfer of assets may have tax consequences that would not arise in a conventionally structured project financing.[43] Although some jurisdictions have implemented specific legislation to avoid such tax consequences,[44] sponsors should work with their tax advisors to identify and alleviate or minimise any such add-on tax duties when structuring a multisource project financing that includes Islamic financing.

Other structural challenges may arise when combining Islamic financing with conventional sources of debt to finance a single project as a result of the restriction on unjust enrichment that is imposed by Islamic law. For example, Islamic financiers are prohibited from earning interest on their investments.[45] While the amounts paid to Islamic financiers under the Islamic finance documents can be constructed in a Sharia-compliant manner that mirrors conventional terms, issues may arise if all of the project's funds are co-mingled in interest bearing project accounts. Depending on the flexibility of a project's other financiers, this can be dealt with by requiring the project to have only non-interest-bearing accounts or separate non-interest-bearing accounts from which Islamic financiers will be paid.[46]

SPONSOR SENIOR DEBT

A multisource project financing may permit sponsors to provide senior debt that is pari passu to the senior debt provided by other financiers (and secured on the same basis as

---

41   *See* Christopher F. Richardson, *Islamic Finance Opportunities in the Oil and Gas Sector: An Introduction to an Emerging Field*, 42 TEXAS INTERNATIONAL LAW REVIEW, 119, 124 (2006–2007).

42   *See* Ferzana Haq and Neil D Miller, *Islamic finance: key principles and recent developments*, PRACTICAL LAW COMPANY, *available at* http://www.practicallaw.com/9-504-3194?q=islamic%20finance.

43   *See* Heike Ruttgers, Mansur A. Noibi PhD, Jacques Bertran de Balanda and Foued Bourabiat, *Tifert: acid test for Islamic and conventionally-financed projects in North Africa*, INFRASTRUCTURE JOURNAL, 9 September 2009 (noting that in the Tifert financing (for a phosphoric acid plant in the south of Tunisia), the structure of the Islamic tranche, which involved acquisition of land by the Islamic financiers from the project company, transfer of the project assets to the Islamic financiers by the project company and sale of the Islamic assets back to the project company, would have triggered triple stamp duty if not for the fact that the Islamic financier was the Islamic Development Bank, which is a multilateral development bank and enjoys a tax exemption in Tunisia).

44   *See* Christopher G. Cross, Craig R. Nethercott, Harjaskaran Rai and Mohammed A. Al-Sheikh, *Islamic Project Finance*, PRACTICAL LAW COMPANY, *available at* http://finance.practicallaw.com/3-501-3312?q=islamic%20finance#a59612. *See also* Heike Ruttgers, Mansur A. Noibi, Jacques Bertran de Balanda and Foued Bourabiat, *Tifert: Acid Test for Islamic and Conventionally-Financed Projects in North America*, INFRASTRUCTURE JOURNAL, 9 September 2009 (noting that an adaptation of certain Tunisian tax legislation (which would result in triple stamp tax for Islamic financiers using common Islamic financing structures) is under consideration).

45   Christopher G. Cross, Craig R. Nethercott, Harjaskaran Rai and Mohammed A. Al-Sheikh, *Islamic Project Finance*, PRACTICAL LAW COMPANY, *available at* http://finance.practicallaw.com/3-501-3312?q=islamic%20finance#a59612.

46   Traditionally, the Islamic principle prohibiting speculation has been interpreted to extend to conventional insurance products. While there is a nascent market for Sharia-compliant insurance products, we are not aware of any multisource financing with an Islamic tranche that has included Sharia-compliant insurance.

such other debt). Such sponsor senior debt may be raised, amongst other reasons, to plug a financing 'gap' where it is not possible to obtain external financing for 100 per cent of the project's financing requirements. Notwithstanding that such sponsor senior debt ranks pari passu with other senior debt, and will share equally in the security granted to the senior creditors, sponsor senior lenders generally will be entitled to limited voting rights on intercreditor decisions.

Structuring and Documenting a Multisource Project Financing

The structuring and documentation of a multisource project financing inevitably gives rise to complexities that do not arise in a single source project financing. However, there are various ways that the intercreditor and other structural issues that arise from combining different sources of debt in one capital structure may be addressed in the finance documents.

In a conventionally-structured project financing that includes only commercial bank debt, the key finance documents typically are:

a) Loan agreement between the borrower and the commercial bank lenders; and
b) Security agreements between the borrower (and other entities providing security) and the commercial bank lenders (or an agent/trustee on their behalf), granting the commercial bank lenders security over relevant project and other assets.

In a multisource project financing, in addition to the agreements between the project financiers and the project sponsors and the borrower, the arrangements between different groups of financiers must be documented, typically in an intercreditor agreement. There often are also 'common' agreements to reflect terms that are applicable to all (or most) sources of debt. The terms contained in (and the names) of these common agreements will vary depending on the type of project (i.e., the industry or sector, geographic location, etc. of the relevant project) and a number of other factors. Set forth below is a brief, high-level overview of some of the key finance documents typically entered into as part of a multisource project financing, the purpose of each such agreement, the parties to it, and certain key terms likely to be included in it.

Common terms agreement[47]

A common terms agreement generally will be executed by the borrower, each of the project financiers (or their agents on their behalf) and the relevant agents and trustees for the financiers. The purpose of a common terms agreement is to set forth the terms that will apply to each of the different sources of funding comprised in the overall multisource project financing. Such common terms typically include common conditions precedent to funding, representations, warranties, covenants and events of default. Where a

---

47   In certain multisource project financings, some of the terms discussed herein may be included in other 'common' agreements such as a common security agreement.

multisource project financing includes a project bond issuance, the extent to which financing terms applicable to the bonds are the same as those applicable to the other sources of debt will vary from deal to deal. As noted above, in some transactions, the project bonds will be subject to all of the same terms and conditions as the other sources of debt. In those transactions, the bond trustee typically will accede to the relevant common agreements on behalf of all bondholders. In other transactions, the project bonds may be subject only to a sub-set of the otherwise common conditions – such as certain terms and conditions relating to the intercreditor arrangements and the shared security package. In those transactions, the documentation may be structured so that the bond trustee accedes only to certain of the common agreements.

Separate facility agreements, indenture and Islamic financing documentation

In addition to the common terms agreement, financiers providing each tranche of debt included within a multisource project financing may enter into separate agreements with the borrower. In the case of commercial banks, ECAs and senior sponsor debt providers, each group of lenders typically will enter into a separate facility agreement with the borrower. Project bondholders and their trustee will enter into an indenture. With respect to Islamic facilities, the documentation will vary depending on the nature of the relevant Sharia-compliant finance product. Each such agreement will set out terms that are relevant to, or required by, only the specific financiers party to that agreement. Such items are in addition to the terms and conditions set out in the common agreements and may include specific additional representations, warranties, covenants, conditions precedent to availability of funding and/or events of default. Examples of such items applicable to certain specific sources of funding include:

ECA facilities

If an ECA is providing tied funding, such ECA typically will require evidence of the procurement to which funding is tied as an additional condition to disbursement of its facility. If an ECA is lending (or providing credit support) for other policy-related reasons (such as supporting imports of natural resources to the ECA's home nation), such ECA may require particular conditions (such as specific events of default or mandatory prepayment obligations) to apply to its facility should the basis for such support no longer apply at any time (e.g., the project no longer will be providing such natural resources to the ECA's home nation, or if a sponsor from the ECA's home country no longer has equity in the project or certain key management functions). ECAs also may require additional representations, warranties, covenants, conditions precedent to availability of funding and/or events of default to satisfy their internal governance rules.[48]

---

48   For an example of such requirements, see http://www.exim.gov/products/guarantee/ebd-p-01.cfm, which sets forth some of the conditions to obtaining a project finance loan from US Exim. US Exim will require certain representations, warranties, covenants, conditions precedent and events of default in its direct loan agreement to ensure that these internal requirements are satisfied by the projects to which it makes direct loans.

Project bonds

Bondholders often do not require additional tranche-specific conditions (in part due to the less active role bondholders take in managing the debt following financial close). However, a number of bondholder specific items not addressed in the common agreements typically are addressed in the bond indenture and related documents (e.g., the terms of the bonds themselves, or the requirements for the purchase agreement with the bond underwriters).

Islamic financing

The documents for an Islamic financing tranche typically will include provisions that have a similar effect to those included in the facility agreements for the other forms of financing. However, certain important differences will be reflected in the Islamic financing documentation to reflect the structure of the relevant Sharia-compliant finance product. As use of Islamic financing in multisource project financings has become more common, there now are numerous precedents for combining Islamic and conventional forms of financing in the capital structure for a single project and therefore many of the structural issues resulting from such combination (some of which are mentioned above) now have commonly applied solutions.

Intercreditor agreement

The intercreditor agreement is central to any multisource project financing. This agreement documents the relationship between the financiers providing all relevant sources of funding, including arrangements with respect to voting on consent, modification or waiver requests and decisions with respect to acceleration of debt and enforcement of security. The parties to the intercreditor agreement typically will include each of the project's financiers (or their agents on their behalf), the common security trustee, the intercreditor agent and the other relevant agents and trustees (including entities such as the accounts banks).

In a multisource project financing, the intercreditor agreement can be used to address items such as voting by individual creditor groups. As noted above, such agreements frequently contain mechanics that act as proxies for bondholder action where a capital structure includes both commercial bank debt and project bonds. This is so that an issuer will have the same flexibility to obtain waivers and consents for anything other than the most fundamental matters (such as releasing security or changing debt maturities or interest rates) as would have been the case if the financing consisted only of a commercial bank tranche (and therefore without the need separately to approach the bondholders for approval). For example, in such a multisource financing the intercreditor provisions may provide that so long as commercial bank loans and ECA supported debt exceeds an agreed threshold (for example, 25 per cent of total project debt), bank lender approval of waivers (other than in respect of agreed fundamental decisions) also will be binding on bondholders. In other cases, the intercreditor provisions may provide that bondholder consent will not be required for certain actions if an appropriate and agreed third party consultant confirms that such amendment or waiver will not materially or adversely affect the bondholders, or if the relevant rating agencies rating the bonds issued by the relevant project confirm that they would reaffirm the debt rating of such bonds if the proposed amendment or waiver were effected. This is beneficial to the project sponsors because, as noted above, it can be extremely difficult to seek votes from potentially large and disparate groups of bondholders.

In a multisource project financing that includes an Islamic tranche, the intercreditor agreement also will set forth the terms governing the relationship between the Islamic financiers and each of the other financiers to the project. Special provisions are required to address issues specific to an Islamic facility such as the Islamic financiers' ownership of the assets they finance. As such an ownership interest (a) is inconsistent with the principles of a multisource project financing where all financiers otherwise do not own the financed assets but share in the security provided by all relevant entities in such assets, and (b) otherwise may provide Islamic financiers with a preferential interest in the relevant assets that they finance and own (in essence, structurally subordinating the other lenders that expect pari passu treatment), the intercreditor arrangements may require the Islamic financiers to grant to the security trustee (for the benefit of all financiers) a security interest in such assets. Consistent with such approach of seeking to treat such assets as part of the general collateral pool for a multisource project financing that includes an Islamic tranche, the Islamic financiers also may be restricted under the intercreditor arrangements from creating any other security interest or third party interest in such assets or from selling, leasing, transferring or otherwise disposing of such assets. The intercreditor agreement also may include a requirement that the Islamic financiers follow the instructions of the security trustee with respect to transferring such assets in connection with any exercise of remedies by all financiers participating in the multisource project financing.

Conclusion

The constantly growing global demand for, and increasing size of, infrastructure and industrial development projects, together with other factors such as the impacts of the global financial crisis on the debt capacity of commercial banks, among other things, has led to the increased use of multisource project financing. The capital cost of certain large-scale infrastructure and industrial projects, together with a variety of external factors, has contributed to the increased use of multisource project financing structures by sponsors that require a fully funded capital plan. However, even for projects that could rely on a single source of debt to meet their capital requirements, there are benefits associated with including multiple sources of funding in a single project financing that also have contributed to increased use of such financing structures. Such benefits include the creation of competition in the marketplace amongst alternative sources of finance in order to obtain the best possible terms from each source of debt used to fund a particular project. In order to obtain and maximize such benefits, there are key considerations for sponsors in selecting which sources of debt to include in a multisource project financing, including structuring, security and intercreditor implications. Although structuring and documenting a multisource project financing may result in complexities that would not arise in a single source financing, with careful planning from the early development stages of a project, the possibility of additional complexity need not deter sponsors from seeking multisource project financing and enjoying the benefits that can be derived from combining multiple sources of debt to fund a single project.

5

The Role and Impact of Export Credit Agencies in Project Finance

TERRY NEWENDORP, JOHN SACHS and JENNIFER HARA
Taylor-DeJongh

The value of export credit agency (ECA) support in international project finance soared in the mid-1990s with the rapid growth of private power investments (IPPs) in the emerging markets. As private developers ventured to build independent power plants in places such as Pakistan, the Philippines, Turkey, India, Colombia and elsewhere, ECA political risk cover was vital for mobilizing capital and for keeping the cost of capital at a level that produced manageable tariffs for the emerging economies. Since 1994, ECAs have provided over US$17bn, as of June 2011, in debt financing, risk mitigation cover and other enhancements for power generation projects globally. But the impact of ECAs was not confined to IPPs. ECAs have also been major catalysts for mobilizing capital for large oil, gas and pipeline projects, such as Qatargas, Ras Laffan, Oman LNG, Nigeria LNG and the BTC pipeline. Since 1996, ECAs have provided US$7.7bn of debt for seven liquefied natural gas (LNG) facilities, both liquefaction and receiving terminals. That financing leveraged an additional US$12.4bn in capital for these LNG projects. ECAs have also provided substantial capacity in the telecoms market, in countries such as the Philippines, India and Kazakhstan. Of the US$22.7bn in financing raised for telecom projects from 1995 to 2005, US$7bn was supported by ECAs.

The range of tools ECAs can bring to bear in project finance transactions includes political risk insurance (PRI), guarantees for commercial debt, and direct lending. Using these financial instruments, ECAs provide both political risk and commercial credit risk coverage that mobilizes commercial bank capacity in many markets. Even where political and credit risk are not a major issue, ECAs can bring additional debt capacity in highly rated markets, such as Qatar and Australia. The industry sectors most benefitted by these instruments include those with the largest capital requirements: LNG, telecoms, petrochemicals, mining and power (both conventional and renewable).

How ECAs Work

TERMS ON OFFER: OECD CONSENSUS

ECAs from OECD countries adhere to a set of guidelines (called the 'OECD Arrangement' or the 'Arrangement'), which is a 'gentlemen's agreement' setting out the most generous export credit terms and conditions that may be provided in respect of the financing of exported goods and services. The key rules as part of the Arrangement include guidelines concerning:

a) size of down payment;
b) local costs;
c) maximum credit terms;
d) other terms and conditions of repayment;
e) minimum interest rates (CIRR) for direct lending;
f) minimum premiums for political risk; and
g) aid-related credits.

Key OECD Arrangement terms for project financing (as of the March 2011 update) are set out below:[1]

- Participating ECAs can cover:
  - Up to 85 per cent of export contract value
  - Local costs up to 30 per cent of export contract value.
- Maximum repayment term of 14 years.[2]
- Weighted average life of the repayment term must be less than or equal to 7.25 years.
- Grace period up to 24 months.
- Capitalization of interest and exposure fees during construction.

Each ECA has its own interpretation of the OECD Arrangement, particularly with respect to the definition of the export contract value. Consequently, for a given export contract value, one ECA may be able to provide a greater level of support than another.

A worked example of an ECA financing under the OECD Arrangement is set out below (Figure 5.1). The project costs US$150, of which US$100 is the value of goods and services exported from the ECA's home country. Local costs are US$50 and financing costs (interest during construction and exposure fees) are US$20. The ECA would be able to cover 85 per cent of the export contract value (US$85), plus local costs up to 30 per cent of the export contract value (minimum of US$50 and US$100*30 per cent, or $30), plus financing costs ($20), for a total of US$135.

There are four main 'models' or groups of ECAs globally - European, North American, Asian and Australia. Each member of each group generally has its own interpretation of the OECD Agreement. Short descriptions of some of the most active are described below.

---

1   OECD Arrangement terms are for emerging market projects. Different terms apply for projects in high income countries.

2   Certain sectors qualify for extended tenors (beyond 14 years). Renewable Energy transactions, for instance, qualify for 18-year tenors.

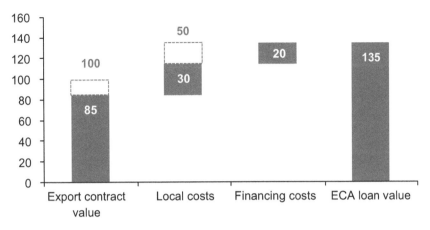

Figure 5.1   Simplified ECA financing model

Source: Taylor-DeJongh

Europe

GERMANY

Euler Hermes is the export credit agency in Germany, and manages the export credit guarantee scheme on behalf of the German government. The Group is 100 per cent privately owned with Allianz as the majority stockholder.

Euler Hermes provides a range of tools that covers the various types of export transactions. It reported a record covered export volume of €32.5bn in 2010, with most of the policies directed towards the aircraft sector. Pertaining to project finance, 2010 also marked an unprecedented year in the number of approved deals. Seven project finance deals were granted cover with a total value of €3.2bn. Besides assuming a €1.8bn cover for the German portion of exports in building a pipeline from Russia to Germany, the remaining projects were in the Middle East. The demand for Hermes cover for project finance deals continued in 2011, as 13 applications valued at €4bn were received at the onset of the year. In addition to transport and infrastructure, Euler Hermes seeks to increasingly focus on power generation projects.

ITALY

SACE SpA, Italy's export credit agency, is one of the most active ECAs globally in project finance, with an average annual project financing volume of US$1bn to US$1.5bn. At year-end 2010, project finance represented approximately 20 per cent of SACE's guarantee portfolio by value. Capital-intensive projects across the entire oil and gas value chain have consistently included an element of Italian procurement, either at the contractor or supplier level, and that procurement is often supported by the SACE buyer's credit programme. SACE is 100 per cent owned by the Ministry of Economy and Finance, and its commitments are guaranteed by the Republic of Italy.

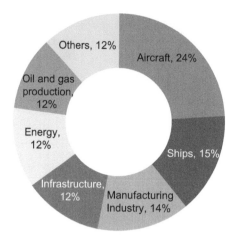

Figure 5.2   Single transaction policies by industrial sector (€m)

Source: Export Credit Guarantee of the Federal Republic of Germany, Annual Report 2010

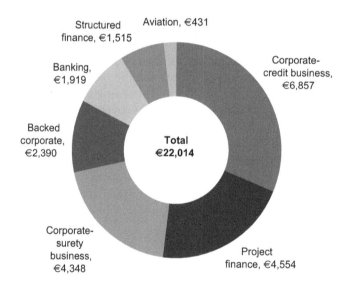

Figure 5.3   SACE guarantee portfolio (€m)

Source: SACE, Annual Report 2010

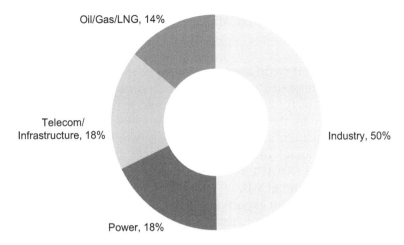

Figure 5.4   COFACE project finance portfolio sector breakdown (€m)

Source: COFACE, Project Finance Activity, November 2011

SACE typically supports project finance transactions through the provision of a guarantee or insurance product for the benefit of commercial banks lending to the project (or bondholders in the case of a project bond). SACE can provide up to 100 per cent coverage against commercial and political risks both for guarantees and for insurance products. The level of coverage can be adjusted to optimize financing costs for the borrower.

The level of SACE support is up to 85 per cent of the value of the contract entered into by the project company and Italian exporters (or joint ventures including Italian companies). In practice, SACE may allow the borrower to borrow against the value of third country procurement (that is procurement neither from Italy nor from the project's home country), provided that such procurement falls within the Italian company's contract scope (and further that SACE support for third country procurement and local content does not exceed its support for Italian procurement). SACE is also able to finance local costs, interest during construction, and exposure premia as per the OECD Agreement. The overall level of Italian procurement and the involvement of Italian sponsors are important factors in determining the level of support that SACE may provide. In addition, for those projects it deems 'strategic,' SACE may be able to extend its level of support.

SACE also offers direct loans in addition to guarantees and insurance products. As an alternative to a SACE guarantee or insurance policy, a borrower may also request a direct loan, which is provided by the Cassa Depositi e Prestiti (CDP), a financing institution 70 per cent owned by the Government of Italy (with the remainder held by a broad group of banks). CDP is able to lend both to the project directly or to provide funding to financial institutions to lend to the project. In practice, the pricing of CDP tends to relatively high (particularly in USD), and it should be considered as an option primarily where the commercial bank capacity is constrained such as in a credit crunch.

FRANCE – THE COMPAGNIE FRANCAISE D'ASSURANCE POUR LE COMMERCE EXTERIEUR (COFACE)

COFACE is the French export credit agency. Founded in 1946 by the French government, it was subsequently privatized in 1994 and is currently owned by the bank group Natixis. In addition to its private sector activities, COFACE also manages export guarantees and other safeguards provided by the French government, designed to promote and support French exports in the medium and long-term (credit over two years). COFACE is paid by the government to manage these procedures, under an agreement, renewed every four years. For several years COFACE's three main co-financing partners have been Euler-Hermes of Germany, SACE and ECGD.

COFACE offers guarantees for exports in foreign currencies, particularly to SMEs, and covers up to 85 per cent of the risk of French exporters defaulting on bonds. In addition, it provides export credit insurance to cover exporters or banks against manufacturing and credit risk in large-scale international project contracts over two years. The value of the contracts covered by COFACE's export credit insurance was €14.9 billion in 2010. The main industry sectors were aeronautics and space, followed by defence and energy.

UK

The Export Credits Guarantee Department (ECGD), the UK's export credit agency is a government department that operates under an act of Parliament, in accordance with financial objectives set by HM Treasury. The ECGD is required by the UK government to operate on a slightly better than break-even basis, charging exporters premia at levels that match the perceived risks and costs in each case.

For lending banks, ECGD provides guarantees rather than insurance. ECGD normally guarantees the financing bank 100 per cent of the loan value and accrued interest. For project sponsors ECGD may be able to provide interest rate support to banks so that bank loans to sponsors can attract officially supported fixed rates of interest. Minimum project size is normally £20m.

Between 2010 and 2011, ECGD supported exports and investments through the issue or renewal of guarantees and insurance policies with an aggregate value of £2.92 billion: Buyer Credit and Supplier Credit financing accounted for £2.86 billion, Supplier Credit Insurance for £21 million, and Overseas Investment Insurance (OII) business for £42 million. This represented a 33 per cent increase on the level of business supported in 2009–2010, with activities in 32 countries spread over 192 guarantees and insurance policies.

ECGD has not been a significant participant in the project finance market in recent years, in large measure due to their strict adherence to the export promotion model. Their recent activity has been primarily linked to aircraft financing, with 61 per cent of financing allocated to this industry sector. However, there has been a recent increase in support for projects in various non-aerospace sectors, including: construction, oil and gas, power, healthcare, water treatment, petrochemicals, industrial processing, satellites and automotives. The wider range of business sectors reflects the rise in demand for official credit support due to reduced lending from commercial banks and the capital markets.

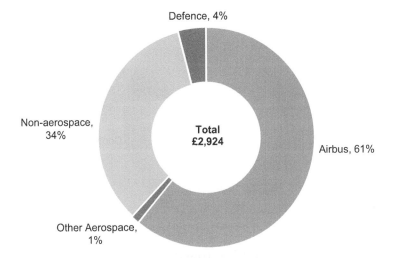

Figure 5.5   ECGD value of business supported by sector (£m)

Source: ECGD, Annual Report and Accounts 2010–2011

North America

UNITED STATES

The Export-Import Bank of the United States (US Ex-Im Bank or Ex-Im) is the official export credit agency of the US. Its stated goal is to supplement and encourage, and not compete with, commercial financing. In 2011, Ex-Im authorized a record $32.7bn to support US exports, marking a 34 per cent increase from the previous fiscal year. Some of the industries of focus were aircraft, oil and gas, power generation, construction, and a range of specialized services. The record year was driven by the increase in authorizations of goods and services towards emerging markets.

The project finance division of US. Ex-Im was created in 1994 and was immediately one of the most prolific project finance leaders for IPPs, LNG and mining ventures in the 1990s. US Ex-Im Bank offers both direct loans and guarantees of loans made by commercial banks and bonds, up to 85 per cent of the total export value from US suppliers. Direct loans are extended to the foreign buyer, not to the US exporter. Loan guarantees are provided to banks financing the export sales of a US supplier. In all cases, US. Ex-Im Bank requires a 'reasonable assurance of repayment,' which in the Structured and Project Finance programme is translated as a 'shadow rating' for a project of investment grade. US Ex-Im has a well-defined process for application, review and negotiation of project finance loans. The process involves the submittal of a commercially and technically complete information package, which is taken on as a formal application. Following a preliminary review by internal staff, US Ex-Im proceeds to select an external financial advisor to assist in expediting the commercial and financial analysis of the project. If lenders' engineers and legal counsel have not yet been agreed, then US Ex-Im also selects these advisors. These advisors work for the benefit of US Ex-Im throughout the review and approval process, but their costs are paid by the applicant.

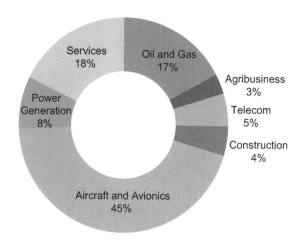

Figure 5.6   US Ex-Im Bank FY 2011 Authorizations in Key Industries ($m)

Source: Ex-Im, 2100 Annual Report

Within 45 days of the acceptance of the application and finalization of financial, technical and legal advisors, US Ex-Im will issue a Preliminary Project Letter (PPL) that encompasses the initial evaluation of issues identified, willingness of US Ex-Im to proceed with the transaction, and terms and conditions of a financing offer. Following the PPL, the applicant and its advisors will engage in a typical project financing negotiation process for term sheets, security package, financing agreement, and related project documentation. US Ex-Im is a strict adherent to the OECD Agreement guidelines with maximum average loan-life of 7.25 years and a maximum tenor of 14 years, with additional beneficial terms for renewable energy and environmental exports. Transaction fees are also part of the cost of the loan; and an exposure fee is based on the risk profile of the host country, the type of borrower or guarantor and the repayment term. On a loan guarantee, a commitment fee of 0.125 per cent per annum is charged on the undisbursed balance.

CANADA

Export Development Canada (EDC), a Crown corporation wholly owned by the Government of Canada, operates on commercial principles and is self-funding. EDC's portfolio in 2010, which had a total business volume of C$84.6bn, was focused primarily on three major sectors: aerospace, extractive industries, and infrastructure. It is highly concentrated in the North America/Caribbean region, with almost two-thirds of its loan exposure in it.

EDC is unique in that the majority of the support it provides is through its 'market window' programme. Under a market window programme, an ECA provides support on market terms (as opposed to OECD Arrangement terms). As a consequence, tenor and pricing can be from terms which would be available under a tied financing. Eligibility requirements may be less stringent under market window than under an OECD

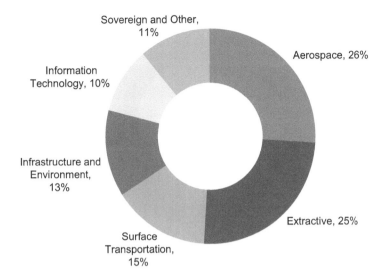

Figure 5.7   EDC total loans and exposure guarantee by sector (Cbn)

Source: EDC Investor Presentation

Arrangement financing. For example, EDC will consider a project under its market window programme based on the potential for the project to generate economic benefit to Canada. Under an OECD Arrangement financing, eligibility would rest on the inclusion of defined Canadian procurement.

EDC is not the only government-owned institution to operate a market window programme; for example, KfW (German development bank) and SACE can provide market window financing.

Asia

JAPAN

Japan has two leading government institutions designed to provide support to exports and investments by Japanese companies, the Japan Bank for International Cooperation (JBIC) and Nippon Export and Investment Insurance (NEXI). JBIC is a government agency, established in 1999 through the merger of the Export and Import Bank of Japan (JEXIM) and Overseas Economic Cooperation Fund (OECF). NEXI is also government owned and was established in 2001, assuming the insurance services operated by the Japanese government (Ministry of Economy and Trade and Industry, METI).

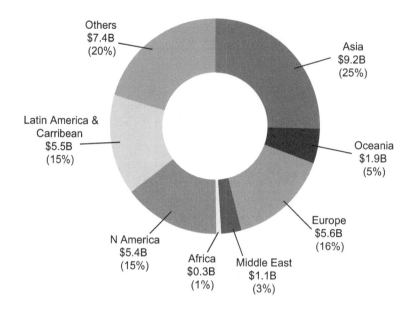

Figure 5.8a JBIC 2009

Source: Taylor-Dejongh and JBIC, 2010 Annual Report

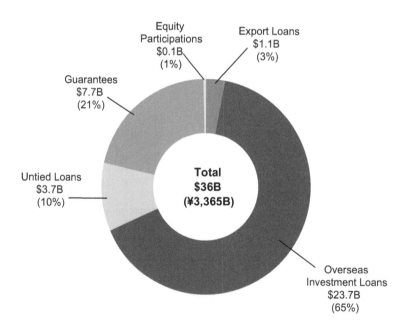

Figure 5.8b JBIC 2009 commitments by purpose of financing

Source: Taylor-Dejongh and JBIC, 2010 Annual Report

Commitments by Region

Between the two agencies, they offer a menu of financial products relevant to typical export and project finance transactions. In addition to the classical trade insurance, buyer's credit and buyer's credit insurance common with other ECAs, JBIC and NEXI offer a number of flexible, untied products suitable for project finance transactions including: the Overseas Investment Credit (OIC); the Energy Natural Resources Finance (ENRF) loan, and an Untied Guarantee in the case of JBIC; and an Overseas Untied Loan Insurance and Investment and Loan Insurance for Natural Resources and Energy projects in the case of NEXI.

JBIC/NEXI's untied support has several unique features related to its flexibility for borrowers, and the long tenors and competitive pricing. The proceeds of the untied loans do not have to be 'tied' to exports from Japan, are not bound by OECD Agreement guidelines for tenor, interest rate, repayment schedule, down payment, etc. As a result, utilizing the Japanese agencies and their untied products may enable sponsors to raise financing for longer tenors than normally available from tied financings or commercial banks.

Table 5.1   JBIC's Energy and Natural Resources – Untied Loan Programme

Advantages of ENRF

Lending capacity
  • Multi-billion dollar facility from single source
  • Can finance up to 70 per cent of the total required debt needed (co-financing with other commercial banks)
Longer tenor and repayment
  • Tenors up to 15-20 years
  • Flexible repayment schedule
Interest rate
  • More competitive than any banks
  • Most favourable among JBIC facilities

Unique conditions

Energy and Natural Resources Must Benefit Japan (examples)
  • Direct control of off-take right by Japanese firm
  • Indirect benefit through swap arrangements may be possible
  • Direct import to Japan
Japanese Involvement (examples)
  • Substantial equity interest project
  • EPC contracts
  • Operation and Maintenance contracts

Both JBIC and NEXI place a high degree of importance on the direct or indirect benefit to Japan. While the support can be untied to direct exports of Japanese goods and services, there must be a clear benefit to Japan or Japanese companies. This may come in the form of one or a combination of the following: equity participation of Japanese companies in the project company (borrower); feedstock supplier; natural resource off-take; future investment from Japan; EPC; end-user; etc. In addition, the project seeking the untied financing needs to be a new or on-going project, and not a refinancing of existing project debt, and satisfy the typical environmental due diligence requirements.

SOUTH KOREA

Established in 1976 under the Export-Import Bank of Korea Act as its national export credit agency, Korea Export-Import Bank's (KEXIM) primary services include export loans, trade finance and guarantee programmes to support the international business development of Korean companies. In addition, KEXIM provides overseas investment credit and import credit. The Korea Trade Insurance Corporation (K-sure), the other official ECA of South Korea, also provides various types of credit insurance and guarantees. Established in 1992, K-sure operates under the Ministry of Knowledge and Economy.

While KEXIM provides many of the traditional ECA products and complies with the OECD Arrangement governing the terms thereof, it also provides more flexible untied Overseas Investment Financing and in particular the increasingly important Natural Resources Development Financing (NRDF) product. These provide project sponsors with sources of flexible financing, long tenors and very competitive pricing, exceeding that which might be found under tied ECA lending or conventional commercial bank lending.

KEXIM has a mandate to promote the Korean national economy and enhance international cooperation through the provision of financial support for the development of overseas natural resources. Since 1979 (KEXIM's first overseas natural resources development project), KEXIM has been supporting the development of natural resources projects and its support has been accelerating in recent years.

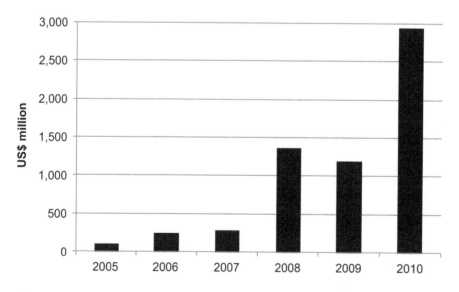

Figure 5.9   KEXIM loan disbursements for natural resource development

Source: KEXIM

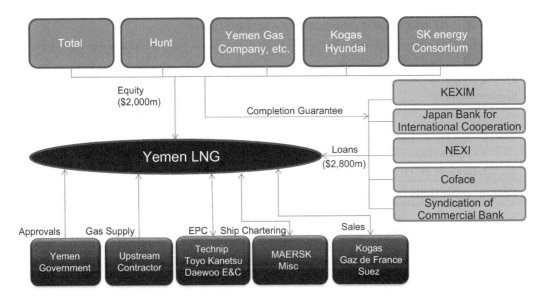

Figure 5.10 Yemen LNG project

Source: Taylor-DeJongh

KEXIM can provide NRDF to Korean companies or to foreign companies in the natural resources industry in which a Korean company has an equity share or an off-take contract. Under NRDF, KEXIM typically requires that there be a contractual connection between the borrower and the participating Korean company.

An example of KEXIM's financial support for large-scale energy and infrastructure projects is its role in the Yemen LNG project. The project included shareholders from Korea, off-take to Korea, as well as a package of loans and guarantees from KEXIM. On Yemen LNG, KEXIM provided funds totalling US$400m split between a direct loan of US$240m and a US$160m insured tranche.

The finance package was designed in part to significantly help secure LNG, an important source of energy in Korea, and further promote Korean companies' participation in natural resources projects and plant projects in the Middle East.

K-sure also provides support for investments and resource development projects. In 2010, K-sure supported project financing of USD 1 billion for the Jubail Refinery and Petrochemical project in Saudi Arabia and USD 890 million for the Jurong Petrochemical complex in Singapore. K-sure expanded its co-financing capabilities with other ECAs and covered local currency loans for the Korean companies involved in these projects.

K-sure's Medium and Long-Term (MLT) Insurance products are financial (MLT Export Credit Insurance, Overseas Business Financing Insurance, Export Bond Insurance, Interest Rate Risk Insurance), which support financing needed for the export of capital goods or EPC projects abroad and insurance (Overseas Construction Works Insurance, Overseas Investment Insurance, Service Export Credit Insurance), which covers risks related to export receivables and overseas investments.

Table 5.2   KEXIM's NRDF programme – Untied loans

Eligibility
Korean company or foreign company with Korean shareholder or at least long-term off-take by Korean company. Sectors: • Agricultural development projects • Forest resources development projects • Gas, oil and mining – all stages
Unique conditions
Borrower: • Korean company • Foreign company with Korean company as shareholder or long-term off-take with Korean company • Foreign governments or companies which make co-investments in a foreign company with a Korean company Repayment: • Maximum term of 30 years and grace period of seven years. (If KEXIM support is based on an offtake contract, then repayment will be bound by the term of the offtake contract.) Coverage: • Up to 100 per cent of the funds required for the project. • Either direct loan or direct loan and guarantee (the guarantee is limited to 45 per cent of total KEXIM support)

CHINA

The Export-Import Bank of China (CEXIM), founded in 1994, has a mandate that includes: facilitating the export and import of key products, equipment and technologies; assisting Chinese companies in their investments, projects and contracts abroad; and promoting China's relationships and trade with other countries.

Like other ECAs, CEXIM offers tied financial products including export buyer's/seller's credit, loans and guarantees, structured finance, trade finance, and transport finance; as well as untied products, such as loans to overseas investment projects. Some of CEXIM's programmes require the borrower to obtain export credit insurance from the China Export and Credit Insurance Corporation (Sinosure) depending on the level of risk exposure of each project.

China's rapid export-driven growth in the past decade has fuelled an expansion of CEXIM's export financing activities. This is demonstrated by the growth in export buyer's credit (illustrated in the Figure 5.11), which has grown from US$1.9bn in 2006 to US$4.9bn in 2010, reflecting an annual growth rate of 27 per cent. Other financing products reflect a similar growth trajectory.

Although CEXIM generally follows the OECD Arrangement for its Export Buyer's Credit operations, China is not a member country of OECD and may lend outside of

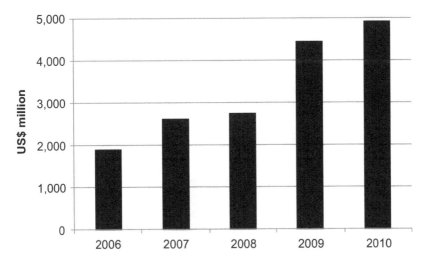

Figure 5.11 China Export-Import Bank disbursements of export buyer's credit

Source: China Ex-Im Bank, Annual Report for 2010

internationally agreed-upon terms and conditions. As a result, the involvement of Chinese components in a project could potentially bring more favourable financing terms, such as longer tenor and reduced costs, compared to those following the OECD Arrangement.

In January 2011, the US Ex-Im Bank, for the first time, agreed to offer financing outside the OECD guidelines to match those of CEXIM for a US$500m rail project which will supply 150 locomotives to Pakistan. US Ex-Im has also urged a dialogue among OECD ECAs to be initiated in order to 'enforce rules against state-created advantages.'[3] This suggests that CEXIM could face increased pressure to comply fully with the OECD Arrangement.

AUSTRALIA

Export Finance and Insurance Corporation (EFIC), Australia's export credit agency, provides finance and insurance services to Australian companies exporting and investing overseas, as well as to foreign companies or projects importing Australian goods and services. EFIC also works closely with commercial financiers in Australia and overseas to support exporters. As with most ECAs, EFIC does not seek to compete directly with the commercial bank market, but to provide complementary capacity to enhance the competitiveness of Australian companies.

In 2011, EFIC entered into over 100 facilities under the Commercial Account worth $593 million, covering exports or contracts worth nearly $3.5 billion. The main sectors were construction, shipbuilding, and wholesale trade.

---

3   'How the US Can Lead the World in Exports: Retooling Our Export Finance Strategy for the 21st Century,' speech by Fred P. Hochberg, Chairman and President of the Export-Import Bank of the United States. June 15, 2011. http://www.exim.gov/about/leadership/hochberg_20110615.cfm.

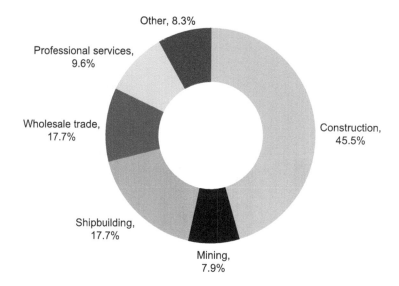

Figure 5.12 EFIC Signings by industry sector supported (AUS$m)

Source: EFIC, Annual Report, 2011

EFIC provides a range of medium to long-term financing facilities to Australian companies exporting or investing overseas. These facilities include loans, guarantees, bonds and insurance products. EFIC generally works on a self-funded basis and when providing loans or guarantees it writes transactions using funds from its commercial account (although all the operations of EFIC are effectively guaranteed by the Government of Australia, which accounts for their AAA credit rating and low cost of funds).

For major projects deemed to be in the national interest, where the size or risk exceeds EFIC's commercial parameters, the Government of Australia may provide additional support through the Ministry of Trade. This support is written to the government's National Interest Account (NIA), whose day-to-day business is managed by EFIC.

A recent example of the use of the NIA is the US$350m 17-year term loan that EFIC provided for the PNG LNG project financing, and which comprised US$100m from EFIC's Commercial Account and US$250m from the National Interest Account.

EFIC is bound by the OECD Agreement, but interprets its mission to support of Australian exporters broadly. For example, its rationale for participating in the PNG LNG project was 'to support Australian exporters in pursuing contracts for the construction phase of the project,' although there was no specifically identified export contract.

Similarly, EFIC is expected to participate in the financing of the current slate of proposed CBM to LNG projects in Queensland, although there will be (by definition) no exports from Australian companies. In these cases, the rationale for EFIC's participation is to support the export of natural resources, and the incremental foreign currency earnings.

The current law governing EFIC's role does not allow it to provide direct loans for projects in Australia (e.g., the CBM to LNG projects), and so its participation would be by way of guarantees. Amending legislation has been drafted to allow EFIC to lend domestically, but has yet to be enacted.

Recent significant project financings supported by EFIC include:

- Papua New Guinea LNG (2009) – US$350m 17-year direct loan.
- Abu Dhabi Aluminium Smelter, Emirates Aluminium (2007) – US$125m 16-year direct loan.
- Lumwana Copper Project (2007) – participation in US$173m 7-year direct loan.
- North Luzon Expressway Refinancing (2006) – US$15m 7-year, 7-month direct loan.
- Kwale Titanium Mineral Sands (2006) – US$180m in loan guarantees (political risk insurance).

Typical ECA Project Finance Structures

TIED FINANCING

'Tied financing' is financing cover from an ECA that is tied to the exports from its home country. ECAs charge a premium (paid upfront or during the construction period and financeable) for the commercial and/or political risks associated with the loan. A key factor in determining the level of premium charged is the country risk of the project.

Figure 5.13 shows the basic structure of a tied financing. The ECA from 'Country X' provides a guarantee to a commercial bank lending to the project on the basis of an EPC contract with a contractor from Country X. In practice, the basis on which the ECA can provide financing support will not be tied to the EPC contract 'headline value,' but rather to the goods and services procured under the EPC contract. In this case, Country X ECA would be able to provide financing on the back of goods and services procured from Country X under the EPC contract, but not goods and services procured from 'Country Y'.

The insurance or guarantee can be 'comprehensive,' which covers commercial risk as well as political risk, or political risk only. In large projects, some banks may also participate with loans that are not covered by an ECA. An example is shown in Figure 5.14.

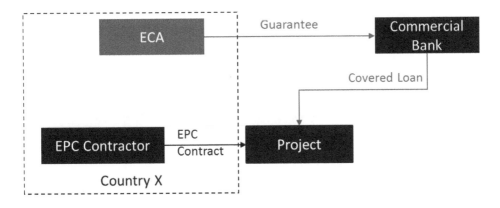

Figure 5.13 ECA tied financing structure

Source: Taylor-DeJongh

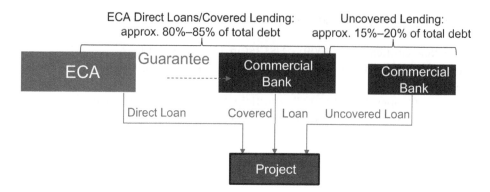

Figure 5.14 ECA financing structure

Source: Taylor-DeJongh

'UNTIED' FINANCING

Certain ECAs can also provide 'untied financing,' that is, financing which is not tied to procurement of home country goods and services. This type of financing is often linked to equity investments by companies from the ECA's home country or import of natural resources to the ECA's home country, or even the prospect of increasing future exports for the home country. Asian country ECAs – such as JBIC and KEXIM – routinely provide financing on the back of imports of natural resources.

Figure 5.15 sets out an indicative untied financing structure. On the left, Country X ECA provides financing on the back of a project investment by a sponsor from Country X. On the right, Country Y ECA provides financing on the back of an offtake agreement with a buyer from Country Y. Under an untied financing, the ECAs are not required to

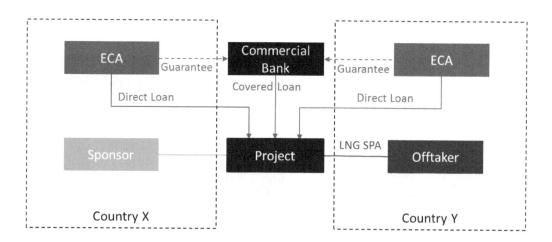

Figure 5.15 ECA financing through offtake and project investment

Source: Taylor-DeJongh

abide by the OECD Arrangement. However, when participating in a financing that also includes tied financing, an ECA providing untied financing often aligns itself with the other ECAs with respect to the major financing terms, including tenor and grace period. The process by which an ECA determines the amount of eligible financing under an untied financing is not clearly defined, and is often determined on a project-by-project basis.

INSURANCE – POLITICAL AND COMMERCIAL RISK COVERAGE

Political risks are generally covered 100 per cent by ECAs. These risks include: creeping or outright expropriation, political violence/standalone terrorism, currency inconvertibility, repossession, and unavailable foreign exchange. Commercial risks can include non-payment by a government, breach of contract, non-performance of asset, and non-payment by offtakers.

Events covered by commercial (or comprehensive coverage) include non-payment, unilateral termination of contract, destruction, requisition, seizure, and unfair call of bonds caused by political or commercial events. Premia are payable on the amount of the insured financing. In most project financings, 100 per cent of the premium can be financed at the same conditions of the underlying commercial contract.

When considering an application for project financing, ECAs approach the risk evaluation in the same way as commercial lenders and will consider (a) stakeholder risk sharing, (b) identity of the sponsors (owners) and their retention of equity interest in the project, (c) financial and technical capability of all project participants, and (d) the overall structure of the collateral security package. Premium rates will also be based on a similar formula of the CIRR plus a premium.

ECA Cost of Debt

The cost of an ECA facility is composed of certain upfront and ongoing fees and an interest rate, which can be fixed or floating. The pricing structure, however, is somewhat unique to ECAs.

EXPOSURE FEE

The borrower is charged an exposure fee, which can be paid upfront or with each drawdown. The pricing of the exposure fee is driven by an OECD country risk rating matrix, in the case of political risk cover. For commercial risk coverage, an analysis of the project's commercial structure, credit strength and forecasted cash flow, sets the exposure fee.

ECAs will finance the exposure fee, and therefore the fee is rolled up into the financing costs, which are covered during the construction period and amortized over the tenor of the loan. The exposure fee is priced separately by each ECA, but in practice the ECAs coordinate closely on pricing.

INTEREST RATES

There are two basic interest rate structures employed under an ECA facility, and the structure employed is largely determined by the type of financing support that the ECA is providing.

Under a direct loan, ECAs charge the Commercial Interest Reference Rate (CIRR), which is defined as the yield on the government bonds corresponding to the currency of the loan plus a fixed margin of 100 basis points. For long-term project financings with a repayment term over 8.5 years, the yield on the seven-year government bond is used. The CIRR is set shortly before financial close and is generally fixed throughout the term of the debt.

Under a guarantee, a commercial bank is providing the actual loan, and the pricing will reflect the bank's cost of funds and profit margin. With a comprehensive guarantee, the commercial bank is effectively taking the credit risk of the ECA's government (as opposed to risk associated with the project or the borrower) and as such, the borrowing cost will be relatively low. Borrowing costs are typically structured as a margin over a base rate (typically LIBOR). If the project is exposed to interest rate risk, the borrower can swap out its floating rate for a fixed rate with the participating banks.

OTHER FEES – COMMITMENT, ARRANGING AND ESTABLISHMENT

ECA facilities are drawn down throughout the construction period in parallel with the procurement of goods and services. Each interest period, the borrower pays commitment fees on the undrawn portions of the facility. Certain upfront fees – arranging or establishment fees – are also typically included in the financing costs. These fees are negotiated with and charged by the commercial banks participating under a guarantee.

Process and Evolution

A lot has changed since the mid-1990s when the ECAs began a concerted effort to participate in project finance transactions in the emerging markets. Twenty years ago the offerings of the ECAs were considerably more formulaic and strict. The role of ECAs was to promote the export of goods and services from the home country. Today, though still complying with the gentleman's agreement of the OECD Arrangement, many of the ECAs operate almost like commercial banks by offering a variety of financial products. The reasons for these enhancements and expansion to the product offerings of the ECAs can be attributed to the recent global liquidity crisis and accompanying worldwide economic contraction, and overall increased international competition for markets.

Japan's JBIC was the first of the ECAs to offer huge direct loans to projects where Japanese companies were either the developer or natural resource offtaker. KEXIM and KEIC followed JBIC's lead by offering similar loans, and SACE introduced its own variation on this theme with its own untied loan programme. In North America, US Ex-Im has always been able to offer very large direct loans, but only with strict export content provisions. Canada's EDC has implemented an even broader range of products. Despite the ECAs being 'lenders of last resort,' they are often used as the necessary top-up in an overall debt package.

Besides the pure financial benefits of adding ECAs to the finance package, there are benefits of including an export credit agency, or other multi-lateral lending institution, to the transaction. The noted 'halo' effect has had mixed results over the past two decades of involvement by the ECAs in large infrastructure and energy project financings.

Does the 'Halo' Effect Work?

In large capital projects, project sponsors often wish to see a diversified lending structure and a widespread group of risk-sharers. Besides the various options of political and commercial covers that directly guarantee or insure certain tranches of capital, it is a general belief that ECA involvement in a project financing can produce a 'halo' effect over the commercial bank tranches that are not directly covered. With strong cross-default provisions prevalent in virtually all multi-source financings, the failure of a borrower to cover some portions of debt service will typically trigger a default with all lenders, thus bringing the weight of the ECAs (and often their home country governments) down upon the defaulting project.

INDONESIA POWER

In 2002, US Ex-Im Bank renegotiated the project agreements and terms and conditions of certain tranches of debt financing for the PT Paiton power project in Indonesia. The project is a 1,230MW coal-fired plant, selling output to PLN, the state-owned utility. It was the first Indonesian IPP to renegotiate its PPA with the government and PLN following the Asia financial crisis in 1997. PT Paiton was developed and owned by the following shareholders: Mission Energy 32.5 per cent, GE Capital 20 per cent, Mitsui 32.5 per cent and BHP 15 per cent. Project financing of US$1.8bn was arranged consisting of an OPIC loan; a direct loan from JEXIM/MITI (JBIC Tranche A); a commercial bank loan covered 75 per cent by JEXIM comprehensive guarantee and 20 per cent by Mitsui corporate guarantee; a 10-year US dollar bond; and a US$540m commercial loan with US Ex-Im PRI cover during construction that was to be converted to a US Ex-Im Direct Loan upon the successful attainment of project commercial operations.

The project failed to meet its completion conditions due to PLN's failure to pay the PPA tariff. US Ex-Im extended the availability of its take-out loan, but the project had still not met the take-out conditions. The PPA with PLN was being renegotiated with a substantially lower tariff, and the fuel supply arrangements were also revised.

During the construction period the project's debt to equity ratio was changed as a result of regional macroeconomic difficulties (the Asian Crisis), with the loans being only partially drawn and additional equity being injected instead. Conversion of the US Ex-Im loan was originally scheduled to occur in October 1999, but the project experienced delays. Even when the project did begin operations, conversion CPs were not satisfied. Among other things, PLN, the offtaker under the power purchase agreement (PPA), attempted to renegotiate the terms of the tariff. PLN made partial payments of the PPA obligations, sufficient to provide for payment of all interest due on the project's senior debt, but not sufficient to provide for the originally scheduled principal repayments.

On February 14, 2003, the US$2.7bn restructuring was closed. Principal repayments were successfully rescheduled without placing the senior debt in default. This successful restructuring was completed as a result of US Ex-Im being involved as an original guarantor of the commercial debt. As part of the restructuring, US Ex-Im created a risk-sharing tranche, where US$308m came from its own books, and the banks, which bought into all tranches on a pro rata basis, kept US$127m. The direct loans now mature in 2013.

Summary

Since the 1990s, ECAs have repeatedly proven to be valuable (and in some cases, necessary) providers and enablers of substantial project finance debt. They have mobilized debt capacity where political risk cover was required; and they have provided large tranches of capacity even in investment grade countries where book markets might have been stretched to their limits.

ECAs have been essential and knowledgeable participants in many sectors: power generation, LNG, pipelines, refineries and petrochemicals, mining and telecommunications. Their versatility in industry sectors, and their knowledge of project credit and structuring issues, have made them one of the most significant capital participants in the past two decades of global project finance.

6 *The Role of Multilateral Banks and ECAs*

BOB SHEPPARD
Teaches project finance at the University of South Carolina and advises the Global Clearinghouse on Development Finance

Multilateral development banks (MDBs), export credit agencies (ECAs), and other official agencies have played a significant role in the financing of developing country projects since the early 1990s, when the current form of international project finance first took shape. These institutions were established to provide financing for governmental and private-sector transactions in countries where political risks often prevent private-sector institutions from lending. Yet, despite the importance of direct funding provided by official agencies, their most important role is their ability to mitigate political risks for private–sector lenders and thereby to attract them to assist in financing developing country projects. In fact, in the three-year period 2008–2010, total debt for projects that featured lending or credit support from MDBs, ECAs, and other official agencies represented more than 47 per cent of total project finance debt for developing country projects.

Multilateral Development Banks

The International Bank for Reconstruction and Development, generally known as the World Bank, was created in 1944 to assist in European reconstruction after the Second World War; however, its mandate evolved into the broader role of promoting economic development globally. Other regional and sub-regional development banks were established throughout the post-war period with similar development mandates. In 1956, the World Bank, which is limited by its charter to lending only when a member government commits to repay the loan, established the International Finance Corporation to conduct private sector lending and investment. Regional and sub-regional MDBs provide loans, guarantees, and, on occasion, equity investments for private sector projects in developing countries. In 1960, the World Bank also established the International Development Association to lend to the world's poorest countries on concessionary terms.

Table 6.1 lists those global, regional, and sub-regional MDBs that are significant participants in the project finance market.

Table 6.1   **Global, regional, and sub-regional MDBs that are significant participants in the project finance market**

Institution	Abbreviation	Year Founded
International Bank for Reconstruction and Development	IBRD	1944
International Finance Corporation	IFC	1956
European Investment Bank	EIB	1958
Inter-American Development Bank	IDB or IADB	1959
International Development Association	IDA	1960
Central American Bank for Economic Integration	CABEI	1960
African Development Bank	AfDB	1963
Asian Development Bank	ADB	1966
Corporación Andina de Fomento	CAF	1968
Islamic Development Bank	IDB or ISDB	1974
Nordic Investment Bank	NIB	1976
European Bank for Reconstruction and Development	EBRD	1991
Black Sea Trade and Development Bank	BSTDB	1999

The shareholders of MDBs are governments – most of the world's governments in the case of the World Bank, IFC and IDA, regional governments, plus certain other governments with a special interest in the region, in the case of regional and sub-regional MDBs.

Export Credit Agencies

ECAs were created to promote exports from the country that owns or controls the ECA. Previously, ECAs were identified with older manufacturing economies in Western Europe and North America, but in recent years, as economic development has led to manufacturing on a global scale, many other countries have created ECAs.

ECAs typically provide short-term trade financing, medium-term financing for capital goods, and political risk insurance for export transactions and long-term investments, but they vary greatly in the extent to which they are active in the project finance market. Only those ECAs based in countries that produce the sort of goods likely to constitute a significant portion of the capital cost of a project will have an opportunity to provide project financing. These ECAs are primarily located in the largest manufacturing economies in Europe, North America, and increasingly, Asia.

Table 6.2 lists those ECAs that are most important in the project finance market, together with their home country. In some countries, the export credit and political risk insurance functions are handled by separate agencies (that are grouped together in the table).

Table 6.2   ECAs that are most important in the project finance market, together with their home country

Institution	Abbreviation	Country
Export Development Canada	EDC	Canada
Export-Import Bank of China	China Eximbank	China
China Export & Credit Insurance Corporation	Sinosure	China
Finnvera	Finnvera	Finland
Compagnie Française d'Assurance pour le Commerce Extérieur	COFACE	France
KfW IPEX-Bank	IPEX	Germany
SACE	SACE	Italy
Japan Bank for International Cooperation	JBIC	Japan
Nippon Export and Investment Insurance	NEXI	Japan
Export-Import Bank of Korea	KEXIM	Korea
Korea Export and Insurance Corporation	KEIC	Korea
Garanti-Instituttet for Eksportkreditt	GEIK	Norway
Export Credits Guarantee Department	ECGD	UK
Export-Import Bank of the United States	US Eximbank	US

Although Coface was privatized in 1994, most ECAs are owned by the government of their home country.

Bilateral Agencies

Bilateral agencies constitute a third type of official agency that is active in the project finance market. Most of these organizations were created with the specific mission of promoting international economic development through loans, guarantees, equity investments, and in some cases, political risk insurance.

Table 6.3 lists the bilateral agencies that are the most significant for the project finance market.

Bilateral agencies are a more heterogeneous group than MDBs or ECAs, and institutions cannot always be rigidly placed in a single group. EDC, for example, often functions in a manner that is more like a bilateral agency than an ECA and, it could reasonably be included on the above table. OPIC's mission is to support foreign investment by US companies, with development following as a corollary. Proparco, DEG, and FMO tend to focus on very difficult economies and to make smaller loans and investments than many of the other official organizations.

Table 6.3   Bilateral agencies that are the most significant for the project finance market

Institution	Abbreviation	Country
Société de Promotion et de Participation pour la Coopération Economique	Proparco	France
KfW Bankengruppe (originally Kreditanstalt für Wiederaufbau)	KfW	Germany
Deutsche Investitions- und Entwicklungsgesellschaft (a subsidiary of KfW)	DEG	Germany
Nederlandse Financierings-Maatschappij voor Ontwikkelingslanden	FMO	Netherlands
Commonwealth Development Corporation	CDC	UK
Overseas Private Investment Corporation	OPIC	USA
United States Agency for International Aid	USAID	USA

Political Risk in Theory

To understand the role of MDBs, ECAs, and other official agencies, it is necessary to understand political risk and the reasons why political risk insurance – a standardized product that is widely available – is often viewed as an inadequate risk mitigation instrument.

Investments in foreign countries are subject to a number of risks that could occur in a developed country but that are far more likely to occur in a developing country. One is the risk that the government of the host country will expropriate the investment without providing adequate compensation. (International law permits a government to expropriate foreign investments but not without providing proper compensation to the foreign owners of the investment.) A second risk is that the assets constituting a foreign investment will be destroyed by politically motivated violence – a civil war, revolution, riots, etc. – in the host country.

A third risk is the possibility that the host country of an investment will run out of foreign exchange. This occurs when a sufficient number of holders of the host country's currency want to exchange it for US dollars (or another hard currency) held in reserve by the host country's central bank. If the central bank of the host country runs out of foreign exchange, foreign investors will be left with local currency revenues that they cannot convert into US dollars.

The reason that holders of local currency wish to exchange it for foreign currency is, of course, that they have come to the conclusion that the host country's currency is overvalued and is being maintained at an artificially high value by the host country's government (primarily through the central bank's purchases of local currency at the prevailing exchange rate). When it becomes apparent to the host government that the current exchange rate cannot be maintained, it will have no choice but to allow the market to determine the rate at which its currency will be exchanged for US dollars and other currencies. Subsequently, more local currency will be required to purchase one US dollar than before the devaluation.

The two most important providers of political risk insurance are OPIC and the Multilateral Investment Guarantee Agency (MIGA), a part of the World Bank Group. Both offer policies covering the three classic forms of political risk: expropriation, political violence, and transfer and convertibility. A fourth type of coverage, breach of contract coverage, is also available on a negotiated basis from both OPIC and MIGA to pay claims for breach by the host government of an explicit contractual undertaking with respect to the investment. Political risk insurance is also available from private insurers, but the basic forms of coverage are those that are offered by OPIC and MIGA.

Political Risk in Practice

Projects located in developing countries also fall into two different categories: (1) those that export their output and are able to require their customers to pay in US dollars, and (2) those that provide a product or service for the host country's domestic market and that receive revenues denominated in local currency. Developing countries typically lack debt markets that provide long-term financing denominated in local currency; as a result, most projects – both export and domestic market – are financed with long-term debt denominated in US dollars.

Export projects are subject to the risk of expropriation and political violence just as are projects with local currency revenues, but their US dollar revenues provide a hedge against the risk of having long-term debt denominated in US dollars. On the other hand, projects with local currency revenues must try to create their own hedge if they are financed with US dollar debt. If they price their output in local currency and adjust prices based on changes in the host country's inflation rate, they can keep their product or service affordable for the public, but the US dollar value of their local currency revenues will fluctuate with changes in the host country's foreign exchange rate. If the value of the host country's currency declines, they may not have enough local currency to buy the US dollars they need to pay their debt service.

Consequently, projects with local currency revenues and US dollar debt have typically sought to enter into output contracts (or to insist upon regulatory regimes) that require output prices denominated in local currency to be adjusted based on changes in the host country's foreign exchange rate. The effect of such contracts, if they continue to be honoured following a devaluation of the host country's currency, is to shield a project from the effects of devaluation. However, the effect of devaluation on such foreign exchange indexed contracts is to raise the price of a project's product or service substantially in excess of the host country's rate of inflation. In practice, enforcement of such contracts has proved difficult for political authorities that are required to stand for election or are otherwise subject to pressure from the public. As a result, foreign exchange indexed contracts have frequently been subject to renegotiation following devaluation of the host country's currency.

This risk, however, is not covered by political risk insurance. If an output purchaser – with or without being compelled to do so by its government – breaches its contractual obligations and demands that the contract be renegotiated, this is viewed as a credit risk, even though it was motivated by devaluation of the host country's currency. Moreover, political risk insurance policies typically provide an explicit exclusion for devaluation, which means that, if the project suffers a financial loss as a result of devaluation of the host country's currency, the project has no ability to bring a claim under a political insurance policy. A related risk is that of changes in the host country's regulatory regime for a particular sector that are brought about as a result of devaluation. These changes usually prevent the public from bearing the full cost of foreign exchange indexed output contracts, but the host government normally has not made any commitments to the foreign investor with respect to such changes; therefore, a foreign investor has no claim under a breach of contract clause in a political risk insurance policy.

Products Offered By MDBs, ECAs, and Other Official Agencies

The products offered by MDBs, ECAs, and other official agencies that are used in project financings can be separated into two categories: (1) risk mitigation instruments that permit project lenders or investors to make a claim and be paid in accordance with the terms of the official agency's contractual undertaking, and (2) financial commitments by the official agency that are intended to have a halo effect that will protect a project from adverse actions by a project's host government but that do not provide payment to lenders and investors if losses occur as a result of political risks.

Political risk insurance is an obvious example of a contractual product, but except for OPIC and MIGA, it is not the principal form of risk mitigation offered by official agencies. Instead, the most widely used forms of risk mitigation are halo effect financing structures.

There are, of course, strong reasons why MDBs, ECAs, and other official agencies should create a halo effect by virtue of their participation in a project financing. As previously noted, each MDB is owned by sovereign governments, many of which are highly rated. In addition, many MDBs[1] have a special status under the Basel II international banking regulatory framework.[2] These MDBs are eligible for a 0 per cent risk weighting with respect to their debt held by private sector banks, and this risk weighting also affects the risk weighting of project finance debt that benefits from their support. Each MDB eligible for a 0 per cent risk weighting is rated Aaa or AAA, as the case may be, by each of the three major international rating agencies.[3]MDBs are also accorded preferred creditor status, a term denoting that their obligations will be given priority access to foreign currency in the event of a foreign exchange crisis and will have priority in the event of a sovereign debt rescheduling. Preferred creditor status is not determined by treaty or other law but rather reflects customary practice as it has evolved in the financial relations between governments and MDBs.

The idea that the participation of an MDB in the financing for a project should provide protection for the project from adverse actions by the host government encompasses other forms of political risk beyond transfer and convertibility. The most obvious is expropriation, but the more practically important is the risk of adverse regulatory actions

---

1   These MDBs are IBRD, IFC, EIB, IADB, AfDB, ADB, ISDB, NIB, EBRD, and certain other supranational organizations that are not active in project finance.

2   This special status has not been altered by the post-financial crisis changes to Basel II that have been termed 'Basel III'.

3   Moody's and Standard and Poor's rate each of the MDBs eligible for a 0 per cent risk weighting. Fitch rates each discussed above, except IFC and NIB.

that have the effect of reducing project revenues and threatening a project's ability to meet its debt service obligations. The types of adverse action that a host government can take are numerous and diverse, a fact which makes it difficult to specify each in drafting a breach of contract clause. Moreover, a political risk insurance claim based on government action normally requires that the action that is the subject of the claim violate international law and discriminate against the foreign investor. Regulatory actions taken in exercising a government's 'police power' to regulate social and economic activities are almost never against international law and need not be discriminatory; yet, they can have severe effects on the economics of a project, especially infrastructure projects that provide an essential service to the public.

The presence of an MDB, ECA, or other official agency is potentially a very cost effective means of addressing a wide range of political risks. The forms that financing provided by official agencies can take vary widely. MDBs and other official agencies can provide senior debt, subordinated debt, or equity financing. Debt can be funded by an MDB, ECA, or other official agency or the agency can provide a guarantee. When an official agency provides a 'comprehensive guarantee', it assumes all of the credit risk of the transaction, and the lender that makes the loan merely provides funding. If the project fails for any reason to make required payments of interest and principal, the lender has a claim against the guarantor.

A/B LOANS

The principal instrument for capitalizing on MDBs' preferred creditor status is the A loan/B loan structure, a form of financing that enables MDBs to attract private sector lenders to transactions led by the MDB. The A loan is the amount of financing provided by the MDB itself, while the B loan(s) are provided by private sector lenders. These lenders are usually commercial banks, but occasionally, institutional investors have been B loan lenders. The MDB providing the A loan is the lender of record for the entire loan (A loan plus B loans). If the amount paid by a borrower is less than the required debt service payment with respect to the entire loan, the amount actually received will be shared pro rata by the A loan and B loan lenders. It is, therefore, impossible for a borrower to remain current with respect to the A loan, while being in default with respect to the B loans.

An important effect of the A/B loan structure is that rating agencies regard it as the functional equivalent of political risk insurance covering transfer and convertibility. Normally, the foreign currency debt rating of a project's debt is limited by the host government's foreign currency debt rating (the sovereign ceiling). Purchase of transfer and convertibility coverage in an amount that the rating agencies regard as sufficient to cover debt service during the longest likely period of inconvertibility (24 months' coverage often being sufficient) removes the host government's foreign currency debt rating as a constraint and permits the project's global scale local currency debt rating to become its foreign currency debt rating. Where a project's global scale local currency debt rating is higher that its foreign currency debt rating (without transfer and convertibility coverage) – as is often the case – the benefit of breaching the sovereign ceiling can be significant. The A/B loan structure enables the project's debt rating to exceed the host government's foreign currency debt rating without the necessity of purchasing political risk insurance.

The IFC originated the A/B loan structure and has been responsible for the largest amount of this lending, but other MDBs also attract private sector lenders to project finance transactions through the use of the structure.

PARI PASSU LENDING

Loans provided to a project by an ECA or a bilateral agency such as OPIC where private sector lenders provide loans on a pari passu basis will not use the A loan/B loan structure, but they will have much the same effect. Typically, all lenders to a transaction – official and private sector – will sign an inter-creditor agreement that will require debt service payments to be shared on a *pro rata* basis. The inter-creditor agreement thus creates a situation identical to the A/B loan in that it is impossible for a borrower to remain current with respect to its loans with official agencies, while defaulting on its loans from private sector lenders.

The protection afforded private sector lenders by the participation of an ECA or other official agency depends to a great extent upon the clout of the official agency. If an ECA or bilateral agency is important in providing financing for the host country, if its home country is an important trade partner, or if its government is important as a donor or has other important relationships with the host government, then transactions in which the ECA or bilateral agency is a lender can be expected to benefit from a halo effect. Pari passu financing by an ECA or bilateral agency is not regarded by rating agencies as the functional equivalent of political risk insurance covering transfer and convertibility.

EQUITY INVESTMENTS

Equity investments in projects by MDBs and other official agencies are much less frequently made than loans and, when they are made, they are for much smaller amounts. Equity investments are not regarded by rating agencies as the functional equivalent of transfer and convertibility coverage. The halo effect of equity investments by official agencies is substantially less than that of A/B loans and pari passu lending, but it is still a positive factor in lenders' evaluation of the credit strength of a project.

PARTIAL CREDIT GUARANTEES

In addition to comprehensive debt guarantees through which an MDB assumes all credit risk, MDBs offer partial credit guarantees (PCGs) that apply only to a portion of a project's debt. The remaining, unguaranteed debt is provided by private sector lenders. PCGs are closer to a form of pari passu lending than to a contractual form of risk mitigation because, just as in the case of a comprehensive guarantee, the guarantor assumes all credit risk with respect to the guaranteed debt and the private sector lender merely provides funding.

PARTIAL RISK GUARANTEES

Unlike comprehensive guarantees and PCGs, partial risk guarantees (PRGs) provide coverage only with respect to certain explicitly defined risks that are within the control of the host government. The World Bank Group includes MIGA, which was specifically established to provide political risk insurance, but regional and sub-regional MDBs do not have a similar affiliate. Nevertheless, each of these MDBs can provide the functional equivalent of political risk insurance by means of a PRG.

PRGs can also be used to cover regulatory risks that in a political risk insurance contract would be covered using a breach of contract clause, or depending upon how the PRG is drafted, other risks – especially regulatory risks – that go beyond the traditional scope of breach of contract clauses. The World Bank has been the most active issuer of PRGs, although other MDBs have also issued them or are prepared to do so. When the World Bank (as opposed to the IFC) issues a PRG, it requires a counter-guarantee from the host government, the effect of which is to enable the Bank to bring a claim against the host-government if the Bank is required to make a payment pursuant to the PRG. Other MDBs may issue PRGs without requiring a counter-guarantee, but it is unlikely they would do so, given the fact that payment would be required only in the event of an action by the host-government.

Constraints in Accessing and Implementing Official Agency Support

MDBs, ECAs, and other official agencies each have explicit and detailed criteria covering the eligibility of projects to obtain support and the terms of that support. While these criteria do not change frequently, they do change and, thus, it is always best to check an agency's web site or contact the agency directly before determining whether it can play a useful role in a proposed project financing.

COMMON CRITERIA

MDBs, ECAs, and other official agencies have criteria for the entities that may be the subject of a financing transaction. These criteria include items such as corporate form, domicile, and capital structure. While these criteria vary from agency to agency, they rarely create a barrier to structuring a project in a manner that permits an official agency to provide support.

MDBs, ECAs, and other official agencies evaluate the credit risk of projects by looking at the same factors as private sector lenders. From the standpoint of construction risk, technology, input and output contracts, operational risk, and the credit strength of counterparties, their standards are essentially the same as those of private sector lenders. Projects are generally required by all official agencies to adhere to environmental standards that are equal to the higher of the host country's standards or those of the World Bank.

DEVELOPMENT CRITERIA

MDBs and those official agencies that have a development agenda require that a project make a contribution to the economic development of the host country. Evaluating a potential development contribution is necessarily a subjective process that provides opportunities for project sponsors and their advisors to demonstrate their ingenuity and advocacy skills. ECAs' mission is export promotion, not development, and development considerations do not factor into their decision-making process.

LOCATION CRITERIA

All MDBs require that a project that is a candidate for their support be located in a host country that is a shareholder. In the case of regional and sub-regional MDBs, the host country must lie within the region served by the MDB. Each ECA and provider of political risk insurance has a list of countries in which it is open, but most countries are included. Countries that are excluded tend to fall into that category for obvious reasons. For example, US Eximbank will not provide financing for a project in Iran, and neither OPIC nor MIGA will write political risk coverage for North Korea. Other official agencies, all of which have a development agenda, select the countries in which they operate on the basis of development considerations.

EXPORT CRITERIA

ECAs will provide financing for a project only if it purchases equipment from the ECA's home country; however, ECA support must be obtained *prior* to the project's making a purchase commitment. ECA support cannot be obtained if a purchase commitment has already been made because, in such a situation, the ECA's support was not necessary to promote the export of this equipment. MDBs and official agencies with a development agenda are not concerned with the location of manufacture of the equipment used in the projects they finance.

TERMS OF FINANCING

The fact that most financing (whether direct loans or guarantees) provided by MDBs and development-oriented official agencies is, in one form or another, intended to attract similar financing from the private sector means that the tenor and pricing of official agency financing tends to reflect current market practice. Pricing with respect to an A loan will be the same as that of the B loan, and substantially different pricing from different lenders to the same transaction is unlikely in practice. MDBs will occasionally provide a tranche of financing with a longer tenor than that provided by private sector co-lenders, but this is not the norm.

MDBs do, however, have explicit policies governing how much debt or equity financing they will provide to a single transaction. The criteria for debt provided by an MDB tend to have two limits: (1) the amount of debt as a percentage of the total cost of the project (typically 25 per cent, but perhaps as much as 50 per cent) and (2) the total amount of debt expressed as a monetary amount.

ECAs are governed by the OECD's Arrangement on Officially Supported Export Credits, a framework established and maintained by the Organization for Economic Co-operation and Development. The framework, generally known as 'the OECD Consensus', is a 'gentlemen's agreement' establishing minimum interest rates and risk fees and maximum repayment terms. The Arrangement is intended to ensure that competition among exporters is based on the price and quality of goods, rather than on the terms of financing.

The participants in the Arrangement are Australia, Canada, the European Community, Japan, South Korea, New Zealand, Norway, Switzerland, and the United States, but historically, the terms of the arrangement have been widely honoured by other country's

ECAs. However, in recent years, certain ECAs have provided borrowers with lines of credit that, on their face, do not commit the borrower to the purchase of goods from the home country of the ECA (although that may be the ultimate outcome). These lines of credit contain terms more favourable to the borrower than those permitted by the arrangement and, thus, have the practical effect of avoiding its provisions.

The principal terms of the OECD Consensus are that:

- Up to 85 per cent of the value of the export contract can be financed, with a sub-limit of 30 per cent of local costs incurred in the host country. The buyer must, therefore, make a minimum cash payment of 15 per cent.
- For developing country transactions that do not qualify as project finance transactions (as defined in Appendix I to Annex X of the Arrangement), loan tenor is limited to 10 years, with an exception allowing up to 12 years for non-nuclear electric power plants. However, the maximum loan tenor is 14 years for projects meeting the Arrangement's definition of a project finance transaction[4] and 18 years for renewable energy projects.
- The default standard for amortization schedules applicable to transactions not meeting the definition of a project financing is equal payments of principal on a semi-annual basis, but for transactions meeting the definition of a project financing, variable principal payments are permitted so long as principal payments during any six-month period do not exceed 25 per cent of the loan; the first principal payment is made within 24 months of the starting point of the credit; no less than 2 per cent of the amount of the credit shall have been repaid 24 months after the start of the credit; the first interest payment occurs no less than six months after the start of the credit and interest payments are made at least every 12 months; and the weighted-average life of the loan does not exceed 7.25 years.
- Interest rates must be equal to at least 1 per cent over the rate of equivalent long-term government bonds in the currency in which the export credit is denominated (known as CIRR rates – Commercial Interest Reference Rates), with a surcharge of 20 basis points for loans with tenors longer than 12 years.

The effect of the requirement that ECA financing is limited by the amount of equipment purchased from the ECA's home country (in combination with the 85 per cent limit and the 30 per cent local content exception) is to prevent ECAs from being able to provide all of the senior debt financing that would be required to produce the level of leverage that is typical of project financings. As a result, project financings with a tranche of ECA debt typically require private sector senior debt as well, and in many cases, financing from other official agencies also.

The Way Forward

Political risk insurance was an effective method of addressing the risks that seemed most significant in the late 1960s and early 1970s. During those years, expropriation was a high risk in the oil and mining industries, and the possibility of political violence was

---

4   The Arrangement provides that the more flexible terms it sets forth for project finance transactions also apply to nuclear power plants and renewable energy projects.

reinforced by insurgencies and civil wars. Similarly, the risk of currency inconvertibility was greater than it is today because there was a greater stigma attached to devaluation then than now. In the last decade and a half, the most significant forms of political risk have shifted towards devaluation and regulatory changes that leave ownership of a project with its original investors but that sharply erode the economic returns that were expected at the time the investment decision was made. The risk mitigation structures offered by official agencies are in theory able to deal with these new developments, but in practice, they have yet to catch up to the changing landscape of political risk.

A/B loans and other forms of pari passu financing have one fundamental limitation: when conditions in financial markets tighten and lenders become more risk adverse, there is no way to change the terms of offer to continue to attract the same volume of private sector financing. When conditions in financial markets tighten, loan pricing can increase and project structures can be required to employ stronger risk mitigation, but the essential function of official agencies is the mitigation of political risk. If lenders have become more concerned about political risk, the terms of A/B loans and other pari passu financing cannot be improved; for an approach based on trust rather than contractual commitments, lack of trust translates into a lack of financing, and, in fact, B loan volumes have historically been quite volatile.

A related issue limiting the expansion of risk mitigation offered by official agencies is the fact that most countries that have below investment grade foreign currency debt ratings also have below investment grade local currency debt ratings. Whether an A/B loan is used to breach the sovereign ceiling or whether this is done by purchasing transfer and convertibility coverage, the value of these forms of risk mitigation is greatly diminished – or in many cases, rendered worthless – if the local currency rating of the transaction is below investment grade.

Since the early 2000s, rating agencies have been reluctant to assign a local currency rating greater than the sovereign's local currency rating to any infrastructure transaction. Infrastructure projects are viewed as being particularly vulnerable to political interference to reduce tariffs for the benefit of consumers, with adverse consequences for all firms involved in the chain of providing the product or service. This form of political risk has resulted in the host government's local currency debt rating serving as a de facto ceiling for the local currency debt ratings of all infrastructure firms. Although ratings change periodically, at any given time, the number of developing country governments with a below investment grade foreign currency rating and an above investment grade local currency rating is usually no more than six to ten.

Prior to Argentina's economic crisis of 2001–2002, institutional investors purchased debt issued by projects in Argentina that received an investment grade rating based on Argentina's investment grade local currency sovereign rating, plus the use of A/B loans or political risk insurance to breach the sovereign ceiling. When Argentina devalued, its government prevented tariffs from rising sufficiently to compensate for the devaluation, with the result that these infrastructure transactions defaulted. Although investors were extremely disappointed, they were reminded by the institutions that provided risk mitigation that they received protection against the risk that Argentina's currency might become inconvertible – which did not occur – but not against the risk of devaluation – which did.

This episode highlights the lack of structures to deal with the risk of devaluation. In 2001, OPIC provided a contingent loan facility it called a 'foreign exchange liquidity facility' that was used to mitigate foreign exchange risk in a US dollar-denominated bond issue for a Brazilian electric power transaction. The bonds received investment grade ratings from Moody's and Fitch at a time when Brazil's sovereign debt ratings were B1 and BB-, respectively. However, the transaction's ratings were dependent upon the power purchaser's having an investment grade local currency rating, and the difficulty of obtaining such ratings in most countries has limited the use of this structure, just as it has the use of A/B loans and political risk insurance as means of attracting institutional investors.

A more recent development to deal with the currency mismatch risk that can lead to devaluation is the promotion of local currency financing, which eliminates currency mismatches for projects with local currency revenues. As previously noted, developing countries normally lack debt markets offering long-term local currency debt, with a corresponding absence of long-term markets for interest rate and currency swaps. However, in 2007, the Currency Exchange Fund (TCX) was established in the Netherlands by a group of MDBs and official development agencies to facilitate transactions in developing countries by providing long-term currency and interest rate swaps and currency forwards.[5] TCX can provide swaps on a fixed or floating rate basis, and interest rates can be fixed up to a tenor of 1.5 times the tenor of the yield curve in the host country debt market. Currently, TCX's limit for transactions in a single currency is US$175m. Counterparties for TCX's transactions are limited to its shareholders and investment-grade institutions that have been vetted by its shareholders. As of the end of 2009, TCX had hedged US$362m in local currency loans in 25 different currencies. Certain restrictions placed on the size of individual transactions have resulted in an average transaction size of approximately US$15 million for the amount of debt hedged in each transaction. Although private sector financial institutions are eligible to become shareholders of TCX, few have yet done so. Nevertheless, TCX represents a significant step forward in dealing with what is the most difficult issue in international project finance.

A final issue that affects the ability of MDBs, ECAs, and other agencies to be effective agents of development is their ability to attract private sector financing to transactions in which they participate. In recent years, some MDBs have been capital constrained and have needed to raise additional funds, and there is clearly not enough capacity in the official agency community to address the developing world's needs without additional participation by the private sector.

In 2008, the total amount of senior debt in project finance transactions with official agency participation was US$50.7bn, according to Thomson Reuters Project Finance International. In 2009, this amount dropped to US$32bn, and in 2010, recovered only to US$40.5bn, an amount 20 per cent below its level two years earlier. While these numbers are perhaps not surprising in view of the fact that they coincide with the global financial crisis, a more disturbing trend is the declining ratio of private sector debt to official agency commitment. In 2008, private sector debt in project finance transaction with official agency participation, divided by the financial commitment of official agencies was 1.13. In 2009, this ratio fell to 0.56 and in 2010, to 0.50.

One of the most effective ways to increase private sector participation is through the use of PRGs, which are able to address the specific concerns of lenders in an individual transaction. The commitment made by the MDB or other official agency that issues a PFG

---

5   Forwards are limited to equity and mezzanine financing.

is contingent, and the liability that it represents is assessed at less that its face value by rating agencies in their evaluation of the issuer. Even if a counter-guarantee is required by the host government, the liability represented by the PRG will be viewed by the IMF and rating agencies as an amount less than its face value because the risk of having the counter-guarantee called lies completely within the hands of the government itself. No other structures exist that offer the same potential to increase the development impact and financial effectiveness of commitments by MDBs and other official agencies.

7 Basel III and its Implications for Project Finance[1]

EDWARD CHAN, a partner, and MATTHEW WORTH an associate, the banking group at
Linklaters LLP

In December 2010, the Basel Committee on Banking Supervision published its report 'Basel III: A Global Regulatory Framework for More Resilient Banks and Banking Systems.' Expressly set out as a response to the global financial crisis, the Basel III framework represents a substantial step forward from its predecessor regime, Basel II. It introduces a package of reforms aimed at strengthening the regulation of both capital and liquidity, to improve the stability and resilience of individual banks and the banking sector as a whole.

Basel III is expected to be adopted worldwide, and will be phased in from 2013 to 2019. It is expected to pose significant challenges for banks. In particular, there will be a marked increase in the quantity of capital – particularly common equity capital – that banks will be required to hold. Individual asset classes or areas of activity, especially on the trading book, are expected to be significantly more expensive for banks in future. Banks will need to meet rigorous funding requirements for their long term asset bases.

All of this will have an impact on those who borrow from banks, as well as on the banks themselves. Stricter capital requirements will cause cost pressures for lenders and therefore for borrowers. The banking landscape may change, as major players scale back in some areas and invest in others, in response to changing capital and liquidity requirements.

In the context of project finance, concerns have been raised about the impact of Basel III, and in particular its treatment of long term lending. Certainly, there may be challenges, as this article explores. However, these must be kept in proportion. While it is too early to draw firm conclusions, it is likely that their impact will be moderated, or accommodated, by innovation in the way that project financings are structured and documented.

This article provides an overview of the content of Basel III, and explores at an early stage some of its potential impact, both in general and on project finance in particular.

---

1   This article was first published in Thomson Reuters Project Finance International (PFI) on June 29th, Issue 460.

Basel III – Background and Overview

The financial crisis was widely seen as exposing a number of weaknesses in the existing global regulatory framework, as embodied in the Basel II regime. In particular, the regulatory capital regime was seen as somewhat too permissive, and the definition of capital too broad; trading book risks and off-balance-sheet exposures as insufficiently covered; and Basel II did not regulate liquidity. To address these and other issues, Basel III introduces five main 'planks' of reform, as follows.

ENHANCING QUALITY AND QUANTITY OF CAPITAL

Regulation of capital has been at the core of the Basel regime since the days of Basel I. Under Basel III, as under its predecessors, banks are required to maintain a minimum ratio of capital, on the one hand, to risk-weighted assets, on the other. This is referred to as the minimum capital ratio. The aim is to maintain stability, by ensuring banks at all times retain enough capital to absorb losses incurred during periods of stress.

Basel III will require that a bank's capital ratio must be 8 per cent at all times, made up as follows.

- At least 6 per cent must consist of Tier 1 capital, of which at least 4.5 per cent must be in the form of common equity, meaning ordinary shares and retained earnings. The remaining 1.5 per cent may be made up of additional going concern capital. The latter is subject to strict conditions to ensure it is equity-like in its ability to absorb losses.
- 2 per cent may consist of Tier 2 capital. This may have more debt-like characteristics than Tier 1 capital, but must nonetheless be deeply subordinated and meet strict criteria as to its loss absorption.

In addition Basel III imposes a capital conservation buffer, which requires another 2.5 per cent of common equity to be maintained. A bank will be constrained from paying dividends or bonuses if this buffer is not maintained, meaning no bank is likely to treat it as optional.

Altogether, Basel III represents a material toughening of capital requirements when compared to Basel II. While the headline minimum capital ratio under Basel II was also 8 per cent, only 2 per cent was required to be common equity. By 2019, including the capital conservation buffer and certain new deductions from capital, banks will need to hold nearly four times the amount of common equity currently required to cover exposures. Additionally, under Basel II, numerous sophisticated 'hybrid instruments' were permitted to count as Tier 1 capital. Under Basel III, these will be phased out.

CHANGES TO RISK COVERAGE AND WEIGHTINGS

A bank's capital ratio is applied to its risk weighted assets. Under the risk weighting scheme, a weighting factor is applied to asset values, such that safer assets are discounted, and can therefore be backed by less capital.

In the wake of the financial crisis, it was widely felt that Basel II failed adequately to capture the risks posed by, among other things, off balance sheet risks, derivatives exposures, and other aspects of a bank's trading book. To address this issue, Basel III puts in place a series of additional capital charges for different risks. The overall effect of this is to increase the relative amount of capital that banks will have to allocate to their trading book, as opposed to their lending book, in future, as shown in Figure 7.1.

REDUCING LEVERAGE

In addition to the minimum capital ratio, Basel III imposes a new gross leverage ratio with which banks must comply. Once fully in force, this will require that banks' capital is at all times equal to at least 3 per cent of their total assets; or, to put it another way, maximum leverage for a bank will be 33.33 times capital.

Assets are not risk weighted for the purposes of the leverage ratio, and collateral is not taken into account. Off balance sheet items are to be included in the test, as are net derivatives exposures.

LIQUIDITY MANAGEMENT

Basel II dealt primarily with capitalization. However, as the financial crisis showed, liquidity or funding issues can be just as challenging to a bank in times of stress, if not more so. Basel III requires banks to demonstrate adequate liquidity in both the short and the medium to long term.

In the short term, the liquidity coverage ratio (LCR) requires that banks have sufficient 'high quality liquid assets' available to enable them to meet anticipated outflows over a 30-day period of acute stress. High quality liquid assets include cash, central bank reserves, and assets of similar quality. The assumed outflows will include a variety of outgoings

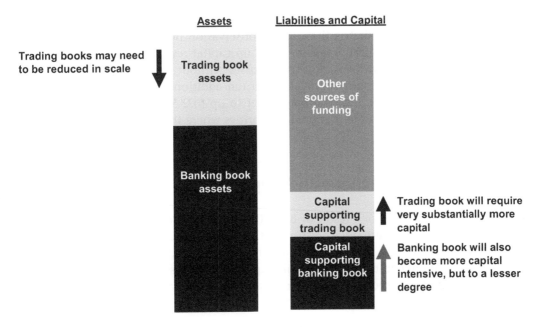

Figure 7.1   Effects of the changes of risk cover

including withdrawals of retail deposits and drawdowns by borrowers on committed loan facilities.

One key feature of the LCR is its differential treatment of undrawn but committed facilities such as revolving loans and liquidity facilities. An undrawn revolving loan will require 10 per cent liquidity cover if made to a non-financial corporate borrower, but 100 per cent cover if made to a special purpose vehicle (SPV). A liquidity facility, however, (i.e., a back-up facility put in place expressly for the purpose of refinancing the debt of a customer in situations where such a customer is unable to obtain its ordinary course of business funding requirements in the financial markets) will always require 100 per cent cover.

The net stable funding requirement (NSFR), on the other hand, requires banks to demonstrate stable funding over the longer term. Broadly speaking, banks will be required to keep funding in place of at least one year in maturity to cover their assets of one year maturity or more. Not all assets will require the same degree of coverage. In particular, high-rated bonds will require a lower proportion of stable funding under the NSFR than similarly-rated loans.

It is not the case that the maturity of funding need precisely match the maturity of the asset, so for instance a 25-year loan need not be backed by a 25-year deposit. Such a requirement would negate the maturity transformation function of the banking sector, namely that it can lend longer than it borrows. However, it is likely that for longer term loans, funding considerably longer than one year in maturity will be sought in future. This, indeed, is the purpose of the NSFR, which seeks to reduce banks' reliance on the volatile wholesale funding markets that dried up so rapidly during the critical phases of the credit crisis.

ADDRESSING PRO-CYCLICALITY

Two additional capital buffer regimes are put in place by Basel III, with the aim of managing cyclicality. The first is the capital conservation buffer, discussed above. The broad idea of this is to require banks to build up capital reserves which can be drawn upon during cyclical downturns, to absorb losses without imperilling the minimum capital ratio. Secondly, a countercyclical buffer (an additional extension to the capital conservation range, of Tier 1 capital equivalent to up to 2.5 per cent of risk weighted assets) may be set by individual national authorities where there is excess credit growth in a particular country.

Some General Reflections and Implications

It is widely expected that one result of Basel III will be an increased cost of lending for banks, and therefore upward price pressure in the loan market. As the chart below shows, under Basel III once fully implemented (and taking into account its various limbs) the quantity of common equity that banks will require to back assets could quadruple. Since common equity is an expensive form of capital, this could have a significant economic impact.

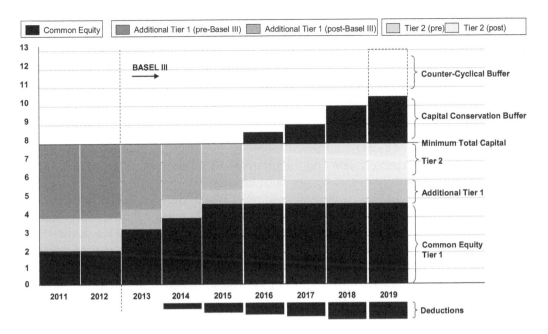

Figure 7.2 Basel III capital requirements phase-in

The capital-hunger of the banking sector can be expected to increase markedly. A McKinsey report[2] recently estimated that the European banking sector is likely to require an additional €1,050bn of capital as a result of Basel III, and the US banking sector a further €600bn. This increased need for equity capital is likely to coincide with a reduction in the availability of central bank funding, while the recovery of wholesale funding markets remains uncertain.

It is widely anticipated that the global banking sector as a whole may have some difficulty raising the amount of capital required. As a result, banks may need to make difficult choices as to how to ration their capital. Given the differential treatment of different types of asset and exposure under Basel III, many banks can be expected to change their business models or seek to exit different product lines. Those banks who wish to operate a large trading book may need to allocate significantly more capital to this than was previously the case.

We may see the entry of non-bank lenders to different segments of the lending market, using their relative regulatory advantages to compete with the banks and meet demand that the banking sector cannot. So far, however, this trend has been slower to develop than some predicted during the financial crisis.

---

2 *"Basel III and European Banking: Its impact, how banks might respond, and the challenges of implementation"*, McKinsey & Company, November 2010.

An Early View of the Implications for Project Finance

As described above, Basel III treats different asset types, and exposures, quite differently. What, then, are the aspects of project finance that will affect its treatment under Basel III and what might be the impact? It is of course very early to be making predictions in respect of a regime which is to be phased in over eight years. However, we are able to explore some of the possible effects.

Early discussions of Basel III in the project finance context have focused on the length of maturity (tenor) of project debt and the interplay with the NSFR. It is true that, under the NSFR, banks are likely to seek longer term funding for long-term debt. The letter of the Basel III requirement is, broadly, that funding of at least one year be in place to match assets of one year's maturity or more. However, were banks to back long term assets with the bare minimum funding – which would have a maturity of, say, 13 months – this would effectively impose a rolling funding requirement from month to month. It seems likely that banks will seek longer term funding, and there is debate as to what longer term will mean. It is not the case, however, that a 25-year project loan will require locked-in 25-year funding.

It is nonetheless likely that banks will seek to manage their commitment to very long term exposures in various ways, and project debt structures may evolve as a result. The current market reflects these trends. Currently, the marketplace of willing lenders does grow smaller at tenors greater than, say, seven to 10 years, particularly for larger loans (above say £100m). However, deals can still be done provided they are well structured and priced. We have seen an increased move towards 'semi-perm' structures, under which the borrower is given incentives to refinance, after several years, through the use of cash sweep mechanisms and increases in margin. Or banks may succeed in persuading sponsors to accept refinancing risk, at perhaps seven or eight years, by structuring loans that mature at that point. Tenor can be expected to remain a key negotiating point for some time, until a new market standard is achieved that accommodates Basel III and other post-crisis concerns.

Certain discrete elements of project financings may be adversely affected, in price terms if nothing else, by Basel III. We mentioned, above, the differential treatment of revolving or working capital facilities under the LCR regime. Since the use of SPV borrowers is very common in project financing, it is likely that working capital facilities in the projects context will require 100 per cent short term liquidity cover, which will make them expensive for banks. Since these types of facility are often a relatively small proportion of a project's overall debt, this may not be a critical issue. More important may be the impact on letters of credit, demand for which is significant in the projects market. Basel III allows national regulators to specify the level of LCR cover they will require for letters of credit, and many, including in the UK, have yet to specify what level they will demand. Liquidity coverage requirements of 25 per cent, 50 per cent or more could make it difficult for banks to provide these products economically. It would probably be too pessimistic to say that letters of credit will disappear, especially given the key role they play in project finance. It is quite likely, however, that banks will tie any offer of a letter of credit facility to concessions from sponsors.

Various changes can be anticipated to loan documentation as a result of Basel III. Perhaps the most significant for sponsors will be an increased focus by banks on transferability. Traditionally, transfer restrictions on banks have been relatively common, and onerous, in project lending compared to other forms of loan. In future however, banks are likely to focus on liquidity across their portfolios, and on the need to be able to adjust their asset base and leverage quickly, including through asset or portfolio disposals. It will be increasingly important to banks both that their loans are readily transferable – without borrower consent – and that the terms of transfer are standardised. The tight-knit "club" of banks who are effectively committed to a project financing right through to maturity may become a thing of the past.

Arguably the most profound shift that is under discussion in the projects market in light of regulatory change is the potential role of project bonds. Highly rated bonds are treated relatively favourably under Basel III in two ways. Firstly, they require a relatively low proportion of stable funding under the NSFR. Secondly, bonds of sufficiently high rating can themselves be used as short term liquidity cover under the LCR, because they qualify as high quality liquid assets.

It is therefore quite likely that project financiers will seek to increase the proportion of debt that is offered in bond form, as opposed to loan. There are a number of challenges to be overcome, however, if the bond market is going to assume this greater role. For example, there can be challenges persuading bondholders to accept construction risk in the early phases of a project, although these may not be insurmountable. Additionally, bondholder voting is an unwieldy way of making key creditor decisions on issues such as waivers, particularly since the retreat of monoline insurers (who used to act as 'coordinating creditors') from the market. It is yet to be seen what market standard will emerge to address this latter issue. It is possible that a 'bondholders' agent' concept will evolve and/or that electronic voting among bondholders will be made workable and efficient.

It should also be noted that it is unclear what impact other regulatory changes – such as 'Solvency II,' the new regulatory regime for European insurers – will have on the project bond market. Overall however, there is cause to be optimistic that the use of project bond structures will to an extent alleviate some of the impact of Basel III on project finance. Perhaps what is required at this stage is a significant 'push' from governments or other infrastructure buyers to get one or two path-finding deals done.

Conclusions

Undoubtedly, Basel III will have an impact on project financing, just as it will on other areas of banking activity. The cost of project debt is likely to be affected by the increased capital-intensity of lending generally. Discussions over tenor can be expected to be complex while banks resolve how to meet the NSFR in respect of long term lending, and debt structures may change. The availability and cost of letters of credit may well be adversely affected. However, there is little need to believe, at this early stage, that the impact will be crippling for the market. Like other forms of loan business, the capital intensity of project lending relative to the trading book may actually decrease, increasing its relative attractiveness to banks. Assuming demand for infrastructure is robust, it seems likely that the project finance market will adapt and evolve, as capital markets tend to, to overcome the challenges posed by Basel III.

8 Déjà Vu or a New Paradigm?

LIAM O'KEEFFE
Head of Project Finance, Global Loan Syndications Group,
Crédit Agricole Corporate & Investment Bank

Just when we thought the loan markets were finally over the worst, a financial storm has blown up in the Eurozone that threatens to engulf the project finance market. Since the start of the Credit Crunch, if we exclude state owned banks, the market has been dominated by Eurozone and Japanese banks.

Take away the eurozone banks and the project finance market would look decidedly sick if not in terminal decline. According to PFI's table of global initial mandated lead arrangers, the eurozone banks accounted for more than one third of total commitments in the first half of 2011. If that amount of liquidity was to disappear overnight, it would represent a major collapse in the market and leave sponsors and governments that rely on banks to fund infrastructure with a major headache.

If that was bad enough, many commentators are suggesting that Basel III will deliver the coup de grace to project lending by banks leaving the market wide open to the bond markets to take over and inject some new market discipline into the product. Is it really possible that a market worth US$200bn annually according to PFI will really disappear more or less overnight? And if the loan market does collapse, what will replace it?

It is surprising that there has recently been so much negative press about the project finance market. After all, it had a comparatively less painful credit crunch than most other loan products. If the crunch started mid-2007, project finance appeared to be oblivious to

#	2010	2009	2008	2007	2006
1	State Bank of India	State Bank of India	RBS	BNPP	RBS
2	Bank of Taiwan	Crédit Agricole CIB	BNPP	RBS	Crédit Agricole CIB
3	IDBI	BNPP	State Bank of India	Dexia	Mizuho
4	Axis Bank	Societe Generale	SMBC	Crédit Agricole CIB	Societe Generale
5	BNPP	SMBC	Crédit Agricole CIB	Mizuho	ABN.Amro
6	Crédit Agricole CIB	IDBI	Dexia	BoS	BNPP
7	IDFC	Mitsubishi UFJ	Mitsubishi UFJ	Societe Generale	BBVA
8	Mitsubishi UFJ	BBVA	WestLB	SMBC	WestLB
9	Societe Generale	Santander	ING	State Bank of India	State Bank of India
10	SMBC	Mizuho	Fortis	Mitsubishi UFJ	Mitsubishi UFJ

Figure 8.1   PFI global mandated league table position

the rising panic as the volume of loans arranged reached an all-time record in the third quarter of 2008 even as the rest of the loan markets were going into freefall.

It was only the collapse of Lehman Bros that brought the party to an end. 2009 saw a 45 per cent fall in global volumes with the market reaching its nadir in the first quarter of that year, two quarters ahead of the global loan markets. Fortunately, project finance bounced back much faster. A bystander might have assumed that project banks had survived their biggest test and come through with flying colours. Perhaps though this time things will be different?

Perhaps not! The speed of the recovery in the project finance loan market was extraordinary and driven by a number of factors, the most important of which is the role of sponsors. In fact many of the so called experts who are predicting the demise of the project finance loan market forget one key fact. It is sponsors that drive the market, not banks. Banks are simply responding to the needs of their clients and providing them with what they need.

After all, it is sponsors that identify the projects, develop them and eventually bring them to market. This involves enormous investment of time and resources and it is only relatively late in the process that lenders start to become heavily involved. Given the high costs of all that effort, it is hard for sponsors to abandon projects, even if those costs are what economists call 'sunk costs' and should have no impact on the final decision to proceed or abandon.

There may also be reputational or relationship considerations that make it almost impossible for a sponsor to walk away from a project. Governments and joint venture partners have long memories and are unlikely to give a second chance to a fickle sponsor who cut and run when the going got tough. Infrastructure is a long term game and only those prepared to take a long term view of investment should get involved. The

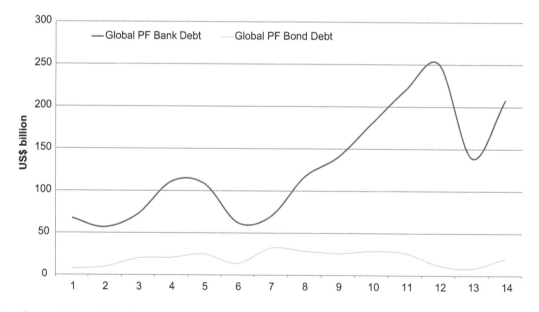

Figure 8.2   Global project finance volumes to 2010

Source: Project Financial International

commercial reality is that sponsors usually remain committed to projects through thick and thin if they want to remain in business.

So, if sponsors are prepared to stick with a project, they also expect their relationship banks to do so too. In essence, project finance is about trust between the various parties and a willingness to confront problems together. Sponsors need to know that the lenders on a project will work with them to ensure the long-term success of the project. Getting to financial close is just the first step in a long process to reaching project completion and the generation of stable cashflows.

While banks can be pressured into supporting transactions by sponsors, they are not altogether unwilling brides. Shy perhaps but the physical asset security and premium pricing relative to corporate loans makes project finance an attractive asset class. In fact, project finance loans could be thought of as the industrial equivalent of a prime mortgage. What could be safer?

During an economic downturn, project finance loans tend to perform better than other asset classes. Ahead of financial close, banks spend months analysing reports, modelling cash flows and negotiating risks. All that effort brings its rewards with investment grade risk profiles but more importantly high levels of recovery in the event of a default. Unlike those fancy pre-credit crunch products like collateralized debt obligations (CDOs) and collateralized loan obligations (CLOs) that have caused so much trouble, project finance arrangers usually retain 'skin' in the game and lenders don't rely on third party ratings to tell them whether it's safe or not to invest. We put our money where our mouth is and take real risk.

All that effort has paid off. In the long run, project finance has served committed banks well with steady earnings growth, healthy returns and the opportunity to cross-sell products like interest rate swaps. Project revenues tend to be uncorrelated with the wider economy and so more resistant to the cycle of boom and bust that can be so painful for banks when their borrowers fall like dominos into financial distress.

It may not be as glamorous as a leveraged buy-out (LBO) but it's certainly a lot safer. Project finance bankers often have to work late into the night for weeks on end in order to close deals but when they do finally get to bed, they sleep soundly dreaming of reinforced concrete, steel and kilometres of tarmac!

So what about the future? So far there are no signs that banks are giving up. It's true that a few banks have left the market. Depfa and IKB have largely exited whilst the Irish banks are selling their portfolios. Alliance & Leicester and Fortis have been swallowed by larger banks. After an initial wobble, it looked as if Dexia had survived the first wave of the crunch only to succumb with the latest round of volatility. Could Dexia be the tip of the iceberg? Perhaps it's just a forerunner of what is to come. A bank swamped by too much long dated paper on its balance sheet that lacked the financial flexibility to adapt to changing market conditions.

Maybe but Dexia is not a typical bank. Most large banks are structured differently to Dexia and have a healthy balance of long and short term paper on their books. Take RBS for example. Although no longer top of the league tables it is still surprisingly active ranking number 14 in PFI's table of global initial mandated loan arrangers for the first half of this year so down but not out! In fact, contrary to popular opinion, it remains the most active British bank in the market admittedly with the help of the British taxpayer. However, the reason is quite simply that RBS is now a client focused bank and many of its clients value its skills as a project finance adviser and arranger.

Just as there have been departures from the top of the league tables we also have new players moving up. Change is in the air reflecting the post credit crunch global economic landscape. It's not just the Japanese banks that are throwing their balance sheets around. BTMU's purchase of the RBS portfolio was a real statement of intent but for the second year running, the PFI global league tables were topped by a non-Japanese, Asian bank: State Bank of India.

Asian banks are becomingly increasingly dominant in the league tables, even if their focus is, for the time being, largely confined to domestic markets. However, we are beginning to see non-Japanese, Asian sponsors and contractors exploring opportunities in the EMEA region. As they begin investing, they will expect their relationship banks to join them. This will significantly increase liquidity in the markets, perhaps at a time when the traditional European lenders are more constrained.

So can the banks really maintain momentum and meet the growing needs of borrowers? Banks are still paying a very high premium for their funding and liquidity costs with long dated paper proportionally higher. There is still a suspicion that there could be more pain to come whether through more losses or regulation. Either way, the markets are not yet ready to give banks the benefit of the doubt.

This is reflected in credit default swap (CDS) prices that remain stubbornly high and very volatile as each new twist in the euro saga sends the market lurching from panic to relief. Although, CDS prices are at best purely indicative they do provide a guide to future bank funding costs. At the moment, we see three implied tiers amongst the main players in the market. The large Spanish and Italian banks have an implied cost of funds at c.300–400bp depending on the time of day. The second tier of banks is represented by the large European banks at c.150–250bp and the third tier is the Japanese banks at c.125–225bp.

On this analysis, one would expect pricing to be directly linked to the size of the loan, all things being equal. Smaller deals should price around the Japanese bank cost of funds with pricing jumping as each tier has to be tapped to achieve a fully funded deal.

However, in practice banks are behaving as if cost of funds is in fact significantly lower. The Gazprom sponsored Nord Stream II closed in February of this year and included Hermes and SACE facilities carrying margins of 110bp and 115bp respectively for a tenor of 10 years. Even though ECA facilities use little capital, margins must still be above funding costs in order to be profitable. Yet these margins are significantly below CDS prices. Nord Stream I has just been repriced in line with its successor.

These two deals were not European anomalies. In the Gulf, the US$4.5bn Qatari deal, Barzan, is due to close with pricing rumoured at pre-completion of 130bp rising to 200bp post-completion on the uncovered and 130bp flat on the ECA tranches. Tenor of the loans is 16 years. If market gossip is correct there is only one eurozone bank in the syndicate proving that they are not indispensable to the market.

Given the eye-watering pricing on these three deals, it would seem that banks have surprising flexibility in how they calculate cost of funds and where they allocate their capital. Strong appetite for project finance loans has clearly resulted in highly competitive pricing but is also driven by very low margins on corporate loans together with a general lack of lending opportunities across all banking products. Not only that, but large sponsors can lean on their relationship banks to squeeze every last basis point out of the banks.

How long the pricing environment will remain so competitive is hard to predict and if the eurozone crisis continues pricing surely must rise. Even without that, the pain of bank regulation is starting to be felt and adding to bank misery. Fortunately though, the picture around regulatory risk is becoming clearer although there is still some uncertainty about the full impact of Basel III or indeed whether regulatory authorities have decided on all the changes to be made. There has also been much speculation that Basel III will change the way banks lend, limiting tenors to less than 10 years, and that will open the way for the bond markets to take over? Well don't bank on it!

Basel III focuses on two elements, capital and liquidity. The changes to capital will require most banks to improve their equity buffers and limit the total assets relative to that buffer. The overall effect will be to constrain balance sheet growth over the period of implementation. The liquidity measures will mainly impact undrawn, short term loans. This was one of the problems identified during the Credit Crunch. The simultaneous and unexpected utilization of back-up facilities by borrowers at a time of crisis created enormous stress on the financial system and stretched liquidity of the financial markets. But note, project finance loans were not directly a problem.

So in summary, the only clear message is that Basel III will require banks to set aside more equity capital either through retention of distributable reserves or rights issues. This will be implemented over the next few years with full compliance by the beginning of 2018. Lending will be constrained but that is not necessarily a bad thing. Provided banks are profitable they should be able to achieve a healthy combination of balance sheet growth, profit retention and dividends to shareholders. Nevertheless, as Basel III is implemented there will undoubtedly be upwards pressure on pricing as dividends to shareholders are reduced and in some cases fresh capital has to be raised.

However, that is only half the story. The main consequences of Basel III should be to make banks safer. Lower risk should eventually translate into a lower cost of capital. Those high CDS prices mentioned earlier should fall significantly from their current levels with a consequent benefit to bank funding costs.

Of course, it is hard to quantify the impact of these changes on the loan markets. Nevertheless, my feeling is that assuming there is no further escalation in global political risk and the Euro countries manage to contain or limit any break-up of the Euro, loan market pricing will gradually trend down until full implementation of Basel III has been achieved and banks are seen to be less risky. The rise in costs due to higher equity buffers will be more than offset by the perceived de-risking of bank balance sheets. Having said that, pricing should remain well above the ultra fine pricing seen in 2006–7 in the run up to the Credit Crunch. It would be nice to think that we have learnt some lessons from then.

In particular, there is one lesson that banks still need to learn. There has been talk of requirements to ensure that banks match balance sheet funding to the life of assets on the balance sheet. Although no rules have as yet been defined, the main object of this exercise appears to be to stop banks funding themselves entirely in the overnight markets. Most banks already match funding to the average life of their portfolios and use internal liquidity charges to penalize longer tenor loans.

Most, but not all. It is likely that this is one of the main factors that finally brought Dexia down. It is always tempting for a bank to use cheap short term borrowing to finance a better paid, long term loan. Playing this game can significantly improve profitability and give a bank a competitive advantage. That works provided short term borrowing remains cheap. Even if short term costs start to rise this need not be a problem provided the loans mature or prepay quickly.

Unfortunately, many project finance loans have tenors in excess of 10 years and locked in pricing that hardly changes. Since the credit crunch, short term borrowing costs have risen steadily to the extent that they are significantly higher than the pricing on long term loans booked before the credit crunch. It is now more than four years since the start of the credit crunch and some banks have been haemorrhaging cash with no end in sight to their pain.

If there is one lesson that project lenders must learn, it is that they must protect their balance sheets from changes in funding costs. In fact we started to see this shortly after Lehmans. Hard and soft mini-perm structures became popular. These provide strong incentives for sponsors to refinance loans whilst at the same time giving them flexibility as to when they do so. Of course, sponsors would rather not have to worry about a refinancing unless it will translate into savings for the project in question.

One possible solution is to look to the capital markets to provide that cheaper long term refinancing solution. Some have claimed that Basel III will force banks to restrict long-term lending to less than 10 years and reduce the role of lenders to providers of medium term bridge loans with a bond take out creating a new paradigm. Banks will provide construction bridge finance whilst bond markets will finance the long term commercial operation of the asset in question. No more long term bank lending.

Although there is no evidence of this as yet, it is certainly true that whereas banks are better at taking construction risk than the bond markets, bond investors are perhaps better placed at taking very long tenors albeit that they generally prefer to see a stronger risk profile than is usually the case for projects.

So will the mighty bond markets step in and sweep the banks aside? The departure of the monoline insurers in 2007/8 was a major blow to the project bond market but appetite is recovering. Bond markets are riding high again and there is excess liquidity driving pricing down. Nevertheless, project bonds remain a rare sight accounting for barely 10 per cent of total project debt raised in the first half of 2011. Outside of the Anglo-Saxon investor base there appears to be little enthusiasm for long term, weak investment grade paper.

Furthermore, there are three barriers to a major shift in the current status quo that will need to be overcome. First, as already mentioned, projects financed through the bond markets account for only perhaps a tenth of total funding requirement. That implies a big shift in human resources from banks to bond investors. That is not impossible but will take time.

Second, and more importantly, bond investors (unlike banks) do not invest on the basis of relationship. Many sponsors are wary of going to the bond markets because of the potential loss of control. This is a key point. Many sponsors will not wish to place infrastructure that is essential to their business at the mercy of the wider financial markets. Project finance may be non-recourse but neither party expects the other to walk when problems inevitably materialize.

Thirdly, most bond investors require third party ratings before they will invest. Whilst the due diligence is more or less the same as that conducted by banks, sponsors may feel they have less control over the process with rating agencies. Banks are more likely to give their clients the benefit of the doubt when due diligence throws up unexpected problems. The public disclosure of sensitive, commercial information can also deter sponsors.

In spite of the above, there is clearly an important role for the bond markets and that role will continue to grow with the market. Hybrid deals such as utilities, ports and airports have been relatively easy for the bond markets to digest and more complex single assets have also been financed although the rating needs to reflect a strong investment grade outlook. Project bonds are here to stay and in the right circumstances provide an efficient and competitive funding solution.

Nevertheless, many sponsors will prefer to stick with the tried and trusted route of the loan markets with the occasional opportunistic foray into the bond markets when liquidity makes it attractive to do so. Refinancing bank debt carries no penalty unlike a bond. A bond is for life whereas a loan need only be for Christmas, to re-cycle a well-known British slogan!

So in conclusion, will the latest round of market changes trigger a new paradigm as banks finance construction and look to the bond markets for their exit route. Many investment bankers would like to think so. Alternatively, the markets will weather the Euro storm and project banks will bounce back much as they did after the collapse of Lehman Bros with non-Eurozone lenders taking advantage of the high margins and the weakness of their European competitors to increase market share.

Whatever the outcome, there will be growing demand for long-term project finance whether provided by banks or bond investors. The global economy is slowly returning to growth and governments everywhere must also provide new or upgrade legacy infrastructure if only to kick-start their exhausted economies back into expansion. Emerging countries are constrained by their ratings and developed countries by their existing borrowing. Then there is the urgent need to drive down carbon emissions.

All this will need capital, much of it in the form of project finance debt. Governments will expect and demand the support of the banking and wider financial community in part as the price for government support during the Credit Crunch. If Basel III is seen to be too draconian, endangering growth and investment, then it is likely the impact will be softened or delayed. Bank debt will be more expensive for some time to come, opening the way for capital markets to compete more effectively but this will be at least partially offset by long-term swapped rates remaining exceptionally low. The combined effect means that the overall cost of debt whether bank or bond will be low enough to encourage sponsors to invest in long-term infrastructure.

I suspect the final result will be more déjà vu than new paradigm but there is no doubting that the door is now open wide for the capital markets to jump in should they want to.

9 *Project Bonds in Project Finance*

JEAN-PIERRE BOUDRIAS
Director investment banking, Credit Suisse
REBECCA KOTIN
Analyst, energy and project finance debt capital markets, Credit Suisse

Traditionally, commercial banks had provided financing for large scale infrastructure projects financed in non-recourse private markets. Beginning in the early 1990s, project sponsors began accessing the bond markets to finance projects. The project bond market was born. Over the past 20 years, capital markets have been accessed to finance multiple types of assets on a non-recourse basis, from oil and gas and power generation assets to infrastructure projects both in developed and emerging markets.

Nowadays, project sponsors will access the bond markets when desiring long-term fixed rate debt with a flexible covenant package. The asset class has proved popular with investors as project notes have experienced amongst the lowest default rates and high recovery rates for the few defaults, according to a study conducted by Standard & Poor's.

What are Project Bonds and How They are Used

Project bond markets include non-recourse project-based bond issuances, generally with long tenors and investment grade ratings, but not necessarily. A typical issuance would be from a project operating company with a long term off-take contract with the debt amortizing fully by the term of the contract. The issue would be rated investment grade by one or more rating agencies. Rating agencies have provided specific guidelines for projects to achieve investment grade ratings (i.e., minimum debt service coverage ratios, minimum requirements for commercial framework, etc.). Historically, project bonds were mostly used to refinance existing indebtedness, as institutional investors and rating agencies were reckoned to have high thresholds to be comfortable with construction risk but, provided the right protections and safeguards, construction projects have been successfully financed in the project bond market.

The project bond market will be ideally suitable for projects, either as the sole indebtedness or with bank debt for larger projects, with the following characteristics:

- large projects (total capital in excess of US$450m)

Year	Total	Sectors
1996	4.8	Power, 2.6; Petrochemicals, 1.4 and; Infrastructure, 0.8
1997	7.5	Infrastructure, 2.4; Power, 1.9; Telecoms, 1.3; Oil & Gas 1.0 and; Mining, 0.9
1998	9.8	Power, 4.5; Telecoms, 2.2; Oil & Gas, 1.3; Infrastructure, 1.3 and Mining, 0.5
1999	19.9	Power, 7.2; Telecoms, 5.2; Infrastructure, 3.7; Oil & Gas, 2.8; Petrochemicals, 0.7 and; Leisure, 0.3
2000	20.8	Power, 11.9; Infrastructure, 3.4; Oil & Gas, 3.3; Telecoms, 2.0 and; Industrial, 0.2
2001	25.0	Power, 17.3; Oil & Gas, 3.8; Infrastructure, 2.4 and; Telecoms, 1.5
2002	13.8	Infrastructure, 6.5; Power, 4.3; Oil & Gas, 2.6; Industrial, 0.3 and; Leisure, 0.1
2003	32.1	Power, 12.3; Infrastructure, 9.8; Oil & Gas, 7.0; Social infrastructure, 2.1 and; Telecoms, 0.9
2004	28.6	Power, 11.4, Infrastructure, 8.0; Oil & Gas, 5.2; Social infrastructure, 3.0; Petrochemicals, 0.7; Mining, 0.2 and; Industrial, 0.1
2005	27.5	Oil & Gas, 9.7, Power, 7.3, Social infrastructure, 5.0; Infrastructure, 4.4; Mining, 0.7 and; Petrochemicals, 0.4
2006	28.7	Oil & Gas, 9.0; Social infrastructure, 8.6; Infrastructure, 6.8; Power, 2.5; Mining, 0.7; Petrochemicals, 0.6 and; Leisure, 0.5
2007	26.8	Infrastructure, 10.3; Power, 7.0; Social infrastructure, 6.1; Oil & Gas, 2.1 and; Leisure, 1.3
2008	11.9	Infrastructure, 6.9; Oil & Gas, 4.5; Power, 0.4 and; Mining, 0.1
2009	8.5	Oil & Gas, 5.5; Power, 1.6; Social infrastructure, 0.9 and; Infrastructure, 0.5
2010	19.8	Infrastructure, 7.7; Power, 4.8; Oil & Gas, 2.5; Social infrastructure, 2.2; Mining, 2.0 and; Leisure, 0.6
2011	22.2	Infrastructure, 6.0; Power, 5.5, Social infrastructure, 5.3; Oil & Gas, 5.1 and; Mining, 0.3

Figure 9.1   Project bonds by sector (US$m)
Source: Thomson Reuters Project Finance International

- operating projects
- long-term contracted cash flows from creditworthy off-takers
- fixed price off-take agreements
- highly-rated project participants

Project sponsors will generally opt to access the project bond markets for large projects that necessitate the depth of the bond market and/or when they desire long-term fixed rate debt which matches the project's contractual and commercial framework. Project bonds have become increasingly more attractive (and utilized) subsequent to the depths of the credit crisis in 2008 as the bond market presented itself as a more liquid source of funding. Prior to this, the bank market had been exceedingly popular given covenant flexibility and prepayability.

As pressures remained on the commercial bank market throughout the early portion of 2009, sponsors increasingly turned to the bond market in an effort to benefit in tandem with broader corporate debt market strength. This was used for financing new projects, as well as refinancing existing projects given the attractive economics of doing so. As mentioned previously, this marked a departure from previous financing precedents, in which the project bond market was generally tapped to refinance rather than bear construction risk through the first few years of the financing term.

144A vs 4(2) Markets

Project bonds are almost exclusively issued via the 144A and 4(2) private placement markets. Though definitive investor bases have developed in each market, significant crossover now exists between the two. The 144A market broadly speaking offers greater liquidity to non-SEC registered offerings, and attracts substantially the same institutional investors as a public offering. Buyers of Rule 144A securities must be Qualified Institutional Buyers (QIBs) with more than US$100m in securities. Foreign buyers may purchase the offering under Regulation S if the offering is conducted in a global format. Securities are thereby freely tradable, subject to certain resale restrictions. As such, the syndication of 144A securities are often syndicated to more expansive investor base, which is further discussed in the following pages.

Much of the decision to pursue one market over another will depend on cost, documentation and disclosure readiness (and willingness). Other factors to be considered in determining the appropriate market are the size and tenor of the offering, as well as desired financing structure. The disclosure requirements also have a large impact on the decision to enter one market over another, as well as the desired execution timeline and distribution. The receipt of a 10b-5 comfort opinion is also demanded for 144A-style offerings, whereas 4(2) offerings entail an assumption of risk by the investors that the information being provided in the offering documents merits investor reliance on transparency and factual accuracy.

Pros and Cons

Project bonds have a number of advantages vs commercial bank financings but also have a few drawbacks as detailed below:

Pros:

- Long tenor and strong capacity to absorb large quantum of debt
- Flexible covenant package (oftentimes incurrence-only)
- Fixed rate
- Streamlined, quick-to-market syndication process subsequent to finalizing documentation and preparation stages

Year	Bonds	Loans	Total	% Bonds to loans
1996	4.8	42.8	47.6	10.0
1997	7.5	67.4	74.9	10.0
1998	9.8	56.6	66.4	14.7
1999	19.9	72.4	92.3	21.6
2000	20.8	110.8	131.6	15.8
2001	25.0	108.5	133.5	18.7
2002	13.8	62.2	76.0	18.1
2003	32.2	69.6	101.8	31.6
2004	28.6	116.4	145.0	19.7
2005	27.5	140.3	167.8	16.4
2006	28.7	180.6	209.3	13.7
2007	26.8	220.0	246.8	10.8
2008	11.8	250.6	262.4	4.5
2009	8.5	139.2	147.7	5.8
2010	19.8	208.2	228.0	8.7
2011	22.2	213.5	235.7	9.4

Figure 9.2   Project financings by type (US$m)
Source: Thomson Reuters Project Finance International

- Current bond market environment is robust with cash looking for stable projects and yield opportunities as compared with historically low rate environment that defines current landscape

Cons:

- Expensive to modify or refinance as soliciting consent from bond holders can be a difficult exercise. Furthermore, bonds lack prepayment flexibility of bank loan market
- Generally require ratings
- Negative carry and risk of prematurely locking in long-term rates
- Generally require more procedural steps to come to market than issuing via the bank market

Investor Base

As previously mentioned, project bonds have been an established funding source for large-scale non-resource undertakings for 20 years. As such, a diversified investor base has developed to support product syndication. Given the structured nature of most project finance transactions and the fact that many are tailored to achieve weak investment grade ratings, the investor base is largely dominated by large insurance companies and money managers with risk appetite commensurate with many project-level financings that may also imply construction risk in addition to any operational risk posed by the project in the initial financing stage. Each class of investor approaches the credit process differently.

LARGE INSURANCE COMPANIES

The most active buyers of investment grade project paper have historically been insurance companies that prior to the emergence of the project bond market had provided long-term fixed-rate financings to projects. Risk appetite for structured project paper can be constrained by investment quality as deemed by the NAIC publicly traded securities listing definitions, but is also diversified by the inherent investment framework under which they operate. In other words, insurance companies are often incentivized to buy across separate portfolios with the investment decision made independently at each. Insurance buyers tend to be more yield focused; given the nature of their business, they are well suited to participate in the long-end of the yield curve given need for extra duration (asset-liability matching):

i.

Private-side portfolios: Generally speaking, more conditioned to 'true' 4(2) private placement offerings whereby the reporting and financial covenants are oftentimes formed through negotiation with a limited club of investors, creating the potential for a tighter covenant package. 4(2) private offerings can be marketed with or without ratings, and typically see little pricing penalty for small/odd tranche sizes or odd maturities allowing issuers to match their cash flow profiles with maturities. That said, however, many insurance companies demand at least one rating from the three major rating agencies in order to arrive at, or sponsor, the offering to be designated as NAIC 1 or 2. This limits the amount of capital they must hold against the security.

ii.

Public portfolio: More traditionally focused on 144A style offerings which afford the offering with a larger investor base composed of Qualified Institutional Buyers (QIBS). This generally implies a more flexible covenant package though documentation and disclosure requirements are stricter. This group of investors typically demand at least two ratings from Moody's, S&P and Fitch in order to participate in the US public (or 144A) capital markets, although some deals have been successfully marketed with only one (albeit with a pricing concession). Private-style offerings, and thereby investors, are more amenable to delayed draw offerings in an effort to provide a means of mitigating negative carry on behalf of the issuer.

Depending on the insurance company, some are conditioned to evaluate the credit only subsequent to the other portfolio doing so. In other words, the broader investment practice of the institution will determine whether only one, or both, may invest in the project bonds under consideration and whether one portfolio must pass on the credit for it to be considered by the second portfolio.

LARGE ASSET MANAGERS

Large asset managers have become increasingly involved in the project finance capital markets in recent years given natural fit vis-à-vis many of these QIB's investment philosophies and reach for additional yield-bearing projects. Recent transactions have seen asset managers establish the anchor bid to the entire offering, thereby driving subsequent price talk and serving as a voice for broader investor appetite. Generally speaking, money managers are more total return focused but remain active across various parts of the capital structure.

PENSION FUNDS

Though pension funds have not trafficked in the space as much as large insurance companies and asset managers, the long-term and stable cash flow profile nature of project bonds make them a natural fit for these types fixed income portfolios. A number of large pension funds have recently taken a more active role in participating in project offerings as they become increasingly comfortable with straightforward construction risk (e.g., wind turbines), as well as highly structured (and covenanted) offerings. Pension funds, similar to other investor classes, have been active across the capital structure, including the participation in tax equity positions.

HEDGE FUNDS

The typical long duration of project bonds and the lack of liquidity in the secondary market often create a mismatch with the investment philosophy and manifested trading strategies of hedge funds. Historically, hedge funds have not taken (or been assigned) an active or anchor role in project financings given the syndication process as well as demonstrated interest. 144A offerings in particular are more typically allocated to buy-and-hold investors, offering stability to the offering in any secondary market that exists in the security.

A typical orderbook will see 70–80 per cent of the bonds allocated to large insurance companies and asset managers, with the vast majority of accounts being allocated sums larger than US$20m of the overall deal, dependent on the net deal size.

Investment Decision Considerations

Investment decisions on behalf of the above mentioned parties are predicated on a number of factors, all of which are both credit and market dependent. These include but are not limited to:

1. Strength of underlying contracts and, thereby, security of the project
2. Credit ratings and outlook
3. Sponsorship of project and credit quality/duration of off-take arrangements

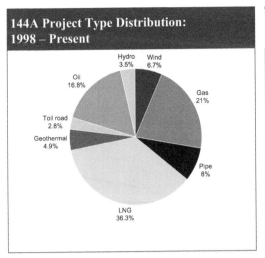

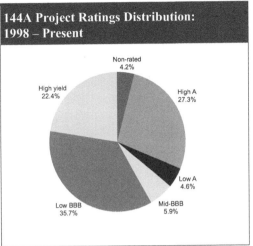

Figure 9.3   114A project type distribution; 1998–present and 114A project ratings distribution: 1998–present

Source: Credit Suisse, Bloomberg

4. Existing exposure to similar projects and the off-take credit
5. Structural enhancements including reserves, collateral package and covenants afforded
6. Sovereign jurisdiction implied by the project's financing arrangements
7. Project cash flow profile and cash waterfall as deemed by reserve arrangements
8. Final life and amortization profile
9. Equity commitment of sponsor and general trust of sponsor's financial discipline and desire to maintain active interest in project throughout the financing term.

Recovery Analysis

Recovery is dependent upon a number of factors for project finance defaults like those in corporate defaults, including the initial quality of the assets, geography and local jurisdiction governing the recovery process.

Investor Demand

Investor demand for structured project bonds noticeably diminishes in times of market weakness; the broader health of the corporate credit market works to bolster demand for project paper. Though still a situation-specific decision, broader market health and corporate supply augment the fixed income project finance pipeline.

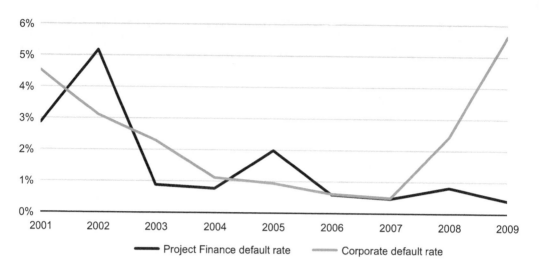

Figure 9.4 Historical annual default rises

Instrument Type	Recovery (%)
All project finance debt	72
All corporate loans/facilities	74
Corporate secured bonds	57
All other corporate bonds	34
Total corporate defaulted instruments	50
*Corporate data is from 1987-2009	

Figure 9.5 Project finance and corporate recovery rates

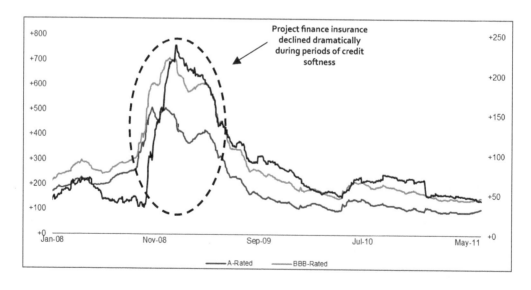

Figure 9.6 A vs BBB spread differential vs project finance issuance

Source: Credit Suisse LUCI Index

Preparation and Process

STAGE 1: PREPARATION

i) Due diligence to access the project's overall bankability and 'financeability':
    a) Hire relevant third parties (e.g., counsel, consultant, independent engineer)
    b) Review political, economic, regulatory and tax issues
    c) Analyse risks and mitigants
    d) Assist in negotiating/reviewing contracts
    e) Develop and maintain financial model
    f) Coordinate site visits, as necessary
ii) Establish funding structure in light of desired financial strategy:
    a) Advise on debt and equity financing options
    b) Draft preliminary Offering Memorandum ('OM')
    c) Appoint lender consultants and finalize reports
    d) Prepare financing plan, term sheet and security package
    e) Shortlist potential arrangers, underwriters and targeted investors
iii) Rating agency process:
    a) Engage rating agencies and develop financing structure that will achieve the desired ratings outcome
    b) Develop and finalize rating agency presentations
    c) Coordinate follow-up with the agencies after presenting the final material and assist them in arriving at the commensurate ratings outcome

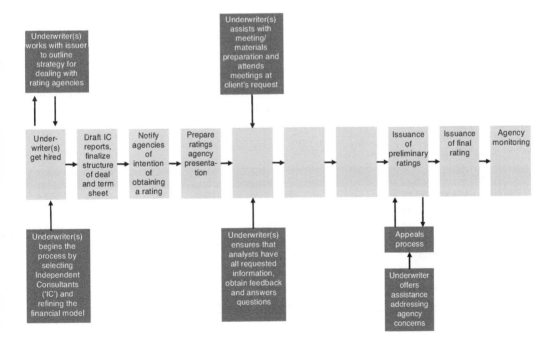

Figure 9.7   Bond in preparation phase

STAGE 2: EXECUTION

i) Finalize financing documents:
   a) Term sheet
   b) Offering Memorandum and auxiliary financing documents including the Independent Engineer's report, as well as Inter-creditor Agreement (as needed)
   c) Receive rating agency confirmation of ratings
ii) Roadshow:
   a) Draft/finalize roadshow presentation and refine marketing highlights
   b) Engage in physical or electronic roadshow as demanded by market conditions and complexity of the transaction
   c) Premarketing: similar to the above mechanics but prior to announcement, proactively educating sales force and marketing leaders on the merits of the offering
iii) Launch, price, fund and close:
   a) Evaluate the market to determine most opportune and appropriate window for market entry
   b) Announce transaction to the market
   c) Marketing: directly after announcement of the transaction, distribute marketing materials and develop early price views in order to introduce unofficial price talk and build an orderbook through value proposition and scarcity perception
   d) Launch: deal publicly launched with official price talk and tranche sizes
   e) Price offering at tightest spread that holds the book together and ensures a successful deal

144A vs International Markets

The US capital markets continue to be the deepest source of liquidity for project issuance. US investors have demonstrated that they are willing to participate in international project financings so long as they are comfortable with the country risk and the structure of the transaction. In fact, from 2004–2006, over half of PF issuance was international

Date	Issuer	Country of Origin	Rating	Amount	Final/AL	Spread
03/29/11	Inkia Energy Ltd	Peru	B1/BB-	300.0	10NC5	+502.4
11/10/10	Odebrecht Drilling Norbe VIII/IX	Brazil	Baa3/BBB-	1,500.0	10/8	+370
11/05/10	AES Dominicana	Dominican Republic	B-/B	284.0	10NC5	+696.7
10/14/10	Lancer Finance	Brazil	Baa3/BBB-	270.0	6/3	+470
07/23/09	Dolphin Energy	UAE	Aa3/A+	1,250.0	10/5.65	+337.5
07/16/09	Ras Laffan LNG 3	Qatar	Aa2/A	1,115.0	5	+312.5
07/15/09	Ras Laffan LNG 3	Qatar	Aa2/A	500.0	3	+300
07/15/09	Ras Laffan LNG 3	Qatar	Aa2/A	6,150.0	10	+325

Note: Data represets 144A non-domestic issuers

Figure 9.8 Select issuance from non-US issuers

Source: Credit Suisse, Bloomberg

Year	Total	Location
1996	4.8	North America, 1.1; Latin America 0.3; Europe, 1.2; Middle East & Africa, 1.4 and; Asia, 0.8
1997	7.5	North America, 2.5; Latin America, 2.6; Europe, 1.1; Australasia, 0.7 and; Asia, 0.6
1998	9.8	North America, 4.3; Latin America, 2.7; Europe, 1.3; Middle East & Africa, 0.3; Australasia, 1.1 and; Asia, 0.1
1999	19.9	North America 14.8; Latin America, 1.3; Europe, 2.4; Middle East & Africa, 0.8; Australasia, 0.5 and; Asia. 0.1
2000	20.8	North America, 11.8; Latin America, 4.2; Europe, 3.2; Middle East & Africa, 0.2 and; Australasia, 1.4
2001	25.0	North America, 16.4; Latin America, 4.7; Europe, 0.9; Middle East & Africa, 0.1; Australasia, 0.5 and; Asia, 2.4
2002	13.8	North America, 3.4; Latin America, 3.7; Europe, 1.9; Middle East & Africa, 0.1; Australasia, 2.8 and; Asia, 1.9
2003	32.1	North America, 10.4; Latin America, 7.1; Europe, 9.1; Middle East & Africa, 0.3; Australasia, 2.9 and; Asia, 2.3
2004	28.6	North America, 8.8; Latin America, 6.3; Europe, 8.1; Middle East & Africa, 0.8; Australasia, 3.0 and; Asia, 1.6
2005	27.5	North America, 14.3; Latin America, 3.1; Europe, 4.7; Middle East & Africa, 2.2; Australasia, 0.8 and; Asia, 2.4
2006	28.7	North America, 7.0; Latin America, 2.2; Europe, 12.1; Middle East & Africa, 2.8; Australasia, 4.2 and; Asia, 0.4
2007	26.8	North America, 10.0; Latin America, 1.6; Europe, 10.5; Australasia, 4.4 and; Asia, 0.3
2008	11.9	North America, 7.0; Latin America, 0.9; Europe, 3.0; Australasia, 0.3 and; Asia, 0.7
2009	8.5	North America, 4.5; Latin America, 0.2; Middle East & Africa, 3.5; Australasia, 0.2 and; Asia, 0.1
2010	19.8	North America, 9.4; Latin America, 0.4; Europe, 3.6; Australasia, 4.6 and; Asia, 1.8
2011	22.2	North America, 8.4; Latin America, 4.7; Europe, 5.5; Middle East & Africa, 1.0; Australasia, 1.0 and; Asia, 1.6

Figure 9.9   Project bonds by location (US$m)
Source: Thomson Reuters Project Finance International

project financings funded in the USS markets. International projects have been financed in the US capital markets since the early 1990s. International issuers have been able to access the market in size at various degrees of the ratings spectrum and continue to diversify country of origin.

Conclusion

As investors continue to allocate funds away from money market funds into yield-bearing products such as corporate bonds, the project bond market has tangentially garnered momentum. Recent transactions have enhanced both structural and pricing precedents in the space. This is occurring simultaneously with a period in which investors are continuing to seek diversity across the capital structure in the project financing arena, thereby expanding the demand for project bonds.

As the pricing of financing in both the bank and bond markets becomes increasingly attractive and corresponding investor appetite diversifies while remaining resilient, project finance issuance is expected to expand in many respects (including funding markets tapped, tenor, position in capital structure, form of security, etc.). Given the fact that most project financings benefit from the existence of one or many long-term contracts that support the revenue stream to the project (which is in turn used to service the debt), strong economic downturns have less of an immediate, tangible effect on the project given the long-term, fixed-price nature of many of the contracts. This is not only reflected in new projects, but also the default (and corresponding recovery) rates of outstanding project bonds. The project bond market is anticipated to maintain strength as investment grade capital market liquidity remains strong vis-à-vis the 2008–2009 timeframe. Strong appetite continues to be manifested in reverse inquiry for project paper as asset classes evolve while demand for low risk, stable cash flow projects remains. A strong technical dynamic coupled with strong historical performance has left the project bond market well-positioned to not only solidify, but expand its current footprint.

CHAPTER **10** *Insurance Principles in Project Finance*

DAVID BORTHWICK
Practice Head, Structured Finance Practice,
Marsh Ltd

Introduction

Insurance is a principal means of risk financing but insurance should never be the first line of defence to any risk scenario. The objective should be to allocate the risk to the party best able to manage the risk with insurance as the fall back solution should something go wrong. In reality however, the availability of insurance does facilitate the transfer of risk by making it more palatable.

Insurance is an integral part of a risk management strategy, its most important function being the financing of risk. But insurance is not a substitute for other forms of risk management such as transfer of risk through contract, mitigation and control. To illustrate the point, it is a principle of insurance that an insured party always acts as if uninsured and an insurer could avoid paying a claim on the grounds that the insured party failed to act prudently to safeguard the property from loss or damage or to mitigate the loss. Some policies have specific undertakings to this effect as a condition precedent to indemnity.

In project finance the lenders have limited recourse against the sponsors of the project company if it is unable to repay the debt and a sponsor has no guarantee that its co-sponsors would step in and rescue the project company should an unfunded, uninsured and unaffordable event occur. Consequently, the project company and its lenders require a risk management strategy that reflects the nature of its business and its financing, and balances the use of insurance to represent the needs of all relevant parties.

Risk Management Philosophies

A risk management strategy follows the organization's philosophy to risk; are they a risk taker or are they risk averse and what is their tolerance (what will the balance sheet absorb) and appetite (despite affordability, what amount of loss are they prepared to bear) for risk?

It is often commented that the interests of the parties (sponsors, lenders and public authority, as applicable) to a project company are aligned and the insurance that would be sought are similar. Well, if you look at insurance in isolation there are some core insurances that would be typically sought by all parties but even then there are invariably differences in the amount and breadth of the cover they require. When you further broaden the review to the overall risk management strategy, there are significant conflicts of interests: The sponsors will have their own risk management philosophies with regard to their investment in the project company and possibly different philosophies where they are a subcontractor, supplier or off-taker to the project company.

Risk Appetite

Lenders tend to be the most risk averse, justified by the fact that they have the least to gain from a successful project and the most to lose from an unsuccessful project. With regard to public private partnerships, the public sector authority would be at the opposite end of the risk appetite spectrum to the lenders, with the sponsors somewhere between the lenders and the authority.

Risk Tolerance

In this regard, a project financed petrochemical business potentially has greater options for dealing with risk than a project financed public private partnership. In the latter case, the service delivery levels and the payment mechanisms are core to the agreement with the authority and there is very limited opportunity to alter the business activities and pricing in order to recover from a catastrophe and the position is further compounded by typically lower margins.

Consequently, the risk philosophies of each party are quite different and they are, therefore, working from different platforms when considering the risk management strategy. This is why the respective parties need their own independent advisers.

Risk Identification and Assessment

In project financing, the lenders are fundamentally interested in the revenue earning capability of the project and therefore, the risk review needs to look at all risks that threaten that revenue. This would obviously include damage to the asset but also external threats such as a loss to a supplier or off-taker or access restrictions. In one project involving on-shore oil fields, processing plant, pipelines and marine terminal, the largest delay in completion of the works risk was a loss to the manufacturing facilities of a key plant manufacturer and in a container terminal port, the largest delay risk was loss of quayside cranes in sea transit to the site.

Identifying and assessing the risks to the project creates a risk profile which enables the respective parties to consider the risk management strategy relevant to them and in particular enables the lenders' independent insurance adviser to overlay the project company's insurance proposal in order to assess the appropriateness and gaps in the insurance programme.

Risk profiles: A road project will obviously be exposed to different risks than to a combined cycle gas turbine power plant project. However, even similar project types will invariably have their own project-specific risks. For instance:

- Brown field versus green field developments.
- Building on flood plains as opposed to dry ground.
- Constructing a road through farm land versus over a high speed train line.
- Constructing and operating onshore and offshore wind farms.

Risk Treatment

Not all risks are insurable, the obvious ones being the deductibles (the first threshold of loss that is excluded from the insurance) and standard policy exclusions. Lenders are even more interested in what is not insured than what is insured as those uninsured risks need to be managed differently. Associated risks may be premium volatility where the cost of insurance can fluctuate over a period, a risk that is particularly relevant to public private partnerships because of their low margins and the contract regulated pricing mechanisms.

Responsibility to Insure

Typically, the project company effects the insurance at their expense. This is preferred by the lenders as it gives them more control over the insurance.

Risk has a cost and transfer, whether to insurance or under contract, comes at a price. The conundrum for the project company, is having paid to transfer the risk to a contractor should they additionally pay to insure it? Arguably, the recipient of the risk i.e., the contractor, should take the insurance position into account when pricing the risk, however, in practice this is not always the case.

In one case, the project company had allocated the fitness for purpose risk to an engineer procure and construct (EPC) contractor and consequently purchased a reduced level of defects, workmanship and material cover under the construction all risks insurance and delay in start-up insurance. At testing and commissioning, the works were found to be defective with very considerable remedial costs and a lengthy delay in completion. The EPC contractor honoured its contractual obligations, remedied the defects at their expense and the liquidated damages were sufficient to service the debt during the delay. Whilst this case had a happy ending for the project company and its lenders, it did highlight that both parties were at the mercy of contract enforcement and the credit risk of the EPC contractor when it could have been insured. The moral of the story is that not only should insurance not be a substitute for risk management but conversely, insurance should not be disregarded merely on the grounds of other forms of risk management, e.g. through allocation. All this potentially does is create new risks as in the scenario cited above.

Principal Insurance Classes

The insurance market is segmented, not only between marine, non-marine, aviation and so on but also within such sectors, with construction insurance typically being underwritten through a separate department to operational insurance.

Both construction and operation insurers are providing insurance for the core risks:

- loss or damage to assets,
- legal liabilities,
- loss of earnings.

However, the difference between them is the nature of the risks that are being insured: The risks arising from constructing the project and the risks arising from operating the project are quite different. For instance, building a hospital has a very different risk profile to operating a hospital.

There would, therefore, be a suite of construction insurance policies and ultimately a suite of operation insurance policies. Theoretically this is straightforward but it is the transition from construction to operation that creates the challenge, because as part of the testing and commissioning process, the project may be in a state of operation even in a reduced capacity. Therefore, whilst contractually, the project is still in its construction phase, practically and for the purpose of insurance, it is now exposed to operational risks so risk under contract and under insurance are out of alignment. Particular attention therefore, needs to be paid to this transition period and the appropriate dovetailing of covers.

Construction Phase

CONSTRUCTION ALL RISKS

The construction all risks insurance insures the works and materials intended for incorporation therein against accidental loss or damage arising out of the works, occurring during the period of insurance, at the site and normally includes elsewhere in the country whilst in transit or temporary storage.

In addition to replacing the works and materials that are lost or damaged, the insurance would include the costs of demolition and removal of debris of the damaged property, the costs of professional fees necessary for its reinstatement and the expediting costs to minimize the lost time, e.g., overtime or airfreight costs.

The insurance has a specific period of insurance being the estimated construction period which will need to be extended if the works duration over runs. The premium is also calculated on the estimated construction cost and is adjusted upon completion at the actual construction cost. A longer construction duration and higher-than-estimated construction cost can therefore attract an additional premium.

In addition to the construction period the insurance will also extend to include an agreed defects liability period usually similar to the defects period in the construction contract but not exceeding three years (longer periods up to five years may be available but may have a reduced level of cover after three years).

The insurance cover provided during the defects liability period is:

- Loss or damage occurring during the defects liability period from a cause arising before practical completion (this can vary and some insurers impose restrictions such as requiring the cause of the defect to occur during the period of insurance and at the site, e.g., would not include pre-works designs or off-site fabrication);
- Loss or damage caused in the course of complying with the obligations under the construction contract, i.e., visiting the site to undertake snagging works or remedy a defect.

DELAY IN START-UP

Delay in start-up insurance covers the loss of earnings as a result of late completion of the works due to the physical damage to the works. A claim under this insurance is conditional upon the Insured's interest in the damaged physical property being insured (save for the operation of a deductible) and many insurers require such physical loss to be insured by them (not someone else) under the construction all risks insurance. In either case, the insurer is seeking to ensure that the loss of earnings claim is not increased due to a delay in repairing the physical damage and for their purpose, the more control they have over both the physical and consequential losses, the better.

There are effectively two limits of liability under the delay in start-up insurance:

1. the sum insured
2. the indemnity period.

The indemnity period is the maximum duration over which the insurers will be liable to indemnify the insured parties. Under the delay in start-up insurance the indemnity period runs from the date from which revenue would have commenced but for the damage rather than from the date of the damage. So if there was a 36 months' indemnity period under the insurance and a loss occurred in March, without which the works would have been completed in October, then the 36 months of indemnity will start from October. This makes sense as there would not have been any earnings between March and October anyway.

Deductibles are typically expressed by way of number of days rather than a monetary amount.

The insurance does not cover fines or penalties and the insurers are reluctant to cover liquidated damages.

The policy can usually be extended to include delay caused by insured damage to the premises of a supplier or damage in the vicinity of the works which prevent access to the site. There needs to be physical damage so mere adverse weather would not be insured.

MARINE CARGO AND MARINE CARGO DELAY IN START-UP

Equipment and materials that are being imported for incorporation in the works would need to be insured under a marine cargo insurance (the construction all risks insurance could cover inland transits but not transits by sea).

The procurement of such insurance would depend on the conditions of purchase where, for instance, if the purchase price includes insurance then the supplier would take out such insurance. In the circumstances where loss or damage to the cargo could result in a delay in completion of the works then typically, in order to purchase marine delay in start-up insurance the insurer would also want to insure the physical damage risk in which case the purchase conditions should be ex-works (meaning from the factory not the building site) and the purchaser insures the transit.

CONSTRUCTION THIRD PARTY LIABILITY

Third party liability insurance indemnifies the insured party for sums that they are legally liable to pay as damages for accidental death or injury to third parties or for damage to third party property arising out of the works and occurring during the period of insurance.

The period of insurance is the same as for the construction all risks but that does not limit the builder's liability where for instance defective works results in injury or damage occurring after the works were completed.

Legal liability is not restricted to negligence – it would include nuisance and breach of statutory duty, i.e., the normal liabilities that exist in common law or civil codes in the country in question. The intention of the policy is to pay damages that arise in common law and not liabilities voluntarily (or involuntarily) accepted by contract and which would not exist in the absence of the contract term. That is a business decision and insurers are not in the business of supporting commercial decisions of that nature or certainly not without very specific written agreement.

The damage or injury needs to be accidental and the insurance will also exclude liability that is an inevitable consequence of the works.

Pollution is excluded although insurers typically cover sudden and accidental pollution. Consideration will need to be given to the need for a broader level of pollution insurance.

CONSTRUCTION INSURANCE STRUCTURES

The above basically categorizes insurance into asset, revenue and liability. In practice, the insurance may be provided through a number of insurance policies to reflect the nature of the project.

In the power sector, an onshore wind farm would have a comparatively simple insurance programme consisting of:

- Construction all risks (albeit it may be separated between the turbine and tower contract and the remaining civil works contract)
- Delay in start-up
- Third party liability (tends to be a modest amount due to the site being remote to neighbours)
- Marine transit
- Marine transit delay in start-up.

Insurance policy deductibles tend to be small. On the other hand an offshore wind farm is complicated by the need for marine works where specialist construction and cable laying vessels are required. A construction third party liability policy would not cover liabilities arising out of the operation of these marine vessels and the marine contractors would procure that liability insurance and removal of wreckage cover should they capsize. If the employer is not able to obtain an indemnity under the marine contractor's liability insurance they may be advised to purchase a 'contingent' marine liability insurance to protect the employer against claims from third parties for things caused by the marine contractor.

A conventional combined cycle gas turbine (CCGT) power plant project presents a significant single asset and revenue risk as opposed to wind farms that are spread over a larger area. Whilst they are also typically at a reasonable distance from neighbours, they nonetheless buy higher levels of liability insurance than wind farms, deductible levels are much higher reflecting the typical size of loss and values insured, and during testing and commissioning the higher risk items of boilers, turbine generators and step-up transformers will have much higher deductibles than testing and commissioning of other items or in respect to loss or damage to such plant from other risks.

Road projects can also have similar insurance considerations. A simple road may be through farmland with no material third party liability exposure. It may not even have an exposure to imports so does not require marine transit insurance.

Roads involving significant tunnelling may have major liability exposures (Cologne sub-way tunnel collapse in 2009) and in some cases the delay in start-up insurance for tunnel collapse might have a very lengthy time deductible.

Submerged tunnels and some bridges will involve the use of marine contractors where the marine liability and removal of wreckage will need to be provided by the marine contractors or else the employer would need to take out some 'contingent' insurance.

Operating Phase

PROPERTY DAMAGE

This insures the property against physical damage caused by a risk that is not otherwise excluded. For instance, war is a standard excluded risk and terrorism is normally separately insured. In addition to repairing the damage the policy would also extend to include debris removal costs, professional fees and the increased costs of complying with a public authority requirement in the reinstatement of the property, e.g., building regulations have changed requiring more expensive materials.

The insurance policy covers the reinstatement cost provided the asset is reinstated (and the sum insured is adequate). If the asset is not reinstated then the insurance switches to an indemnity settlement where wear and tear is deducted from the claim and would also impact on any possible business interruption claim (see below). The principle here is that one should not profit from insurance. This is a potential issue to lenders who may wish to invoke a head for the hills clause; they may now get less from the insurance than had the damage been reinstated.

BUSINESS INTERRUPTION

Business interruption insurance covers the loss of earnings consequent upon physical damage to the asset and again follows the material damage insurance requiring the insured's interest in the asset to be insured and insurers would normally require the physical loss to be insured by such insurers so that they can fully control both the physical damage loss and the business interruption loss.

The indemnity period is the maximum duration of the insurers' liability following the damage and would be set for the duration of time expected to get the business back into the same position it was in prior to the damage, not just to completion of any repair or reinstatement. Under the delay in start-up insurance the indemnity period runs from the date which but for the damage, the works would have been completed whereas under the operational business interruption insurance the indemnity period runs from the date of damage obviously because the economic consequences of the damage is typically felt immediately.

Typical extensions to the cover would be:

- Denial of access – damage in the vicinity that prevents access to the site;
- Infectious diseases – outbreaks at and in the vicinity of the site;
- Suppliers – damage at their premises that results in a consequential loss to the project;
- Customers – damage at their premises that results in a consequential loss to the project;
- Utilities – damage to a public utility premises that results in a consequential loss to the project.

If the damage is not reinstated, all claims under this insurance will cease to be payable.

PUBLIC AND PRODUCTS LIABILITY

Public and products liability insurance is substantially the same as for construction except that it deals with operational risks and the supply of products.

The insurance covers legal liabilities that exist in common law or civil codes provided that it arises from injury to third parties or damage to third party property. As for construction public liability, the insurers are not in the business of insuring liabilities voluntarily accepted under contract that do not exist in the absence of that contract term.

OPERATIONAL INSURANCE STRUCTURES

Projects involving any significant amount of plant such as power generation, energy, petrochemical, paper and board mills, etc. will purchase insurance against damage through breakdown and steam pressure explosion (where applicable) in addition to the normal risks of loss or damage.

Operational projects potentially have significant external risks which may be difficult to insure and are best managed through contingency plans where practicable. A petrochemical plant may be exposed to a single feedstock supplier and the issue to the plant and their insurers, is not having any control over the risk nor the reinstatement of supply capabilities if the risk materialized. Consequently, the insurers may not be prepared to provide a sufficient amount of insurance and may also offer a more limited cover than 'all-risks'.

Insurance cover for overhead power cables is very limited, typically 1000 metres from the generation plant. The plant might be exposed to distribution through a single substation which belongs to the distribution company but which may be possible to insure as a customer extension to a business interruption insurance.

Suppliers of products will need to purchase liability insurance against injury or damage caused by defects in those products (products liability insurance) and if they are chartering vessels to export their goods, they will need to purchase ship charterer's liability insurance.

So in operation, some additional insurance will be necessary.

Also, the quantum of insurance may well be different. For instance, you would not typically purchase a full reinstatement sum insured for a road or railway during operation if it is not possible to incur such a loss. Instead, the project would purchase a loss limit which reflects the estimated maximum loss.

A road in operation may have a lower liability exposure than in construction if for instance we are no longer encroaching on a railway whereas the liability exposure to a hospital or a school increases significantly when occupied by patients and students.

Lender Security Package

The insurance policies and the proceeds receivable are an asset of the business over which the lenders will take security in the same way as any other asset of the project. In addition to assignment of the insurance rights there is a fairly standard suite of lender requirements that are applied to internationally financed projects. These requirements are largely based on English law but most of them have application globally, however some are unnecessary due to local insurance law but still regarded as good practice and some and not legal by local laws or might attract stamp duties (from cut-through agreements or assignments, see below) so are not advisable. Depending on which endorsements the insurers will agree to, it may not be advisable to require others. For instance, if the insurers do not agree to include a non-vitiation clause (see below), do not agree to waive the lenders' duty of disclosure nor waive the lenders liability for the premium, then the lenders might be best advised not to be an insured party (those things can only apply to insured parties) and simply rely on loss payee provisions.

Insurance policies are not contracts of insurance, they evidence that an insurance contract exists and the overall contract includes the provisions of the insurance laws of the relevant country governing the policy and all disclosures made in the course of procuring the insurance. Insurance policies are also policies of indemnity, that is, they indemnify the insured parties for their legally recognized insurable interest in the risk that is insured. As will be seen below, simply being a named insured does not automatically entitle that person to make a claim if they do not hold the insurable interest. For instance, the lender's insurable interest in the asset is the outstanding debt.

For the purpose of this chapter we will address the English law position.

CO-INSURED AND INDEMNITY

The lenders will require to be named as an insured party under the principal insurance policies and by doing so the insurers undertake to indemnify them in respect of their insurable interest in the insurance. By being an insured party all the terms and conditions, implied and actual, may equally apply to each insured party such as be jointly and severally liable for the premium. This can vary where for instance aviation insurance policies typically differentiate between principal insured and additional insured where the additional insured are exempt from certain conditions such as the payment of the premium. So depending on the structure of the policy, being an insured party has its benefits but also has its risks, one of them being that each insured may be equally capable of invalidating the insurance for the other parties.

Lenders are also required to be an insured party in the liability insurance. As will be seen above, a liability policy indemnifies the insured party for their liability at law arising out of the insured business (design, build, finance and operate the project). It is difficult to see how a lender will be held liable for the acts and omissions of the borrower in building or operating the project so being a co-insured under the liability insurance has no real practical benefit save for some comfort that if someone tried to join the lenders in an action, the lenders would be entitled to the benefit of the policy.

DISCLOSURE

As stated above all insured parties have a duty to disclose all material facts, which are those facts that would influence the mind of a prudent underwriter whether to underwrite the risk and on what terms. Project companies are typically special purpose companies established as the vehicle for procuring and financing the project and they subcontract the activities to builders and operators. The project company would typically arrange the insurance and are, therefore, dependent on the builder or operator, as appropriate, to provide the underwriting information. Failure to disclose material information may enable the insurer to avoid the claim or even void the policy in its entirety from its beginning. It is a standard practice for the lenders to have their duty of disclosure waived under the insurance. This is crucial for the lenders because they are insured parties and rely on the insurance. They however, are not party to the actual procurement of the insurance yet they have a considerable amount of information on the project including reports from technical advisers, insurance advisers and lawyers. The lenders would not want their interest in the insurance to be undermined because another insured party failed to disclose a material fact.

LIABILITY FOR PREMIUM

All insured parties are potentially jointly and severally liable for the premium. This is unpalatable to the lenders so they would require the insurance to be endorsed to remove them from this liability. As there is no insurance contract if the premium is not paid, the lenders reserve the right to pay the premium but as a right not an obligation.

NON-VITIATION

The ability for insurers to avoid a claim from one insured party due to a breach of the policy by another insured party varies by local laws and policy structure and conditions. Regardless, it is standard practice in project finance to endorse the policy so that the insurers agree that the insurable interests of the parties that are innocent of the breach are not prejudiced. Some insurers retain the right to recover their loss from the vitiating party where but for the non-vitiation clause, they would have been able to avoid the claim. The issue to the lender is that the party who vitiated the insurance may have been the borrower and in which case, if the lender is able to make a claim for its insurable interest, the insurer could then claw it back by exercising its subrogation rights.

Further, merely being an insured party does not necessarily entitle another insured party to step in and make the claim. As stated above, lenders are co-insured under the liability policy. As the policy is indemnifying the insured parties for their legal liability arising out of the business, then unless the lenders are also held legally liable, they would not be able to step in and make the claim even though their borrower now has an uninsured liability. This is because the policy is covering the legal liabilities of the insured parties not the lenders' credit risk in the borrower.

ASSIGNMENT

The insurance policies and the proceeds under them are assets of the project company and lenders will take security over them through an assignment agreement. Insurance policies are not freely assignable (with minor exception such as marine cargo policies) and therefore, such assignment is not valid under the insurance unless agreed by the insurers. Consequently, an endorsement on the policy is an agreement to the assignment by the insurers. That will deal with insurance policy but it is normal practice to also serve a notice of assignment on the insurers which is to satisfy UK property law, not insurance law.

Assignment is a legal process requiring legal advice but could also be a tax issue where in some territories it could attract stamp duties as a transfer of property.

In territories where insurance regulations require insurance with local insurers but those insurers do not have sufficient credit ratings to satisfy the lenders it would be normal to require the insurance to be reinsured into the international reinsurance market to the maximum amount permitted and lenders would seek assignment of the reinsurance proceeds. Again, local regulations or solvency laws may not permit direct payment to the lenders.

LOSS PAYEE

Insurance policies indemnify the insured parties for their insurable interest in the thing being insured. Lenders will want to regulate all receipts of the project company and consequently will require the insurers to agree to pay all proceeds to certain bank accounts except with regard to liability insurance, where they will agree that the insurers may pay the injured party directly. This overcomes the issue that whilst the lender may not have the insurable interest in the entire claim and, therefore, are not entitled to the full amount from the insurers, they are able to control those proceeds. Again, local laws or tax considerations may prevent payment of proceeds in this manner.

PRIMARY INSURANCE

Where the same insurable interest in the same risk is insured under more than one policy of insurance there may be local rules as to which policy pays the loss or how the loss is shared by those policies. This is not acceptable to lenders as they have provided a loan on the basis of a specific set of insurance policies, they have vetted those policies, accepted the insurers, may have approved the reinsurance and taken security over them. To find that all or part of the loss is now to be pursued through a 'non-compliant' insurance would undermine their security. Consequently lenders would require the project insurers to agree that their policy is primary and would not seek contribution from other insurance policies before paying the claim.

NOTIFICATIONS

The loan agreement would impose obligations on the borrower to notify the lenders in the event that the insurance is cancelled, suspended or adversely altered. Lenders also require the insurer and reinsurer where applicable, to notify the lenders in such circumstances and require a minimum amount of notice. In the event that the insurer is giving notice for non-payment of the premium, the lenders may cause it to be paid or pay it themselves and recover from the borrower. For other reasons of cancellation or suspension, the lenders can consult and monitor the borrower's effort to replace the insurance.

In the case of breach of the borrower's insurance obligations the lenders have the right to step in and affect the insurance, but that is not as easy as it sounds!

Lenders usually include an obligation for the insurer to notify lenders if the policy is lapsed. Typically, insurers do not agree to that and only agree to notify things that happen during the policy period, not at the end of it. Lenders need to ensure that they receive evidence that the insurance is renewed at the end of each policy term, prior to the insurance cover running out.

Typically, but not in all territories, the borrower employs the services of an insurance broker to negotiate and arrange the insurance as agent of the borrower. In those cases, the lenders will also require the broker to undertake to give similar notifications to the lenders. See broker letter of undertaking below.

INSURER SECURITY

Probably every country in the world has regulations controlling who can transact insurance in the country and insurance that is required by law tends to be more tightly controlled. Commonly, insurance needs to be purchased from insurers in the country in which the project is sited. In Europe, the European Union freedom of services legislation permits, with some conditions and exceptions, persons in one member state to insure with insurers in another member state. Insurers, however, would typically have greater freedom to arrange reinsurance in the international insurance markets. This is for practical purposes where the local insurers may not have the capacity to retain all the risks that they underwrite and need to cede some of the risk to other insurers, i.e., re-insure.

Where the local insurer does not meet their minimum credit rating level the lenders would require reinsurance with international reinsurers who do meet their minimum standards. They would want the reinsurance to be project specific (known as facultative reinsurance) rather than under the insurer's general reinsurance arrangements (reinsurance treaties). The lenders' reason for requiring international reinsurance may not be restricted to the liquidity of the insurer but may also be for exchange control purposes where the proceeds are paid into an 'offshore' bank account (some countries require reinsurance proceeds to be paid to the local insurer).

Where permitted by law and provided that it does not have tax implications, e.g., stamp duty, lenders will take security over the reinsurance with similar provisions as for the local insurance such as the notification requirements, loss payee provisions, primary insurance and suchlike. Where possible they may take assignment of the reinsurance. As the reinsurance is a contract between the insurer and the reinsurer the lenders will need to enter an assignment with the insurer and the insurer will have to agree it with the reinsurer.

BROKER LETTER OF UNDERTAKING

The status of the insurance broker is that they are normally an agent of the insured, not the insurer. The broker will enter a service agreement with the borrower under which he may or may not limit his liability.

The role of the broker is much wider than just arranging the insurance. He collects the premium from the borrower and pays the insurers (there may be several) and also may collect claims proceeds and pay the borrower. Some insurers such as Lloyd's Underwriters in Lloyd's of London, can only operate through the Lloyd's broker so in practice they are not able to notify the lenders of cancellation, etc., and as for loss payee they can only cause the broker to pay the proceeds into the designated bank account.

The broker letter of undertaking creates a legal relationship between the broker and the lenders under which the broker commits to the lenders various notification obligations, money handling commitments, provide evidence of the insurance and confirm that to the best of their knowledge the insurers are solvent and the cover is in full force and effect. The broker cannot warrant that the insurer is solvent nor can they warrant that the insurance is in force because unknown to the broker the borrower may have failed to disclose material information thereby undermining the validity of the insurance. The broker may or may not cap his liability under that letter.

Reinsurance is a separate agreement between the insurer and the reinsurer and there would be a service agreement between the reinsurance broker (who may be the same as the broker) and the insurer. Consequently, as the lenders will be relying on the more robust reinsurance, they would also need to obtain a reinsurance broker letter of undertaking along the same lines as the broker letter of undertaking.

ROLE OF INSURANCE/REINSURANCE BROKER

Typically, the project company would employ the services of an insurance broker to advise them on their risk management strategy including insurance needs, design the insurance programme, tender the insurance, negotiate the terms for them and place the insurance. The broker would then have an on-going role to agree the policy wordings, advise on changes throughout the period of insurance and may be engaged to advise on claims under the policies. This is not always the case and in some territories the project company deals directly with the insurers.

In some territories the local insurers do not have the ability or desire to retain the entire risk or, regardless of the local insurer risk management strategy, the lenders or project company may require more robust security and cause the insurer to reinsure with more acceptable reinsurers.

Contractually, the insurance broker is an agent of the project company arranging the insurance with the insurer. The insurer would then employ a reinsurance broker as its agent to arrange the reinsurance with the reinsurer. In practice the price and cover under the insurance is driven by the availability and price of the reinsurance so the reinsurance broker would actually design the insurance programme and seek project-specific reinsurance to satisfy the needs of the project company and their lenders. Then the insurer can offer their insurance to the project company. This is why the reinsurance broker and the insurance broker are normally from the same firm as the two roles are far more synchronized than the contract structure would suggest.

ROLE OF LENDER INSURANCE ADVISER

Fundamentally, the project company is presenting its business case to the lenders including its proposal for insuring the project. In the same way that the lenders' technical adviser reviews the design and working methods, etc. for building and operating the project, the lender insurance adviser reviews the risk management proposal of the borrower. It is not the role of the lender insurance adviser to design the insurance solutions.

The lender insurance adviser should review the risks to the project recognizing the nature of the debt and how those risks have been allocated under the principal contracts. Having undertaken that risk profile, the lender insurance adviser can review and benchmark the project company's insurance proposals in order to opine as to whether it is appropriate and if not, to negotiate or recommend improvements. Lenders also want to know what risks are not covered so that they can ensure that the risks are managed through contract, contingency or otherwise as outlined at the beginning of this chapter. The lender insurance adviser would liaise with the legal and technical advisers as well as with the lenders and the project company in order to carry out its services. Having agreed the minimum insurance requirements and which aspects of the lenders security package are to be applied to the respective insurance policies, the lender insurance adviser would liaise with the lawyers to document those requirements into the loan agreement and subcontracts. Prior to financial close, the project company would submit evidence of the insurance and reinsurance, the broker and reinsurance broker would provide their letters of undertaking and the lender insurance adviser would audit them against the loan agreement and complete their final report to the lenders summarizing all of the above and confirming that the insurance documentation complies with the loan agreement. The lender insurance adviser would normally be retained to review the insurance when they move from construction into operation and at each renewal date until the loan is repaid. The lender insurance adviser should be an integral party to the diligence team. Their sole duty of care would be to the lenders.

11 *The Equator Principles – The Global Standard*

SUELLEN LAZARUS
Independent consultant

When 10 international banks announced their commitment to adopt the Equator Principles (EPs) in June 2003, it signalled a dramatic change in the international banking community's approach to environmental and social issues in their project finance lending. The decision to apply a comprehensive set of environmental and social standards to a high profile and often core business-line began a process of coordination among financial institutions in monitoring, managing and mitigating environmental and social risk that was unprecedented. Within one year, 25 financial institutions in 14 countries had adopted the EPs. Eight years later, there are 72 Equator Principles Financial Institutions (EPFIs) representing all continents, including banks in Africa and China, and a broad range of financial institutions including export credit agencies and development finance institutions.

The transformation in bank thinking on environmental and social issues stands in sharp contrast to their previous attitude. While not disregarding environmental and social issues, most banks saw this area as the responsibility of borrowers. Before the EPs, most banks treated environmental and social risks in projects on an ad hoc basis, if at all. A deal turned down by the credit committee of one bank due to concerns of high environmental or social risk was likely to be financed by the bank up the street. Banks did not have an agreed basis by which to evaluate environmental and social risk in projects; they had limited leverage with borrowers to implement a standard; and environmental covenants that were included in loan documentation were largely unenforceable. This hands-off approach left it to borrowers to set, implement and monitor the environmental and social standards to which they would adhere. With the adoption of the Equator Principles, this changed and financial institutions took responsibility for setting clear and consistent rules for environmental and social risk management in project finance lending.

With impressive speed upon its initial launch, the EPs became the new market standard for project finance. Project sponsors planning to raise funds in the international financial markets recognized that they had to structure their projects to meet the requirements of the EPs. Today, successful and broad international syndication of a project finance deal means EP compliance is expected. The fact that this has happened is testimony to the change that has occurred in financial markets. Environmental and social stewardship is not just seen as something that is nice to do. It is an essential component of risk management and of good business.

Historical Context

The EPs were conceived at a time when banks were facing tremendous pressure to follow their major clients to increasingly remote locations to invest in large, complex projects, particularly in the oil and gas and mining sectors. In these frontier markets, environmental and social regulations may be minimal with little, if any, government enforcement capacity. For international banks financing these long-term, expensive and high-profile projects, the risks were very high. Beyond the environmental and social risk, reputation risk was substantial and lasting. No bank wanted to be associated with displacing 1.2m people, killing whales, uprooting indigenous people, destroying the rainforest, employing child labour or contaminating ground water, to name some of the acquisitions levelled against banks. Yet banks lacked capacity to respond to these accusations since they had no consistent framework for evaluating social or environmental risk or for determining the conditions under which they could proceed with an investment. As pressure from non-governmental organizations (NGOs) mounted and questions were increasingly raised about some high profile projects, the banks faced the potential of pulling out of project finance lending in emerging markets, particularly in the extractive industries.

Thus, the creation of the EPs as a voluntary initiative in 2003 was a watershed achievement for the banking industry. For the first time, banks asserted their responsibility for environmental and social outcomes in the projects they were financing. The EPs provided a language around issues of environmental and social risk management and a reputable and consistent platform for engaging clients on these issues. The EP framework allowed banks to evaluate, manage and monitor difficult cross border project finance deals in emerging markets.

Changing Market Conditions

Since the EPs were launched, there have been fundamental changes in the financial industry and the economic climate in which the EPFIs operate. During this period, global project finance activity grew from about US$70bn in 2003 to US$250bn in 2008, but then declined to US$139bn in 2009 following the global financial crisis (see Figure 11.1). The market gained strength in 2010 reaching US$208bn, although a US$12bn project in Taiwan and the increasing Indian market accounted for much of this growth.

Membership in the EPs has grown consistently since 2003, continuing to expand during the crisis despite some consolidation in membership associated with bank mergers. The regional concentration of projects also has shifted as the Asian markets – especially Indian and Chinese banks – play a more prominent role in financing projects in their home countries. Of the 10 leading project finance banks in 2010, four were Indian and projects in India represented 26 per cent of the total project finance market (22 per cent in 2009). For the most part, Indian banks have financed Indian projects with little participation from international banks (see Figure 11.1).

EP membership has evolved as some of the early adopting EPFIs have merged with other banks; others have decreased their project finance activity opting instead to lend shorter-term or to limit their project finance lending to developed rather than developing countries. Despite the growth of project finance activity in emerging markets, and an increased number of EPFIs based in emerging markets, there currently are no domestic

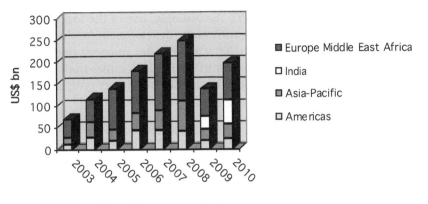

Figure 11.1 Global project finance market

Source: Project Finance International

Table 11.1 Top loan arrangers 2003 and 2010

Rank	Global Mandated Arrangers (2003)	US$m	No of Deals	Head Office	Global Mandated Arrangers (2010)	US$m	No of Deals	Head Office
1	Credit Agricole-Credit Lyonnais	3864.1	36	France	State Bank of India	21136.9	55	India
2	Royal Bank of Scotland	3256.8	27	Scotland	Bank of Taiwan	12005.1	1	Taiwan
3	BNP Paribas	2986.5	29	France	IDBI	11019.4	25	India
4	SMBC	2638.1	21	Japan	Axis Bank	8512.2	24	India
5	Societe Generale	2614.1	21	France	BNP Paribas	8338.5	69	France
6	Westdeutsche Landesbank	2268.3	22	Germany	Credit Agricole	7614.5	82	France
7	Citigroup	2100.8	17	US	IDFC	7371.1	30	India
8	Mitsubishi Tokyo Financial Group	2003.5	24	Japan	Mitsubishi UFJ Financial	6000.5	69	Japan
9	Korea Development Bank	1947.8	6	Korea	Societe Generale	5487.4	55	France
10	Barclays Capital	1940.3	28	UK	SMBC	4589.7	41	Japan

Source: Project Finance International

Indian EPFIs and only one Chinese EPFI. Accordingly, five of the top 10 project finance banks in 2010 were not EPFIs. This is a problematic development for the EPs. If we assume simply that those projects in India and Taiwan were not financed under the EPs, those alone account for 32 per cent of the market in 2010. Thus, rather than growing stronger, it can be argued that the global influence of the EPs on project outcomes has lost some ground.

Principles, Policies, Procedures

More than a declaration of intent, the EPs were designed to have teeth. From the preamble of the EPs, banks commit to 'not provide loans to projects where the borrower will not or is unable to comply with our respective social and environmental policies and procedures that implement the Equator Principles.'

As a voluntary standard, the EPs distinguish themselves in going beyond a statement of intent to provide policies and procedures for assessing, managing and monitoring environmental and social risk in project finance lending. They include a set of baseline policy requirements, quantitative environmental guidelines and process steps to facilitate application of these policies and guidelines. The social and environmental policies and guidelines are drawn from the World Bank Group while the process steps are contained in the Equator Principles themselves. The International Finance Corporation's (IFC's) Performance Standards (PS) are the basis of the policy standards that the borrower is to meet throughout the life of the project and cover cross cutting environmental and social issues as follows:

PS 1 – Social and Environmental Assessment and Management System
PS 2 – Labour and Working Conditions
PS 3 – Pollution Prevention and Abatement
PS 4 – Community Health, Safety and Security
PS 5 – Land Acquisition and Involuntary Resettlement
PS 6 – Biodiversity, Conservation and Sustainable Natural Resource Management
PS 7 – Indigenous Peoples
PS 8 – Cultural Heritage

The World Bank Group Environmental, Health and Safety Guidelines (EHS Guidelines) form the core of the EPs' quantitative environmental guidelines. The EHS Guidelines provide general and industry-specific technical specifications on pollution prevention and abatement including acceptable performance levels and measures that are considered achievable. When host country regulations differ from the levels in the EHS Guidelines, projects are expected to achieve whichever is more stringent. The EHS Guidelines include 62 industry specific guidelines and a General EHS Guidelines applicable to all projects as well as those projects without a specific industry guideline. The advantage of utilizing the World Bank Group's policies and procedures was their broad scope and the experience of applying them over many years in the emerging market context. (The detailed process steps of the EPs are set out in Table 11.2.)

APPLICATION

The EPs apply to project finance transactions only, and those with a capital cost of US$10m or more. They also apply to advisory assignments, which simply means that banks encourage clients to consider the EPs when structuring projects; and they apply to expansions and refinancing when there is expected to be significant environmental and social impact.

Table 11.2 Equator principles: process steps

Principle 1 – Review and Categorization	Based on an initial review of impacts, EPFIs categorize all projects into one of three categories: • High Impact (Category A): Significant adverse social or environmental impacts beyond the project site, difficult to mitigate • Medium Impact (Category B): Site-specific impacts, largely reversible and mitigation measure are readily available • Low Impact (Category C): Minimal or no adverse social or environmental impacts.
Principle 2 – Social and environmental assessment	For Category A and B projects, the borrower is expected to prepare a Social and Environmental Assessment addressing the relevant social and environmental impacts and risks of the project and proposed mitigation measures. The borrower, consultants or external experts may prepare the Assessment but it must be 'adequate, accurate and objective.' Issues to be covered might include protection of human rights, protection of biodiversity, labour issues, socio-economic issues, involuntary resettlement, impacts on affected communities and indigenous people, and efficient production and use of energy.
Principle 3 – Applicable standards	Projects located in High-Income Organization for Economic Co-operation and Development (OECD) countries (defined by World Bank Development Indicators) are expected to meet local or national standards. Those in Non-OECD countries or in OECD countries that are not High-Income must meet the Performance Standards and the applicable industry EHS Guidelines.
Principle 4 – Action plan and management system	For Categories A and B projects in low and middle income countries, the borrower is expected to develop an Action Plan setting out how the mitigation measures identified in the Assessment will be achieved. Borrowers also must establish a Social and Environmental Management System to address on-going management of impacts and corrective actions needed to comply with applicable standards.
Principle 5 – Consultation and disclosure	For Categories A and B projects borrowers must consult with affected communities about project-related impacts. Assessment documents are to be made available to the public and borrowers are expected to consider feedback from affected communities and adapt projects as needed.
Principle 6 – Grievance mechanism	For Category A projects and Category B, as appropriate, the borrower is expected to establish a grievance mechanism to facilitate resolution of concerns raised by project-affected communities.

Principle 7 – Independent review	For Category A and, as appropriate, for Category B projects, an independent social and/or environmental expert not directly associated with the borrower is expected to review the Social and Environmental Assessment, Action Plan and consultation process.
Principle 8 – Covenants	The loan documentation for Categories A and B projects should contain covenants that the project will comply with relevant host country social and environmental laws and with the Action Plan, will provide periodic reports documenting social and environmental compliance, and will decommission the project according to an agreed plan.
Principle 9 – Independent monitoring and reporting	For Category A and, as appropriate, for Category B projects, an independent social and/or environmental expert will verify monitoring information.
Principle 10 – Reporting	Each EPFI commits to report publicly at least annually on its EP implementation processes and experience, subject to confidentiality constraints.

IMPLEMENTATION

Ideally, when a financial institution moves from adoption of the EPs to implementation, a change process occurs within that institution. The first step is to evaluate what activities and staff are affected by the EPs, how the new procedures will be incorporated into existing operations and what department will have responsibility or authority for overseeing EP implementation. Models vary within banks with some having a centralized group function that covers environmental and social risk often reporting to the head of risk management; for others, EP responsibility is embedded more broadly in the business line. Regardless of the model, an EP manager needs to be identified or recruited.

Credit procedures need to be revised and steps developed for managing high-risk cases and issues of non-compliance. Training of key staff is essential since they will need to know how to categorize projects, identify risks and supervise technical experts. Understanding that successful EP implementation depends on the cooperation of a number of parties within an institution, financial institutions are training project finance professionals, credit officers, public affairs managers, lawyers and even Board members. Tracking procedures need to be put in place to ensure that EP monitoring and reporting is in place. Internal audit procedures may be adapted to monitor compliance with these new policies.

Successes

The question that is often asked of EPFIs is whether they are turning down deals as a result of adopting the EPs. Yes, they are, but this is probably not the right question. Projects turned down by one bank are likely to get financing by another bank, perhaps one that is not an EPFI. Thus, under this scenario the environmentally dodgy deal is still being done. More importantly, the question that needs to be asked is whether projects are being structured more sustainably as a result of the EPs; are the environmental and social risks reduced and better managed? The new procedures place emphasis on impact categorization and assessment of sponsor capacity to effectively manage environmental and social risks. High impact projects with high-risk sponsors are warning signs that a project will require considerable effort to get it right and continuing high-level attention among the banks financing the deal. While the riskiest deals need and should be turned down, the majority of deals should benefit from the careful risk assessment and mitigation approach provided by the EPs.

The EPs have fostered cooperation among bankers who are otherwise competitors and not accustomed to working across institutions unless in the context of a deal. Having agreed to provide a level playing field on environmental and social standards, the EPFIs have demonstrated considerable strength of purpose in actively working together to promote best practice in implementation of the EPs. Regular coordination meetings are held to facilitate implementation. The recently completed update of IFC's Performance Standards is a case in point. The EPFI Steering Committee worked closely to provide a comprehensive and forceful response to IFC's draft standards and to encourage IFC to go further on such issues as climate change and human rights.[1]

> We provide this feedback believing that it is in all our interests that the IFC's standards continue to remain best in class.
>
> As we have highlighted to the IFC before, climate change is one of the EPFIs' greatest priorities. In order for the IFC to maintain its standard setting role, the EPFIs recommend that the IFC is more assertive and innovative with regards to climate change than is currently proposed in its revised drafts.
>
> The EPFIs would request the IFC consider … [to] include language (or a specific brief human rights section) related to Government's Duty to Protect, and to the private sector's Responsibility to Respect Human Rights in PS 1.

In light of civil society's interest in successful implementation and monitoring results of the EPs, the EPFIs hold regular meetings with representatives of these organizations.

Once a bank begins systematically considering environmental and social issues in its project finance business, inevitably it should begin looking at these issues in other aspects of its business. Adapting EP or incorporating other mechanisms to manage environmental and social issues in corporate finance, export finance, equity investments, mergers and acquisitions, IPOs and corporate bond underwritings is an important benefit of the EPs that is underway in some EPFIs.

The EPs have set in motion a movement towards a globally recognized environmental and social standard that has as its basis IFC's Performance Standards and EHS Guidelines. Following the example of the EPs, 15 European development finance institutions and 32 export credit agencies (ECAs) from the OECD refer to the Performance Standards in their operations, and in its 2008 update, the European Bank for Reconstruction and Development (EBRD) modelled its Performance Requirements on IFC's Performance

---

1   28 July 2010, 'EPFI Steering Committee's Letter Submission to the IFC Regarding the Phase II Consultation of IFC Performance Standards Review and Update,' http://equator-principles.com/resources/EPFI_Letter_to_IFC_Jul2010.pdf.

Standards.[2] This consistency will result in better project outcomes and reduced costs, while above all promoting sustainability.

Challenges

In October 2010, the EPFIs embarked on a Strategic Review process to 'produce a multi-year strategic vision to ensure the EPs continue to be viewed as the "gold standard" in environmental and social risk management for project finance within the financial sector.' The review was undertaken against the backdrop of the update of IFC Performance Standards and the necessity of also revising the EPs to reflect the changes in the Performance Standards. Shawn Miller, Chair of the EP Association and Managing Director of Environmental and Social Risk Management at Citi, noted:

> Through seven years of proven success and impressive growth, the Equator Principles (EPs) framework has served us well. During this period, the financial sector's landscape has changed considerably, while society's attention and focus on environmental and social issues has increased. Our goal is to ensure the EPs continue to be the 'go-to' environmental and social risk management standard for the financial sector and our clients. We encourage all stakeholders to provide their candid feedback during the Review process so that the EPs continue to help us manage our risk effectively while respecting people and planet.[3]

The Strategic Review completed in May 2011 by independent consultants, outlines the successes and challenges faced by EPs, and provides a set of recommendations.[4] While accepting some of the recommendation, most will be considered in the context of the EP III update process.[5]

RELEVANCE

Among the pressing issues facing the EPFIs, one of the most urgent is the question of relevance. With economic growth in China and India, there is high demand for improved infrastructure and a vast number of projects generated by these countries. Domestic banks have the capacity to fund these projects, yet only one Chinese bank is an EPFI. For the EPs to remain relevant, it is a priority that more of these banks become EPFIs, but this is challenging. For EPFIs in emerging markets, generally all of their projects are financed in emerging markets versus approximately 40 per cent of transactions for banks in High-Income OECD countries. As noted in Table 11.2, Principle 3, the EP process used in emerging markets is more robust than that in High-Income countries due to the expectation that High-Income countries have sufficient environmental and social standards and regulatory

2   12 May 2011, 'IFC Updates Environmental and Social Standards, Strengthening Commitment to Sustainability and Transparency,' IFC Press Release, http://www.ifc.org/ifcext/media.nsf/content/home.

3   The Equator Principles Strategic Review, http://equator-principles.com/index.php/governance-management/the-equator-principles-strategic-review.

4   17 February 2011, Suellen Lazarus and Alan Feldbaum, 'Equator Principles Strategic Review, Final Report,' http://equator-principles.com/resources/exec-summary_appendix_strategic_review_report.pdf.

5   The Equator Principles Strategic Review, http://equator-principles.com/resources/ep_association_summary_response_strategic_review.pdf.

regimes. Whereas banks in China and India (and other emerging markets) face greater responsibilities under the EPs, they may have less capacity for implementation.

The EPs need to embark on a more targeted outreach effort for India and China, and should consider if they can accommodate these banks through a somewhat more flexible implementation regime. For example, a tiered membership structure might allow financial institutions in emerging markets to apply the EPs to projects with a larger size limit, say $25 million instead of $10 million. In addition, the EPs should consider offering targeted training packages for emerging market institutions.

SCOPE

The limit of the EPs strictly to project finance may create credibility problems for the EPFIs since different banks define 'project finance' differently. Thus, one bank may treat a deal as a project financing whereas another may handle it as a corporate loan. The result is that different standards are applied to the same loan. But regardless of what it is called, the social and environmental risks remain the same. Rather than sticking to terminology, it may be more effective to apply the EPs when the majority of financing in a deal is targeted to a clearly identifiable physical asset.

IMPLEMENTATION

There is inconsistency in how rigorously EPFIs implement the EPs. With each EPFI responsible for its own implementation and as the number of EPFIs has expanded to different continents and countries, disparity in implementation has increased. Inconsistency is born both of different interpretation of requirements and of lack of capacity in some banks. In some markets, clients may have little experience with the EPs and there is a shortage of consultants with the requisite EP skills. Improving implementation requires more knowledge sharing among EPFIs, standardized training programmes, better and more consistent disclosure and development of a standardized independent audit methodology. Ultimately, implementation will improve when membership is dependent upon a demonstrated base level of implementation capacity and the potential to be delisted for failure to implement properly.

EP MANAGEMENT

The EP Association has limited funding and staffing, and relies on the volunteer efforts of its members. There is no annual report and, until just recently, the website was difficult to navigate. Accordingly, others have largely told the EP story. This approach has meant that progress is often slow and that others have controlled the EPs' message. The organization is now mature enough and has an ambitious enough agenda that it needs to be put on a more secure footing and assert its leadership position.

The Equator Principles Association needs to advance as an organization and create a sustainable platform for its success and continued development. It must excel at delivering its core mission, as contained in its Preamble, of ensuring that the projects that its members finance are developed in a socially responsible manner and using sound environmental management practices. At the same time, it must expand its membership to encompass new entrants in the project finance market, broaden its scope to accommodate the greater ambitions of its members, and address evolving environmental and social risk management needs.[6]

The creation and broad adoption of the EPs is a great achievement for the banking industry. They have played an essential role in catalyzing better environmental and social risk management within banks. Within a few years, the EPs have become the global standard for sustainability in project finance. It is now incumbent upon the EPFIs to build on this success to create a sustaining future.

---

6   17 February 2011, Suellen Lazarus and Alan Feldbaum, 'Equator Principles Strategic Review, Final Report,' http://equator-principles.com/resources/exec-summary_appendix_strategic_review_report.pdf.

12 Chinese and Korean Contractors in Large Project Finance Transactions

CLARE RHODES JAMES
Divisional Director, Mott MacDonald

Introduction

Chinese and Korean contractors are increasingly part of large infrastructure developments globally. The reasons put forward for their ambition, their increased presence and its impact are various and much discussed. This chapter examines some of these reasons – from falling domestic opportunity through to linkage with tactics to access useful commodities – and the impacts they are having on the market.

Project finance transactions span many sectors – rail rolling stock, mining equipment, LNG terminals, electricity transmission lines, toll roads, cement plants, hydropower plants, airports and communications satellites to name a few. This chapter draws examples from the power generation sector.

Power generation is reasonably representative of large project-financed infrastructure: it covers both the combined civil engineering and equipment driven development typical in hydropower as well as the more purely equipment dominated thermal, solar and wind generation. The transactions are sizeable and rely on global equipment suppliers in a sector relatively consolidated in the west which is quickly being challenged by suppliers from Korea, China, (and domestically in India). Many of the arguments apply to other sectors – for example mining and minerals investments are lumpy and incorporate specialist equipment. In the transport sector – other than rail – there is generally a smaller role for electrical and mechanical equipment so the factors that lead to selection of contractors are more related to issues such as funding and competitive construction than on globally deployed technologies. However, construction is a significant element in power generation also, especially in hydropower. In addition, project finance in power is very mature, being one of the first sectors to adopt this approach to delivering infrastructure.

Electrical transmission and distribution is not a focus of this chapter, except for grid lines being developed as part of power generation projects. However, brief comment is made here because of the growing role of Chinese and Korean players both as owner-operators and as equipment suppliers.

The chapter first examines key technical issues central to any internationally financed project finance transaction (Section 2). This provides some context for an assessment of whether any different issues apply when Chinese and Korean contractors are involved. Section 3 shows the status of Chinese and Korean suppliers within the power sector. A brief description of some of the commonly discussed motivations for Korean and Chinese companies to seek to grow their share of the international infrastructure market is then made in Section 4. The examples are drawn largely from thermal general and hydropower. Similar arguments can be made for the other technologies: whilst wind turbines are less sophisticated than gas turbines many of the same trends apply and the solar market is also evolving based on development of panel manufacture.

It is often implied in discussions amongst western participants in the infrastructure business that Chinese contractors buy their way in through bringing cheap finance with few conditions and cheap labour. The reality is more complicated. Section 5 examines some of the tactics contractors, including the Chinese and Koreans, have used to grow their market share outside their domestic market and Section 6 discusses some of the implications of this growing position. Comment in the chapter considers the technical and commercial angles particularly in relation to lending to project finance transactions, as these are the experience of the author, rather than any financial or legal matters.

Section 2 – The Technical Perspective

Many details need to be sorted out for project finance transactions to be closed. However, for lenders the technical issues are all related either to the limited- or non-recourse nature of the finance provided or to the reputation risk potentially associated with these large developments.

The non-recourse or limited recourse nature of the transactions means lenders rely predominantly or solely on the project's cash flows to repay the loans. Thus the project's technical performance is critical to its financial viability. Firstly, there needs to be confidence in the projected capex and the programme to bring the plant into commercial operation. Cover ratios and thus the viability of a project are particularly sensitive to delays in the start of commercial operations and extended capital spend. Similarly, it is evident that a clear view of performance in operations is needed – for opex, availability and generation capacity over a period often of 10 to 25 years. For all these parameters a consensus on project 'pessimistic' scenarios is critical to enable bank funding on a non-recourse basis.

There are always issues in a project which call into question the expected capital costs, schedule or performance. These are typically dealt with in one of four ways: they are designed out, allocated to the contractor (or another party) through the contract(s), insured against or contingency (or other support) is added to the project. In the case of reputation risk, the usual reference is international standards as a means of understanding whether good practice has been followed.

The key principles are set out below.

(I) CONFIDENCE IN THE CAPITAL COSTS

The first technical requirement for non-recourse project finance to be possible is to have confidence that the capital cost estimates are firm. Having a single strong contract on an Engineer Procure and Construct (EPC) basis – or in some cases a small number of EPC contracts – is key to achieving this. Strong EPC contracts provide a brief functional requirement for a project and leave it to the contractor to design and deliver it. Transfer of design and delivery risks to the Contractor removes key sources of cost overrun from the project company. Reducing the work to a single contract also removes the cost uncertainty associated with managing interfaces. In practice, there is very significant scrutiny of EPC contracts to gain confidence that the allocation of risks is fully understood and that the owner's requirements are appropriate and functionally stated. This is to avoid the need for changes after contract signature to remove ambiguity, correct mistakes or adjust for the conditions encountered.

In a number of parts of the industry there are parties trying to move away from the model of a single EPC contract and in some cases this has been forced where no one party is willing to take on all the delivery risk. There is not space to debate the specific issues here, however, it is clear that there is a price premium attached to an EPC contract as the contractor needs to take responsibility for a range of uncertain scenarios. Some owners are keen to keep this premium instead as a contingency, especially where the owner feels experienced in project management or where the price premium is perceived to be very high.

(II) CONFIDENCE IN THE PROGRAMME

Achieving commercial operations on time is generally critical to project viability as interest on the construction loans compounds if the start of revenue generation is delayed. It is typical to include in the EPC contracts 'liquidated damage' mechanisms. These aim to hold the owner whole in the event of late completion – i.e., to provide compensation such that they are financially no worse off than if the project had completed on time. Such liquidated damages provide a strong incentive to the contractor to observe the planned schedule.

Separate to the examination of the contracts it is important to have confidence that the contractor – and importantly the team the contractor is allocating to the project – have the right experience in delivery of projects of a similar nature. Experience should be demonstrated across all parts of the supply chain for critical equipment, including the manufacture or key components and the logistics of transportation as well as construction, assembly and commissioning. Incentives are of no value if the contractor is unable to deliver. Equally, there are always caps on liquidated damages – both in the daily rate and in the aggregate amount payable. The project company needs to demonstrate either that it can deliver the project, even under pessimistic scenarios, before the aggregate cap on damages is reached or to provide a form of contingency to cover the impacts of any further delay.

(III) CONFIDENCE IN PERFORMANCE AND OPEX

Assuming a suitable agreement for power purchase is in place, the project's cash flows and ability to service its debt are driven by the availability of the plant, its technical capability and on-going operational and maintenance costs. Operation and maintenance agreements (OMA) typically do not transfer significant risk to the operator. This is because contracts are often only around 5 years in duration and therefore it can lead to a skewed incentive to reduce maintenance spend, to deliver profit not while putting at risk longer term project performance. The main sources of comfort in the operational performance are therefore:

- The robustness of the plant delivered by the EPC contractor – its longevity
- The suitability of the performance testing in the EPC contract
- The competence of the operator and the ability to replace them, if necessary, for a similarly competent party at a similar fee level
- Availability of funds for on-going maintenance and a suitable programme.

In passing over to the EPC contractor the responsibility to design the plant, the owner has less control over the plant which is delivered. Performance tests should show the plant's ability to deliver the capacity and flexibility specified in the short term but they do not guarantee long-term performance. Confidence in longer term robustness comes from the standards applied to the design and construction. These are not always easy to measure – especially in the case of civil engineering works. Where civil works are particularly significant, more prescriptive requirements are often included in the contracts. This may dilute the transfer of the design risk to the contractor, and hence increase the risk of cost increases to the project during construction. The balance of longer term robustness versus confidence in capital costs is assessed prior to EPC signature and financial close so documents can be adjusted as appropriate.

(IV) REPUTATION

In addition to these broadly financial indicators, reputation risk is a key aspect considered by international project finance lenders as well as by some developers and contractors. Large infrastructure projects often have significant impacts on local communities and attract the attention of wider stakeholder groups who may be vocal if their voice is not being heard. When poorly designed and developed, such projects can cause significant harm. In addition, failure to engage early on with stakeholders can lead to delay and additional cost which compound the problems.

Standards have evolved which cover best practice in identifying, mitigating and managing environmental and social impacts. The Equator Principles is a set of 10 principles [reference] broadly based on IFC (International Finance Corporation) performance standards, which is currently adopted on a voluntary basis by the majority of international banks. Even banks who are not signatories tend to consider the Equator Principles as they will need to show that projects are compliant in order to attract other lenders.

Locally developed and funded projects are usually developed in line with local environmental and social standards. The move to international standards needs to be considered early on in a project's development. There are often some differences in environmental standards on particular pollutants between international and local standards, however, the most significant difference is often in the area of public consultation.

Section 3 – Current Status in the Power Sector

The power sector, and in particular thermal power, provides an interesting example of the dominant incumbents starting to be challenged. The industry has consolidated over the past few decades. In thermal generation, and often in wind and solar power, the equipment suppliers are the key players also in EPC contracts. In the case of hydropower, the plant is not the majority of the EPC value and therefore equipment suppliers do not usually act as lead contractors. Separate contracts for civil works and for mechanical and electrical equipment are, however, quite common so the equipment suppliers contract with the project company.

Figure 12.1 shows the equipment suppliers' share of the global thermal power generation market in 2010 (whole market, not just project finance). With the top four suppliers holding 60 per cent of the market, this is still a concentrated market but this has fallen from 76 per cent in 2001. The growth of the Indian, Korean and Chinese in the

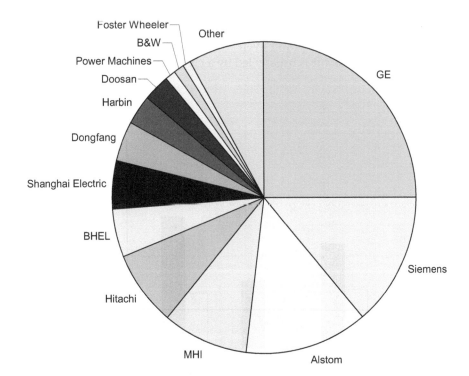

Figure 12.1 Share of global power generation equipment market 2010

Source: Redburn Partners
Note: China: Shanghai Electric, Dongfang, Harbin. Korea: Doosan

past five to 10 years has been huge and is set to continue. BHEL of India is in a category of its own in growing strongly but being very absorbed by a fast growing domestic market. Shanghai Electric, Dongfang, Harbin, Doosan and Power Machines (Russia) have collectively shown a compound annual growth of 22 per cent over the past decade and sales are expected to continue to increase over the next decade from around €20bn in 2010 to around €27bn in 2012 (based on Redburn Partners analysis).

The Chinese domestic market is continuing to demand large additional capacity each year, however, from 2009 to 2010 the level reduced for the first time, by about 14 per cent. This is providing added impetus to their export and is evidenced in the comparison between their 2010 revenue and their 2010 orders (see Figure 12.2). In power generation there is a lag between orders and revenue which depends on the technology (longest for nuclear but still often two to three years for coal plant) which explains the spread in the graph. For example, in the case of Shanghai Electric, 19 per cent of its 2010 revenues were from non-Chinese business whereas 34 per cent of its 2010 orders were from outside China.

China and Korea are currently achieving only modest success in markets with more developed environmental standards – mostly the western markets. Demand comes from a combination of GDP growth and replacement of aged assets. The most significant growth is in the markets with less evolved environmental standards but the current 'big 4' thermal suppliers are continuing to supply into the more gas turbine dominated established western markets where asset replacement is needed due to the age of current power plant and tightening environmental regulation across areas such as the EU.

For hydropower a different set of contractors is involved. As noted above, split EPC contracts are common in hydropower even when project finance is involved and when there is a single EPC contract it is usually led by a civil contractor. This is a field with few

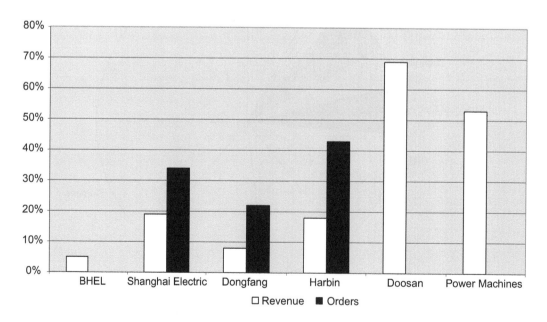

Figure 12.2 External activity as a per cent of total activity

Source: Redburn Partners. *Note*: Orders data not available for BHEL, Doosan, Power Machines.

global players and much less concentration – even international contractors tend to focus on particular relationships or a restricted geography. In this context China Three Gorges, China Gezouba and Sinohydro are very significant players. CNEEC, CMEC and Guangzi are also highly active in addition to the equipment manufacturers shown above.

Korean contractors are becoming more involved in hydropower and are looking for opportunities to develop projects as a precursor to taking on EPC roles in all parts of the power sector. Players now include Sambu, Samsung, Posco, KOMIPO, Daewoo and Hyundai. These companies are bringing in partners to assist with hydropower expertise or operations in some cases and treating the opportunities as general contracting. Their general activity and ambition in power is across the technologies – for example, recent Samsung activities include wind power in Ontario, large Saudi thermal projects, a joint venture with KEPCO (Korean power utility) in Mexico, 50 MW solar in Indonesia, the Kexim (Korean export credit) supported USD$800m Shuweihat 2 project in Abu Dhabi, a US$2.5bn thermal plant of 1200 to 1500MW in Kazakhstan led by KEPCO and a confidential 50MW hydropower project in SE Asia.

Section 4 – Reasons Behind the Growth

It could be argued that contractors' decisions to increase exports are based on economic factors – greater opportunity externally than domestically for their particular services. However, once export credit (government-backed support for contractors and suppliers exporting, usually to cover unpalatable risks such as political risk) is involved, political dimension is usually introduced. China has taken this a few steps further in exporting construction labour overseas and in using infrastructure projects to position itself to secure scarce resources. Korea is less complex but is still very active in pursuing opportunities outside its home market to sustain demand for its factories.

In the case of the power sector, growth in Indian suppliers is also highly significant. However, the Indian suppliers are focused on the domestic market because of its sustained high growth levels so the per cent share of exports in the Indian companies' revenues is actually falling despite growth in external activity. Whereas the Chinese domestic market is flat or slightly declining, in India a three-fold increase in demand is projected over the next few years and India is a very significant customer for Chinese contractors, including having placed the largest ever power plant contract with a Chinese contractor in 2010 (ca. €8bn).

PART OF A LONG-TERM PLAN TO ACCESS COMMODITIES

China's ambition to access primary commodities and foodstuffs is well documented. Development of infrastructure plays a role in meeting this aim in several ways. Firstly, new infrastructure can directly help in accessing mines, etc.; it can provide the power and water to enable extraction, irrigation or general development. In some cases, a bartering arrangement is set up in which primary commodities are used as payment for the infrastructure put in place. Such arrangements are part of a national strategy and backed by state resources including potentially low cost finance for the Chinese contractors involved.

MAINTAIN DOMESTIC ECONOMIC ACTIVITY

Projects can also benefit the provider by providing orders for domestic factories in the case of electromechanical equipment and in the case of Chinese contractors who bring their own workforce, also bring jobs for construction workers previously engaged on construction sites at home. China has been delivering 90,000MW per year but this rate is declining as noted above so companies are looking outside China to sustain factory orders and employment. Korea is similarly keen to maintain economic activity by creating project opportunities overseas and has needed to push this sooner than China because of the local economic situation. The figures above showing Doosan's exports making up nearly 70 per cent of its business are evidence of this.

The role of Chinese contractors on projects outside China is evolving and where they tender for work on funded projects they are free to source from anywhere. However, for projects where they are expected to bring the finance, China Exim or China Development Bank are often involved. Such institutions often require insurance to be taken out with Sinosure and Sinosure requires a minimum threshold 60 per cent to 70 per cent of Chinese content across the supply chain of a project.

PRIVATE SECTOR MOTIVATIONS TO SEEK MORE FAVOURABLE MARKET CONDITIONS AND LEARN ABOUT COMPETITIVE MARKETS

The Chinese market is currently highly regulated and investors achieve modest returns. Reported return on assets for the five major state owned power generating groups in China were all well under 2 per cent (Platts Power in Asia, September 2010). The government is starting to make some tentative steps towards competition, for example testing out bilateral trading for power purchase and two state-owned grid companies have lost their role as monopoly electricity buyers and sellers. However, generators still have the undesirable position of being exposed to market fuel prices while retail prices and wholesale tariffs are controlled by the state. In this context, quite apart from any considerations of maintaining industrial demand or securing primary resources, there are good reasons for Chinese power sector players to invest outside China. Chinese contractors need not necessarily be part of this type of investment; recent investments have included acquisitions – for example Tuas Power in Singapore – rather than just greenfield projects. However, Chinese contractors along with Chinese funding can be part of the strategy of investing outside China.

Section 5 – Means of Growing the External Market Share

China's advantage is built on a lower labour cost and Korea also has a cost advantage. However, this is not enough to succeed in international contracts. There is a combination of factors that have enabled their advance:

- lower cost of finance
- availability of finance
- strategic national relationships
- flexibility to local conditions

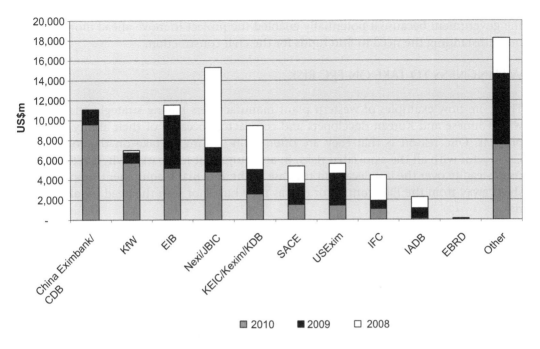

Figure 12.3 Multilateral exposure 2008–2010

Source: Project Finance International

- willingness to take on EPC risk
- joint ventures to build a credible supply chain.

The export credit agencies China Exim and Kexim for China and Korea respectively and their development banks CDB and KDB account for a significant volume of the external contractor activity. Figure 12.3 therefore gives an indication of the success of the strategy.

LOWER COST OF FINANCE

It is Chinese contractors rather than project developers who tend to source finance for projects. Cost of finance can be as low as 2 per cent which is highly competitive.

AVAILABILITY OF FINANCE

Availability of finance is used as a way to secure contracts. It is not just the amount available but the speed or ease with which finance can be put in place that enables Chinese contractors in particular to win work. There are a number of recent examples, some publicised, others less known where contracts have been won despite processes awarding the work to others. For example, for Gibe III hydropower in Ethiopia, due diligence by European Investment Bank and African Development Bank was extensive because of the environmental and social issues to be covered. This caused delay to the timetable desired by the government. An offer was made from China of funding tied to selection of a Chinese contractor for the power plant equipment. This was attractive to the government because it potentially enabled the project to move ahead more quickly, notwithstanding the need to find funds for the civil construction.

WILLINGNESS TO TAKE ON EPC RISK

There are now examples of western plant manufacturers having strategic relationships with Chinese and Korean developers and contractors because of their ability to secure projects. One reason is that they are often more willing to take on the role of EPC Contractor with all the associated risks. In an equipment-led market where returns have risen steadily over the last decade in the case of thermal plant, equipment suppliers have shied away from the EPC contractor role as they have not seen the need to take on this risk.

JOINT VENTURES, ETC. TO BUILD CREDIBLE SUPPLY CHAIN

A number of significant equipment providers have formed joint ventures which has assisted in sharing know-how and cost base.

EXAMPLES OF JOINT VENTURES

Dongfang Guangzhou, gas (China) – Mitsubishi (Japan)

Dongfang Guangdong, nuclear (China) – Alstom (France)

BHEL, nuclear (India) – Alstom (France)

Shanghai Electric (China) – Siemens (Germany)

Power Machines (Russia) – Siemens (Germany)

Kvaerner Hangfa – GE (USA)

Harbin – GE (USA)

Source: Redburn Parters

In addition to the joint ventures, there has been significant development in the supply chain with recognition of the quality needed in international contracts and growing experience in seeking to meet this.

STRATEGIC NATIONAL PARTNERSHIPS

Relationships are forged government to government as a precursor for some investment in infrastructure. These relationships may relate to regional interests (for example Pakistan) or as part of a strategy to secure access to primary commodities (various examples in Africa). As noted previously bartering is used in some cases where infrastructure finance, for projects implemented by Chinese contractors is exchanged for commodities. One of the features of Chinese government relations is that they are generally economic in focus and do not impose any particular standards. Funding therefore does not require any Chinese or international standards to be applied – local standards are sufficient.

Section 6 – Evolution and Impacts on the Market

The emergence of the Chinese and Korean contractors as major players in the market is having an impact. This is not just because it challenges the other regional and international incumbents but because they take some slightly different approaches. Some of these differences are becoming less marked but the impact on the market will remain.

INTERNATIONAL LENDERS ARE BEING SUPPLANTED FOR SOME TRANSACTIONS

The combination of good value contractors and available finance at competitive rates makes it more challenging for international or other multilateral lenders to compete. This is particularly the case since the Chinese do not require application of Equator Principles or other reference to international standards.

CHINESE FUNDERS OFTEN REQUIRE GUARANTEES

So, the onus is on the guarantor rather than the lender to get comfortable with the risk profile. In the case of Chinese funding, there is less focus on the typical points of due diligence compared to other internationally project financed transactions. The contracts are less scrutinized and there is less attention given to the expected capex and delivery schedule. This is because the finance is typically given on the condition that there are strong guarantees in place from the contractor or developer. This places the onus for due diligence less on the lenders and more on the guarantor.

CHINESE ATTITUDE TO ENVIRONMENTAL AND SOCIAL IMPACTS IS DISTINCTIVE BUT EVOLVING

Chinese foreign policy is publicly economic and not political. Thus relationships are forged with economic objectives in mind and funding does not require anything other than the application of local standards. This makes Chinese money and support attractive to some countries as projects can be faster to implement. This is also a strong difference to many multilaterals and commercial lenders for whom environment and social standards are important to manage reputation risk as well as to fit with organizational principles.

The market currently accessible to Chinese manufacturers is limited by their experience in delivering to tight environmental standards. Currently the target market largely excludes countries with the tighter standards. This is not particularly restricting since an increasing proportion of the installed power generation base will be in Asia (expected to be up to around 40 per cent by 2030 from about 30 per cent in 2010) where currently environmental standards are lower than in Europe and the USA.

Environmental regulation in China is, however, developing. China Exim developed an environmental policy in 2004 which was released in 2007 and guidance on environmental and social impact assessment was developed in 2008. Whilst standards are not at levels current in IFC guidelines there have been developments in social impact assessment as a result on learning on recent large projects. Thus, whilst this is an area of difference to other multilaterals, the difference may well decrease.

As an example, Lom Pangar Dam in Cameroon had Chinese funding for part of the US$200m. China International Water and Electric Corporation was appointed as contractor. EIB was expected at the time of writing to commit to funding, suggesting that international standards had been met.

INTERNATIONAL STANDARDS, HEALTH AND SAFETY AND CONSTRUCTION QUALITY

Korean contractors are developing their experience in working on international contracts. Many Chinese contractors are following this but have yet to perform to international standards including in construction quality and in the area of health and safety. There are challenges in the short term in understanding the quality delivered and in verifying performance on construction sites. This extends up the supply chain as quality control varies significantly between different manufacturers who may all supply the same part to a single supplier – i.e., it depends on which week you place an order as to which sub-supplier takes up the order.

COST ADVANTAGE IN CHINA IS REDUCING BUT CONTRACTORS ARE BECOMING MORE DEPENDENT ON THE CHINESE SUPPLY CHAIN

Boston Consulting Group predicts that by 2015 the cost advantage currently enjoyed by Chinese suppliers will have been eroded as a result of wage inflation (reportedly 70 per cent over the last few years). However the combination of the current cost advantage and the Sinosure requirements to source Chinese is meaning that alternative supply chains are becoming less viable. It is quite possible that when the cost advantage has gone, there will be gaps in alternative supply chains which are hard to fill so the Chinese suppliers will continue to be chosen.

It is also becoming less clear on what we mean by Chinese or Korean supply as many large international players located outside the region are forging joint ventures or developing their own supply chain in China and Korea.

THE CHINESE AND KOREANS ARE TAKING INCREASINGLY DIVERSE ROLES ON A GREATER RANGE OF PROJECTS

The stereotype of Chinese and Korean involvement on projects being purely through contractors who are low price is outdated. Both are increasingly looking to provide funding but also to get involved in project development. JVs are more common with a range of nationalities and there are examples of Chinese developers taking on non-Chinese contractors.

Conclusions

The power sector has been used to illustrate the dynamics in international project finance arising as a result of the increasing role played by Chinese and Korean contractors. The power sector is not entirely representative of all sectors but includes both manufacturing and construction contracting. Korean contractors are already substantially outward facing and with the decline in the build rate in the Chinese power sector, there is increased impetus for the Chinese contractors to be active externally. Data from manufacturers suggests this change is happening.

Some of the usual rules of project finance do not apply when Chinese funding is in place, because Chinese funders may require guarantees from either a contractor or developer. Also, because Chinese funders require only compliance with local environmental and social standards, one of the other hallmarks of international project finance – Equator Principles compliance – is not an issue. There is some evolution in Chinese environmental and social standards and unless China and Korea decide they do not wish to supply into the EU and US, there could be further development in the standards.

Korean and Chinese players are becoming more active across a range of roles in projects including funding, developing, contracting and equipment supply and are increasingly working with partners. Although the cost advantage enjoyed in the region is likely to be eroded within five years, it is possible that the supply chain will be relied upon as the supply chain elsewhere may have developed gaps.

We can therefore expect to see a growing role for these players.

2 Sectors

13 *Financing Renewable Energy*

MARK HENDERSON
LDC (Lloyds Development Capital), head of Cleantech &
Environmental

Renewable energy is perhaps the youngest sector within the project finance and infrastructure world. Which probably also makes it the most dynamic, as technologies evolve, regulations change and risks (or perspectives on risk) rise and fall. For these reasons, writing about the project financing of renewable energy projects is a daunting task, given that the norm today could be the exception tomorrow. Whole sub-sectors may appear – hopefully not disappear – in a very short period of time.

What I will therefore endeavour to describe in this chapter are the current features of the main technologies being project financed in the renewable energy market. By highlighting the key issues and risks, like any good project finance assessment, one can then determine how a project should be structured, the risks mitigated (where possible) and allocated to the parties best placed to manage them. The finance facilities can then be structured to take account of these risks and issues – although that is not to say that the market is perfect and some projects and renewable energy financings can be accused of being less than ideal structures for the risks of the projects. As a result, I have felt obliged to describe how certain renewable technologies are being financed, even though I do not believe these to be in the sector's interest. Where I believe the prevailing project finance market can be improved, I have made these comments, not for my own satisfaction, but in the hope that people reading this book with a view to financing projects themselves can form their own view on how their project can be best financed. If they are in the fortunate position of being able to design their own financing structure, then this viewpoint may be of some use.

How Did We Get Here?

But first, let us look at how the renewable energy sector has evolved. Some would say that the rapid growth of the sector over the last decade could be called a revolution, rather than an evolution. It is certainly true that the current scale of developments is impressive, by any yardstick. Total annual investment in renewable energy has now overtaken that for conventional, fossil-fuel power. In 2010 the annual investment in renewable energy was over US$200 billion, up from US$160 billion in 2009. Annual growth rates over the five-year period ending in 2009 range from 10 to 60 per cent for the various technologies.

However, as the various sub-sectors within the renewable energy market tend to be financed in a standard, or consistent, manner, it is useful to understand why they have adopted certain principles and structures. This is where a bit of history is useful – or as someone clever once said: 'If you don't know where you are coming from, how do you know where you are going?'

People within the renewable energy sector like to point out, with a mix of pride and also a pained sense of injustice, that theirs is the only source of electricity that has not been developed by governments with all the public sector resource that entails. And, of course, they are right. The coal-fired power plants that were the bedrock of electricity generation were rolled out by governments and, later, state-owned utilities; the gas-turbine was developed originally for jet propulsion in the arms race run-up to the Second World War, and then began to be deployed in the generation of electricity; nuclear power (which is low carbon power rather than renewable energy) has a multitude of government backed Cold War scientists to thank for its creation.

By contrast, much of the renewable energy market could be classified as a cottage industry, with development being undertaken ad hoc by a diverse group of engineers, enthusiasts and idealists. This began to change around 1973–4 when the then oil crisis drove companies and governments to consider and explore alternative, non-fossil fuel, energy sources. After some progress, some failures and some changes of heart, the fledgling industry only really began to take off in the late 1990s and early 21st century as fears over oil supply again arose, this time being reinforced by new concerns: energy security and, more controversially, global warming and climate change.

So, why is all this important or relevant to today's renewable energy market? Put simply, the answer is that it has shaped the market through the characteristics of the companies and projects that have been developed; it has created a need for new and evolving regulations to promote the projects; and it goes a long way to explain the technologies that have been – and still are being – developed. Before looking at the individual sectors, let us briefly look at these three areas.

Renewables – The Companies and Projects

As a general observation there is a pattern of evolution of the market's players which is common across all renewable energy sectors. The companies who begin developing renewable energy projects tend to be smaller, entrepreneurial ventures. A number are pure developers, but at the beginning of almost all renewable energy sub-sectors, the pioneers are frequently technology-led manufacturers. Gradually, as the technologies become more established and there is more of a market pull, or demand, for these projects, the technology companies focus on manufacturing and a separate development market forms. At this stage the technology companies seek capital to expand and/or merge with other manufacturers. Developers tend to be specialist developers and the projects are small as the equipment is still small-scale per unit and the developers are cash constrained.

The next stage of evolution is the entrance of deeper pocketed developers. This is normally the introduction of financial investors, such as private equity or infrastructure

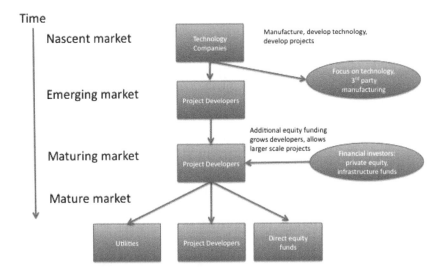

Figure 13.1 Renewable market evolution

funds, either investing directly, where they buy into or inject capital into existing development companies, or indirectly, through a dedicated fund. This category of investor is return-driven and they want a short to medium term investment, which they can sell on to a long-term asset-holder. This long-term investor is typically a utility although pension funds have recently begun to invest significant amounts in the sector, either through long-term funds, but increasingly in their own right as primary asset purchasers.

The other category of deep-pocketed investor is the utility company. Utilities are not typically early-stage developers but prefer to acquire assets when the technologies and projects are proven and they can acquire large, meaningful portfolios. As a result, the utilities can be seen as aggregators of assets, who leave the development risk to the smaller, early stage, project developers.

Whilst the smaller project development companies and financial investors use considerable amounts of project finance debt, the utilities have not, historically, been so active. This is because project finance is no longer deemed to be 'off-balance sheet' for utilities, so it counts towards their total debt, and the high credit rating of utilities means that they can raise cheaper corporate debt through their normal treasury funding, than the project finance market. The scale of this is enormous – of the more than 4,000MW of onshore wind commissioned to date in the UK, only 18 per cent – less than 1,000MW – is project financed. The rest has been financed by utilities on their own balance sheets.

One can therefore conclude that the nature of the renewable energy market's participants, from small developer to short term funds and ultimately highly creditworthy pension funds and utilities will influence the demand for, and structure of, project finance for the relevant participants' projects.

Regulation

As renewable energy is the new kid in the power generation playground, it suffers from being a relatively 'new product'. Three problems that arise for any new product are: it is relatively expensive, it needs further development and it has to win market share. This means that there is little mass-market 'pull' for renewable energy projects in a liberated, unregulated market. As a result, governments need to give it a market 'push'. This is the reason behind the plethora of regulatory change in most active renewable energy markets.

However, one corollary to this market push is that anyone trying to finance projects in the renewable energy sector has to live with a greater degree of political, regulatory and tariff price risk than most other infrastructure sectors. As new technologies come to the fore and existing technologies become better (and cheaper), so regulations need to be adapted, to encourage the use of these new technologies and to reduce the cost to the consumer of the maturing technologies. Consequently, the changing regulations creates a risk that will not go away for some time and is at the mercy of the ever-shifting winds of political change, bias, prejudice and government budgets. As we shall see, this has caused significant problems for the renewable energy market, particularly in recent years.

Technologies

The most prevalent renewable energy sector is that of wind.[1] Historically, it was certainly the first distinct, widespread, renewable energy technology, the poster child of the industry. However, the history also illustrates the problems of developing technologies: there were a number of competing technologies, debates as to which was best, so it took a number of years before today's typical wind turbine became entrenched as the market standard. This diversity of approach has the problem of hampering cost reductions and improvements in performance, as it takes longer to create supply chains, efficiencies of scale and enhancements of design when there is a lack of co-ordinated research and development and pooling of knowledge as competing designs are developed.

If this diversity and internal competition appears unique to the wind industry, it is unfortunately still a major issue for the wave and tidal sectors as well as the waste to energy sector – and a continuing issue in the wind industry as it develops vertical axis turbines, direct drive turbines and other innovations.

While this is a feature of the renewable energy market that can be argued is essential – innovation and improvement surely being a good thing for any industry – when taken with the above observations on market regulation and market pull, one can perhaps see the issues. In other words, if a new style of wind turbine is created, and a market has a fixed tariff for all onshore wind projects, unless this new turbine is immediately at a competitive level (which is unlikely), either it will not be competitive or the regulations will need to be amended to distinguish between this turbine and the more established turbines.

---

1   Some may argue that hydro power is older and more widespread, but I would argue against this as it has not developed as a widespread, distinct, industry but rather a part of utilities' portfolios with limited geographic application.

For this reason, the evolution of renewable energy technologies will be prone to having long lead times as prototypes are developed, a 'standard' technology takes shape and the projects can then be developed with appropriate regulatory support. Nevertheless, project financiers are – rightly – extremely wary of technology risks, which will also hamper the evolution of the market as early-stage technologies struggle to attract bank debt and have to finance the first projects on an all-equity basis. This will, in turn, tend to dictate that the projects are very small to begin with, only growing in scale through a combination of improved technical efficiencies and a slow trickle of equity and debt financings.

This concludes my review of the broad history of the development of the renewable energy market and the consequences of it. Some might say the lessons of it as the patterns we have seen for the onshore wind, offshore wind and solar photovoltaic markets, look to be repeating themselves for other renewable energy sectors such as biomass, waste to energy, wave and tidal.

Let us now look at these sectors individually, from a banker's perspective. Below I will set out the key features, risks and issues, and describe how a banker will view them, assess them, and structure a financing around them. As mentioned earlier, this will be a practical description of how such projects are being evaluated and financed, which may not be seen as the optimum way that these projects should be evaluated and financed! While project developers will always have cause to disagree with a banker's perspective, by and large the very successful track record of project financings means that lenders are doing something right. Let us remember that banks are typically very highly exposed to the projects (typically financing 75–85 per cent of a project's cost), and only have a fixed rate of return. Equity has a much lower commitment and, if the project goes well, stands to make a much higher return.

Wind

Table 13.1 Wind

Risk	Level
Permitting	1
Technology	½
Construction	½
Operation	½
Fuel supply	1
Power sales	¼
Financing issues	½

INTRODUCTION

Wind is the most prevalent renewable energy source and has been developed longer than any other as a specific industry. That said, to many it is not necessarily the best renewable energy technology as it has certain inherent weaknesses, which we describe below. That said, because there is now such a significant international wind energy industry, and it is currently the most economic renewable energy source, it will remain a major sub-sector for some time to come.

Some of the most important risks and issues to consider, from a project financing perspective, are the following:

PERMITTING

Wind projects suffer from being highly visible, spread over a large area and therefore in areas that people consider to be unspoilt and of natural beauty. If they are closer to communities, then people near the turbines may complain of being too close and the visual impairment of this, noise from the blades turning and even snow and ice being thrown off the blades, if it is in a cold area. As a result, whilst there can be much popular support for the concept of wind projects, there can be strong local opposition to them. One acronym for this effect is NIMBY-ism (Not In My Back Yard); although there are also those who oppose the projects in their totality, who can also be called BANANAs (Build Absolutely Nothing, Anywhere, Near Anyone)!

In addition to the human complaints, wind projects suffer from a number of potential environmental threats to their permitting, the main ones being the potential damage to birds and bats. The potential to damage birds is now less of a practical issue as the larger turbines typically used today rotate much more slowly and evenly than earlier, smaller turbines, so if any bird were to be struck by a blade, some might suggest that it was an appropriately Darwinian improvement to the gene pool! Nevertheless, the emotive nature of the issue and the string opposition that some people have to these projects, still means that much time and cost is taken up with projects at a preliminary stage undertaking detailed environmental studies.

Another permitting and development issue is that of land rights. Sometimes the land that the project is to be built on is bought freehold by the project developer. For most projects, particularly larger ones, this is not a practical solution due to the large acreage over which a wind farm is built and the access needed to it, so leaseholds or access rights are needed. These can involve a number of different parties and so be a time-consuming and costly exercise before the project's construction can commence.

As a result, banks typically lend to a project at the end of the development period when all permits and planning consents have been obtained. The risk of getting to this stage is normally borne by equity, which is one reason why the projects in the wind sector began small and have only grown in size as financially larger developers have invested in the industry.

TECHNOLOGY

As with all technologies, in the wind sector it has to be proven. There are now over two decades' worth of precedent and therefore an established, standard format of wind turbine (three blades on a horizontal axis, affixed to a tubular tower), should be fairly predictable. However, this is not the case as there are still evolutions of models as manufacturers of wind turbines seek to increase the size of each individual turbine, improve efficiencies, adapt to sites with lower wind speeds and increase reliability. On a small scale there are also firms which are re-visiting some of the basic structures and experimenting with some of the early concepts: one- or two-blade turbines, vertical axis rotation and even unmounted, kite-style prototypes. These are, on the whole, small scale so let us focus on the evolved, established structures.

Perhaps the biggest technical concern, for a lender, is the gearbox. Over the years there have been issues with these working, reliably, for long periods of time and there have been many reports of more frequent maintenance and early replacements being required. This has improved of late but it will be important to consider if there are key components of a turbine that are being procured from a third party and, if necessary, that they are only procured from a reputable, reliable and creditworthy third party who is in turn providing warranties for their performance, to the principal turbine manufacturer.

Turbines constantly evolve in size: 600kW used to be the standard size, then 1MW, 1.5MW and now 2MW and 3MW are standard, with larger models underway, driven by the offshore wind industry. As these models grow, it is not unusual for a manufacturer to claim that, for example, their new 3MW turbine is proven as it is essentially the 2MW model with longer blades. This should not be acceptable and a lender will want to see the 3MW model having worked, in numbers (ie not just one prototype), for at least a year, before being willing to finance it. Even then it will be important to check that the new turbine can be fully insured and, if necessary, the manufacturer stand behind it with warranties for the percentage of time that it is available to generate (typically 95 per cent to 97 per cent of a year, less in the first year as teething issues are resolved), and warranties for the 'power curve'. The power curve is the amount of power produced for the level of wind speed.

Where there are residual concerns or uncertainties, then the lenders can consider a lower percentage of debt being provided to the project, in order to increase the debt service cover ratio and so the buffer of cashflow expected to be generated and the debt service; and/or establishing a maintenance reserve account (MRA). An MRA can be used to cover additional work on repairing the turbines, but should not be a proxy for a fundamentally unproven turbine, where a fleet-wide flaw could financially ruin the project.

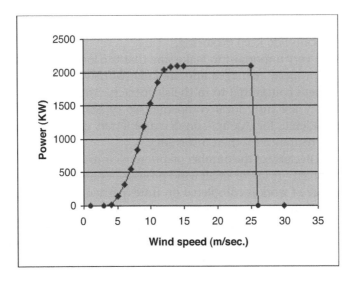

Figure 13.2 The power curve

CONSTRUCTION

For most project financings the ideal commercial structure governing the construction of the project is a lump sum, turnkey engineering procurement construction, or EPC contract. This is where the contractor assumes all of the risk of delivering the entire project, for a fixed price. Because of the historical beginnings of wind projects, where the projects were put together by small contractors and on a small scale, the EPC contracting approach was not used. Instead, they tend, even today, to be built on a multi-contract approach, with separate contracts being given for the wind turbines (sometimes abbreviated to WTG, or Wind Turbine Generator), the connection to – or construction of – the electrical substation which in turn connects to the grid, and then a 'balance of plant' contract, or set of contracts, which can involve any combination of all the peripheral work. This includes the construction of access roads to the wind turbine sites (remember, these are normally built at high altitude, away from communities so access is usually needing to be created); the foundations and civil works on site for the turbines; and the electrical work on the site.

The potential issues, which a developer and financier will wish to protect against, are, in general terms, the standard ones of delay and cost over-run. In the construction period this typically arises through poor workmanship, interface issues and site-specific issues. Briefly these are caused by:

- Poor workmanship – Admittedly this is an issue for any construction project, but can be exacerbated in wind projects because of the multi-contract approach and consequently certain packages of work, particularly in the balance of plant, being given to small, local contractors who can lack the experience and ability to perform to the required standard and timeframe. The attraction of using local contractors is that it can be cheaper than using national or international firms, and it provides employment to the local community. Given the problems with local opposition to wind projects (see the Permitting section above), this involvement of local contractors is frequently an intent of project developers – or even an undertaking given to the local community in order to assist their approval of the project – and so the consequential problems it can cause do keep occurring.

  It is therefore very important to make sure that the local contractors have relevant experience, are properly managed and are creditworthy for their warranties and/or liquidated damages committed to in their contracts. Their creditworthiness is often a problem if they are truly local companies, so typical credit enhancements may need to be considered, for example on-demand letters of credit, third party or bank guarantees and insurance for their insolvency.

- Interface issues – Because of the number of different contracts and different contractors that can be involved – even for small wind projects – there can be difficulties ensuring that each package of work is completed on time (particularly where another package of work is reliant on the previous package being completed before they can begin). Poor workmanship can also have consequential effects on a package of work reliant on it, for example if the foundations are not to the correct specification, then the reliability of the towers could be at risk. Finally, there is an obfuscation of overall responsibility, as the blame for a time or cost overrun will be passed from one contractor to another if it is not clear who was responsible for each package and the overall project management did not identify the responsibility and issues as they arose.

- Site-specific issues – Due to the remoteness of a wind turbine site and the large distance over which the turbines are deployed, there can be an increased risk of site problems. These are typically geotechnical, as the foundations need to be checked to ensure the ground is not solid granite or too soft or even that there are underground caves, as are found in porous rock. The biggest delaying factor for a wind project, and so a double revenue hit as it can cause additional costs whilst teams have to stay on site for longer and a loss of income generation, is perhaps very obviously: excessive wind! This problem arises as the sites are, one would hope, naturally very windy and the wind turbine needs to be assembled by crane, lifting the tower in sections, the nacelle at the top of the turbine and the blades. Due to the required precision this can only be done at low/no wind speeds.

Unfortunately, this last risk cannot be contracted against, but it is possible to factor weather windows into the construction programme and obligate the contractors to deliver their packages of work within this time, or suffer higher liabilities or penalties through the liquidated damages within their contracts. Insurance can also be taken out for 'advanced loss of profits' or delay, although the cost of this for wind delay is naturally not going to be without a cost for a wind project. Consequently, a certain level of contingency, both of time and cost, should be factored into a construction schedule.

OPERATION

The operation of wind farms is relatively simple, especially compared to fossil-fuel power plants. The issue is that, with a number of wind turbines, there is a greater probability of one or more of them having a fault at some time that prevents it from operating (an outage). As this usually only comes to light when the wind turbine should be turning, it follows that any outage is a direct loss of revenue – and with a wind turbine only operating around 25 per cent of the year, then any outage causes a disproportionately high percentage of lost revenue for a wind project compared to a fossil-fuel power plant that is expected to operate at over 95 per cent of the year. Remember also, that wind projects are normally situated in remote locations, so even a rapid response can take several, valuable hours, just to reach the site.

It is therefore essential to have a strong contract O&M (operation and maintenance), with a company who can respond quickly and effectively to faults. In the early years of a project's operation this is usually undertaken by the wind turbine manufacturer, although larger developers and utilities may have their own internal teams who do this work, relying on the turbine manufacturer's warranties in the early years for financial compensation, where relevant. Insurance can be obtained for certain faults, but it is not a remedy for poor technology, casual supervision or slow response times.

It is therefore important that, in addition to a strong technical ability, companies undertaking the O&M for a project, even internal ones, have bases located near the wind turbines, 24-hour supervision and monitoring, and are of sufficient credit standing that they can meet claims, where applicable, for loss of earnings. As the wind turbine manufacturer can also be liable, directly so in the early warranty period (typically two to five years post construction), then their long-term financial standing is a relevant assessment by the lenders during the initial due diligence work.

FUEL SUPPLY, WIND RESOURCE

This is probably the most critical aspect of a wind power project, as it has the most significant bearing on a project's ability to repay the debt facility. There are now several armies of consultants who have a variety of sophisticated wind measurement apparatuses and software methods of analysing data and forecasting future wind resource and energy production. Sadly, this merely reduces the risk and does not eliminate it. How do bankers therefore assess it? Typically by ensuring that there is a reliable, long-term set of wind resource data.

Put simply, this requires having data taken from the proposed project site, be for at least a year and be at hub height (i.e., the height of the wind turbine's nacelle). Unfortunately this cannot always be possible or practical (for example, given the height of wind turbines, having a mast at 80–100m for over a year is difficult and/or expensive), but where it is not possible, then lenders should consider some ways of protecting themselves. This is not usually done, but suggestions would be:

- Reducing the gearing, so equity takes more risk. This also has the benefit of increasing the debt service cover ratio (DSCR), providing more cushion to the numbers;
- Having a larger debt service reserve account (DSRA), which can protect or top up a shortfall in debt service; and
- Having a flexible repayment structure, such as 'upside sharing'. This is actually an old concept, but rarely seen these days as equity pushes for more aggressive terms. It is simply an additional level of repayment above the scheduled debt service, if the cashflow in any period is above a particular level of equity return. It is not a cash sweep as such (as this is usually a sweep of cash which reduces equity return), instead it is a sweep of cash above a return level. This protects the equity return, but reduces the debt exposure and risk of poor wind in later years.

When sizing debt, lenders require that the wind forecasts show the annual production according to a probability of exceeding the number shown, typically 90 per cent (P90) or 50 per cent (P50), with 75 per cent (P75) also being used. In other words, with P50 there is only a 50 per cent chance of the wind production exceeding this forecast, but P90 is more conservative, as there would be a 90 per cent chance of the actual wind figures exceeding the forecast. P50 is the norm used by project sponsors for equity returns, banks did use it when lending became more aggressive up to 2008, but since the financial crisis they have tended back towards the P90.

These forecasts are typically for a 10-year forecast horizon, which means that in any one year there could be a significant variation from this annual forecast, as it would be expected to be made up over the other years. As a result, it is possible to have different horizons and if lenders wish to be conservative, or test their models for downside sensitivities, then a one-year forecast is sometimes used. As a break-even analysis it is standard practice amongst some banks to have a one-year P99 test, in order to size the debt and structure the repayments.

POWER SALES

As the unpredictability of precisely when wind will blow, and for how long, makes forecasting very difficult, one would expect the ability to sell the resultant power to be difficult. However, for this reason, wind power sales almost have priority of despatch – in other words, as soon as they can generate, they will and be the first power despatched into the grid system.

As a result, whether the revenue system is governed by a long-term power purchase agreement, a feed-in tariff or green certificates, a project has the security of knowing that, as long as the wind blows and the turbines work, they will be paid the price of x per megawatt hour (MWh) of production. Of course there is a regulatory or political risk that the pricing regime or payment method will change over time, but this is a more macro risk and issue.

FINANCING ISSUES

Wind power is now an established and mainstream project sector, so finance is relatively easy to obtain, on competitive terms, providing the project has no unusual flaws or risks. Debt is sized in a standard way, looking at the revenues produced and back-solving from these cashflows to obtain the desired DSCR (usually 1.3 times the cash available for debt service). In other words, if there is £130 of cash in a period, that would support a debt service (principal and interest) of £100.

This sounds simple enough, but what of seasonality? In any region there are generally varying seasons when the wind blows more or less – autumn and winter in the UK being much more windy than summer. Therefore it is important to tailor the repayment amounts for the cashflows expected in the season and either have very different repayment amounts, if the repayment schedule falls at the end of a high or low wind period, or the repayment dates should be adjusted if a more consistent and even repayment schedule is desired.

One final consideration for a financier is the risk of decommissioning the project. Some landlords or lessors stipulate in the lease or concession that the project site must be returned to its natural state at the end of the lease or concession period. As this can be for a period of 20 or 25 years, it is not much longer than some projects' debt tenors. Given the uncertainty of earnings, there is a possibility that the debt repayments may even be stretched so that there is a large decommissioning cost at the end of the debt repayment period. To cover for this, it is not unusual to have a decommissioning reserve account established, which can be built up towards the end of the debt period.

CONCLUSION

Given the number of issues surrounding a wind power project: they are difficult to permit, need careful care and maintenance and the earnings are volatile; one might be forgiven for wondering why develop them, particularly compared to other technologies such as solar PV. The reason is that the volatility of earnings and the difference between equity's P50 wind forecast assumptions and lenders' more conservative P90 forecasts, do provide the potential for good equity returns.

They can also be deployed on scale as projects can be much larger and, on a portfolio basis, the variance between sites can be reduced – particularly for those project developers with international operations. The cost is also reducing with technologies being reasonably proven, so the risks reduce, including that of political or regulatory risk – the closer one is to the delivered cost of fossil fuels, the less likelihood there is for political interference and tariff reductions.

Solar PV

Table 13.2 Solar PV

Risk	Level
Permitting	½
Technology	¼
Construction	¼
Operation	¼
Fuel supply	¼
Power sales	¾
Financing issues	¼

Solar PV (or photovoltaic, to differentiate it from solar thermal projects) technology consists of arrays of solar panels being deployed in large scale on the ground, or on smaller arrays on large roof areas (such as warehouses), or small arrays on domestic houses. Overall, it is perhaps the simplest technology to build and operate and there have been very large numbers of solar projects developed in the last few years, albeit typically on a very small scale (in MW terms). Germany alone installed over 7,000MW in 2010 and Italy around 3,000MW in 2010.

The Achilles heel of solar PV is that the cost per MW is very high, around three times as expensive as onshore wind, although it is dropping rapidly. Therefore the risk of political interference and regulatory change is high as countries change their tariff regimes to keep step with the reducing costs.

The primary risk areas can be summarized as follows:

PERMITTING

Like any large scale, visible power technology, developers can have problems obtaining consents to build. Unlike wind, solar PV arrays are not so visible, especially those on roofs. Where there are issues are when large, multi-MW arrays are being deployed in the countryside.

TECHNOLOGY

Solar PV technology benefits greatly from having no moving parts. Photovoltaic panels consist of cells that convert daylight (not necessarily bright sunlight – although this helps: the brighter the more power produced) into electricity. Generally, there are two types of solar PV technology: thin film and crystalline silicon. Thin film is generally used on buildings, as it is lighter; crystalline silicon is cheaper and more robust, so is better for large, field arrays.

The panels are generally long wearing, for at least 20 to 25 years. In the recent rush to build solar PV projects, a number of new manufacturers began operations and the quality of certain of these was poor. Now that the initial rush has largely subsided and the more credible panel producers have been able to expand their production capabilities, there should not be a need to acquire or finance panels that are otherwise not proven, from reputable manufacturers and who can guarantee their products for the project life.

Two technical issues do need to be considered, first is the efficiency of production, as the electricity generating potential of panels do degrade over time, usually by about 0.5 per cent to 1 per cent per annum. For modelling purposes, lenders tend to assume 1 per cent pa. The second technical issue are the inverters. These convert the electricity generated from the panel from direct to alternating current, or DC to AC. Inverters do not last as long as panels and need to be replaced, both on a major maintenance upgrade after, say, 15 years, although if not sourced from a good manufacturer or are not kept in a cool, ventilated state, can need replacing much earlier and much more frequently. This needs checking with the lenders' technical adviser and, if necessary, allowance made for more spares to be kept and/or a maintenance reserve account to be established.

CONSTRUCTION

Solar PV arrays, whether on roofs or ground-mounted, can be swiftly built on little more than a secure metal (even wooden) foundation, with the panels affixed to them. Perhaps the only issue needing special consideration is the security of the units. As they are located in exposed areas, there is the opportunity for panels to be stolen, so a secure protection system is required.

OPERATION

As stated above, there are no moving parts to solar PV projects. Therefore, apart from the issue of inverters, they should operate with relative predictability over time. The primary concern that can arise is a reduced performance of the panels due to the build-up of dirt, snow or shadows that can arise from neighbouring foliage or buildings. The latter should be considered in the project's initial design but the maintenance programme should allow for regular cleaning and removal of natural growth.

FUEL SUPPLY, IRRADIATION LEVELS

The level of irradiation that a site receives is well mapped and can be judged from satellite surveys. Given that it is the level of natural light that is important rather than the specific amount of direct sunlight, it is not necessary to establish on-site direct data collection like wind projects. This greater predictability of resource levels allows the hours of production to be much more predictable, with very little volatility.

POWER SALES

Solar PV, like wind, is sold under a variety of feed-in tariffs and green certificate mechanisms. Importantly like wind, solar PV also benefits from priority of despatch in most jurisdictions, so again a project sponsor and lender have the comfort of knowing that whatever power is produced, is despatched and sold.

FINANCING ISSUES

As mentioned in the introduction to this section, the issue with solar PV sales is the high cost of production, and therefore the sector is exposed more than most to political and regulatory change. From 2010 to 2011 many countries introduced quite sudden changes to the price they paid for solar PV projects, amongst them the three biggest countries by installation: Germany, Spain and Italy, as well as France, the UK and Czech Republic. It is therefore important to ensure that, where there is a tariff deadline, the contractors can install within the timeframe required and have strong liquidated damages in their contract which can make up a significant part of any reduced income.

Lenders may also consider sizing their debt on the future, lower tariff, to protect themselves against the relevant deadline not being met. Should the project be completed in time to achieve the higher tariff, then there can be an additional debt drawdown made to reflect these economics. The important point is that it is equity that carries the risk.

CONCLUSION

Given the relative ease and reduced risk of developing and constructing solar PV projects, one may wonder why any other renewable technology is developed. There are two simple answers: one is return, as it is very stable, but relatively low (equity returns of 10–12 per cent re the norm), the other is the scale of the projects. They are much smaller in MW size than other renewable technologies and, whilst the high panel cost made it a high capital outlay, this is now reducing.

Biomass (and Energy from Waste)

Table 13.3   Biomass (and energy from waste)

Risk	Level
Permitting	½
Technology	1
Construction	½
Operation	½
Fuel supply	1
Power sales	¼
Financing issues	¾

INTRODUCTION

Biomass is the last section, it shares many of the same issues and characteristics as Energy from Waste (EfW), which is why mention is made in the heading, so the comments I make about biomass can be taken to be applied, generally, to EfW as well. Where there are relevant and material differences between the two areas, this will be mentioned.

Biomass is the production of heat and electricity from the combustion of sustainable natural crops. In the case of EfW the fuel is municipal and commercial waste and/or waste materials such as wood that has been treated, used (typically in building) and has to be disposed of.

The major issues are the sourcing of the fuel and the technologies. Due to the difficulty of sourcing a large, long-term scale of fuel, most biomass projects are small scale (under 50MW) and developed by local development teams.

PERMITTING

As most biomass and EfW plants involve the incineration of the fuel supply, this can cause a lot of local concern and objection, particularly where waste is concerned, as local communities can be concerned about noxious smells and pollution. In Europe the European Union has also laid down very strict emission levels, which can be difficult to comply with, hence prototype plants are often built first to demonstrate the technology.

Where biomass fuels, such as wood chip, pellets are being imported from any distance, which is frequently the case, then there are many more permits and approvals that must be obtained. It can therefore take quite considerable periods of time to develop these projects.

TECHNOLOGY

In its simplest form, biomass projects are very simple, proven technologies. Just like a coal-fired power plant, the wood chip is loaded into a boiler, is incinerated and the heat drives a steam turbine. Ash is removed and disposed of. This is the case in Scandinavia and Germany where there are a large number of straightforward, usually very small-scale biomass projects successfully operating.

The problem is elsewhere, where either the wood source is not so plentiful, and/ or the scale of the project is much larger, or where more novel forms of fuel are being used. In this regard there are straw burning projects, chicken litter and anything else combustible and considered a waste source, from olive residues to by-products of whiskey distilling.

In these cases there are three questions a lender should ask:

1. Is the technology proven? Is there another plant successfully operating, for over a year, without major incident, using the same technology as the one proposed?
2. If yes, is the proven plant the same size as the one proposed? It is not uncommon for initial, smaller scale prototypes to be built, then developers approach project financiers for finance on the large-scale version. This overlooks any number of technical issues that can arise and should generally be avoided. An exception could be a project that comprises a multiple of units the same size as the proven project, although the interface risk would still need to be checked carefully.
3. If still yes, is the proven plant using the same fuel as that proposed for the new project? It may seem obvious, but just because a boiler works with one fuel, does not mean it will work with a different one. Even fuel crops grown in different areas will have different chemical compositions that can affect the combustion, emissions and the longevity of the boiler lining. The composition of waste is even more variable.

CONSTRUCTION

Once the technology is established, the construction of a biomass project is relatively straightforward and mirrors a coal-fired project on a much smaller scale. It should be possible to obtain the contract on a fixed lump sum, turnkey contract, which provides a high degree of confidence on the price of the project and the interface issues.

A problem that can arise with smaller contracts is that the contractors do not have large balance sheets, and therefore it may be necessary to seek additional security, such as letters of credit, bank guarantees, or parent company guarantees, should the contractor be part of a larger group.

OPERATION

Again, the comparison with conventional steam plants means that the operation of biomass projects should be relatively standard. The problems arise, in the main, from the fuel handling. This can be particularly relevant for EfW projects as there has to be a lot of manual sorting of the waste and the actual transportation system can therefore be resource intensive and not entirely efficient – only one scaffolding pipe or gas cylinder can evade detection for there to be a big problem with the boiler.

With biomass fuels, there can also be issues, albeit of a different nature. Typically the fuel can be wet (from being transported in open trucks and stored outside), so the moisture levels need to be monitored, and experienced personnel are needed to mix the fuel to obtain a consistent quality and moisture of fuel being fed into the boiler.

The actual boiler itself may need to be repaired more frequently, or even be cleaned more frequently, depending on the calorific value of the fuel, its emissions and the ash it produces. All such outages not only cost more in repairs, but the time the boiler is out of service prevents any revenue being produced, so it is a double negative effect on the project revenues.

FUEL SUPPLY

For most biomass projects the fuel supply is a major financing issue. Project financiers wish to see long-term contracts (for at least the term of the debt plus a 'tail' of one to two years), with the following features:

- the required volume to operate the power plant;
- at a fixed price, indexed if appropriate, e.g., to inflation, and
- for a specific quality.

The quality usually states a range of calorific values, so the biomass plant can be certain that the volume of fuel supply will produce the required amount of power. As energy crops and wood are often stored outside and transported in open trucks, it is also important to agree a maximum moisture content. The final point on quality is to ensure that the fuel will not generate too much ash within the boiler, as it can be costly to dispose of.

Unfortunately, it is very rare to be able to find long-term fuel supply contracts with these three features. Volume and quantity are usually possible, but price rarely is. In EfW contracts the waste fuel is usually a source of revenue (called gate fees), as the counterparty disposing of the waste would normally have to pay landfill taxes (in the UK), or other penalties to dispose of their fuel. This makes the economics of EfW projects extremely attractive, but there is a risk that these prices will decrease, possibly dramatically, even to being a cost in the long term. As a consequence, any financial model should test for lower gate fees, or even none, to see if the power generation revenues alone can sustain the project.

Pure biomass projects are therefore forced to find ways to structure around this uncertainty of fuel supply. Three suggested approaches are:

- Secure your own fuel source: either own or lease the woodland or energy crop fields. This may be possible for smaller projects, difficult for larger ones unless the sponsor has significant financial resource (a UK coal fired plant is converting to run on biomass – the utility is growing its own fuel in the southern United States. A neat solution, but beyond the ability of most project sponsors).
- Locate your project in an area with abundant fuel resource. This is not a perfect solution, as it still requires the lenders taking a risk on fuel prices. It also introduces an issue into the creditworthiness of the fuel suppliers, as they will tend to be farmers or co-operatives with little financial standing and a high risk of not supplying the fuel for the long term. Nevertheless, a variety of contracts may be achievable.
- Become a 'captive' plant for the fuel source. If the fuel is coming from one source, such as a pulp and paper mill, chicken farm or whiskey distillery, by building the

plant adjacent to it, one not only reduces the transportation cost but also typically can sell the heat and electricity to the host, with additional power being sold to the grid. The fuel price can then be linked to the sales of heat and electricity that the host contracts for, in a tolling style of contract.

Whilst this last solution has the benefit of securing supply and possibly price certainty as well, it can also introduce the risk of the host fuel supplier's industry and their own creditworthiness. In other words, if the host is a paper mill, then the business cycle of the paper industry will affect the host's financial performance and possibly their demand for heat and electricity will vary as well. In such circumstances lenders will need to assess this risk, which they may not feel able to do if it is an unfamiliar or highly risky industry. Alternative fuel suppliers and power offtakers should also be identified.

Finally, the last fuel supply issue is the question of logistics. How does one transport the fuel to the project? Clearly, location is everything and the more options the better: be located next to a deep-water port with rail access and a major road system passing nearby. If not, then consider what is required and, from a lender's perspective, is this risk acceptable, bearing in mind the power project will be operating pretty much 24 hours every day of the year (except during scheduled maintenance). There are projects that the author has witnessed where the fuel was expected to be supplied by trucks over long distances, on a small, poorly maintained road network, through a town, six per hour. That is every 10 minutes, come rain or snow! Even if that were possible, which personally I doubt, the town is unlikely to approve such traffic, particularly at night and so it would be unlikely to achieve environmental clearance.

POWER SALES

If fuel supply is the greatest issue for biomass and waste projects, power sales are a great strength. Unlike other renewable energy projects, these ones can run as full-time baseload power plants with certainty of despatch. Accordingly they can secure long-term power purchase agreements for the electricity and, if applicable or desirable, can also sell heat to neighbouring industries or municipalities. The heat sales make the projects much more energy efficient, and in many countries the projects can secure greater revenue from these sales (in the UK, for example, such projects can secure two renewable obligation certificates, ROCs, rather than 1.5 ROCs or less for pure electricity sales).

FINANCING ISSUES

The financing issues centre on the fuel supply contracts, as highlighted in that section above, the potential technology issues and the lack of creditworthy counterparts that are typically involved in these projects. The biomass projects tend to be small scale but this does not detract from the risks and should not make higher risk counterparties acceptable to lenders.

Important features in a project financing of a biomass and/or EfW waste project include:

- A lower gearing level, so that the sponsors share more of the risk

- A shorter tenor, so the technology and operational risk is reduced, perhaps having a cash sweep after a certain period of operation
- Major maintenance reserve accounts
- Fuel supply reserves, which can be either a requirement to store more fuel at site, or a financial reserve to protect against higher than expected fuel costs (although this latter is effectively covered by a higher DSCR as a result of lower gearing)
- A rolling potential cash sweep.

This last structure, a rolling potential cash sweep, is a structure to address the issue of achieving long term fuel supply contracts. In some cases it is possible to contract for a shorter period, say five years. In which case, lenders can structure a longer repayment period, say 10–12 years, and require that the project sponsors contract their fuel supply for 5 years out. Therefore, whenever one year is ended, then they contract the next year five (now sixth year of operation). If the market suddenly changes and becomes much more expensive, or it is no longer possible to contract for this period, then the financing facility triggers a cash sweep of all surplus cash after paying for the project's costs. This may not be enough in the remaining four years of the contracted period to fully mature the debt, but it should be enough to reduce it down to an acceptably low level for the lenders now that the project has higher fuel costs and lower cash available for debt service.

CONCLUSION

Biomass and EfW projects are the subject of much discussion but not many make it to a full project financing. In the UK there has been renewed interest in both these areas, assisted in the case of EfW by the European Union's waste directive, reducing the amount of waste that can go to landfill and the higher financial penalties for doing so. The UK government has also provided greater incentives through the ROC system for biomass projects, which has caused some very large projects to be developed. The extent to which these can be realized by smaller developers (as opposed to utilities, who are unlikely to project finance them given the issues) will depend on the creation of a bankable fuel supply chain and the presence of creditworthy contractors and operators.

Conclusion

There are many different renewable energy projects and to describe all of them and their particular features would take a book in its own right. What I have tried to do in this chapter is to cover the three primary technologies being financed at present and, by doing this in some detail, provide a template for assessing the risks, issues and potential solutions to common features. For example, if considering the finance for a mini hydro project, the fuel supply – in this case the water flow and predictability – will clearly be an issue not unlike the wind resource in wind projects, so how can it be assessed, how can bankers build flexibility into their loans to accommodate it? The same resource problems will arise for wave energy projects and tidal projects (to a lesser extent), in addition to the technology, its reliability and long term maintenance, where the comparison to the biomass technology risks will be pertinent.

As global power consumption increases and governments grapple with the 'trilemma' of security of supply, low cost power and low carbon power, renewable energy technologies will continue to be in demand and will continue to evolve and add to the global energy mix. The next decade requires £200bn of investment in the UK's electricity sector alone, so there should be ample work for project developers, investors and financiers.

Long may the lights be on!

14 *Financing Offshore Wind*

JÉRÔME GUILLET
Managing Director, Green Giraffe Energy Bankers

With investments in the offshore wind sector set to increase from a few hundred million euros to tens of billions per year, the question of where the money will come from has been at the forefront of industry preoccupations. This article examines how equity investors and potential lenders look at the sector and in what ways they can be expected to contribute. The article focusses on Europe, as the US are still at the pioneer stage, whilst Chinese projects are likely to be funded under specific local conditions.

The Market to Date

Industry growth so far has largely been achieved by utilities, alone or in small partnerships, financing and building their own projects and keeping them on their balance sheet.

There are, however, other possibilities. Non-utility projects, undertaken by independent power producers (IPPs), may call on non-recourse debt financing from banks, particularly during the construction phase. As of end 2010, just over 10 per cent of operational capacity (and a similar percentage of capacity under construction) had benefitted from non-recourse debt financing, with a smaller percentage having been refinanced through debt after completion:

(End 2010)	Capacity (MW)	In %
Total operational offshore wind farms	2946	100%
Q7	120	4%
C-Power phase 1	30	1%
Belwind	165	7%
Non-recourse construction debt	315	12%
Lynn & Inner Dowsing	194	6%
Non-recourse debt (operational projects)	509	18%
(End 2010)	Capacity (MW)	In %
Total offshore wind farms in construction	3,300	100%
C-Power phases 2-3	295	9%

Borkum West 2	200	6%
Non-recourse debt (projects under construction)	495	15%

In parallel to debt transactions, a number of equity transactions have taken place. Beyond utilities sharing risk on a given project, new buyers such as pension and private equity funds have emerged as contributors of additional non-utility finance:

(End 2010)	Financial owner	Capacity (MW)	In %
Total operational offshore wind farms		2946	100%
North Hoyle (67%)	Englefield/FIIA	40	1%
Nysted (50%)	PensionDanmark	83	3%
Lynn & Inner Dowsing (50%)	TCW	97	3%
Belwind (22%)	Rabo/Meewind	36	1%
Financial investors		256	9%
Total offshore wind farms in construction		3,300	100%
London Array phase 1 (20%)	Masdar	126	4%
Walney 1 & 2 (25%)	PGGM/Ampere	92	3%
Nysted 2 (50%)	PensionDanmark	103	3%
Anholt (50%)	PensionDanmark/DKA	200	6%
Gunfleet Sands (50%)	Marubeni	86	3%
Financial investors		607	18%

A number of interesting conclusions may be drawn at this point. One is that there are alternative sources to utilities for investment in offshore wind. Another is that banks show willingness to take construction risk (via debt), preferably, so far, in non-utility projects. Meanwhile, financial investors (via equity) tend rather to seek a stake in already operational projects. These conclusions also point to the most likely routes for utilities looking for external sources of funding:

- Recycling of project equity via the sale of (typically minority) stakes in operating projects; non-recourse financing of IPP projects prior to completion;
- Non-recourse refinancing of utility projects once they are operational.

Financial Investors

In the long run, it is quite likely that offshore wind will be a very attractive asset class for a certain type of investor: with very stable, heavily regulated, long term cash flows, its revenue profile fits the needs of pension and similar funds with very long investment horizons. The various regulatory frameworks will offer investors fine-tuning according to specific preferences (fixed revenues in countries with feed-in regimes like Germany, access to some market upside in countries with green certificate regimes and grey power sold on the market, inflation mitigation in countries where support mechanisms are indexed, like the ROCs in the UK, etc. ...) and to diversify 'political' risk exposure within a consistent and broadly stable European policy framework.

Such investment will follow the move into onshore wind, and volumes available are likely to be significant, as offshore wind offers the additional advantage of making large size tickets possible.

The big obstacles to date, of course, have been the lack of precedents in the market, and the perceived high risk of construction. Several years of operational data from the pioneer projects, and the current large build-up of assets, is resolving the first problem, as it appears that offshore wind farms are indeed able (sometimes after some teething problems) to perform at high levels of availability. Construction risk is still an issue, which explains why the transactions that have taken place to date have mostly been post-completion, when the assets are operational. Operational assets are sold at low double-digit returns today and will in all probability find investors happy with high single digits in the near future.

It is likely that this will last – a majority of investors will probably remain unwilling to take any construction risk, and the developers able and willing to take that risk will certainly be glad to be able to sell their projects – or a fraction thereof – at a premium once they have successfully completed them.

This will thus provide, via recycling of the investments of early developers, a steady source of capital for the sector, with investors focussing on the different portions of the development cycle – permitting, contracting, building and operating. Utilities will be able to keep operational control of the assets whilst carrying a smaller fraction of the initial cost on their balance sheet, and long-term investors will get access to the long term revenue stream offered by the industry under the current regulatory framework.

Project Finance

Moving on to consider non-recourse debt financing, it seems clear today that two markets have been developing side by side: one for completed projects, the other for projects to be built. The first is centred on London, following the initial refinancing by Centrica of its Lynn and Inner Dowsing assets (the Boreas transaction) in 2009, whilst the other has been focussed on continental Europe, and in particular on the Benelux countries, where a series of deals including construction risk were closed by banks between 2006 and 2010.

At the heart of these different trajectories are construction risks, and how they are perceived and managed by utilities (which dominate the UK market) and IPPs (which have been more active on the continent).

Given London's traditional dominance in project finance activities, it is not surprising to come across media coverage suggesting that banks are unable or unwilling to take construction risk, and this has been a source of frustration and angst for developers. A series of delays on new transactions, and relatively minor mishaps on operational turbines (notably the infamous grouting issue) have kept a negative spotlight on the industry in the UK and created a perception that it was de facto impossible to finance offshore wind farms. The continental experience shows that this could not be further from the truth, and suggests that it is worth discussing in more detail how the UK and continental markets differ and what that means for future project finance transactions.

Unusually High Construction Risk

Offshore wind construction presents a unique combination of challenges:

1. It is an inherently risky endeavour, with large scale construction and high precision work to be carried out in hostile conditions (the best sites for offshore wind farms are, well, windy, and thus naturally the least favourable to construction work). Weather risk is intrinsic, serious and unavoidable; it can cause delays in construction if the site is not accessible, and, in the worst cases, incidents.
2. The sector is at the intersection of industries that were previously distinct (wind turbine manufacturing and marine construction), with each industry representing a similar share of the overall construction budget and thus neither able to naturally take the lead on projects (unlike onshore projects, where turbines represent most of the cost and thus turbine manufacturers are more easily able to take responsibility for the ancillary tasks like civil works); turbine manufacturers were not familiar with work at sea; marine contractors – including those from the oil industry – were not used to the serial and very precise erection work required over many individual sites in a short period; no contractor from one group will willingly bear financial commitments in respect of work it does not really control by the other contractors.
3. As a brand new industry, offshore wind had initially to make do with equipment not specifically designed for its needs – existing jackup vessels, cranes and other marine equipment were borrowed on an ad hoc basis; turbines were onshore versions with more or less comprehensive attempts at marinization: it was neither easy nor even desirable to replicate what was done on the early projects. This is changing fast as specialized vessels and turbines specifically designed for offshore conditions are brought to market; but it means that there are few precedents and few experienced people.
4. In an attempt at minimizing installation costs, the industry has systematically tried to install the largest turbines available on the market, meaning that these were typically new designs with little or no track record of operations and which presented real risks of 'teething problems'. With many new entrants on the market, it means that a large portion of the turbines available to the sector are still untested.

So the risks are high, and nobody is in a natural position to bear these risks single-handedly. This means that risks must be allocated with the agreement of all interested parties, interfaces between contractors understood better than usual, and potential snowball effects identified. This generates complexity and a need for strong project management competence (something not usually available in the onshore wind industry, where it was not really required, or available in other industries, but in people unfamiliar with the particulars of wind turbines). As a result, occasional spectacular incidents or problems have caused severe losses for a number of parties in the budding industry.

Despite this, many offshore wind developers are counting on lenders to bear construction risk without any completion guarantee, making this one of the few industrial sectors where banks would have to manage multi-contract structures without a dominant counter-party. Banks don't usually take such risks even in sectors they already know well!

A Risk-adverse Banking Market

Additionally, this comes at a particularly difficult time for the banking market.

Following the financial crisis of 2007–08, we are going through a period when there is no syndication market, something which seems likely to last for a while yet. In practice, it means that banks will only commit €50–75m per individual transaction on a 'take-and-hold' basis. Offshore wind projects, given their current scale (say 300–500MW), would require billion-euro scale financings. In this market context, that means setting up large club deals involving at least 10–15 banks, or bringing in multilaterals, with their specific requirements and constraints. This makes offshore wind deals inherently complex and difficult to pull off today. Furthermore, post-crisis, banks are generally more conservative and risk-adverse, and as they lack relevant precedents in this sector they are thus particularly prudent in what they are willing to offer to offshore wind developers. If you need to bring in 15 banks and put together all their disparate sets of restrictive conditions, you're likely to end up with a rather uncompetitive financing structure, effectively the worst of all worlds.

To add to the grim picture in the medium term, Basel 3 rules are likely to make long-term funding more expensive for commercial banks, something that they will have to pass on to clients, in particular in the project finance world, which requires such long maturities. Whilst not applying to current deals yet, this is seen as a serious medium-term threat to the competitivity of project finance for offshore wind.

And yet, despite all this, deals have happened, and more are in the works, at terms and conditions which have been seen as sufficiently attractive for very diverse groups of investors, including utilities (Centrica in Boreas, EDF and RWE in C-Power) or financial investors (TCW in Boreas, Blackstone in Meerwind).

Utility vs Non-utility Projects

The crux of the matter, and the big difference between the UK and continental approaches, is that the UK market is dominated by utilities to a much greater degree than the continental market, and utilities approach these risks differently from independent power producers and from banks.

For utilities, offshore wind farms are, first and foremost, just another power plant. They have the in-house management capacity to deal with the complexity of such projects, and to manage the cheaper multi-contracting route. It also means that they want to keep control of the project, and avoid unnecessary interference from outsiders, especially bankers and their multiple advisors. Offshore wind also offers utilities the possibility to deal with large industrial suppliers (like Siemens, Areva or GE) with which they have much more extensive dealings (this is different from onshore wind where there are many competitive 'pure player' turbine manufacturers). With such familiar counterparties, they don't need to rely on detailed contractual terms but can manage these projects as part of a bilateral relationship with a supplier for whom they are a strategic client – the corporate ties are worth as much as any formal warranty package. They will also tend to take a slightly more conservative route and go for 'safe' turbines coming from a big name or with a large track record (as can be seen in the string of contracts Siemens earned with its workhorse 3.6MW turbine).

In that context, project finance was seen as too much trouble (interference in contract negotiation, more complexity, more risks of delays) and, given the favourable corporate bond market in the past couple of years, it was also more expensive and unneeded.

Conversely, smaller developers have a different approach: for them, project finance is vital, and its requirements cannot be avoided. The project structure, and the contracts, should be 'bankable,' and everything is driven by that fact. Non-recourse projects need to work on a stand-alone basis, and contracts, and in particular warranties, need to work without any reference to any possible commitment by any party beyond its formal obligations, or additional support from an outside party. Contracts thus need to be a lot more detailed and, in a multi-contract framework, interfaces need to be looked at much more closely. As banks tend to focus on downside scenarios, commercial negotiations also have to focus on slightly different issues, as banks don't really care about wringing out a few more percentage points of upside, but absolutely want to avoid the risk of catastrophic failure or delay. That typically means trying to transfer more risks to counterparties, which can have a cost, and impose cumbersome contracts to deal with all the 'what if' scenarios wary bankers can come up with.

Advantages of Bank Involvement

The good news is that bringing the banks into the commercial negotiations can also have an upside. Given that developers can credibly tell their suppliers that the project (and the associated industrial orders) will not happen unless banks are satisfied with the contracts, they often have more leverage than utilities with such contractors, and they can actually obtain better terms with respect to warranties and risk allocation. Also, by bringing a third party into play, it is possible to get out of the zero-sum game typical of one-on-one negotiations: as long as banks are well protected against downside scenarios, they can be more relaxed about other things and accept more aggressive base scenarios; by increasing leverage, lenders can increase the returns for the project by more than the developer needs to give up to purchase the downside warranties from the suppliers.

Interestingly, it would also appear that non-recourse finance and its intrusive due diligence, through the discipline it brings to a project, is an effective way to deal with multi-contracting risks. In this industry, banks know that corporate warranties do not eliminate interface risks; by imposing checks on all 'hard' interfaces, irrespective of whether they are between contracts or between sub-contractors within a broader contract, they make sure that the risk is well understood and allocated. In fact, it can be argued that a well-designed multi-contract structure is less risky than a full EPC contract with a large general contractor, which will typically reject requests for due diligence on its subcontractors and work timetable. Recent experience in the offshore wind sector has shown that such EPC contractors can experience severe failures and cost overruns, whether they are turbine manufacturers, marine contractors or general contractors, whereas, so far (and on the basis of an admittedly still small sample), project financed wind farms have been built within the budget and timetable agreed with the banks at financial close.

As of today, it can be argued that banks, through their intrusive review of all contracts and project plans, can provide a *de facto* 'wrap' for multiple contracts more cheaply and more effectively than external contractors.

Looking Ahead

Utilities, which have not allowed banks such an extensive role in their projects so far, have been frustrated by the project finance market refusal to take construction risk on the basis of their internal contractual negotiation skills and project management capabilities. On-going transactions suggest that banks might be willing to take construction risk on utility-negotiated projects on the basis of massive contingency budgets underwritten by the utilities. This is not particularly cost-effective, of course – indeed, contingencies in such transactions appear to be roughly double the size of contingencies in projects where project financiers have been involved in structuring and negotiating the project contracts.

The lesson from this is that, in all likelihood, for the next few years, construction risk project finance will be reserved for independent power producers which have no choice but to accept the early involvement of project financiers and advisors in their project deal, and utilities which deliberately take the same route – and which do in fact listen to these advisors. There will be a larger market for non-recourse refinancings of operational projects, taking place either jointly with the sale of (all or part of) such projects or as independent endeavours launched by the asset owners.

Current market trends suggest that pricing, maturity and other commercial terms for financings are not that different for pre-construction or post-completion financings (typically, the margin is 50bp higher during the construction period than during the early years of operation) and tend to be driven by other factors, such as the quality of the project team, the strength of the entities owning the project and the discipline and transparency imposed in the contract negotiation phase to ensure full bankability of the project. Without going to the extremes of the Belwind example, where the financing closed despite the bankruptcy of the original sponsor, thanks to a capable project team which was able to remain on board as a new group of sponsors was created, it should be reassuring to project developers that project finance is not reserved only to the biggest players, and that high quality in project development and structuring can justify an external financing.

Looking further ahead, one can imagine that banks will at some point find again their appetite for junior or mezzanine tranches (which are currently mostly avoided), and that refinancings of operating assets may at some point be financed through the bond market, but construction risk is likely to remain the realm of traditional project finance.

15 *International Renewable Incentives*

SIMON CURRIE
Partner and global head of energy
Norton Rose LLP[1]

This chapter is written in interesting times. Governments in both developed and developing countries are reeling from the cost of the financial crisis and are attempting to tread a fine line between 'just enough' and 'too much' funding for renewable technology deployment. Many countries are cutting back support or redesigning renewables incentives models, despite the importance for investors of policy certainty in this area. In the EU there is an extensive discussion, if not a battle, in respect of the European Commission's Roadmap for moving to a competitive low carbon economy in 2050 and moving towards a 30 per cent emissions reduction target. The Fukushima disaster in Japan has also caused many to reassess the role of nuclear in avoiding the threat of dangerous climate change and ensuring energy security.

Progress towards securing a legally binding international deal in respect of climate change is happening glacially slowly, but the deployment of renewable energy is nevertheless moving on apace. The Cancun climate summit which took place in December 2010, together with its surrounding side events and business conferences, had a somewhat split personality. It showcased both the hesitant nature of discussions in this area, and also the strides that are being made by both developed and, perhaps more importantly, developing countries, in rolling out a low carbon future. Much, though not all, progress in the implementation of renewable energy, is underscored by incentives regimes based around 'renewable portfolio standards' (RPS) or 'feed-in tariffs' (FIT). Legal and regulatory certainty in this area is therefore vital.

In general, RPS impose a purchase requirement on an obliged entity (consumers, producers or suppliers) to derive an increasing proportion of their total electricity from renewable sources. This obligation is often (but not necessarily) combined with tradable green certificates (TGCs) which are issued to generators on production of a unit of electricity and which may be traded together with or disassociated from the output they represent. The revenue available to renewable electricity generators under this mechanism is the aggregate of the market price for the electricity produced and the price

1   Written in conjunction with Juan I. Gonzalez Ruiz of Uria Menendez and Kathryn Emmett of Norton Rose LLP and Kathryn Emmet of Norton Rose LLP in mid 2011.

of the TGC. The value of the TGC represents a subsidy, the value of which is determined by the interaction of supply and demand.

Whereas RPSs are volume-based mechanisms, FITs are price-based, setting a regulated price and allowing the market to determine the quantity supplied. The design of FIT regimes also varies. Fixed FITs provide renewable electricity generators with a guaranteed long-term total price per megawatt hour (MWh) of electricity. Premium FITs provide producers with a bonus on top of revenues earned by the generator by selling its electrical output into the wholesale market for a fixed period. A contract for difference (CfD) FIT is a contract to pay or be paid the difference between a notional market reference price and an agreed 'strike price' (so that if the generator can sell its electricity into the wholesale market at the notional reference market price, it will receive in aggregate a revenue stream equal to the strike price). FIT schemes usually offer technology specific tariff levels, thereby incentivising a range of technologies. In general, FITs have been more widely adopted than RPS schemes.

By 2010, at least 83 countries had some type of policy to promote renewable power generation, with at least 50 countries and 25 states or provinces having FITs, more than half of which had been adopted since 2005. Equally, RPS had been put into place by 10 national governments and 46 state or provincial governments.[2] Other renewables incentives on offer include capital subsidies, grants and tax breaks. They are too numerous to describe in one short chapter. Together, these incentives serve, in particular, to underpin investment by the private sector both in low carbon technologies more generally and in low carbon projects themselves, often under project finance structures.

An Evolving Area

The use of FITs and RPS is still evolving. For example, EU jurisdictions have implemented a variety of support schemes under the Renewable Energy Directive, which sets out legally binding targets for the use of renewable energy to be met by each Member State but which does not specify how such targets should be met. South Africa, the host of this year's climate conference in Durban, is currently finalizing its Renewable Feed-in Tariff (REFIT) programme.

Many jurisdictions have had renewable support schemes for so long that they are now involved in extensive exercises of review and modification, as regulators move into a second phase of incentivization. Examples include the UK, where the Renewables Obligation is likely to be replaced for new projects by a FIT mechanism which is likely to have a CfD structure. Italy is moving away from TGCs under an RPS towards a FIT. South Korea, which had implemented FITs, is now moving towards a TGCs-based RPS model.

Another common theme is the rebalancing of the level of incentives available. The renewables market has been rocked by a number of changes in government policy which have been driven partly by governments' failure to properly take account of the potential costs of such incentives and to design them in ways that adequately pass on these cost to consumers. Spain is often singled out for criticism in this regard. Equally, governments are trying to ensure that FITs and RPS are designed in the most economically efficient manner. For example, South Africa is currently reviewing the implementation of its REFIT

---

2   REN21, Renewables Global Status Report 2010.

scheme before finalizing FIT rates, and solar photovoltaic (PV) investment in the UK has suffered a bumpy ride following the review of small scale FITs.

Italy

In Italy, the scheme that promotes renewable electricity generation (excluding solar) has been the legal framework for green certificates. Generators and importers of conventional power have an obligation to purchase a certain amount of green certificates every year.

In 2008, various significant amendments were made to the green certificates system, including the introduction of a price determination system and a buyback scheme which supported the price of certificates. Important changes were mooted in 2010 and partially implemented. Crucially, the certificate buyback mechanism was threatened to be withdrawn, but was eventually maintained. Nonetheless, a cap was placed on the financial commitment of the buyback mechanism.

However, the publication of the Romani Decree, approved by the Italian government on 3 March 2011, has heralded the replacement of green certificates in Italy with a new system based on tariffs and auctions for renewable capacity, the detail of which has yet to be fully fleshed out. This has created uncertainties for project developers and lenders.

The switch to the new system of support will occur by the end of 2012 and specific provisions are set out to ensure the continuing support of existing projects as well as the deployment of fresh projects before the new system is in place. A transitional period will be applicable to existing plants, as well as those commencing operation before 31 December 2012. These plants will receive green certificates until 31 December 2015, and will thereafter migrate to a tariff-based mechanism.

Under the new mechanism for projects commissioned after December 2012, support will be differentiated by plant size and/or technology. Fixed tariffs will be provided for plants below 5MW. All types of plants with an installed capacity above 5MW will get incentives set through public auctions. A predetermined capacity will be auctioned in separate sessions for each technology. Auctions will be structured on a 'reverse' basis, with bids opening at a ceiling value and then dropping to the value at which the auction will clear. The final tariff will be granted for the average useful lifetime of the plant.

It is still unclear whether the tariffs will be 'premium' or 'all-inclusive', and whether the incentive will be fixed in nominal or real terms. If the incentive is a premium on wholesale electricity prices, investors may face the electricity price risk (with resulting higher uncertainty on the economic conditions for project financing). If the level of the premium is not related to the wholesale electricity price (for example through a cap and floor mechanism) high electricity prices may result in over-remuneration of new projects, whilst low electricity prices may result in insufficient revenues for such projects. Project developers and financiers are grappling with the implications of these changes. As is the case in the UK, the detail will need to be available before their full implications changes can be assessed. The structuring of long-term financing for projects has been made more difficult pending the publication of implementing regulations.

In the wake of the Romani Decree, the Conto Energia IV has been introduced. This establishes the incentive tariffs payable to PV plants commencing operations between 1 June 2011 and 31 December 2016. The Conto Energia IV progressively (and significantly) reduces FITs as compared to those set out in its predecessor, the Conto Energia III. It also introduces expense budgets for specific time periods for the incentives that may be paid during such periods and foresees the transition from a premium FIT, where the incentive tariff is payable in addition to the revenues that can be received from the sale of energy, to a fixed FIT system, based on the payment of an overall tariff that includes both the premium and the remuneration of the sale of energy into the grid.

Spain

The generation of electricity through renewable technologies in Spain has been traditionally fostered by the award of incentives in the form of FITs, additional premiums and other incentives. Starting in April 2010, when the Spanish government declared its intention to revise the economic regime for facilities already in commercial operation by adjusting the level of tariffs and incentives available, regulations on renewable technologies have gone through substantial changes. This is especially the case in respect of PV projects, which were targeted as the technology benefiting from some of the most generous tariffs but contributing only a relatively low portion of renewable electricity output.

A new Royal Decree was approved in August 2010 requesting PV facilities to produce certain limited documentation to evidence that their facilities had been properly put into operation by 29 September 2008, a deadline after which the remuneration of PV facilities changed substantially. As a result of the August 2010 measures and the indiscriminate application of very strict rules, several solar PV facilities have seen their FIT entitlement suspended. The intention of the August 2010 measures was to expurgate PV facilities improperly and belatedly commissioned such that the impact on the total amount of subsidies borne by Spanish electricity rate payers could be reduced. A sort of limited amnesty was offered to sponsors of PV facilities who came forwards, but the results were very disappointing.

As a result, a new raft of regulations was introduced in November 2010, which caused a substantial reduction in FITs for new PV projects (up to 45 per cent for new ground-based facilities) and the introduction of additional technical requirements (e.g., voltage dipping protection equipment) that added another cost for such facilities. Interestingly, the FIT entitlement of PV facilities was limited to 25 years (even for existing facilities). Concentrated solar power (CSP) projects and wind projects also suffered as, amongst other provisions, a cap on the number of operating hours remunerated at the FITs was introduced. Interestingly, this was the first time that legislative measures with a retroactive flavour were implemented. This cap affects projects already commissioned and those under construction.

The last nail in the coffin for PV projects in Spain was a set of rules approved on Christmas Eve of 2010. As had happened with CSP and wind, a cap on the operating number of hours payable at the feed-in tariff prices was put in place. Facilities that had entered into operation on or before 29 September 2008 (note the retroactive effect here) were subject to a three-year special and extra reduction in their feed-in tariffs. That extra reduction is said to have been devised to hurt only the equity providers of solar PV projects rather than lenders, but the impact on lenders is still being analysed. International funds have already taken the step of bringing international legal action against the Kingdom of Spain through an LCIA arbitration.

It can be disputed whether the steps taken by the Spanish Government are absolutely legal and constitutional, but undoubtedly such steps are an example of bad regulation.

The UK

The UK Renewables Obligation (RO) has been the main support mechanism in the UK for the development of renewable electricity generation. The UK coalition Government which came into power in mid-2010 announced that it intended to implement a system of feed-in tariffs in electricity as well as maintaining the RO. This announcement culminated in the publication of Electricity Market Reform (EMR) in December 2010. With 25 per cent of the UK's generating capacity due for closure in this decade, and with demand expected to increase, the EMR is intended to exploit a unique opportunity to overhaul the British energy market and shift it decisively towards renewable energy. To achieve this, four principle incentives are encapsulated within the EMR: the introduction of FITs, the deployment of capacity payments, the introduction of a Carbon Price Support tax, and establishing an emissions performance standard (EPS).

A key part of the package of measures proposed is the replacement of the RO for all new projects from 2017, by the introduction of FITs and the extension of this financial support to all large scale low-carbon electricity generation: nuclear power and coal-fired generation with carbon capture and storage (CCS) as well as renewable energy. The Government consulted on a Fixed FIT, a Premium FIT and a CfD FIT, with a stated preference for a CfD model. The introduction of FITs is intended to stimulate investment in low carbon generation at lower cost to the consumer by providing greater certainty for investors both in respect of the price that can be obtained for low-carbon electricity and in the ability of the FIT policy to withstand political change.

How and the extent to which revenue certainty for generators is achieved will depend on the type of FIT adopted. In the Government White Paper on EMR, it has proposed a CfD model. However, the level of revenue certainty offered will depend on its detailed design, particularly the mechanism for setting a strike price and a market reference price for different low carbon technologies.

Following but in parallel to the introduction of the RO, the UK introduced small-scale FITs in April 2010, aimed at both the domestic and commercial sectors, although individual projects were capped at 5MW. The tariff applicable when a project came online was guaranteed to it for 20 years, and rises in line with the Retail Price Index (a widely used measure of inflation in the UK), to which FITs are index-linked. The levels of the tariffs were originally scheduled for review in 2012 at the earliest, but the government announced a fast-track review of FITs for solar installations much earlier, in response to fears that large-scale solar 'farms' were monopolizing the FIT funding pot. In the review, the tariffs for all PV installations above 50kW were slashed.

This has, to say the least, been badly received by the solar industry, with a mix of companies and individuals petitioning the High Court for judicial review to overturn the government's sudden decision. The government's standing with the industry has, as a result, been badly damaged. Moreover, the decision has not sent the right message to investors. In order to commit to an industry, investors need to have long term certainty as to the regulatory environment surrounding it, so they can objectively assess any potential investment. The pre-emption of the stated review date has raised serious concerns amongst investors that this certainty may be lacking in the UK.

China

More renewable energy is coming online in China than anywhere else in the world. It is estimated that 130 gWh of wind power is in the pipeline, more than 130 gWh of hydropower is operational, 2010 saw solar energy and offshore wind gathering momentum. It is now difficult to identify decent onshore sites for wind, prompting more outward-looking investment.

Since August 2009, China has implemented tariffs for wind, hydropower, biomass and solar energy. Solar tariffs have been reduced from CNY4.00 per kWh in 2007 to around CNY0.90 for recent projects. Power purchase agreements for most renewable projects are for a one-year term and in theory could be terminated at the end of the year. In practice, the agreement is rolled over automatically each year. In the case of wind projects, there had been a 30,000 hour limit on the tariff duration. However, fixed tariffs for all wind projects approved after 1 August 2009 have now been imposed, going from CNY0.51/ kWh to CNY 0.61/kWh. The 30,000 hour limit no longer applies.

South Africa

South Africa's Renewable Feed-in Tariff (REFIT) programme was announced in 2009. As with a typical FIT, the National Energy Regulator of SA (NERSA) will set up-front tariff levels. Independent power producers (IPP) are able to sell electricity to an offtaker, which is currently Eskom. IPPs tender for contracts to supply electricity to Eskom.

The renewable energy industry has deployed significant amounts of development capital, estimated to be in excess of R500million, in preparing for the REFIT programme. However, the South African Department of Energy and National Treasury has recently stated that the REFIT programme is unlawful and has questioned NERSA's authority to set upfront tariff determinations. This has delayed the implementation of REFIT which was hoped to take place from March 2011. A final decision is hoped to be imminent.

South Korea

South Korea also implemented a FIT structure, with legislation placing an obligation on Korea Electric Power Corporation (Kepco), South Korea's electricity utility, to purchase all electricity generated from renewable sources at a fixed price. On the back of this structure, in the three years up to mid-2008, PV had an exceptional growth rate with a total of 99 mWh of capacity being installed. However, the FIT was slashed in October 2008 by between 8 per cent and 30 per cent (depending on installation size).

South Korea has now introduced a RPS, similar to those in Italy and the UK, which will gradually replace FITs as the key solar incentive. Under the RPS, 14 state-run and private power companies will be required to produce specified percentages of energy from renewable power. These rise from 4 per cent in 2015 to 10 per cent by 2022. The government also provides tax incentives to encourage investment in renewables.

Not Just RPS and FITs

Despite the prevalence of FITs and RPS, there is evidence to show that, at least in developing countries, investment in renewables will forge ahead even without the complexities of FITs and RPS. Brazil, until recently considered to be resource poor in fossil fuels, pioneered renewable energy long before many developed economies. Today, hydro-power provides roughly 80 per cent of Brazil's electricity, and renewables overall meet nearly 45 per cent of the country's energy needs.

For the future, Brazil is reputed to have approved a large new hydro dam, the Belo Monte hydro project in the Amazon, which would become the third biggest in the world on completion. It is also trying to diversify its renewables portfolio. In 2009, Brazil held its first wind-only energy auction, which was very well subscribed and contracted around 1,800MW of generation. This is expected to lead to some 70 different wind farms, with the earliest completions scheduled for July 2012.

Funding the Future

Given some of the difficulties that funding and passing on the cost of fixed price FITs have posed, it is possible that there will be a move towards adopting systems of RPS, as in South Korea, which can be more sensitive to supply and demand. Conversely, it is likely that the UK moves in the opposite direction, but relying on the CfD element of a FIT to ensure its sensitivity to market prices. Italy is also moving away from the RPS model. However, both kinds of support mechanisms appear to be on the rise in developing countries, which should be keen to learn from the experiences of their forerunners. In choosing between different renewables structures, governments must carefully weigh the problems of bedding in new regimes against the temptation to modify schemes, in order to make them as attractive as possible to investors.

Equally likely is that, particularly in mature markets with good or even 'excessive' renewables penetration, or which can no longer afford to offer previous levels of support, there are reductions in the levels of support schemes, or modifications to regimes which make them less attractive. Maximum capacity thresholds for attracting support, as have been implemented in Italy and South Korea, are likely to become prevalent.

Investors should also be wary of 'left field' thinking on behalf of legislators who are keen to limit 'solar booms' or 'dashes for wind'. Such 'innovations', where reductions in tariffs are off limits or could be subject to legal challenge, can include the imposition of taxes on 'excessive' profits, periods for 'tariffs amnesties' during which projects can declare their non-compliance with support scheme eligibility criteria or face being found out later and stripped of all benefits, ad hoc taxes that can be imposed to claw back 'windfall' profits and the imposition of onerous conditions that reduce the attractiveness of investment.

International Funding

Turning back to the international discussions which were referred to at the start of this chapter, it is important to bear in mind that the cost of mitigating and adapting to climate change internationally is estimated to be in the region of several hundred billions of euros per year, way beyond the current contemplated budget of most countries. Under the Decisions adopted at the Cancun climate conference in December 2010, commitments to 'mobilize' US$100bn per year by 2020 under the Copenhagen Accord were restated and confirmed as part of the international negotiating process. FITs and RPS are clearly an important part of this mobilisation of finance. However, in jurisdictions where energy costs have been kept artificially low, or reflect historic investment that has now been fully repaid, funding such initiatives by passing costs onto the consumer is unlikely to be practicable.

A potential part solution lies in the establishment of the Green Climate Fund (GCF), in relation to the GCF which was agreed to at Cancun. Discussions are on-going in respect of a variety of areas, including how the GCF should be different to the existing Climate Investment Funds set up under the auspices of the World Bank and implemented with the support of a variety of Multilateral Development Banks (MDB). Whatever the outcome of discussions, it seems likely that FITs and RPS will form only part of a complex matrix of sources of climate funding for the implementation of projects in developing countries. They are likely to be supported by a broad and complex range of instruments, including loans and grants from MDBs, support from Development Finance Institutions (DFIS), guarantees, structured finance solutions and any available funds from climate funds such as the Green Climate Fund. 'Green' or 'climate' bonds are also being developed to drive renewable investment and the international community is looking to raise funds by way of novel sources of finance such as the imposition of levies on shipping and aviation fuels.

In developed countries, as the scope and scale of the ramping up of renewable energy is fully addressed and energy prices start to fully reflect the cost of carbon, it will be increasingly challenging for governments to reconcile their short-term costs with long-term benefits, which are often not readily perceived by the electorate. This is likely to lead to increasing opposition to the costs of renewables support regimes. The kinds of legal challenges that have been raised in Spain and the UK may become more prevalent, whilst governments are likely to focus on making changes to their implementation of support schemes less susceptible to legal challenge.

Conclusions

It is clear that despite increasing use of renewables incentive regimes throughout the international community, such incentives raise a number of political and economic challenges. These are likely to increase with time unless public support for the deployment of renewable energy increases. However, despite failures within the international climate negotiations process, governments appear to be going their own way in deploying renewables and the mechanisms to spur their growth. More broadly, the financial architecture for the deployment of low carbon technologies in developing countries will have to be improved. Lessons should be learnt from experiences with RPS and FITs, but wider-reaching and more innovative sources of finance will also be required. Facing up to the future architecture of renewable finance will require a detailed understanding of the financial sources available.

16 *Project Financing LNG Projects*

DAVID LEDESMA[1]
South-Court Ltd

The earliest examples of the financing of energy projects, using project finance, are in the USA where oil and gas projects have been financed this way since the 1960s. However, it was the UK that saw limited recourse lending take off in the 1970s. Lenders at this time started to make debt available through project finance for the development of oil and gas fields offshore of the UK, this then extended to projects in the Danish and Norwegian sectors on the North Sea. The 1980s saw the project financing of power and infrastructure projects in the UK. In the 1980s and 1990s liquefied natural gas (LNG) projects started using limited recourse financing, for example Woodside's share of the North West Shelf in Australia (1985), Indonesia Bontang (1991) and Malaysia Dua (1993), but in reality there was considerable recourse to shareholders in those early deals. The real growth in project finance for LNG projects was in the mid-2000s with the growth of LNG production in Qatar.

This chapter will give an overview of the LNG business, to give the reader an understanding of the complexities of the sector, the factors driving the development of LNG projects and therefore the risks facing lenders. The chapter will then examine why project finance is frequently used as a source of finance for LNG projects and then examine the risks faced by lenders in lending and how these risks can be mitigated. Specific project financing examples will be given from three financings. The chapter will conclude with an opinion of the future of project finance in the development of LNG projects.

1   David would like to thank his friends and colleagues in the project financing sector for their help and support in writing this chapter. David Ledesma is an independent consultant with over 20 years' LNG experience gained through the development of LNG projects in Asia and the Middle East. David provides commercial, financing and strategic support to national and international energy companies globally. He also gives commercial training courses on LNG and is a Fellow of the Oxford Institute for Energy Studies and has co-authored two books on Asian and Middle Eastern gas, published by the Institute.

LNG overview

WHY LNG?

Gas reserves are increasingly being found in remote areas, away from established markets and major population centres. Unlike oil, which has a high energy to volume ratio and can be relatively easily handled and transported, gas requires significant infrastructure to be constructed to move it to market. The commercialization of gas reserves can take several forms, use in the domestic market, using the gas to enhance oil production, converting the gas to another product such as gas to liquids[2] or by exporting it to another market. Moving the gas to another market can either be by pipeline or by LNG. Although the capital investment required to construct an LNG chain is considerable, US$10–US$20bn for an 11 BCMA (8mtpa) LNG project, traditional industry assumptions are that LNG is the more economic alternative compared with pipeline for distances in excess of 2,000 to 3,000 miles (less if a subsea pipeline). These distances are indications only. More importantly, LNG enables gas to be moved to market without crossing through any third party country and many countries see this political driver as a key factor in providing security of energy supply. LNG may also be economic where topography or water depth presents obstacles to pipeline development. LNG is, therefore, a means of transporting gas – a pipeline in a tanker, moving gas to gas-importing countries.

BRIEF HISTORY OF THE LNG INDUSTRY

The LNG industry was born in the USA in the 1950s with the first deliveries to the UK in 1959 and the first major commercial deliveries from Algeria to the UK and France in 1964 and 1965. It was the development of Japan as an LNG buyer from 1968, initially from Alaska and Brunei, then later from Indonesia, Malaysia, Australia and Abu Dhabi, that underpinned the major growth in the LNG industry.

In the Atlantic Basin, first deliveries of Algerian LNG to the USA were in 1972, where four US receiving terminals were constructed (Cove Point, Elba Island, Everett and Lake Charles). Sales of LNG to the USA collapsed during the 1980s and 1990s as US tax incentives encouraged exploration for domestic gas supply, and didn't pick up again until 2000. The 1980s and 1990s saw further LNG demand growth in Asia (Korea and Taiwan) and in Europe (Belgium, France and Italy).

The late 1990s and 2000s have seen the entry of new LNG markets in Europe – Portugal, Turkey and UK and in Asia, China and India. More recently the South America countries of Brazil, Argentina and Chile and Middle East countries of Kuwait and Dubai have started importing LNG. To meet this demand, new production facilities have been developed, most notably in Qatar which, as at May 2011, has a production capacity of 105 BCMA (77 mtpa) – 30 per cent of world LNG production capacity.

The LNG sector has seen annual average growth over the past 30 years of 7–8 per cent pa and it is the author's view that these growth rates will be maintained.

---

2 Gas to liquids is a refinery process to convert natural gas or other gaseous hydrocarbons into longer-chain hydrocarbons such as gasoline or diesel fuel. Methane-rich gases are converted into liquid fuels either via direct conversion or via syngas as an intermediate.

Gas →	Liquefaction	→	Shipping	→	Regasification	→	Gas Market

% Investment	75%	15%	10%
Capex	$6-10 bn	$1-2 bn	$0.6-1.5bn
Unit Cost ($/MMBtu)	$3.0-4.5	$0.8-1.5	$0.4-0.8
Gas Usage	10-14%	1.5-3.5%	$1-2%

Note: Upstream capex ~ $1-3 bn ($0.5-1.5/MMBtu)

Figure 16.1 Project financing[3]

Source: Author

THE STRUCTURE OF THE LNG CHAIN

Each LNG project consists of a set of interlinked activities that connect upstream gas production to the gas user.

LNG projects typically require in excess of 10 tcf[4] (280bcm) gas, able to produce gas at plateau level for at least 20 years. Gas quality is also important; if gas contains natural gas liquids (C3, C4 and C5) then these liquids provide additional revenue for the development of the project. Often this credit is kept by the upstream and, in the case of Oman and the initial Qatar project, the liquids revenue effectively paid for the upstream development. If gas contains impurities (e.g., H2S, Mercury, etc.) then these have to be removed before liquefaction, which means additional capital costs. Gas reserves for LNG projects are dedicated to that project (a requirement of LNG buyers and financiers) with the gas reserve amount independently assessed. Often gas is produced from several fields (giving some gas quality and cost issues). Qatar has the benefit of producing gas from one field (the North Field) with a common specification and operational facilities.

Liquefaction units are often referred to as LNG trains, with most LNG plants using between two and eight (Indonesia). Some projects do have individual trains, but the reason there are usually several trains is technical – to produce more LNG than the train can produce then a second train is needed. Operationally, projects like more than one train as it gives production flexibility and security of output.

There are two main processes for liquefying gas, the multi-component refrigerant process and the Phillips Cascade Process. The liquefaction part of the value chain makes up approximately 60–75 per cent of the investment. As such it is important to keep the liquefaction plant fully operational, and achieving utilization of over 90 per cent. The capacity of other parts of the chain are designed to ensure this continuous production.

---

3   Indicative only, numbers can vary by project.

4   tcf = trillion cubic feet of gas.

A challenge currently facing the industry is the rising cost of LNG production due to increasing costs of raw materials (nickel and steel) and shortages of manpower resources and contractor capacity. The industry compares liquefaction costs using an indices of US$ million/metric tonne installed capacity (i.e., the capital cost of a project divided by its capacity). Whereas in the period up to 2005 liquefaction costs were US$300–US$600/metric tonne installed capacity (MTIC), newer projects are proceeding at far higher costs. Over the past few years projects have taken investment decisions on the basis of capacity costs in the region US$1000–US$1400/MTIC (with expansion projects US$700–US$900/MTIC). These higher costs mean that markets must pay higher prices for the LNG in order for the project to proceed and buyers may have to guarantee a floor price that covers capital and financing costs.

LNG is carried at atmospheric pressure in specially designed tankers. Most of the 361 LNG vessels operational in May 2010 have a capacity of 122,000 to 165,000 cubic metres, though the Qataris have constructed 24 larger vessels (209,200 to 265,000 cubic metres). Ships either use the Kvaerner-Moss design (vessels with independent storage spheres mounted in the body of a tanker) or one of two membrane designs (where the LNG storage tanks are an integral part of the vessel). The most popular ship design is the membrane. A 165,000 cubic metre vessel currently costs ~US$200m–US$250m.

Whilst loaded on the LNG vessel the LNG boils-off, with the cargo reducing by 0.10–0.20 per cent per day. This boil-off gas is usually used to fuel the ship. The amount of boil-off generally depends on the age of the vessel. In the case of some of the newer vessels, including the new Qatari vessels, the gas is re-liquefied on board and the vessels are fuelled by oil. Some ship-owners are ordering ships with on-board re-liquefiers.

LNG is unloaded from ships at specially designed LNG receiving terminals. These terminals store LNG (not under pressure) and regasify the LNG (by adding heat) and distribute the gas to end-users. Typically 1–3 per cent of the gas is used in the regasification process. Capital costs of regasification terminals vary considerably by location, in the range US$0.7–1.0bn. South America has recently started importing LNG using vessels with on-board regasification, through floating terminals.

SALES OF LNG

With the high capital cost of the LNG chain, LNG sellers have sought security of LNG offtake whilst, at the same time, buyers in markets such as Japan and Korea with no other gas supply source (such as domestic gas production or pipeline gas supply) have also sought security of gas supply. The LNG business has, therefore, evolved around a regional structure with, in 2010, 80 per cent of LNG being sold on long-term 15–20 year LNG sales agreements and the balance 20 per cent being sold under shorter term contracts with variations in pricing based on which market the cargo is discharged into. This enables LNG suppliers, who have surplus capacity in the system, to take advantage of global pricing differentials.

The LNG trade is therefore structured in two ways:

1. A long-term basis where sellers structure contracts on a pricing basis that provides reliable revenues to the project, often with price protection should prices fall too low in the case of new LNG projects. For financing, the majority of LNG volume needs to be committed on a long-term basis to support the project cashflows, so spot/short-

term LNG volumes from base production will be lower. For older projects (20 years+) this is not the case and an LNG seller can take more risk and sell a greater portion in the spot market.

2. A shorter term basis where LNG sellers and buyers seek to sell/buy surplus cargoes into higher priced markets, sometimes diverting cargoes that were previously destined for one market to another to optimize revenues.

It is the growth of Middle East LNG production that has acted as a catalyst to develop a global LNG trade as a result of its physical location equidistant from the Asian and Atlantic Basin markets (the distance from Qatar to Tokyo Bay and North-West Europe is approximately similar). Middle East producers therefore have the ability to ship cargoes to Asian, European or US markets and be cost competitive in all major market regions. With the growth of regasification capacity in the European and US markets, LNG suppliers will increasingly be able to interplay between markets on a short-term basis and to exercise the choice between the different markets when pursuing long term contracts, reflecting their view of which will offer the highest returns.

Qatar is unique, endowed with the combination of geographical location, low upstream production costs and economies of scale in liquefaction and shipping. This gives it greater flexibility than most other LNG suppliers to optimize their supply position between markets.

It is this market structure (a mixture of flexible and firm markets), the cost of moving LNG, and the nature of the product (in that it 'boils off' in transit and in storage) that has resulted in the market structure seen today. This structure includes a blend of long, medium and short-term contracts, but with only 19 per cent global LNG traded on short-term basis in 2010.

Why do LNG projects frequently attract project financing?

The LNG chain is highly capital intensive, and each of its elements has been financed through project finance, either together (such as in the case of Qatargas II) or separately. However, it is mainly the liquefaction and regasification part of the chain that is project financed, as the shipping segment tends to attract other types of finance. Some projects have used the capital markets (e.g., RasGas), using bonds to raise finance for their expansions. Financing of LNG projects is therefore through a combination of equity and third party loans with the project itself raising finance against the security of its own revenues – the quality of the LNG buyers is therefore key.

The LNG chain can be complex and carries risks, but the risks can be identified, quantified and mitigated through due diligence. Lenders can get themselves comfortable with the level of risk that they are taking. In the case of more risky projects, export credit agencies can cover political and some commercial risks. This was particularly the case for the PNG LNG project in Papua New Guinea, which reached financial close in March 2010, during the 2008–10 financial crisis.

Project financing for LNG projects has both advantages and disadvantages. It gives a project the ability to generate large debt capacity whilst passing the project risk to the lenders, with the sponsors able to assume limited recourse, after project start-up and in many cases enjoy flexibility of loan repayment to improve the overall project economics. Often LNG projects have governments, as well as domestic and international companies as shareholders, who all have different credit ratings. The international companies, who often have the highest credit rating, do not want to use their rating to support the weaker

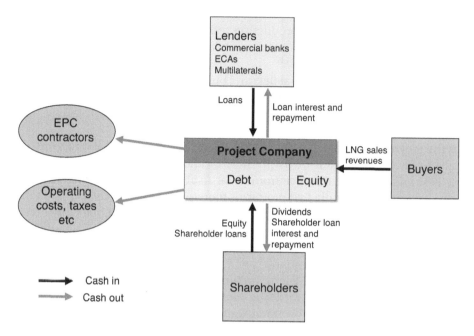

Figure 16.2 Project financing

EPC = Engineering Procurement Contract

Source: South-Court Analysis

shareholders. Through the establishment of a project company[5] that constructs and operates the LNG facility, and more importantly is the commercial entity that funds the project development, project finance allows the project, not the individual shareholders, to be the borrower. The revenue to the project comes from the LNG buyer (or the capacity users in the case of a tolling facility). There are also disadvantages to raising finance this way; higher interest rates, it takes more time and costs more to put together a project finance deal as well as the constant involvement of the lenders during the loan period; project shareholders prefer this non-recourse structure as it ensures that if the project were to default then there would be no recourse to the individual shareholder companies. An example of this structure is set out in Figure 16.2.

Lenders, therefore, see good projects as those with strong sponsors, strong governments who support the development of the project and strong buyers with good credit ratings. The project itself must also make commercial sense with strong economics that are resilient to market changes and are structured correctly with good project documentation.

The history of project finance for LNG projects is, therefore, good as seen in Figure 16.3.

Prior to 2003 the amount of finance raised by project finance was limited, often with considerable shareholder support. In 1985 Woodside raised debt for its one-sixth share of the North-West Shelf project against its LNG sales revenue and in 1991 and 1993 Indonesia (Bontang) and Malaysia LNG Dua raised limited recourse debt (Malaysia was later refinanced after start-up). It was, however, the financings of the Qatar large LNG

---

5   Financing special purpose vehicle.

In USD billion

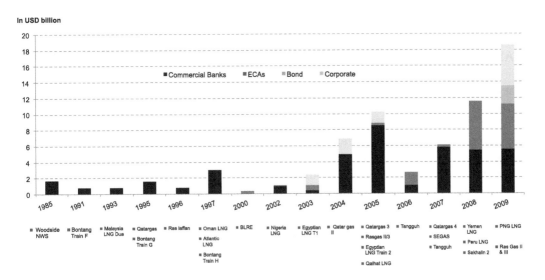

Figure 16.3 Project financing
Sources: Societe Generale, Dealogic

trains, 2004–07 that really increased the volume of third party debt and by 2009 Qatar decided to expand the debt into the bond market. These later financings also included less recourse to shareholders as banks became familiar with LNG project debt and projects (especially Qatar) were able to negotiate better terms.

Understanding and Managing Project Risks is Key

With banks assuming the project risk it is key that they can understand and quantify the risks in the project in order to maximize debt in the project. Since 2000 project financing of LNG projects has increasingly been accepted by the banks, and with it their understanding of the risks that have to be managed.

Each part of the chain is linked by an agreement and lenders review the contracts in detail to ensure that there is a flow through of liabilities such that the risks are taken by the correct party – usually the party that can best control them. Lenders want to ensure that the economic rent is freely distributed along the chain and that each part of the chain earns a fair return to ensure that it will be a reliable part of the chain and will not undermine the flow of revenues from the LNG buyers. Lenders also want to ensure that the liabilities and force majeure clauses are structured such that in the case of project default, liability payments will be sufficient to meet debt obligations.

Key Project Risks

GAS SUPPLY

There needs to be sufficient recoverable gas reserves to produce sufficient LNG over the period of the LNG sales and the gas must be delivered to the plant at a rate that supports LNG production on a daily basis. Often the companies that own and operate the gas supply are different to the shareholders in the liquefaction plant. If this is the case, then the gas has to be sold, and in this case the gas sales and purchase agreement becomes a key document. Lenders will seek assurances from the gas owner that there are sufficient reserves[6] and that the gas is dedicated to the LNG project and cannot be used for other purposes. It will also look to independent consultants to carry out a review of available gas reserves to confirm that there is sufficient gas available to cover the period of the LNG sales and purchase agreements plus a few years. The gas has to be proven with a 90 per cent probability that it can be recovered (P90). If the gas cannot be proven to this level of certainty, the banks could seek additional assurances from the host government, and the shareholders, that additional reserves will be dedicated to the project.

Lenders will also seek assurances that there are no environmental risks, the facilities will be completed on time to ensure prompt start-up of the liquefaction plant and that there are sufficient production facilities are in place to deliver the gas on a reliable and regular basis.

LIQUEFACTION

The liquefaction part of the chain is a key element and, as with the gas supply, the lenders will want to make sure that the plant is constructed and delivered on time to ensure no delay in start-up and sales of LNG to buyers (and flow of revenues from the market). Lenders will, therefore, look for fixed price turnkey construction contracts with clear performance guarantees. Prior to completion of the plant and to the completion tests being carried out (when the engineering and guarantees become effective), lenders will expect shareholder pre-completion guarantees. This may at times be an issue if the shareholders are of different credit ratings and one shareholder, who could be a government company, cannot give sufficient financial guarantees. In this case, lenders could seek export credit agency (ECA) guarantees or insurance cover.

Lenders will be particularly concerned if the facility is using a new technology (such as larger LNG processing trains, a new process or floating LNG). In the case of new technology the lenders will probably seek assurances and guarantees from the provider and the shareholders. Lenders will also look for reports from independent consultants on the technical and operational plans for the project.

Lenders will focus on who will operate the plant and insist that an experienced company be used and defined training schemes are put in place to train up local staff. Experience in operating LNG plants is a real strength that international companies, such

---

6   Reserves – The amount of gas underground that can be commercially recovered – reserves are normally quantified in trillions of cubic feet (Tcf) or billions of cubic metres (BCM). The amount of gas in place underground is normally defined as a percentage of certainty that the gas can be commercially recovered.

as BP, ExxonMobil and Shell bring to a project, hence the importance to many new projects to include a company with experience in LNG in its shareholder structure.

SHIPPING

Whether the LNG is sold FOB[7] or ex-ship[8] the lenders will want to understand the details as to who will be arranging the shipping and what ships will be used. This may include the construction of new ships, and in this case, the lenders will seek to understand and mitigate vessel construction risk. Where vessels are to be chartered, the charter-parties will need to be reviewed to ensure that the lenders are comfortable with them. Lenders will also want to ensure that the vessels are to be operated by an experienced shipping company and, as with liquefaction, this is often an area where international companies bring skills and therefore their involvement in the project. That said, national oil companies, joint-venture projects and ship-owners are developing their skills, often being trained by the international companies – for example, when China wanted to develop its LNG ship construction facilities and LNG ships operations skills, BP and Shell agreed to assist. All vessels are flagged[9] by a particular country, and the lenders will want to ensure that the country of flagging is reputable and has suitable shipping regulations.

In the case of the vessels being owned by the project, lenders will want to know the vessel payment terms to ensure that the project cashflows are not being unduly stretched. They will also want to understand when the vessel payments are to be made and to ensure that if the project is not able to use the ships (e.g., in the case of plant problems) that they could be redeployed and at what cost.

REGASIFICATION AND MARKET

The performance of the LNG buyer is a major risk as it is the LNG sales revenue that forms the main security for lending money to a liquefaction project. Considerable due diligence will, therefore, be carried out, using market consultants. The LNG buyer needs to understand the market and whether it is able to sell the gas to earn sufficient revenue to pay for the LNG. This due diligence will examine the long-term market to ensure that, in signing a long-term contract to buy LNG, the buyer will continue to have a reliable market into the future. For both FOB and ex-ship sales, lenders will also want to understand what regasification facilities the LNG buyer intends to use, who is constructing them, who the operator will be, and what guarantees are there that the facilities will be in place for start-up of the LNG supply. And, in the case of late completion, is there an alternative market into which the LNG can be sold?

Lenders may also seek to understand the political risks of the market and if there are any risks that could stop the market being available for the LNG during the period of the contract.

---

7   FOB = Free on board where the LNG sold to the buyer at the load port and title and risk passes at the flange at the load port. The LNG sales price does not include freight.

8   Ex-ship (or delivered) = LNG is sold to the buyer at the discharge port and title and risk passes at the flange at the discharge port. The LNG sales price includes freight.

9   The flag state of a commercial vessel is the state under whose laws the vessel is registered or licenced. The flag state has the authority and responsibility to enforce regulations over vessels registered under its flag, including those relating to inspection, certification, and issuance of safety and pollution prevention documents (*Source*: Wikipedia).

REGULATORY RISKS

Along all parts of the chain the lenders will want to understand the legal and regulatory risks such as are consents, permits, concession agreements and other laws in place to ensure that the cash flow from the project will not be threatened. Laws and regulations are, of course, set by central and local governments and are often subject to regional rules, such as those set by the European Union. Lenders will, therefore, seek to mitigate this risk through a clear understanding of all applicable rules and regulations.

Risk Mitigation

Managing and allocating risk is key to a successful project financing. Lenders will carry out detailed due diligence with support from lenders' consultants[10], to understand the risks in each part of the chain and how the links of the chain operate and where, if any, the weaknesses are and how they can be mitigated.

Figure 16.4 summarizes project risks and mitigants.

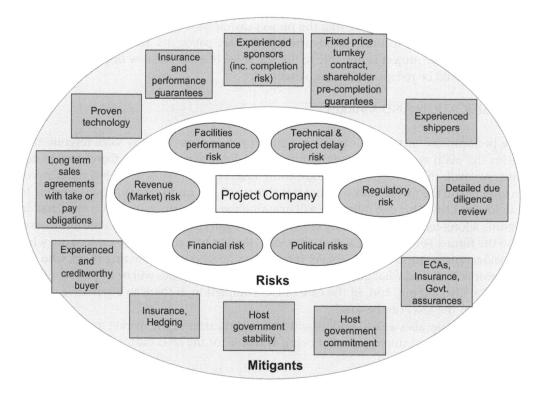

Figure 16.4 Project risks and mitigants
Source: South-Court Research

---

10   Lenders will appoint independent consultant in areas such as technical, shipping, market, environmental analysis and insurance.

MARKET

Since a key revenue risk is the revenues from the market, long-term LNG sales and purchase agreements with take or pay commitments are very important. But this is only contractual support, so to make sure that payment is made and cashflow received, stability of the LNG offtaker and the LNG offtaker's country is key. The purchasing country's commitment to the long-term LNG purchase is often required, and many long-term LNG sales need political support between the government of the LNG supply and LNG buying countries.

Lenders will also insist on letters of credit or parent company guarantees if the LNG buyer is not of sufficient financial standing. Lenders will also seek to prioritize the funds when they are received by the project company, with payment of operating cost and taxes taking precedent over loan service and repayments but ahead of any shareholder dividends being paid. This prioritization is usually set out in the loan documentation as the cash waterfall. In some projects, lenders may insist that the LNG sales revenues be paid to an offshore agent – Escrow account – and the agent disperses the funds to the correct part of the cash waterfall.

SPONSORS

Lenders, and LNG buyers, will look to the quality of the sponsors of the LNG export project (including the host government) to ensure that the project will proceed and that

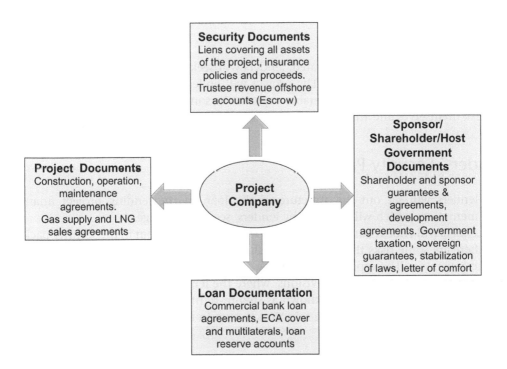

Figure 16.5 Project documentation
Source: South-Court Research

it will be operated safely and correctly. Having a sponsor with LNG experience as a major shareholder will clearly mitigate this risk. Using experienced shippers, with sponsor support if required, will mitigate any shipper risk that lenders may have. Lenders can only rely on revenues if the LNG chain operates effectively, and this can only happen if all links of the LNG chain are completed and operate as designed. Prior to completion, sponsors will be asked to give guarantees (completion guarantees), which only expire once the part of the chain that the guarantee covers has passed stringent completion tests to the satisfaction of the lenders and the lenders' consultants. Lenders will also insist that sponsors' equity is paid prior to any loan being paid. This ensures that the sponsors are fully committed and bound to the project in case of problems.

TECHNOLOGY

Lenders will have concerns if the project seeks to use new technology, such as larger LNG trains or floating LNG, and will seek assurances such as supplier/contractor guarantees or shareholder financial support to mitigate this risk. Lenders will also seek performance guarantees on the equipment during the period of plant operation.

HOST GOVERNMENT

Lenders will seek support from the host government of the supplying country (and maybe the buying country). This could also be related to the stability of the tax regime as well as other regulations related to the LNG export project.

INSURANCE

For any risk that cannot be mitigated, lenders will seek insurance to be taken out by the project or the project sponsors. The project will endeavour to minimize the insurance cover as this represents a considerable expense. In some cases the sponsors may absorb the risk themselves and this has been the case in some projects.

Lenders' Security Package

The lenders will set out the structure of the loan in the lending project financing documentation, which will include the lenders' security package.

Lenders will endeavour to minimize the risks and set them out in the security package. But there are some risks that will be difficult to quantify – project cost estimation, how project revenue will be applied and changing government policy. The loan documentation will therefore include default provisions, where the lenders would have the right to step in and operate the project (also known as step-in-rights). These theoretically give banks protection, but in reality they are reluctant to step in and in reality they have not been used.

Conclusions

Project finance has been used very effectively in supporting the development of LNG export projects and providing a useful source of debt for finance and the development of LNG projects that potentially would not have been developed due to the partner structure and project risks. Even during the financial crisis of 2008–10 projects could be financed, albeit with greater ECA cover.

There are many challenges facing the future growth of LNG, but one thing is certain, with increased growth of gas as a preferred fuel for efficiency and environmental reasons, and the growth of countries that are seeking to import LNG to cover shortfalls in gas supply or for security of supply reasons, new sources of LNG supply will be required. The pace of growth of this new supply will depend on a variety of factors, availability of feedgas, economic growth, demand for gas in exporting countries and government policy in both the supplier and buyer countries. One thing is clear though, the costs of LNG projects are high and the companies who seek to be shareholders in the projects do not have large enough balance sheets to fund the projects themselves so they will seek third party debt. Project finance as a proven source of finance to the energy sector will therefore be the preferred source of third-party debt, and as long as the risks remain manageable and all stakeholders accept where that risk should lie, then the future of project finance in the LNG sector should be good.

EXAMPLE 1

Papua New Guinea LNG

(Shareholders: ExxonMobil: 33.2 per cent; Oil Search: 29.0 per cent; Independent Public Business Corp: 16.6 per cent; Santos: 13.5 per cent; Nippon Oil: 4.7 per cent; PNG landowner interests: 2.8 per cent; Petromin PBG Oil: 0.2 per cent)

Table 16.1 Project financing

	$bn
Project cost	18.50
Financing:	
ECA portion*	8.30
Commercial loan (59% with political and commercial risk cover**	1.95
ExxonMobil shareholder loan	3.75
Total financing (balance equity)	14.00 (75% gearing)

*US Exim (US$3.0bn), Japan Exim (US$1.8bn), Australia Export Finance (US$0.5bn), China Exim and SACE (US$3.0bn).

** Nippon Export & Import Insurance providing 100 per cent political risk and 97.5 per cent commercial risk insurance to $0.95bn.

Source: South-Court Research

The ExxonMobil sponsored PNG LNG project was developed in a country with a poor credit rating and with no LNG project experience. This caused many banks many concerns. The shareholding structure is such that ExxonMobil was the only shareholder with a AAA credit rating. The country has a Standard & Poors B+ credit rating, non-investment grade, with a stable outlook, Santos has a rating of BBB+ and Oil Search is unrated. In May 2009, Santos raised US$3bn through the sales of additional shares to meet its equity obligations[11] and Oil Search has said that it will fund its equity from existing funds and future cashflows.[12]

The project reached financial close in Match 2010 after the final LNG sales and purchase agreement was signed with the buyers: Sinopec (China) 2.7 BCMA; CPC (Taiwan) 1.6 BCMA; Tokyo Electric (Japan) 2.5 BCMA and Osaka Gas (Japan) 2.0 BCMA.

The project achieved a 75 per cent gearing, due in part to the LNG project experience and balance sheet of ExxonMobil, as well as the credit strength of the LNG buyers. The interesting point with this project is how the debt was structured with the export credit agencies covering 67 per cent of the total debt, ExxonMobil providing shareholder loans for 27 per cent debt, meaning that uncovered commercial debt (i.e., debt from commercial banks that did not have an political risk insurance from the ECAs) was only 7 per cent of the debt portion.

EXAMPLE 2

Qatargas II

(Shareholders: Train 1 – Qatar Petroleum: 70.0 per cent; ExxonMobil: 30.0 per cent. Train 2 – Qatar Petroleum: 65.0 per cent; ExxonMobil: 18.3 per cent; Total: 16.7 per cent)

Table 16.2 Project financing

	US$bn
Development, construction and start-up costs	a) US$9.3bn upstream and LNG liquefaction facilities in Qatar b) US$0.75bn LNG import terminal (South Hook)
Upstream facilities Third party debt and debt/equity ratio	Equity US$2.8bn ExxonMobil loan US$1.9bn Commercial loans US$3.6bn ECAs US$1.0bn Third party debt/equity: 50/50*

---

11   http://www.theage.com.au/business/oil-search-no-to-cash-raising-20090512-b20x.html.
12   Business Spectator, 13th January 2011 'S&P affirms Santos credit rating'.

Regasification terminal Third party debt and debt/equity ratio	Equity US$0.14bn ExxonMobil loan US$0.18bn Commercial loans US$0.43bn Third party debt/equity: 57/43**
Loan tenor	Upstream and liquefaction: 15–16 years LNG terminal: 25 years

* 70/30 with EM inc. as debt
** 80/20 with EM inc. as debt

The 15mtpa (20.5 BCMA) two train Qatargas II LNG project is an integrated project where the shareholders have a common interest along all parts of the chain. Originally, the shareholders were Qatar Petroleum 70 per cent and ExxonMobil 30 per cent. Total later joined the second train with a 16.7 per cent interest. This gave Total an 8.35 per cent interest in the South Hook regasification terminal in the UK.[13] The Qatargas II project was developed based on selling the output to the UK market.

Qatar Petroleum and ExxonMobil were targeting a debt/equity ratio of 55–60 per cent with no recourse to shareholders after start-up. The financing had real challenges: the project cost was ~US$10bn, and the base market was the UK, where the imports from Qatar were going to represent over 20 per cent of UK gas demand. In the UK the price of gas (and therefore the price of the LNG) is based on the National Balancing Point Hub price, and the Qatargas II project was the first LNG project to sell Its LNG based on hub based versus oil related pricing. The Qatargas II project was also the first to use the 7.8mtpa (10.5 BCMA) mega-trains and large LNG ships (216,000–265,000BCMA) LNG ships.

These market and technology risks caused lenders some concerns, but after considerable due diligence in December 2004 the project was able to secure 50 per cent debt cover in the upstream and liquefaction portion of the chain (70 per cent debt if ExxonMobil shareholder loan is included as debt) and 57 per cent debt in the regasification terminal portion (80 per cent debt if ExxonMobil shareholder loan is included as debt). A primary reason for the banks' support was the high quality of the sponsors, especially ExxonMobil who lent over US$2bn to the project as shareholder loans and gave LNG experience to the project. The export credit agencies' US$1.0bn cover was also important.

Qatar, a stable country, had a proven track record of developing and operating LNG projects. The Qatargas II project financing was a real success and formed the basis of the financing of the Qatargas III (Qatar Petroleum/ConocoPhillips) and Qatargas IV (Qatar Petroleum/Shell) projects.

---

13   i.e. Total received a 50 per cent interest in the South Hook terminal as it only had a shareholding in half the Qatargas II liquefaction capacity. This interest in South Hook is believed to be in the terminal itself and not the capacity.

EXAMPLE 3

Sabine Pass LNG regasification terminal

Table 16.3   Project financing

Project cost	US$1.0bn
Debt	US$0.8bn
Debt/equity	80/20

The Sabine Pass LNG terminal in the Gulf Coast of the USA was developed as an independent LNG regasification facility by Cheniere and was the first greenfield regasification terminal to be financed. The project came to the market in 2004, at a time when the US banks were reluctant to lend to energy projects as they had experienced problems lending into the power sector in previous years. The banks therefore had to educate the lenders about the LNG sector and the risk structure of the LNG regasification portion of the LNG chain. Lenders were also concerned about the US market and due diligence set out the key market factors and the role of LNG in meeting US gas supply.[14] Cheniere did not have a strong balance sheet but used the payments from the two long-term 25 year sale of regasification capacity (set out in binding terminal use agreements with Chevron and Total for 1 bcf/day[15] each) as the cash flow to develop the project on which to base the financing. It has been reported that each of the companies is paying in the region of US$100m–US$120m pa for the capacity. Lenders were happy with the strong balance sheets of these two capacity offtakers and lent US$822m, meaning that the project was able to secure a debt/equity of 80/20.

Cheniere was able to further reduce the project risk through fixed price engineering and procurement contracts with Bechtel and the physical location of the terminal, close to pipeline infrastructure to evacuate the gas to market gave further confidence to the lenders.

---

14   In the 2005 US Energy Information Administration's annual outlook, it estimated that the USA would import 130 mtpa (140 BCMA) in 2025. This estimate dropped to 7 mtpa (10 BCMA) in its 2011 outlook due to the growth in Shale Gas in North America.

15   1 bcf/day equivalent to 7.8 mtpa or 10.7 BCMA.

17 RBL in the Oil and Gas Sector

KEITH O'DONNELL
Head, global ebergy team, KBC

Reserve based lending (RBL) refers to an asset based financing technique that is unique to the oil and gas sector. It is secured lending where the collateral is the revenue stream that the borrower has from oil exploitation contracts. The lender bases the amount of the loan on its assessment of the present value of the expected cashflows that it considers the borrower is capable of repatriating to accounts typically held by the lending bank(s). Critical to this assessment will be nature and location of the hydrocarbons, the production forecast, the price deck and the portfolio spread of assets available as security. Also notable is that the lenders are looking at a specific subset of assets that are considered acceptable security. Outside this sphere the parent may have other activities that are uninterrupted by the RBL structure.

Who Uses RBL Sructures?

RBL structures are typically used by independent oil and gas companies although, exceptionally, larger players (Tullow to fund its expansion in Africa) have tapped this market and even super majors (BP used the product in its efforts to raise liquid funding following the Mocondo disaster) have used the technique from time to time. Apart from generating liquidity, in its typical market, the RBL is a very effective means for a growing oil company to release cash from 'de-risked assets' that may be re-invested in higher risk expansion opportunities that accelerate growth. By de-risked assets is meant discoveries that have been proven and developed to the production phase. Although cash is released by the financing (possibly all cash equity) the oil company retains the upside. Re-investment may take place outside the RBL structure. The benefit is a leveraged balance sheet optimizing more diverse portfolio growth strategies and enhanced equity returns.

Who Provides RBL Structures?

RBL structures are provided by international commercial banks, regional commercial banks and multilateral institutions particularly the International Finance Corporation (IFC). The key players tend to be the international commercial banks as they have the technology and human resources to implement the financing structures. Regional banks can be very effective in their local markets and multilateral institutions bring capacity in underdeveloped markets that would otherwise not attract commercial bank funding. Financings are generally for between US$100m and US$500m but the markets capacity has proven that capacity exists to complete transactions up to US$2.5bn – Tullow, Perenco and BP have all completed transactions at this level in recent years. As we will see later this is a highly specialized industry subsector and the most serious players all have specialist teams that include industry experts with commercial, modelling and engineering skills. In banking terms the business is considered to be in the 'high risk high return' category.

In a typical transaction the funds are provided by a consortium of banks. Decisions are generally by majority lenders and there will be an agent bank to handle the interface between the consortium and the borrower. There will also be a technical bank(s) and a security trustee acting on behalf of all lenders.

Common Features of an RBL Structure

RBL structures take account of the fact that effective direct security over concessions is not possible and they are tailored to the specific requirements of a transaction. But given the high risk nature of the transactions lenders usually seek a comprehensive security package and reserve discretions that ensure lenders have adequate control over the behaviour of the borrower, thus ensuring the security is protected.

SECURITY

Primary recourse of an RBL transaction is to the underlying asset or, more likely, portfolio of assets. Normally when contemplating secured lending banks think about real assets and contracts that compensate the owner for the use or benefit from the assets. For example, in the case of a power project the security would comprise the land, connections and the plant itself whilst the key contract would be the power sale agreement. In respect to real estate banks could look to land, buildings and occupational leases to entities using the premises. Banks are able to take real security over real assets that in a worst case scenario can be sold on the open market.

Upstream is fundamentally different as, rather than supplying a service to the state (e.g., power generation) for which it pays, the state is supplying access to its resources for which it expects the oil company to pay (committed work programme and share of any discovery). With only limited exceptions host countries own the hydrocarbons through until the point of sale and they do not grant any other entity ownership or security interest in any circumstances. Exploration and exploitation concessions are contracts from host authorities to oil companies giving the right, under

> **Representations, warranties, covenants and undertakings:**
> - Corporate Standing and Authority
> - Documentation properly Authorized and binding
> - Good Title to the Assets
> - Necessary Approvals obtained
> - Documents give first ranking security interest
> - All information is accurate
> - No other security Interest
> - No other debt
> - No change of control

strict circumstances, to explore subject areas and exploit discoveries. The concession contracts place strict obligations on the holder to undertake minimal exploration activity and to develop discoveries within agreed timeframes whilst also maintaining industry standards. Failure by the concession holder may result in forfeiture (loss of lenders' security) but any benefit from a concession is shared with the host authority (paid before lenders). Any party wanting to sell its interest in a concession is likely to need the approval of the host country. Given its strategic importance most producing countries form separate ministries and national oil companies to manage their hydrocarbon interests (host authority).

In the vast majority of cases independent oil companies prefer to share concession risks with others. Thus consortia are formed and an operator is appointed with significant discretion to manage and develop the concession. Operatorship brings benefits and obligations that are significant from a lender's perspective. On the one hand the borrower is able to control the pace of the project to suit its and its lender's sensitivities. On the other hand the operator has duties to its partners and to the host authority that may have significant financial impact. The greatest exposure is to Health, Safety and Environmental obligations and the largest risk is offshore in developed economies where the obligations and penalties are greatest. At a minimum the operator is required to post multimillion dollar security deposits against its obligations and in a worst case it may face clean-up obligations resulting from blowout or spillage.

SHARE PLEDGE

As a direct security interest is not possible banks will seek share pledge security over all the group entities holding concessions (obligors) on which the borrowing base facility is structured. This allows lenders to indirectly control ownership of the concession and in certain circumstances it may provide the route to dispose of a concession interest without requiring the consent of a host authority especially if it is a minority non-operated interest. The structure is less robust than direct security and therefore lenders require certain representations and warranties at the outset to give reassurance that the assets offered are clean and

> **Representations, warranties covenants and undertakings:**
> - Share pledge
> - Fixed and floating charges
> - No change in ownership
> - No concession disposals

represent good value from a security perspective. Lenders will also likely take fixed and floating charges to mop up any other assets held by obligors (ex stock, office equipment, pipelines) but this will have little value in the financial analysis. Finally, there will be a range of reserve discretions designed to ensure the assets are preserved as good security.

BANK ACCOUNTS AND CASH WATERFALL

Lenders are advancing loans based on the present value of net expected income from exploitation concessions. Therefore, the banks want to be able to measure the income flows and they want to be able to control how the cash is applied. Operating Accounts (OA) are opened with the security trustee and there will be significant restrictions in respect to the management of cash through these accounts. To the extent that the income and expenditure is substantially in line with the base case the borrower may have discretion to apply the funds but in any case it is likely that any application is in the following order:

1. Expenditure relating to the borrowing base assets including operating costs, royalties, taxes, allocation of G&A and other concession expenses;
2. Fees costs and expenses relating to the facility;
3. Interest relating to the facility (may include hedging);
4. Payments to or from the debt service reserve Account (DSRA);
5. Scheduled repayments (may include hedging termination);
6. Unallocated G&A;
7. Cash sweep; and
8. Release for general corporate use or distribution (possibly with additional group level restrictions).

> **Representations, warranties, covenants and undertakings**
> - All revenue paid to OA
> - Release consistent with forecast or with approval of Security Trustee
> - Maintain DSRA
> - Hedging Obligation
> - Provide monthly performance updates
> - Provide Semi-annual certificates of cashflow
> - Group Liquidity Tests

Commodity hedging may be permitted or required and in such case the hydrocarbon hedging settlement may take place at the top of the cash waterfall or even before the revenue hits the account. In addition, in many cases the Security Trustee will hold a DSRA into which is placed an amount equivalent to 6 months' debt service. A cash sweep may or may not apply depending on the circumstances.

Senior debt providers may restrict hedging counterparties and may add conditionality to the standard hedging documents to reflect the lenders' interest in the revenue stream.

COMMITMENT AND AVAILABILITY

The transaction is sized according to the capacity of the borrowing base assets to support the proposed debt. The first step in the process is to generate a base case cashflow which requires production, hydrocarbon price, operating cost, royalty costs, abandonment and administration cost and taxation forecasts, all of which are factored into a computer model for the life of each borrowing base asset. Specialist lending teams require a great deal of information and input in respect to the control and management of the assets.

The production forecast is an engineering forecast usually prepared in the first place by the borrower. The leading banks in the sector usually have their own geologists and reservoir engineers who will review and validate the technical assumptions. In addition, lenders will normally require an independent reserve report to be prepared by an internationally recognized firm. Next, banks and the borrower's commercial decision makers consider the forecast prices for

> **Representations, warranties, covenants and undertakings**
> - Monthly production reports
> - Copies of operators' reports/budgets
> - Copies of Operating Committee Meetings minutes
> - Copies of all official notices
> - Copies of all HSE events
> - Copies of all capital expenditure budgets
> - Annual Independent Reserve Reports
> - Semi-annual financial statements
> - Annual financial statements
> - Annual strategy update

each producing asset. It seems obvious but banks consider it much easier to evaluate the likely price of oil delivered to Sullom Voe compared to gas delivered to the domestic market in, say, Russia. The forecast prices applied will be linked to leading benchmarks but take account of the nature of the hydrocarbon (oil is more easily transported and marketed compared to gas and certain crudes are more attractive than others given certain physical characteristics), location of sale, currency exchange risk and the currency transfer risk. Consideration is given to abandonment date and abandonment cost. Depending on circumstances this might be offset against the decommissioning value of the infrastructure. Clearly, the previous production and economic assumptions impact the economic life of the field so there is some circularity in determining the date and net decommissioning cost to be factored into the forecast. Nevertheless, it is essential to make best estimates. Finally it is necessary to include a charge for the borrower's general and administration costs and to make assumptions about how these might increase over time. At this point the borrower has a base case estimate of its revenues for the full economic life of the fields.

> **Representations, warranties, covenants and undertakings**
> - Semi-annual financial forecast
> - Loan Life Cover Ratio
> - Field Life Cover Ratio
> - Reserve Tail Date

Banks will apply an appropriate discount factor to these flows to give a net present value. The discount factor is subject to negotiation but it should reflect the volatility of the forecast which is driven by the extent and nature of the underlying asset portfolio. However, the margin is intended to reflect the same risk and often the discount factor is similar to the total interest payable on the debt but with a minimum rate of around 10 per cent.

The lenders now have a net present value (NPV) of the underlying assets which might otherwise be referred to as the value of the assets. But senior debt providers do not normally lend the full value of the underlying assets, preferring to see risk equity invested ahead of debt. The loan that banks are usually prepared to extend is determined by taking the lower of the loan life cover ratio (LLCR) and the field life cover ratio (FLCR).

The LLCR is a factor applied to the NPV of the cashflows up to the final repayment date of the loan facility. The ratio applied is transaction specific but it would not be unusual for it to be in the region of 1.4 times. For example, if the NPV is US$100m then the LLCR would determine that the maximum availability should not exceed US$66.67m. As is implied, the FLCR factor is applied to the NPV of the cashflows over the full life of the field through and including abandonment. Again, the ratio is transaction specific but it would not be unusual for the ratio to be in the order of 1.7 times. In such case assuming a Field Life NPV of say US$150m the availability should not exceed US$88.24m. Lenders take the lowest figure, in this case US$66.67m.

The loan commitment and availability is sized in this way but the repayment (minimum reduction to commitments) may be sculpted to take account of the fact or expectation that a successful borrower will at least replace production with new reserves each year. A borrower might structure a loan with a five-year tenor but no repayments in the first year and significant repayments back ended to the last 18 months of the loan. As long as new reserves are added the availability will remain or could even grow; however, if reserves fall the opposite will happen and the availability will fall sweeping all cashflow to loan reductions.

Lenders avoid assets that are coming close to the end of their economic lives. At this stage the period of remaining cashflow is becoming short and evaluation of abandonment costs is critical which adds volatility reducing attractiveness from a senior debt perspective. Lenders also fear the risk that they might need to enforce security at a time when the borrower is about to incur abandonment costs and take on the related environmental risks. For this reason many lenders will include a covenant control to the effect that the 'reserve tail' must be at least 25 per cent, meaning that at least 25 per cent of the hydrocarbon reserves must still be in the ground when the debt is finally repaid and if necessary (in the case of a reserve downgrade) the repayment profile needs to be accelerated to achieve this outcome.

There is close follow-up by the banking teams to ensure that the forecasts are robust technically and economically. This is manifest in semi-annual re-determinations when the technical and economic assumptions are all revisited and a new economic forecast prepared leading to a new availability for the succeeding period and so on. The structure responds quickly to positive and negative news to ensure that the Borrower and Lenders maintain their relationship status.

Recent Trends

RBL structures have been used since the early 1970s when BP first used the concept to finance the Forties Field. Structures constantly evolve in response to economic conditions and client needs. We set out below a number of the more recent trends.

LIQUIDITY TESTING

In the aftermath of the crisis in 2009 a number of independent oil and gas companies experienced a severe squeeze on their liquidity. The economic conditions changed, accelerating abandonment dates and cutting NPV calculations dramatically. However, companies that suffered most were those that had entered long term contracts (often outside the borrowing Base Group on the assumption of strong cashflows and even new increased bank facilities. These companies found themselves severely constrained and in some cases were forced into insolvency. As a result, lenders began to look more closely at the wider activities of group companies linked to the RBL structure but, possibly, outside the security package. Liquidity testing was introduced to demonstrate that the wider group is capable of meeting all contractual obligations from existing available resources.

CAPEX ADDBACK

Capital expenditure into new discoveries and developments are the lifeblood of RBL structures and an essential ingredient of a successful independent oil and gas company. Within the portfolio of borrowing base assets a borrower may have investment opportunities that are uncertain and not assumed to be realized in the production forecast. Equally, the financial forecast takes account of all expenses including capital expenditure and so the NPV is reduced by the capital expenditure on the RBL portfolio. As a result, the borrower has a strong disincentive to invest in the RBL portfolio (lenders' security) which could ultimately be to the detriment of the banks and the borrower.

Lenders have recognized this and accepted the concept of capex addback which allows certain forecast capital expenditure (up to no more than 12 months and not linked to the production forecast) to be added back for a period thus neutralizing the negative NPV impact. This facilitates investment but is for a relatively short period that can be quickly controlled in no new reserves result.

PRE-DEVELOPMENT FINANCING

RBL structures usually only include fields that are proven and already in production (occasionally fields in advanced development but pre-production might be included as part of a wider portfolio but this would be limited in scale). It has been possible to raise modest amounts of senior debt against assets that are proven undeveloped and pre the final development plan approval. Such finance is considered to be at the higher end of the risk scale and likely to be for relatively short tenor with bullet repayment. The repayment obligation is a significant burden if the borrower is not able to move the asset into its operating phase which would support longer term finance.

DEBTOR FINANCING

RBL structures by their very nature are only measuring cashflow from the date of the financial forecast forwards for the life of the loan. However, on the date of the forecast the Borrower may already have debtors in respect to sales/deliveries over the previous accounting period. The existing debtors are already caught by the security structure around the RBL facility so external sources of funding are excluded. Assuming that it is possible to establish that the debtors are credible, the currency risk is modest and the transaction is in the normal course of business it is possible to have the RBL loan facility increased to provide finance for a proportion of the receivable. In return the lenders will require additional reporting of debtor ageing and receivables may be fully discounted after a certain ageing period.

18 *Non-recourse Financing for Mines*

EERO RAUTALAHTI
Partner, Edwards Wildman

A sustained period of high metal prices invariably brings out a surge in new mining projects. But high metal prices can prove a red herring: they enhance profitability projections and valuation models and make a project much more attractive to investors and lenders. But it takes 12–48 months from the investment decision before a new mining project will start generating cash flow, and nobody can predict commodity prices in three years' time. Moreover, most metal mines do not actually produce metal. Their product is sand – albeit with a high metal content – which must be treated, refined, processed and transported before it becomes the metal that is traded on the world's commodity exchanges.

Financiers considering lending to mining projects need to understand how these mines generate cash flow, even more so when the lending is on a non-recourse basis, secured with project assets and cash flow. In addition to the cost of investment and production, overheads and other items affecting any industrial project, mine revenue is also affected by a number of factors that are unique to the mining industry. These include the chemical composition of the concentrate, supply and demand of concentrates of a particular type, supply and demand of processing capacity of smelters and refineries as well as metal content recovery rates.

The recent extended period of high metal prices has encouraged a number of new mining projects – many of which might not have proceeded at lower price levels – and many of them are likely to come on-stream at a time when prices have fallen from their historic highs. Ironically, the drop in prices is often a direct result of the over-supply engendered by new projects.

This chapter discusses the special characteristics of mine development projects, with the aim of helping lenders and investors to understand how these projects differ from other industrial projects and how mines produce the cash flow needed to repay the financing.

Introduction

The mining industry is divided into segments that have little or nothing in common beyond the basic extractive nature of their business. In one end of the spectrum are coal and uranium in the energy sector, with perhaps closer similarities to oil and gas than metals mining. In the other end are precious metals (gold, silver), gemstones and small volume but valuable rare earths and special metals. Half-way between these extremes is the traditional large-volume mining of base metals: iron, copper, zinc, nickel and aluminium. The operators in each segment tend to be closely linked, often bound together by a web of supply and purchase agreements. This chapter will mainly focus on base metals, but same or similar general principles apply across the industry.

The mining industry is divided vertically between exploration and mining, and mining is often integrated with the downstream activities of smelting, refining and metals trading. Major international mining companies invariably operate in all of these segments. On the other hand, there are also businesses that restrict their operations to one segment or two segments only.

The market for each metal and mineral has its own specific characteristics, often influenced by historic factors and competitive dynamics. For example, almost all aluminium mining is vertically integrated with processing plants. As a result, there is little free trading in unprocessed alumina, and the producers have developed highly complex methods for swapping quantities of material between themselves. The function and effect of such swaps are essentially similar to the trading arrangements for copper and zinc, but the mechanisms are completely different.

Historically, the discovery and development of a major deposit of ore (the orebody) has often led into downstream expansion as the mine seeks to capture a bigger portion of the revenue stream originating from the mine. Downstream operations tend to have a longer lifespan than the mine, so that they continue operating with raw materials from other sources after the mine has been exhausted.

Concentrate is what a base metal mine normally produces. Once extracted, metal ore typically contains 1–10 per cent metal.[1] Ore cannot be transported economically beyond the limits of the mine compound. It needs to be crushed and treated to reach a metal content of 10–70 per cent. The resulting mix is called concentrate, which looks like sand and can be shipped to a smelter even in another continent, provided that this can be done by rail and ship without too many transshipments.

A stand-alone mine normally sells all its concentrate production to a smelter. The smelter refines[2] the concentrate into pure metal that can be traded in commodity exchanges or sold directly to customers. Integrated mining and smelting companies sell and buy concentrates even when they could cover the entire feed requirements of their smelters with concentrates from their own mines. This initially surprising situation is explained by the variable chemical composition of concentrates produced by individual mines. Ores from different mines have different chemical composition, which vary and change within a single mine over its life as the extraction progresses across the orebody. Smelters, on the other hand, have been designed for a specific chemical mix of concentrates, and they need to buy in material in order to reach the optimal raw material feed mix.

---

1   As regards commercial viability, the lower limit for ore metal content varies from metal to metal: for example, copper deposits with even less than 0.5 per cent metal content can still be mined economically, whilst bauxite ore is expected to have 25–30 per cent aluminium content before it can be utilized commercially.

2   In some metals like copper and nickel, the outcome of the smelting process is an intermediary metal product which still needs to be refined in a separate process in order to reach pure metal. There are both integrated and independent copper smelters and refineries.

All widely traded metals are quoted on one or more commodity exchanges. The London Metal Exchange (LME) quotes non-ferrous metals such as aluminium, copper, nickel, tin, zinc, lead, molybdenum and cobalt. The Chicago Mercantile Exchange quotes precious metals gold, silver, platinum, palladium and also copper. The New York Mercantile Exchange and its COMEX division quote palladium, platinum, uranium, aluminium, copper, gold and silver. In recent years, The Shanghai Metals Exchanges (copper, aluminium, gold, lead, zinc, steel wire rods and reinforcing bars) and other Chinese commodity exchanges have gained importance for pricing.

The Life Span of a Mine Development Project

Mining projects require substantial investment over several years before anything is produced and accordingly, the payback time tends to be long. The lifespan of a mine is entirely dependent on the size and quality of the orebody. After the mine has closed, there is the further cost of environmental regeneration and ensuring that the disused mine does not become dangerous to the surrounding area.

Many mining projects are located in relatively inhospitable parts of the world. This is partly because easily accessible orebodies in industrialized countries have been long since exhausted and partly because the inherently disruptive nature of mining prevents opening new mines in densely populated areas. Mining projects are vulnerable to country risks, as the business cannot be relocated if the relations with the government sour. Should a new regime in the country decide to impose higher taxes on profits from the extraction of its natural resources, the company operating the mine faces a stark selection of choices between paying the taxes, selling out or closing down the mine. Because of their disruptive nature, mining operations can also become PR disasters where they cause damage to the livelihoods of the local population or offend their beliefs, or if there is substantial environmental damage.

As mentioned, a base metal mine construction project commenced today will take 12–48 months before it generates any cash flow. After that, it will take years before the financing has been paid and the equity investors can fully enjoy a return on their investments.

(A) SECURING RIGHTS TO THE OREBODY

All mining projects start from the discovery of the orebody. Prospecting and exploration is a highly speculative business and whilst most major mining companies have exploration divisions, most orebodies have been discovered by independent exploration companies – in some cases by amateur geologists.

Geological drillings give an idea of the size, orientation and chemical composition of the ore, but it is not commercially feasible to map out the orebody completely beforehand.[3] As a result, the industry expects mining projects to have undiscovered upside potential. This does not always work – in one instance, two promising zinc discoveries were made in

---

3   Geological data from the Former Soviet States that dates back to the Soviet Union is an exception: geological data based on drillings in Soviet times tends to be quite exhaustive, which means that orebodies based on such data are less likely to have unexpected upside, and should be valued on this basis.

Ireland in the 1960s on two sides of a river. Each project set out to develop a mine, only to realize much later that both discoveries were part of the same orebody lying at an angle so that one end of the ore surfaced on one side of the river whilst most of the ore was on the other side, together with all the upside potential.

In addition to rights to the orebody, it is also important to secure other rights that are necessary for commercial utilization of the ore, such as water and access rights. The processes used in mines and concentrate plants require a great deal of water and access to water can be crucial for mines located in arid areas.

(B) PROJECT PLANNING PHASE UNTIL INVESTMENT DECISION

As soon as the rights to the orebody have been secured, the project planning can commence. Early important decisions are the choice of technology and selection of the supplier of technology. This choice tends to be driven by the chemical composition of the orebody. The London-listed mining company Talvivaara Mining has recently developed a major mine from a large but relatively low grade orebody discovered in 1983. This orebody could not be extracted profitably using traditional methods, but Talvivaara Mining chose bioheapleaching, a relatively untested new technology, which is suited to the characteristics of the ore. The construction of the mine was started in 2007 and it is currently producing 22,000–28,000 tonnes of nickel annually.[4]

The project planning normally progresses through three stages: scoping, pre-feasibility study and bankable feasibility study. The financial viability of the project is assessed at the conclusion of each stage, before moving on to the next stage. It is imperative to analyse both project and production costs against expected future competition. When the unpredictability of the metal prices makes it difficult to project future cash flows, the planning phase tends to focus on cost: a cost-competitive project can be expected to perform better than its peers even at times of low metal prices.

Access to non-recourse financing pre-supposes that the mining project is a bankable project on a limited recourse basis. It also requires that the construction of the mine is completed within agreed timescales. Although the project financing will be non-recourse in the sense that there will be no shareholder guarantees, banks will not wish to take the risk of non-completion. The sponsors will then have to provide some form of undertaking to ensure that equity is subscribed and the mine is brought on stream within an acceptable time limit. This document often requires careful negotiation given the risks of government intervention and other factors.

The sponsors may also be required to provide other forms of support, such as take or pay contracts to secure the cash flow. Banks will also be concerned to ensure that the company obtains any necessary derogations from local exchange control regulations, thus ensuring that the financing obligations can be serviced in hard currency.

Different streams of project preparation proceed concurrently, such as mine design, commercial preparations, securing financing, environmental impact studies, permitting and negotiations with suppliers and contractors. All these processes aim towards the investment decision, which can only be taken when the permitting has been completed and the contracts for construction, technology licences, financing as well as 80–90 per cent of the product sale has been negotiated and committed, all subject only to the

---

4   Talvivaara Mining Company plc revised production guidance for 2011 announced on 7th May 2011.

investment decision. It is imperative that the project management reviews the profitability forecasts at this point when the project cost can be estimated relatively reliably against the latest metal price forecasts.

When developing a new non-integrated mine, negotiations on product supply contracts should commence during the early stages of project preparation. The aim of these negotiations is to gradually establish a position for the new player on the market. Lenders usually also require that the long-term sales/purchase contracts are negotiated at an early stage, before the financing for the building of the mine or smelter is committed.

(C) BUILDING PHASE FROM INVESTMENT DECISION TO FIRST DELIVERY OF CONCENTRATE

The path to the investment decision can be long and tortuous. There is an industry saying that 'the third owner builds the mine' – in many cases, the initial owner runs out of resources before they reach the building phase.

Once the investment decision has been made, the contracts become unconditional and construction starts. The construction of a base metals mine takes usually 1–4 years, including the mine facilities, concentration plant and ancillary facilities.

(D) LOGISTICS: NECESSITY FOR TRANSPORT LINKS

Apart from precious metals and gem stone mines or some rare minerals operations, mines tend to require access to rail and shipping facilities. Base metal concentrates are too bulky and have too low an intrinsic value to be transported economically by any other means than rail and ship. So the mine development cost usually includes the investment in building a rail connection from the mine to the closest mainline railway network that gives access to a harbour with facilities for handling bulk commodities.

In some cases it can be viable to build a pipeline from the mine to the harbour. The concentrate is pumped through the pipeline as a slurry, and the water is separated from the concentrates at the harbour before loading on a ship. This alternative can be viable for distances up to 400–500 kilometres, assuming that there is no suitable railway connection.

Once the concentrate is on a ship, it can be transported economically to any harbour in the world, as long as it does not need reloading to another vessel. So ideally, you would want your concentration plant next to the mine and connected with a conveyor belt to a railway line, which will take the product to the harbour, where it is off-loaded onto a conveyor belt that takes the concentrate onto a ship. In the destination harbour, the material is again transferred to railway cars via conveyor belt and taken by rail to a smelter. If the smelter is located very close to the harbour (or has its own harbour), concentrates can be transported by a conveyor belt directly from the ship to the plant.

(E) OPERATION PHASE

Once at full capacity, the mine can operate until the orebody is exhausted. This timespan can range from a few years to several decades.

The decision to close down a mine is a judgement call that in many respects resembles the investment decision. The decision is based on an evaluation of how much additional ore can be extracted at a cost that is still commercially viable, with a view to the short and medium term forecast on metal prices. Once the close-down decision is taken, reopening a decommissioned mine can involve huge cost and, accordingly, it is seldom financially viable. Only at times of exceptionally high metal prices, can there be an economic justification for reopening certain closed mines.

(F) CLOSING DOWN AND DECOMMISSIONING PHASE

Closing down a mine involves an additional cost of decommissioning and securing the site. When the mine has been closed down, the disused subterranean mine shafts tend to fill with water. This can initially lead to land subsidence but water eventually stabilizes the ground around the shafts. There will be continuous need to ensure that access to the disused mine shafts is prevented and that there are no environmentally damaging substances leaking from the disused installations. Open-cast mines may require substantial environmental repairs before the land can be taken into another use. Remote mines with a long operating history tend to have substantial communities develop around them, which lose the very reason of their existence when the mine closes down.

There is a school of thought in the mining industry that decommissioning and related costs should be included in the mine's initial investment budget at the time of the investment decision. In practice, this only happens with small mines that have a short projected operating life (3–5 years). The longer the mine operates, the harder it is to estimate what the cost may be when the mine is closed down 10, 20 or 80 years later.

Customers: To Whom and How do Mines sell Concentrates?

By definition, a mine has a limited customer base. Concentrates are a bulk product that must be sold in large quantities. Non-integrated mines sell their concentrates either to smelters or traders. In an integrated operation, a large proportion of the mine's output is used by the group's own smelter(s), but not all. Smelters are designed to operate with a concentrate feed that meets a given range of chemical specification. A smelter operator normally purchases concentrates from several mines and mixes them together to produce a raw material mix with a chemical composition that enables the plant to optimize its operation.

Spreading the supply between several mines and smelters reduces the risk of stoppages in case a mine or a smelter is closed down due to circumstances of force majeure, such as strikes, accidents or technical problems. No mine can afford to be dependent on a single customer and no smelter can rely on a single supplier. Prudent industry practice dictates that an operation should not place more than 20 per cent of its concentrate supply with one supplier or customer.

Smelters usually buy most of their concentrates under long-term supply contracts typically concluded for a term of 3–10 years. Critical commercial terms, however, are re-negotiated at regular intervals to reflect the prevailing market conditions. The negotiation of commercial terms normally takes place once or twice a year.

A concentrate contract can also be structured as a toll processing contract, where the smelter agrees to process material supplied by the mine, and return the resulting metal to the mine owner. Title to the material remains with the mine throughout the process. In reality, the mine delivers concentrate to the smelter, which mixes it with other raw materials and delivers refined metal to the mine. The essential difference to a normal concentrate contract is that in toll processing the metal price risk remains with the mine. The smelter's risk exposure is limited to technical and production risks, and it need not finance the working capital for the material in the process.

(A) LONG-TERM VERSUS SPOT

Long-term concentrate supply contracts have a significant stabilizing effect on both mines and smelters. Most importantly, they ensure that the mine has an outlet for its production and a secure cash flow to off-set the cost of investment during early stages of the operation. They also secure the raw material feed for the smelter and allow it to be run close to economic and technical optimum.

A mine or smelter that chooses to operate without long-term concentrate contracts has to sell/purchase all its material requirements on the spot markets. By operating on the spot market, the mine can take advantage of the peak prices but is exposed to low prices. The same applies to the smelter in reverse. In addition to the price risk, a smelter is also vulnerable to shortages of concentrate, which could force it to reduce production or even temporarily close down. Major smelter operators consider it prudent to fix 70–90 per cent of their feed through long-term contracts and fill the rest from the spot market. Similarly, a mine operating exclusively on the spot market is vulnerable if smelter stoppages result in an over-supply of concentrates.

Long-term concentrate contracts were originally developed to regulate sales and purchases between integrated mine-smelter operators, who needed to swap concentrate quantities with other producers in order to reach an optimal feed mix for their plants. These agreements became even more important when the non-integrated smelter business expanded in the 1950s and 60s as part of the post-war industrial revival in Western Europe and Japan. Over the decades, long term concentrates contracts have developed into extremely elaborate commercial arrangements which regulate most of the concentrate supply from mines to smelters globally.

Despite this, concentrate contracts generally receive little attention from financiers, lawyers and consultants. This is partly because they are normally written and negotiated by in-house commercial experts who deal with these contracts all the time and who know the inner workings of their market thoroughly. Only a handful of experts in the world are fully initiated into the inner workings of these complex contracts.

These experts are few in number, and even a major integrated mining and metals group would normally have no more than between one and four concentrates experts per metal. Their expertise is metal-specific, so whilst the broad principles may be similar, a copper specialist for instance seldom feels comfortable dealing in nickel. These experts know all their counterparts in the industry and they negotiate new contracts and renegotiate the annual pricing terms. They both develop and interpret the Byzantine web of trade customs and etiquette that regulates concentrates sales and deliveries.

Recruiting a sales director with all this expertise may be one of most important decisions for a new non-integrated mine, especially as this expertise is needed from early on during the planning phase of the project, so that the new mine can ease itself into the market.

(B) MARKET PRACTICE AND RELATIONS BETWEEN SUPPLIERS AND CUSTOMERS

Market practice and the mutual trust between major industry players are often more important than the legally binding agreements between them. What underpins all of concentrate business is the fact that no major mining or smelting company is prepared to risk its position in the market by unreasonable behaviour. Long-standing business relations ensure that parties virtually always settle their differences in an amicable fashion.

This trusting approach is further strengthened by commercial managers who negotiate the contracts. As they are few in number, they tend to know their counterparts in other mining and smelting companies. This does not mean that the concentrate market is not fiercely competitive, but that the competition is confined to the clearly defined boundaries of established trade customs – a player can be as ruthless as possible within these boundaries but seldom breaks the rules because that jeopardizes the business relationship.

(C) PRICING OF BASE METAL CONCENTRATES

All concentrates are priced with reference to the metal price. The pricing formulae vary from metal to metal, but the underlying mechanism is always the same. The price for a delivery of concentrates is calculated by multiplying the assayed quantity of metal content delivered with a price that has been arrived at by subtracting agreed deductions from the metal price (LME or another commodity exchange) averaged over an agreed period of time.

As metal prices are quoted for refined metal delivered to a warehouse of the commodity exchange, the price for concentrates and intermediary products is calculated by deducting items that reflect the various steps of the smelting and refinery process. It is also necessary to allow for variations in the chemical composition, substances that complicate the processing and side products recovered in processing.

(i) Physical aspects: establishing weight and metal content

The first step in pricing is to establish the weight and metal content in the concentrates. Concentrates are measured by the weight of metal content, not by reference to the weight of the concentrate itself. The quantity of supply is normally expressed as an annual tonnage, although occasionally at times of undersupply, a new mine may be able to conclude agreements based on the supply of a given percentage of its annual production.

Each delivery of concentrates is weighed at dispatch and delivery, and each of the supplier and the buyer takes samples of the material. Every sample is divided into three portions, one for the seller, one for the buyer and the third reserved for an independent umpire. Both the seller and the buyer obtain laboratory analyses of the chemical composition of their samples. Should the results vary, a third laboratory will be appointed to act as umpire.

(ii) Metal price: reference quotation, quotational period, averaging

Commodity exchanges quote metals daily. The price of a delivery of concentrate (whether under a long-term contract or spot) is calculated for a specified metals price on a given day or averaged over a period of time. Most widely traded metals like copper and gold are quoted on several commodity exchanges so the buyer and the seller need to agree which reference price is used.

The prices are usually averaged over a period of time, which acts as an in-built hedge mechanism against metal price fluctuation. When the metal prices used in determining the price of a concentrate delivery are averaged over a period of time (quotation period), this evens out some of the price peaks and lows. The longer the quotation period is, the more hedging effect it has. In practice, most concentrate contracts apply a quotation period of one to two months. For example, the metal price may be averaged over the two first full months after the date when the concentrates arrived in the port of destination.

(iii) Deductions and additions based on the characteristics of the concentrate

Many concentrates contain other metals in quantities that can be extracted in the refinery process and sold as by-products. For example, zinc ore often contains also lead and copper as well as smaller quantities of tin, silver, gold, cadmium, bismuth, antimony, indium, mercury and germanium. These metals need to be removed in the processing and if the quantities are sufficient, the processor may sell them to the market. Significant quantities of by-product metals are usually priced separately by reference to a calculation similar to that applied to the main metal.

On the other hand, the concentrates may also contain substances that complicate the processing. For example, copper concentrates often contain arsenic, chlorine and fluorine as well as antimony, bismuth, lead, zinc, mercury, nickel and cobalt. The impact of these substances is taken into account as penalties deducted from the concentrate price. The penalties are usually calculated as monetary amounts per dry metric ton.

A mine owner can use insurance in situations where the harmful substances cannot be covered by the penalty element. Technical risk insurance can be used to secure the future cash flow of the mine against the risk that the chemical composition of the ore results in concentrates with such high content of harmful elements that no customer can process them in a commercially viable way.

Metal deduction (also called free metal) is based on a trade custom specific to zinc. The free metal component reflects the historic rates of loss decades ago, that far exceed the actual rate of loss of metal in the modern production process. Almost entirely detached from its original justification, free metal now exists purely to reflect the competitive balance between supply and demand of mining and smelting capacity in zinc.

(iv) Deductions and additions based on market dynamics

The final and perhaps most important pricing elements are treatment and refining charges. Technically, these deductions are designed to reflect the cost of recovering the metal from the concentrate:

- *Treatment charge* – Discount that reflects the value added by smelting or otherwise processing the concentrate into unrefined metal.
- *Refining charge* – Additional discount for metals that require a secondary processing (such as copper that is first processed in a smelter and then further refined through electrolytic processing).

In practice, these charges are detached furthest from the actual cost of production. They are determined entirely by the supply and demand on the concentrates market – when concentrates are in short supply, treatment and refining charges fall, and at times of over-supply they go up. They reflect not only metal price (and thus the supply and demand of the underlying metal) but also the supply and demand in mining and smelter/ refinery capacity. Additional capacity on either is likely to impact treatment and refining charges.

Treatment and refining charges are often bound to the metal price through an escalator/de-escalator, which automatically adjusts the charges when metal prices change. This mechanism allows smelters to get a slice of the mines' profits at times of exceptionally high metal prices but works in reverse at times of low prices.

(D) CONTROLLING THE METAL PRICE RISK

The metal price risk can be hedged with futures contracts traded at LME and other commodity exchanges.

Base metal producers traditionally hedge a major part of their price risk. The smelting industry traditionally considers metal price an item that is passed through to the customers further down the production chain, and smelting industries tend to focus on the gross margin excluding the metal value.

Gross margin is an accurate method for valuing tolling contracts, because the toll operator assumes no risk on metal prices. In all other parts of the concentrate business, the metal price is an integral part of the business: when the prices go up, so do the profits of the mines and smelters. Conversely, the more prices drop, the more they are bound to lose on the metal value, unless the price risk is covered by hedging on the London Metal Exchange (LME) or another commodity exchange.

The precious metals industry looks at metal prices from a completely different angle. For example, gold is almost a pure investment product with virtually no industrial use beyond jewellery production. Producers hedge gold price only for speculative purposes: they fix the price of their production when they believe the gold price has reached its peak. Sometimes this gamble pays off, sometimes it does not.

Long-term contracts focus on operational and financial stability instead of fast profits. In a business environment where short-term profits do matter, long-term contracts can be seen as an impediment against taking full benefit from undersupply and ensuing high metal prices. This has resulted in some changes in concentrate markets: quotation periods have got shorter, and the renegotiation of commercial terms has become more frequent – key terms are now increasingly revised every six months instead of the traditional annual re-negotiation. So whilst the mechanism continues untouched, the long-term market now follows spot market movements more closely than before.

There is also an increasing tendency for stock markets to look at mining and smelting companies not as industrial investments but as investments in the metal they produce.

According to this school of thought, an investor buying shares in a copper mine is actually taking an investment position in copper, and speculating on how copper prices will develop in the future. Such an investor would not look favourably on any arrangements that dilute the impact of the copper price and hence on the value of his investment.

Conclusions

Many mining projects are capital intensive, vulnerable to country and political risk and have a long pay-back time. The perennial dream of the exploration business is to strike gold (literally or metaphorically) and develop a non-integrated, stand-alone mining operation. In reality this not easy to achieve in a closely-knit industry where the major players tend to be integrated. It is not surprising that most exploration projects are sold to major mining companies who eventually develop them as a part of their bigger business.

Any lender considering financing a mining project should understand the risks involved, and carefully evaluate the commercial plans and projections of the project. Also, lenders should pay attention to whether the project company has sufficient industry-specific commercial expertise to realize the project's revenue projections. Lenders should carefully review the metal price assumptions used in such projections, and ensure that project revenue is sufficient to service the loans even when metal prices drop.

It may be prudent for the lenders to require that a new mine hedges all or substantially all of its metal price risk until the financing has been repaid. This may reduce the mine owner's profits, but it helps to secure the cash flow during the critical initial years of production.

Increased investor interest in commodities is changing the metal markets. Just five years ago the metal markets were still primarily serving the needs of the industry. Now the metal prices are much affected by investor sentiment and demand from financial investors. Industry experts believe this has contributed to the current protracted period of high metal prices, keeping the metal prices at levels that supply and demand cannot justify. As a result, metal prices are even more difficult to predict than before, and this makes the hedging of metal prices risk even more essential for the lenders.

19 *The Evolving Market and Models for PPPs in Europe*

JAMES NEAL
Global Head of Project Finance at Ernst & Young

Introduction

The PFI model which developed primarily in the UK and Portuguese markets in the 1990s has evolved into the broader public private partnership (PPP) models which we now see today. The countries which had steady and consistent private finance initiative (PFI) programmes, such as the UK, attempted to standardize the approach and documentation in order to improve efficiency. However, through a mixture of economic pressure and political change, combined with changing financial markets and regional prioritization, we are now seeing some fundamental changes to the way PPP is approached. These range from trying to attract non-traditional sources of funding to trying to create models that can be flexible to future change. These issues are discussed in this chapter.

Rationale for PPP

The main drivers for the PPP model have been typically centred on improving value for money and enabling public infrastructure projects to be funded where there are funding constraints in the public sector. There has been a strong track record of delivering projects on time and to budget, reinforcing the belief that PPP is a more efficient delivery model than traditional public sector procurement. Indeed, the UK has signed in excess of 700 PFI projects over the last 12 years with only a very small number failing. Despite this, PPP is coming under increasing scrutiny and challenge in the UK whilst at the same time it is gathering pace elsewhere in the world. The UK challenge is an interesting one and is likely to lead to the emergence of new models, which could well influence how PPPs are carried out in other parts of the world.

Evolving PPP Models

Traditionally, PPP programmes tend to focus on infrastructure that has the greatest economic benefit and the least political resistance. This is why transport schemes tend to feature heavily (for example the experience in Portugal, Spain, France, UK and USA) and are then followed by social infrastructure such as schools, hospitals and other public accommodation type projects. Once the major projects have been done then the focus is on the delivery of programmes of schools or hospitals or whatever. This is when PPP becomes harder since flexibility needs to be built in and this brings the challenge of meeting the value for money tests.

In the UK the complex models for Local Improvement Finance Trusts (LIFTS) for healthcare and Local Education Partnerships (LEP) for education were developed to try and achieve this flexibility. These models use centralized tendering for a programme of investments with incentive based payments under a strategic partnering agreement between the private and public sector parties. The LIFT model has certainly been very successful in delivering projects over the last 10 years involving 87 Primary Care Trusts and 78 local authorities. The 47 LIFT companies have generated over £1.5bn of investment to develop more than 225 integrated community facilities.

The LEP structure used in the Building Schools for the Future programme is a 10-year strategic partnership between a local authority, private sector company and Building Schools for the Future Investments (BSFI), the funding arm of the BSF programme.

The LEP and LIFT models have however been open to criticism since there is a potential conflict of interest between the private sector partner as both manager of the programme and potential implementer of the work. The UK Government has effectively now dropped the BSF programme in favour of developing a new approach.

LABV Model

More recently another variant has emerged and that is the Local Asset Based Vehicle (LABV). Under this joint venture, the public sector contributes land and/or property assets with the private sector partner acting as developer and manager of those property assets, with the profits being shared. This of course works best during a buoyant economy. A typical structure would be a 15-year joint venture partnership where the LABV is set up as a 50:50 corporate entity between the public sector body and the private sector partner.

In order to be successful, LABV schemes need to make commercial sense. They need to be affordable and realistic and need to be able to generate surpluses that will adequately reward the partners. Being less complex than PFI these schemes can be delivered more rapidly.

There have been a steady number of such LABV schemes over the last few years and the model is continuing to develop in terms of flexibility and markets. It is now being used and considered in the healthcare, education, regeneration, extra care and energy sectors. It is a natural development of the more rigid PFI structures, providing a more balanced partnership approach. In essence this is about risk sharing rather than risk transfer. One great advantage is that commercial deals can be structured on a tailored basis rather than being locked into a rigid standard model such as in the traditional PFI model.

NPDO Model

In Scotland, a particular PPP model has developed to deal with specific Scottish political requirements and that is the Non-Profit Distributing Organization (NPDO). This is like a traditional PFI except that there is minimal equity which is owned by a charitable trust. In effect, the performance risk is passed back to the lenders and is not carried by equity investors. This model evolved for a schools project but is now being used more widely, for example in the education sector. The NDPO structure provides an alternative to traditional PFI structures for public sector bodies seeking a greater level of stakeholder involvement in project operations. The fact that private sector upside returns are capped is politically attractive. This type of structure works especially well where downside risks are well understood and can be effectively allocated.

The NPDO model is structured in such a way that there are in effect no shareholders in the project company, only senior and junior debt providers. Any surplus profits generated by the project company are given to a specially created charity rather than distributed to shareholders. Junior debt providers earn a capped coupon and hold seats on the NPDO board along with an independent director and a stakeholder director appointed by the charity.

The contractual arrangements are illustrated in Figure 19.1.

Table 19.1 sets out the areas in which the NPDO model differs from a traditional equity-based PPP:

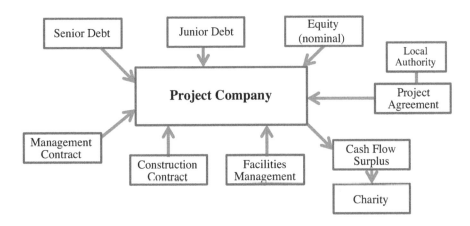

Figure 19.1 NPDO contractual model

Table 19.1 Differentiating the NPDO model from a traditional equity-based PPP

Topic	Traditional PPP	NPDO
Finance	Provided by senior debt and equity or shareholder loans.	Provided by senior debt and fixed rate junior debt. There is a nominal amount of equity owned by the junior lenders with no rights to dividends or other distributions.

Topic	Traditional PPP	NPDO
Profits	Profits, including those generated by efficiencies or windfalls, are taken by the equity shareholders.	Junior debt with a fixed return provides the risk-bearing element of the funding in its entirety. Profits after paying the required capped junior loan return are passed down through the NPDO to the charity. However, there is an effect on unitary charge payments since lenders require a 'tail' of extra cash flow in the last few years of the project to absorb risk exposure and to allow 'lost' coupon to be recovered where possible. The lack of equity shareholders might suggest there is no impetus for the SPV to generate surpluses due to the lack of shareholder pressure. However, it is in the lenders' interest for surpluses to be generated in order to improve their security.
Compensation on termination	Needs to provide for repayment of shareholders' equity.	Needs to provide for repayment of subordinated debt.
Refinancing gains	Only available on senior debt.	Available on both senior and junior debt. There is greater scope for refinancing junior debt after the construction period (when most project risk is present) has been completed.
Governance	The equity interest acts as a control over directors to ensure the SPV operates efficiently so that distributions can be made from any profits in the SPV.	The NPDO board will have directors appointed by the junior lender as well as an independent director and a stakeholder director appointed by the charity. The SPV Articles of Association prevent the lender directors voting on areas of potential conflict such as where lenders might wish to use surplus cash to improve their security position rather than distribute legitimate surpluses to the charity.

RAB Model

The Regulated Asset Base (RAB) model has been used effectively to govern investment in utilities (electricity, gas and water) and in the railway sector and is now being examined as a potential model for PPP infrastructure. In essence it tries to deal with delivery performance, risk transfer and cost of capital. Under the RAB model, investor returns are regulated by an independent regulator and the cost of investment is funded by the consumer over an extended period of time. The price review would typically take place every five years and would consider the value of the asset base, the cost of capital and the return to investors with a focus on preserving the value of the assets. To adapt this for the PPP market, the management and procurement of the assets, or portfolio of assets, passes to the private sector which is paid for its services through a user charging system regulated by an independent arbiter to ensure efficient delivery and control of investor returns. So, unlike the traditional PPP model, procurement will be managed by the owner of the asset but returns will be regulated. It will be complex to adopt this model more broadly for PPP, particularly given the issues that accrued on the London Underground PPP where a similar structure was put in place. That said, toll roads in Italy are now being structured where the traffic risk is taken by the concessionaire but in certain circumstances the concession holder can request a tariff adjustment based on the level of traffic. The RAB-type formula allows mitigation of the risk of uncertain traffic volumes and effectively balances out road performance from one road concession to another across a portfolio. A key feature is that there is in effect a profit cap.

HUB Model

Scotland's PPP model is centred around a Hub approach, under which public sector organizations and trusts in the same geographic areas form joint ventures to deliver projects. Whilst this is quite similar to the LIFT model it differs in that the local authorities are equal shareholders in the joint vehicle. The Hub model is planned to be used on £1bn of community infrastructure over the next decade. A Hubco consists of the local authority shareholders and a private sector development partner. Depending on project circumstances, the projects will be implemented either as design and build using public capital, or as concession agreements using project finance, with the public and private shareholders sharing the financial returns. The type of social infrastructure covered by this arrangement will include: education services, social care, social housing, special needs housing, residential and library services. Each Hubco is expected to take a strategic, long-term planning approach to the development of community infrastructure and services.

OFTO Model

An interesting development of the PPP model has been the structure which has evolved for the issuing of licences for the ownership and management of the transmission assets constructed by the developers of various offshore UK wind generation projects. The first round of tenders involved nine projects with a total value of approximately £1.1bn. In return for purchasing the transmission assets from the offshore wind generator and operating them in accordance with the requirements of the offshore transmission licence, the successful bidder receives a 20-year regulated revenue stream. The Offshore Transmission Owner (OFTO) will own and manage the transmission assets between the offshore point of connection with the generator and the point of connection with the onshore network. The revenue stream is RPI linked and calculated on the required return on investment on the transfer value and the on-going cost of financing, operating and managing the asset. During the licence period there is no automatic periodic price review and the revenue stream is not dependent on utilization but rather on availability. The revenue stream may be adjusted during the operation phase due to performance incentives and penalties, any increase in transmission line capacity and a pass through of certain predictable but uncertain costs such as decommissioning and lease costs. The outline contractual structure is set out in Figure 19.2.

So, apart from the traditional model, there are quite a number of variants. In looking forwards at the models that will be used in the future, these are going to be increasingly

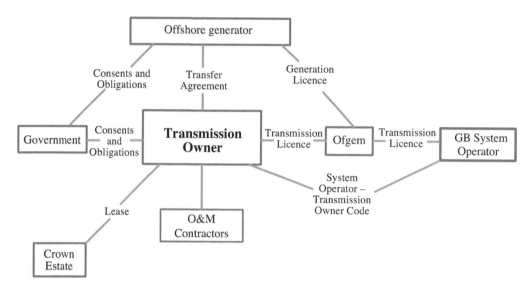

Figure 19.2 OFTO contractual model

influenced by the constraints and requirements of the funders and the level of risk they are prepared to take.

A key issue in developing PPP models in the current market with more restricted funding available is to match the needs of prospective funders to the risk profile of projects. The higher risk construction component is, for example, difficult for many funders such as multilateral agencies or pension funds to fund without third-party guarantees, whereas the deemed lower risked post construction period is likely to attract a broader range of funders. In France this has been addressed recently by the French Government guaranteeing the funding during construction, with the guarantee falling away post construction. This type of pragmatic approach to assisting in stimulating the market is one that other countries might heed.

Sources of Funding

Historically PFI and PPP projects have relied on banks and monoline insurers to take the construction period risk. This worked well whilst there was plenty of liquidity but has now clearly changed with the demise of the monoline insurers and fewer banks prepared to take the project risk or provide long term finance. As a result, there is a strong need to open up the market to multilateral financial institutions, pension funds and insurers, amongst others.

The European Investment Bank (EIB) is an important source of funding. Over the last 20 years EIB has broadened its geographic and sectoral spread of its PPP lending, making it one of Europe's foremost funders of PPP with a portfolio of over 120 projects and investment in excess of €25bn. EIB has a number of facilities relevant to the PPP market. These include:

- The loan Guarantee Investment for Trans European Network (TEN) transport projects, taking traffic revenue ramp-up risk in the early years of TEN's projects. This provides up to 20 per cent of senior debt in the form of mezzanine debt.
- Investment in equity funds which in turn take equity participations in infrastructure investments. These include the Marguerite Fund which is targeted at the transport and renewable energy sectors.

JESSICA

JESSICA (Joint European Support for Sustainable Investment in City Areas) is an initiative developed by the European Commission to contribute to making the EU Cohesion Policy more efficient and sustainable. The JESSICA mechanism is based on cooperation established between the Commission, the EIB and the Council of Europe Development Bank and supports investment in sustainable urban development and regeneration. This includes housing projects and the renovation of urban infrastructure.

This initiative, designed to increase the use of financial engineering instruments, allows EU member states to use some of their European Structural Funds allocations to invest in revolving funds rather than once-off grant financing. By doing so they can recycle financial resources in order to enhance and accelerate investment in urban areas. These investments, which may take the form of equity, loans and/or guarantees, are delivered to projects via Urban Development Funds and, if required, holding funds.

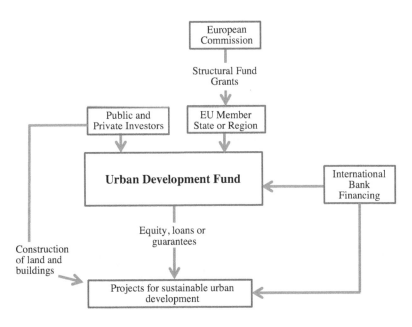

Figure 19.3 JESSICA contractual model

TIF

Tax Incremental Finance (TIF) is a relatively new concept for funding infrastructure in the UK although it has been used effectively in the USA to fund community and redevelopment programmes. It is a means of funding public sector infrastructure which can unlock regeneration which may be unaffordable to local authorities. It uses future additional revenue gains from taxes to finance borrowing to fund improvements that will create those gains. In the UK, TIF allows local authorities to raise finance from the Public Works Loan Board to fund the up-front infrastructure works with the private sector partner providing the finance to fund the subsequent commercial development. The local authority debt is then repaid from the uplift in business rates from the resulting development. So, for example, improving transport infrastructure would enable the development of an industrial park, the resulting investment generating increased tax revenue.

Whilst TIF is a useful approach for the regeneration sector it is not without its risks. The local authority becomes the prime risk taker in the early stages of development and any external funder is reliant on the market and on the future tax uplift. It is also more appropriate for economic infrastructure rather than social infrastructure such as schools or housing.

In order to gain access to the volumes of finance required and to meet the long-term funding that PPP project demand, a way needs to be found to unlock funding from the pension fund and insurance markets. These markets have been constrained by a combination of the lack of appetite for construction risks and a lack of people resource to deal with the transactions. Once a way is found to deal with these two issues then it should be possible to unlock large amounts of financing.

One way to achieve this is the incorporation of a mezzanine debt tranche which should have the effect of enhancing the overall risk profile of the transaction. Hadrian's Wall Capital is an example of a private fund set up specifically to deal with this. It has agreed a strategic partnership with Aviva and EIB which will enable it to provide enhancement to the senior debt.

The increased use of junior debt should also have the benefit of shifting the risk profile such that bond finance can be entertained. In the past, access to the bond markets has been dependent on the now defunct monoline insurers. PPP projects have traditionally been rated low – sub investment grade. However, if this can be moved well into the investment grade category (e.g., A–) then large amounts of debt funding should become available.

FCT

Some interesting work is currently being explored in France to try and unlock broader institutional investment. The proposal is to create a securitization vehicle (*fonds commun de titrisation* or FCT) which is dedicated to PPPs in France. This is designed to encourage investment by both French and foreign institutional investors, such as pension funds and insurers, who would invest by subscribing to bonds issued by the FCT. The FCT itself would be divided into segments, each of which would be dedicated to a specific PPP transaction. Structurally, the FCT would be acquiring project receivables which approximate to sovereign or quasi sovereign debt. FCT will cover up to 80 per cent of the debt of PPPs and will transfer some of the PPP risk away from private developers.

In Spain this is being tackled in a slightly different way. The state owned credit agency Instituto Credito Oficial (ICO) has launched an infrastructure fund, FES Infraestructuras, to invest stakes of 10–49 per cent in PPP concessions as well as offer subordinated debt. Minimum amounts per project will be €10m and maximum €100m. This should act as a catalyst to attract senior lenders by changing the projects' risk profiles. Also, countries such as Russia are recognizing the need for stronger Government support for major projects and this is now being evidenced by the provision of grant funding. Indeed, Russia has recently announced the formation of a closed direct investment fund designed to co-invest in development projects with the private sector. It will be capitalized at around $10bn funded by the federal budget.

In the UK the Government has announced the formation of a Green Investment Bank (GIB) with some £3bn of government funding. The GIB is due to become operational in 2012 and will focus on leveraging private sector investment in 'green' projects.

In the medium term, funding for partnership projects is going to need a pro-active role from Governments in supporting funding, an increase in the use of multilateral funding, more involvement of the natural long term investors such as the pension funds and insurers, and a shifting of the risk profile to allow increased use of the bond markets.

The Way Forwards

It is clear that there is no single 'one-size-fits-all' model but rather that any model needs to be tailor made to the political and economic environment in which it sits. The key requirements of successful future models will be: the need to build in flexibility; the need to encompass a procurement process that is streamlined; and the need to be realistic about the transfer of risk in order to meet the requirements of the funding markets. This is bound to result in interesting changes for the better in how partnership programmes are put together and delivered.

20 *Emerging Markets Project Finance*

KATHARINE BARAGONA

Senior infrastructure specialist, World Bank Financial Solutions Group

Emerging markets[1] are countries in transition; moving from a closed economy to an open market economy. They are generally in the process of implementing reforms and legislation designed to attract foreign investment. Often, an emerging market economy is one that was previously centrally planned, typically with a long-standing one-party political and socioeconomic system. An emerging market economy may also be one that is emerging from poverty or economic sanctions. Such countries account for approximately 80 per cent of the global population, and represent about 20 per cent of the world's economics.[2] Countries that fall into the emerging market category vary in size but are usually considered emerging because of their developments and reforms.

Emerging markets tend to be more volatile than established markets. The potential rewards of a successful project financing in an emerging market are considerable. Emerging markets have high potential as well as high risk.

To bridge the gap between available public funds and the growing need for new infrastructure and energy assets, governments in emerging markets are increasingly turning to private sector financing. In developing countries, project finance is commonly used as a vehicle for private participation. This chapter looks at some of the challenges facing project financings in emerging markets where, given the current economic and financial environment, governments face significant challenges to finance projects. It also highlights some of the actions governments can take to ease investor reticence and attract project financing.

Project Financing

As a financing method, project financing is costly to implement and the financial structures used to establish the necessary contractual relationships are complicated. Using project finance to develop projects is only justifiable for large-scale projects, such as major infrastructure or energy facilities and is best suited for long-term, tangible, revenue

---

1   The term 'emerging market' was coined in 1981 by Antoine W. Van Agtmael of the International Finance Corporation of the World Bank.

2   World Bank Market Data, 2010.

producing assets whose development cycle can be separated into a construction phase (including start-up and testing) and operating phase.

Project financing is structured on a non-recourse or limited recourse basis, where all of a project's debt and equity are paid from the project's cash-flows, allowing the projects to be highly leveraged. To secure financing, project sponsors pledge the project's assets and revenue-producing contracts to the project's financial creditors. In exchange, the creditors agree to look to the project's cash-flows and assets, rather than the sponsors and their balance sheets. As part of their security package, lenders receive liens on all project assets, and have the right to assume control of the project if the special purpose project company fails to comply with the project's loan terms.

Unlike a corporate financing, the purpose of a project financing is to complete development of specific assets that make up the project. Therefore, although the investment term is long (20+ years) it has a limited life-span.

The kinds of assets that are best suited to project finance are large-scale infrastructure, energy, and transportation. Until recently, assets of this type were most often developed by governments as public sector projects, using public funds. Going forwards, development of these high-risk, high up-front expense projects, will challenge governments to source financing through other means, whether as an alternative to, or in conjunction with, public funds. It is against this backdrop that project financing has grown steadily in emerging markets.

Parties to a Project Financing

Project financing brings together a cast of characters with distinct roles. These parties work together shepherding the project through its preparation phase (culminating in financial close), its physical construction and finally, the management and operation of its commercial operations. A special-purpose project company is usually established as the vehicle to bring all these contractual relationships together.

The process is often described as a marriage, and the project as the offspring of the union. These references allude to and illustrate the challenges and achievements associated with project development but also warn of the folly of entering into project financing with thoughts of quick or easy money. The process is long and arduous and not for the easily dissuaded or dismayed.

Key participants in a project financing are:

- *Project sponsors*, who provide equity to the project. The project sponsors will often include a lead sponsor with experience in the particular area of project focus. Lenders and the government take comfort if there is a high correlation between the lead sponsors' core area of expertise and the project focus, attributing a higher chance of success where there is a high degree of relevance. In emerging markets, lenders and the government will also want to see that the engineering, procurement and construction (EPC) contractor is a member of the project sponsor team with an equity stake in the project, often referred to as having 'skin in the game'. The idea that the EPC contractor has money at risk, in addition to fees earned on the project EPC works, gives parties comfort that the contractor will work more diligently to secure its own equity returns from the project.

- *Third party contractors*
    - The EPC contractor who accepts responsibility for delivering a fully operational facility on a date-certain, fixed-price basis;
    - The Operation and Maintenance (O&M) operator, who will operate and maintain the project assets upon completion of construction and the entering into commercial operation. The operator may or may not also be a member of the project sponsor group, but is always a party with particular expertise operating and maintaining assets similar to the project.
- *Lenders* to the project – Lenders want to ensure that the risks allocated to the project company, to which they are lending, are in turn passed on as much as possible to the various subcontractors who will build and operate the project facility. The lenders therefore have a strong interest in the financial strength and technical capability of the subcontractors, in addition to the terms of the project contracts. The availability of banks willing and able to provide project financing and the availability of strong and capable contractors go hand in hand. There may also be a direct contractual relationship between the public sector and the lenders, such as a mechanism to govern the project if the lenders need to 'step into' the shoes of the project company in the event that the contractors do not perform and alternative contractor arrangements are required.
- *The off-taker*, usually a governmental entity such as a utility, that will provide the cash revenues upon which the project financing is based. The primary issue in respect of the off-taker will be its creditworthiness. Lenders want assurances that the cash-flow they look to for repayment of their loans will be readily available in full and on time. In emerging markets, where market structures are new or in transition, external credit support will often be required to underpin the creditworthiness of the off-taker and mitigate the risk of non-payment.
- *The end-users* – often thought to be government, but in actuality the ultimate beneficiaries of the project are the tax payers or as in the case of tolls roads, the actual users of the completed asset.
- The relevant market regulator or governmental entity providing market oversight. Regulation can occur by contract, by law or by appointment of an industry regulator. Typically, the more developed a market, the more likely it will have an experienced system of regulatory oversight. In emerging markets, the regulatory process is usually in its infancy. Even if a regulatory system has been designed, its body of experience will be limited and there will be greater emphasis on the contractual arrangements between the parties.
- *Donor organizations*. In emerging markets, it can become particularly confusing when the same parties play multiple roles and the web of interrelationships amongst the parties is not readily transparent. In such situations it doesn't mean there is corruption per se, but it is the area where rent-seeking and political interference can most readily occur and easily operate.

Setting the Framework

Governments wanting to include private financing in their development plans will need to invest time and effort into laying the right foundations by establishing a clear policy rationale, a legal framework, an investment framework along with a well-organized operating framework. The upfront effort to establish a proper framework will ensure a much better private sector response when project procurements are launched.

Given the particular characteristics of emerging market developments, governments wanting to support project financing will need to make public sector resources available for the high upfront costs required for feasibility studies and project preparations. Investing resources, time and effort up front in laying the right foundations can have a positive impact on a project's ability to attract project financing. In countries where public sector processes and institutional capacity are weak, managing the complex project finance process, together with the risks of project development, is especially challenging.

Legal Framework

When considering a project finance investment, lenders will want to examine the legal framework where the project will operate and ensure the effectiveness of long-term contracts. In markets where infrastructure and public services have previously been developed using public funds, legislation may be needed to allow private participants to charge and collect user fees for formerly public sector activities or convert and expatriate hard currency. Specific laws may also be required to allow the public sector to contract with private bodies for the delivery of services previously provided by government.

Investors and lenders involved in project financing have a strong preference for certainty, detail, and clarity in the legislative and legal framework. They will want to know whether:

- The investor's rights at all stages of the project cycle but especially during operation and upon termination, are predictable, enforceable and well established;
- Repatriation of profits is allowed, and what restrictions, if any, will be placed on the use of expatriate personnel;
- The lenders' ability to take security over the contract or take over management of the asset when enforcing security and other rights are established and enforceable;
- Contract disputes can be resolved in a predictable and reliable manner, and what rights and obligations are required of either party if the project does not go according to plan;
- Sales or value-added taxes on construction costs or service payments will be taxed under the project;
- Government support is available for certain risks and in what form;
- The public sector will continue to be involved in the project and how that involvement will be defined;
- The process for tariff setting has been established and a transparent regulatory environment exists; and
- A framework for contractual changes exists and what compensation mechanisms are available.

Operating Framework

Whilst many governments understand the need for a strong legal and investment framework, investors also want assurances that the operating framework within government is capable of managing a project development process that involves private participation. They want to confirm that the project can be delivered under a project financing model.

Project Scope and Requirements

The need for a project's outputs may be obvious and the project itself may even be part of an existing higher-level development programme, with a decision to proceed having already been made at a policy level. Such decisions, however, do not necessarily mean that a project has been properly sized for financial and economical viability.

One of the fundamental causes of project failure in emerging markets is a lack of clarity regarding the exact scope and requirements of the project. Lack of clarity usually results in change later on. If the change happens during the project identification and procurement phase, then the level of private sector interest may be significantly reduced or procurement drawn out, causing higher costs and delays for all parties. If change takes place during the construction or operating phases, this too may lead to significantly higher costs. Clarity of scope is fundamental to successful project financing, particularly where the participation of private debt capital is sought. Project financing requires the long-term contractual relationships that make up the project and the outputs needed from the project be clearly established from the start.

Economic and Financial Viability

Economic viability looks at the level and structure of the project's overall revenue requirements in relation to the capacity of end-users, whether consumers or a public authority, to pay for the project's output. This requires a clear understanding of the expected operating and maintenance costs of the project, together with the levels of cash flow that will be required to repay the loans and provide a return to investors.

A project financial model is developed using the best estimates of capital, operating, and maintenance costs, appropriate cost escalation indexes, and assumed financing structure and terms. The financial model projects cash flows over the term of the proposed project contracts. At the early stages of project development, the financial model is developed at a high level. As the project progresses, increasing levels of detail are included.

Once the project's expected revenue requirements have been established, the capacity and willingness of end-users to pay for the project outputs needs to be examined. For an electricity generation project, this may require significant reform to existing tariff levels. The risks of such reform may be unacceptable to private investors, or the private party may be prepared to assume such risks but will add the cost of the risk to project costs, further affecting the level of tariff required. If private participants are unwilling to accept the risk, governmental guarantees or up-front payments may be required.

For availability-based projects, where a public authority, not the end-user, makes payments under a long-term power purchase agreement (PPA), assessing affordability is one of the most important aspects when considering deliverability of a project. Long-term payment obligations present significant challenges to newly formed state owned entities (SOEs), which in turn affect both the scope and level of services in the project design. In markets where tariffs have traditionally been subsidized by government, a realistic assessment of the true costs of a subsidy often reveals that either a higher level of government support or significant tariff reform is needed. Both of these issues imply significant risk for project financing.

Project lenders want to participate in projects where the source and level of revenue covering the project's costs are clear and predictable. Projects that lack necessary preparation, where the project sponsors have not invested the required technical and financial resources into project development, are inherently more risky and less predictable. Therefore, they will be considered unattractive to both lenders.

Risk Analysis and Allocation

In addition to understanding the revenue sources supporting a project's economic viability, an investor considering a project financing in an emerging market needs a clear picture of the political and market risks associated with the project. In project financing, risks are allocated and apportioned across the spectrum of project participants – sponsors, lenders, third-party contractors, state-owned enterprises, and the government as end user – on the basis of who is best positioned to manage them efficiently.

- *Risk analysis.* Early in the project process, the participants need to identify the risks relevant to the project and group them according to the various phases of the project (e.g., pre-project preparation, construction, and operation).
- *Risk allocation.* The goal is to allocate each risk to the party best able to control its occurrence and consequences as well as to the party in the best position to assess information about the likelihood of the risk within the context of what is likely to be commercially acceptable. Sharing responsibility for the consequences of each risk is fundamental to project financing. Ultimately, there are only three parties to whom the risks can be allocated: investors (the private sector), end-users or rate payers and tax payers (through the government).

  Risks associated with design, technology, construction, and commercial operations are typically allocated to the private sector (either the project sponsors, the EPC contractor or project subcontractors), that is usually more efficient at controlling and managing them. Other risks may be better managed by the public sector, such as project availability and project siting, regulatory, environmental, and foreign exchange risks, or may be shared, such as demand or change-of-law risks.
- *Risk mitigation.* It is important to reduce the likelihood of risks and their consequences for the risk taker. A change in project scope or the inclusion of government support and guarantees can sometimes reduce risk or favourably change the risk profile. Risk does not disappear through contractual structuring or reallocations amongst the parties; it is simply mitigated.

Political Risk

In emerging markets, the private sector is particularly concerned about political risks that arise from the potential impact of governmental, legislative, judicial and political acts. It is difficult to avoid some overlap with other types of risks since political influence can be so pervasive, particularly in emerging markets where institutions and policies may be evolving.

The following types of political risks are most worrisome to investors:

- *Convertibility and transferability* – Monetary regulation can limit the extent to which local currency (capital, interest, principal, profits, royalties, or other monetary benefits) can be converted to foreign currency and to which local and foreign currency can be transferred out of the country. These restrictions cause significant problems for foreign investors and lenders who will want to have access to distributions and debt service in foreign currencies and to service their debt abroad.
- *Devaluation* – Certain countries govern conversion of the local currency into foreign currency by legally or administratively fixing the rate or terms of exchange.
- *Expropriation, confiscation and nationalization* – If a government decides that assets currently owned by or under management of the private sector would be better managed by the public sector it can nationalize those assets through confiscation or expropriation. Most countries have the right to expropriate any asset located in their jurisdictions, subject to restrictions and processes. Most countries (and international law) require the government pay compensation for the seized assets, but issues arise as to what constitutes fair compensation and how long it takes for payments to be made.
- *Political violence (including war and civil disturbance)* – Political decisions may result in destruction, disappearance, or physical damage to assets caused by politically motivated acts, whether by formal declarations of war or acts of civil disobedience.
- *Failure to provide (or revocation of) licences, approvals and consents* – Investments in infrastructure require a number of permissions from political entities from different levels of government, involving often heavily decentralized decision processes.
- *Regulatory decisions* – Risks arise in relation to the discretion granted to regulators (often subject to political influence) over issues key to the investment, in particular pricing (such as tariffs or tolls), standards of performance and who is entitled to receive services. Currency risk is a regulatory risk, which is normally treated separately by guarantees.
- *Change in law or tax* – Legislative powers may be used to change laws or pass new laws inconsistent with the arrangements the investor is relying on for his return on investment. Changes in law or tax may also result in gradual deterioration of a project's sustainability, a form of loss referred to as 'creeping expropriation.'
- *Governmental contract breaches* – Risks that arise in relation to the non-payment of amounts due under contract, including fees for services, tariff shortfall compensation, damages, penalties, termination amounts, subsidies, and compensation for change in law or failure to provide licences, approvals or permits, as well as frustration of contractual arbitration processes.

Market Risk

There are also risks related to market influences that create uncertainties around the financial fundamentals of the project. These risks are not necessarily under the direct control of any of the participants and therefore are often the most difficult to manage in emerging market projects.

- *Foreign exchange rate* – Where the local currency floats freely against other currencies, the currency markets define the relative value of the local currency. Foreign exchange rate risk arises where the local currency's value decreases relative to the currency of investment or debt, which then increases the cost of debt in local currency and decreases the return on investment in the currency of investment.
- *Resource availability* – Project profitability will rely on the availability of project resources. Resource availability risk is tied to the availability and quality of project resources relied upon when developing the project development plan. If the character and quantity of project resources change in a way that affects the viability or sustainability of the project, it can be detrimental to the expected returns of the project.
- *Interest rate changes* – Projects financed with variable rate debt are subject to the risk that the interest rate charged (based on the market cost of money) will increase more than anticipated, increasing the cost of debt and reducing return on investment. Given the volatility of interest rates, most privately financed infrastructure projects seek fixed rate lending.
- *Access to financing* – Infrastructure requires large, long-term investments, usually 10 to 20 years. It is often difficult to access large amounts of long tenor debt in emerging markets. Project sponsors looking to finance infrastructure projects with debt bear the risk of the liquidity and depth of the local financial markets. Where the local financial markets are insufficiently liquid or deep, the project sponsor will borrow abroad, with the associated cost and currency mismatch risks.
- *Demand* – A variety of market influences affect demand for the output of the project, including demographic changes, competition and changing technology. Where demand falls, revenues may not reach anticipated levels and profits may suffer.
- *Default risk* – Underlying most risks are the lenders' concerns that the project, as borrower, will default on its repayment of debt. Default risk also takes into account the lenders' qualitative assessment of the borrower's credit risk, including perceptions of quality of management, market position of the borrower and the effectiveness of governance mechanisms.

Interface Risk

For projects relying on the purchase of its output by a utility, investors pay close attention to the terms of any purchase agreement and the reliability and creditworthiness of the interface party (often a state-owned entity). If the connecting infrastructure is not in place or needs to be built or rehabilitated, investors want to know how this will be addressed, which, in turn, raises questions about who is responsible, where the funding will come from, whether the required infrastructure will be available when needed by the project, and what conditions will attach in the event it is not.

Investors and lenders need to analyse all the risks of the immediate project as well as those of other projects on which the primary project is dependent for sales (that is, the external interface risks). It is for this reason that project sponsors in emerging markets will often design the project as an integrated whole. The private sector is often better than government at managing the risks of integrating such different components of a project.

Funding and Foreign Currency Risk

Projects without foreign currency revenue are likely to face significant constraints in a number of countries due to the limited availability of long-term local-currency finance.

Local capital markets in some emerging markets are developing rapidly, as evidenced by the increasing number of recent issues of local-currency financial instruments with terms of up to 15 years. Coupled with strong investor appetite for infrastructure investment, this suggests that long-term sources of local-currency funding may increasingly be a realistic source of funding for some well-structured projects in some emerging markets.

Bankability

The majority of third-party funding for project financings normally consists of long-term debt, which typically varies from 70 per cent to as much as 90 per cent of the total funding requirement, depending on the perceived risks of the project. Debt is a cheaper source of funding than equity, as it carries relatively less risk. Project financing looks to the cash flows of the project as the principal source of security, which is quite different from corporate financing where lenders rely on the value of the company's assets.

Project finance lenders will take a strong interest in the projected and actual performance of the project on which repayment of their loans depends. The involvement of lenders also plays a useful role in reviewing the financial viability – bankability – of the project on which their decision to lend will be based (a process known as due diligence) and in helping to ensure that the project is constructed and subsequently operated on time and on budget. In some markets and projects, the lenders may receive additional guarantees in light of the perceived risks. The availability of such guarantees in emerging markets must be considered carefully, as they transfer risk back to the public sector and may weaken the incentive of lenders to care about the performance of the project. Guarantees also create potential fiscal liabilities for the public sector that should be carefully considered before being made available.

The currency of the project's cash flow must match the currency of the debt service, or the risk of any mismatch must be credibly covered either through hedging or by government taking the risk. As these options are either difficult or very expensive to obtain for long-term debt in many emerging markets, one of the early considerations in assessing bankability is the availability of long-term funding that matches the currency of the project revenue.

The tenure of the debt also has an impact on the affordability of the project: longer-term debt implies lower annual capital repayments and therefore lower annual costs. A clear understanding of how potential lenders perceive the risks of the project is required from the very early stages of project preparation in order to establish the most likely available terms of funding, including its tenure and currency.

Apart from the debt, the balance of funding consists of equity, usually made available by the public authority, the project sponsor/developer, the main project contractors or by third-party financial investors. Equity plays a useful role in absorbing project risk and facilitating debt funding. Equity funding is needed because lenders require some cushion between the cash flow available from the project and the margin required to service the debt. The return on equity depends on the performance of the project after construction and operating costs. The return on equity is only received after the debt has been serviced, usually later in the life of the project, resulting in a higher level of risk that is compensated with higher returns.

Mitigating Risks

The allocation of risks does not cause them to go away. The best that can happen is that the risks are managed or mitigated. Risk mitigation instruments incorporated in the project's contractual and financial arrangements do not need to be unlimited and all-encompassing to provide the levels of comfort investors and lenders require. Commitments may be limited in scope (restricted to geological risk, labour and equipment productivity, operation and maintenance, market demand, or force majeure), amount (limited to a percentage of project debt or capital costs, contract price, or operating budget), and duration (applicable only during construction, performance testing, start-up, operation, or on failure to achieve certain milestone dates or operational or financial indicators).

During a project's construction phase, three primary types of instruments are used to mitigate risk:

- Contractual arrangements and associated guarantees;
- Lines of credit and contingency funds to cover unexpected cost increases or specific contingencies, and
- Insurance.

The emerging market instruments used to mitigate risks during the operating phase are:

- Contractual arrangements, such as take-or-pay, put-or-pay, and pass-through structures;
- Contingency reserves to cover debt service or extraordinary maintenance;
- Cash traps – where the cash-flow margins or debt service cash reserve account (DSCR – typically defined on a pre-tax basis as gross revenues minus operating expenses

divided by interest and principal payments) is insufficient to cover the margins lenders require;

- Insurance for property damage, loss of revenue from machinery breakdown and business interruption from property damage, and
- Third-party guarantees.

Role of Development Institutions, Regional Investors and Donors

In emerging markets, multilateral development agencies, (MDAs) can play an important role in the preparation of projects by acting as a sounding board for the project's structure and commercial viability as well as being an important source and catalyst of long-term funding.

MDAs can also provide early endorsement of a project, issuing indicative and conditional terms of finance that potential private sector partners may incorporate into their funding structures. Whilst such institutions usually provide only a proportion of the likely funding required, their participation can significantly improve the credibility of a project and provide greater assurance and comfort for the other providers of long-term finance, investors, and contractors, particularly with regard to perceived political risks. Some MDAs also have guarantee instruments that provide a degree of protection for private sector parties with regard to public sector payment and other political risks. Some MDA funding can also help to mitigate foreign exchange risks, by providing local-currency finance.

21 Forecasting Traffic on Infrastructure Schemes

CHARLES RUSSELL
Director, Steer Davies Gleave

First the disclaimers!

There may be textbooks (see Willumsen and Ortuzar, *Modelling Transport*, 2001 for the true guide), university courses, official guidelines – and practitioners, thousands of them world-wide – but traffic forecasting is not a precise science. The true relationships between an individual and his or her decision to drive a car down a particular route are truly so complex and depend on so many behavioural and contextual factors that they cannot be mapped or predicted with complete reliability.

Traffic forecasts must always depend on a very wide range of what we might call exogenous or external factors. How much traffic there will be on a particular road will depend on how the population grows and how the geographical distribution of employment grows; then it will depend on how the behaviour of that population changes – will people make more trips for longer distances; and then how will the travel opportunities evolve over time. For each of these factors – depending as they do on the national and local economy, planning decisions, public and private investment, etc. – a shared set of forecasts has to be developed.

These forecasts have to be prepared not just for the short or even medium term – but sometimes for what I have seen referred to as the deep future – often 30–40 years and sometimes as much as 70. Can anything truly be predicted over such a period?

However, relying on techniques and tools which have been well tested over a long time, and applying judgement based on good analysis and experience, we can produce useful – and hopefully reliable – forecasts. But we must all know what these forecasts are; their strengths and weaknesses, their reliability and what they can be used for. It must be then up to the investor to treat them with the respect but also the caution that they demand.

Forecasts Fit for Purpose

Because of these constraints it is unreasonable to expect that a portmanteau approach will provide the most helpful analysis. It is possible, of course, to prepare a forecasting system that will start from the beginning and work right through to the end – to cover every stage of the forecasting process, address all of the different aspects and cover as wide a geographical range as you like. We now have the computing power to model the world (even Dallas Fort Worth in Texas where they told me that they had the world's largest model ...), but the real power comes through focussing. Focussing on those decisions which are really important and really impact on the traffic and revenue of the scheme we are addressing. When we understand these, we can in turn understand more about how traffic might change in the future.

We can do this at the outset by understanding what those key questions actually are – and by then developing an approach which is properly attuned to understand those questions. Take for example the different requirements of greenfield and brownfield projects. For a greenfield project – be it road, rail or air – the first question will always be what would that facility be carrying today if it were in operation? What role would that infrastructure play – who would use it at what price, and then would the existence of that infrastructure change?

For a brownfield project, we already know the answer to that question. We know who is travelling on that facility now (or we should do as this is certainly the starting point). So the question then is how will that demand change into the future.

It would of course be possible to develop exactly the same approach for the second as the first question – to build the major network models which provide the first estimate of usage of the facility and then use these models to look at the future. And, of course, you could be confident that your model was doing a good job analysing what is happening today. But does that give us understanding of the change from now on – the true questions of the assignment. In our view not.

In our view, we should be developing different approaches which really help us to understand what might be happening as we move forwards.

The Context

Of course, part of this understanding of the project reflects an understanding of the context. Within our world, forecasts are not generally produced academically; we are not preparing forecasts for themselves. They are produced for investors and lenders who need to know how the outputs impact on them. Why do you care about traffic growth if you are taking no traffic risk? What are the triggers for expansion – and when will the project reach these triggers?

Part of the specifying of the modelling approach must depend on a proper analysis of the contract and of any special conditions it imposes in order that the forecasts serve a useful purpose.

And finally – but certainly importantly – the forecasters and their clients must share their understanding of the precision of the forecasts that are required. The forecaster cannot make the judgement of the investor on the risk they are prepared to take. We can only set out what we believe are the likely outcomes – and the envelope of uncertainty around them. We cannot properly follow the client in their demands for certainty – either the certainty of the central forecasts themselves or the ranges of certainty around them. The siren calls of formal risk analysis – of quantified distributions of uncertainty and confidence limits – have to be resisted.

The Different Approaches

In looking at traffic and revenue analysis, the investor will have come across two general approaches.

The four stage network model is the more formal of the two – relying on the same laborious and lengthy approach traditionally adopted across the transport planning industry. The spreadsheet model is the more simplified but focussed approach – probably developed across the last 20 years in the face of the often time and data constrained needs of the project finance industry.

Of course, nothing in this world is that simple – different approaches are adopted either combining elements from these two approaches or relying on different, usually statistical, tools – but familiarity with these two main approaches will provide the tools to understand most of the analysis presented to the lender and the investor.

The Four Stage (Network) Model

At the heart of traditional transport modelling is the four stage model. This encompasses four key steps – trip generation, trip distribution, mode choice and assignment. Whilst it will be very rare for this full formal approach to be adopted within the project finance sphere, its principles lie behind much of our analysis. Those working closely with the public sector in the USA – and relying on models developed there by the Metropolitan Planning Organizations – will already be familiar with this approach.

TRIP GENERATION, TRIP DISTRIBUTION AND MODE CHOICE

The first three stages concern the construction of the picture of the basic travel demand patterns across the zone of influence of our target infrastructure. This allows us to estimate how many trips of what sort will be generated in each zone, where are those trips going to and by what mode. This matrix (trip-table) will generally form the input to the toll road traffic and revenue modelling.

In summary, the first two stages of these models relate the numbers of trips generated in and attracted to each zone to a number of socio-economic and demographic factors (such as numbers of residents and jobs). Then they use a gravity model to establish the distribution of those trips (who is going where).

The third stage determines what mode each of those trip makers will take. In this analysis, the (generalized) cost of making those trips by each of the available modes (car, transit etc.) will be estimated – and the different trips then assigned to the modes in line with the relative costs.

Generally – in an analysis of a toll road either in an urban or an inter-urban context – these first stages will not be explicitly covered. Instead, we may be able to rely on earlier analysis of this nature to have prepared a matrix – which we will then update/validate with new revealed movement (OD) data collected for the project. Otherwise, if no such matrix exists, we will be required to build our own matrix from scratch – again with the collection of new data rather than reaching all the way back to the trip generation and attraction stage. This is not to sideline the role of the first stage, however, as this analysis might be relied on in preparing estimates of how traffic will grow into the future.

ASSIGNMENT

The final stage – and one that should be familiar to all those relying on traffic and revenue estimates – is determining what routes each of the trips might make in travelling between their origins and destinations. Traditionally this is done though the schematic representation of the actual road (and/or transit) network within a modelling package – describing each link in the network in terms of its length and its characteristics which allow a set of programmed algorithms to determine how long it will take to transit each link at different levels of traffic. Finally, relying on one of a number of methodologies, the model then estimates the times (generalized costs) of travel between each zone pair – and assigns traffic in an iterative manner to the cheapest route available.

These models have been developed to allow a complex analysis which can take into account simultaneously the behaviour of different classes of traffic (each with their own definition of cheapest) as well as considering the interrelations between the assignment of more or less traffic to each link and the performance of that link.

BUILDING THE MATRICES FROM TRAFFIC SURVEYS

As noted above, in most studies the matrices will be developed not (or not solely) from the matrix build described above – but also from new revealed data collected as part of the study. A quick detour therefore to discuss this data collection.

ROAD-SIDE INTERVIEWS

In order to collect full information about travel, the obvious approach is to stop travellers – and ask them questions about where they are travelling and why. However, the conduct of such surveys is always expensive and time consuming; on many occasions they are practically impossible.

New approaches are therefore being developed which rely on the new technologies associated either with video recognition of number plates or with the possible tracking of vehicles through GSM/GPRS or via bluetooth. However, it must be noted that at this time the full, and likely potent, potential of these techniques has not yet been fully realized.

TRAFFIC COUNTS

Traffic counts, on the other hand, are easy and relatively cheap to deliver – and can be of real value in traffic analysis. First, they provide up-to-date data on what is happening today – and, hopefully, allow analysis of how that has changed over the recent past. They also provide the measuring points against which the effectiveness of the models in predicting today's behaviour can be judged along with insight into the temporal variability of traffic, more and more important in these days of peak pricing and the early stages of dynamic tolling and demand management.

TRAFFIC TIME SURVEYS

Similarly, a key input into an analysis of the competition between roads will depend on the time taken to transit each of them. This will be an output from the network models – but again it is always valuable, and in our view highly recommended, to find out what is actually happening today, both to validate the models and provide a proper understanding of the situation, and the choices available to users.

BEHAVIOURAL ANALYSIS

The final area of new data collection relates to creating/updating an understanding of what people want in the trip making, how they (dis)value time of travel and delay and how much they are prepared to pay to avoid the costs of time and delay. This is a very complex area – and one which really deserves a far wider analysis which we discuss below.

The Spreadsheet Model

INTRODUCTION

As discussed, the formal network modelling approach described above requires very substantial data collection and analysis – and the building of models which describe the present situation which can then be used to predict the future. Much effort seems to focus on building the models – and introducing a wide range of analysis which in truth is at best only incidental to the questions we are exploring.

In the face of this, a new approach has been developed which seems to allow a simpler modelling framework – and a focus not on the model but on its outputs.

However, it must be noted that this approach must always rely on a range of simplifying assumptions – assumptions which necessarily have to be based in experience and judgement. Human elements which of course, should form the basis of all forecasting.

In round terms, with a spreadsheet modelling approach, one must define the traffic that might be affected by/might choose to use the infrastructure under consideration (this we first defined as In-Scope traffic when looking at the proposed toll roads in the UK some 20 years ago).

We then frame the choice which this traffic faces – which defines whether this traffic will choose to use the target infrastructure or whether it will (continue to) use the competing alternatives. The decision will reflect – in some way – the costs and attractiveness of each of the alternatives – in terms of how users perceive their costs, time, reliability, comfort, etc.

This approach is most appropriate when the decisions being modelled are comparatively simple – when the choice is binary and there are few if any feedback loops that need to be considered. I would argue that it would be the obvious approach to use to look at possible traffic and revenue growth on an existing highway: only under certain circumstances might you adopt the approach for looking at the development of a new ring (loop) road, complex urban route with multiple alternatives or transit link.

THE IN-SCOPE TRAFFIC

To follow this approach, it is essential to understand the total volumes of traffic which *might* use the target facility – for which the facility might present an alternative. For an inter-urban toll road, this will be the traffic already using the corridor – with some allowance for any traffic that might be diverted into the corridor with the new facility. For an airport rail link this will be the – essentially – the air passengers travelling between the airport and the city centre location of the terminal.

It is important to understand as much about this traffic as possible – perhaps the purpose of the trip (although it doesn't seem that this is always as important as traditional modelling might suggest), frequency of the trip, familiarity with the route and the routeing decisions, etc. All this information is useful in then understanding how that traffic will behave in the face of the new alternative, or in the face in the change in the level of service or cost that that alternative offers.

On many occasions the first basis for the definition of this In-Scope traffic will be a traditional network model. In our analysis, for example, of the possible usage of the I635 managed toll lanes in Texas, we first relied on the network model developed by the North Central Texas Council of Governance (NCTCoG) model – to define the traffic levels and trip distributions across the corridor.

This output we can interrogate further – moving perhaps from a 24-hour analysis through to the 15 minutes model required for managed lanes or adding further disaggregation for those factors (including income) which might be important in the choice analysis.

Because this is the base data for all the on-going analysis – and indeed incorporates the actual traffic flows which are the only data on which we can absolutely rely – it is really important to carry out as much quality work as possible to make sure this data is as reliable as possible.

ORIGIN AND DESTINATION DATA

If no network model exists – or if you have little confidence in the analysis coming out of that model either because of inherent weaknesses in the modelling or because (as is often the case) the lack of robust up-to-date data to support that model – it will be important to try and collect new data on which to base an understanding of the traffic patterns of the In-Scope traffic.

Traditionally such data is collected through carrying out a programme of roadside interview surveys – where traffic is stopped and drivers are asked a range of questions about themselves and their journey. However, it is often (always?) difficult to carry out such surveys – especially on freeways or on a complex and congested urban highway. Even when it is legal to stop traffic in this way, the organization of such a programme will be tortuous, including certainly the active support of the local police. Because of this, many forecasts on which important decisions have been made rely not on real, observed activity but on modelled and estimated matrices based on data collected many years before.

On one major highway on which Steer Davies Gleave worked, the public model on which all the teams based their initial analysis relied on data actually collected 15 years before – and this might perhaps have been a contributing factor to the over-estimation that was then observed in the actual outcomes.

As already discussed above there are new techniques being developed which ought to make the collection of information of traffic patterns more simple (and potentially almost automated allowing on-going monitoring and model updates) – although as ever, interrogation of the data and understanding of the asset context will remain essential.

DIVERSION CURVES

In a network model the analysis of traffic assignment (how traffic will travel through a road system) will be carried out within one of the transport modelling packages (EMME, TransCad, Cube, Vissum etc.).

In the spreadsheet model the assignment is more explicit. Here the decision to use the target infrastructure, or, instead continue to use the competing (free) highways is defined as a binary choice. For each component of the traffic, the cost for making a particular journey using the target infrastructure and using the best alternative is defined. That traffic is then assigned to either of the two routes according to these costs – and the cost differences.

This assignment commonly rests on a *logit* distribution – this formally describes the mathematical formulation of the curve which relates the difference in costs of the competing routes to the probability of either particular choice being made, and thus the proportion of the total traffic making that journey which will choose the target road thus allowing for the imperfect choice process of a proportion of human users.

GENERALIZED COSTS

The costs of making the trip by each of the routes, on which the decisions are based, do not merely reflect the out of pocket expenses associated with making the trip. Instead, these costs (commonly called 'generalized costs') will reflect as far as possible each of the different components of disutility that a traveller faces. As well as tolls and, perhaps, vehicle operating costs, these generalized costs will commonly also include the time consumed as well as some factor representing comfort and safety and, possibly, reliability. Each of these different disutilities has to be converted into a single base – so, for example, the benefit of an hour saved can be measured against a US$10 toll paid.

VALUE OF TIME

A (the most?) very important component of the benefit of a new highway will be the travel time that will be saved. New toll roads will generally only be successful in carrying significant volumes of traffic and generating substantial revenue when the competing routes are congested and the time saved through the use of the toll road significant. Whilst other costs can be important, time saving will almost always be the most important factor.

Converting minutes saved into value requires some estimation of the value of time to the traveller. The simple (and commonly used) fall back assumption is that each minute saved has an observable value – and that this value per minute will remain constant the number of minutes saved. Then the value of time saved – to be used as a key input into the generalized cost – can simply be estimated by multiplying the time saved by the unit price of that time.

This is, of course, a simplifying assumption – but, in the context of toll road forecasting, one that has been used successfully and simply over a number of years. However, as we discuss a little in the next section, new analysis is suggesting that this assumption should be treated with some care.

STATED PREFERENCE RESEARCH

As a first approximation, it might be considered that the value of time will relate directly to the income of the traveller. Indeed, good relationships have been established which show how, in any one country, the value of time of travellers can be estimated as a direct function of the per capita income of that country.

However, it is now generally felt that it is helpful to establish the value of time on each separate occasion – relying usually on a market research technique known as Stated Preference analysis. This technique relies on the conduct of specially designed interviews with users which allow the researcher to identify, for each individual, how they trade off time saved against toll paid (as well as investigating the impact of other factors such as reliability and comfort).

Whilst this is clearly a powerful technique, it is my personal view that that Stated Preference is often relied on as a *wonder drug.* Poorly and mechanistically developed, and simplistically applied, this research does not necessarily create any wider understanding of the factors underlying the choices made – and cannot therefore be helpful in determining the likely behaviour in the future. Instead, whilst there are of course problems in formally expanding the results obtained, I believe that carefully organized qualitative interviews and focus groups provide a better understanding on which to base interpretation of estimated values of time.

TRAVEL TIME AND DELAY

The second important component in establishing the competitive position of each of the two possible routes is determining exactly how long it will take to make the journey by each of the two routes.

Again, this is one of the key factors that can be measured – for the competing route and, if this is a brownfield project, on the target road itself. Even if these times are estimated within a network model, we would always recommend that it was worthwhile to spend time on the road – across the day if possible – to understand how the existing network was actually performing.

It is my experience that it is very common for an observer to over-estimate the time lost on a journey through congestion (the impact of how we perceive negative occurrences). Insofar as the route choice is in fact based on the actual travel times, then it is important to get this right. (Remember, on a 60 km journey, if one travels at 120kph – a standard speed limit – the journey takes 30 minutes. If the average speed drops to 100kph – the additional time taken is only 6 minutes. Further, if generally the road is free flowing (at 120kph) but for some reason for 10 minutes the speed drops to 60kph then the total transit time will rise only to 35 minutes).

Up until now – relying on the approach commonly adopted in the traditional network modelling approach – our analysis has commonly rested on the assumption that drivers make their assumptions on the basis of the actual time it will take them to transit the system. Clearly, this can only represent an approximation – but, in the context of the normal toll road analysis, this assumption would seem to be robust. However, on the managed lanes now being proposed in the US, where tolls might be significantly higher and varying frequently in response to rapidly changing traffic conditions, we believe that this simple assumption requires reappraisal.

CONGESTION AND RELIABILITY

Recent work – especially that focussed on new capacity within a very congested urban system – has made it clear that drivers value not only the time that they save under normal circumstances – but also the certainty about the time a trip will take. This we believe is very important in the new analysis of managed lanes – where travellers are invited to pay substantial amounts to bypass the congested freeway and use a tolled lane which provides not only speed but certainty.

Although many forecasters are introducing special factors to allow for this (such as attaching a higher notional value of time to the delay caused by congestion), there remains little concrete assessment of how this issue should be dealt with. Whilst good approaches are being developed, the forecasts obtained should always be treated with some caution until more thought has been invested.

CONSIDERING GROWTH

In both greenfield and brownfield projects, a key part of the analysis will be how traffic (and revenue) will grow into the future – although it must be said that, for a greenfield project the uncertainty around estimating the opening year position will normally drown out doubts about onward growth!

Again – and as discussed – in the traditional four-stage approach (still adopted in public sector appraisal such as the development of mobility plans), traffic growth is forecast through the input of new estimates of socio-economic factors into the generation and distribution modules. However, on occasion we believe that a more controlled appraisal can be achieved through the simpler application of a Fratar or Furness technique – which expands the matrix directly in line with the differential growth of housing and employment in each of the zones.

For most inter-urban projects, however – and especially for many of the toll road brownfield studies – growth estimates are developed/applied directly to the measured flows. In this case, it is common to use recent historic performance to provide the basis for estimating growth – often relying on establishing simple econometric models which relate past growth to other exogenous factors such as economic development.

Whilst it is obviously correct that traffic growth rates will be related to economic growth, and possibly correct that traffic growth will vary directly with economic growth, this relationship is clearly complex. This should be (but is usually not) reflected in the econometric models proposed; nor indeed is the theoretical development of these models very robust.

Whilst therefore we believe that this GDP-based approach IS useful – again the results should be treated with judgement, especially in present times where the macro-economic performance across many countries is certainly outside the trends we have observed over the past 40 years.

RISKS AND RISK ANALYSIS

I hope that my belief that traffic forecasting cannot be too mechanistic and that judgement must always be applied can be seen in what I have written above.

Within this context it should then be obvious that I have significant concerns about the strict application of formal risk analysis modelling techniques to the forecasts we prepare. Throughout the modelling process we rely on approximations and judgements, with underspecified definition of travellers' potential behaviour and unspecified measurement uncertainties.

We can try to understand an envelope of risk – which we share with our clients. This will be based essentially on understanding what key factors the forecast actually rely on – and exploring the impact of variations in those factors. *In my view*, we cannot – except spuriously – attached formal probability ranges to our output.

Conclusions

I have on a number of occasions given presentations to potential investors and lenders on the approaches we as forecasters adopt in our work. Then, as now, I recognized what a body of theory and practice forecasters draw on, and what a common language of concept and jargon we share. What we are doing is essentially simple; however, given the computing power now at our disposal, the temptation to add complexity, and try to quantify all influences, in order to accommodate all the different aspects appears to become irresistible.

It is my belief that, as advisors to potential investors lenders, our responsibility is to *simplify*: to get to the big picture and show – as robustly as we can – what our traffic projections are based on and how they might vary as outside conditions change. It cannot be our job for us to decide on what risk is acceptable; instead we should be able to explain in numbers and words to our client not only what we believe is a likely outcome, but also what we believe is the likelihood of other outputs.

Finally, we must always remember it is not the elegance of our models and our modelling methodology that matters – it is the actual-world reliability of our forecasts.

22 *Light Rail – The Issues*[1]

ROBERT LEWIN
Director of project & infrastructure finance, Investec

City planners see light rapid transit (LRT) as an efficient form of transport offering an attractive solution to many of the challenges faced by our congested cities. LRT, ranging from mainly segregated light rail to mainly on-street trams, has proven to be successful at getting people out of their cars, has zero emissions at point of use and has been shown to encourage regeneration of run-down areas.

Public private partnerships (PPPs) for LRTs have proven to be something more of a challenge to public promoters, private investors and financiers alike, with the number of successful projects being outweighed by those which have run into difficulties, either in procurement or in implementation.

Why should this be so? Are LRT PPPs a step too far? Are there solutions to successfully bring in private finance? This chapter examines these issues.

Some Unique Characteristics

Clearly, LRTs undertaken by way of PPPs share many characteristics of other major capital projects, but are in certain respects unique in that:

- They are in large part built in the centre of our congested cities, rather than on a defined and largely ring-fenced site, meaning that there are a far greater number of interfaces to be managed than most projects.
- Depending upon how the PPP is structured, bidders need to bring together a wide range of multi-disciplined consortia, including participants with a different appreciation of, and appetite for, different risks.
- Systems integration and completion issues are greater, particularly where there are on-street sectors.
- Farebox and associated revenues have proven to be more difficult to accurately forecast and are more sensitive to influence by factors beyond the control of the concessionaire.

These characteristics are explored in greater detail below.

---

1   This article first appeared in 'Infrastructure Finance – The Road Ahead' published by Project Finance International.

Multiple Interfaces

Designing and building an LRT within a major city requires interaction with a huge number of third parties. Some examples are:

- Agreements will need to be reached with perhaps hundreds of landowners or occupants affected directly or indirectly by the construction and/or operation of the LRT;
- The route may run through different planning authorities or municipalities;
- The assets of dozens of utilities may be affected;
- Highway junctions may need to be redesigned;
- Construction may result in major traffic disruption, requiring work areas and methods to be carefully planned to avoid traffic chaos.

Additionally, LRT schemes tend to have a wider socio-economic and regenerative impact on the communities they serve, again giving rise to interfaces between the promoters (usually the public transport authority), the private sector and elected officials.

A well prepared LRT project will have had a large number of these issues solved by the public sector promoter prior to inviting tenders from the private sector (although all too often, far too much is still open on publication of the tender documents). Ideally, preparatory work should include securing agreements with affected landowners, agreeing an outline design with municipalities, reaching agreement with highways authorities on matters such as junction design, traffic control priorities, and siting of stations and depots.

Even when a considerable amount of early work is undertaken before tender publication, the private sector bidder and successful concessionaire will still need to manage the interfaces throughout the bid and construction process (and, of course, then on into operation). Typically, a tender will need to specify a precise alignment within the promoter's defined limits of deviation. This precise alignment may have implications not considered previously, requiring further input from planners and highways authorities. Works on relocating utility diversions may impact on construction timetables (or in older cities, unmarked utilities may be found). Highways authorities may change their requirements (or fail to make consequential changes).

An area that has been of particular concern is the interaction with planning and highways authorities for the agreement of final designs. It has not been unknown for planners to require changes to the scope and/or quality of the on-street works and finishes within the project. Naturally, these changes usually represent a betterment, as opposed to a (usually) cheaper like-for-like replacement, of affected public assets/services. Since these authorities are rarely party to the PPP concession contract, it is impossible to tie them into the outline design, so making detailed approvals more of a formality.

Multi-discipline Consortia

To date, most LRTs have been procured under a single concession contract entered into with multi-discipline consortia comprising civil contractors, mechanical and electrical

(M&E) and rolling stock suppliers, operators and investors. The principal reasons promoters have adopted this approach include:

- single point responsibility and minimum risk interfaces left with the public sector;
- whole-life costings of all inputs;
- full funder due diligence on all aspects;
- bidders resolve contractor/operator interface.

Since PPPs tend to require a turnkey construction contract with single point responsibility, most projects require different skills to be applied: for example, a hospital requires civil contractor, medical equipment supplier and a facility maintenance supplier. However, in most hospital PPPs these roles have been compartmentalized. Even where not, and the main civil contractor has to rely on the medical equipment supplier to achieve completion, there is a scale difference between the two and the actual interface may be quite limited. With LRTs the M&E equipment and civil works packages might be similar in size and both will rely on the chosen operator to achieve completion.

This inter-reliance creates complexity and fault lines. Each party is exposed to risks with which it is not familiar and some which it normally would not wish to take. This can mean that construction prices become inflated as parties price in additional contingencies for an unfamiliar risk they are being asked to share. It can also mean unstable consortia, since the turnkey contract will normally be split into two separate sub-contracts (civils, M&E) with a fault allocation arrangement between the parties. This agreement can lead to one subcontractor making a profit but the other taking a bath, an outcome that fails to encourage long term co-operation.

Systems Integration/Completion Risk

These problems become most acute at the point where completion has to be achieved to satisfy the requirements of both promoter and funders.

Completion risk can arise from a variety of sources, although typically would result from deficiencies in the design, construction, integration management or commissioning of the system or operation performance. In particular, LRT systems with on-street sections have to manage all those interfaces with all manner of third parties, who can either have an effect upon LRT operation (for example, road traffic, pedestrians, junction management, illegally parked vehicles), or be affected by operation of the LRT (for example, access to properties, noise and vibration in properties in the street).

As with other projects, concession contracts and finance documents will require specified completion tests to demonstrate that the 'as constructed' system can perform to an acceptable level. Typically, such tests are designed to show that, inter alia:

- the system can perform to timetable over a defined period;
- where there is a performance payment/penalty regime, that this works to an acceptable minimum level;
- in-service environmental conditions (such as noise and vibration) are within defined limits.

Lenders require that they are adequately protected against the failure of such tests, including a sufficient level of liquidated damages to cover the financial consequences of failing to achieve completion on time to the required performance level and/or the cost of replacing the contractor to enable the works to be completed. These tests can be made even more important where the public sector promoters are paying for part of the project partly with capital grants (as has been common with such projects) and make a final grant payment conditional on a performance test.

Whilst the use of construction milestone payments by the promoter reduces the cost of borrowing, linking the final milestone payment to the concessionaire demonstrating a period of successful running exacerbates the financial risk the concessionaire faces in this critical post commissioning phase. This is because the concessionaire would already be at risk from losing farebox revenue and/or incurring performance deductions against an availability payment if it failed to deliver the required service.

There are three basic options for addressing completion risk in a PPP:

1. *Turnkey contractor responsibility* – The turnkey contractor takes responsibility for achieving completion, with the necessary operational services being provided under subcontract or key drivers initially employed by the contractor.
2. *Shared responsibility* – The responsibility for achieving completion is shared between the turnkey contractor and the operator. Each party would bear the financial consequences for a failure to achieve completion on time according to which one is at fault.
3. *Concessionaire responsibility* – Either the financing structure and/or the shareholders take the risk through standby capital and/or completion guarantees.

Unfortunately, as explained below, none of these solutions is easy.

Turnkey contractors can be unwilling to accept sole responsibility, arguing that it is possible to demonstrate compliance of the technical performance of the system at the end of a test running period and, accordingly, that its prime responsibilities are completed once physical completion has been achieved, and the main activities during the performance testing period are to check the operational aspects of the system. As a result, the turnkey contractor argues it should not have to cover the liabilities of the operator during shadow running. Furthermore, civil contractors within the turnkey contract may argue that any failure during shadow running will either be the fault of the M&E supplier or the operator, and that therefore it should not share in the liability.

A shared responsibility structure has sometimes been put forwards as an alternative to the first option. Under this, both the contractor and the operator would have defined responsibilities during performance testing and would provide sufficient liability limits within their contracts to meet funders' requirements. The main obstacle with this option is that the financial consequences of failing to achieve completion are usually far higher than the value of the operating services provided during this period and, accordingly, the liability cap for the operator would need to be significantly more than a year's operating costs, and many years' of his margin. To round things off, the operator will usually argue that if faults occur during the performance tests, then these are the fault of the system design or consortium, not his inability to operate.

Alternatively, it can be argued that the operator should accept liability up to a cap within its contract, with any liability above this being taken by the M&E supplier, turnkey contractor, the concessionaire or its shareholders directly.

If neither of the above approaches can be made to work, the concessionaire could accept the responsibility of delay through putting in place standby facilities (equity and/or debt) to provide the necessary funding for additional costs and delayed receipt in revenues. Typically, the equity providers may be required to provide completion guarantees, such that if completion is not achieved by a certain date, then equity is responsible for repaying the senior debt. Third party equity will not normally be willing to provide support for the completion risk. Furthermore, even should there be no requirement for third party equity, the lenders would require a significantly higher level of equity in the funding plan and the cost of debt would be higher. This solution will tend to price the bid out of the competition.

Patronage and Revenue Risk

LRTs share the same patronage and revenue risks as other transportation projects but there are several characteristics which can make the forecasting of ridership numbers and farebox yield much more difficult to predict.

As with other transport modes, ridership and revenue forecasts require the development of complex models to assess current travel patterns along a corridor, the choices people make between modes, how sensitive this is to price changes and how the number of trips will grow over time.

By way of contrast, a new road or bridge crossing relies (simplistically) on what alternatives are available (mode choice), and often these might be quite limited. It will be necessary to understand how the surrounding road network may be developed over time and the concessionaire may seek some protection from the development of competing routes if these are seen to be a risk to usage.

For an LRT, however, mode choice is much more complex. Not only are the choices much wider (car, bus – sometimes different quality buses – walking, cycling, heavy rail) but comfort also has an influence. Indeed, it is generally accepted that passengers prefer light rail to bus and accordingly most forecasting assumes a bias towards the former (for example, given a choice of a bus journey of equivalent duration, the passenger will prefer light rail even if it is a bit more expensive). Additionally, road networks in cities are more complex and journey times may be impacted by congestion and traffic management measures. Where LRTs are to be the part of a plan to regenerate an area (a common objective), the volume, diversity, scale and relative timing of potential development proposals can be a significant forecasting challenge. Finally, it has proven to be very difficult to determine how quickly passengers will recognize the benefits of the new transport mode, leading to slower and much longer ramp-up periods than expected.

Critically, however, LRTs can greatly be affected by public transport policy, and whilst it may be less difficult for transport authorities to give certain protections to a concessionaire for a total freeway, bridge or airport (for example), this is much more of a challenge for public transport in cities. Patronage and revenues on a light rail system can be dramatically impacted by a wide range of matters usually controlled by the public sector, including:

- Policies which may impact upon the ease of car use within a city, including car parking policies, pedestrianization and, for the future, congestion charging or road pricing.
- Bus policies, including removing (or not) competing bus services or providing (or not) feeder bus services which may deliver additional passengers to the LRT.
- Fare policies which may cover not just competing bus services but the LRT itself.
- For on-street systems, the priority they receive at road junctions and future traffic management measures.
- Future decisions on regeneration investment and property zoning.

No public transport authority will easily give up its freedom to make changes to such areas.

All of these factors can make bidders, and certainly their funders, far more cautious about LRT revenue forecasts. The level of revenue downsides that their funders will require the financial model to be able to withstand have, in the past, been such that in some cases the amount of debt that can be included in the funding is so small as to make its value questionable. All of this can mean that a private financing, with marked revenue risk, does not provide the public sector with good value for money.

Some Solutions

Much thought by many different parties around the world has been put into solving some of the problems described above, including:

- mitigating the interface issues through greater early design by promoters, minimizing betterment issues and tying municipalities into the concession contract structure;
- unpicking some of the issues around the need for multi-discipline consortia and the problems this causes during completion;
- sharing revenue risks.

Mitigating the Interfaces

Whilst it is clearly not possible to reduce the complexity and number of interfaces involved in the planning, design, construction and operation of an LRT system, a number of measures can be taken to mitigate their impact.

As alluded to above, promoters can and should seek to simplify the bidding process through undertaking a much higher level of design before publishing tenders. This should be completed with wide consultation amongst potential contractors, suppliers and operators to ensure the buildability, commerciality and operability of designs. Promoters should try to resist the temptation to include too many mandatory variants or shirk hard decisions by 'allowing the market to decide'.

Several LRT scheme promoters have recognized this and have procured a greater level of design in-house before procurement has started. This approach also strengthens the robustness of the scheme's cost estimate but at the expense of higher promoter sunk costs.

Taken to its extreme, it is possible for promoters to procure substantially all design aspects in-house and seek to novate the solution to the concessionaire to construct, albeit having allowed bidders the opportunity to engage with the promoters' design team throughout the procurement phases. Creating a greater degree of certainty over the final physical form of the LRT system will allow bidders to price the works with a greater level of confidence, reducing the potential for excessive cost contingencies being included.

Whether such an extreme approach can work in practice depends upon the willingness of the concessionaire's contractors to accept the design since it will bear the direct risk as to whether the design is fit for purpose.

A casualty of this approach is the potential loss of innovative design and construction proposals from the private sector that may result from a reduced level of bidder engagement in the design process and completion pressures.

Third parties, including municipalities and highways authorities should be tied into the process, either through them being parties to the concession contracts or entering into design agreements so that the cost of any changes to the design beyond a pre-agreed set of standards to meet increased planning requirements with the public sector. The permitting process needs to be clear with established review and approvals timeframes, standard in most PPPs with a single client, but hard to achieve with LRTs.

Separation of Activities

As noted above, one of the problems of past LRTs has been the fact that concessions have tended to be let as single contracts requiring multi-disciplined contractors and concessionaires, which leaves the disparate parties taking responsibility for risks with which they may be unfamiliar, in with the contractor-operator interface being particularly difficult to resolve.

Other significant additional disadvantages arise from the fact that bidding consortia tend to be dominated by contractors and suppliers, whose main interest is short-term (i.e., construction only) and the influence of the operator on the concession may be very limited. In addition, self-selecting consortia may result in a mixture of companies which are both good and bad from the promoter's perspective. In addition, some bidders have withdrawn from the market due to an unwillingness to take some of the unfamiliar risks.

Accordingly, greater focus is now being placed on separation of procurement of the delivery of the infrastructure from the operating services, and possibly also procurement of the rolling stock, with the infrastructure provider either being paid directly against milestones or through an availability payment structure. Some of the advantages of such a separation may include:

- It allows the promoter to select separately the best infrastructure provider and the best operator.
- It could allow early operator involvement (enabling the operator to contribute to the design of the system, to improve operability, alignment design and system simplicity.
- Through decoupling provision of the infrastructure from the revenue risk, this creates a financing based largely on system performance and availability, more similar to mainstream PPP projects. This should allow cheaper and longer-term finance to be varied for the provision of the infrastructure.

- Network expansion should be easier (no need for early termination of the infrastructure provider, more easily allowing phased expansion).

However, one of the main potential benefits is the mitigation of completion risk, which is discussed further below.

Completion/Integration Risk

Clearly, separation of the provision of the system from the operation is attractive to the private sector, since removing the contractor-operator interface reduces risk and cost, so long as the promoter devises seamless completion tests or assumes the ultimate risk itself. And therein lies the rub for the promoter. Since it seems to currently be beyond the wit of man to devise a structure that satisfies both contractor and operator (e.g., physical completion tests are as good as extended performance tests), the promoter will have to pick up the pieces. This is not necessarily a big ask since, at the end of the day, the promoter bears the ultimate risk that the LRT system is unable to provide the necessary services.

Certain promoters have recognized this and developed alternative contracting structures – e.g., where the constituent suppliers remain liable for their own works and agree to work in a collaborative manner to ensure that the system is commissioned successfully, with each party participating in the attribution of responsibility for any commissioning defects and hence rectification costs amongst the panel members. This requires an intelligent client base as well as a strong incentive for suppliers to align their individual commercial aspirations with the wider project objectives held by the promoter; neither of which may be present in reality.

Ultimately, however, the ability of the promoter to retain all or some completion risk is dictated by the balance between the amount of contingency that can be removed from contractors' and suppliers' costs and the potential cost exposure the promoter may face if completion risk were to materialize.

However, many promoters consider that the public sector must not be exposed to completion risk at all: the public sector could have an active role in ensuring that the tests are properly controlled and managed but must not as a result be exposed to the risk. Accordingly, some different approaches are being trialled, which aim to achieve some of the advantages of separate procurement but still leave completion risk with the concessionaire:

- separate procurement of the main contract packages, followed by a 'shotgun wedding' of the parties to create a single entity;
- separation of infrastructure provider and operator after completion ('early divorce'?).

It remains to be seen whether either of these approaches represent the future. Putting together commercial organizations to create a made-in-heaven consortium from the promoter's perspective could be a living hell for companies with no history of co-operating together. But, if the long-term alignment of interests (through an equity shareholding in the concession) of the construction and operating parts of a consortium are no longer there, through the separation of contracts after completion, will agreement of the roles of the parties during completion be harder to achieve? Probably so.

Revenue Risk Sharing

Given that leaving the full revenue risk with the private sector might not be possible or, at best, may offer poor value for money, promoters have increasingly looked to alternative approaches.

The separation of project implementation into different concessions for the provision of the system and its operation clearly protects the funders of the construction works from revenue risk. In theory, revenue risk remains with the operator but, in practice, operators tend to establish thinly capitalized companies for such projects with little ability or appetite to bear much risk, leaving the ultimate risk with the promoters. Accordingly, the level of revenue risk under separate concessions is more of an incentive to the operator to grow revenues or minimize fare evasion.

Such structures do not work where the promoter is looking to raise some of the funding for the project from farebox and associated revenues and is unable to borrow itself against these. In such circumstances mechanisms that share revenue risk are more appropriate.

Revenue risk sharing can be achieved in a wide variety of ways but may include the provision of a minimum revenue floor percentage sharing of revenue downsides within different bands, or simply an effective underpinning of the concessionaire's debt. Typically, promoters will also require a sharing in higher than expected revenues, to compensate for taking part of the downside.

Revenue risk sharing can have many benefits for all parties, not just improving the funding amounts and terms that can be achieved. Sharing of risks means that the interests of the public and private sectors are more closely aligned than when one party is fully protected. Indeed, the public sector will be incentivized to adopt policies that will help the LRT to thrive and to think twice about introducing measures that might damage LRT revenues.

Conclusion

Although the history of LRT public private partnerships has not always been a glorious one, people have been learning from past mistakes. Different contractual structures and forms of risk sharing are being tried, recognizing the unique challenges of LRT projects. As an example of progress, in the UK public transport authorities, operators and private sector participants (through the Light Rapid Transit Forum) have come together to form UKTram, a body set up to address the issues that have been holding back tram schemes in the UK, including scheme costing and procurement processes. It is hoped that through identifying and applying best practice to future schemes, a future article on this subject will be able to point to a much more positive record of successes.

23 UK Waste Sector – An Assessment

MELVILLE HAGGARD[1]
Quartermain Advisers

The past eight years have seen an accelerating rate of change in the UK waste management sector. Following a Cabinet Office report in 2003, Defra established the Waste Implementation Programme (WIP) to spur investment to meet England's EU landfill diversion targets. This led to the establishment of a Challenge Fund to provide grants to local authorities in support of 'front-end' waste recycling and collection activity whilst an investment gap analysis conducted by Defra's Waste Infrastructure Delivery Programme (WIDP)[2] in 2006 identified the need for an additional £10bn of investment in capital intensive 'back end' waste treatment infrastructure to enable England to meet its 2013 and 2020 landfill diversion targets.

The Energy White Paper 2007 made a significant breakthrough by providing official recognition that:

> *Generating energy from that portion of waste that cannot be prevented, reused or recycled has both energy and waste policy benefits. Energy generated either directly from waste or through the use of a refuse derived fuel has benefits for security of supply. In addition, the biodegradable fraction of waste is a renewable resource.[3]*

Spurred by £3bn of waste PFI credits and the waste hierarchy principles embodied in the Revised Waste Framework Directive, these combined actions have initiated a transformation of the industry from a logistics and landfill model, with some EfW, towards a process engineering model focussed on recyclate extraction, preparation of waste derived fuel and recovery of energy as electricity and heat. Out of a total constituency of some 47 PFI and PPP projects over 50 per cent had reached financial close by March 2011 with some 18 projects at advanced stages of procurement. This broadened range of commercially viable waste management solutions has instigated a market for solid, liquid and gaseous

---

1   Melville Haggard is Managing Director, Quartermain Advisers Limited; member of the Advisory Group on the UK Government's Green Investment Bank; and Chairman of the Investment Committee of the London Waste and Recycling Board. He was Markets Development Adviser to the Waste Infrastructure Delivery Programme, at the UK Department for Environment Food and Rural Affairs ('DEFRA') from 2005 to 2011.

2   Waste Infrastructure Delivery Programme combining resources from DEFRA, Partnerships UK and Local Partnerships.

3   DTI: Energy White Paper 2007, Meeting the Energy Challenge, page 152, paragraph 5.3.44.

fuels with bioenergy content whilst delivering value for money through competition and choice. Some notable features of this unfolding waste market transformation are:

- By December 2010, Defra's Waste Infrastructure Delivery Programme had achieved financial close on sufficient 'base load' waste treatment capacity from the waste PFI and PPP programmes to meet the UK's 2020 EU landfill diversion targets.
- The introduction of a range of waste treatment technologies including MBT, AD, autoclave, EfW electricity-only, EfW with CHP, advanced conversion technologies (ACT); but
- Recognition that 'new' technologies alone may not provide 'the answer' but new combinations of fully commercialized technologies can do so.
- The need to treat a range of waste feedstocks apart from MSW, in particular C&I and C&D wastes, waste wood and farm wastes.
- An expanded range of outputs including SRF, bio-derived liquids and gases, electricity and heat in addition to recyclates differentiated by quality.
- Significant steps towards reflecting waste's renewable energy potential within the Renewables Obligation ('RO') and Renewable Heat Incentive ('RHI') with further progress pending the finalization of current regulatory reviews.
- The arrival of the 'fuel producer/fuel user' (MBT/SRF) model enabling waste management to structure itself as a resource creating industry.
- The emergence of a fuel supply/logistics industry with associated processing capacity based around waste and non-waste biomass fuels.
- New entrant contractors giving an expanded range of bidders for municipal waste contracts with greater financial, technical and human resource than available five years previously.
- Utilization of Competitive Dialogue to ensure competitive tension throughout the procurement process.
- The formation of bidding consortia comprising more than one company in order to combine expertise in energy recovery, waste management, CHP and carbon abatement.
- A progressive shift towards balance sheet financing of bids as well as project finance
- The gradual emergence of efficiency metrics for heat and electricity generation as well as waste treatment.

The convergence of the energy and waste sectors is now supported by a plethora of policy drivers but frequent changes to the energy market's regulatory architecture mean there is now an urgent need to re-introduce some 'fixed certainties'; and to reduce complexity which has become a constraint to business.

The foregoing gives a sense of where the now inextricably twinned waste management and renewable energy industries are heading, with the proviso that the business environment will remain uncertain until the current regulatory reform overhang is resolved. That overhang includes the RO 2013 banding review[4]; confirmation of the sustainability criteria for biomass; re-design of the carbon reduction commitment (CRC);

4   http://www.decc.gov.uk/en/content/cms/consultations/cons_ro_review/cons_ro_review.aspx.

implementation of Phase 1 of the renewable heat incentive (RHI)[5] with Phase 2 to follow in 2012 and last but not least Electricity Market Reform (EMR).[6] These developments augur well for a more holistic approach to the role of waste within the broader energy spectrum but the suspense will leave investors sitting on their hands until some fixed certainties are re-established.

Technologies

Government Review of Waste Policy in England 2011[7] provided strong support for the 'fuel producer/fuel user' model and the use of energy recovery when using the 'right fuel, [in the] right place and right time'[8]. It recognized that EfW is a multiplicity of things, not one thing, and that its role within the waste hierarchy is much more nuanced than reflected in previous policy statements. It is now the task of other inter-locking regulatory reforms to optimize renewable energy potential from all waste and non-waste feedstocks; and to take measures that support the development of fuel supply chains for gaseous, liquid or solid fuels from renewable sources.

Market activity already reflects these changes as evidenced by investment in fuel preparation and supply infrastructure via MBT/SRF plants under the PFI and PPP programmes; investment by transport and logistics groups in biomass fuel supply businesses[9]; power generators seeking to access sources of renewable fuels under long term contracts[10]; and waste management companies looking to use waste for the production of bio-fuels.

The Enpure/TEG component in Viridor Laing's solution for Greater Manchester is an example of how AD can be deployed as one part of an integrated waste management solution whilst the Welsh waste programme demonstrates how investment in AD can be secured on the back of long term local authority municipal waste contracts. Strenuous efforts are being made to deploy more AD in a 'stand-alone' on-farm context in England but the financing model is more complex in the absence of long term municipal feedstock supply contracts; and compounded by financially weak project sponsors, high due diligence costs for small projects and lack firm digestate disposal outlets.

Autoclave, like all intermediate treatment technologies, needs outlets for its sterilized fibre and is probably most appropriately deployed as part of a multi-technology solution sponsored by a corporate with the financial, human and technical resources to bid for a long-term waste supply contract – and the resulting SRF off take – as was attempted at Wakefield.

5   http://www.decc.gov.uk/assets/decc/What%20we%20do/UK%20energy%20supply/Energy%20mix/Renewable %20energy/policy/renewableheat/1387-renewable-heat-incentive.pdf.

6   http://www.decc.gov.uk/en/content/cms/consultations/emr/emr.aspx.

7   http://www.defra.gov.uk/publications/files/pb13540-waste-policy-review110614.pdf.

8   Ibid., page 62.

9   Stobart Group.

10   The 3SE consortium comprising Scottish and Southern Energy plc and Shanks plc were awarded Preferred Bidder status for Barnsley, Doncaster and Rotherham's waste management contract. The solution involves the production of SRF for use in a new multi-fuel electricity generating plant next to S&SE's existing coal-fired power station at Ferrybridge.

Bio-energy Feedstocks

Integrity of fuel supply in terms of the financial covenant of the fuel supplier and the quality and reliability of fuel specification remains a pre-condition for the financing and construction of any fuel use facility, whether a conventional thermal combustion plant or a transformational technology turning solid feedstock into bio-liquids. It is the case that a local authority waste feedstock contract is likely to be stronger and more bankable than its pure biomass counterpart which suggests that bio-energy developers using off-balance sheet project finance may need to use an initial block of waste derived fuel attracting a gate fee in order to secure finance, commence operation and reduce debt to a level sufficient to allow access to shorter term or spot biomass supply contracts. This requires business models to be able to switch between gate fee based economics and ROC-based economics where the former supports debt repayment and the latter returns to equity investors.

Prospects for fuel supply from waste sources are more promising than might be generally recognized. A recent review of PFI and PPP waste management projects due to deliver treatment capacity by 2013 and 2020 showed that of those due to deliver by 2013, 50 per cent had elected MBT/SRF as their preferred option; and 40 per cent for those delivering capacity by 2020. There was concern for much of the last decade about disposal routes for SRF estimated to be up to 5m tonnes per annum by 2015. Interest has now turned to accessing bio-content from whatever source as the sheer scale of the UK's renewable energy requirement has become clear; and the need to replace some 20GW of time-expired generating capacity by 2020 becomes ever more pressing.

The feedstock supply challenge remains considerable in terms of tonnage, composition and delivery logistics when you consider that a 100MW SRF/waste wood fired combustion plant may require up to 800,000 tonnes of material a year. As we shift away from coal and into other forms of continuous renewable energy generation, the enduring importance of the rail network for bulk fuel supply becomes apparent. Finding a rail head at both the source of fuel production and fuel use will prove challenging but is the key to a sustainable solution embodying the best energy efficiency and carbon footprint principles.

The quantity of biomass feedstocks needed to support the UK's renewable energy ambition is likely to focus attention on feedstock supply from sources other than municipal waste, notably commercial and industrial (C&I) sources and the waste wood component from the construction and demolition (C&D) sector.

The publication in December 2010 of Defra's Survey of Commercial and Industrial Waste Arisings tracked the evolution of C&I waste over the period 2002/3 to 2009[11] and was an important step in delineating this emerging market segment. The report noted that total C&I waste arisings fell by 29.3 per cent over the period to 48m tonnes but that recycling rates rose by 10 per cent and use of thermal treatments increased by 9 per cent over the same period – the latter being the single largest positive percentage change in waste management method apart from land recovery.

Increasing investment in C&I and C&D waste treatment infrastructure is a priority but is constrained by short term feedstock supply contracts and the financial profile of many SME operators which makes it difficult to raise finance for new investment, in particular from banks. The arrival of the UK Government's Green Investment Bank is

---

11   Defra/Government Statistical Service: Survey of Commercial and Industrial Waste Arisings 2010.

significant as two of the three initial priority sectors it will address are waste and non-domestic energy efficiency. These two sectors have the potential to stimulate the fuel chain building needed to achieve the UK's 2020 renewable energy generation targets by supporting investment models for new C&I and C&D waste treatment infrastructure, thereby adding to the supply of waste derived fuels.

Energy Outputs

The arrival of the RHI should help to accelerate the use of SRF and waste derived bio-fuels as industrial energy users see this as a practical way of getting the 'R' into their heat use, reducing reliance on imported fossil fuels and exposure to fossil price volatility. This will encourage waste preparation technologies like MT and MBT to become more nuanced and reliable in the range and composition of waste fuel outputs. Initial beneficiaries are likely to be large volume heat users in the chemical, pulp and paper industries.

Whilst waste fuels are a flexible way of delivering biomass content in volume to multiple users, the RHI can also encourage heat use via fixed pipe from energy from waste plants, particularly where there are adjacent public sector entities with long term, stable heat loads. Prisons, MoD establishments, schools, hospitals and other public buildings have good heat profiles but linking up heat production and heat use across different parts of the public sector has not proved to be an easy task. It is against such good quality anchor heat loads that energy service companies (ESCOs) will deploy capital to build skeleton heat distribution networks onto which private sector commercial and residential users can connect over time.

There is a significant opportunity for ESCOs with experience of managing heat use portfolios in continental Europe to enter the nascent UK market. But, it requires a 'utility-style' business model predicated on long term, predictable returns – and one more suited to corporate rather than project finance in its early stages.

This direction of travel received an encouraging boost in 2011 when South Devon Waste Partnership awarded preferred bidder status to a solution that included long term heat supply to the adjacent Devonport naval dockyard. A similar scheme is in prospect in Staffordshire where an EfW plant is being built within striking distance of HMP Featherstone and it is to be hoped that such anchor contracts will spawn further heat use through the addition of incremental district heating schemes. District heating scheme outcomes need to be measured in decades rather than years as illustrated in Sheffield where the build out of the present scheme commenced in 1987 and is still on-going. But that is the nature of the ESCO business building opportunity – and is quite distinct from the business model of the merchant developer.

The attractiveness of the RHI and RO options for heat use hang in the balance until the RO 2013 Review and the RHI Large Biomass band remain are concluded. Developers are concerned that long lead time projects may achieve accreditation at a point in DECC's funding cycle when the RHI pot is empty – a risk that does not affect the RO with its cost pass-through to consumers.

Not far behind the developments described above are the producers of bio-methane – especially from AD – keen to use existing gas transmission and distribution networks to bring renewable content to a wider range of commercial and residential heat users. The economics of this approach are likely to require greater 'socialization' of gas cleanup and grid connection costs than currently envisaged; but the major advantage of this route – as with electricity to grid – is that it avoids a project's exposure to the bankruptcy risk of a single energy user.

Contractors

The arrival of new entrant contractors bringing different interests and skills into the market is contributing greatly to the transformation of the waste industry in the UK. These include energy companies seeking long-term sources of fuel with renewable content; PFI specialists wanting to redeploy expertise into a new growth sector; civil and building contractors with build-operate-transfer expertise; EfW operators looking for new markets; and CHP specialists. Very few of these were active in the UK waste management business in any meaningful way in the early 2000s.

Other significant features are the growing use of consortia to provide the waste management, energy, technology, financing and carbon abatement skills needed to win contracts in an increasingly energy-linked environment; and the need for a single entity to 'front' these increasingly complex arrangements. There is also a growing list of equipment suppliers and sub-suppliers (most of them located overseas) too long to enumerate here – and, of course, a fluctuating field of financiers notable for those joining and leaving the sector.

The complex nature of waste management contracts means that large-scale PFI waste procurements are handled under competitive dialogue procedures.

Financing

Recent discussion in UK political circles around the role of PFI has been an unfortunate distraction. Critics use the PFI acronym to confuse three different inter-linked elements, namely (a) project finance as a method of financing waste infrastructure (b) the role of long-term contracts and (c) the transfer of resource from central Government to local authorities to support local government projects.

Long-term contracts from good quality counterparties are a well tried and tested means of *financing* capital intensive infrastructure. They provide the 'fixed certainty' against which commercial banks advance finance. Critics of PFI tend to overlook the fact that you can have (a) and (b) without PFI credit transfers implicit in (c) – as illustrated by the many successful public private partnerships (PPPs) in the waste and transportation sectors.

The principal concern with PFI credits was that departments did not have to prioritize this *funding* against other areas of spending; and that it incentivized authorities to structure projects to ensure they were eligible for additional central government funding. This has now been changed and from April 2011, new local authority PFI projects will need to pay the grant funding from their own Resource Budgets; and to compare calls on these budgets on a like-for-like basis.

A significant recent development is the arrival of corporate project sponsors favouring balance sheet financing solutions over project finance in response to tighter credit conditions, higher pricing and banks' increasing appetite for shorter term construction finance in response to constrained access to cost effective funding and new capital adequacy requirements. As a result, the number of banks offering long maturities has scaled back from the high water mark in 2007 when project financiers active in the waste sector numbered around 20.

For all the concerns expressed about long term contracts and the PFI model, the fact remains that the PFI and PPP project pipelines supported by Defra's Waste Infrastructure Delivery Programme are on track to deliver by 2020 waste treatment capacity sufficient to meet England's 2020 EU municipal waste diversion target. It was confidence in this outcome that led Defra to withdraw PFI credits from several authorities in UK's Spending Review 2010 – a statement of the market transformation that has taken place in the waste sector in little more than half a decade – and testament to the success of the WIDP model.

Policy/Business Models

Both WIDP and its predecessor the Waste Implementation Programme were organizational structures designed to deal with an urgent policy implementation issue. The speed of response was impressive as it took little more than a couple of months to assemble a multi-disciplinary group with experience in consultancy, banking, industry, waste technology, renewable energy incentives, local government and third sector activity.

WIDP's pipeline of projects is in many ways the praxis of waste policy – the translation of policy intent into projects on the ground. One important caveat is that policy and practice are never perfectly aligned because long project lead times inevitably straddle changing policy cycles. In consequence, outcomes are incremental not final – but if you wait for perfection, nothing happens!

Access to a live project pipeline is a helpful and immediate way of informing policy. Longer continuity in post in complex policy areas like energy and waste is desirable in view of long development cycles needed to implement energy incentive frameworks. It is a model that could be strengthened further with more cross-fertilization between private and public sectors from inward and outward secondments to/from a relevant industry sector, particularly at middle management level.

Both my secondment experiences in Government involved working closely with the private sector. WIDP provided the opportunity to see Government acting proactively to implement a specific aspect of policy and doing so in an area notorious for the sensitivities that can arise between central and local government. WIDP is an atypical model within the UK Civil Service but there is no doubt that the programme's Janus-like ability to look outwards to the markets and inwardly across government departments has been a significant contributor to the speed of transformation across the waste sector in the UK.

Acronyms and Abbreviations

AD	Anaerobic Digestion
C&D waste	Construction and demolition waste
C&I waste	Commercial and industrial waste
Defra	Department for Environment, Food and Rural Affairs
EMR	Electricity Market Reform
GIB	Green Investment Bank
MBT	Mechanical and Biological Treatment
PFI	Private Finance Initiative
PPP	Public Private Partnership
RHI	Renewable Heat Incentive
RO	Renewables Obligation
SRF	Solid Recovered Fuel
WIDP	Waste Infrastructure Delivery Programme
WIP	Waste Implementation Programme

Countries

CHAPTER

24 *Project Finance in Emerging Markets*

ATIF ANSAR
BT Centre for Major Programme Management, Saïd Business School, University of Oxford

The number and volume of non-recourse project finance deals in emerging markets (hereafter EM), as reported by the Thomson Reuters PFI database, were at an all-time high in 2010. The momentum in emerging markets project finance (EMPF) has propelled the State Bank of India as the global No. 1 Mandated Lead Arranger as of the first quarter of 2011. Over 200 deals with a total value of over US$130bn were signed in 2010 across the BRICs (Brazil, Russia, India, and China), emerging Europe, and the next frontier markets in Asia, the Gulf, Africa, and Latin America. This makes the project finance market nearly twice as large as the market for initial public offerings (IPOs) in emerging markets.[1]

The robust project finance volumes in EM from 2006–Q1 of 2011 (see Figure 24.1) are surprising. Global economies have suffered one of the worst financial crises in history during this period leading to significant reduction in gross capital inflows in emerging countries.[2] What explains the expanding use of non-recourse project finance in EM? Despite the upward trend in EMPF in recent years, the longer term year-on-year growth in total value and number of EMPF deals has been anything but steady (see Figure 24.1). Increases in 1996–1997 and 2000 were followed by precipitous declines. Is the record volume of EMPF deals in 2010 slated for a similar slowdown or will project finance remain in vogue in emerging markets going forwards? Why might project finance, despite typically higher cost of funding, be attractive in emerging markets?

In addressing these questions this chapter will argue that project finance is here to stay as one of the most significant sources of long-dated financing in EM. Underpinning the expanding importance of project finance in emerging countries is a critical shift. Instead of a reliance on foreign arrangers, home-grown, and often State-backed, intermediaries such as State Bank of India, Bank of China, China Construction Bank, VEB in Russia, and BNDES in Brazil are assuming a central role in making project finance deals happen. Similarly, domestic institutional investors and banks – and not foreign investors – are becoming the proportionally largest source of capital for many EMPF transactions. Home-grown intermediaries, from an investor relationship perspective, are aided in their ability

---

1   Ernst & Young, 2011, Global IPO Trends 2011. Available at http://www.ey.com/Publication/vwLUAssets/Global-IPO-trends_2011/$FILE/Global%20IPO%20trends%202011.pdf [Accessed 4 July 2011].

2   Bank of International Settlements, 2010, 1.

Figure 24.1 Emerging market project finances transactions 1991–2010 (US$m)

Source: Thomson Reuters PFI database at www.pfie.com. 2011 forecast is the author's estimate[3]

to arrange the transactions. If the legal and regulatory frameworks in emerging markets keep pace, EMPF volumes can be expected to grow strongly in coming years, outpacing developed countries.[3]

The chapter is organized as follows. The first section analyses trends in EMPF by breaking down the data in Figure 24.1 further by country and sector. The second section looks at the general characteristics of project finance in emerging markets and how these differ from project finance in developed countries. The third section also looks at what makes project finance particularly suitable to emerging markets. Several case examples are discussed. The final section concludes with some thoughts about the future of project finance in emerging countries.

Trends in Emerging Markets Project Finances (EMPF) by Region and Sector

East and South Asia have led the way in EMPF since 1991 (see Figure 24.2a and b). In recent years India has led the way with a number of flagship deals. These range from the recently closed Mumbai Metro 2 being developed by Reliance Energy and SNC Lavlin to the 3,960MW Krishnapatnam Ultra Mega Power Plant Project being developed by Reliance Power at a cost of over US$3.6bn. Similarly, China (including Hong Kong) hosts several innovative PF deals each year. In recent years, PF deals in China have been of a smaller scale on the mainland such as the Gansu Guazhou Ganhekou No. 8 Wind Farm or the Beijing Gao-an-tun Waste to Energy Project. Hong Kong's US$5.6bn, Hong Kong

---

3   Note that all data reported here come from Thomson Reuters' PFI database at www.pfie.com. Any errors in the data ought to be reported directly to Thomson Reuters' data team.

– Zhuhai – Macao Bridge Hong Kong Link, however, is amongst the largest road projects ever financed using non-recourse debt. The dominance of Asia is also aided by robust deal volumes in South Korea, Taiwan, Indonesia, Thailand, Malaysia, and Singapore. All of these Asian countries are amongst top 15 emerging markets in terms of total volume of project finance deals closed since 1991.

Despite the importance of project finance in Asia, some of the largest deals have happened elsewhere. For example the Yamal Gas Pipeline in Russia, the Jubail and Rabigh refineries in Saudi Arabia, or Qatargas' LNG projects. The scale of relatively fewer but larger deals in oil and gas and petrochemicals, in particular, that propel the Middle East and North Africa (MENA) as a runner-up to East Asia in term of project finance volumes since 1991.

Latin America and the Caribbean (LAC) are, however, not far behind. In fact, since 2007, LAC, led by Brazil, has seen nearly twice as much PF volume as MENA. This is partly explained by the fact that MENA had by 2007 embarked on some very large refining and LNG projects and many foreign investors were up against country limits of how much they could lend in MENA. In terms of deal size the oil and gas has also been important in Brazil. But equally important has been the electricity generation sector. Brazil's largest-ever deal, for instance, is the Jirau Hydroelectric dam. The financing for the dam closed in 2009 with US$5.4bn raised from the markets.

Brazil's lead in LAC is relatively recent. Mexico has in the past been the leading PF market in Latin America in part also owing to significant oil and gas deals (e.g., Ku-Maloob-Zaap Oil Field Development or the Manzanillo LNG Project). One of the more intriguing areas in Mexican project finance has, however, been privately developed toll

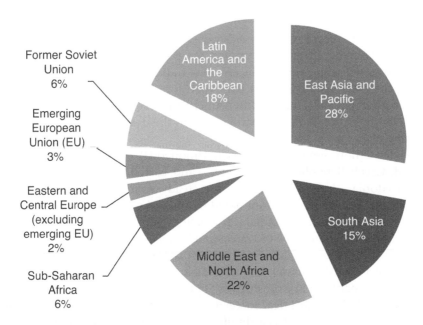

Figure 24.2(a) Where are the project finance deals in emerging markets? 1991–2010, Cumulatively, by region

Source: Thomson Reuters PFI database at www.pfie.com

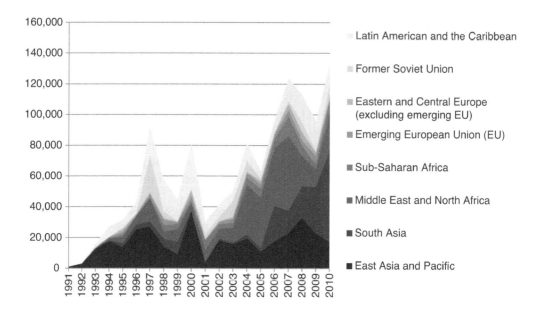

Figure 24.2(b) Where are the project finance deals in emerging markets? 1991–2010, Annually, by region (US$m)

Source: Thomson Reuters PFI database at www.pfie.com

roads. Between 1989 and 1994, during the first wave of private highway development in Mexico, over 50 toll road concessions were granted. Many of these toll-road-concessionaires collapsed in mid-1990s due to adverse economic conditions and were nationalized. By late 1990s as conditions approved these roads were re-privatized. With deeper operational experience and a general uplift in the economy, the economics of these roads improved, credit quality increased, and soon significant new transactions followed. The largest of these has been the 2007 deal to support the expansion, operation, and maintenance of 558km of toll roads in Guadalajara. The Inter-American Development Bank, a multilateral organization like the World Bank, also participated in the deal by *providing a partial credit guarantee to support the bond issuance.*

Former Soviet Union, emerging European Union (EU) – which includes countries such as Poland, Czech Republic, Hungary etc. – and Eastern Europe – such as Turkey, Croatia, or Macedonia – have also seen low but steady volumes of non-recourse deals. Russia is clearly the leading market dominated by oil and gas transaction sponsored by State-operated companies (e.g., the Yamal Gas Pipeline). A recent development in Russian PF market has been the emergence of transport PPPs. The approx. US$2bn Moscow–St Petersburg Motorway PPP concession won by Vinci is one such flagship deal that closed in 2010. This deal is seen by many as a harbinger for a more robust deal pipeline in Russia. Vnesheconombank (VEB) – the Russian State-development bank – played a critical and enabling role in helping this deal succeed. Such a role of State-led intermediaries is increasing in emerging markets. It is a significant development because it helps reduce risk in the deals by aligning the governments' interest with those of foreign investors and concessionaires.

In terms of sectoral trends, oil and gas deals – development of new fields, oil refineries, LNG terminals, and pipelines – are clearly a front-runner, accounting for nearly a quarter of all EMPF transaction by volume since 1991 (see Figure 24.3). The closely related sector of petrochemicals also accounts for a large share. Both these sectors require vast amounts of capital, relatively long development horizons, and extensive technical competence. It is no surprise that the world's largest national and international oil companies (NOCs and IOCs) sponsor such deals.[4] Because of the strategic nature of oil and gas, government involvement in these deals is paramount even when the government, or a state-owned enterprise, is not amongst the sponsors.

Equally important is the greenfield power generation and transmission sector (see Figure 24.3) for which PF has been the single most important source of funding in developing countries. For the majority of power generation deals, such as the recently closed Kondapalli gas-fired combined cycle power plant in India or the Konin combined heat and power coal-fired power plant in Poland, the debt involves direct finance or credit enhancement from export credit agencies and/or multilateral development banks. This is usually because of the large slice of imported equipment inherent to power generation.

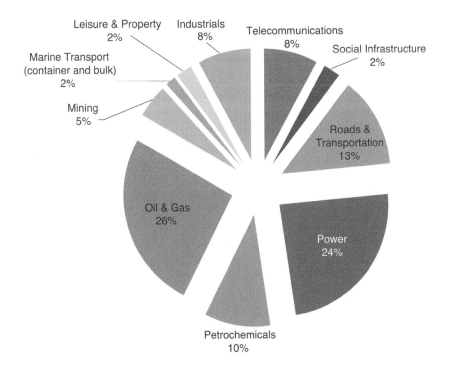

Figure 24.3 The sectoral trends in emerging markets project finance, 1991–2010

Source: Thomson Reuters PFI database at www.pfie.com

_____

4   A national oil company (NOC) is an oil company fully or in the majority owned by a national government. According to the United States Energy Information Administration, NOCs accounted for 52 per cent global oil production and controlled 88 per cent of proven oil reserves in 2007. Major NOCs include: Abu Dhabi National Oil Company; China National Offshore Oil Company (CNOOC); Petrobras; Rosneft; Saudi Arabian Oil Company (Aramco). International oil companies (IOCs) include oil majors such as ExxonMobil, BP, Chevron, Total, or Shell.

Development time for power deals average two to three years, and even shorter in countries with a mature legal and regulatory framework to deal with independent power production. The shorter duration required for power projects makes these deals attractive to a broader set of project sponsors and investors.

Roads and transport deals are also a consistent component of EMPF as examples from Hong Kong, Russia, and Mexico show. Because most of the project finance roads in developing countries are financed from user fees rather than general tax revenues or shadow tolls, this has an important disciplining force. If, for example, traffic projections turn out to be too optimistic, it is the investors rather than the government which bear the financial distress. From many capital-poor countries this is a welcome way of risk sharing. The art of road pricing, however, remains in its infancy. Many tolled roads face competition from non-tolled roads making it difficult to project future traffic volumes. Evidence suggests that in order to get projects financed, forecasters often overstate the traffic. Whilst data are currently not available, concession and debt renegotiations appear more pervasive in the road sector than in the oil and gas or power sectors.

Note that formal Public-Private Partnerships (PPP) accounted for 4.3 per cent across a variety of sectors. The involvement of governments in EMPF is, however, considerably higher as the next section will discuss.

General Characteristics of Project Finance in Emerging Markets

Projects, i.e., temporary endeavours undertaken to meet specific benefit targets, financed through project finance have the following general characteristics. These projects tend to be large-scale investments. The average size of EMPF projects between 1991 and 2010 is US$598.7m (median is US$247.2m) in nominal dollars. The average for developed countries is US$ 381.3m (median is US$148.9m). These projects go through three distinct step-changes: planning, delivery (or construction) across a specified schedule, and operation. The project finance is typically put in place towards the end of the planning phase and the only purpose of the financing is to complete the delivery of the project and graduate it to the operational phase. The planning and delivery phases consume cash, whereas positive cash flows ensue during the operation phase, which pay-off the incurred outlays and their cost of financing. If all goes to plan, any remaining positive cash flows (denominated in the currency in which the output is sold during operation) accrue to the equity holders until the life of the project expires at which point it is sold for scrap value. The forecasted project performance, against which the financing is secured, can be thought of in terms of i) scope of work, ii) schedule, iii) upfront and operational costs, and iv) output/benefits yielded during operation. On the one hand, cost overruns, poor estimates of demand for eventual output, adverse interest rate or exchange rate movements, or other risks can turn a good planned investment idea into a financial disaster. On the other hand, higher-than-expected volume or price of the output yielded during the operational phase, with costs remaining in line with projections, can create substantial profits for sponsors. Due to extreme focus on specific out and in-cash flows of a project, project finance is conceptually far more transparent than the black box of corporation finance. In providing corporate finance, investors sign up to an ill-defined buffet of investment ideas the managers of the corporation may cook up. Project finance takes an à la carte approach. This conceptual simplicity of project finance is of considerable value in emerging markets.

The ring-fencing of a project and its specific cash flow profile requires the creation of a special purpose vehicle – SPV – (also often called the project company). This legal entity has a limited and independent life, and is the formal borrower under all loan documents so that, in the event of default, sponsors are not directly responsible before financial creditors. Instead, their legal claims are against the SPV assets. In return for enjoying a hedge against future financial distress in case a project goes awry, the sponsors also have to give up considerable operational freedom by binding themselves to certain types of contractual obligations (under a variety of commercial, financial, and construction contracts) that define the terms of action throughout the life of the project. In-take and off-take agreements, project completion guarantees, or long-term equipment service agreements are thus an integral feature of project finance. At a practical level, project finance deals with core theoretical concerns regarding future 'hold up' (or opportunism) inherent to making relationship specific investments. Project finance is equally adept at addressing the theoretical problems of information asymmetry and principal-agent problem between investors and their managers. By tightly structuring the project around its cash flows, investors reduce their dependence on managerial capture.

TYPES OF SPONSORS

There are three types of sponsors who use project finance in emerging markets.

1. Multinational corporations (multinationals also often bring other parties, e.g., construction contractors or equipment manufacturers into the deal, which can be called a sub category of 'piggybacking foreign sponsors').
2. Host country governments, and government-backed enterprises.
3. Domestic firms, particularly relative newcomers to the capital markets. In many cases project finance is the debut transaction of some scale for the sponsors backing the project. Often successful projects are later restructured into a corporate holding and sold to the market on a stock exchange public offering. This evolution from project finance to corporate finance helps to bring down the cost of funds for future projects but only once the entrepreneur or sponsor backing the projects has proved his or her track record.

It is difficult to describe with precision how many of the EMPF deals in the last 20 years have been done by which type of a sponsor. Much of this is attributable to the bespoke nature of EMPF deals in which various types of sponsors form complex relationships in order to execute the project. For instance, the Dabhol power project in India involved three multinationals (Enron, Bechtel, and GE) and the State Government of Maharashtra as the project sponsors. Similarly, the sponsors for the Nghe An Tate & Lyle Sugar project in Vietnam closed in 1998 included Tate & Lyle – a multinational – in partnership with a Thailand based sugar firm, a Dublin-listed private equity fund, and a local Vietnamese partner. The government of Vietnam was also instrumental throughout the process.[5]

---

5   See Esty, B. (2004) *Modern project finance: A case book.* New York, John Wiley & Sons.

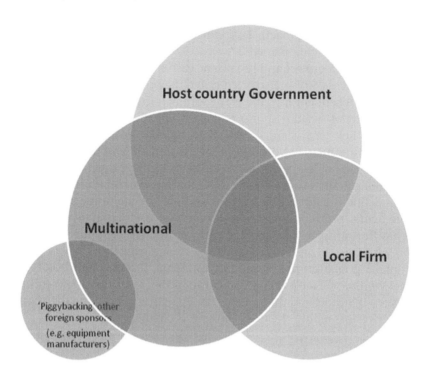

Figure 24.4 Sponsor type in emerging markets projects finance

Source: Author's impressionistic view

Figure 24.4 provides an impressionistic view of which of the sponsor types are often in the lead in promoting an EMPF deal and how these sponsors often overlap.

Text cloud, tag cloud, and word tree analysis of over 2,000 EMPF deals signed since 1991 suggests that in emerging markets there is a great emphasis on co-partnering across the three main types of sponsors – i.e., multinationals, local firms, and host country central or local level governments or enterprises set up by the governments. Such risk sharing is of importance. The multinationals often bring technology, seed equity capital, and access to global marketing/customers. Multinationals, however, seek to limit their exposure to the country, commercial, and financing risks inherent to large-scale investments in EM. In such cases the multinational sponsors share these risks with local partners, local governments, foreign and local banks, export credit agencies (ECAs), multilateral agencies, and relatively rarely the capital markets. A local partner in EM is often important because it has access to the local pool of labour, unencumbered land, local customers, and usually local pools of finance. Finally, host country governments, which can be a source of considerable expropriation, tax, and legislative risk when they act capriciously, are often included in the projects. Governments in many countries also tightly control rights to natural resources (e.g., oil, mines, or water) and land. In such instances it is also necessary to include the government in the project as a sponsor in order to align the interests of private investors with the public sector.

TYPES OF CONTRACTS

When the sponsor is the host Government of an emerging economy, the longest-established and most widespread method of project financing is BOT (Build Operate and Transfer). BOT structure involves the granting of a concession (sometimes called an authorization or a licence) by a properly empowered governmental authority (the grantor) to a special purpose company (the concessionaire). Under the concession, the concessionaire would agree to finance, build, control and operate a facility for a limited time, typically 20 to 35 years, after which responsibility for the facility is transferred to the government, usually free of charge. The concessionaires typically assume primary responsibility for constructing the project, arranging financing, performing maintenance, and collect tolls, whilst the public sector retains legal ownership. In most projects design responsibility is shared, with the public sector taking the lead in the preliminary design (including route alignment, number of lanes, interchanges, and other high-level design specifications) and the private sector completing the detailed design, subject to government approval. A typical BOT structure looks like as follows (see Figure 24.5).

There are several variants of BOT (see Table 24.1).

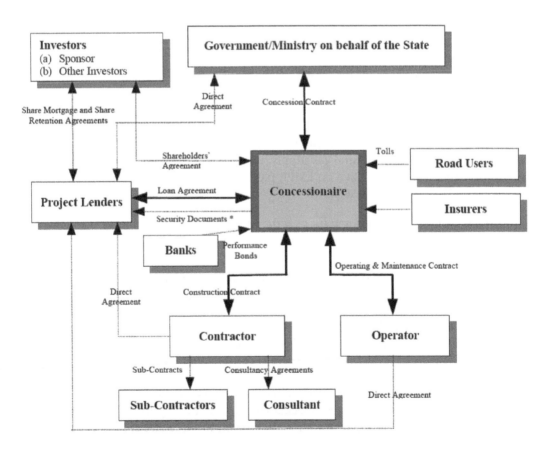

Figure 24.5 A typical BOT structure

Source: World Bank

Table 24.1 Contract types

BOO	Build Operate Own
BOT	Build Operate Transfer
BOOT	Build Own Operate Transfer
DBFO	Design Build Finance Operate
BTO	Build Transfer Operate
BLT	Build Lease Transfer

Source: Gatti (2008)[6]

A shared aspect of all of these forms of contracts is their long-term nature. Contractually, durability is necessary to match the durability of investments being rendered. However, precisely because of their long-term nature, these contracts suffer from the risk of mispricing. It is not uncommon for a concession to be awarded for too high or too low a bid. On the one hand, a concession with generous terms for the private party can become a political liability for a government. On the other hand, overpaying to clinch a deal can quickly lead to financial distress for private investors. A solution to this risk of mispricing has been greater reliance on derivative contracts such as futures, over-the-counter instruments, and swaps.

Another problem of long-term contracts is that they act to forestall competition. For example, long-term supply contracts between a few large iron ore mining companies and a few large steel processing companies would make it difficult for other steel producers to enter the market. Competition regulators have begun to take notice of this problem. For example, some influential voices in the US and Europe are calling for a potential ban on long-term contracts in the natural gas supply, which will also apply to power generation. The impact such a ban may have on EMPF, particularly in gas producing countries such as Russia or Qatar, is yet to be seen.

HOW DOES PROJECT FINANCE IN EMERGING MARKETS DIFFER FROM DEVELOPED COUNTRIES?

The essential structure of project finance is the same in developed or emerging markets. There is, of course, considerable variation in terms of average deal size, funding costs, number of corporate sponsors, credit ratings, reliance on banks versus bond markets, cost of insurance, etc. Such variations are, however, more appropriately looked at a country-by-country level. I ought to mention that project finance in developed countries is dominated by the Anglo-American model, whereas there is considerably more variation in emerging markets. The US, UK, Australia/NZ, Canada, and Ireland account for nearly two-thirds of the total project finance volume amongst developed countries. The dominance of the Anglo-American model may provide a few speculative clues as to why India and Hong Kong, which have a strong common law tradition, have been so successful at project finance.

---

6   Gatti, S. (2008) *Project finance in theory and practice: designing, structuring, and financing private and public projects.* Burlington, Academic Press.

Apart from some structural variations, there are a few more generalized differences between project finance in developed versus emerging countries.

First, as seen above, there is greater discretionary governmental interaction in developing countries, even when a government, or a state-owned enterprise, is not explicitly part of a deal. The ability to get deals done in emerging markets is highly correlated with the entrepreneurialism of the host government; and ability of a foreign or local sponsor to 'relationally' contract with the state. Such discretionary contracting has pros and cons. The pros are that there is great flexibility of how the project can be structured; the government may be able to provide land, flexible taxation, or non-pecuniary support to aid a project to succeed. The serious drawback is, however, the threat of corruption. There is little reliable research into the extent of graft in EMPF but industry practitioners do acknowledge this to be a problem.

Second, there is considerable involvement of intermediaries such as multilateral institutions (World Bank, IFC, EBRD) and ECAs. One of the main financial products of multilateral institutions is the A loan/B loan structure, in which a multilateral institution funds the A loan and syndicates the B loan to private sector financial institutions. The multilateral bank is the 'lender of record' for the B loan and all loan payments are shared pro rata between the multilateral bank and the B loan lenders. A borrower cannot default on a B loan without also defaulting on the A loan, thereby jeopardizing the host country's relationship with the multilateral institution.[7]

ECAs do not offer formal A loan/B loan structures. Instead, ECAs act as an intermediary between national governments and exporters to issue export financing. The financing can take the form of direct lending to the importer, loans to a financial intermediary in the importing country, credit insurance and/or guarantees to the exporter. ECAs currently finance or underwrite about US$430bn of business abroad – about US$55bn of which goes towards project finance in emerging markets. ECAs, in this regard, are larger than multilateral sources of finance. The ability of private sector lenders to fund side by side an ECA is viewed favourably amongst private sector investors.

Third, government-backed development banks such as State Bank of India, the Bank of China and China Construction Bank, BNDES in Brazil, VEB in Russia. All of these banks command substantial financial resources and are in a pivotal position to facilitate project finance deals in their respective countries. Owing to the backing from the state, these development banks also have the highest credit rating within their respective jurisdictions. This gives them the ability to issue 'benchmark setting' bonds at competitive rates, which then helps price loans for rest of the market. As intermediaries with a deep pool of global and local competencies, these institutions also act as informal go-betweens linking the host country's politicians and foreign investors.

The state-development banks are also increasingly complemented with a variety of sovereign wealth funds, and public-private infrastructure funds. The Macquarie-Renaissance infrastructure fund in Russia, for example, has contributions from the two private sponsors, VEB, IFC, EBRD, and a broader set of global investors. Similarly, IDFC or IL&FS are innovative funds in India. The rise of such state-backed development banks and public-private funds is a welcome development that has contributed significantly to increasing EMPF volumes. Furthermore, due to increased involvement of local financial

---

7   For further discussion and data, see Sheppard, R. (2011) Effectiveness of mulitlaterals. *Project Finance International*, March 9, Issue 452.

intermediaries, the relative reliance on foreign intermediaries and investors is declining. This too is a welcome development because until recently foreign investors were exposed to several risks, such as the local currency or creeping political expropriation, which they were the inappropriate party to absorb. With greater pools of local capital and expertise, there are greater options to share risks in an appropriate fashion. By the same token, sponsors now have the ability to raise a slice of funds required in local currency terms from the host country's financial markets. Frontier Asian and African markets ought to particularly take note of these developments in more mature emerging markets.

What Makes Project Finance Particularly Suitable to Emerging Markets?

The drivers for interest in non-recourse project finance in EM are manifold but three factors merit particular attention.

First, EM are currently experiencing strong demand for new capital formation (such as for transport and energy infrastructure or natural resource extraction). Currently, more than 20 per cent of global economic activity takes place as projects, and in some emerging economies it exceeds 30 per cent. 'World Bank (2009) data indicate that 22 per cent of the world's US$48tr gross domestic product (GDP) is gross capital formation, which is almost entirely project-based. In India it is 34 per cent, and in China it is 45 per cent of GDP' writes Christophe Bredillet.[8]

Second, traditional corporate financing channels in many EM remain relatively weak when compared to developed economies. Corporate bond market in India, for example, is only 1 per cent of the country's GDP. Corporate bond market is 111.8 per cent of the US GDP, for instance, or 42.4 per cent in Japan.[9] Part of the weakness of traditional corporate financing options in EM can be attributed to relatively poor corporate governance, information asymmetries, and uncertainty regarding the rights of minority shareholders and creditors.[10]

Third, project finance structures are more robust in dealing with risks associated with large projects in emerging markets. The risk mitigation role of project finance comes into its own in emerging markets due to the limited operational track record of many of the project sponsors, magnified macroeconomic and contractual risks. The weakness of traditional corporate financing channels in emerging markets in fact turns out to be a blessing in disguise. Due to the rigour of project finance transactions, EM project managers have less leeway to make mistakes. Cost overruns, poor estimates of demand, or other risks can turn a good investment idea into a liability. It is more difficult for investors to scrutinize large investments financed via traditional corporate finance with respect to their investment performance; whereas project finance provides for greater transparency, which is of particular value in emerging markets.

8   Bredillet, C. (2010) Blowing Hot and Cold on Project Management, *Project Management Journal* 41:3 (2010): 4. Also see, Scranton, P. (2011) *Projects as Business History: Surveying the Landscape*. Rutgers University.

9   ICMA Centre, 2008. The Development of India's Corporate Debt Market. http://217.154.230.218/NR/rdonlyres/98998CB3-DAE9-460A-9193-451F6A53FCED/0/IndiaCDM.pdf Accessed 2 June 2011, p. 27.

10   See, for instance Klapper, L. F. and Love, I. 2004. Corporate Governance, investor protection, and performance in emerging markets. *Journal of Corporate Finance*. Vol. 10(5), 703–728.

Fourth, project finance allows for public and private sector collaboration in innovative ways in emerging markets. For instance, many government programmes in physical or social infrastructure can be implemented via non-recourse techniques. This allows for these programmes to benefit from greater scrutiny of costs and benefits. It also lightens the burden on the balance sheet of the public sector. Since many emerging markets need to accelerate new capital formation, project finance offers a clearer way to prioritize projects with the highest value and hence economic impact.

Concluding Thoughts

Project finance is here to stay as one of the most significant sources of long-dated financing in emerging markets. If the legal and regulatory frameworks in emerging markets keep pace, emerging markets project finance volumes can be expected to grow strongly in coming years, outpacing developed countries. Oil and gas, and petrochemicals, power, and the road and transport sector will likely remain leading sectors. Mining and metals, particularly steel and aluminium, will also remain active areas for project finance. Underpinning the expanding importance of project finance in emerging countries is a critical shift. Instead of a reliance on foreign arrangers, home-grown, and often state-backed, intermediaries such as State Bank of India, Bank of China, China Construction Bank, VEB in Russia, and BNDES in Brazil are assuming a central role in making project finance deals happen. Similarly, domestic institutional investors and banks – and not foreign investors – are becoming the proportionally largest source of capital for many transactions. Foreign sponsors and investors, interested in exposure to emerging market project finance, need to take into account this shifting landscape to capitalize on arising opportunities.

25 *Project Finance in Australia*

PHILLIP CORNWELL, Partner
ROB WATT, Partner
BEN FARNSWORTH, Senior Associate
HUGH BOYLAN, Lawyer
Allens Arthur Robinson

Project finance activity has recently made a marked recovery in Australia. The sector is experiencing a period of growth driven not just by the resources boom but also by social and economic infrastructure projects (in particular public private partnerships). As the effects of the global financial crisis fade, evidence of Australia's upcoming project pipeline is a clear indication of this turnaround in activity and investment appetite.

The combined capital expenditure (capex) of Australia's advanced minerals and energy projects was a record AUS\$173.5bn in April 2011, 31 per cent higher than in October 2010. The latest figures on mining investment from the Australian Bureau of Agricultural and Resource Economics and Sciences (ABARES) indicate that mining companies are expected to increase spending by as much as 83.5 per cent. Much of this activity is in Western Australia, and figures for April 2011 show that 63 per cent of total advanced capital investment in mining is in that state.[1]

The AUS\$173.5bn figure represents 94 projects at an advanced stage of development (committed or under construction) and includes 35 energy projects, 35 mineral mining projects, 20 infrastructure projects and four minerals and energy processing projects. According to ABARES, the commodities attracting the most investment are oil and gas, iron ore and coal and associated infrastructure, which collectively account for around 92 per cent of all committed capex.[2]

---

1   Australian Bureau of Agricultural and Resource Economics and Sciences, Minerals and Energy – Major Development Projects, April 2011 Listing, p 1.

2   Australian Bureau of Agricultural and Resource Economics and Sciences, Minerals and Energy – Major Development Projects, April 2011 Listing, p 1.

Infrastructure

PUBLIC PRIVATE PARTNERSHIPS

Public private partnerships (PPPs) continue to play a significant role in financing Australian infrastructure. Infrastructure Projects Australia has estimated that approximately AUS$400bn will be spent on Australian infrastructure in the next decade, and that investment in PPPs will constitute 10–15 per cent of that market.[3]

SOCIAL INFRASTRUCTURE

There are currently a large number of projects within the health sector at various stages of procurement. The 2011–12 Federal Budget designated AUS$1.33bn from the Health and Hospitals Fund[4] to fund 63 regional health infrastructure projects. This portfolio, and other current health sector projects include significant developments such as:

The New Royal Adelaide Hospital (SA): this is the largest PPP deal of 2011, and was won by the SA Health Partners consortium (Macquarie Capital, Leighton Contractors, Hansen Yuncken and Spotless). This project involves the construction of an 800-bed hospital on North Terrace in the Adelaide CBD. The project's cost will be approximately AUS$2.6bn and, once completed, the hospital will be one of the most environmentally friendly social infrastructure projects of recent years.[5]

The Sunshine Coast University Hospital (QLD) project is a PPP for the construction of a AUS$2.03bn facility. Expressions of interest have been received and are currently being evaluated. The hospital will have 450 beds by 2016, and will grow to a 738-bed facility by 2021. The Queensland Government has also recently announced that the successful bidder to construct a private hospital also located on the Sunshine Coast University Campus is Ramsay Health Care, an Australian company operating over 100 medical facilities worldwide. Construction is scheduled to commence in 2012 and the design-build team includes construction firm John Holland and architects Phillips Smith Conwell. Akalan Projects will be Project Manager. The Queensland government is also financing a AUS$1.4bn, 400-bed new Royal Children's Hospital in Brisbane (partly financed by the proceeds of an agreement for Tattersall's to manage Golden Casket and to operate lotteries).

Other health sector projects include the Royal North Shore Hospital Redevelopment (NSW), Orange Hospital Redevelopment (NSW), Wagga Wagga Hospital Redevelopment (NSW), Royal Hobart Hospital (TAS), Fiona Stanley Hospital (WA), QEII Medical Centre Redevelopment (WA), Midland Health Campus (WA), Monash Children's Hospital, Bendigo Hospital (VIC) and the Parkville Cancer Centre (VIC) – with three consortia; Plenary Health, the Nexus Partnership and Aptus Health.

---

3   See Infrastructure Projects Australia: *Performance of PPPs and Traditional Procurement in Australia*, November 2007.

4   The Health and Hospitals Fund was set up with the aims of investing in major health infrastructure programmes that will make significant progress towards achieving the Commonwealth's health reform targets; and make strategic investments in the health system that will underpin major improvements in efficiency, access or outcomes of health care. The HHF is governed by the *Nation-building Funds Act 2008* (Cth).

5   Measures include use of rain water, high efficiency water fittings and a tri-generation system (with absorption chillers) will utilize waste heat from energy generators to provide heating and cooling to the building. For further information on the hospital's 'green initiatives' see www.sahealth.sa.gov.au.

There are also a number of projects planned to provide custodial services, including the Doug Owston Correctional Centre (NT), a AUS$23m development of the Eastern Goldfields Prison (WA), Young Adults Prison (WA), as well as opportunities in government housing provision. The major players in Australia are also active in NZ, with bids due for the Wiri prison, South Auckland in August 2011.

ECONOMIC INFRASTRUCTURE

Australian economic infrastructure projects are usually very large in scale and so tend to dominate the project finance market. There are numerous road and rail projects underway and the 2011–12 Federal Budget commits AUS$1bn of funding for major transport projects.

a) *Public transport* – There have been some well publicized difficulties for existing Australian toll road projects. Brisbane's Airport Link toll road has not yet reached completion, and has already produced substantial losses for its builder Leightons. There are fears that its actual traffic flows once opened will not meet projections, following recent difficulties for RiverCity Motorway in Brisbane and the Lane Cove and Cross-City tunnels in Sydney (each having gone into receivership). In the toll road space, the Peninsula Link project financed by the Victorian Government and the Southern Way Consortium (by way of a nine-bank club facility debt provision with equity provided by Bilfinger Berger Project Investments, State Super, Officers Super Fund and Prime Super) may show the way forwards. There are also developments in rail services, including Brisbane's Cross River Rail and the Melbourne Metro Rail Tunnel.

   The Federal Government has recently taken steps to increase the appeal of funding airport developments. In May 2011, the Government publicized its intention to extend the term of the series of tripartite deeds currently applying to Australia's 12 privatized airports. The deeds provide greater certainty to financiers in the event of a government-leased privatized airport becoming insolvent by providing limited step in rights to the financiers in circumstances where the airport lease is terminated. The deeds also grant secured financiers the ability to claim the debt owed to them against the Commonwealth which is required to pay that amount out of any funds it obtains from selling on the lease. The extension of the deeds comes in response to the expression of concern by airport operators and the Australian Airports Association that development will become prohibitively expensive without the comfort afforded to lenders by the deeds. The Minister for Infrastructure and Transport has reported that Aus$9b is expected to be invested in Australian airport development over the next 10 years.[6]

b) *Resource infrastructure* – The Newcastle Coal and Infrastructure Group (NCIG) Coal Terminal is noteworthy. Stage 1 of the project was the largest single stage development of a coal terminal of its size in the world. The project has now reached Stage 3, and the terminal capacity on completion is estimated to be 66m tonnes per annum. The members of NCIG are BHP Billiton (BHP), Centennial Coal, Donaldson Coal, Peabody

---

6   See www.minister.infrastructure.gov. au. This figure was included in a media statement issued by the Hon Anthony Albanese on 24 May 2011.

Energy, Yancoal and Whitehaven Coal and are all significant coal producers with an interest in ensuring the on-going development of relevant infrastructure apparatus.

The privatizations of Port of Brisbane (Morgan Stanley Infrastructure Fund and Global Infrastructure Partners), Queensland Rail and the Abbott Point Coal Terminal by Indian company Adani (a further example of export infrastructure) have also been the subject of national headlines over the previous year.

Significant proposed rail projects include the Oakajee Port and Rail Project in Western Australia and the Surat Basin Rail. The latter rail project will be accessible to general freight, and its construction will make possible the opening up of 16 new coal mines which the project sponsors, Surat Basin Rail Pty Ltd, report will facilitate the mining of approximately 6.3bn tonnes of coal reserves in the Surat Basin.

CHALLENGES

Overly optimistic long-term patronage forecasting continues to present challenges to transport infrastructure projects. A failure to meet traffic forecasts has seen three privately financed toll roads (Sydney's Cross City and Lane Cove Tunnels and Brisbane's River City Motorway) plus the Alice Springs to Darwin Railway go into receivership. This has soured the private sector's appetite for financing toll roads and similar projects. The Peninsula Link roadway in Victoria provides an alternative Australian toll roads model, where the Victorian Government agreed to an availability fee structure that removes the private sector's exposure to patronage risk.

The construction and operation of the Brisbane Airport Link exposes a further challenge. Promoted by the Brisbane City Council and under construction by a joint venture between Theiss and John Holland Group, 24 per cent of this project's funding relied on the equity raised through BrisConnections' initial public offering which lost value dramatically after listing. The World Economic Forum has reinforced the need for greater transparency (using this as an example), as well as the requirement for realistic projections of usage and simplification of the financial structures used in toll road financing.[7]

A wider concern for all infrastructure projects is the risk of cost overruns. Statistics provided by Infrastructure Partnerships Australia however, indicate that the chance of an overrun in the instance of a PPP is greatly reduced. In a study of 21 PPPs and 33 traditional procurement projects Infrastructure Partnerships Australia found that, on a contracted AUS$4.9bn of PPPs, net overrun was AUS$58m, whereas for AUS$4.5bn of traditional procurement, net overrun amounted to AUS$673m.[8] PPPs have the disadvantage of exposure to political risk, as seen in the cancellation, well into the bid process after short-listing, of the Sydney CBD Metro (noting, however, that bidders are to be at least partly compensated for bid costs).

---

7   World Economic Forum and PriceWaterhouseCoopers, *Paving the Way: Maximising the Value of Private Finance in Infrastructure*, August 2010.

8   Infrastructure Projects Australia, *Performance of PPPs and Traditional Procurement in Australia*, November 2007, p 1.

FUTURE FUNDING SOURCES

The Federal Government has recognized the important role Australian superannuation funds and private investors can play in funding infrastructure, with significant tax incentives announced in the 2011–12 Federal Budget. Private investment has the obvious advantage of freeing up government capital for other projects, whilst the long-term investment appetite and sheer quantum of equity held by superannuation funds sets them apart as prime investors for infrastructure projects.

One possible means of such participation would be investment in infrastructure bonds. This argument was floated by the Liberal Party in the lead up to the 2010 election. Under such a scheme, private infrastructure projects could issue bonds to be purchased by super funds or retail investors who would then receive a tax rebate on dividend received from the bonds. Following a survey, Ernst & Young has suggested the creation of an IBX (Infrastructure Bond Exchange) to inform the market of super funds' demand for the bonds. Under Ernst & Young's model, bonds would be issued according to infrastructure asset class, giving investors the opportunity to purchase solely in a particular industry.[9]

Another possible method of finance would involve the revival of Australia's domestic bond market. Australia's corporate bond market is underdeveloped and large Australian companies prefer to issue bonds in the US or European markets. Development of an Australian retail bond market is hampered by over-regulation, however, post-GFC, there is strengthening issuer demand for alternative funding sources, as evidenced by the increasing number of Australian corporates issuing in foreign debt markets. The popular pre-GFC use of credit wraps provided by monoline insurers to finance infrastructure projects is no longer available. Monoline insurance enabled companies to access AAA credit ratings for projects that would otherwise have had a lower rating, affording them cheaper finance. The collapse of the monolines has stripped the infrastructure sector of an important avenue for finance and it will be necessary for Australian project financiers to find new ways to bridge these funding gaps.

There are a number of challenges to be overcome. However, the re-opening of Australia's domestic bonds market to infrastructure projects and the introduction of infrastructure bonds would provide an ideal method of funding for long-term PPPs due to the layer tenors available in the debt markets and possible reductions in refinancing expenses.

Oil and Gas

LIQUEFIED NATURAL GAS

The combined capex of Australian liquefied natural gas (LNG) projects in differing stages of construction is approximately AUS$200bn, with Australia expected to become the world's largest LNG provider (behind Qatar) by 2015–16. Australia is also uniquely positioned within the Asia Pacific LNG market, as short shipment times coupled with an increase in regional demand will reduce Asia's reliance on the Gulf states as its primary LNG source.

---

9   Ernst & Young, *The Trillion Dollar Question: Can superannuation boost investment in Australia's infrastructure?*, 2009. The authors provide the examples of health, road and heavy rail.

LNG projects currently underway include Gorgon LNG (Chevron, Exxon Mobil Shell, Osaka Gas, Tokyo Gas and Chubu Electric Power), the Ichthys LNG Project (INPEX Browse Ltd and Total E&P Australia), Wheatstone LNG (Chevron, Apache Corporation and Kuwait Foreign Petroleum Exploration Company), Woodside's Pluto Project (Woodside, Tokyo Gas and Kansai Electric), and the Browse LNG Project (Woodside, BHP, BP Developments Australia Pty Ltd, Chevron Australia and Shell Development Australia). Chevron recently sought Federal Government approval to boost production of LNG from its Gorgon project by 33 per cent to 20m tonnes per year. Chevron will require a fourth processing unit at the site to meet this target.

There are also developments in floating LNG. Floating LNG refers to the production, storage and offloading of LNG on a floating vessel. Floating production storage and offloading vessels (FPSOs) are more commonly used in the production and storage of oil. The world's first LNG FPSOs are currently under construction, including Shell's FPSO project development, Prelude, centring on a 500m vessel off the coast of Western Australia. Shell is likely to fund the project almost entirely by way of equity finance, as the relatively young FLNG project market has yet to engender necessary lender confidence. Shell's international executive director has reported that the project is likely to cost between US$3bn and US$3.5bn per million tonnes of production (an investment of between US$10.8bn and US$12.6bn). The project is set to commence operating in 2016. There are reportedly 150 gas fields which could be harvested by FLNG and Australia is high on the list of potential sources.

Despite worldwide acknowledgement that LNG is a 'greener' source of energy than other fossil fuels, the proposed carbon tax agreed under the Labour Government's former emissions trading scheme[10] poses a particular challenge to LNG producers. Industry leaders claim that the application of this proposed regime to LNG producers has the potential to cripple the AUS$90bn of LNG projects expected to be in progress at the time the new tax is enacted and threatens the ability of Australian producers to compete in the global market. The Australian Federal Government has recognized the significant changes in the LNG industry since the 2009 agreement and has agreed to enter into talks with the industry to re-assess the current treatment.

COAL SEAM GAS

Coal seam gas (CSG) (also known as coal seam methane or coal bed methane) occurs when coal is formed deep underground by a process of heating and compressing plant matter. In usable form, it is the same as conventional LNG. Coal seam gas is trapped in the coal in tiny fractures, known as seams or cleats, typically 300–600 metres underground. The gas is held in place by water pressure and is extracted via wells drilled through the coal seams. When the water pressure is reduced, natural gas is released from the coal. The gas is then processed to remove water and piped to compression plants for injection into gas transmission pipelines.

---

10   The Carbon Pollution Reduction Scheme. Under the terms of the Scheme, LNG companies were due to receive free carbon credits for 66 per cent of their emissions – as well as a six-point recession buffer. At the time of the Scheme's development, only two major LNG projects were underway in Australia, and the CSG industry expansion was not accounted for.

LNG and CSG usage in Australia is expected to grow by 3.4 per cent per year until 2030, largely driven by a growing demand from the electricity generation sector.[11] This increase in production will be facilitated by numerous development projects, many of which are already underway.

There has been significant activity in the international and Australian CSG markets in the past few years. CSG production in Queensland and New South Wales is projected to increase from 118 petajoules in 2007–08 to 2507 petajoules by 2029–30.[12] By 2015 it is likely that CSG will be converted to LNG. Currently, there are several proposed CSG to LNG projects with a potential capacity to produce up to 43m tonnes (2312 petajoules) per year by 2020. Those projects include Australia Pacific LNG (APLNG) (Origin, ConocoPhillips and Sinopec), Gladstone LNG Project and the Fisherman's Landing Project (Santos, KOGAS, Petronas, Kansai Energy and Tokyo Gas) and Queensland Curtis LNG (BG Group, CNOOC, Tokyo Gas).

China's Sinopec has entered into a US$90bn, 20-year supply agreement with Origin and Conoco regarding the APLNG project, in which Sinopec will buy 4.3m tonnes of LNG a year for 20 years. Sinopec has also acquired a 15 per cent stake in the APLNG project with plans to export Queensland CSG to Asia. This mirrors a long-term supply deal struck between Santos and Total in 2010, in which Santos sold a 15 per cent stake in its Gladstone LNG project to Total, which also contracted to purchase 1.5m tonnes of LNG a year for 20 years.

SHALE GAS

Shale gas refers to natural gas that is trapped within shale formations (fine-grained sedimentary rocks that can be rich sources of petroleum and natural gas). Over the past decade, a combination of horizontal drilling and hydraulic fracturing (or 'fracking') has facilitated access to large volumes of shale gas that were previously uneconomical to produce. The growing role of shale gas in the US and Asian markets is steering Australia towards greater investment in its production.[13]

Typically found alongside conventional gas reserves, companies with rights over current reserves stand to profit from the processing of shale. Beach Energy, which has a large stake in the Cooper Basin (across north-east South Australia and south-west Queensland), has joined with Canada's ATCO to assess shale reserves. Santos, which also has rights in the Cooper Basin, may follow suit. Australian Worldwide Exploration and Norwest are both targeting shale in key regions of Western Australia.

Shale gas and CSG production has been argued to have a reduced carbon footprint from that of other energy sources (see below), and technological advances are now lessening the difficulties associated with extraction. Shale exploration companies have also noted that deposits are generally large enough to offset higher extraction costs.[14] It is

---

11   Syed et al., *Australian Energy Projections to 2029–2030, Australian Bureau of Agricultural and Resource Economics*, March 2010, 1.

12   Syed et al., *Australian Energy Projections to 2029–2030, Australian Bureau of Agricultural and Resource Economics*, March 2010, p 2.

13   We note that both the United States and China have substantial shale gas deposits. In relation to China, it is possible that these extensive reserves may decrease the country's reliance on Australian LNG.

14   Cant, W, quoting Sam Willis of New Standard Energy, 'Australian Shale Gas could be the Next Big Thing', *Oil & Gas Australia*, April 2010, 10.

also possible that production will increase in the next decade as Australia's LNG providers struggle to meet export demand.

OIL

One of the most significant developments is that of Exxon Mobil, Esso Australia, BHP and Santos' Kipper Tuna Turrum project, which involves both the construction of new facilities and the redevelopment of existing facilities to extract and process gas and oil. The Turrum field holds approximately 110m barrels of oil and gas liquids. With regard to oil processing, the redevelopment includes the building of a new platform (Marlin B) to be linked to the Marlin A platform in the Bass Strait (the first of such projects in the strait for over a decade). The new platform will process additional oil to be piped back to Longford via the pre-existing pipeline.

The Turrum development is part of the Gippsland Basin joint venture between BHP and Esso. The Tuna reservoir will continue to process oil and is being developed to produce gas and other liquids available from the field. BHP has recently announced an increase in its share of the capex for this segment of the project to US$1.35b (up from US$625m), and the project will not begin operating until 2013. BHP has cited cost overruns and the discovery of mercury, as well as design and fabrication problems, as the cause of delay and capex overrun.

OIL AND GAS SECTOR CHALLENGES

Cost overruns and delays to timelines have the ability to significantly reduce the viability of any project, perpetuated by the imposition of potentially unattainable deadlines and the large production requirements characteristic of this market. For example, over US$70bn has been invested in Queensland projects with 4000 wells to be drilled between now and 2015. In 2010, only 435 wells were drilled and it is estimated that in order to deliver expected LNG capacity, Queensland providers will need to produce 33m tons of LNG from 2014 to 2020.[15]

CSG and shale gas are extracted by fracking, which requires large amounts of water and accordingly impacts upon the subterranean water table, notably Australia's Great Artesian Basin. If mismanaged, hydraulic fracturing fluid (which may contain potentially hazardous chemicals) can be released by spills or leaks and contaminate surrounding areas. The extraction process is also proven to raise salinity in the water table and produces large amounts of wastewater, which may contain dissolved chemicals and other contaminants that require treatment before disposal or reuse. The amount of water used and the complexities inherent in treating some of the wastewater components makes treatment and disposal important and challenging issues for the industry. It has also been reported that the fracking process may lead to increased seismic activity.[16]

There has also been significant debate regarding whether CSG and shale gas are 'cleaner' forms of energy than coal. Deutsche Bank, Climate Change Advisors and the Worldwatch

---

15   Stojkovic, M., *Cost, risk management key to CSG-LNG success*, Energy News Bulletin, 12 April 2011.

16   This has been reported in Canada, Switzerland and the United States. See Deutsche Bank Climate Change Advisers and the Worldwatch Institute, Natural Gas and Renewables: A Secure Low Carbon Future Energy Plan for the United States, November 2010.

Institute expect that data will be released over the next 12–18 months which will help to better conduct life-cycle analysis of unconventional natural gas production and assist in addressing some environmental concerns.[17] The same organizations have also drawn attention to the urgent need for more robust empirical data quantifying the life-cycle greenhouse gas emissions from electricity produced from coal and both conventional and unconventional natural gas, and have warned analysts and stakeholders against drawing premature conclusions.[18]

The Greens have raised considerable opposition to gas developments, with particular reference to the water issues highlighted above, as well as the impact on Queensland's agricultural sector (according to the Greens agricultural production in the area is worth between AUS$1.5bn and AUS$2bn) as significant concerns.[19] A recent gas leak at one of Arrow Energy's CSG wells has also contributed to anti-industry sentiment. A variety of anti-CSG groups have been established throughout Australia representing various interest groups, notably farmers and conservationists. In May 2011, New South Wales announced a 60-day moratorium on new coal, petroleum and CSG exploration licences.

Litigation has been launched in the US and Canada, whilst in Australia the New South Wales Environmental Defenders Office has lodged an appeal against two decisions of the Planning Assessment Commission (PAC) to approve the concept plan and stage one of the Gloucester CSG project. The case will focus on the PAC's consideration of the environmental impact of the Gloucester project.

The projects are large scale, and foreign export credit agencies (ECAs) have bridged funding gaps. In February 2011, the Japan Bank for International Co-operation (JBIC) provided US$102m of funding to Chevron's Gorgon LNG project by way of a loan agreement with Tokyo Gas Gorgon LNG in order for it to acquire a stake in the project and participate in the project's development. Also, China Eximbank (the Export-Import Bank of China) and Australia's Westpac Bank have recently entered into a general co-operation agreement in order to jointly pursue major energy, infrastructure, mineral and agriculture projects.

Whilst not limited to the oil and gas sectors, there is a Foreign Investment Review Board issue (the FIRB is the body established by the Foreign Acquisitions and Takeovers Act 1975 (Cth) (the FATA)) evident in, for example, JBIC's role in the Gorgon LNG project. Whilst the FATA provides an exception to notification requirements to the FIRB for foreign money lending institutions, recent amendments to Australia's foreign investments policy highlight that enforcing a security is a 'direct investment', and 'foreign governments or related entities' (being entities in which a foreign government owns a larger than 15 per cent share) are required to notify FIRB of their investments. Government-sponsored export credit agencies (ECAs) may therefore face difficulty enforcing a security where there is a failure to notify the FIRB of the provision of finance to a project.

An unincorporated joint venture is a popular structure in Australian project finance where the scale of many projects necessitates apportioning risk between sponsors. Whilst it has been contended that the unincorporated joint venture is an appealing financial

17   Deutsche Bank Climate Change Advisers and the Worldwatch Institute, Comparing Life Cycle Greenhouse Gas Emissions from Natural Gas and Coal, March 2011.

18   Ibid.

19   Australian Greens Policy Initiative: *Protecting our farms; protecting our water, Regulating the coal seam gas industry*, 2010.

structure to foreign investors, it is arguable that the lack of familiarity with such a structure operates as a disincentive for some financiers. For example, the unincorporated joint venture can subordinate a financier's security interests over a participant's assets to the interests of another joint venturer. It also saddles participants with unlimited several liability, and the lack of regulation governing them means that common law provides most guidance, posing difficulty to financiers from non-common law jurisdictions. Single corporate management structures are more familiar to foreign sponsors, and accordingly, at the very least, the incorporated joint venture with its 'management committee' will likely be more attractive. It has also been recently noted that tax liabilities under Australia's incoming Minerals Resources Rent Tax (MRRT) may affect the use of the joint venture structure in coal and iron ore projects.

Multiple joint ventures between the same parties over Australian resources is not uncommon. For example, Shell's FLNG project, Prelude, is close to the Browse Basin where Shell is a participant in a joint venture with Chevron, BHP, BP and Woodside. That joint venture has faced difficulties on many fronts, from party disagreements to land rights claims, whilst Shell's historical solo FLNG project is proceeding smoothly. It is apparent that where parties have capacity to undertake a project on their own, it may end up being more economical doing so, despite taking on the additional risk. This could lead to large asset re-shuffles and joint venture buy-outs across the resources landscape as individual players with an eye on private LNG projects shift investments across the board.

Resources

IRON ORE

Australia has the second largest accessible iron ore reserve in the world.[20] Rapidly developing Asian economies have created an Australian resources boom, and the largest buyer of Australia's iron ore is China,[21] whose demand outstrips its domestic reserves. To meet the increasing demand, mining projects abound and the sector remains one of Australia's most profitable, despite a seeming duopoly comprising mining giants BHP and Rio Tinto who together control 80 per cent of the country's iron ore production.

BHP's Rapid Growth Project 5 is presently underway, which will increase the company's production capacity to around 205 million tonnes per annum (mtpa) by late 2011. Rio and FMG plan to expand their projects in the Pilbara (the expansions will raise Rio's production capacity to approximately 283 mtpa by 2013, and FMG's will rise to 155 mtpa). CITIC Pacific Mining is developing the country's first magnetite mine, where currently all Australian iron ore mines are hematite.[22]

Other proposed projects, mainly in the Pilbara and mid-west regions of WA, are at various stages of planning and design. Overall, the investment projects already committed

---

20   Defined by Geoscience Australia as accessible economic demonstrated resources. Ukraine (18 per cent of global total) has the largest reserves of iron ore, *Reserve Bank of Australia Bulletin*, March Quarter, 2011.

21   Almost 70 per cent of ore exports were to China in 2010, *Reserve Bank of Australia Bulletin*, March Quarter, 2011.

22   *Reserve Bank of Australia Bulletin*, March Quarter, 2011.

– which total around AUS$35bn – suggest that Australia's iron ore production and exports are likely to increase by around 50 per cent over the next four years.[23]

Other iron ore projects include WPG Resources' South Australian Peculiar Knob Iron Ore project (intended to be a Direct Shipping Ore project transporting 3.3 mtpa to Asian markets), Crosslands Resources' expansion of its Jack Hills Iron Ore Project (from 2 mtpa to 35 mtpa, this mine will be a major user of the Oakajee port and rail project described above), and Hancock Prospecting's Roy Hill Iron Ore Project (the deposit contains in excess of 2.4bn tonnes of low phosphorous iron ore and exports from this region are currently 300 mtpa). Aquila Resources and US-based American Metal and Coal International have launched an AUS$4bn joint venture project to extract 500m tonnes of iron ore from the Pilbara. This will involve the construction of a 275km heavy haulage railway and a new deepwater port at Anketell Point near Karratha; yet another example of the flourishing export resources infrastructure sector that has developed with the resources boom. A plethora of other projects are in varying stages of development.

There also remains a significant demand for other Australian minerals, including gold and copper.

COAL

The black coal mining industry is expected to generate revenue of AUS$57.32bn in 2010–11, compared with AUS$36.16bn five years earlier. Despite flooding in the major coal mining areas of Queensland, industry revenue is expected to grow by nearly 27 per cent in 2010–11.[24] Whilst coal is used to generate 76 per cent of Australia's domestic electricity, three quarters of the country's black coal is exported, with Australia accounting for 6 per cent of the world's black coal production. Foreign demand for Australian coal continues to increase and accordingly there are a number of projects in various stages of development.

The Arckaringa Project, a large joint venture between subsidiaries of Altona Energy and CNOOC, is a AUS$3bn coal-to-liquids project for which CNOOC recently received FIRB approval. MacArthur Coal and Gloucester Coal's AUS$170m Middlemount Coal Project in Queensland commences operations this year, and AMCI (Alpha) Pty Ltd and Bandanna Energy's South Galilee Coal project has recently received positive feasibility study results (and is likely to commence in around 2016). Hancock and Waratah Coal also have future Galilee projects, and the existing facilities at Xstrata and Mitsubishi Development Corporation's Ulan Coal Mine) are being further developed. The Queensland Government and Xstrata are conducting feasibility studies and environmental assessments to determine the viability of the AUS$6b Wandoan Coal project. Further projects in the pipeline for the next five years include Anglo-American's AUS$1.1bn Grosvenor Underground; BHP's AUS$4 billion Peak Downs project, Hancock's AUS$3.4bn Tad's Corner project; Aquila Resources' AUS$2.8bn Belvedere underground development and Anglo Amer's AUS$1.3bn Moranbah South underground development will both commence.

---

23   *Reserve Bank of Australia Bulletin*, March Quarter, 2011.

24   IBISWorld, Black Coal Mining in Australia – An Industry Report, 6 May 2011.

CHALLENGES

(a) Minerals Resources Rent Tax

The MRRT is a project-based tax that, from 1 July 2012, will apply to iron ore and coal extraction projects.[25] A 'project' encompasses extraction activities related to iron ore or coal up to the taxing point. However, producers with less than AUS$50m in resource profits in an income year will be exempt from the MRRT. Entities consolidated for income tax purposes will be able to elect to be consolidated for MRRT purposes. The head company of a consolidated group that makes that election will be responsible for paying the MRRT of the entire group, but each entity in the group will be jointly and severally liable for the group's unpaid MRRT.

The rate of tax imposed by the MRRT is 30 per cent of the taxable profit. However, in recognition of the contribution that miners' expertise makes to profits, projects will be entitled to a 25 per cent extraction allowance, which effectively reduces the real rate of tax to 22.5 per cent. The MRRT will be deductible for income tax purposes. Miners with existing projects as at 1 May 2010 can claim MRRT deductions for a 'starting base' for those projects. An entity can choose to calculate starting base deductions based on either book value or market value for each interest the entity holds in a project or other mining tenement that was in existence at 1 May 2010.

There remain ambiguities in the MRRT legislation. The first of these is the definition of 'project'. As the MRRT is a project-based tax, determining how a project is defined, the treatment of multiple interests in a project and a single interest in multiple projects will be key issues in practice. There are also issues associated with valuing a resource to determine taxable revenue: where there is not an arm's length sale at the taxing point, issues arise as to determining how to value the resource at the time it leaves the run of the mine stockpile (i.e. the taxing point). In certain cases, a 'safe harbour' valuation method may be available. There may also be problems determining what costs are 'necessarily incurred' in carrying on mining operations upstream of the taxing point, and therefore deductible. This will not always be straightforward (e.g. financing costs will generally not be deductible).

(b) Funding issues

As described above in relation to the oil and gas sector, the scale of funding required in developing mining projects provides a series of challenges (including, as above, enabling ECA involvement in transactions). Recently, the low rates on US government bonds have resulted in buyers seeking higher returns on corporate bonds, and miners are taking advantage of this development. Unrated junior and mid-tier miners have displayed a preference for sourcing finance by issuing high yield bonds; Midwest Vanadium and Boart Longyear are examples – both companies issued high yield bonds in excess of AUS$300m last year. This follows an increase in the big players' use of debt finance, with Fortescue

---

[25] We note that onshore oil and gas projects in Australia will be brought within the existing Petroleum Rent Resource Tax that already applies to offshore oil and gas projects.

Metals' AUS$2.05bn high yield bond issue (making it the seventh largest issuer in the US bond market in 2010[26]).

Intierra has also highlighted another problem faced by junior miners – whilst many institutions will provide them with equity finance, significantly fewer will provider debt finance to single mine companies looking for AUS$20-AUS$200m. Intierra reports from its database that, since April 2009, 63 listed companies have raised between AUS$20m and AUS$200m by way of loans or convertible notes. Thirty-seven of those transactions were to fund the development of a mine (to place this figure in perspective, there are more than 950 projects in feasibility or pre-feasibility). Only eight of those 37 transactions involved major banks.[27]

(c) Labour shortages

All existing Australian energy and resources projects currently face labour shortages. In Western Australia it has been forecast that 119,500 people will need to work in the minerals and energy sector to meet 2012 demands. In 2009, there were 75,600 people working in the sector. The Gorgon Gas project, combined with expansions at BHP's Pilbara, will contribute significantly to this increase in demand for labour – as will the now booming Queensland energy sectors. Labour shortages in Queensland will likely be worsened by the number of people already required for the State's rebuilding programme following the 2010–2011 floods.

(d) Environmental challenges

The mining industry also battles environmental groups who express concern over the potential damage caused by large scale projects. Vasse Coal Management's proposal to mine coal near Margaret River in Western Australia was recently rejected by the Government Environmental Protection Agency because of possible damage to local aquifers as well as concerns relating to noise, dust and waste. The EPA has no authority to prevent a project from going ahead; however, its reports are used to advise ministers as to the correct course of action, and an unfavourable report (along with public protest) is likely to guide the minister to halt the project.

The alleged mutual exclusivity of agricultural and mining interests in the same land has also raised its head in southern Queensland, where Xstrata's AUS$6bn Wandoan coalmine faces a legislative agenda aimed at reclassifying the site as prime agricultural land – which would prevent Xstrata from continuing with the project. The Queensland Government has proposed Strategic Cropping Land Legislation, which will impose a Trigger Map (which designates certain land as strategic cropping land), a Protection Area (Central) and Protection Area (Southern) (areas requiring the highest protection) and Protection Areas and Management Areas (areas outside of the Protection Areas that will also receive protection). A similar process of land classification is also said to be underway in New South Wales.

---

26   Bloomberg Businessweek, *Harmony May Sell Bonds to Fund Share of $3 Billion Mine*, 7 April 2011.

27   Intierra Resource Intelligence, Intierra Spotlight: A Debt Gap?, 14 June 2011.

The introduction of carbon pricing has created uncertainty for Victoria's brown coal manufacturers – manufacturing brown coal creates 40 per cent more carbon dioxide than black coal. However, under the Labour Government's 2009 scheme, coal manufacturers were to receive reimbursement based on the intensity of emissions in an attempt to lessen the sting of the new laws, which has the bizarre outcome of providing the greatest polluters with the most money, allowing them to remain competitive to the detriment of smaller black coal miners. This issue has been subject to considerable debate on a state and national level. Despite the uncertainty, however, one of Victoria's largest brown coal power stations (Loy Yang) has recently received a $500 million refinancing package from its existing investors and a syndicate of Japanese banks as well as a long-term electricity hedging agreement with Alcoa.

Energy

GOVERNMENT POLICY

Environmental concerns and political incentives are changing the face of Australia's energy markets. The country's climate change policy is subject to heated political debate, with Australia currently attempting to tackle climate change by way of a Renewable Energy Target (RET) (implemented in August 2009) to promote investment in the sector, and by enacting legislation aimed at reducing carbon emissions by placing a price on them. The RET aims to cut carbon emissions by 20 per cent by 2020. The RET scheme creates tradeable Renewable Energy Certificates (RECs) to foster a market in renewable energy production.

Although the proposed carbon price scheme faces significant opposition both politically and from powerful industry groups, the Gillard Government has indicated that implementation may begin as early as July 2012. By way of summary, it is set to operate in two phases:

a) The fixed price phase – under the first phase, the price for emissions permits will be fixed in the first year and increase for each subsequent year. Liable entities will be required to purchase emissions permits sufficient to cover their greenhouse gas emissions at the fixed price for each year during this phase. This phase will last for three to five years.

b) The flexible price phase or 'cap and trade' phase – following the fixed price phase, emissions will be capped at an annually decreasing rate that will be determined with reference to Australia's 2020 emissions reduction target. Liable entities will be required to acquire emissions permits sufficient to cover their greenhouse gas emissions at government-run auctions or on the secondary market.

Whilst it is not identical to the Government's previous greenhouse gas emissions trading proposal (the Carbon Pollution Reduction Scheme (CPRS)), due to the on-going debate and lack of certainty regarding the content of the new proposed scheme, interested parties should review the CPRS for guidance. Despite the uncertainty there has been growth in the number of renewable energy projects.

WIND FARM DEVELOPMENTS

Since 2009, 1091MW of wind capacity has been commissioned, more than three times the capacity commissioned in the two years prior to the RET. An additional 742MW of wind capacity is likely to seek financing in 2011.[28] In addition to its 116 turbine project at Mt Gellibrand, Acciona Energy is currently seeking a permit for the construction of a 114MW, 97 generator windfarm at Mortlake. An Australian subsidiary of Meridian Energy Limited is developing a wind farm with a 113MW capacity at Mt Mercer in Victoria. A sample of other projects include Infigen Energy's Woodlawn Windfarm, Mitsui Bald Hills Windfarm, Meridian and AGL's Macarthur Windfarm, Silverton Windfarm, Transfield's Collector Windfarm, Renewable Energy Systems Australia's Ararat Windfarm, Pacific Wind Farm's Nilgen Windfarm, EPURON's Gullen Range Wind Farm, Roaring 40s Renewable Energy's Musselroe Wind Farm and Verve Energy's Mumbida Windfarm.

THE SOLAR FLAGSHIP PROGRAMME

As part of its AUS$5bn Clean Energy Initiative, the Government has committed AUS$1.5bn to support the construction of up to four large-scale solar plants. Eight projects were placed on a shortlist to receive funding[29] and the announcement is imminent. Another solar development includes the Greenough River Solar Farm, a PPP between Verve Energy and the Western Australian Government to build a 10MW solar photovoltaic facility near Ellendale.

GEOTHERMAL DEVELOPMENTS

Australia has large deposits of 'hot-rock' geothermal energy. In 2008 the Geothermal Industry Development Framework (the Framework) was implemented to identify strategies to exploit Australia's significant geothermal resources. Exploration leases have been taken out for land near to Adelaide, Melbourne, Hobart and Geelong. The Framework was set up to complement the Australian Geothermal Industry Technology Roadmap which identifies key technological difficulties facing the industry. Whilst the majority of projects are in their early stages, if they are able to demonstrate the commercial viability of geothermal energy use, there will likely be an increase in investment in the sector (as yet no one has demonstrated the commercial viability of using geothermal energy to produce electricity for supply to the National Energy Market (NEM)). Development is also assisted by government grants issues under the Federal Government's Renewable Energy Demonstration Programme and Geothermal Drilling Programme. The Victorian Government has also provided funding for a development project.

Considerable investment is required for development in this area. Commercial viability in using the energy to produce electricity must be ascertained (geothermal energy is rarely traded in its primary form), and government funding will play a key role in financing projects. ABARES reports that it is not yet possible to determine whether current technology is sufficient to facilitate commercially viable production.[30] There are

---

28   *AEMO Statement of Opportunities 2010*, as cited in Project Finance International, issue 453, 23 March 2011, p 49.

29   Shortlisted sponsors are AGL, BP Solar, Infigen, TRUenergy, Solar Dawn, Solar Flair Alliance, Transfield.

30   Geoscience Australia and ABARE, *Australian Energy Resource Assessment*, 2010.

also potential problems associated with the location of geothermal sources and electricity generation plants: heat is lost when the water or gas is moved and there are associated environmental issues including a small risk of increased seismic activity.

There are currently a number of projects seeking to harness Australia's geothermal reserves. The Geodynamics Ltd project in South Australia's Cooper Basin is the largest project in Australia. Geodynamics completed a proof-of-concept for its Hanabero project in 2009 and is also drilling holes at its Savin and Jolokia prospects. Geodynamics' tenements in the Cooper Basin contain in excess of 400,000 petajoules of high-grade thermal energy. Geodynamics has also commenced development of a 25MW Commercial Demonstration project, and in 2009 the company was granted AUS$90m to assist with the development.[31]

The Paralana project, a joint venture between Petratherm Ltd, Beach Petroleum and TRUenergy, is a 7.5MW pilot plant seeking to supply power to nearby uranium mines and then to scale up to a 30MW demonstration plant connected to the NEM grid. In April 2009, Petratherm Ltd was awarded a AUS$7m geothermal drilling programme grant, and in November 2009 was awarded a AUS$62.75m renewable energy demonstration programme grant to assist with the development of its demonstration project.[32]

Panax Geothermal Ltd started drilling the Salamander 1 well at the Penola Hot Sedimentary Aquifer project having received a AUS$7m grant from Round 1 of the geothermal drilling programme. Panax Geothermal Ltd has announced plans for the rapid development of a 59MW commercial plant at its Penola project in the Limestone Coast area of South Australia.[33] Other projects include Torrens Energy Ltd's development in the Parachilna project area, Green Rock Energy Ltd's work in the Olympic Dam project area, and KUTh Energy Ltd's drilling in its Central Tasmania project area.

POWER STATIONS

There are currently many proposals for both gas- and coal-fired power stations. Whilst the proposed coal-fired power stations will use the latest technology to reduce carbon emissions, they still face considerable opposition from environmentalists. In Western Australia, Aviva is constructing Coolimba (a 450MW station) and Verve Energy and Inalco Energy are upgrading and recommissioning the previously mothballed Muja coal-fired power station.

TRUenergy has proposals for two gas-fired power stations (GFPS); one in Gippsland, Victoria (Yallourn Power Station, 1000MW, next to its existing coal-fired facility) and one as an extension to its existing Tallawarra Power Station in New South Wales (400MW). The Northern Territory Government has recently announced plans to build an AUS$17 million GFPS in Wadeye, an Aboriginal community south-west of Darwin. ERM Power Pty Limited is looking to develop two GFPSs: Braemar 3 (520MW), which will include a high-pressure gas pipeline network, and Wellington Power Station (640MW). Queensland Gas Company and ANZ Infrastructure Services are developing Condamine, a 135MW

---

31   All project descriptions are sourced from Geoscience Australia and ABARE, *Australian Energy Resource Assessment*, 2010.

32   All project descriptions are sourced from Geoscience Australia and ABARE, *Australian Energy Resource Assessment*, 2010.

33   All project descriptions are sourced from Geoscience Australia and ABARE, *Australian Energy Resource Assessment*, 2010.

GFPS. Merredin Energy Holdings also plans to build a 70 MW diesel-fired peaking power station in Western Australia.

CHALLENGES

In addition to the considerable opposition facing the government programmes promoting it, the renewable energy sector is plagued with difficulties. Designed to facilitate investment in the sector, the price of RECs was depressed by the introduction of residential solar incentive schemes in 2010, diminishing the feasibility of large energy projects. Whilst the REC system was originally set up for large enterprises, when domestic RECs became available to retail customers (for items such as solar hot water heaters and photovoltaic panels), the market was flooded with RECs, which depressed their price. In an attempt to combat this, legislation was passed in 2010, dividing the RET into the Large Scale Renewable Energy Target and the Small Scale Renewable Energy Scheme, creating two markets and thereby preventing movements in one scheme from impacting the other. Together, the two schemes are expected to deliver more renewable energy than the Council of Australian Government's 2020 target of 45,000MW.

A further challenge is posed by geography. Many locations in which it would be appropriate to develop renewable energy are not accessible by the national power grid. For example, the country's best solar resources are in areas of central and north-west Australia that cannot access the grid. Remedying this situation will require significant infrastructure investment. The grid will need to be decentralized and extended to more remote parts of Australia where some of the best renewable energy may be harnessed.

The introduction of carbon pricing has created uncertainty for Victoria's brown coal fired power stations – burning brown coal creates 40 per cent more carbon dioxide than black coal. However, under the Labour Government's 2009 carbon reduction scheme, coal miners were to receive reimbursement based on the intensity of emissions in an attempt to lessen the sting of the new laws, allowing them to remain competitive.

This issue has been subject to considerable debate on a state and national level. Despite the uncertainty, however, one of Victoria's largest brown coal power stations (Loy Yang A) has recently achieved a AUS$455m refinancing package from its existing investors and a syndicate of local and international banks, as well as a long-term electricity hedging agreement with Alcoa.

26 *Vietnam Infrastructure: Needs and Challenges*

JAMES HARRIS, Managing Partner, Vietnam and
Singapore
STANLEY BOOTS, Consultant, Vietnam and Hong Kong
Hogan Lovells

Vietnam needs infrastructure. At its Mid-term Consultative Group Meeting for 2011, EuroCham Vietnam estimated that the country will require nearly US$160 billion in infrastructure investments by 2020 to meet the needs of its growing economy, particularly in the power, water, transport (rail, airports and road) as waste treatment sectors.[1]

This chapter discusses Vietnam's infrastructure needs with particular focus on the evolving regulatory environment chosen to attract private sector investment. This chapter is divided amongst the following topics which provide a snapshot of the current state of Vietnam infrastructure development, the framework for addressing these needs and the challenges faced in implementing the infrastructure projects in Vietnam, as follows:

- Part 1 – The challenge of investment efficiency
- Part 2 – The Role of Master Plans
  – Examples from transportation
  – Examples from energy and power
- Part 3 – Decree 108 and the BOT model
- Part 4 – Decision 71 and the PPP model
- Part 5 – Conclusion, challenges to financing.

The authors of this [chapter] have advised on several large infrastructure projects in Vietnam that were implemented between 2002 and the present and therefore have witnessed Vietnam's legal framework for infrastructure investment evolve from a series of ad hoc decisions towards a promise of a fully-fledged PPP model. This chapter is written under the premise that Vietnam's legal framework for infrastructure investment will continue to evolve and must eventually address, with clarity, a practicable risk sharing between investors and government and the government's scope of support

---

1   Vietnam Business Forum held in Hanoi on 27 May 2011.

for projects (particularly, viability gap funding), if Vietnam is to attract sustained investment.

Part 1 – The Challenge of Investment Efficiency

Investment in Vietnam infrastructure is estimated to comprise more than 10 per cent of the nation's GDP, a figure reflective of a high growth economy. Authors Nguyen XuanThanh and David Dapice of the Harvard Kennedy School's Ash Institute for Democratic Governance and Innovation identify that a key challenge in directing investment in Vietnam infrastructure arises due to the mismatch between projects identified politically as preferred investment targets and those that would otherwise be chosen by investors on the basis of economic viability. Nguyen and Dapice illustrate their assertion with the following anecdote:

> An example of how politics can tend to lead to bad infrastructure decisions is that of the North-South Road link. In 2000, the government decided to construct the US$1bn Ho Chi Minh highway which is parallel to Highway 1 but cuts through mountains of central Vietnam, tracing the path of the famous wartime Ho Chi Minh Trail. The rationale for the project is that Vietnam needs a second North-South highway as sections of Highway 1 are often affected by tropical storms and the poor regions in the northwest and the central highlands need a modern road for poverty alleviation. The first stage of the Ho Chi Minh highway, 1,230km in length, is now near completion with actual costs rising to more than US$2bn. With the road nearly devoid of traffic, it is clear that connecting a poor province with another poor province does not create a lot of new traffic. Furthermore, the horrendous nature of the highland regions that the highway goes through means that it is more easily damaged by floods than Highway 1. Vietnam's geography is such that it is very cost effective to build a limited-access highway and a railway that can go through all major coastal towns. Feeder roads can be constructed to connect poorer areas in the highlands to the richer ones in the coast.

Whilst the above anecdote highlights the tension between political selection of projects and their actual economic viability, it also illustrates some of the challenges of developing large scale infrastructure projects without a robust legal framework to guide such projects. In 2000 when the Ho Chi Minh highway was chosen and implemented, Vietnam had not yet developed a body of law specifically designed to support large scale infrastructure investment. Infrastructure projects were selected for political reasons and were governed by ad hoc rules or decisions to address the various investor and lender issues being raised at the time. As a consequence, the Vietnam government found itself committing greater support to projects than it may have originally intended or desired. Today, Vietnam has in place an evolving body of legislation aimed at guiding the project selection process, tendering for qualified investors and allocation of rights and responsibilities during the implementation of such projects. However, the tension between politically driven projects and investors' needs for project viability continues to influence the implementation (or lack thereof) of large scale infrastructure projects in Vietnam.

Part 2 – The Role of Master Plan

The Vietnamese government periodically develops master plans for each key infrastructure sector and publishes lists of projects that are to be developed within the scope of those master plans. Despite Vietnam's urgent need for more infrastructure to sustain its economic growth, and despite the lofty targets of various sector master plans (as discussed below), progress continues to be slow in the actual development and implementation of infrastructure projects across the country. In the recent years, Vietnam's Prime Minister has issued many decisions for the approval of master plans to develop infrastructure status with a vision to 2020 and beyond as far to 2030. Such master plans include:

- Decision 1734 of December 2008 for development of high-speed road transportation systems (Decision 1734)
- Decision 1436 of September 2009 for development of railway systems (Decision 1436)
- Decision 21 of January 2009 for development of air transportation (Decision 21)
- Decision 2190 of December 2009 for development of seaports systems (Decision 2190)
- in January 2011, Decision 05, Decision 06 and Decision 07 of the Prime Minister addressing the transportation systems in the North, the South and the Central areas of Vietnam, respectively.

In the market one often hears allusions to specific projects or project types contemplated in a master plan, as if the master plan has a binding effect on the public or private sector or otherwise lends certainty to specific goals or projects of the government. It is more realistic to view the various master plans as setting general but non-binding targets, aimed at identifying key developmental needs and attracting investment in towards such targets. A master plan provides a 'near' future vision for development and investment, with terms of five or 10 years, with longer term extension of up to 20 years. Certainly, a master plan does not impose any strict legal obligations on any government organizations, agencies or individuals but acts more akin to guidelines for the ministries, industrial agencies and/or Provincial local authorities to develop their specific developmental plans in accordance with the relevant master plan.

Despite the urgency of infrastructure development in general in Vietnam and the targets set by the various master plans, no single infrastructure sector is currently marked as fast track or deemed a priority over other sectors.

The authors note that the transportation and power are particularly constrained and in need of rapid investment. To provide an example of Vietnam's infrastructure needs, the following illustrates the current status and needs of the transportation and energy sectors, although many examples could be drawn from other sectors as well.

TRANSPORT

a) Airports

Vietnam has a total of 23 airports of which nine are deemed international airports due to serving flights to and from other countries. However, in practice NoiBai International Airport (Hanoi) and Tan Son Nhat International Airport (Ho Chi Minh City) operate the vast majority of international flights, serving 47 airlines and connecting Vietnam with 22 countries and territories. A larger international airport, to be called Long Thanh International Airport, is currently under construction in Dong Nai Province, approximately 60km from Ho Chi Minh City. All other international airports are slated to be upgraded in coming years. The Ministry of Transport, Vietnam estimates the total investment in air transport to require approximately US$13.4bn by 2020.[2]

b) Rail[3]

Decision 1436 (master plan for railway development) contemplates the development of new railway transport systems including a new 1700km North-South route between Hanoi and Ho Chi Minh City to replace the existing route which is ageing and poses various dangers as it passes through residential urban areas. In June 2009, the National Assembly rejected a proposed high-speed railway option for the North-South route (sought by Japanese investors) on grounds of the project's high estimated costs approaching US$56bn. At the time the proposed project appeared to be gaining political moment, some potential lenders expressed to the authors their concerns that high speed rail projects require continual precision maintenance to keep the line accident free, which could pose significant challenges and costs in Vietnam due to the length of the route and the lack of local maintenance skill for such a project. Little progress seems to have been made in respect of a North-South rail project following the National Assembly's rejection of the proposal.

c) Roads

Roads have recently become a key component of Vietnam's development of a public private partnership (PPP) programme, with the World Bank assisting the Ministry of Transport to implement projects under the PPP model, which would offer an alternative to the established BOT model that has been favoured to date. There are approximately 20 highway projects at present to be invested under a BOT or PPP model. A persistent hurdle facing Vietnam highway projects, regardless of the choice of BOT or PPP model, is how to bridge the viability gap where user fees are insufficient and government support is not readily offered. To date many road projects have supported ODA loans, adding the Vietnam's public debt which has approached 56 per cent of the country's GDP in 2010. It is the authors' observation that PPP has been viewed by some in government as a way to stem reliance on ODA by asking the private sector to fund and build necessary road projects (in return for revenue of course). However, viability gap funding will continue to be raised as a key concern and requirement of investors and lenders on Vietnam highway projects, and government may nonetheless find itself having to take on greater debt to cover this concern.

---

2   Green Book 2011 – EU Commercial Counsellors report on Vietnam.
3   Green Book 2011 – EU Commercial Counsellors report on Vietnam.

d) Metros/subways

During 2007 and 2008, the Prime Minister issued Decision 80[4] and Decision 101[5] calling for 11 metro/subway lines to be installed in Hanoi and Ho Chi Minh City. Five lines are anticipated for Hanoi and six for Ho Chi Minh City by 2020. Only a few lines are under construction, such as the Cat Linh – Ha Dong line in Hanoi and the Ben Thanh – ThamLuong and Ben Thanh –- SuoiTien lines in Ho Chi Minh City. The remaining eight lines are still under planning or investor selection. The above decisions further contemplate monorail lines (mass transport systems) to connect the various subway lines.

e) Seaports

Vietnam boasts a 3,260km coastline but few seaports capable of handling deep draught vessels. Decision 2190 (seaport master plan) contemplates the construction of 30 seaports by 2020, comprising international ports, national ports, local ports and special ports (i.e., ports designated for import and export of coal). In early 2011, CaiMep International Port (Ba Ria – Vung Tau Province – South Vietnam) came into operation, becoming the country's first deepwater port as well as the largest port in Vietnam, financed with Japanese loans. The LachHuyen port project (HaiPhong Province – North Vietnam) is under development as a Japanese sponsored bilateral PPP model at an estimated cost of US$1.6 billion.

ENERGY AND POWER

Primary energy and power demands are growing inexorably year on year in Vietnam to meet the needs of this rapidly expanding economy. Between years 2000 and 2009, primary energy demand (i.e. coal, oil, gas and power) grew an average 6.54 per cent per year.

The Vietnam Academy of Science and Technology forecasts that the total energy demand of the country will more than triple between 2010 and 2030 as shown in Table 26.1:[6]

Table 26.1   Energy demand growth

Years	Total energy demand (Million TOE[7])
2010	52,16
2015	72,77
2020	100,86
2025	129,09
2030	169,82

4   Decision 80/2008/QD-TTg.
5   Decision 101/2007/QD-TTg.
6   ibid.
7   Tonne of oil equivalent.

a) Power

Power weighs heavily in Vietnam's continued economic growth. In 2007 with the implementation of Decree 78, Vietnam's initial regulations governing build operate and transfer projects, the government identified 24 specific power projects to be developed across the country, as well as proposed the need for an addition 114 gigawatts (GW) to be developed by 2025. By way of comparison, Vietnam had 9GW of installed power in 2004.

Vietnam Electricity (EVN) is the state utility but does not have the capability to develop all of the proposed projects. Accordingly, in 2008, EVN rejected 13 of the suggested power projects opening their development to the private sector, as shown in Table 26.2:

Table 26.2 Private sector prospects

No.	Coal Fired Project	Capacity	Expected time to start operations	Location	Estimated capital	Proposed Investor (by the Ministry of Planning and Investment and subject to the Prime Minister's final approval)	Prime Minister's Decision (No.7469/VPCP-KTN on 3 November 2008)
1	Duyen Hai[8] 2	1,200	2013, 2014	Tra Vinh Province (South Vietnam)	About US$4 billion for Duyen Hai projects US$1.5 billion for Duyen Hai 2	International tender process	Janakuasa Group (Malaysia)
2	Duyen Hai 3.1	1,000	2014				Pending for final decision
3	Duyen Hai 3.2	1,000	2015				
4	Soc Trang[9] 3.1	1,000	2015	Soc Trang Province (South Vietnam)	About US$5 billion for Soc Trang projects	International tender process	Petro Vietnam (No.3266/ VPCP-KTN on 18 May 2010)
5	Soc Trang 3.2	1,000	2015				
6	Vinh Tan 3.1	1,000	2013	Binh Thuan Province (Central Vietnam)	US$2.6 billion for Vinh Tan 3 projects	EVN	Consortium: EVN, One Energy, Pacific Corporation
7	Vinh Tan 3.2	1,000	2014				

---

8   It was assumed that: the former name of Duyen Hai project listed in Decision 110/2007/QD-TTg dated 18/7/2007 is Tra Vinh project.

9   It was assumed that: the current name of the Soc Trang project listed in Decision 110/2007/QD-TTg fated 18/7/2007 is Long Phu project for investment purposes.

No.	Coal Fired Project	Capacity	Expected time to start operations	Location	Estimated capital	Proposed Investor (by the Ministry of Planning and Investment and subject to the Prime Minister's final approval)	Prime Minister's Decision (No.7469/VPCP-KTN on 3 November 2008)
8	Hai Phong 3.1	600	2013, 2014	Hai Phong City (North Vietnam)	About US$650 million for Hai Phong 3 projects	Vinacomin	Vinacomin
9	Hai Phong 3.2	1,200	2014				
10	Hai Phong 3.3	1,200	2015				
11	Vung Ang 3.1	1,200	2015	Ha Tinh Province (Central Vietnam)	About US$4 billion for Vung Ang projects	Petro Vietnam	International tender process
12	Vung Ang 3.2	1,200	2015				
13	Quang Trach 1, 2[10]	2,400	2015	Quang Binh Province (Central Vietnam)	About US$1.82 billion for Quang Trach projects		International tender process

Of the projects listed above, only a handful have been signed up to date. Negotiation of these projects has been slow and therefore the start of operation dates stated above are generally delayed. The majority of power projects currently under development in Vietnam are fuelled by coal, with a growing number of projects looking to imported coal despite Vietnam's rich coal fields.

b) Renewables

Renewable energy is considered by the Vietnamese government as a long term developmental goal. Vietnam plans to increase the rate of renewable energy to 5 per cent by 2020 and to 11 per cent by 2050[11].

The prevailing view observed by the authors holds that primary energy demands must be satisfied by the lowest cost means as quickly as possible. This favours coal over

---

10   Quang Trach power project was developed with Quang Trach 1 and Quang Trach 2 before, when 13 projects were refused by EVN to invest into. Quang Trach had been proposed as Quang Trach with only 1,200MW of capacity with estimated capital is US$1bn.

11   Decision 1855/QD-TTg dated 27 December 2007 of Prime Minister approving Vietnam's national energy development strategy until 2020 with vision to 2050.

other renewable energy sources, except to a small extent hydro-power. Vietnam currently generates about 35 per cent of its power by hydropower but faces significant annual losses in generation during the dry season. Hydropower production is anticipated to grow 4.9 per cent annually through 2030, whilst in comparison, coal and natural gas are expected to grow 6.9 per cent and 7.3 per cent respectively during the same period to meet immediate and growing base load demand.

Summary – So far, sector development has generally proceeded slower than anticipated in the master plans. A key challenge to the timely implementation of the master plans has been a persistent lack of capacity within the government to tender or award and then negotiate the projects set forth in the various sector project lists. The government lacks sufficient trained human resources to move those projects along at the pace anticipated in the master plans. As noted in the Nguyen and Dapice anecdote above, the projects set forth in the government projects lists are chosen through political processes rather than on the basis of economic viability. To date, the private sector has not been invited to participate in project selection. Rather, the private sector must wait for the invitation to bid for listed projects or must lobby to win specific projects on a negotiated basis.

Part 3 – Decree 108: The BOT Model

The majority of privately invested infrastructure projects in Vietnam have been developed on a concession basis under the build operate and transfer (BOT) model. Other concession models such a build transfer operate (BTO), build transfer (BT) and build own operate (BOO) are in use to a lesser extent in Vietnam.

Currently, Decree 108[12] which came into effect 15 January 2010 regulates concession rights in large scale infrastructure projects in Vietnam, such as ports, rail and road transportation, power, water and waste and other similar projects. It should be noted, however, that Decree 108 does not cover BOO projects, which are still regulated under various legislation including:

- Law on Investment (as the basic law)
- Law on Electricity
- Decree 105 guiding the Law on Electricity
- Decision 30/2006/QD-BCN of Ministry of Industry (now (Ministry of Trade & Industry MOIT)) on IPP projects.

Decree 108 replaced the former Decree 78[13] which was often referred to as the BOT Law. As discussed in the next section of this [chapter], the PPP Framework came into effect on 15 January 2011 and sits alongside Decree 108 to govern certain pilot projects selected for development under a PPP regulatory scheme.

Decree 108 has evolved significantly since the promulgation of the former BOT Law, partly in response to various issues uncovered by the parties in negotiating BOT projects under the former BOT Law which were either unclear or simply not addressed under that former decree. Accordingly, Decree 108 attempts to rectify several gaps found under the

12   Decree 108–2009-ND-CP on Investment on the Basis of BOT, BTO, BT Contracts, effective 15 January 2010.
13   Decree 78–2007-ND-CP on Investment on the Basis of BOT, BTO, BT Contracts, 2007.

former BOT Law, such as the minimum equity requirements placed on concessionaires, the scope of the authorised state body (ASB) to negotiate an extension or reduction in the term of the concession, the rights of lenders to step into projects on the default of the project enterprise and the minimum performance security required of project enterprises, amongst others.

Decree 108[14] must be interpreted by way of more detailed provisions set out in the Circulars to Decree 108–2009-ND-CP (Circulars). Circular 03/2011/TT-BKHDT dated 27 January 2011 of MPI sets forth the guidelines for implementation of a number of articles of Decree 108. This Circular came into effect on 1 April 2011.

SCOPE OF DECREE 108

Decree 108 encourages the implementation of large scale infrastructure projects to support Vietnam's development requirements. The government's current policy seeks to have such infrastructure projects developed by private sector investment through granting concessions, generally on a tender basis (subject to some exceptions), in the form of BOT, BTO or BT projects. Most projects under Decree 108 would be implemented on a BOT basis.

The vast scope of Decree 108 provides significant investment opportunity for project developers entering Vietnam, across a broad range of sectors. For instance, projects in the following sectors fall under Decree 108:[15]

*   Roads, bridges, tunnels and road ferry landings
*   Railways, rail bridges and tunnels
*   Airports, seaports and river-ports
*   Water plants; drainage systems, and waste and sewage treatment systems
*   Power plants and transmission lines
*   Other infrastructure facilities as decided by the Prime Minister.

Each January, the relevant ministries and Provincial People's Committee are required to announce a list of projects (on the relevant websites or by way of the Tendering Newsletter) that are available for investment.[16] When Decree 108 was promulgated, it called for a list of 59 projects to be implemented under BOT, BT and BTO forms, as follows:

*   Roads, bridges, tunnels and road ferry landings: three projects
*   Railways, rail tunnels: 15 projects
*   Airports, seaports and river-ports (including channel): eight projects
*   Power plants: six projects
*   Road projects (including highway/expressway, ring road): 25 projects
*   Economic/industrial zone infrastructure: two projects.

---

14   Decree 108 was amended by Decree 24/2011/ND-CP dated 5 April 2011 by the Government (Amending Articles 4, 8, 11 and 12 of Decree 108). Decree 24 came into effect on 20 May 2011.

15   Decree 108, Article 4.

16   Decree 108, Article 10.

Since then, the list of available projects has changed somewhat but the overall number of projects remains quite large.

THE ROLE OF THE AUTHORIZED STATE BODY

Projects under Decree 108 are implemented by the Authorized State Body (ASB), which is a government ministry or Provincial People's Committee empowered under the act to represent the government to enter into and implement the project contracts in respect of the project.[17] The ASB negotiates directly with the investors and has authority to commit the government to all obligations specified in the BOT/BTO/BT contract.

The nature and size of a project determines who shall act as the ASB. In general, the following parties act as the ASB in the sectors listed below:

• Roads, bridges, tunnels and road ferry landings – Ministry of Transport (MOT)
• Railways, rail bridges and tunnels – MOT
• Airports, seaports and river-ports – MOT
• Water plants; drainage systems, and waste and sewage treatment systems: Provincial People's Committee
• Power plants and transmission lines – Ministry of Industry and Trade.

It is important to note that the ASB seeks approval from other ministries in the government during the course of project negotiation on specific issues relevant to such ministries. Therefore, investors may find that issues previously agreed during negotiation are sometime revisited or reopened as a result of review and comment from other ministries. Prior to the enactment of Decree 108, participation and review by ministries other than the ASB was rather ad hoc, on an as-needed basis. Decree 108 attempts to bring more structure to the role of other ministries by strengthening the provisions of an 'Inter-branch Working Group' whose role is to provide formalized input and assistance from relevant ministries. The role of the Inter-branch Working Group is discussed below.

In addition to the ASB, the investor must also reach an agreement with the relevant off-taker. It is a common misconception that the ASB, as the party empowered to implement a project, has the authority to dictate the commercial terms of the project to the off-taker. The full scope of the ASB's authority is not specified in Decree 108. Therefore, investors must be aware that the ASB cannot dictate commercial terms to the off-takers, although it may express its views on such issues and attempt to obtain agreement from the off-taker. In practice the investor runs simultaneous negotiations with the ASB regarding the terms of the concession agreement and with the off-taker regarding the terms of the off-take contract. The investor faces the challenge of trying to ensure the interests of both the ASB and the off-taker are generally aligned on key commercial interests, in order to avoid having agreed points reopened or stalled.

INTER-BRANCH WORKING GROUP

Behind the scenes during the negotiation of a BOT project, the ASB seeks the input of several key ministries and local authorities with interests in the project. Typically, the

---

17   Decree 108, Article 3.

investor should expect the ASB to seek second opinions from the Ministry of Justice and Ministry of Finance on issues such as the enforcement of security and guarantee provisions, change of law provisions, minimum performance security, etc. In past transactions, these issues were fielded to the relevant ministries as requests for comment in a rather unclear and time consuming process. Decree 108 seeks to streamline this process by providing for an Inter-branch Working Group for each project comprised of members from the ASB, members from relevant ministries and local committees and independent legal, technical and/or financial experts (as determined by the ASB).[18] The purpose of the Inter-branch Working Group is to assist the ASB with issues under negotiation, assist the resolution of matters arising during implementation of the project and to assist with other issues determined by the ASB. In the authors' recent discussions with the MOIT about how the Inter-branch Working Group will function in future deals, we understand that this panel will likely meet more frequently during the negotiation stage to circulate issues amongst the group members for more open, consensus-like decision making. The authors doubt, though, that independent consultants will take a significant role, if any, in the meetings of the Inter-branch Working Group. However, according to the MOIT, advisor opinions will be sought on key issues under deliberation by the group.

If the function of the Inter-branch Working Group is well managed by the ASB, the overall capacity of the ASB negotiating team should naturally increase from deal to deal, and upcoming deals will benefit from the greater overall knowledge base of the group members, particularly if group members participate over the course of several deals.

A couple of challenges, however, still face the effective performance of the Inter-branch Working Group. Firstly, Decree 108 does not clarify whether a budget will be established to permit the participation of independent advisors in the Inter-branch Working Group. This raises a potential stumbling block to the desired function of the group, as meaningful advisor participation would require significant time commitments and therefore a reasonable allocated budget to cover their fees. Secondly, Decree 108 does not provide that investors may approach or participate in meetings of the Inter-branch Working Group. Investors may therefore need to rely on the ASB to fully and properly convey to the other inter-branch working group members the issues under discussion. In the authors' experience, it is good practice in Vietnam for investors to provide to the ASB clear and concise explanations and rationale for key issues under debate, bearing always in mind that such explanations greatly facilitate the ASB's ability to reach a decision with the other members of the Inter-branch Working Group and/or obtain approval from other ministries on issues outside of its authority.

INVESTOR SELECTION

Investors are selected for projects by way of open competitive bidding or through direct awards by the implementing agencies (i.e., 'negotiated deals'). Although the presumption under Decree 108 is that most awards will be made on the basis of open competitive bidding, the negotiated deals seem to be progressing faster towards signing and financial close. For example, in the power sector the Nghi Son 2 coal fired power project was open to competitive bidding but faced significant delays during the tender process such that 'later' projects have progressed to negotiation ahead of Nghi Son 2. At this point,

---

18   Decree108, Article 7.

the project will not reach commercial operations by the 2012–2013 start date that was anticipated when Decree 108 was enacted. By comparison, the Van Phong coal fired power project has already moved into negotiations on the project documents, even though commercial operations for Van Phong were aimed for 2015, significantly later than Nghi Son 2.

Although the government favours competitive bidding, the tendering process requires significantly more work from the working team of the ASB to address numerous, varying bidder (and their lenders) comments to the project documentation and other variables, which stress the operating capacity of the ASB responsible for the bid project. Effective competitive bidding will continue to be hampered unless the government allocates greater human and financial resources to the relevant ASB teams or the ASB develops uniform project documents (particularly the concession agreement, the off-take contract and form of guarantee) applicable to all BOT/BTO/BT projects within the sector.

Decree 108 provides that a potential investor may propose a project outside of the official list of projects, e.g., an 'unsolicited project'.[19] Most investors with whom the authors have spoken are not fully satisfied with Decree 108's approach to unsolicited projects. They typically point out that a potential investor loses the benefit of being a front runner in developing a project because Decree 108 requires the unsolicited project to go to competitive bidding if other parties are interested in pursuing the project.[20] Neither Decree 108 nor the Circulars specify the method by which bids for unsolicited projects will be evaluated and/or weighted. Accordingly, there is little incentive for a potential investor to undertake the initial development and feasibility study for an unsolicited project.

MINIMUM EQUITY INVESTMENT AND MINIMUM SECURITY

Decree 108 sets out minimum equity requirements for BOT projects, which vary according to the size of the total investment capital of the project. For projects up to 1500bn dong (approximately US$75m), the minimum equity invested by the project enterprise must not be lower than 15 per cent of the total investment capital of such project.[21] For projects with a total investment capital exceeding 1500b dong (approximately US$75m), the project enterprise must hold at least 15 per cent equity for the portion up to such 1500bn dong and at least 10 per cent for the portion in excess of 1500bn dong.[22]

It should be noted that the ASB may request the project enterprise to invest greater equity than the minimum equity requirements set out in Decree 108. In practice, however, lenders are likely to require a greater overall equity commitment from the project enterprise for the initial financing of large scale projects, and therefore the minimum equity requirements of Decree 108 are more likely to be at issue when negotiating the rights of the investors to seek refinancing and reduction of equity at a later stage in the project's life.

---

19   Decree 108, Article 11.
20   Decree 108, Article 11(4).
21   Decree 108, Article 5(2).
22   Decree 108, Article 5(3).

SECURITY

Decree 108 also specifies the scope and quantum of security to be provided to secure the performance of the project contract. Particularly, security is required for all projects to cover implementation from the date of signing the project contracts until the date of completion of the project works.[23] Similar to the calculation of minimum equity requirement above, the amount of such security is determined in two portions. For the portion of the investment capital up to 1500bn dong (approximately US$75m), the security must not be less than 2 per cent of such portion and for the portion of investment capital above 1500bn dong, the security must not be less than 1 per cent of that portion.[24] For example, in a US$1bn BOT project, the investors would need to arrange security for the financing and construction phase of the project of approximately, US$10.75m.

COST OF FEASIBILITY STUDY AND ASB ADVISORS

Decree 108 provides that investors shall reimburse the ASB for the cost of preparing and evaluating feasibility reports.[25] In addition to bearing the costs of the project's feasibility study, the current practice in BOT power projects has investors bearing some or all of the ASB's costs for retaining independent advisors, although Decree 108 does not make this a legal requirement of Vietnam BOT projects.

Whilst investors may be surprised by this and may be tempted to demand the legal basis for such requirement under Decree 108 or other Vietnam law, they should recognise that previous deals such as Mong Duong 2 have set a de facto pattern where sponsors bear the ASB's legal costs simply as a part of getting the deal done. Unfortunately, Decree 108 does not specify that funds will be allocated to the ASB to cover the costs of its independent advisors. As a result, the ASB has a very limited budget allocated to cover its advisory costs, and thus far the allocated budget tends to be insufficient to cover the typical costs of specialist advisors.

Accordingly, the MOIT as the ASB for BOT power projects, has established a practice where it requires the project sponsor to bear the costs of its advisors, particularly the legal advisors. Admittedly this is not an ideal situation from the perspective of investors, or even the ASB's independent advisor in the middle, as it adds costs and also raises the spectre of a potential conflict of interests.

LENDER ISSUES

Decree 108 addresses several lender and financing related issues that arose during actual negotiations under the former BOT Law. For instance, Decree 108 permits the project enterprise to assign its rights and obligations pursuant to the project contract.[26] This right permits investors to make the usual assignments necessary to finance the project. Further, lenders are given the express right to step into a project, pursuant to the loan agreement,

---

23   Decree 108, Article 23.

24   Decree 108, Article 23.

25   Decree 108, Article 8.

26   Decree 108, Article 18.

in order to take over the rights and obligations of a project enterprise (the borrower) where it fails to discharge its obligations under the project contract or loan agreement.[27]

GOVERNMENT GUARANTEE

Perhaps second in importance only to the tariff or user fee for a given project, potential investors and lenders want clarity on the extent of Vietnam's guarantee for BOT projects. Decree 108 addresses the government guarantee as follows:

> *Where necessary and depending on the nature of a project, the government shall appoint an authorized body to provide a guarantee for loans, provision of raw materials, sale of products and other contractual obligations to the investor, project enterprise or enterprises participating in the implementation of the project and a guarantee for obligations of State enterprises selling raw materials and/or purchasing products and services of the project enterprise.*[28]

This clause does not assure investors or lenders that a guarantee will be provided or the scope or size of any guarantee, if provided. Recently, the MPI has stated publicly that it seeks to reduce the scope and quantum of any guarantee it would provide on projects. The issue of whether the government will give a guarantee for BOT and PPP projects is currently hotly debated in Vietnam, and, therefore, investors and lenders should expect that any guarantees will be granted only on a case by case basis.

Part 4 – Decision 71 and the PPP Model

On 9 November 2010, Vietnam's Prime Minister, Nguyen Tan Dung, approved the much anticipated legal framework for PPP in Vietnam. Promulgated as Decision No. 71/2010QD-TTg (Regulation on pilot investment using Public-Private Partnership model), this 'PPP Framework' which took effect on 15 January 2011 is expected to promote the development of PPP projects in Vietnam for the next three to five years.

Vietnam's MPI leads the development of the PPP Framework with the goal of improving the legal basis for investments in Vietnam's infrastructure on a PPP basis. The PPP Framework is intended to promote pilot projects across a wide range of much needed infrastructure sectors, including:

- Roads, bridges, tunnels, ferries
- Railways, railway bridges, railway tunnels
- Urban transport
- Airports, seaports, river ports
- Fresh water supply systems
- Power plants
- Healthcare (hospitals in particular)
- Environment (waste treatment plants in particular
- Other infrastructure needs identified by the Prime Minister.

---

27   Decree 108, Article 17.
28   Decree 108, Article 40.

It could be said that 2010 was the 'Year of PPP' in Vietnam when one considers the numerous workshops, forums and articles on this issue, as well as the voluminous advice the Vietnamese government has received from foreign governments and private sector players. The approval of the PPP Framework indicates that the government has summoned the political will to move beyond the early questions of 'What is PPP and is it good for Vietnam?' With a PPP Framework in place at last, leading questions shift to 'How does Vietnam implement the PPP Framework and will it achieve its intended results?'

Proper implementation of the PPP Framework will be key to ensuring Vietnam's successful adoption of the PPP model. Worldwide, there are numerous examples of PPP programmes successfully delivering large scale infrastructure on time and on budget, when compared to traditional public procurement.

Certain elements tend to be present in successfully implemented PPP projects, regardless of where they are located. These include:

- Political will and support for the PPP programme
- An adequate legal framework
- Projects selected on the basis of their suitability for PPP
- Proper pre-selection of bidders to ensure the project will be well managed
- Adequate preparation, training and institutional support for the government's PPP unit overseeing the project.

For the PPP Framework to achieve its stated goals, the elements listed above will need to be present, and in addition, a variety of investor and lender concerns will need to be adequately addressed.

ADEQUACY OF LEGAL FRAMEWORK

A number of observers have already commented on the scope and adequacy of the PPP Framework. Admittedly, this new law is a bit thin from a lawyer's point of view and will require fleshing out as it is actually implemented. Looking at the continuing development of Decree 78 (2007) and Decree 108 (2009) on BOT projects, one can observe an evolutionary process taking place in Vietnam with the legal framework for infrastructure projects as more deals are actually negotiated. For example, certain gaps in the law the parties faced whilst negotiating the Mong Duong 2 power project under Decree 78 were later addressed in Decree 108, indicating the law is evolving as the government gains greater experience in implementing transactions. It is reasonable to assume that the PPP Framework will also evolve to reflect lessons learned in implementing the first pilot projects. However, certain issues must be addressed up front and cannot wait for the law to catch up, such as the need for implementing regulations, the preparation of standardized project documentation and the establishment and capacity building of the PPP unit. These issues are addressed as follows.

IMPLEMENTING REGULATIONS

The MPI has publicly stated that there will be no implementing regulations (ie, circulars) for the PPP Framework. Their stated intent is to learn by doing. This approach may surprise potential investors who fear becoming a test case in early PPP pilot projects. However, given that the PPP Framework itself gives little guidance beyond project selection and tendering provisions, investors will need to focus on the terms of the PPP contract as the 'law of the project'.

THOROUGH PREPARATION AND STANDARDIZED DOCUMENTATION

The PPP Framework provides that once an investor is selected, the ASB will negotiate and execute a PPP contract with such investor within 30 days of the investor selection. This provision of the PPP Framework reflects the tension discussed in Part 1 of the [chapter] between political ideals and the practicalities of the given project. Billion dollar deals are not generally negotiated in one month. However, it is obvious the government seeks to close deals quickly and let investors get down to the actual implementation of the project. In order for the ASB to achieve finalization of the project documentation of a PPP project in the least amount of time following investor selection, all project preparations will need to be thorough and complete prior to issuance of bid requests for the project. To meet such a tight negotiation schedule, issues for clarification and negotiation must be minimized. To minimize the number of commercial, technical, legal and financial issues left for negotiation, the project documentation must be up to the best international standards and be readily bankable on its face. Further, all technical requirements and the scope of government support must be clearly and thoroughly presented to investors with the request for proposals. Currently, the MPI is just initiating this exercise with its advisors – developing tender criteria, procedures and documentation aimed to achieve efficiency in negotiating the PPP pilot projects. It remains to be seen how this will pan out in practice.

CAPACITY BUILDING

In addition to strong documentation and preparation, it is essential that prior to issuance of bid requests the government has in place a trained PPP unit with sufficient human resources and budget to manage the preparation and implementation of the project. With sufficient preparation on the part of the ASB, bids may be evaluated on the basis of the bidder's conformance with the standardized agreements, pricing and technical solution for the project.

Having made sufficient institutional preparations for the PPP programme, including the elements discussed above, the government will need to grapple with several key investor concerns. Amongst the values that investors bring to a PPP programme are innovation, relevant skill, efficiency and funding. Funding is probably the largest driver of investor issues, as investors cannot obtain funding of an expensive large scale infrastructure project unless lenders are satisfied that all material risks affecting the success of the project are managed. There will be a number of investor and lender concerns to projects implemented under the PPP Framework. Some of the more significant of these include clarifying investment preparation costs, ensuring currency conversion and coming to grips with the extent of government financial support, as discussed below.

INVESTMENT PREPARATION COSTS

At issue in some of the current Vietnam infrastructure projects is the scope of the ASB's costs to be borne by the investor. The PPP Framework suggests that investors may be required to bear the investment preparation costs, but the scope and quantum of the obligation is not clear. This and other costing provisions in the PPP Framework require clarification so that potential investors can adequately predict the cost of investing in Vietnam. As cost is a key commercial consideration, ambiguity on the scope of cost to be borne by investors or funded by lenders in the PPP Framework will naturally require negotiation which may delay the implementation of a project. In the worst case, lenders could refuse to fund a project where costs appear unpredictable and uncapped.

FOREIGN CURRENCY CONVERSION

The foreign currency conversion provisions of the PPP Framework are nearly identical to those found under Decree 108. These provisions appear designed to offer comfort to investors and their lenders that project revenues (and other project related monies) may be converted to hard currency and remitted abroad. It is said that parties negotiating some current BOT projects are facing severe issues in respect of interpreting the equivalent provisions under Decree 108. In particular, lenders to some of the current BOT projects comment that the government has not assured that all of the revenues may be convertible into hard currency, but rather has indicated that only a percentage of revenues can be assured to be convertible. This is a core concern affecting the bankability of large scale infrastructure projects and must be resolved clearly if the Vietnam PPP pilot deals are to find the necessary funding.

GOVERNMENT GUARANTEE

There is little difference between the government guarantee provision of Decree 108 (Art 40) and the one found in the PPP Framework. As suggested in the previous comments regarding currency conversion, investors and lenders have valid concerns about the interpretation of provisions appearing to offer hope of government support for a project, where such provisions may subsequently be interpreted to water down any such support. Although the government has legitimate reasons to avoid adding more debt to its balance sheet, it in turn must recognize that investors and lenders need clarity as to the true level of commitment and support the government will offer in respect of costly infrastructure projects, such as those contemplated under the PPP Framework. Where two jurisdictions offer similar opportunities for investment, but one of those jurisdictions offers better risk hedging (e.g. government guarantees, guaranteed currency conversion, etc.), the investor will normally follow the path of least resistance and go with the safer, easier jurisdiction.

In sum, the PPP Framework is a welcome piece of legislation that has been eagerly anticipated by international investors with an interest in Vietnam's various infrastructure sectors. The PPP Framework is another step in the evolution of Vietnam's regulatory regime for private investment in much needed projects that will benefit the economy and people of Vietnam. With the PPP Framework now in place, the MPI faces the crucial next step to put into place a well devised, workable PPP programme that works for Vietnam and the investors it seeks to attract. Now the real work begins.

Part 5: Conclusion, Challenges to Financing

The main challenges to financing of much needed infrastructure projects in Vietnam remain the same as ever, namely:

- Lender appetite for the country
- Alignment of government, sponsor and lender risk appetite for individual projects
- Other political risks
- Return for risks taken
- Lack of capacity of the ASB to negotiate deals in an efficient and timely manner

Vietnam has made tremendous progress since the ad hoc regulatory environment facing the early BOT power deals in 2001/2002 (i.e., the Phu My deals) to establish a workable framework governing investment in the nation's infrastructure. Decree 108 is a significant step in the natural evolution of Vietnam's infrastructure investment laws. If the past is any indication, one may anticipate that this legal framework will be revisited within the next few years as more of the 59 projects contained in the government's projects list are negotiated and implemented and as the PPP pilot projects are implemented and drive the formulation of a comprehensive PPP law.

27 *Indonesia, the Future*

ANDREW KINLOCH, Managing Director
Logie Group Limited

Why Indonesia?

'Indonesia is the country of the future...and will always remain so.' French President Charles de Gaulle was actually speaking of another major emerging market, Brazil, more than 50 years ago but his sentiments could have applied just as much to Indonesia ever since. However, in recent years, that potential has been attracting increased attention from investors and their governments from elsewhere in Asia; the Government of Indonesia (GoI) is taking steps to address longstanding blockages to deal flow; and market players are again hopeful that more of that potential can be translated into actuality than has been in the past. Consider the following:

Firstly, Indonesia is big: at 235m, it is the world's fourth most populous country. This population's need for infrastructure is also big: for example, in the power sector, only 66 per cent of the population is connected to the grid compared to 99 per cent in neighbouring Malaysia and Thailand and 86 per cent in the Philippines. In the water sector, only 31 per cent of the population of urban areas has access to fresh water supply – and only 2 per cent to sewerage services. And in urban transport, Jakarta (and elsewhere) lags almost all south east Asian capital cities. The government cannot afford to build this infrastructure itself; local investors and lenders alone cannot meet the bill; and expertise is much needed across all disciplines.

Appropriately big numbers for foreign direct investment are being bandied about like never before:

- GoI is hoping that two thirds of the US$157bn which it plans to be invested in infrastructure by 2014 will come from the private sector. In the power sector alone, over the next five years it is seeking US$31bn for 22GW (gigawatt) of new generation, US$7bn for 17,000km of transmission lines and US$5bn for distribution networks.
- In January 2011, Japan and Indonesia signed an MoU to spend some US$24bn across all infrastructure sectors in the so-called metropolitan priority area of greater Jakarta, i.e. Jakarta itself, Bogor, Depok, Tangerang and Bekasi collectively known as Jabodetabek; in all, Japan has committed some US$53bn to investment in Indonesia over the next 15 years; Mitsubishi Corp alone is planning to invest US$20bn by 2020.
- Also in January 2011, India and Indonesia signed 18 MOUs worth US$15bn covering a wide range of sectors.

- And in April 2011, Chinese sovereign wealth fund CIC announced plans to enter the market, earmarking US$4bn for loans to Indonesian infrastructure.

Secondly, there is reason today to be more optimistic about this potential than perhaps previously. Politically, Indonesia is increasingly stable. Susilo Bambang Yudhoyono was comfortably re-elected as president in 2009. He may not have been as bold in his reforms as some would have liked but remember that, in the aftermath of Suharto's ouster only 12 years ago, it was widely considered that Indonesia risked breaking apart as a country. Indonesia has the largest population of Muslims and moderate ones too so, post the terrorist attacks of 9/11, it has been paid increased attention by the West. It served as a member of the UN Security Council in 2006–08 and is the only south east Asian member of the G20. Economically, recent news has been good too: Indonesia is benefitting from the boom in coal and other commodities; and it largely missed the global financial crisis of 2008 if only because it is less connected to the outside world than some. Government finances are in comparatively good health with government debt at a manageable 29 per cent of GDP and an exchange rate that has strengthened modestly since 2008. In April 2011, Standard & Poor's duly followed other ratings agencies in raising its foreign long term sovereign rating to BB+ with positive outlook, only one notch off investment grade. The Indonesian Investment Coordinating Board (BKPM) has been promoting a wide range of prospects. New legislation, including Presidential Regulation (Perpres) 13/2010 which updated the framework for Public Private Partnerships (PPPs), and some implementing regulations have been enacted.

On the other hand, Indonesia has a long track record of over-promising and under-delivering in that the flow of deals actually consummated to date has been but a fraction of that potential. When it comes to making infrastructure happen, all the difficulties found elsewhere are to be found in Indonesia: opaque organization of the economy; weak legal/regulatory enabling environments; an inability of government to acquire and clear land at a sensible cost in a sensible time frame; decision making distorted by corruption; lack of properly prepared projects; and indecision over appropriate government support for both offtakers from projects and for projects themselves.

Indonesia has some difficulties all of its own: any country spread across more than 17,500 islands is going to struggle when building national power grids or road networks. Indonesia also has the full suite of national disasters to cope with: the Indian Ocean tsunami of 2004 killed 170,000; and 'Lusi', the mud volcano at Sidoarjo in East Java, has been spewing out a million cubic feet per day for the past five years and could carry on doing so for the next 30 years.

Lastly, in a country where the public sector remains active in many industries, Indonesia is interesting to project financiers because it has been prepared to experiment with different techniques for implementing government support for projects.

If the government can take some difficult decisions in consultation with counterparties and implement policies which it has been mulling for some time, it will be able to realize a higher fraction of that potential leading to a significantly greater deal flow across all industry sectors for the benefit of foreign and domestic investors, lenders and users alike.

Figure 27.1 Indonesia

Sector Review

CONVENTIONAL POWER GENERATION

Historically, independent power producers (IPPs) have been the most active sector for project finance. The electricity industry is regulated by the Ministry of Energy and Mineral Resources (MEMR). Total installed power generation capacity is about 31GW. Of this, 27GW is owned by PT Perusahaan Listrik Negara (PLN) which, as a Persero, is a limited liability company wholly owned by the Ministry of State Owned Enterprises (MSOE); a further 4GW is owned by some 21 IPPs. In aggregate, this represents only 109MW (megawatt) of capacity per million of population, lower than Vietnam, Thailand or the Philippines; much of this capacity is concentrated in the main Java-Madura-Bali (Jamali) grid with much less elsewhere; as mentioned, the electrification rate is only 66 per cent so no less than 80 million people have no access to the grid; yet demand is forecast to grow at 7–9 per cent p.a.

IPPs were first contemplated in the 1985 Electricity Law. These featured a conventional long term take-or-pay power purchase agreement (PPA) which passed through to PLN substantially all demand, fuel price and currency risk. However, PLN's ability to pass these risks through to its customers is severely curtailed by the fact that it charges widely different tariffs to different categories of user and these tariffs are set for it by the DPR (Parliament), often at less than cost. For example, current prices are in the order of 11–12 US cents per KWh for industrial and commercial users but only 6 US cents for retail customers. This and operational inefficiencies have resulted in PLN making sustained losses and being dependent on the Ministry of Finance (MOF) for a significant subsidy, currently some US$5.5bn per annum.

On the other hand, selling electricity at below cost constitutes providing 'a function of public benefit' and, if the government requires a State Owned Enterprise (SOE) such as

PLN to perform this Public Service Obligation (PSO), Law 19/2003 requires it to compensate the SOE. Crucially, the amount of subsidy is not the difference between the tariff imposed on PLN for each category of customer and the tariff it would otherwise have sold at; it is instead the difference (when negative) between the tariff and the total cost of supply for that tariff category plus a margin, set subsequently at 5 per cent in 2009. This has the effect of passing all major risk through to the government. PLN's accounts may look uncreditworthy when viewed on a standalone basis but, as a result of the PSO support, its counterparty credit risk is effectively the same as MOF's so long as i) the monthly reimbursement mechanism from MOF to PLN functions as intended (it has since 2006); ii) ironically, the government does not set PLN's tariffs above cost in each tariff category, at which point the PSO would fall away; iii) the law does not change. Fundamentally, one needs to ask, would the government walk away from its power industry?

Indonesia was hit hard by the Asian crisis in 1997/98. President Suharto was ousted after 32 years of rule amidst widespread unrest, GDP contracted 13 per cent and the rupiah collapsed from 2,500 to the US$ to as low as 18,000. Neither PLN nor MOF could afford to pay a seven-fold increase in the price of its power! PLN cancelled some proposed IPPs and purchased or renegotiated the terms of others. It paid operational IPPs only according to the pre-crisis exchange rate, i.e., a partial payment default. Several years of 'contract rationalization' and litigation later, projects such as Paiton Energy and Jawa Power went ahead with slightly longer debt tenors and reduced, but still positive, equity returns; much-needed assets got built; and these are now generating to international levels of availability and efficiency – for their sponsors and lenders alike, not a bad outcome for a catastrophic downside sensitivity!

PLN's obligations to these IPPs were supported by comfort letters issued by MOF. In subsequent arbitral proceedings, however, a key sentence in these comfort letters was held to be a binding obligation on MOF to ensure that PLN could meet its obligations as they fell due.

Little progress was made during the post-Suharto Reformasi era in 1998–2004. Indeed, no new IPP of size was signed for the next 12 years. A new Electricity Law in 2002 was ruled unconstitutional by the Constitutional Court two years later. Perpres 67/2005 set a framework for Public Private Partnerships (PPPs) generally but it was unclear whether or not this applied to IPPs (This is what Perpres 13/2010 updated). Supposed model projects such as Pasaruan fell by the wayside, for want of gas supply in Pasaruan's case.

In 2006, MOF signed a Memorandum of Mutual Understanding (MOMU) with the historically most active of the export credit agencies (ECAs), namely JBIC, intending to issue for each Japanese-sponsored project a letter acknowledging the support which MOF gave PLN for fulfilling its Public Service Obligations. However, only one acknowledgement letter was issued under the JBIC MOMU (in March 2010 for the 815MW coal fired Paiton expansion (Paiton 3)) and no other ECA or multilateral signed a comparable MOMU. In the same month, Marubeni et al. signed the financing for the 660 MW coal fired Cirebon project but they had been appointed preferred bidder before the JBIC MOMU was signed.

A third model for government support of IPPs is now underway in the form of the long-awaited Central Jawa IPP. Seven bidders have been shortlisted for this 2,000 MW coal fired plant which is estimated to cost some US$3 billion. The bidders include two Chinese-led consortia (China Shenhua and CNTI-Guangdong Yudean) who are bidding for the first time to take IPP risk rather than MOF-guaranteed PLN EPC risk (see below). The World Bank's IFC has been advising PLN since 2006. It is intended that PLN's obligations under the 25 year PPA will be supported by the newly established and still evolving Indonesian Infrastructure Guarantee Facility (IIGF), more of which later.

In 2006, with the IPP programme progressing only slowly, the President issued Perpres 71/2006 to launch the Fast Track Programme, under which MOF would guarantee PLN's obligations under engineer, procure and construct (EPC) contracts for 10,000MW of capacity. Ten projects totalling 7,460MW would be built on Java and 23 much smaller projects totalling 2,513MW on other islands. All would burn low sulphur coal which PLN would source domestically, the intention being as much to tilt PLN's fuel mix away from a reliance on oil as to increase aggregate capacity. PLN would then operate the plants. The contractors were foreign/domestic joint ventures with all but one foreigner being Chinese. Offshore funding (principally from the Chinese state via China Exim, Bank of China and Sinosure) was raised alongside a domestic tranche on a project-by-project basis. Counterparty payment risk was not at a project level, though, but at the PLN corporate level guaranteed by MOF. MOF contingent liabilities had been brought under control in the aftermath of the Asian crisis and, conceptually, throwing guarantees at the problem was not unreasonable. As at December 2010, finance had been raised and construction was underway on 9,521MW of capacity. Some hiccups can be expected if completion is late or over budget as the EPC contracts were signed subject to a condition subsequent that financing be put in place within a year which did not happen. Further, the mines were required to undertake significant expansion then transport the volumes of coal required if the new plants were to be fuelled. Even in the event that there is some delay and a further contribution to costs is negotiated, though, PLN would be getting additional capacity more cheaply than it would have from western or Japanese suppliers.

Encouraged by the comparative success of Fast Track 1, Perpres 4/2010 launched a second 10,000MW of capacity to benefit from MOF guarantees. 21 projects totalling 5GW have been listed for PLN to build at a cost of perhaps US$5bn; and 72 projects, also totalling about 5GW, are listed for development as IPPs at a cost of perhaps US$11bn. This time around, the emphasis was to be on (more expensive) renewables rather than coal fired plant. A MOF guarantee of PLN obligations represented a fourth model for government support of IPPs.

Industrial users have built some 13GW of captive generation in Indonesia. Various additions are planned.

Historically, PLN has had a monopoly over transmission and distribution. The 2009 Electricity Act, which has attracted some controversy, and its implementing regulations which are still underway, contemplate a relaxation of this and various other privileges. PLN has used export credits from time to time to finance the purchase of transmission equipment and has various plans for domestic and cross border interconnectors.

RENEWABLES

In Indonesia, renewable has to date primarily meant geothermal. Being on the Rim of Fire, potential capacity is huge at 28GW (40 per cent of the world's) although less than 2GW has actually been built.

As elsewhere, the size and shape of the resource of a geothermal field needs to be first determined, a risk more familiar to the oil and gas sector than to power utilities. The tariff usually needs to be a feed – in one, i.e. subsidized, but who pays for this, how much do they pay and for how long?

In Indonesia, sponsors have been expected to negotiate a deal with the owner of the resource, usually the state-owned oil and gas company Pertamina, before negotiating a tariff with PLN. This is because Geothermal Law 27/2003 addresses the production of steam whereas generation of electricity therefrom is governed by the 2009 Electricity Law. There has been the perennial issue of PLN's creditworthiness. And implementation of the carbon credit scheme pursuant to the Kyoto Protocol's Clean Development Mechanism has been slow.

In the private sector, Chevron operates the 377MW Salak and 260MW Darajat plants, both on Java (plus two smaller ones); and Star Energy operates the 227MW Wayang Windu plant, also on Java (In 2010, Wayang Windu raised US$350m via a five year project bond, a rare event in Indonesia). Sponsors Itochu, Kyushu Electric, Medco International and Ormat have shortlisted banks for the US$1.25bn/18 year debt facility for a 330MW geothermal plant at Sarulla in North Sumatra. Government support comes from a pre-Asian crisis comfort letter. Otherwise, though, progress was hampered by, inter alia, no feed-in tariff. However, MEMR has recently announced that PLN would pay a headline price of 9.7 US cents/KWh (kilowatt hour). It remains to be seen whether this will be enough to kick-start some 30 waiting projects.

Indonesia has some 3GW of installed hydro-electric capacity but has not built large dams the way that Malaysia, for example, has. Challenges include acquiring then clearing the land as well as building the required transmission lines.

Being close to the equator, Indonesia may not be especially suitable for other renewable technologies such as wind or tide; nor can it afford them yet.

NATURAL RESOURCES

As elsewhere, natural resources projects benefit from revenues being denominated in hard currency; sponsors/offtakers having deep pockets; locations being stand alone, often remote, i.e., more able to be controlled by sponsors; and capital expenditure requirements which are both large and which need a significant proportion sourced from offshore, making them attractive to ECAs. Significantly, there is not the need for government support that there is in other sectors. Resource projects also bring heightened environmental and social responsibilities, of course, under the 2009 Environment Law and other legislation.

Key legislation for oil and gas is Law 22/2001. BPMIGAS regulates upstream activities and BPH MIGAS downstream ones.

In terms of oil, Indonesia produced about 950,000 bbl/day in 2009, down 32 per cent from 2000 levels. It became a net importer in 2004 and withdrew from OPEC in 2008. Pertamina is no longer a monopoly but it is still a major player, operating all nine of the country's refineries, for example. Oil products are still sold to domestic consumers at subsidized prices. Private sector opportunities are more at the corporate level: Chevron operates the two largest oil fields, Minas and Duri whilst ExxonMobil is developing the new Cepu block. Going forwards, there may be discrete opportunities for pipelines, storage or even coal-to-liquids.

In terms of gas, Indonesia has some 112 tcf (trillion cubic feet) of proven reserves, the tenth largest in the world. Pertamina and a number of foreign operators dominate the market. Majority state-owned PT Perusahaan Gas Negara (PGN) operates a network of pipelines. Three LNG (liquified natural gas) liquefaction projects are in operation. The most recent, Tangguh in West Papua, is led by BP and raised US$3.5bn of debt in 2006/07. Interestingly, the sponsors tried initially for recourse on one tranche to be limited to the project but eventually they went for the cheaper funding and less intrusiveness of all tranches having recourse to the sponsors on a several basis. Next up is Donggi Senoro in Central Sulawesi. Sponsored by Mitsubishi Corp, Korea Gas Corp, Pertamina and Medco International and with the debt led as usual by JBIC, it will cost US$2.8bn and produce 2 mtpa of LNG and 47,000 barrels of condensate a year. Future opportunities include coal bed methane (CBM): Indonesia is estimated to have three times as much CBM as it has conventional natural gas.

In the mining sector, Indonesia is the world's second largest exporter of coal, principally thermal coal for the booming power industries of China, India and elsewhere; as well as copper, gold, tin and nickel. A new Law on Mineral and Coal Mining 4/2009 replaced the well-established contracts of work with three categories of mining licence. Reaction has been mixed, however, and some implementing regulations are still awaited. Mining activities will always need to address environmental considerations, of course: GoI has recently draughted rules for a two-year ban on permits for forest clearing after signing a US$1bn climate aid deal with Norway aimed at avoiding greenhouse gas emissions from deforestation. These rules will impact eight mining projects worth at least US$14bn, though. Again, investing and lending opportunities are more corporate than project in nature. Just two current examples are:

- Posco of Korea and state owned Krakatau Steel are progressing a US$2.7bn integrated steel mill project with an annual production capacity of 6 mtpa.
- Aneka Tambang (Antam) and Showa Denko of Japan are in documentation for the US$400m Tayan alumina mining project.

TRANSPORT

Indonesia has one of the lowest road densities in south east Asia, whether measured in terms of length per 100 people or per square km, whether paved or all roads. There are only 693km of toll roads, 72 per cent of which are operated by Jasa Marga which is 70 per cent owned by GoI.

Road projects in Indonesia bring two significant issues. Firstly, they have been hobbled by GoI's inability to exercise its powers of eminent domain and forcibly purchase the required land at a reasonable price in a reasonable time frame then clear it of legal and illegal occupants. Instead, land on the route chosen has been purchased by connected parties ahead of the announcement; prices have escalated subsequently; delays have been extensive; the government has been unable to clear the land of legal or illegal occupiers; contracts have been awarded to parties with no wherewithal to perform; and contracts have been let subject to raising finance within, typically, 12 months – when this did not occur, the contracts should have lapsed but this has often been difficult to enforce for political reasons.

A Land Procurement Bill has been making its way through the DPR for some time. Implementing regulations then need to follow. Fundamentally, the compulsory acquisition process needs to be put onto a much more rigorous basis so this legislation needs to be both robust and implemented robustly – neither will be easy or quick. GoI is also planning a Land Revolving Fund to take some of the price escalation risk (see below).

Secondly, roads bring traffic risk, of course. Countries such as Australia have recently demonstrated how difficult it is to forecast traffic numbers. If these cannot be forecast with some degree of confidence, then it is surely more sensible/cheaper in the long run for the government to retain this risk. It can do so via viability gap funding, i.e. contributing enough to upfront costs such that project revenues divided by the now reduced upfront costs represent a reasonable return for the project, as has been done in India. Alternatively – and quite possibly more cheaply – the government can undertake to the project to top up revenues in the event that they fall below a pre-agreed level (minimum revenue guarantees). Revenue collars allow for the government, in return, to share in the upside benefit too. Such structures have been implemented in South Korea. The government can also share downside and upside risk by paying shadow tolls to the road operator, i.e. payments which may be more or less than the tolls which the operator charges actual users of the road and which it then hands over to the government.

Some of these ideas are being mulled over by GoI. In the meantime, the Ministry of Public Works is preparing to put up for tender five toll road projects totalling US$2bn as public private partnership (PPP) schemes although it is not yet clear what risk profiles are contemplated.

Rail projects in Indonesia face similar issues. Heavy rail is dominated by state-owned Kereta Api and likely to remain so. However, two exceptions are currently being promoted by GoI. Both offer challenging risk profiles and both will require considerable GoI support, recent announcements notwithstanding:

- The US$2.2bn Puruk Cahu-Bangkuang railway in central Kalimantan is intended to link a number of coal mines in the interior to the coast, 185km away. The mines will only commit to expansion if they are confident that the rail line will go ahead and the builders of the rail line will only go ahead if they are confident that the mines will be expanded. Such significant mutual performance risk can be addressed only by the central government standing in the middle. This is possible, though: take the example of the MRT lines being proposed by the Thai government for Bangkok where it will let separate EPC and operations and maintenance (O&M) contracts such that (sensibly) it is the government which takes the risk of ground conditions and traffic volumes.
- The US$1.1bn Sukarno Hatta airport rail link is intended to connect Jakarta's main airport to downtown Manggarai. Three bidders have been shortlisted. However, rail links to airports worldwide compete with other modes of transport, principally taxis, so tend to make money only if subsidized directly by government or via the development of associated real estate; and connections for onward travel are crucial, often involving considerably more capital expenditure, so these need to be sorted out at the Manggarai end.

Urban rail, whether heavy, light or mono (a politically connected unsolicited bid in Jakarta did not proceed) faces issues of cost, land acquisition and coordination with other modes of transport. Jakarta has some heavy rail operated by Kereta Api but, in comparison to cities such as Bangkok or Manila, has no mass rapid transit, light rail or subway. Instead, Jakarta has introduced several Bus Rapid Transit routes, i.e. lanes on main roads dedicated to buses. These need to be connected to covered footpaths so that passengers can complete their journeys in a modicum of comfort; and squeezing the other traffic into, say, two lanes instead of three, leads to significant congestion for them; but BRT schemes are, at least, more affordable.

There has been little, if any, private sector involvement in ports (Hutchison has a stake in Tanjung Priok in Jakarta) or airports to date but GoI is exploring how best to introduce PPPs.

WATER

Back in 1998, France's Ondeo/Palyja and the UK's Thames Water won fresh water distribution franchises in Jakarta. However, both have struggled, Thames sold out in 2006 and no further franchises have been let.

Several new prospects are being examined. For example, AusAid has been leading renewed attempts to finance the Umbulan Springs fresh water pipe from the foothills of Mount Bromo to the conurbation of greater Surabaya. This typifies the issues which need to be addressed in so many water projects: uncreditworthy PDAMs (municipality-owned water distribution companies) (some progress has been made in this respect), the PDAMs' need to build out their distribution networks so as to take delivery from the pipe; how to clean up their water from other sources before it is mixed with the clean water from Umbulan Springs; uncertainty over ownership rights; and, in particular, a political reluctance to increase tariffs to consumers so as to cover full cost.

When the political will is there, wonders can be achieved in the water sector: between 1993 and 2006, the publicly owned Phnom Penh Water Supply Authority in Cambodia cut non-revenue water from 72 per cent to 6 per cent (developed market levels); increased its coverage area from 25 per cent to 90 per cent of the city and collection rates from 48 per cent to 99 per cent; and transformed itself from needing a heavy subsidy to covering full cost.

TELECOMS

Majority state-owned Telkom Indonesia is the incumbent fixed line provider. Fixed line teledensity, mostly fixed-wireless, remains low in Indonesia at about 15 per cent. On the other hand, the mobile subscriber base passed 150 million in 2010, a penetration rate of 65 per cent, and continues to grow at some 20 per cent p.a. 3G technology, mostly from Telkom-owned Telkomsel, accounted for perhaps 7 per cent of this.

Investing and lending opportunities are mainly at the corporate level with mobile carriers. With these growth rates, they have made money. They face the usual risks of changing technology and stiff competition but there is political risk too. In 2007, the Commission for the Supervision of Business Competition (KPPU) forced STT Telemedia to sell its stake in Indosat, alleging that because it and Singapore Telecom, which held a stake in another carrier Telkomsel, were both partly owned by the Singapore sovereign wealth fund Temasek, then they must be colluding to drive up prices to consumers. The ruling overlooked the fact that the Singaporeans controlled neither carrier, that GoI had approved STT buying into Indosat, that GoI itself also owned indirect stakes in both carriers and that there was plenty of competition from other operators.

SOCIAL INFRASTRUCTURE

In due course, hospitals, schools, prisons and other municipal infrastructure could be financed on the basis that facilities are made available to the government which then operates them. Indonesia can learn lessons from elsewhere as to how best to finance this risk profile and there are plenty of bilateral and multilateral partners eager to assist with advice and/or funding.

Government Support

GoI experimentation with different levels of support for government-owned offtakers from projects has, to date, been almost exclusively concerned with PLN. Different counterparties have taken very different views of PLN risk:

- As explained above, all PLN activities benefit from MOF support via the PSO mechanism.
- Historically, this PSO support has been sufficient for the ratings agencies to rate PLN the same as the sovereign. The capital markets essentially view PLN as sovereign risk but with an extra 105–115 b.p. of yield in that PLN has issued domestic and offshore bonds for maturities out to 30 years with no further MOF support.
- This PSO support alone has also been sufficient for smaller scale IPPs with domestic players which are not considered here.
- In terms of PLN's obligations to larger IPPs, JBIC took a supportive stance via its MOMU but others did not follow. Now, all nationalities bidding on Central Jawa are doing so under the IIGF-led regime.
- At the same time, PLN had the option of developing plants on an EPC basis under the first Fast Track programme but these required MOF guarantees of PLN's obligations.
- Now Indonesian IPPs are being offered to the market on three different bases: the IIGF-led regime (on Central Jawa with more expected to follow); MOF guarantees (on Fast Track 2); and PSO only (on everything else).
- In doing so, PLN and MOF need to address two conceptual issues:
- Which method of support should be offered for which IPP? Who makes this decision?
- How should PLN decide whether to proceed with a project as an IPP or on an EPC basis?

INDONESIAN INFRASTRUCTURE GUARANTEE FACILITY (IIGF)

Perpres 13/2010 not only updated Perpres 67/2005 but also established SMI (see below) and set up PT Penjaminan Infrastruktur Indonesia (PT PII) also known as the Indonesian Infrastructure Guarantee Facility (IIGF). The fund will provide guarantees in support of performance and payment obligations by state owned counterparties to PPPs. The fund was initially seeded with Rp1tr (US$115m) from MOF with a further Rp1tr per annum intended out to 2014. The World Bank is contributing a US$500m facility. The proposed structure has been shown to counterparties for the first time on the Central Jawa IPP which is currently being bid (see above) so details are variously yet to be made public, yet to be sorted out or yet to be agreed by counterparties.

For Central Jawa, it is currently proposed that the first loss of Rp300bn (US$35m) caused by PLN default under its PPA with the project proponent shall be borne by IIGF – so sponsors benefit as well as lenders. Losses in excess of this would be met by MOF and from the World Bank facility with the IIGF acting as a 'single window' for all three.

The rationale for establishing a guarantor separate to MOF stemmed firstly from MOF payouts needing DPR approval, a process which is both slow and politically fraught. Secondly, IIGF could bring a quicker and more rigorous appraisal of projects at the financing stage than had earlier initiatives such as the Risk Management Unit (RMU) in MOF, the Inter- Ministerial Committee for the Acceleration Programme [of PPPs] (KKPPI) or the PPP Central Unit (P3CU) in Bappenas, the planning ministry.

Issues remain with the IIGF:

- How transparent/reliable/politically independent will the IIGF claims payment procedure be? It will certainly be untested.
- US$35m would be exhausted in less than a week on Central Jawa. How automatic will be the mechanisms to access the MOF and World Bank funds? Will these be paid directly to the project proponent or to IIGF which must then agree to pass them onto the project proponent?
- What is a reasonable gearing ratio in terms of volume of guarantees to be issued versus funds available? After all, any ratio greater than 1.0 runs a theoretical risk of the fund running out of money; claims are likely to be correlated; and counterparties learned in the global financial crisis to be more cautious when assessing long tail probabilities such as these.
- No matter how conservative the gearing ratio, what happens in the event that the fund runs out of money?
- How can investments be structured so as to minimize the strain on IIGF/GoI finances? For example, ceteris paribus, it is better to pay out a claim over time than in one lump sum upfront.
- Ultimately, the story needs to be told to the ratings agencies and all counterparties that IIGF risk is essentially the same as MOF risk but with enhanced liquidity.
- Less significantly, which party will the IIGF charge for issuing its guarantee and how much will it charge?
- Once the IIGF-led regime has been sorted out on Central Java, GoI will apply it to not just further IPPs but GoI obligations in other sectors. The IIGF could again guarantee performance by state-owned counterparties; or it could provide support directly to projects, such as the minimum revenue guarantees and collars needed on roads.

INDONESIAN INFRASTRUCTURE FINANCING FACILITY (IIFF)

Perpres 13/2010 also set up the government-owned PT Sarana Multi Infrastruktur (SMI) which, in turn, invested alongside the IFC, Germany's DEG and the Asian Development Bank in PT Infrastruktur Financing (Indonesian Infrastructure Financing Facility or IIFF). Initial debt and equity funds committed were Rp3tr (US$345m). Modelled on India's IDFC, on the asset side IIFF will invest equity, mezzanine and senior debt across the full range of PPP sectors where appetite is not forthcoming from the private sector, i.e., longer maturities, no political risk cover, etc. On the liabilities side, it aims to develop the long term domestic currency market via issuance of bonds. It also intends to advise on pathfinder transactions. However, like the private sector, the IIFF is waiting for properly prepared projects to be brought forwards ready for the financing phase to commence. It has also recently lost its senior staff.

In April 2011, GoI announced that it would be contributing US$120m to a US$485m pan-ASEAN infrastructure fund. Again, details are not yet available as to the fund's risk appetite, criteria for prioritization of opportunities or plans to expand its funding sources.

LAND REVOLVING FUND (LRF)

The LRF is aimed specifically at the difficulties faced by road operators in purchasing the required land. It is intended that it will provide bridging finance to private sector operators whilst they negotiate the purchase of remaining lots of land. GoI has also floated the idea of land capping whereby it would bear the risk of the price of land exceeding, say, 10 per cent of an agreed price. GoI had allocated US$150m by 2009 with more promised. However, both initiatives appear to address the symptom rather than the cause of the problem; and both could be prohibitively expensive.

Conclusion

Indonesia has long had the potential for a significant flow of project finance deals across all sectors. There is more reason today than perhaps ever before to be optimistic about converting more of that potential to actuality. But much remains to be done.

28 *Key Challenges in India*

L VISWANATHAN, Partner
Amarchand & Mangaldas & Suresh A. Shroff & Co.

Infrastructure development in India continues to face various legal challenges. This chapter focusses on some of the key legal concerns that surround infrastructure development in India.

Private Participation in Infrastructure

All large scale infrastructure projects in India are primarily implemented through a private-public partnership (PPP) model which often takes the form of a concession or a licence granted by the government or a regulatory authority designated for a particular sector (for instance, the National Highways Authority of India (NHAI) for all national highway projects, the Telecom Regulatory Authority of India for telecom sector, the Department of Shipping for major ports in India). As per the policies of the Government of India, competitive bidding must be followed whilst granting concessions and licences to a private sector participant for development in the infrastructure sector. In general, the process of grant of concession and licences to the private sector must be fair and transparent under Article 14 (Right to Equality) of the Constitution of India.

Most projects are awarded through a two-stage bidding process involving a qualification stage (evaluation of both technical and financial parameters) and a bid stage. The nature of the concession varies across sectors, including models like 'build own operate', 'build own operate transfer' or 'build own transfer'. The rights of the concessionaire and the fundamental challenges depend largely on the nature of the concessions granted in each sector. However, one common feature across various sectors is the standard form of concession documents, with little or no scope for any negotiations given to the private developer. In some instances, these documents create uncertainty and ambiguity with little or no clarification forthcoming from the authorities.

Most bid documents have stringent requirements to ensure that there is no conflict of interest between various bidders. For instance, in national highway projects, two bidders would be disqualified if they or any of their constituents have any common shareholders holding more than a prescribed percentage of shares (recently increased to 26 per cent), directly or indirectly or have a relationship which puts them in a position to influence the bids. This is an issue for large conglomerates and financial investors.

Most infrastructure projects in India are implemented by forming special purpose companies, for obtaining non-recourse/limited financing and many times due to specific requirements of regulators in many sectors. For instance, the NHAI requires all national highway projects to be implemented by special purpose companies. Consequently, all such projects have stringent change in control/shareholding/ownership restrictions. As an illustration, NHAI prohibits dilution below 51 per cent during the construction of the project and for a period of two years thereafter. This is to ensure that the entity whose qualifications have been relied upon for a successful bid continues to be responsible for the project. Consequently, the exit options are limited and will have to be in compliance with the shareholding restrictions. Certain authorities like NHAI also restrict any change in control of the shareholders of the project company until financial closure of the projects. Additionally, in the road sector any acquisition of equity in the special purpose company exceeding 15 per cent of the equity of the company requires prior consent from a national security and public interest perspective. Consequently, even inter se share acquisitions amongst the existing shareholders are restricted. Perhaps this is unintended; however, no clarifications are available currently. In certain sectors, the government/regulatory authorities retain some ownership in the project companies and have affirmative rights in relation to key decision making in relation to such projects. For instance, in all airport projects the government/designated authority of the government typically retains 26 per cent shareholding in the project company. Additionally, there are stringent shareholding restrictions in most airport concessions which prevent divestment by private entities for a period up to seven years except for limited divestment in favour of financial investors and inter se share transfer.

Termination Payment

Many public infrastructure projects (like ports and national highway projects) guarantee a termination payment to the financiers as well as the developers in the event a concession/licence is terminated before its expiry. Such termination payments are calculated as a percentage of the equity infused in the project and the debt which is due to the lenders. During construction, the risk of the project is borne by the developer. 100 per cent of the debt of the lenders is assured, usually when the termination is as a result of the default of the authority. However, 100 per cent debt is not guaranteed by the authorities in case the termination is as a consequence of a developer's default. In light of this, most road and port projects in India require some form of support/guarantee from the sponsors who are required to undertake the payment of any shortfall in debt amount which the concessioning authority will not compensate under the concession/licence agreements. A typical non-recourse financing is often not the case.

There is no guarantee on the returns for the developer for a project. In road or port projects, although the returns largely depend on the traffic volumes, no assurance of traffic or monetary compensation is provided in the event the traffic does not meet the projections stipulated by the authorities.

Offtake

Under the tariff policies of the Government of India, long term purchase agreements (PPA) are to be entered into by following a competitive bid. Developers of power projects typically enter into long term PPAs with distribution licensees for long term sale of power. Such PPAs typically take the form of a take or pay contract whereby the purchaser agrees to purchase a minimum quantum of power or pay to the seller fixed/capacity charges. Forex variation risk is taken by the developer. In case of bilateral PPAs, the cost plus tariff approach is followed. Calculations of fixed/capacity charges take into account loan, depreciation, operation and maintenance expenses, return on equity, income tax and interest on working capital. Certain fixed charges (usually for three months) are also payable in the event the PPA is terminated by the purchaser on account of his default. Additionally, the distribution licensees undertake to purchase the power at the project bus bar, thus mitigating any risks in relation to transmission of power with the generator. However, in the event the power is sold to private entities or over the power exchange on a short term basis, there are no guaranteed fixed/capacity charges payable to the generator, who is responsible for making all necessary transmission arrangements. Lenders financing a power project would normally require existence of a binding long term PPA for tie up of at least 50–65 per cent of the power before financial closure of the project or within one or two years from financial closure of the project.

Fuel

Procurement of fuel for power projects is an issue of significant concern in India currently. The supply of domestic coal is regulated heavily. The Ministry of Coal allots a certain quantity of domestic coal by way of a letter of allotment and then a fuel supply agreement is executed. There is no assurance from the government that the quantity of allocated domestic coal shall cover the entire requirement of fuel for the life of the project. If fuel allotment is linked to 60–90 per cent of coal requirement, the Government of India requires the developer to blend the domestic coal with imported coal. In some instances, captive coal blocks are allotted jointly to several developers.

Consequently, the project companies have to rely on imported coal to meet the balance fuel supply requirements. Such fuel supply contracts involving imported coal not only lead to an escalation of fuel cost for the project but also a possible mismatch of the variable cost in tariff for the sale of power, which is usually fixed under the PPA with some escalation.

Government Support

Although concessions are granted by authorities established by the central government, the developers depend on the state government and local government authorities for procuring clearances, licences and infrastructure facilities and there is no single window clearance available for projects. State Governments often agree to provide a certain amount of assistance for the projects, in the form of state support agreements; however, there is no firm assurance provided for granting all clearances, tax exemptions or access to infrastructure facilities/utilities. Typically, the State Government's obligations are on a best efforts basis.

In relation to financial support, the Government of India provides Viability Gap Funding (VGF) for all economically essential PPP projects imposed by the Central

Ministries, State Governments and statutory authorities, as the case may be, which owns the underlying assets.[1] VGF is being used by the Government as a major initiative to complement the financing requirements of a PPP infrastructure project; for instance the Government or statutory entity that owns the project may, if it so decides, provide additional grants out of its budget but not exceeding 20 per cent of the total project cost. A private sector company is eligible for VGF only if is selected on the basis of open competitive bidding, is undertaking a project in specified infrastructure sectors (including airports, roads, seaports, special economic zones) and is responsible for the financing, construction, maintenance and operation of the project during the concession period. The project should provide a service against payment of a pre-determined tariff or user charge. Having said that, in the recent past, developers have agreed to quote and offer a premium to the concessioning authority rather than seek VGF to win bids on a competitive basis.

Project Financing and Security Creation

Although the recent trend has seen an increasing number of foreign lenders, infrastructure project financing in India is largely supported by domestic lenders. Most infrastructure projects in India still require some form of support from the sponsors, which includes cost overrun support, limited financial guarantees from the sponsor at least until the completion of construction of the project.

Security

The following types of security are usually created:

a) Mortgage of immovable property;
b) Hypothecation or charge of all movable (tangible and intangible) assets including receivables of the borrower;
c) Assignment by way of security of all rights of the borrower under the project documents;
d) Charge over all bank accounts and receivables of the borrower.

Security is usually held in favour of a trustee appointed by the lenders financing the project, for the benefit of all the lenders. This ensures that the security is administered by a trustee.

Most contracts in the public infrastructure projects (roads, ports, airports) are awarded by the regulator by way of a concession or a licence, which varies between 15 to 30 years. At the end of the concession period, the developer is required to hand over the project to the government. These concession agreements do not grant any ownership rights over the infrastructure asset to the developer. Typically, the licence granted is limited to the right to develop, finance, design, construct, operate and maintain the infrastructure asset

---

1   Scheme and Guidelines for Financial Support to Public Private Partnership in Infrastructure, Ministry of Finance, Department of Economic Affairs, Government of India (2008).

and to levy, collect and appropriate charges from the users. These concessions restrict creation of security on the project assets by the developer. Recently, in light of concerns expressed by various banks and financial institutions financing road projects, NHAI has permitted the developer to assign its rights under a road concession by way of security in favour of lenders financing the project. Step-in rights or substitution rights of the lenders pursuant to such assignment is recognized through the execution of separate tripartite agreements amongst NHAI, the project company and the lenders. However, entity to which the project can be transferred upon enforcement will have to be approved by NHAI.

Although security can be created by way of a pledge over shares of the project company, the enforcement of such pledge may breach change in control/ownership restrictions under the concession and will require prior approval of the concessionaire. For instance, NHAI requires the consortium members to retain 51 per cent of the shareholding for 2 years post completion of construction.

Security creation over private infrastructure assets (e.g. power projects) where the private developer owns the assets including the land in its name (freehold or leasehold interest in land) is not restricted. Creation of security over forest land requires specific approval from the authorities, which approvals are often not granted.

STAMP DUTY

Stamp duty is required to be paid on all documents creating the security interest at the time of execution of the said documents. Stamp duty payable varies significantly in different states in India and differential stamp duty is payable if a document is required to be enforced in a state which has a higher stamp duty. Since stamp duty payable is high in certain states, security package may become complex. Inadequate stamping or non-stamping of a document results in such a document being inadmissible as evidence in a court of law in India.

OTHER CONCERNS

Project finance lenders also usually require an assignment by way of security over all rights and interest of the borrower on all project-related documents with adequate rights to substitute the borrower in case of a default. State utilities often do not agree to enter into a 'full fledged' direct agreement. Contractors are more amenable to enter into direct agreements.

ENFORCEMENT OF SECURITY

Enforcement of security usually requires intervention of the court. Private remedies by way of a private sale by the lender of secured assets are available only when security over any immovable asset is created by way of a registered mortgage. Security enforcement with the intervention of courts can be a time-consuming process. The Government has taken steps to enable faster enforcement of security through the establishment of Debt Recovery Tribunals (DRTs) under the Recovery of Debts Due to Banks and Financial Institutions Act, 1993 (DRT Act), the enactment of the Securitization and Reconstruction of Financial Assets and Enforcement of Security Interest Act, 2002 (SARFAESI Act) and the proposed establishment of 'fast track' commercial courts pursuant to the Commercial Division of High Courts Bill 2009 (Commercial Courts Bill). For the purposes of the DRT Act, 'banks' include those banks that have a licence to operate under the Banking Regulation Act, 1949 and have branches in India. Financial institutions inter alia, include securitization companies and reconstruction companies incorporated in India and those institutions as are notified by the Central Government as financial institutions. The SARFAESI Act grants special remedies to secured creditors in whose favour a security interest by way of mortgage, hypothecation, charge, etc. have been created to secure repayment by the borrower of any financial assistance. The remedies available to secured creditors under the SARFAESI may be availed of upon fulfilment of certain conditions. Foreign banks/ financial institutions cannot have recourse under the DRT Act and the SARFAESI Act, unless notified as a financial institution by the Central Government.

Although security is common for the Indian lenders and the foreign lenders, enforcement of such security by both Indian and foreign lenders will be in different fora. In light of this, foreign lenders may often have to rely on enforcement by the Indian lenders with the proceeds being distributed thereafter amongst all the lenders, since proceedings in the DRT are 'fast track' compared to civil courts. Also Indian law will invalidate an absolute restriction on the rights of the lenders to take enforcement action. These issues are usually dealt with by the lenders in an inter-creditor agreement executed between all the lenders, wherein they agree to take all actions in a coordinated and consolidated manner. The Borrower is not a party to intercreditor agreement and is required to acknowledge it will be bound by it.

Land Acquisition and Environmental Consents

Land required for the project can be acquired in two ways: (i) by way of a private negotiation between private landowners and project developers and (ii) alternatively, land can also be acquired by the government under the Land Acquisition Act, 1894 (LA Act) and handed over to the developer on payment of requisite charges. Under the LA Act, the Indian Government has the right of acquisition of landis for 'public purposes'

Acquisition of any forest land, land from a tribal area or near a wildlife reserve requires specific consent of the government under different legislations. In some cases ownership of the land must remain with the Government. The exercise by the government of its powers to acquire land for public purpose has been questioned in courts often due to inadequate compensation and deprivation of livelihood. Furthermore, the recent judicial trend is to consider 'public purpose' more narrowly.

One of the key clearances required for all infrastructure projects is clearances from the Ministry of Environment and Forests (MoEF), Government of India. MoEF is the nodal governing executive authority for environmental matters. All major projects need the environmental clearance from the MoEF before they can be implemented and in certain cases an environmental impact assessment is required to be undertaken. Clearance granted can be challenged in appellate authority/courts. The appeal issues can result in additional conditions which may have cost implications.

In addition to the abovementioned environmental clearances, several other clearances need to be obtained (for instance clearance under the coastal regulatory zone for a project near coastal areas, geology and mining clearance, clearances from defence and airport authorities) under different legislations for different projects before construction and the operation stages.

Foreign Investment in Infrastructure Projects

Foreign investment is permitted in most infrastructure sectors under the automatic route. However, there are certain specific guidelines/compliances stipulated by the Foreign Investment Promotion Board (FIPB) and the Reserve Bank of India which will have to be complied with for foreign investment in India.

External Commercial Borrowings

Infrastructure projects in India are currently being financed by both domestic debt as well as foreign currency borrowings. Foreign currency borrowings in infrastructure projects are subject to certain end use restrictions, all-in cost ceilings and other conditions applicable to foreign currency loans as specified by the RBI which is the central bank of India as well as the exchange control regulator.

External Commercial Borrowings (ECBs) cannot be used for (i) on lending or investment in capital markets or for acquisition of a company in India, (ii) investment in real estate, (iii) working capital, general corporate purpose or repayment of existing rupee loans. ECBs cannot be used for the real estate sector (including acquisition of land in India), for working capital or general corporate purpose or for refinancing of existing rupee loans.

Additionally, ECBs are subject to all-in cost ceilings which include a cap on the amount of interest and other fees which the lender is entitled to charge in relation to the facility. ECBs are also subject to certain minimum average maturity periods and hence such loans cannot be prepaid by the borrower before expiry of the minimum average maturity.

Conclusion

Despite all challenges, India is a booming economy with interest in the infrastructure sector growing significantly in the last few decades. The legal framework has been witnessing significant change on a continuing basis, to address various concerns of private developers. The liberalization of the regulatory environment and reforms in India since 1991 have been a key focus of the Indian government. Foreign interest in infrastructure development in India is increasing immensely. Most of the challenges faced today are not unique to the Indian economy.

The growth of several Infrastructure Companies riding the wave of infrastructure development in India will offer a platform for future investments.

29 *Project Finance in Turkey*

YEŞIM BEZEN, Partner
BANU ASLAN, Associate
Bezen & Partners

Turkey, with its diversified economy and geographical location next to Europe and the Middle East, draws the attention of many foreign investors, either for investments directly into Turkey or for investments through Turkey as a gate between Europe and the Middle East. Although traditional agriculture is still an important income for Turkey's economy, a shift to industry in western provinces of the country is clearly notable. Key sectors are energy, automotive, construction, textiles, banking, home appliances, oil refining, petrochemical products, food, mining, iron and steel, ship construction and machine industry.

Turkey's Crisis Experience

Turkey has undergone a crisis in 2001 which made it (due to lessons learned) easier for the country to sustain its economy during the last global economic crisis. However, the global economic circumstances in 2008/2009 still affected the Turkish project finance market. Banks as well as finance institutions were more cautious and their interest towards project finance transactions was replaced by a more demanding structural approach classifying everything as a risk factor (i.e., safe-guarding against the slightest risk). The projects that were financed in 2009 through syndications were led by international finance institutions (such as IFC, EBRD and EIB) rather than commercial banks. Following the world's recovery from the global economic crisis, the deal volume in project finance also began to increase in Turkey.

Turkey's Figure – An Outline

(A) GDP

Apart from the fact that Turkey is the 16th largest economy in the world, the gross domestic product (GDP) figures also indicate Turkey's booming economy. Further, by forecasting an annual average real GDP of 6.7 per cent between 2011 and 2017, Turkey is placed as one of the fastest growing economies amongst the OECD countries.[1] As Figure 29.1 below shows, in 2008, there was a decrease in Turkey's GDP ensuing from the economic crisis which also affected Turkey's economy during 2009.

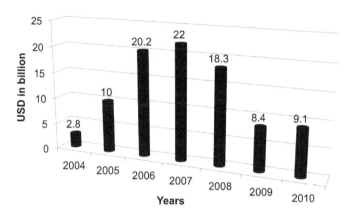

Figure 29.1 Foreign direct investments

(B) FOREIGN DIRECT INVESTMENTS

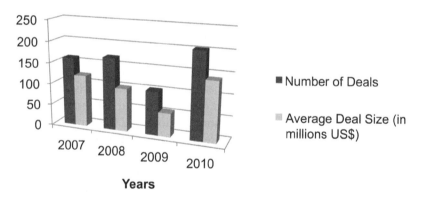

Figure 29.2 Turkey's transaction volume

According to the recent report published by YASED, the Turkish International Investors Association, foreign direct investment reached US$4bn in the first quarter of 2011 corresponding to an increase of 1.5 times compared to the same period in 2010.[2] A total foreign direct investment of US$10bn is expected by the end of 2011. Spain (with an investment of US$2.081m), Belgium (with an investment of US$1.365m) and France (with an investment of US$715m) are amongst the countries that invested the most in

1   http://www.invest.gov.tr/en-US/investmentguide/Pages/10Reasons.aspx.
2   http://www.yased.org.tr/webportal/Turkish/Yayinlar/Documents/UDYRaporu-may2011-2011-I.ceyrek.pdf.

Turkey compared to other countries and rank at the top of the foreign direct investment list.[3]

Turkey's Transaction Volume 2010

(A) MERGERS AND ACQUISITIONS (M&A)

In 2010, the M&A transaction volume in Turkey reached 203 deals with a total volume of US$29bn. Compared with the M&A transaction volume of 2009, the deal number increased almost two-fold in 2010. This deal volume is the highest since 2005.[4]

Privatization transactions made up a high proportion of the M&A transaction volume with a total volume of US$14.6bn.[5] The sale of electricity distribution companies contributed a high proportion to these overall figures.

Private equity involvement in the Turkish M&A sector totalled US$850m comprising 24 deals. In particular, the healthcare, entertainment, food and beverage sectors drew and still draw investors' attention.

The year 2011 is also expected to be a year where M&A activities will boom taking into account not only the increase of private M&A activity but also the forthcoming privatization projects.

(B) PRIVATIZATION

The privatization process is mainly led by two bodies. Firstly, there is the decision-making body which is the Privatization High Council (Council). The Council is headed by the Prime Minister and is responsible for making the ultimate decisions. In addition, there is the executive body which is the Privatization Administration (PA). Its main responsibility is to report to the Prime Minister. Depending on the sector to be privatized, certain state entities are also involved; e.g. privatization in the banking sector would involve the Banking Regulation and Supervision Agency, privatization in the energy sector would involve the Energy Market Regulatory Authority. Turkey's Competition Authority is responsible for granting approval to privatizations as another 'perfection' requirement following which the Council will finally consent to such privatizations.

Privatization is on Turkey's agenda since 1984. Apart from minimizing the State's control in the economy through privatizations, privatization has been developed as a new source for investment. The principles, procedures and any other matters in relation to privatization are regulated by the Privatization Law No 4046 dated 24 November 1994.[6] Privatization can be based on certain models – i.e., share sale, asset sale, leasing, granting operational rights (e.g. based on a concession agreement) and property rights (other than ownership), and the profit sharing model are frequently used.

---

3   http://www.yased.org.tr/webportal/Turkish/Yayinlar/Documents/UDYRaporu-may2011-2011-I.ceyrek.pdf.

4   http://www.deloitte.com/assets/Dcom-Turkey/Localpercent20Assets/Documents/turkey-tr_kf_birlesmesatinalmara poru_210111.pdf.

5   http://www.deloitte.com/assets/Dcom-Turkey/Localpercent20Assets/Documents/turkey-tr_kf_birlesmesatinalmara poru_210111.pdf.

6   The Law No. 4046 was published in the Official Gazette No. 22124 dated 27 November 1994.

Once the tender is won by the highest bidder, the bid amount needs to be submitted to the PA and the successful bidder has to comply with any other conditions specified in the tender documents. The PA grants a certain time period for such payment and satisfaction of such other conditions which can under normal circumstances be extended. However, when such time period (or extension) has passed and the successful bidder does not fulfil its payment obligations and/or satisfies any further conditions, the PA will cash in the bid bond submitted by the successful bidder during the tender stage.

This was recently seen in the privatization tender of Başkent Doğalgaz Dağıtım AŞ where the successful bidder could not comply with its obligation to pay the bid amount in the total amount of US$bn to the PA within the designated time period (which included an extension of 60 days). As a result, the PA cashed in the bid bond in the total amount of US$92,600,000 submitted by the successful bidder as part of the tender participation requirement.

In 2010, 35 privatization tenders took place. The total figure of privatized assets is equal to US$14.6bn which makes 50 per cent of the deal volume of 2010 (see Figure 29.3).[7] In this context, it is notable that all these privatization tenders were won by Turkish companies. Most of the privatizations were related to the energy sector. The tenders were comprised of the following assets: 18 generation assets owned by the Electricity Generation Joint-Stock Company (EÜAŞ), 11 electricity distribution companies, 3 geothermal reserves and 1 natural gas distribution company.[8]

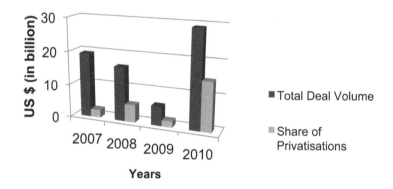

Figure 29.3 Privatization volume[9]

(C) INFRASTRUCTURE

The overall investment in the infrastructure sector between 2008 and 2012 is expected to reach more than US$25bn.[10] In this sector big ticket investments are/were made. One

7   http://www.deloitte.com/assets/Dcom-Turkey/Localpercent20Assets/Documents/turkey-tr_kf_birlesmesatinalmara poru_210111.pdf.

8   http://www.deloitte.com/assets/Dcom-Turkey/Localpercent20Assets/Documents/turkey-tr_kf_birlesmesatinalmara poru_210111.pdf.

9   Table generated by B&P based on numbers set out in: http://www.deloitte.com/assets/Dcom-Turkey/Local per cent20Assets/Documents/turkey-tr_kf_birlesmesatinalmaraporu_210111.pdf.

10   http://www.invest.gov.tr/en-us/sectors/pages/infrastructure.aspx.

infrastructure project of importance is the tender held in 2008 for the construction of the Kadıköy-Kartal metro line on the Asian side of Istanbul which was won by a consortium in 2008 for the total price of €751m.[11] In the same year the Marmaray project was put to tender which also required high investment amounts by interested companies. The main focus of the Marmaray project is the undersea rail project, i.e., construction of an undersea rail tunnel with a total length of 76.5km crossing the Bosporus Strait which will link the two railway lines on the Pan-European Transport Corridor.[12] The major financing of this project is undertaken by The Japan International Cooperation Agency lending Yen111bn (as of April 2006) and the European Investment Bank lending €1.05bn (as of April 2006). The total cost of the project is expected to be approximately US$2.5bn. As of late 2009, costs were expected to increase by approximately US$500m due to archaeological findings which were discovered during the construction works and the consequential delays resulting from the preservation of such findings.[13] Another big ticket infrastructure project worth noting is the İzmit Bay Bridge which, upon finalization of construction, will be the second largest suspension bridge in the world. The respective tender took place in 2009, whereas the agreements were signed in 2010. This project is currently worth US$11bn.

(D) FINANCIAL SERVICE INSTITUTIONS

In 2010, 15 deals were disclosed with a total value of US$6.384bn. Two transactions accounting to almost the entire total value are of utmost importance, namely the share acquisition of 24.9 per cent of Garanti bank shares by General Electric for US$5.8bn and the acquisition of Fiba Sigorta for US$323m by Sompo Japan Insurance and the European Bank for Reconstruction and Development.[14]

(E) CAPITAL MARKETS

Twenty-two initial public offerings (IPOs) were held in Turkey amounting to US$2.1bn in 2010.[15] As of June 2011, for the year 2011, 38[16] IPOs are carried out/announced/planned with an expected volume of a total of US$10.6bn. This figure is of course bound to increase further until year-end.

---

11   http://www.turkeyfinancial.com/news/2008/01/18/astaldi-wins-istanbul per centE2 per cent80 per cent99s-metro-line-tender-worth-e-751-m/.

12   http://www.eib.org/projects/news/bosphorus-tunnel-building-a-milestone-link-between-europe-and-asia.htm.

13   http://en.wikipedia.org/wiki/Marmaray.

14   http://www.deloitte.com/assets/Dcom-Turkey/Localpercent20Assets/Documents/turkey-tr_kf_birlesmesatinalmara poru_210111.pdf.

15   http://spk.gov.tr/indexpage.aspx?pageid=733&showfull=yes&submenuheader=3.

16   http://spk.gov.tr/indexpage.aspx?pageid=777&showfull=yes&submenuheader=3.

Early Developments for the Designation of Project Investment Models

One of the key sectors in Turkey is the energy sector. Any development in the energy sector (including attempts to liberalize such sector) were frontrunners for similar developments in other sectors.

Until 1984, the Turkish electricity market was controlled by the State. The Turkish Electricity Authority (TEK) was the only player in the market. Turkey's intention to open the market to the private sector led to a battle between Turkey's Supreme Courts and Turkey's governments. The Constitutional Court, as the guardian of the Turkish Constitution, had already expressed its view on this matter in 1974. It had ruled that providing electricity is a public service and foreign investors must not take part in the supply of electricity.

In 1984, Law No. 3096 welcomed the private sector to the market. The law introduced the generation, wholesale, auto production and distribution of electricity by the private sector alongside TEK. Once Law No. 3096 was enacted, the Constitutional Court softened its stance but found that under Law No 3096 the nature of the agreements between the State and the private sector were concession agreements. Accordingly, such agreements could not be governed by private law but must be governed by administrative law and submitted to the jurisdiction of the Council of State (Danıştay) – Turkey's Supreme Administrative Court.

In 1994, Law No 3996 was enacted. Law No 3996 deals with private sector investments in certain areas, including electricity by means of Law No 3096, under build-operate-transfer (BOT). In terms of the electricity sector, the law redefines the type of agreements between the State and private sector as private law agreements instead of concession agreements. However, despite the government's efforts in amending the then existent legal framework to further private investments, the Constitutional Court ruled that such provision of the law, which aimed at redefining the legal relationship between the public and the private sector, was against the Constitution, since public services can only be provided by the State. If the State wished to transfer these services to the private sector, it could be done by way of concession agreements only.

The government saw only one way out: to initiate the amendment of the Constitution to counter further legal challenges. Finally, in 1999, the Constitution was amended. By the amended version of Article 47 of the Constitution, the legislator has been given power to determine which services can be conducted by the private sector under private law. Following the constitutional amendment, the Constitutional Court changed its view in favour of private investors. In recent decisions the Court ruled that performing public services by the private sector under private law provisions is no longer against the Constitution. In a decision of the Constitutional Court, (E 2002/47, K2006/1) which was published on 7 October 2006 in the Official Gazette, the Court presented its new liberal approach. The case before the Court was about the setting aside of Article 15 of the Privatization Law (Law No 4046). The provision simply states that public services can be performed by the private sector under private law. The Council of State (Danıştay) also confirmed the latest view of the Constitutional Court in a number of judgments.

In addition to such development, the Council of State's intervention right in respect of agreements between the private sector investor and the State also decreased. The

Council of State was no longer authorized to review the respective agreement (and hence request amendments to be made to such) but only to opine on such agreement.

The constitutional amendment also meant that disputes between the State and the private sector could henceforth be settled by international commercial arbitration. Accordingly, in 2001, the United Nations Commission on International Trade Law (UNCITRAL) Model Law was adopted as the Turkish International Arbitration Law by Law No 4501, paving the way for such disputes to be settled by arbitration.

Turkish Project Investment

Foreign investors face certain models for the realization of projects in Turkey which are specific to the Turkish project sector.

- *Build-operate-transfer (BOT)* – This model was first used during the construction of the Suez Canal when that part of the world was under the Ottoman regime. Some say that this is a Turkish invention and others say that the model was already used but that Turkey's former Prime Minister Turgut Özal gave it its name.[17]

    Any matter in relation to BOT is addressed in the BOT Law No. 3996 dated 8 June 1994.[18] The law defines the assets that can be operated through the BOT model and dictates the terms and conditions of BOT agreements. According to the BOT Law, a BOT agreement can only be executed for a term up to 49 years where the state entity grants the private entity a concession right to build and operate the project facility for a maximum of 49 years. BOT means that the private legal entity constructs the project facility and operates it for a certain time period. Upon expiry of such term, the ownership of the project facility will be transferred to the public sector. Having said this, it is important to emphasize that the responsibility for financing, constructing and operating the project facility rests with the private sector.[19]

    The private entity will be granted usufruct rights over the project facility and is also entitled to grant security over such facility. A usufruct right means a proprietary right of limited duration in respect of the facility/asset in question in favour of an entity which is not the owner of such facility/asset. The holder of such proprietary right has a right to use and enjoy the facility/asset (and hence the right to receive the profits of such facility/asset). For instance, the İzmit Bay Crossing Project and certain port projects (İzmir Karaburun, Tekirdağ, Karasu and Avşa Island port) are based on the BOT model.
- *Build-operate-own (BOO)* – The difference between the BOT model and the BOO model is that once the private sector entity has concluded the construction of the project, it is not only entitled to operate the project but also to own it. As there is no transfer to the public sector following the expiry of a certain concession period, any operating revenue risk rests with the private sector operator. The BOOT model is a hybrid between the BOT model and the BOO model. In the BOOT model, the facility/asset in question is transferred to the public sector upon expiry of a certain 'concession'

---

17   Turgut Özal was Turkey's Prime Minister between 13 December 1983 and 31 October 1989.

18   Law No. 3996 was published in the Official Gazette No. 21959 dated 13 June 1994.

19   Jeffrey Delmon, 'Private Sector Investment in Infrastructure,' 2nd edition p. 93. Kluwer Law International.

period but during such period is owned outright and entirely by the private sector operator. Ownership rights are of course stronger proprietary rights than usufruct rights. Accordingly, the private sector operator of the BOO or BOOT model is entitled to grant security which is more satisfactory to lenders than a private sector operator involved in a project based on the BOT model.

- *Transfer of operational rights (TOR)* means that an existing project facility belonging to the public sector will be operated by a private legal entity for a certain concession period. Upon expiry of such concession period, the facility will be re-transferred to the public sector. The private sector operator has no proprietary rights and cannot grant any proprietary security (i.e. a mortgage) in respect of the respective facility. The risk of a judicial challenge and a stay of execution is an added risk factor for private sector operators of the TOR model (please see below). The privatization of Turkey's entire motorway network and the two Istanbul Bosporus bridges is based on the TOR model.

- *Public private partnership (PPP)* is not regulated by a separate legislation but comprised in various laws. By way of historical background, in 2006, the government established a committee to have regard to PPP systems and laws in other countries so that a Turkish PPP law can be draughted which is in line with European and international standards. A draught law was then prepared by the State Planning Organization. Various public bodies were consulted in respect of the current draught in 2007. However, to date, no further progress is made with regards to the PPP draught law. The PPP draught law is intended to act as an 'umbrella' legislation for various current laws, such as Law No. 3096 (regarding energy investments), Law No. 3996 (regarding the application of the Build-Operate-Transfer (BOT) model) and to redefine the existing models (i.e., BOT, BO, BOO etc.) used in infrastructure projects. The main provisions of the current draught are as follows:

  - The private sector entity will be chosen by way of tender.
  - A joint stock company is then established by the State and such private sector entity for conducting the project (the State's shareholding in such joint stock company is not to exceed 49 per cent).
  - The life of the project cannot exceed 49 years.
  - Treasury guarantees and purchase guarantees will be available for investments coming within the scope of the PPP law. A risk account will be opened for such guarantees; however, what proportion of the amount guaranteed is to be put aside is still unknown.
  - Turkish law will apply to the contracts to be signed with the government entities. In solving disputes between the parties, the state courts will be authorized; however, the parties may resort to arbitration (the Turkish Arbitration Law is in line with the UNCITRAL model law).

There are certain important issues raised by financiers which are relevant to all these project models:

a) The involvement of state entities entails that the agreement to be executed between the State and the private sector operator could be regarded as a concession. This results in the fact that the Council of State is entitled to review such agreement and hence, subject to satisfaction of certain conditions, there is a risk that the Council of State grants a stay of execution upon a judicial challenge which means that the project is halted. As the completion of a project in accordance with the pre-designated milestones is of essence, in particular, where the project is financed by banks or finance institutions, a stay of execution is obviously a high project risk. From a contractual point of view, the parties try to avoid this risk by expressly designating the agreement between the State and the private sector operator as a 'private law agreement.'

b) The lender's focus will also lie on the credibility of the state entity contracting with the private sector operator. If such state entity does not possess an independent budget or is not linked to an entity that has its own budget or revenue flow, then the lenders will question the financial credibility of such state entity and will demand security to ensure that the payment obligations of such state entity under the agreement between such state entity and the private sector operator are met. There is a separate regulation in respect of Treasury guarantees – the so-called Regulation on the Terms and Principles applicable to Payment to be made by way of a Treasury Guarantee published in the Official Gazette dated 21 December 2002 and numbered 24970. This regulation specifies for what kind of projects such a guarantee can be submitted. These are BOT, BOO, TOR and other similar project models. The main aim of such Treasury guarantee is to guarantee the obligations of the state entity in question and against certain other (political) risks. However, although such regulation is still effective, the Treasury is no longer providing guarantees unless this is expressly dictated by law.

c) As any construction is associated with the obtaining of the respective licences, permits, approvals and consents from various public authorities, financiers (i) request that such are obtained as conditions precedent for the drawdown of the financing, and (ii) if such are not in the form and/or content satisfactory to such financiers, ask for additional comfort in the form of so-called comfort letters from the relevant authorities. This is a sensitive matter since most (if not, all) authorities are used to granting the relevant licence, permit, approval or consent in a specific and standard form. If there are certain issues not dealt with in such document, the respective authority generally pinpoints to the laws and regulations in force to 'fill the details' and/or the established court practice to ascertain its stance in certain situations.

Project finance à la Turkey

Although project financing was never non-recourse in Turkey, the more generally accepted limited recourse project financing structure has shifted to a rather full recourse project financing structure during the recent economic crisis, albeit that such full recourse project financing is disguised in documentation which was previously used for limited recourse project financing. Accordingly, banks and finance institutions do not only focus on project assets or on project cash flow to secure and ensure the repayment of their loans but also on the assets and creditworthiness of the sponsors (i.e. the parents or shareholders of the project company).

(I) STANDARD PROJECT FINANCE SECURITY PACKAGE

According to Article 2 of the Turkish Private International Procedure Law (PIPL), parties are permitted to choose the law that shall govern the relevant agreement provided that certain criteria are met. However, Turkey has exclusive jurisdiction in certain areas which are specified in the PIPL. For example, jurisdiction over movables and immovables situated in Turkey is one of these areas and, pursuant to Article 21 of the PIPL, subject to Turkish law. Accordingly, any security comprising movables or immovables situated in Turkey has to be governed by Turkish law.

A basic security package is comprised of the following security documents: commercial enterprise pledge (which comes close to an English law governing fixed and floating debenture), share pledge, onshore account pledge, mortgage agreement, assignment of receivables (either by way of an absolute assignment or a security assignment) and assignment of shareholder loan receivables as an addition to a subordination arrangement (if applicable).

(II) ENFORCEMENT ISSUES

Any assets located in Turkey are subject to foreclosure proceedings pursuant to Turkish law. Accordingly, any typical English law security provisions (e.g., mortgagee in possession rights) will not be applicable and hence not enforceable in Turkey. Further, given the fact that enforcement under Turkish law is a very complex procedure, foreign financiers are often worried about enforcing their Turkish law governed security. Foreclosure proceedings under Turkish law follow a rigid procedure. Only execution offices have the exclusive authority to conduct foreclosure proceedings. The creditor (upon a default of the borrower and the consequential acceleration of the loan) needs to take an action before the execution office by filing an execution request rather than taking any self-remedy action itself.

There is no concept of the rights of a mortgagee in possession. Any contractual provision providing that the secured party shall become owner of the collateral if the debt is not paid is null and void. Further, under Turkish law secured assets are generally sold by way of public auction and the sale proceeds are then distributed to the beneficiaries.

In this context, the concept developed in respect of share pledges is notable. In generic terms, under Turkish law, share pledges are established by way of a written agreement and perfected by transfer of the pledged share certificates bearing endorsements in favour of the pledgee. Enforcement of a standard share pledge (disregarding any contractual requirement, for instance, to serve notices) needs to be undertaken by the respective execution office by way of the statutory enforcement mechanism. Further, due to the fact that shares are classified as moveable assets, the enforcement of a share pledge can be conducted in two ways: either a public auction will be initiated or a negotiated sale will be conducted (i.e. sale of the pledged asset/s without entailing a bidding process as it is the case in the public auction).

In this context, a distinction needs to be drawn between pledge and blank endorsements: (i) a pledge endorsement is the conventional type of endorsement where the pledgor annotates on the back of the share certificate the security interest and the name of the pledgee; and (ii) a blank endorsement where the holder of a share certificate annotates onto the back of such share certificate that it has endorsed it, with no indication of a security interest on the face of it or the name of the beneficiary.

A pledgee in possession of share certificates with blank endorsements is entitled to sell the shares privately – i.e., without going through the formal foreclosure proceedings under Turkish law. The advantage of such private sale seems to be avoiding the lengthy foreclosure proceedings and mitigating the risk that the shares will be sold below their actual market value. Although this seems to be a practical and favourable route from a lender's point of view, there are risks associated with a potential private sale. The mere fact that there is a share pledge agreement in existence suggests that the parties' intention was to create a security interest over the respective shares. This in turn makes the sale of the shares subject to mandatory rules under Turkish law – i.e., foreclosure proceedings before the Turkish execution offices/courts. Accordingly, it is not clear as to whether a private sale will in fact be upheld by a Turkish court if and when the pledgor objects to such private sale by filing a court case. Such a scenario has not yet been tested before the Turkish courts and to form a factual opinion on this is therefore quite a challenge. However, the worst case scenario is that the pledgee could be held liable for breach of fiduciary duty and trust and hence for payment of damages pursuant to the provisions of the Turkish Civil Code (Law No 4721).

(III) STEP-IN RIGHTS/DIRECT AGREEMENTS

Step-in rights are an essential part of international project finance transactions. As the project company is generally a special purpose entity (i.e., an empty shell with no assets other than the project assets), in case of a default by the project company, the lenders, in order to ensure that the project is completed on time and commences/continues generating cash flow for debt service purposes, try to somehow take control of the project. For such purpose the step-in right concept was developed. This concept entitles the lenders or any appointee of the lenders to 'step into the shoes' of the project company. In order to ensure that such step-in functions properly so that the project can be continued without interruption, direct agreements are executed with (preferably) all third party project participants. Accordingly, direct agreements allow the lenders or any appointee of the lenders to replace the project company and assume the project company's rights and obligations.

Enforcement of step-in rights is problematic under Turkish law although appropriate wording allowing such (or a similar) concept was seen in certain privatization transactions – i.e., for instance, certain port privatizations. A further example is also the implementation of the step-in right concept in Article 5 of the Electricity Licence Regulation dated 1 March 2009, according to which banks or financial institutions that provide limited or non-recourse project financing have the right to request from the Energy Market Regulatory Authority that a replacement entity be granted a new licence which will then assume all the responsibilities of the original licensee. This stipulates somehow a quasi 'step-in right.' However, how this will work in practice is ambiguous and has to be put to the test.

Novation is an effective means to transfer rights and obligations from one party to the other. However, as to whether a party active in a regulated sector – such as the electricity sector – can in fact transfer its rights and obligations ensuing from a particular project to a third party entity appointed or designated by the lenders financing such a project is questionable. Such transferee would need to comply with the legal requirements of the relevant legislation and would hence need to be approved by the respective regulator. This entails a regulatory procedure which is in addition to a contractual re-arrangement to give effect to the lenders' so-called 'step-in rights.'

(IV) SUBORDINATION ARRANGEMENTS

The execution of a subordination agreement is effective; however, it is doubtful as to whether such can be enforced in insolvency proceedings. The market has therefore developed the execution of assignments of receivables by way of security in addition to subordination agreements. If the subordination agreement fails during insolvency, then it is thought that an assignment of receivables by way of security can assist in designating the assignee at least as 'secured creditor,' ranking above any unsecured creditors of the insolvent estate.

The Execution and Bankruptcy Law No. 2004 stipulates mandatory provisions which cannot be contracted out. Its main aim is to ensure an equal distribution between all creditors of the insolvent company. The Execution and Bankruptcy Law differentiates between secured and unsecured creditors. However, it recognizes only certain agreements as security, such as a mortgage agreement, a commercial enterprise pledge, a share pledge and an account pledge. An assignment of receivables by way of security is not recognized by the Execution and Bankruptcy Law as a means of security. Hence, the beneficiaries under an assignment of receivables by way of security are in fact not regarded as 'secured creditors.' Nonetheless, security assignments were and still are executed within the security package in project finance transactions in Turkey and have somehow become common practice. However, if lenders wish to execute an additional assignment of receivables to guarantee that a subordination arrangement also works in insolvency, it is advisable to do this by way of an absolute assignment where the receivables become the property of the assignee on 'day 1' or upon the occurrence of an event of default. This has the legal effect of taking the receivables out of the 'insolvency pot' since they are no longer owned by the insolvent entity.

(V) STATE INVOLVEMENT

State involvement is also a factor which makes most lenders anxious. In order to overcome any political risk, the focus lies in obtaining comfort from state entities involved in the project. Thus, a trend has developed in demanding undertakings from Turkish state entities. The purpose of such requirement is to safeguard against the slightest risk that could potentially arise. The financiers' main concern is to ensure that the relevant state entity will not interfere in the project (i.e., by revoking or terminating any licences, permits, approvals and consents (Permit)). As a matter of course, Turkish state entities are not willing to give such undertakings as it is not within their competence to do so. Any Permit has to be in line with applicable law. Accordingly, no state entity is legally entitled to sign any other document, especially an undertaking, which tries to extend the legal scope of a Permit. Any extension of grace periods or conditions for termination or revocation of a Permit cannot be granted by way of an undertaking but must be prescribed in the Permit or regulated by law. As is the case in all constitutional states, Turkish state entities are bound by the relevant laws and regulations and do not have discretion to grant something in contravention of the legal framework. It is therefore of no real surprise when such demand is not well received by the respective state entities.

Turkey's Future Deal Potential

(I) PRIVATIZATION

Following successful years in the privatization sector, the privatization of state entities/ assets remains on the agenda. Investors focus on big ticket privatizations such as Turkey's entire motorway network, the Bosporus bridges, the National Lottery and energy entities/ assets. On the port front, the Istanbul Port (also the so-called Galataport) will attract the interest of many foreign investors. The Istanbul Port is envisaged to be the largest cruise port in Turkey with a total area of 100,000 m^2.[20] It is expected that this port will be put on the privatization agenda based on the BOT model with an operation period of 50 years.[21]

(II) ENERGY

In order to meet Turkey's energy demand by 2023 a total investment amount of approximately US$130bn has to be made.[22] The fact that Turkey offers various alternatives of energy sources (e.g. wind, sun and water) makes Turkey more interesting for investors. In the wind sector, only 15 per cent of Turkey's potential has been utilized to date, however, Turkey ranks first in the world in respect of the highest growth rate in wind energy power plant projects.[23] Not only the renewable energy sector of Turkey is developing but the execution of an intergovernmental agreement for the construction of the first nuclear power plant in Turkey shows that Turkey is also opting for other alternatives. In addition, the number of rivers and lakes with an energy potential of approximately 36,000MW offers investors the possibility for small, mid and large-scale investments.[24]

Pipeline projects where Turkey acts as a transit country will also increase in the future. Due to its strategic location connecting Asia and Europe, Turkey will be of particular interest and part of 'transit projects' (e.g. the Pars Pipeline[25]). The Nabucco pipeline project is one of the major projects in this category. This pipeline will draw gas from the Caspian region – Azerbaijan, Turkmenistan and Kazakhstan – as well as Georgia and Iraq.[26] Furthermore, the Turkey-Greece-Italy Natural Gas Pipeline Project (ITGI), also known as the Southern Europe Gas Ring Project, was developed for the transportation of natural gas supplied from the Caspian Basin, Russian Federation, the Middle East, Southern Mediterranean countries, and other international sources through Turkey and Greece within the scope of the INOGATE Programme (Interstate Oil and Gas Transport to Europe) of the EU Commission.[27] Turkey's involvement in this project consists of a 17km off-shore section and a line with a length of 209km crossing the country.[28] There is also the Egypt-Turkey Natural Gas Pipeline Project. The two governments signed a framework

---

20   http://www.galataport.org/.

21   http://www.galataport.org/.

22   http://www.invest.gov.tr/en-US/sectors/Pages/Energy.aspx.

23   http://www.invest.gov.tr/en-US/sectors/Pages/Energy.aspx.

24   http://www.invest.gov.tr/en-US/sectors/Pages/Energy.aspx.

25   The 1,740 km Pars pipeline will run through Turkey on to Europe. (http://pipelinesinternational.com/news/ pipeline_projects_in_the_middle_east/040183/).

26   http://pipelinesinternational.com/news/pipeline_projects_in_the_middle_east/040183/.

27   http://www.botas.gov.tr/index.asp.

28   http://www.botas.gov.tr/index.asp.

agreement in 2004 in Cairo as regards the import of natural gas by BOTAŞ from the Egypt Natural Gas Company, EGAS. In addition, it is agreed that Egypt transmits gas to Europe through Turkey. Egypt can export between 2 and 4bn m³ of natural gas to Turkey and between 2 and 6bn m³ to Europe through Turkey.[29]

(III) INFRASTRUCTURE

Apart from the fact that certain parts of the infrastructure are envisaged to be privatized, construction tenders for the expansion of the current infrastructure network are expected in the future. The focus which was in past years on Istanbul in particular is shifting to other large to medium sized cities. For instance, certain airport construction projects will be undertaken/finalized in the coming years (Kütahya-Zafer Airport, Iğdır Airport, Or-Gi Airport and Çukurova Airport).

Important here again is the İzmit Gebze Bay Crossing Project which will include a steel suspension bridge with a length of 1688m. Currently, the agreement executed between the project company and the General Directorate of Highways is worth approximately US$6.3bn and overall construction is expected to be completed by 2018.[30]

Furthermore, the construction tender for the third Bosporus Bridge expected to be held this year will be one of the big ticket investments for foreign investors.

(IV) HEALTH COMPLEXES

The interest in the current tenders for the construction of health complexes reflects that this is also a sector of growth. A focus was and still is on the health complexes in Elazığ, Kayseri, Istanbul-İkitelli, Ankara-Etlik, Ankara-Bilkent, and Gaziantep. Accordingly, it is expected that further projects will be put out for tender.

---

29   http://www.botas.gov.tr/index.asp.

30   http://www.yuksel.net/index.php?option=com_content&view=article&id=543percent3Agebzezmir-motorway-and-zmit-bay-crossing-concession&catid=71&Itemid=277&lang=en.

30 *Project Finance in Russia*

MARC PARTRIDGE

Co-head, Project and structured finance department, Gazprombank

It is, to this day, very common to hear at project finance conferences that 'there is no Project Finance in Russia, only the financing of projects.' This was certainly true in the 1990s as many obstacles came in the way of would-be project financiers in the country, despite the obvious tremendous need for capital expenditure in the country. This however, is not true today as there are many examples of non-recourse or limited-recourse financing in Russia, both with international lenders and on a purely domestic basis.

Indeed, sponsors, public and private, Russian and international, more than ever before recognisz the added value that limited recourse finance can bring to their projects in Russia. An admittedly small group of Russian lenders has developed a significant portfolio of project financing, and some international banks have focussed on Russia. The technique is now perceived as crucial to the funding of the capital expenditure requirements of many sectors of the Russia economy, from oil and gas to infrastructure and industrial projects.

However, the perception that Russia is a challenging environment for project finance persists, and like many perceptions, it is certainly not devoid of truth. The paradox of Russia is that it is both one of the most tantalizing and rewarding markets for project finance and one of the trickiest to approach for international project financiers. This is clearly perceived by the government circles in Russia, and there is a consensus on the need to improve the legal, political, and regulatory environment to attract more foreign investment in Russia, although there are significant differences of opinion between those who emphasize the need for stability, and those who, on the contrary, push for a forceful evolution and full privatization of the economy.

Investment Needs and the Case for Project Finance

INVESTMENTS NEEDS

Almost all sectors of the Russian economy face huge capital expenditure requirements in the next decades. Some sectors, notably oil and gas, did enjoy high levels of investments in the years since the collapse of the Soviet Union, but still need more, whilst others such as infrastructures still rely on Soviet-era assets. Others, such as the power sector, need modernization and new capacity, and many industries such as railroads need to answer the challenges of a modern economy.

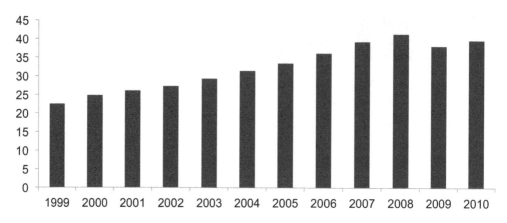

Figure 30.1 Russian GDP in 2008, trillion RUR

Faced with an alarmingly crumbling infrastructure, Russian authorities embarked in the mid-2000s on a US$1tr construction programme, passing laws to allow public private partnerships (PPP) and concessions, but then got caught in thralls of the financial crisis of 2008–2009, and are only now pushing forwards with renewed energy. That became easier to do in view of the responsibilities assumed in connection with such high profile events as the Sochi Winter Olympic Games, the Kazan Olympiad, the Soccer World Championship as well as the World Hockey Cup recently brought into the agenda. Having taken on the obligation to renovate the existing airport network, roads, railways and other infrastructure assets, the Russian Government will be looking into the potential for new forms of financing.

The oil and gas industry will need at least US$800bn in investments to answer the challenges of the near future: in 2011, Gazprom alone has decided to increase its capex programme from US$41bn to reportedly over US$57bn, up sharply from US$27bn in 2010. No slowdown can be expected in the coming years as the development of new fields, of the transport infrastructure, and the distribution and power infrastructure will come at increasingly high prices. A project like Shtokman is expected to cost north of US$25bn for example. Russia needs new refineries, new oil pipelines, and the development of new fields. The country's power-generating companies will spend over US$40bn in the next few years. Metallurgy plants, satellites, cement facilities, the new 4G telecom infrastructure, etc. will all cost billions of dollars.

FROM AN EASY FINANCING CULTURE TO THE AWARENESS OF PROJECT FINANCE

As recently as 2008, just before the financial crisis, it was common to hear from Russian CFOs that project finance did not make sense for them: it was expensive, complicated, long to structure, and anyway often led to consolidation into the balance sheet because of IFRS requirements or Russian legal peculiarities. The financial crisis of 2008–2009 showed that Russian corporates relied on short term debt, often in foreign currency as rates were much cheaper than RUR rates, and the ruble kept appreciating anyway, to fund acquisitions, capital expenditures, and other long term investments. The amounts were huge. A limited number of Russian corporates had realized that despite all the limitations of project finance, this allowed them to better manage their risks: by project-financing those cases that were project-financeable, they preserved funds for those investments that were not. This became painfully clear to all through the crisis, and we see today a much stronger focus on the use of limited-recourse finance.

The Project Finance Challenges

LEGAL ENVIRONMENT

However, it is true that there are specific Russian challenges in using limited recourse finance schemes in Russia. Many of those challenges have to do with the legal environment. It is difficult to do a lending syndicate under Russian law as security cannot be shared amongst lenders. Pledges of accounts are not effective as it is legally impossible to prevent a borrower from withdrawing funds from an account it owns, even if that account is pledged. Russian law does allow a borrower, or even any obligor including guarantors, to

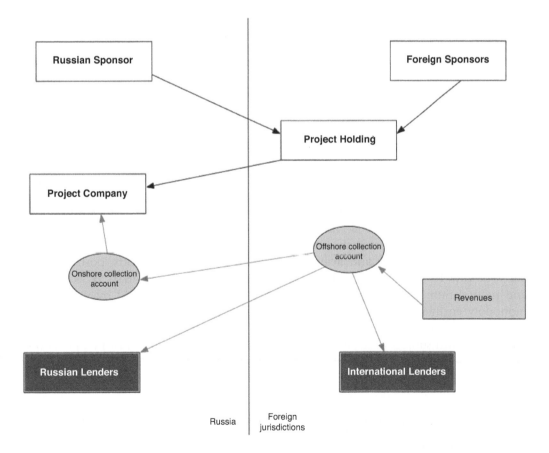

Figure 30.2 Russian project financing uses a delicate balance of onshore and offshore companies and accounts

keep foreign sales proceeds abroad to pledge them in favour of lenders, but that faculty is reserved to borrowers, not exporters in general, and only for loans provided by foreign lenders for more than two years. These and other restrictions explain why it is common to structure facilities under English law (but this requires the participation of at least one foreign entity) and why, as detailed below, specific Russian solutions have been devised over the years. One has to be careful, however, in implementing such solutions: the need for foreign holding companies has the unrelated result of promoting in effect capital flight and the temptation of opaque structures. That may be very effective from an equity and project finance perspective (ability to pledge shares, use of trust mechanisms), but attract unwelcome reactions from regulators or the authorities, sometimes at a later stage, even if all legal requirements have been met. For example, in early 2011, following the terrorist attack at Domodedovo airport in Moscow, the authorities noted that the ownership and management structure of the airport was based abroad and opaque, raising potential risks in managing security. In practice, this is likely to cause potential bidders for privatized airports to think twice about the appropriate ownership structures to be implemented.

Other types of restrictions can make the life of project finance lenders difficult. For example, the 'State Secret' and 'Commercial Secret' statuses can severely restrict the ability of would-be sponsors to share vital information with potential lenders or even advisors.

SPECIAL REGIMES

Some types of projects operate under specific rules. Natural resources and some sectors can be considered of 'Federal Significance' and therefore be of restricted access to foreign investors, particularly if state-owned. The Federal Significance status can depend on the characteristics of a field and therefore become such as a result of exploration work.

The Continental Shelf can only be explored by Rosneft and Gazprom, and Gazprom has a legal monopoly on the export of gas. This, however, should not be interpreted as meaning that Gazprom can prevent at will the export of gas from other companies as this could be perceived as a violation of its obligations. Rather, it means that Gazprom must always be involved in the procedure through mechanisms that respect that principle.

More generally, this is part of the concept of 'Natural Monopolies' which are defined and regulated through Federal Law FZ 147 passed in August 2005. These cover a wide range of economic activities (transportation of oil, refined products, and gas via pipelines; transmission of electricity and heat, railroad, terminals, ports, airports, postal services etc...The law is 'intended to achieve a balance between the interests of consumers and natural monopoly entities which ensures that commodities sold by said natural monopoly entities will be accessible to consumers, and likewise that the said natural monopoly entities operate efficiently.' However, the definition of Natural Monopolies is quite wide[1] and subject to debate. The mechanisms for regulation must be understood as they have significant consequences on the economics of projects. The regulators, for

---

1   'Natural monopoly is the condition of a commodity market under which the satisfaction of the demand in this market is more efficient in the absence of competition by virtue of the technological peculiarities of the production process (because of a significant reduction of the cost per commodity item as the output increases), and the commodities produced by the holders of natural monopolies cannot be substituted for in consumption by other commodities, so that the demand in this market for the commodities produced by the holders of natural monopolies is less dependent on the variations in the price of this commodity than in that of other commodities.' (Federal Law FZ 147, art. 3)

example, must approve tariffs charged by airports, so any business plan must take into account the timing and regulatory risk elements involved.

These and other special circumstances must be understood and taken into account in arranging project finance in Russia.

PSAs

There are at this point only three PSAs in Russia, two in Sakhalin, and one for the Kariaga oil field. PSA have not been favoured by the Russian government in the past few years, but could make sense for some future projects. In December 2010, Energy Minister, Sergey Shmatko predicted that PSAs could enjoy a rebirth to attract the funds needed for geological exploration. The PSA status of Sakhalin II, for example, has both allowed certain forms of project financing to be implemented more easily, and required sensitive negotiations to ensure the Russian party was correctly compensated for the changes in the project costs and structure. Lessons can certainly be drawn for the history of these projects.

REGULATORY ASPECTS

There are many regulatory aspects that need to be taken into account for Russian projects, beyond what has been mentioned above, the permitting regime for many projects requires careful planning depending on the industry. Tariffs for pipelines, airport fees, road tolls, property rights, construction, operation and many other aspects of economic life are regulated and must be understood. There is a deregulation process going on in the gas and power industries which is profoundly changing the landscape and prospects for investment. A good understanding of the process and the constraints are key to successful project planning.

THE CONTROL PARADOX

The State in Russia for various reasons chooses to retain more control over some projects that it would seem necessary to do from a project perspective. This imposes constraints on the potential lenders, prompting them to ask for state guarantees in return. This is true on land rights, for example, complication PPPs. The experience in toll road projects as well as in housing and communal services sector shows that project WACC usually exceeds 18 per cent in RUR denominated cash flows. As senior lenders end up requiring the State to cover specific risks with government compensation for any event of default in both the construction and operation stages, the risk-reward profile becomes actually very attractive for the private partners. Even taking into account the RUR inflation rates, returns are still high, sometimes in the range of 25–30 per cent or even higher levels. As time passes, however, and new projects appear, the compensation terms seem to become less and less favourable to new investors.

RUSSIA AND FOREIGNERS

Russia has long sought to attract foreign direct investment, and even to make an international financial centre out of Moscow. The country has adapted its legislation to ensure that the needs of foreign investors and foreign lenders are taken into account (allowing offshore accounts for loans provided by foreign lenders for example). There are protectionist interests in Russia, and the long negotiations concerning the WTO access to Russia, whilst in good part the result of delaying tactics by existing members, also reflect the uncertainty in Russia about the access to be given to foreign entities to national assets. Russian sponsors therefore often prefer to work in the framework of partnerships, which ensure that benefits are shared.

FOREIGNERS AND RUSSIA

Foreign companies are indeed big players at all levels (investors, contractors, lenders, operators...) in Russia. There remain, however, specificities to the Russian market that require a very good understanding of, and preferably a strong presence in, the country. Russia still suffers from a reputation as a difficult place to do business, and foreign investors can be baffled at first by the barriers of language, bureaucracy, and infrastructures. However, those companies that have invested in understanding Russia have often identified the country as one of their most promising markets.

Although the financial crisis originated in the US and Western Europe, Western lenders suddenly withheld refinancing of existing facilities to Russian borrowers, causing a major funding crisis in Russia. The Russian reliance on foreign funding eventually resulted in a deep (over 9 per cent) drop in GDP, in the need for urgent injection of liquidities into the Russian banking system by the Government, and in the use of accumulated reserves.

As major projects relied on international funding and investment, many came to a halt until they could either attract foreign partners and funders again (St Petersburg projects, but often led then by strong Russian players), or had to turn to purely domestic solutions (M1 toll road).

Russian Solutions

Over the past 20 years, experience has been accumulated and the players in the Russian capital expenditure market have developed specific solutions that answer the challenges of Russian financing. This has allowed the limited recourse finance of projects with international revenues in Russia such as Sakhalin II, and purely domestic projects such as Yuzho-Russkoe or the M1 toll road. These solutions involve a wide array of techniques such as specific indemnities, the use of 'Veksels' (promissory notes) to create security, access to termination rights, various legal clauses, holding companies abroad, e.g., Cyprus, and other structural answers. It also includes addressing certain markets such as pension funds for long term ruble resources, segmenting the banking environment, or defining RUR fixed rate regimes that are compatible with international floating rate tranches.

Funding Sources for Russian Projects

INTERNATIONAL COMMERCIAL BANKS

International banks have traditionally shown a strong interest in working with the large corporates and banks. Some banks have developed a strong presence in Russia, whilst others prefer to work from abroad. International banks operating in Russia must work through a Russian subsidiary (or a limited representative office), not through branches. This means the subsidiaries are technically Russian banks, but are generally relatively small and have limited access to RUR funding. However, the international money market banks have a strong advantage in cost of funds for euro or dollar financing over Russian banks and have tended to dominate the market for large facilities to big names with whom they developed strong relationships. They remain the core of any strategy for project financing of export-based projects, and play a significant role in at least the advisory of major projects, even RUR based. They have a harder time providing the loans for Ruble tranches or to smaller borrowers. The difficulty in obtaining RUR resources and competing for deposits with large domestic banks has actually led some international banks to give up retail operations in Russia in the recent past, at least for now.

MULTILATERALS

Multilaterals, notably EBRD, the IFC, and EIB play a significant role in both international and Ruble lending in Russia. They have certain unique capabilities, but also certain limitations that prevent them from playing a role in a number of projects. Their detailed and sometimes long due diligence processes, lack of Ruble funding, except to some extent on a MosPrime basis, and political influence have been obstacles in the past. (MosPrime is a floating rate index that is insufficiently representative to prove useful at the current time. The Russian market therefore prefers fixed rates). However, as major funding needs for sophisticated projects loom, those institutions, sometimes working together with Vnesheconombank (VEB) the Russian State Development Bank, can provide leadership in structuring project financing, covering energy efficiency standards, or providing assurances to new international players in Russia.

ECAS

As a significant proportion of equipment is imported in Russia, and as Russia is considered a strong risk by export credit agencies (ECAs), there is a significant role for ECAs in Russia. ECA-backed loans provide advantageously-priced funding to Russian banks who can then offer more favourable terms to their clients in the country. For major projects, ECA tranches on a limited-recourse basis make it acceptable to international banks to provide more funds on an uncovered basis in parallel.

Furthermore, because the project finance teams of major ECAs have good experience in negotiating structures, it can make sense to agree on structures with ECAs first, and then enlarge the arranging efforts to mandated lead arrangers amongst international commercial banks with a term sheet that has been approved by ECAs.

Russian Lenders

BANKS

There are more than a thousand banks in Russia. Of these, though, only a small number are willing and capable to provide limited recourse facilities for significant amounts. This is because many banks are small, or tied to specific industrial groups or sectors, and many lack the expertise and experience necessary. For the larger projects in particular, only Sberbank, VTB and Gazprombank are regular players. As the cost of funding of Russian banks for foreign currencies is higher than that of foreign banks, they typically do not focus on the euro or US$ requirements of the largest names who are served by international banks. However, Russian banks can be competitive in Rubles, for specific types of structured facilities, and for clients that the international banks find more difficult to understand.

Before the financial crisis of 2008–2009, Russian corporates borrowed heavily in US$ or euros, not only because they were courted by international banks and could borrow on their balance sheet easily, because the rates were much cheaper in these currencies than in Russian Rubles. In 2011, many Russian borrowers have chosen instead to refinance foreign currency loans with RUR fixed rate loans, that taking into account inflation, rates and swap rates have become more attractive.

GOVERNMENT INSTITUTIONS

Through careful management of the budget surpluses experienced in the years of high oil prices prior to the financial crisis (2001–2008), foreign built solid foreign currency reserves, and accumulated over US$150bn in the Stabilization Fund created in 2004 to provide for rainy days. In 2008 the fund was split into a National Reserve fund succeeding to the Stabilization Fund in its mission and has been used mostly to cover budget deficits, and a National Welfare Fund, that can invest in infrastructure projects. Grants from the National Welfare Fund and local budgets can support projects of national significance, such as the Western High Speed Diameter road in St Petersburg.

The Russian State Development Bank, VEB, plays a crucial role in supporting the Russian economy. VEB represented a lifeline for Russian corporates that could not refinance their international loans during the 2008–2009 crisis, and covers important aspects from developing Public Private Partnerships (PPP) to overseeing the Russian export credit efforts. VEB is a key partner for large projects that require long tenors and/or large amounts in Rubles. VEB is working alongside multilaterals and commercial banks, not in competition with them.

Other specialized government institutions such as Roseximbank can also play a role in structuring projects.

PENSION FUNDS

Along with the State pension fund, managed by VEB, there are in Russia many private pension funds, some of which are quite large, that have long-term ruble liabilities and are seeking corresponding long-term ruble assets. The ageing population of Russia ensures

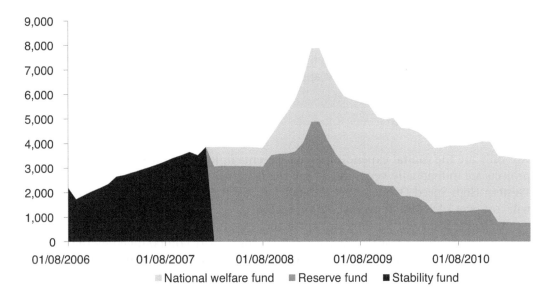

Figure 30.3 Amounts in billion RUR

that pension funds will play an increasingly significant role in funding quality long-term assets in Russia.

It is, however, necessary to ensure that the quality and/or rating of the assets is consistent with the regulation and the investment policies of these pension funds. This requires focussing on certain types of infrastructure projects, and/or enhancing the rating of such projects to meet those standards. There are certain guarantee programmes, or the use of ECA coverage that can help meet those requirements. Furthermore, pension funds are sensitive to protection against inflation and the evolution of the economy through growth rates.

CAPITAL MARKETS

Capital markets have long been an attractive – but elusive – source of funding for project finance. However, relatively few projects have been able to secure significant funding on capital markets for a variety of reasons: Projects can be too complex to explain to investors, the liquidity window may or may not be there at the moment of funding, intercreditor issues can prove tricky if there are other funding sources, etc. Add to this the Russian risk element, and the tasks can appear daunting. Not that Russian issuers have not accessed capital markets, far from there as there are many successful corporate issuers in Russia, but the combination of the elements is the main difficulty.

What about domestic capital markets, then? Russian investors should understand more easily the Russian dimension of projects. And indeed, this is proving to be a promising source of funding for the future projects: already the M1 toll road was financed on a project basis through a RUR bond issue. These bonds appeal to pension funds and other investors with long-term RUR resources. We can expect that infrastructure projects in particular will find significant funding in the next few years from Russian capital markets.

International capital markets, though, will also likely prove to be a source of funding for high quality, rated, export-oriented projects, notably in the natural resources area. The volatility of the markets, however, means that as in other parts of the world, projects will need to take an opportunistic approach to capital markets funding on a limited recourse basis.

WORKING TOGETHER

Not only are the capital expenditure requirements in Russia immense, but many of the projects are individually very large to say the least: some infrastructure projects such as Western High Speed Diameter are estimated at over US$5bn, some oil and gas projects will cost over US$10bn or even US$20bn each.

No single source of funding can cover such needs. Projects that are challenging for technical, regulatory or other reasons see their complexity compounded by the need to bring together several funding sources. Certainly, it is quite common to have multiple tranches of financing within a project financing. However, the truly huge projects in Russia bring issues of their own:

i) Sources of cash flows, such as offtake contracts or completion guarantees, that are considered strong and creditworthy for 'normal' amounts can reach single-project limits and/or stretch their debt capacity beyond the reasonable;
ii) Some institutions impose country limits, industry limits, or single-project limits. If a given sponsor is frequently seeking funding for a series of projects, credit limits could become tight relative to the funding needs;
iii) In order to reach the needed amounts, it may be necessary to bring together many lenders of different types. Experience shows that once you have several ECAs, some IFIs, and commercial banks, it becomes very difficult to manage a lender's group.

Furthermore, there are legal and market obstacles to bringing together different lenders in Russia. There are many signs, however, that this is progressing, and some of the recent projects, including Pulkovo, Yuzhnoye-Russkoye, Sakhalin Energy, or some satellite financing, have indeed been arranged with many funding sources working together, both Russian and international.

Reconciling Russian realities and international project finance practices and culture is the true challenge of Russian project finance.

31 *Unleashing Africa's Infrastructure Potential*

RAVI SURI AND SIMON LASSMAN
Standard Chartered Bank[1]

RAVI SURI AND SIMON LASSMAN
Standard Chartered Bank[1]

Like so much in Africa, project finance exists on two planes. The one lush, verdant and blossoming, the other dry, cut-off and starved.

The resources sphere, most notably, oil and gas, amounted to 80 per cent of project financings by value. These were large scale and successfully syndicated. Taken together, with metals and mining, almost 90 per cent of project financings were in the resources sphere. Resource projects cast a towering shadow over other sectors. This is even starker considering that these statistics exclude the majority of the Chinese investment in African resources that is often bilateral at a governmental level.

This picture is indicative of the macro economic situation of Africa. The resources sector is flourishing and driving much of the feted GDP growth on the continent. However, the current growth rates belie the iceberg shape of the African infrastructure sector. Currently only a small proportion of projects are seen closing. Yet, the quantum and impetus of those projects beneath the surface that have a strong commercial rationale, and with the right structuring and regulatory environment, could close, is exponentially larger. Meanwhile, over much of the continent, per capita standard of living is, at best, stagnant if not falling. Intra-regional connectivity is low, whether measured in transcontinental highway links, power interconnectors, or fibre-optic backbones.[2] This is as true of resource-rich countries, which also lack accessibility to services despite their wealth.[3]

The purpose of this article is to study the role for privatization in unleashing the potential for infrastructure financings and try to navigate the trend of newly formed regulators and the likely impact this will have on project finance in Africa over the next decade. The study is structured into three parts. The first section gives a brief summary of the need for projects in the infrastructure sector, those sectors ripe for privatization and the dynamics needed to finance them along with the relevance of project finance and what privatization does and should mean for Africa. It also explores the importance of navigating the regulatory process; the realization that private money is required needs to be accompanied by judicious deployment.

---

1   This article represents only the views of the authors and does not represent the views of Standard Chartered Bank.

2   Africa's Infrastructure, *A Time for Transformation*, Editors: Vivien Foster and Cecilia Briceno-Garmendia, A co-publication of the Agence Française de Développement and the World Bank

3   *Ibid.*

Secondly, there is a look at the general dynamics of deal structuring in Africa including the use of development finance institutions (DFI), mini perm structures and political risk insurance.

Thirdly, there is an exploration of liquidity. Just as the continent suffers frequent droughts despite its copious rainfall, financial liquidity is abundant in the form of the DFIs and World Bank funding but to access that liquidity requires extensive planning and structuring. Ultimately, the oxygen of any financial system – liquidity – needs working economic organs to service. Establishing the underlying systems is the challenge. This section looks at the potential for an increasing presence of commercial banks and what is needed for them to take on more 'Africa risk' outside the resources sphere.

The Infrastructure Need

Project finance can be described as risk allocation engineering and is an important solution to meet the infrastructure needs of Africa. Cash and corporate lending alone, without fair risk allocations, cannot secure sustainable infrastructure upgrades. A major precept is that the right party takes the risk it is most competent to handle, mitigating the risks of other parties necessary to complete the deal through mechanisms of risk transfer. For example, construction risk can be partially mitigated by bringing a reputed engineer procure and contrast (EPC) contractor with a robust security package and bonus/penalty provisions. An operations and maintenance (O&M) operator taking operation risk allows lenders to take more market risk. The transfer mechanisms inherent in project finance have facilitated countless projects that could not otherwise have been funded by banks.

This is particularly true in power and infrastructure. But in Africa, financings in these sectors are negligible relative to demand and need. Whilst ideas and entrepreneurs are not in short supply, and many projects do pass a feasibility stage, few reach financial close. Many others that do raise financing, often take excruciating years to do so. Whilst part of the reason is scale, especially in fields such as cement and steel, the projects are too small. For other projects, the opposite is true; the ideas are too ambitious or rely on unproven technology.

Whilst big resource development projects often have an infrastructure element, be it a captive power or desalination plant, the incremental benefit to the wider community in terms of accessibility to services and efficiencies is almost invariably limited. Captive infrastructure development should not be confused with large scale infrastructure development. Whilst the former often facilitates a high profile export deal, such as a mine, it serves a specific project and is rarely connected into a larger grid or network. The latter has an exponential effect by unlocking inefficiencies and facilitating enterprise.

Lack of access to power is pervasive across most of Africa. In approximately half of countries it is at 25 per cent or below (see Table 31.1) and in Nigeria, set to become Africa's largest country both in terms of population and GDP (currently second behind South Africa), less than 50 per cent of the population have access to electricity.

Moreover, power consumption in Africa is currently falling because population growth exceeds growth in new supply. The extremely low per capita consumption is 1 per cent of the typical consumption in high income countries. In Nigeria for example, the total grid capacity is only sufficient to run one fridge for every 30 people.

Table 31.1 Lack of access to electricity

Percentage of Population Access to Electricity		
Range	**Country**	**Percentage**
75%–51%	South Africa	75.0
	Ghana	54.0
50%–26%	Cote d'Ivoire	47.3
	Nigeria	46.8
	Botswana	45.4
	Senegal	42.0
	Zimbabwe	41.5
	Gabon	36.7
	Namibia	34.0
	Eritrea	32.0
	Sudan	31.4
	Rep. of Congo	30.0
	Cameroon	29.4
	Angola	26.2
25%–11%	Benin	24.8
	Togo	20.0
	Madagascar	19.0
	Zambia	18.8
	Lesotho	16.0
	Ethiopia	15.3
	Kenya	15.0
	Mozambique	11.7
	Tanzania	11.5
	D.R. of Congo	11.1
>10%	Burkina Faso	10.0
	Malawi	9.0
	Uganda	9.0

The repercussions of this situation are pervasive; lack of access to reliable and affordable power is an impediment to corporate growth; Africa's firms lose over 5 per cent of sales owing to power outages. For the informal sector, losses are 20 per cent given backup generation facilities are not affordable.

The reasons why project financings in power are few and far between is firstly because the cost of power production is relatively high and rising owing to small scale and reliance on expensive oil based generation; historic average cost US$0.18 pkWh, average tariff US$0.14 pkWh versus US$0.04 pkWh and US$0.07 pkWh in South and East Asia respectively.

Secondly, one of the perennial issues for financings in the power sector is the fact that most of the utilities in Africa are effectively bankrupt. A PPA with a utility guarantee would normally be considered strong. But in Africa the creditworthiness of the utility is often in doubt.

Short term solutions are often pushed through, for example diesel power plants which are quick to erect and usually only active for a short time. Because of their relatively small capital cost they are expensive in the long run and tend to be polluting; a veritable false economy, which does not address local inefficiencies. They tend to be financed on a corporate basis because the IPPs tend to be short term and lack strong government guarantees.

Security of electricity supply is an important strategic and economic asset. Power is vital to fuel the more advanced stages of industrialization. The African small and medium sized industrial sector has no chance of getting off the ground in a meaningful way without reliable access to power. Large scale enterprises can take off because they have the capacity to build captive power. Traditionally, privatization of generation of the power sector is at the forefront of regulatory reform because it is relatively easy to set up the framework for the generation business. Moreover, and this is particularly true in Africa, the need is particularly acute.

The following section looks at the solutions to harness the available resources to bridge the infrastructure gap and break away from the short term solutions.

PRIVATIZATION AS A PRELUDE TO PROJECT FINANCING

At one extreme, privatization is an often misunderstood buzzword whilst at the other extreme it is at times perceived as a panacea for all ills. However, it is actually a journey; a means to an end, not an end in itself.

Privatization processes, be they unbundling, performance controls, audits and revenue models to address under-collection or distribution losses, need to be undertaken well before private capital is deployed. Outsourcing can be a useful interim measure to prepare for a transition to privatization. Hence timing and preparation are critical. Governments that have set up these processes well in advance – and have used the quest for efficiency as a guiding principle – have been more efficient in attracting capital at the best terms with regards to both pricing and tenor. Many Middle Eastern countries are good examples of this and their experience and sequence can be emulated in the African context.

UNBUNDLING

It is critical that before any privatization process is started with a view to deploying private capital, that infrastructure is 'unbundled' correctly. Broadly defined, unbundling involves breaking monopolies by offering new entrants access to existing facilities that are hard to recreate. It is possible, and desirable, to separate or unbundle different elements of an infrastructure chain. Governments should lower prices by creating competition in that element of the chain where the barriers to entry are high, for example, power generation. Moreover, power generation may represent an attractive opportunity for a private investor only if government handles the intricacies of transmission and distribution. Generation is furthest removed from the end customer and the traditional starting point for privatization. Private investors do not want to enter impoverished homes to collect electricity bills. This will also serve government's interest in lowering prices by creating competition in that element of the chain where the barriers to entry are high but the social complexities are lower. Infrastructure assets should be unbundled and regulation should be imposed only on that element of the chain that is monopolistic (e.g., transmission in the power sector).

Unbundling, therefore, serves as an important means of testing economies of scale on a gradual and incremental basis. Privatization within a flawed or ill-conceived framework actually produces poorer performance. To understand the concept of unbundling, it is best to look at two vital sectors of infrastructure; power and rail transport.

The political and social importance of power compound the challenge of privatization. Yet, today, there is substantial international experience about what to do and what to avoid. The nature of the power industry in many African countries is broadly a monopoly covering generation, transmission and distribution. Often utilities try to privatize when they are undertaking all three operations. This often results in failure. They need to 'unbundle' i.e., break up generation, transmission and distribution into separate corporations or special purpose vehicles (SPVs) to attract the right capital at different points of this chain.

It is extremely important to decide how to unbundle; horizontal as opposed to vertical unbundling. The very different experiences of rail privatization in Argentina and Britain are illustrative.

Argentina unbundled the rail sector horizontally. Horizontal unbundling is separation of markets – either geographically or by a group of related services. Telecom and rail lend themselves to this method well. In the Argentinean context, this involved breaking up the privatization of rail into various regions and giving the operation of the rolling stock, signals and track to one operator in each region.

Britain, on the other hand, followed the process of vertical unbundling. In this method, two or more interdependent inputs are separated and run separately. In UK rail privatization this translated into each constituent part, tracks, signals and rolling stock, were given to a different operator.

Despite Argentina's macro-economic situation, its rail privatization is considered a success whilst that of the UK bequeathed manifold service and safety issues. The reason was that in Britain there was no clear cross-service accountability. The rolling stock operator blamed the track operator for poor infrastructure and vice versa resulting in delays and traffic accidents.

Hence it is critical to unbundle infrastructure correctly. Many countries in Africa have taken a step towards correct unbundling but more needs to be done.

The next important area which Africa needs to focus on to attract private capital is regulation. It is critical to understand what element of the infrastructure chain to regulate and how to regulate. Only that element of the chain where barriers to entry are high should be regulated i.e., distribution and transmission in the power sector. Where the barriers to entry are low, i.e., generation, it is important that the free market determines the price and not regulation. Many countries have lost a decade or two in trying to attract private capital by trying to regulate the wrong part of the infrastructure chain. Africa can learn from these examples and by so doing can potentially improve the terms on which it raises capital.

After having looked at the what to regulate, let's now focus on the how to regulate. Two types of methods are possible; the 'US type cost push' method or the UK style CPI-X linked method. For Africa, the CPI-X linked method would be more sustainable.

Once the how and what to regulate are understood, independent regulators who have 'teeth' should be set up. This is vital in order to gain the confidence of the international finance community.

Many countries have taken a step in the right direction with regards to regulation, however, a lot more needs to be done on this score if the infrastructure needs of Africa are to be met.

THE ROLE OF CONCESSIONS

A concession is a frequent and flexible means to implement a partial privatization. It can be broadly defined as a business operated under a contract, often with a degree of exclusivity within a certain area and for a limited time frame – typically 20 to 50 years. It is often seen in the port, airport and road sector, as well as the power sector in the form of a power purchase agreement. At the end of the concession period government usually has an option of not renewing the concession and can take advantage of the skills and know-how transferred by a private operator during the concession period. Usually, however, concessions are renewed and government can extract another upfront concession payment, making it a sustainable, as opposed to a one-off, source of income. In an independent power plant (IPP), a utility bids out a plant and can maintain a substantial shareholding. Project financings work best where government maintains some sort of involvement and economic benefit from the success of the project.

Demonstrations of commitment and predictability from government are valuable. Concessions, if draughted well and include standard guarantees and commitments from credit worthy and credible concession granting authorities, represent a powerful capital raising tool, especially if they including step in rights through a direct agreement with lenders. In a step in situation, lenders would have the right but not the obligation to effectively take over the concession in the event of an extended default until such time a new qualified concessionaire can be selected.

It is important that concessions are awarded only after the unbundling strategy has been put in place.

Deal Structuring and Liquidity

Even after successfully unbundling, privatizing, regulating and granting bankable PPAs/concessions, Africa will for some time need credit enhancements. ECAs from developed countries have long been active offering commercial and political risk cover. In recent years, Chinese and Korean ECAs have also become more active. Multilaterals such as the World Bank through political risk insurance, issued by MIGA, cover contract frustration, non-honouring of sovereign obligations, transferability and convertibility risk and civil disturbance. Banks will lend against this cover. Availability of these credit enhancements is not the issue at the moment, but could become an issue as projects proliferate and limits become stretched.

Credit enhancement alone is not sufficient. There is also a need for liquidity enhancement and to involve more local banks. Ironically, it is the local banks which are best placed to understand and manage the long term risks, but are not being utilized to the full, constrained by liquidity related tenor pressures. A mini perm type structure, supported by a host government and enhanced by counterparties such as multilaterals or DFIs effectively allows banks to take a shorter tenor view, typically five to seven years because of a guaranteed refinancing. Yet, the project still benefits from the longer tenor because of the refinancing commitment, which allows for more robust cover ratios. This is achieved by a put option at a fixed date for the project company to government. The use of these structures in Africa is embryonic, but offers a potentially powerful tool to extend tenor, create more flexible funding pools and potentially reduce cost.

In the absence of liquidity enhancers as of now, the DFIs including the African Development Bank (AfDB) and International Finance Corporation (IFC) have anchored most infrastructure deals and commercial banks have played a relatively smaller role, largely in meeting the needs of the ECAs.

The availability of new liquidity pools are important for any market as the 'usual suspect' banks become more exposed. There are several channels; commercial banks, Islamic institutions and eventually capital markets will need to play a more significant role. Furthermore, there are already a number of funds that have become active in Africa in recent years, seeking higher yields. The Islamic banks are also keen to expand into Africa given the large Muslim populations especially in the north and west of the continent. The Islamic political risk insurance arm ICIEC has an understanding with MIGA that can allow much larger investment and debt cover if there is both a conventional and an Islamic component. The power of sovereign wealth funds will undoubtedly also make a large impact. This may be partly inspired by the Chinese.

Capital market participation is possible but not in the short or medium term. There has been much talk about the potential positive impact of project bonds and the development of a liquid capital market, a mainstay of US project financing on global financing. In Africa, this would need to be preceded by development of local capital markets.

The pace of the above processes will depend on privatization and regulatory progress.

However, it is a given that sooner or later, the pace of bank debt will pick up, reducing the dependency on DFIs. The trajectory of the changing nature of lenders is illustrated in the graph overleaf, Figure 31.1.

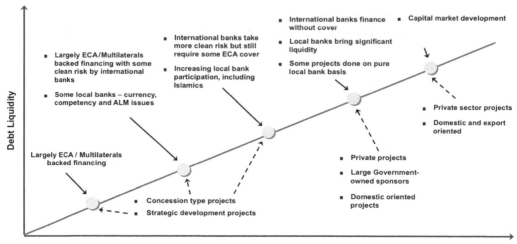

Figure 31.1 The gradual transformation of debt liquidity sources

Conclusion

Africa today is at a crossroads. Whilst the resources sector is raising capital, infrastructure financings, relative to their need, are sporadic.

Project finance as a tool is important because of its ability to apportion risks to the party best able and most appropriately incentivized to manage specific areas. It will play a key role in future to meet Africa's infrastructure needs.

However, for it to be effective, Africa must unbundle its infrastructure correctly and put in place effective regulations. This is also important to grow future liquidity pools, beyond those of DFIs and ECAs.

For the above to happen, privatization needs to be undertaken on a war footing but not without military style planning of the peculiarities of the lie of the land.

32 *Public Private Partnerships in France*

MARIE BOUVET-GUIRAMAND, Avocate au Barreau de
Paris, Senior Associate
Gide Loyrette Nouel Paris

JULIEN BRUSAU CUELLO, Avocat au Barreau de Paris and
Solicitor of the Senior Courts of England and Wales,
Associate
Gide Loyrette Nouel Paris

Introduction

With prospects estimated at €60bn by the French PPP unit MAPPP (Mission d'Appui aux Partenariats Publics-Privés),[1] including the major investment needed for the upgrade and construction of sporting venues ahead of the Euro 2016 football tournament, and a long-standing tradition of using traditional public service concession schemes, the French public-private partnerships (PPP) market is generally considered as one of the most active and promising markets in Europe.

The French PPP market is a very specific one which has long been dominated by French major public groups. That situation has significantly evolved in the past few years as a result of the transposition of European Union (EU) Directives into French Law and the implementation of European Court of Justice (ECJ) rulings supporting free trade and competition in the EU zone.

This progressive opening of the French PPP market constitutes an excellent opportunity for international players willing to enter the French PPP market, both in greenfield projects and brownfield projects.

The objective of this chapter will be to introduce international sponsors and investors to the main features of the French PPP market, focussing on the principal specificities of its legal framework and economy. The most common forms of PPP financing structures will also be presented in broad terms to better understand the specificity of some financial instruments widely used in French PPP, such as Dailly Law assignment.

---

1   AFP press release '*The Government plans 60 billion Euros of public-private partnerships by 2020,*' 17 January 2011.

French Concept of PPP

GENERAL

French law recognizes a multiplicity of contracts for public infrastructures or services which would fall into the market definition of PPP. Depending on whether such contracts imply (i) the performance of a 'Service Public'[2] and (ii) a material part of the remuneration of the private partner based on the commercial profitability of the project, these contracts may be allocated into two main categories: public service delegation (Délégation de Service Public) or partnership contract (Contrat de Partenariat).

In short, if a PPP contract satisfies both (i) and (ii), such contract would fall into the public service delegation (PSD) category. Alternatively, if a PPP contract does not satisfy (i) or (ii), such contract would fall into the partnership contract category.

As a side remark, it should be noted that public procurement is generally not included in the French definition of PPP, even though the fact that EU Directives[3] define French partnership contracts as public procurements could be confusing in that respect.

PUBLIC SERVICE DELEGATION

Under a PSD contract, the commercial risk of the public service operation is substantially transferred to the private partner who is entitled to collect revenues from the operation of the project (e.g., through tariffs levied on users of the facility or infrastructure). The most famous form of PSD is probably the concession, the regime of which is essentially based on administrative case law and the Loi Sapin enacted in 1993.[4] Along with concessions, other forms of PSD include affermages (lease with public investment) or régie intéressée (bonus given to administrator based on revenue from public property).

Traditionally, a concession under French law implied (i) the delegation of a public service, (ii) an integral transfer of the commercial risks to the private sponsor, and in some sectors, (iii) a financing based on the cash-flows coming from the existing infrastructures (e.g., the revenues from the old section of the motorway finance the new section) (adossement).

However, in the 1990s and 2000s the concession regime evolved and moved towards more modern practices, with a more sophisticated transfer of risks, an increase of the financial commitment of the public sector (e.g., construction subsidies) and the use of project finance techniques. Thanks to these improvements, the concession scheme has

---

2   The concept of *Service Public* is very specific to French Law and often considered by authors as the '*cornerstone*' of French administrative law. Indeed, this concept is considered since 1873 as the criterion founding the competence of the administrative judge, another particularity of French Law, and may be defined as an activity considered by the Government as being performed in the general interest of the population and subject to a derogatory legal regime (public law instead of private law). In comparison, the EU concept of '*service of general interest*' is less precise than the French concept of *Service Public* as it sometimes refers to the fact that a service is offered to the general public, sometimes highlights that a service has been assigned a specific role in the public interest, or sometimes refers to the ownership or status of the entity providing the service.

3   Directive 2004/17/EC of 31 March 2004 *coordinating the procurement procedures of entities operating in the water, energy, transport and postal services sectors* and Directive 2004/18/EC of 31 March 2004 *on the coordination of procedures for the award of public works contracts, public supply contracts and public service contracts.*

4   Law No. 93–122 of 29 January 1993 *on the prevention of corruption and transparency of economic life and public procedures.*

been very often used for large scale infrastructure projects, especially in the transport sector in the past few years (e.g., A28, A19, A41, A65, A88 motorway concessions).

Despite this evolution, the concession regime continued to bear significant limits. These limits were not compatible with a number of projects and thus contributed to the need for a new mechanism in order to acknowledge that the private partner is not always in charge of the public service itself (e.g. transfer of hospital financing, construction and maintenance but not of healthcare) and to allow the public sector to make deferred payments (prohibited by French administrative courts under 'the State gets what it pays for' principle).

PARTNERSHIP CONTRACTS

This new mechanism is embodied by the partnership contract enacted in France in 2004.[5]

Partnership contracts are administrative contracts by which a public entity grants to a private entity a mission which includes (i) the financing of the construction necessary to the public service, (ii) the design or conversion of such construction and (iii) the maintenance and management of such construction. The term of the partnership contract is determined in consideration of the amortization of the investments or of the financing. As for the remuneration due to the private partner, it is paid by the public entity until the term of the contract and covers investment and financing costs and maintenance remuneration based on performance objectives.

The use of partnership contracts is subject to a procedure of prior evaluation in order to assess the urgency of the PPP project, its complexity or its financial relevance (value for money). This is achieved by a comparison of the merits of the implementation of the project through a partnership contract with the merits of other contractual structures (e.g. public procurement, concession).

We can see how the new partnership contract differs from concession as it implies that (i) there is no delegation of the public service aspect of the project, (ii) there is no full transfer of commercial risks on the private sector but rather a mix between commercial and performance/availability risks and (iii) part of the financing may be guaranteed by government payments.

Further, this mechanism brings long-awaited innovations to the French PPP framework such as the use of performance or output-based criteria, the possibility for the public sector to make deferred payments and the introduction in French law of the EU concept of competitive dialogue[6] which allows the bidders to participate in the definition of the project's scope.[7]

This new type of French PPPs can also be implemented via other public contracts; mainly long-term leases (bail emphytéotique administratif or BEA, autorisation d'occupation temporaire with location avec option d'achat or AOT/LOA). The allocation of risks under BEA and AOT/LOA projects is the same as under partnership contract

---

5   Ordinance n° 2004–559, 17 June 2004 on partnership contracts – http://www.ppp.bercy.gouv.fr/ordonnance 2004-559_ang.pdf.

6   Directive 2004/18/EC of 31 March 2004.

7   It should be noted, however, that the EU concept of 'competitive dialogue' was originally inspired by the old French procedure of 'appel d'offres sur performance' (performance based tender) provided in the French Public Procurement Code.

projects. These other types of contracts are used mainly in hospital projects and projects relating to police services, under specific sectorial legislations.

French PPP Market

OVERVIEW

France has seen a significant rise of its PPP market over the last few years, with major projects being launched in a wide range of sectors.

This trend is unlikely to stop as France has a huge need for infrastructure projects, with prospects estimated at €60bn,[8] including the major investment needed for the upgrade and construction of sporting venues ahead of the Euro 2016 football tournament recently awarded to France.

Amongst the different forms of PPP described earlier, the two most active forms are probably the concession and the partnership contract. Partnership contracts are increasingly used by the State, local councils and municipalities as an efficient and innovative tool to meet their infrastructure needs. Moreover, partnership contracts allow them to amortise their payments during a longer period and contribute to more flexible public budgets management. To date, the number of partnership contracts procedures launched since 2004 reached around 450, out of which nearly 90 have reached the final notification (i.e., entry into force of the project) stage.[9] That number is expected to rise significantly in the coming years, especially in the local PPP market.[10]

Concession remains a very popular tool for implementing various PPP projects. Indeed, some of the major transport projects use a concession structure. This is the case for the Tours-Bordeaux high-speed line (LGV SEA) and also for the latest closed motorway transaction (A63 motorway). Indeed, France has a long story of using concession schemes for transport projects dating back to the 19th century (railways) and the introduction of project finance methods in the late 1990s has helped the development of this sector. In addition, concession is now used for innovative projects, such as the MMArena Stadium and the Lyon or Reims tramways.

RECENT PPP PROJECTS

In the past few years, the French PPP market has been especially active in transport and public building projects. As an illustration, such contracts represent 40 per cent of all partnership contracts granted since 2004 (in number of contracts).

Indeed, major transport PPP projects have recently been implemented, or are under tender process, for motorways,[11] railways,[12] airports[13] or even fluvial connections.[14]

---

8   See AFP press release above.

9   Source: French PPP Unit 'MAPPP' website – http://www.ppp.bercy.gouv.fr/liste_projets_extract_boamp.pdf.

10   See next page.

11   Ex: A63 motorway concession, A150 Rouen-Le Havre toll road concession or A355 motorway concession.

12   Ex: €7.8bn Tours-Bordeaux high-speed rail concession or €3.4bn Brittany to Loire-Valley rail PPP.

13   Ex: €450 million Notre-Dame-des-Landes airport concession.

14   Ex: €4.2bn 106km Canal Seine-Nord Europe PPP.

Major PPP projects have also been implemented for governmental buildings,[15] tribunals,[16] prisons,[17] universities,[18] hospitals[19] or sports venues.[20] Amongst these sectors, the most promising markets for public buildings PPPs are probably the stadium and arena sector, the prison sector (in July 2010 the French government launched an ambitious national programme to construct or renovate more than 40 prisons in the next five years under PPP contracts[21]), and the university sector (with the launch in 2008 by the French government of an ambitious national programme (Plan Campus) to invest €5bn in the construction and renovation of French university campuses[22]).

Besides transport and public building infrastructures, PPP is also often used in France for a wider variety of projects. Examples include the 1 billion Euros worth Ecotax PPP project, involving the implementation of a tax collection system for trucks for using national roads, the €250m worth communication systems PPP launched by the Ministry of Defence to update the army and air force communications systems (RDIP) or the GSM equipment on French rail infrastructure (GSM-R). PPPs may also be implemented for defence equipment such as helicopters,[23] satellites (Nectar) or military ships (BSAH).

It should be noted, however, that along with these major projects which are often strongly supported by the French government itself, such as the Tours-Bordeaux high-speed rail concession, which is one of the major projects of the Grenelle de l'Environnement programme, most PPP projects are implemented throughout France by local councils and municipalities in various sectors such as street lighting,[24] schools[25] or energy performance contracts.

Even though these projects are often much smaller in size than those major projects implemented by the government, the local PPP market has always been very active. Indeed, 75 per cent of all partnership contracts have been passed by local councils and municipalities since 2004, the vast majority of such projects representing less than €30m initial investment.[26]

The local PPP market is expected to rise significantly in the coming years due to the growing interest of local councils and municipalities in PPP mechanisms to meet their infrastructure needs, especially in the urban equipment sector (e.g. heating systems, public lighting, bicycle sharing systems successfully implemented in Paris and Lyon).

---

15   Ex: Ministry of Defence Headquarters PPP with the development of 90,000m² of real estate.

16   Ex: Paris TGI PPP or Caen new courthouse PPP.

17   Ex: first prison PPP programme launched in 2004–2006.

18   Ex: Toulouse Le Mirail University PPP, Grenoble University PPP or Lille University campus PPP.

19   Ex: Rennes, Annemasse and CHSF Hospital PPPs.

20   Ex: €217m Nice stadium concession, Lille *Grand Stade* PPP, Le Mans MMA Stadium concession, Paris *Parc des Princes* Stadium PPP or Marseille Vélodrome Extension PPP project.

21   Source: French Ministry of Justice website – http://www.justice.gouv.fr/le-garde-des-sceaux-10016/un-plan-sans-precedent-pour-moderniser-les-prisons-20062.html.

22   Source: French Ministry of *Enseignement Supérieur* – http://www.enseignementsup-recherche.gouv.fr/pid20637/l-operation-campus.html.

23   Dax Helicopter Training Center PPP (2008).

24   Ex: Maubeuge streetlighting concession for the installation of street lighting equipment, traffic lights and lighting for car parks, or Rouen streetlighting PPP project.

25   Ex: Montigny-Les-Metz secondary school reconstruction and extension PPP sponsored by the regional authority of Lorraine, or Jarny secondary school PPP for the financing, design, demolition and reconstruction, operating, maintenance and renewal of equipment for a total of €64.2m project costs.

26   Source: French PPP Unit 'MAPPP' website – http://www.ppp.bercy.gouv.fr/liste_projets_extract_boamp.pdf.

Further to these greenfield projects, significant opportunities also exist in brownfield projects with the renewal of major concessions which were originally granted to French major public companies. In that respect, the French hydropower sector, the second most important in Europe in terms of capacity, provides a good illustration. Indeed, a vast majority of French hydropower plants (80 per cent) are currently operated by French ex-national electricity provider Electricité de France (EDF) privatized in 2004. Due to the fact that 25 per cent of hydropower concessions in France are scheduled to be renewed between 2011 and 2020, and in order to comply with EU rules on free trade and competition, the French government decided, in its Grenelle de l'Environnement programme, to simplify the renewal procedure of 10 hydropower concessions in order to facilitate the entry of new players in the French market, constituting therefore a major opportunity for them.

Besides hydropower projects, the French wind energy PPP market constitutes another opportunity in the renewable energy sector for investors. This market is indeed taking off significantly with the upcoming launch by the French government of mega offshore wind projects, such as the €10bn investment offshore farms project with a capacity of 6,000MW to be located on the Atlantic and Northern coasts between Saint-Nazaire and Le Treport.

MAIN ACTORS

Generally speaking, the French PPP market is dominated by three major French infrastructure developers, namely Vinci, Bouygues and Eiffage. These three companies participate to tender procedures either in their own name or through consortia.

Despite the domination of these three major players, other independent infrastructure developers are gradually managing to get a share of the PPP market. Examples include: Spie Batignolles, Demathieu & Bard, NGE and Malet. These independent infrastructure developers often bid in consortia in order to improve their chances against the Big 3 (e.g., on the first road partnership contract signed in July 2010 to design, build and maintain the Tarbes bypass).

Besides O&M subsidiaries of the Big 3, operators such as GDF-Suez, Veolia, Dalkia and Egis are also very active.

On the investor side, the number of infrastructure funds active on the French market is expanding (AXA Investment Managers, FIDEPPP, Barclays Infrastructure, Meridiam, InfraRed etc.). In addition, the Caisse des Depots et Consignations (CDC) has been strongly involved in the French PPP market for a long time.

Through its subsidiary CDC Infrastructure, CDC may invest in equity in infrastructure assets that are critical for the French economic development and the attractiveness of its economy. In 2010, CDC Infrastructure's portfolio represented an investment of €600m in nine PPP projects participations, including the emblematic Millau Viaduc project. CDC expects to increase these numbers significantly in the coming years to reach a portfolio worth €1.5bn in 2015.[27] CDC may also act as lender, notably through the Saving Funds Directorate (DFE), which was required by the government to affect up to €8bn to PPP financings under the 2009 French recovery plan.

---

27   Source: CDC website – http://www.caissedesdepots.fr/fileadmin/Communiqu per centC3 per centA9s per cent20de per cent20presse/Tarbes.pdf.

On the financing side, all French banks are active on the PPP market (BNP Paribas, Credit Agricole-CIB, CIC-CM, CNCE-CFF, Natixis, Société Générale), along with foreign banks such as HSBC which has a long history in France. Over the last couple of years, the market has seen the arrival of many Spanish and German banks. European Investment Bank (EIB) is also a very important financier on transport projects.

Finally, the MAPPP is worth citing as an emblematic institution strongly involved in the development of PPPs. MAPPP is a governmental PPP unit which was established in 2005 to support the implementation of the new partnership contracts procedure. Its primary role is assessing partnership contract projects before they receive approval from the Ministry of Budget. MAPPP provides the methodology for evaluating partnership contract projects and validates feasibility studies prepared by the authorities for governmental approval. Once a project has been proposed as a partnership contract, MAPPP's role is to review and validate the preliminary assessment to ensure that it has been completed correctly from a legal, financial and qualitative perspective.

Since 2004, the main impact of MAPPP on the PPP market has probably been the production of PPP 'best practice guides' which contribute to the improvement of PPP expertise in the market, especially in local councils and municipalities.

PPP Financial Structuring

PRELIMINARY REMARKS ON DAILLY LAW ASSIGNMENT AND STATE GUARANTEE IN PPP

Before we describe the typical PPP financial structures prevailing in France, we will describe two instruments which are specific to the French PPP market: the Dailly Law Assignment and the French State Guarantee for PPP projects.

The Dailly Law Assignment, whose name comes from the name of the senator who originated the law in 1981, is a special mechanism designed to facilitate the granting of loans by credit institutions to companies and is commonly used in all types of financings.[28]

It may be used either as a purchase of receivables (cession Dailly à titre d'escompte) or as assignment of receivables by way of security for a loan (cession Dailly à titre de garantie). In both cases, the Dailly Law Assignment operates a transfer of the full ownership of the assigned receivables to the credit institution as well as the rights attached to the receivables, regardless of the origination date, maturity date or due date of the receivables.

The Dailly Law Assignment is used in all French financing structures for PPP transactions, in particular for partnership contracts. As security to the loan granted to it, the project company assigns its remuneration receivables arising from the PPP contract to the lenders.

In 2004, the French legislator introduced an article in the Dailly Law[29] specific to Dailly Law transfers made over receivables arising from partnership contracts or hospital

---

28   Law dated 2 January, 1981 which is now codified in articles L. 313–23 and subsequent of the French Monetary and Financial Code.

29   Article L. 313–29–1 of the French Monetary and Financial Code.

long-term leases (BEA). Its object was to facilitate the use of the acceptation (acceptance) of Dailly Law Assignments in PPPs.

The acceptance of the Dailly Law assignment is a direct undertaking of the assigned debtor which procures very strong protection to the lenders. As from the acceptance of the Dailly Law assignment, the assigned public debtor is unconditionally committed to pay the assigned remuneration due to the project company under the PPP contract directly into the hands of the assignee (the lenders) and can no longer invoke against the assignee any exception based on his personal relationship with the assignor, such as set off with penalties, nullity, rescission or termination of the PPP contract. The only limit is that 'the global undertaking of the public legal entity in respect of such acceptance shall not exceed 80 per cent of the remuneration due in respect of investments costs and financing costs.'

Dailly Law acceptance mechanism has significantly contributed to lowering the risk profile of PPP financing and has been extensively used in nearly all partnership contract projects (on rents paid by the administration) and in some concession projects (on subsidies).

Besides the Dailly mechanism, from 2009[30] the French government was permitted to grant state guarantees to any financing within the limit of 80 per cent of the total project financings, in order to support the PPP market during the credit crunch. Besides the comfort this tool may have given to the market, it has been greatly appreciated as a possible basis for infra bonds, after the disappearance of monolines. The French State Guarantee may be granted either for the construction or the operating phase.

The French State Guarantee was set to apply only to specific PPP transactions signed before 31 December 2010 or selected before 10 November 2010, such as the Tours-Bordeaux high-speed rail project.

TYPICAL STRUCTURE OF THE FINANCING

A typical partnership contract transaction financing structure can be summarized as follows:

During the construction phase, the financing granted to the special purpose Project Company is generally split in three main facilities, each facility being secured by a specific security interest:

- The equity bridge facility, which pre-finances the equity contributions during the construction phase;
- The VAT bridge facility, which finances the payments of VAT and is reimbursed upon reception by the project company of any VAT reimbursement from the French Treasury; and
- The long-term facility, which is granted to the project company and is reimbursed during the operation phase. This facility is secured by several guarantees (e.g., pledge over the project bank accounts, pledge over the shares of the project company, assignment of all receivables), including by way of a Dailly assignment of indemnities due to the project company under the PPP contract.

---

30   French *Loi de Finance Modificative* dated 4 February 2009.

In addition, appropriate hedging mechanisms to cover rate risks are systematically put in place by the project company in order to satisfy the public entity's demand to disburse a fixed remuneration for the duration of the project.

During the operation phase, the long-term facility is reimbursed by the remuneration received by the project company from the public entity under the PPP contract. In order to reflect the risks associated with the project, the long-term facility may be split into a project facility (representing a project risk) and a Dailly facility (secured by a Dailly Law assignment of part of the remuneration to be paid by the public entity and accepted by the public entity, representing a pure public risk due to the legal effects of the Dailly acceptance, as already discussed).

During that phase, the lenders bear either a project risk and/or a pure public risk. The long-term facility is secured by a Dailly Law assignment of the payments owed by the public entity as from the delivery date and until the end of the PPP contract. The assignment of part of such remuneration is accepted by the public entity under the Dailly Law. As explained above, as from the acceptance of the assignment, the public entity cannot oppose to the assignees (i.e., the lenders) any defence it may have against the Project Company. The assignees are therefore protected against any performance risks of the project company.

However, the acceptance by the public legal entity of the assignment of payments shall not exceed 80 per cent of such payments owed by the public entity. As a consequence, the other financing resources (e.g., equity contributions, subsidies, remaining portion of the long term facility which is not secured by the Dailly acceptance of the assignment of the government receivables) bear a project risk.

In addition to this, it should be noted that a growing number of PPP projects now include a real estate development programme to be implemented in the vicinity of the infrastructure object of the PPP. Such a source of additional revenues has been implemented lately in the Lille, Nice and Marseille Stadia projects, as well as in the Balard project (new headquarters of the Ministry of Defence).

PROJECT BONDS FOR FRENCH INFRA?[31]

To date, very few French PPP transactions have been directly financed by the issuance of bonds (i.e., the Stade de France concession in 1995 and the A28 motorway concession in 2001).

Yet the financial crisis leading to an increase in funding costs, as well as recent international regulations, such as Basel III, has put even more constraints on banks' liquidity obligations. This, combined with the arrival of larger French infrastructure projects and numerous previous deals due to reach the operational phase over the coming years, has contributed to the increasing interest for project bonds in the French PPP market.

The French government launched an initiative in July 2010 to foster the use of capital markets for infrastructure projects in France. This initiative aimed at creating, along with more traditional bank loans, a national securitization vehicle dedicated to strategic PPPs and capable of issuing long-term bonds to be placed with French and international

---

31   For a more detailed account of the French Project Bond market see C. Van Gallebaert and J. Brusau Cuello, 'French bonds – Marrying infra to bonds,' PFI Magazine, 20 April 2011.

investors (insurance companies, pension funds, etc.). This PPP securitization vehicle would intervene, either at the end of the construction phase of a project when commercial operation begins (through a refinancing by the Dailly Law assignments held by banks on the project), or upon the entry into force of the PPP contract to refinance construction loans benefiting from the State guarantee.

In this light, it should be noted that under French Law, several existing structures may currently be used to issue project bonds: Fonds Commun de Titrisation (securitization vehicle without legal personality), securitization vehicle company, Sociétés de Crédit Foncier (using covered bonds), etc.

Despite the existence of such structures, the French PPP market is still reluctant to use project bonds as it often perceives the inclusion of project bond financing or refinancing as potentially raising specific financial issues (e.g., negative carry, make whole provisions). More importantly, a sound structuring of banking loans based on Dailly Law assignment, together with a strong offer from commercial banks and pricing at a satisfactory level, have, until now, proved sufficient to absorb the financing needs of the French PPP market.

The French PPP market is, however, becoming increasingly aware of the potentialities of project bonds as a credible solution for the refinancing of any existing or future projects after completion of the construction phase and occurrence of the effective delivery date of the infrastructure, addressing sponsors and banks' needs for refinancing tools.

Therefore, project bonds are generally considered as the field most likely to undergo further developments in the French PPP market in the coming years.

33 *Fixing US Infrastructure*

JOHN SELLERS, a Principal
Yavapai Regional Capital Inc

Over the very same 30 years in which the US economy slid into a level of debt to GDP approaching ratings downgrade potential, US infrastructure quality has deteriorated commensurately. Ironically, it was here in the US that the seeds of global privatization were sown in the power industry in the early 1980s following the passage of PURPA. This promoted private sector competition which sponsored a global revolution in electrical generating infrastructure. Different observers have different definitions of infrastructure, but as considered here, we've excluded the power sector because of its relative efficiency but included transportation systems (highways, roads, air, water, and rail), water utilities, and some other kinds of public facilities (schools, postal facilities, and prisons). In the US Mountain West where we operate, there are also some infrastructure components that are somewhat special, such as flood control and dams, which have also been largely neglected.

The Seeds of the Problem

Unfortunately, with over 30,000 municipal issuers, the efficiencies generated in the utility sector never materialized in the highly fragmented public sector. The US dollar, as reserve currency, promoted complacency. House prices would rise forever, impact fees would never disappear, people would continue to move westwards and pay ever-increasing house prices that filled state and local coffers. The US political system simply would not tolerate change because the very same public employees who benefited also had sway via their unions over politicians and hence significant control over negotiating their own pensions. The myth was perpetrated that tax-exempt debt always produced cheaper financing. The background to all this was that generally apathetic US voters was far too busy buying electronics and boats to notice the managerial and financial decay of local government, and certainly not astute enough to notice the build-up of the now ticking time bomb: Public pensions. The result was highly inefficient government combined with an infrastructure financing system that never could keep up with what was needed to compete globally and in many cases, couldn't even provide necessary maintenance.

We now recognize that the needs are enormous. The Society of Civil Engineers quotes a US$1.6tr need over the next five years merely to bring US infrastructure up to standard. We think the number is greater than that because unless you've witnessed it with your own eyes, the real needs are hard to comprehend. For instance, there are 14,000 water companies in the US – double the number of banks. Many regulate themselves and some represent real healthcare challenges and water utility black holes with understated renewal costs.

The 2008 Financial Crisis

As a result of the financial crisis, much has changed, although the dawning of the real problem has been death by a thousand cuts in the public sector. Early on, we wrote of the possibilities for rebuilding both the US economy and US Mountain States infrastructure using private capital. This was only weeks after the 2008 fiscal crisis, a 'financial Pearl Harbour.' Unfortunately, the denial at the time, much of which still remains in certain quarters, did not serve to douse the flames on the burning battleships or motivate the troops to load up with ammo and mobilize to fight the good fight. Instead, a lukewarm stimulus soup was spread unevenly over the embers, with little lasting effect other than more national debt and a lot of lethargy. This slow death is now creeping closer and can be felt by all.

Anyone familiar with international crises could see the pattern unfolding – and it did. Creditors are not stupid. After 30 years of filling the porous cheese of the American economy with every imaginable type of debt from overseas, the excess was sucked out with a whoosh overnight. It was replaced by the sound of the constant drip of the Fed pumping money into the economy – QE1 and QE2. Two years ago, expressing concern about the US credit rating was almost treason; today it's conventional wisdom. To quote John Boehner: 'The country's broke.'

As expected, cities and states were to a greater or lesser degree ring-fenced by the credit markets, especially as the Greece-like, hidden off balance-sheet debt related to public sector pensions began to make news. Some still believe that things will be fine in the muni market; default rates are still low, so what's the big deal? This is reminiscent of Walt Wriston's famous adage in the '70s that 'countries don't go bankrupt.' He later modified that to add – they just don't pay you back!

As bankers, we were taught to observe how countries fight wars to see how they deal with financial crises. For a nation like the US, used to relying on technology and overwhelming force, the analogy I like is the Battle of the Bulge. The air cover (Washington) has disappeared. It's now hand-to-hand in foxholes. It's inspiring to watch some public officials as they battle on without support from Federal or even State capitals, casting off shackles and taking initiative.

Unfortunately, in the intervening two years, not much has happened from a public private partnership (PPP) deal standpoint except the bankruptcy in San Diego of a private toll road. In hindsight, this was not a case of lessons to be learned but, instead, what were all the lessons and basic principles readily available at the time that were overlooked in the eagerness to do a deal?

This is not over and the doomsday machine is ticking in Washington.

Why the US is Lagging

The US is the obvious final market for private capital to make its mark in infrastructure, representing the last and biggest bastion to embrace public-private-partnerships. Why is the market not taking off? First of all, we believe it is although it is only apparent in small pockets of activity, some of the factors at work are:

LACK OF RISK TAKERS

The shock of the financial crisis and the slow dawning realization that the stimulus did little is having a debilitating effect at all levels, individual, personal, business, and political, of course. Traditional American risk-taking and optimism has almost, but not quite, disappeared. This is most apparent in the financial sector. Seasoned bankers like us are astonished by the disappearance of the US banking industry as a credible, risk-taking system of intermediation between investors and borrowers. The culture of professional banking has been lost; a new generation of bankers will be needed to fix that, – the kind that don't want to sit in front of a computer screen all day.

PUBLIC FINANCE VS PROJECT FINANCE

Anyone familiar with the evolution of Export Finance into Project Finance in international markets will recognize the parallels between Public Finance and PPPs in the US.

Project Financing is the long-term financing of a project based upon the projected cash flows of the project rather than the balance sheets of the project sponsors or taxation revenues pledged by a government entity. Most commonly known as non-recourse loans, these are secured by project assets including the revenue-producing contracts, and paid entirely from project cash flow supported by financial modelling. Project lenders are given a lien on all of these assets, and are able to assume control of a project if the project company does not comply with loan terms. Usually, refinancing occurs post completion, which means that project finance is essentially a highly structured form of construction lending. Risk identification and allocation are key components. This business is much more about risk management than relationships.

Public Finance, on the other hand, essentially revolves around bonding on a long-term basis of various types of taxation revenues that a government pledges to lenders. The essential difference between project finance and public finance is the risk profile. With a few exceptions the bondholders of tax-exempt debt are insulated from the risks of project construction and completion. Public debt financing in the US is much more of a relationship business and depends on the ability of politicians to squeeze taxation revenues from their voter base which can then be securitized.

Although tax-exempt bonds produce nominally low rates because of tax benefits, it's a little analogous to a private business being restricted to factoring its receivables. If you are a business or a city trying to beat the average growth expectations, you are denied financing markets such as equity and debt which want to pick winners. Would Google exist if it had relied on factoring its receivables?

The nirvana, of course, is to use private capital to finance and bring greater discipline to the construction cycle, then use nominal tax savings from tax-exempt debt as a takeout. This is achievable but requires some adjustment amongst financial players as discussed below. This also requires us to remember the lessons of the international arena. Traditional public finance and new PPP/project finance sources must collaborate – not compete.

The essential difference, difficult to explain to public officials, is the impact of behavioural change triggered by a new private, and very different, financing process. The risk profile with a project financed transaction is such that the finance is not simply a source of money but a whole new process of ensuring that construction is on time and budget. It's an iterative process, with lots of balls in the air at once rather than slow linear steps, a process perceived as highly risky for public officials because it means taking decisions that are conditional–the 'conditional waltz' as we call it.

In the power industry, the effect that this construction financing discipline had on overall construction costs led to 40% savings. The effect will be repeated for PPPs, especially when private sector creativity can bring more efficient technology to solutions, dramatically reducing costs through innovation.

LACK OF PROJECT FINANCE CAPABILITY IN US BANKS

US banks led the charge into project finance lending in the 1970s. Any other country that has had an infrastructure boom has seen its banking industry first participate and then change and adapt, faced with what are usually large capital needs. This occurred first with UK banks with North Sea Oil in the 70s. The Australian banks followed in the 80s, as well as the Japanese, because of their mutual energy import/export situations. The same eventually happened with the European banks in the 90s to the point where those banks now dominate the lending market.

As a well-researched recent Standard & Poor's study points out, US banks did the reverse. They engaged in a disastrous march out of this business in the 80s, abandoning a US$1.9tr asset class that project finance professionals knew deserved investment grade ratings. Project finance loans were much less risky because of the fundamentals of the due diligence involved. Over the intervening 20 years, this would have been a highly attractive business for US banks on a risk-adjusted basis. They preferred securitizing sub-prime mortgages instead.

The question now arises as to how to get US banks to re-enter the market, without offering subsidies, grants, or other incentives such as the relaxed capital or lending requirements that caused Fannie and Freddie to collapse. Put another way, how to avoid creating an 'Infrannie', either due to insufficient capital or moral hazard risk?

We have suggested to Washington that the results of this S&P study be pointed out more forcibly to US banks' senior management and to regulators, so far without success. The emerging National Infrastructure Bank, now the proposed American Infrastructure Finance Authority (AIFA) can play a significant jawboning role here, well beyond its likely US$10bn of initial capital. In the meantime, we continue to plug away at the local level with regional banks, using projects as examples of good lending opportunities. With relatively lower capital requirements relative to large banks in the future, they are the natural motors of project lending.

FAILURE OF THE EXISTING FINANCIAL INSTITUTIONS TO ADAPT

One of the best arguments for a National Infrastructure Bank is that there is no one existing institution that has the ingredients for success in the US infrastructure space. Even if we had such an institution, we believe it would have to be geographically organized along the lines of the Federal Reserve Board, with strong regional groupings connecting states with common needs into manageable blocks. We bill ourselves as a 'regional infrastructure merchant bank' for that very reason – tying in the common needs of the Mountain States.

This is best exemplified by the current financial actors with some, but not all, having the needed skill sets:

i)   *Money centre banks* – They have no real regional presence, retired from project lending years ago, lost their lending culture, and are only interested in securities intermediation. They are likely to be hampered by higher capital needs as they are deemed 'systemic' because their balance sheets exceed US$50bn.

ii) *Regional commercial banks* – They have great relationships, but are still stuck on how to build loan volume in their traditional markets of real estate, credit card, and retail lending. They are not ready for project finance yet and are more likely to expand their loan books by cannibalistic acquisitions.

iii) *Public finance firms* – They have even better regional relationships, especially for the regional firms because they have an immense client network of public officials. But in general, they are territied of PPP's because, not only do they lack the transactional skill sets, but these very transactions require grappling with issues in potentially confrontational, complex negotiating settings. Being completely relationship-driven, they are fearful of the loss of bread and butter business this could bring.

iv) *Foreign banks* – These dominate the project lending business globally and in the US, but they have little or no regional presence. My own experience based in a Europe Head Office tells me their senior managements are also very fearful as to what happens to your risk profile when you step into a world they perceive as very dangerous – US state and local government.

We see serious consolidation opportunities here for public finance, project finance and regional commercial banks with balance sheets to come together. Otherwise, where is the loan growth?

INAPPLICABILITY OF THE OVERSEAS MODEL

The US is different from the rest of the world, especially with its decentralized political and independent political system. It is shocking how few people understand state and local governments' workings. With trust being in short supply across the board, there is a need for new models of mixed ownership for infrastructure assets and decision making, independent of politics, tailored to the unique features of the US market. At its core, this includes the special needs of transparency and 'buy-in' at the grass-roots level. Otherwise, deals will never close. What this means for seasoned international PPP practitioners is:

i)   Do not expect to win mandates in this business the old-fashioned way – in the local Ritz Carlton. It's not going to happen. Be visible throughout the community. Some of the most creative work we do is with local officials in small offices designing some unique structures.

ii) Do not attend any east coast investment conferences where people lament the lack of deal flow – if you do, you are part of the problem.

iii) Get to really understand transparency and ensure via broad-based public outreach that project-affected officials and communities see you practicing it. An American who doesn't know or trust what his government 'is up to' is an army of one who can kill local buy-in on anything.

The typical PPP model, where a government hires an adviser, runs a beauty competition, and then picks a winner with their financial model wrapped up in a bundled black box, is unnatural in American local politics. It's like an arranged marriage. Take a lesson from the energy industry: think joint ventures.

Assume every government official is risk-averse. Give cover to those braver ones by presenting the compelling project benefits that their constituents will enjoy. You just have to spot and support the more entrepreneurial players.

IMPACT FEES

One of the most inefficient means of financing infrastructure in the US is impact fees. Essentially, private developers hand over money for government to build or improve infrastructure as a condition of private development approval. This has a couple of disadvantages in that costs are being loaded into house prices, which is fine if house prices and starts are growing. But it feeds public coffers with a revenue source that is ephemeral as it's based on housing starts. Which banker would lend over 30 years based effectively upon a stream of real estate commissions? This is also not good for regional cooperation because the competition for those impact fees kills genuine regional cooperation for projects needing regional breadth. Governments may say that they play the cooperation game but privately, the knives are out competing with their neighbours for the impact fees associated with development.

A better system is for regional improvement districts or joint powers authorities that levy reasonable long-term user charges that then provide the long-term revenue base for longer-term financing. Arizona's recent passage of HB2003 is a good example of this, proving that public officials are starting to understand this concept.

SECTOR APPROACHES

One cannot ignore sectorial differences in figuring out issues retarding project development. And there is no more contentious issue than the first of these in the dry Mountain State's region in which we operate.

(i) Water

Putting aside the gorilla in the room, i.e., the severe underpricing of water because of lack of market pricing, the biggest impediment we have seen is the use of the word privatization. What has not been fully appreciated is the need for a true partnership in water – not an outright sale to the private sector. The model we like is to retain the public agency as the interface with the retail water users with the long-term infrastructure contract between the relevant City or Municipality Enterprise Fund and the PPP project entity. To keep the public counterparty creditworthy, of course, the long-term tariff structure to the retail users' needs explaining. The good news here for retail users is that they have price certainty over say 30 years for their water. The bad news is that there is a need for price escalation, albeit not full CPI and certainly lower than some recent predatory increases from unscrupulous providers. This is analogous to persuading airlines to hedge fuel cost in the 80s. They would love to do it, but not be the first and certainly not the last, for fear of being a long-term more expensive place to live if somewhere else does not raise rates. On the other hand, try explaining that to the retail water users in Anthem, Arizona, who have been hit by violent water price increases that could repeat next year and the year after that, etc.

(ii) Transport

Transport is the big dollar driver of infrastructure and the sector most capable of creating jobs. In most states, it also is an often neglected means of achieving regional cooperation. Public officials will enter the room in a water context with daggers drawn. In a regional transport context, those same officials can be seen chatting over cocktails. Therefore, getting a really successful transport project off the ground in most states would be a huge impetus.

The issue we see here is not just the voter's disposition against tolls. Most public officials secretly understand people can be persuaded to pay them if value for money is apparent. The issue is how to create this. The model we favour is not to import the traditional black box model where a beauty competition awards the winner the concession. We saw the perverse effects of that internationally when the World Bank relaxed its procurement competition rules for bundled PPP consortia concession bids. We prefer an open book, completely transparent model where each cost component is built up separately to generate the user charges. Then, even an unsolicited proposal might produce an offer that could not be matched. We are presently in the throes of testing this model with a Financial Model that was immediately made a public record – before award. So far it's working. A couple of prerequisites are to make sure every potential player understands there are no cozy deals, and a first-rate detailed financial model that tells you instantly the effect on financeability of on-going contract award and pricing decisions.

THERE IS NO SEED CAPITAL

The challenge, of course, is how to build the tsunami of projects to create jobs and remedy widespread infrastructure weakness. You need an earthquake to start a tsunami, but when government has no money, who will kick-start initiative and seed the initial investment?

Without that, the result is a blocked pipeline that cries out to be unblocked. The textbook tells you that government backed by political will needs to seed the early stages of a project. The problem is this seed capital is simply not available and is unlikely to return any time soon, if at all. There is a gap in the market need to finance the revolution that is coming. To finance this, we at Yavapai Regional Capital decided we must help create a new investment asset class, effectively infrastructure venture capital. A relatively few dollars can kick-start projects where return-hungry, conflict-free investors co-invest alongside local investors and governments ready to contribute their own value-added time. In the latter case, if you're looking for political will, we believe this government sweat equity meets the political will test and frankly it's all that's on the table.

This is not a financing structure for the faint-hearted, but investors bemoaning inadequate returns should delight in it. Why would you expect superior returns financing the sale of an existing infrastructure asset, where by definition the goal—to maximize the sales price – works against your return? Early-stage development equity can control new builds with new cost paradigms and efficiencies. This can generate competitive user charges that consumers might find impossible to refuse. If users actually want the product, investors should think of these as attractive assets from a risk standpoint.

The major risk to private development equity will be local political risk. But internationally, we found ways to split commercial/political risk and insure the latter. If we can do that in the US, by getting governments to self-insure the political risk, i.e., insure themselves, who would not invest, if the economics look sound?

In short, these modest investments in new projects, where the cost savings achieved from the start assure users of competitive charges, can bring venture capital returns over the same short two-year time horizon, and in the process, unblock the pipeline.

A National Infrastructure Bank

With the re-emergence of the National Infrastructure Bank as AIFA, Washington appears decided for once to concentrate on something that the market can't easily supply: project finance debt, commercial bank style. In so doing, it will push private project development to the forefront. Project professionals know projects carry on the way they start. Getting transparent, hungry, private development equity involved early offers the prospect of an early-stage, transparent, pork-free, consultant- and endless-studies-free (almost) environment. Bringing this no-nonsense project discipline will be revolutionary and the revolution is already here in the small pockets that always germinate them.

A Leadership Vacuum

First, there is absolutely no shortage of good projects – people are surfacing them. Some, having been on the drawing boards with insufficient money for years, represent basic needs, and therefore extraordinary opportunities. But the commodity in short supply is leadership. Where are those few Marines prepared to ride into the valley of death? The key is to find the winners. In the Mountain States, these are often the smaller municipal kids on the block, who are used to being the low guy on the regional totem pole. Elsewhere, be prepared for resistance from Dinosaurus Governicus, accustomed to regional dominance and ready funding. Some of these might never 'get it,' so it's a case of picking the champions.

Regionality is also becoming more critical. When money was unlimited, everyone could have their own project and go it alone. Now, regional joint ventures are starting to take hold, because there is no alternative. These present a perfect opportunity to create the integrated, multi-community outreach programmes needed for up-front buy-in.

Despite the above, Arizona, Colorado, Nevada, New Mexico, and Utah, a 'Mountain Mega' as defined by Brookings and ASU, are experiencing some of the fastest growth anywhere in the US. They have a vision, and these states could associate with huge regional investment ramifications.

Conclusions

Two entrepreneurial politicians were seen recently separately 'riding into the valley of death' in the press on the same day championing farsighted infrastructure developments. Winston Churchill said, 'The US eventually gets it right.' We're amongst those who still believe that. The US is eventually going to realise that with 14m unemployed, US$14tr of government debt and US$2tr of corporate cash on the sidelines, private capital is going to be used to fix jobs and infrastructure without adding to the deficit. Betting against the revolutionaries we see moving projects forwards in a new way is effectively betting against the American psyche. Who'd take that bet?

CHAPTER 34 *Brazil – For the Future*

CHRISTOPHER RYAN
Shearman & Sterling LLP, Washington DC
HOWARD M. STEINBERG
Shearman & Sterling LLP, New York
JEAN-LOUIS NEVES MANDELLI
Shearman & Sterling LLP, London
JOSÉ VIRGÍLIO LOPES ENEI
Machado, Meyer, Sendacz e Opice, São Paulo; Paulo Meira Lins, International Finance Corporation, Washington DC
MATHIAS VON BERNUTH
Shearman & Sterling LLP, São Paulo
PAULO DE MEIRA LINS
International Finance Corporation, Washington DC

For decades the sobriquet that hung on South America's resource rich and largest nation was 'Brazil – Land of the Future … But Not of Today.' No longer. Today Brazil's future may finally be here.

One of the world's largest countries by land mass, Brazil's infrastructure demands and plans are massive. Banco do Brasil anticipates that more than US$85bn in financing is required by 2020. President Dilma Rousseff has renewed Brazil's commitment to its Programa de Aceleração do Crescimento or so-called 'PAC II' infrastructure development programme (proposed by her predecessor Luiz Inacio Lula da Silva when she was his chief minister). This Herculean programme earmarks over US$500bn for infrastructure support through 2014 and some US$350bn thereafter.

Infrastructure demands are heightened by the forthcoming 2014 World Cup to be hosted in 12 Brazilian cities and the 2016 Olympics centred in Rio de Janeiro. These events demand major investments in sport-related facilities, urban renovation and transportation and only a small part of that investment is contemplated in PAC II. Additionally, another US$25bn of governmental support has been pledged for infrastructure by local governments and the Federal Government.

Brazil's needs stretch far off-shore. Its pre-salt deep water oil and gas reserves appear to require more than US$300bn to facilitate commercial production of reserves that may add well beyond 50bn barrels of oil to its proven reserves.

BNDES

Much financial support for the mammoth PAC II initiative is likely to come from Brazil's development bank – Banco Nacional de Desenvolvimento Econômico e Social (BNDES). Founded in 1952 and owned entirely by Brazil's treasury, BNDES disbursed over US$100bn in loans in 2010 alone of which infrastructure and energy accounted for almost 40 per cent. Since 2003, BNDES has backed more than 350 power projects in Latin America, accounting for over 28,000 megawatts of new electric generation capacity.

Other Project Finance Players

Although BNDES plays the lead role, other governmental entities, multilaterals and institutional investors are also active in Brazil's project finance initiatives.

Banco do Nordeste do Brasil (BNB), also controlled by the Federal Government but focussed on the northeast region, has provided loans to infrastructure and energy projects on terms often more favourable than those offered by BNDES. Recent examples are a major road system concession and the country's first hospital public private partnership (PPP), both in the northeastern State of Bahia. Many wind generation projects, for instance, have favourable interest rates and capital structures that can achieve as much as a 90 per cent debt-to-equity ratio.

The International Finance Corporation (IFC) and the International Development Bank (IDB) continue to support infrastructure efforts such as São Paulo Metro Line Four, Brazil's first (PPP), and the São Paulo ringroad segment granted under a concession to CCR, both of which were financed by the IDB, together with the Japanese Bank for International Cooperation (JBIC) and commercial lenders.

As part of the same legislation that originally approved the first PAC in 2007, Fundo de Infraestrutura do Fundo de Garantia por Tempo de Serviço (FI-FGTS), managed by Caixa Econômica Federal, was created to invest in infrastructure projects by funnelling surpluses accumulated in the general workers retirement fund accounts managed by Caixa Econômica Federal. Investments to date have exceeded Reais20bn. The FI-FGTS portfolio itself is authorized to invest in the real estate and sanitation projects.

In the private sector, commercial banks and private equity funds show growing interest in infrastructure opportunities, including project finance and mezzanine lending. The Brazilian banking system is formidable, with institutions such as Bradesco, Itaú and Banco do Brasil garnering the top positions in Latin America's bank rankings. Most international banks deal with Brazil on a cross-border basis or through local subsidiaries whose doors have been open in Brazil for many years (including Citibank, JP Morgan, HSBC and Santander).

Given that traditional financing sources such as BNDES cannot shoulder the necessary infrastructure investment, the Federal Government has sought to stimulate the participation of private banks in long-term financing. With Provisional Measure 517, published in late 2010, financing lines with tax benefits and incentives for capital-raising instruments, such as financial bills (Letras Financeiras – LFs) which are exempt from reserve requirements, have been created. As a result, markets eagerly await issuances of so-called 'project debentures', known in the international market as 'project bonds', which have linked credit support such as the backing of receivables and real estate. These long-term debt instruments, with terms of up to 30 years, offer security pari passu to that project owners must grant to BNDES.

Public Private Partnerships

Federal Law 11,079 of 2004, the Public Private Partnership (PPP) Law, governs PPP projects at the federal level and provides a general framework for PPP projects sponsored by states and municipalities. It is important to point out that PPP under the Brazilian PPP law are restrictively defined as public concessions requiring partial or full public payments and Brazil already has a concessions law which sets forth basis terms and conditions for public concessions. The PPP Law provides for construction and operation of infrastructure facilities by private companies on a long-term basis (from five to 35 years) by means of a concession agreement. Execution of these concessions must be preceded by a bidding procedure. Mandatory provisions are required to be included in invitations to bidders.

The first PPP transaction, São Paulo Metro Line 4 (Via Quatro), is a 30-year partnership for operation and maintenance of a subway. This transaction won financing of approximately US$350 million from BNDES, IDB and other banks for acquisition of rolling stock and operation and is believed to be the first project financing of a PPP in Brazil.

Soon a decade will have passed since formation of PPPs in Brazil. During the first years, few PPPs were completed, since the innovative character of the law spawned scepticism and caution. Recently, the number of PPP projects has grown. New subway lines, urban trains, highways, prisons, hospitals, administrative centres, football stadia, multi-purpose arenas, water and sewage treatment stations, urban cleaning, disposal of solid residue, data centres, public projects for the irrigation and revitalization of large urban centres, are now examples of successful PPPs.

Experience accumulated in these PPPs offers important lessons.

- Different frameworks have been allowed to meet the needs of different projects. In the Federal District Data Center Project, for example, reimbursement of 80 per cent of the cost of the work immediately after its conclusion and not in a linear manner throughout operation, was approved. In the Pontal Irrigation Project in the Semi-Arid region, public counter-performance was divided into three phases, triggered by distinct events: first, upon conclusion of the irrigation infrastructure; second, upon conclusion of the agricultural occupation; and, finally, upon availability of the irrigation service.
- Frequently, sponsors' main challenge has been to try to anticipate revenue to see if it can match financial costs so as to minimize lenders' requirements to maintain cash reserves in case revenues do not cover their periodic debt service. Many expect that legislation will evolve to allow for governmental contributions to initial project investments (currently prohibited by Section 7 of the PPP Law).
- Creative solutions could offer governmental funds without impacting Brazil's budget or future collections, such as CEPACs, securitization of overdue tax liabilities, payments in instalments, and real estate and tax incentives.
- Adequate structuring of a PPP may also reduce or eliminate impact of the project on the 3 per cent limit of current net revenue of the respective federative entity, or even

repeal the need to consolidate into the public statements of the Treasury, the assets and liabilities of the private partner (which is required pursuant to Ordinance 614 of the National Treasury).

To date, the Federal Government has not succeeded in contracting out any PPP except through Banco do Brasil and Caixa Econômica Federal for the Brasilia Datacenter. Nevertheless, states and municipalities have closed on more than 20 projects in critical areas such as subways, intercity trains, toll roads, hospitals, urban renovation, public buildings, prisons, sport arenas, soccer stadia, water treatment and waste management. Just like the UK precedent, many expect that these activities will grow exponentially in the near future. Much remains to be done to encourage proliferation of PPPs to allow them to make a meaningful contribution to the infrastructure 'underspend' in Brazil. Healthcare, education and waste should be leading sectors in PPP transactions of Brazilian sub-nationals.

Current Mega Projects

With injunctions now lifted on Brazil's gigantic Belo Monte hydroelectric project in Pará State on the Xingu River in the Amazon Region (to be the third largest hydroelectric project in the world after China's Three Gorges Dam and Brazil and Paraguay's Itaipu Dam), BNDES and Banco do Brasil are expected to support the approximately US$15bn project. The concession was granted to Norte Energia SA (NESA), a consortium formed by public and private corporations, led by the public utilities Electronorte, Eletrobras and CHESF. Engineering and design are being carried out by a design consortium of Brazilian engineering firms led by Intertechne and including Engevix and PCE. Construction and equipment supply contracts are being negotiated by NESA with a group of Brazilian contractors.

The Santo Antonio (3,150MW) and Jirau (3,300MW) hydroelectric plants in the Rio Madeira River in the North Amazon Region, were awarded in 2008 to consortia led by Odebrecht and Furnas for Santo Antonio and Suez and Camargo Correa, amongst others, for Jirau. Operations may commence this year. Together, these projects involve investments in excess of US$15bn. The plants are designed to operate with state-of-the-art bulb hydro turbines demanding much smaller reservoirs and thus reducing environmental impacts.

In 2010, the Teles Pires hydroelectric plant, with a projected installed capacity of 1,920MW, in the State of Mato Grosso, was awarded to a consortium led by Neoenergia. Operations are planned for 2015 and total investments may exceed US$3bn. This will be the largest plant on the Teles Pires River and may be supplemented by up to four additional plants.

In November 2009, Argentina and Brazil entered into an agreement to explore construction of the bi-national Garabi dam. This project, with a predicted installed capacity of 2,300MW, would be constructed on the Uruguay River. Feasibility studies are underway. Other large hydroelectric projects are being considered. On the Tapajós River in Para State, for example, up to five separate hydroelectric plants are being studied with combined installed capacity that may exceed 10,000MW.

Other colossal projects such as the first leg of the planned high-speed rail backbone in southern Brazil to connect Rio de Janeiro and São Paulo (discussed below) are in the bidding stages. Cost of this first rail link alone is estimated at more than US$20bn.

Natural and Economic Resources vs Obstacles

With phenomenal natural resources, hydraulic cascade and reservoir potential, off-shore oil and gas, and the largest economy in Latin America, Brazil is poised to dominate the project finance arena. But several obstacles must be surmounted.

Obstacles

Brazil's currency is relatively volatile. Foreign entrants tend to be at a disadvantage compared to indigenous sponsors when considering that most revenues and loans are Reais based. Brazil's national debt is about half of gross domestic product and BNDES's loans are accumulating losses for the Federal Government.[1] Commercial loans in Brazil command high interest rates and tenors which generally do not stretch long enough to support project financing. Few projects are financed in Brazil without the support of development banks, multilateral or export agencies or vendor financing or institutional investors (such as pension funds) as part or all of their debt capital structure.

Many projects are implemented through the PPP structure as joint ventures between governmental and private parties. Given the 'public' nature of these lending sources, the path to borrowing can be long, further straining project capital costs and investors' returns.

Nevertheless, the capital market as an alternative for raising project finance is becoming a feasible and attractive solution for both new and expansion projects (although this option is still limited to a select few of the largest sponsors in only a few sectors).

Despite current economic complications of private project financing for projects in Brazil, in general, the legal and regulatory framework is already in place to support project financing in most major infrastructure sectors.

Project Bonds

Capital markets in Brazil had traditionally been reluctant to accept the types of risk inherent in lending to a company with only one project which is yet to be constructed and could be subject to cost and schedule overruns and unknown operating costs. The remarkable initial public offering (IPO) of OGX, one of Eike Batista's companies that is part of the so-called X Group dedicated to oil and gas exploration and production

---

1   Although BNDES is a profitable bank on a stand-alone basis, the Brazilian Government has been raising debt (used for general purposes including for injecting capital into BNDES) at higher interest rates (the SELIC rate) than those charged by BNDES in its loans (the TJLP rate). Considering that a relevant part of BNDES loans are made to the so-called national champions, i.e., Brazilian companies that are leaders in their segments, criticism has been levelled that taxpayers are indirectly funding these companies. Others, however, argue that the Federal Government must help Brazilian companies to compete on a global scale.

changed this perception when its offering in 2008 raised the most equity ever raised in a primary IPO in the Brazilian market at the time. OGX's IPO was completed with investors relying only on OGX's planned projects and their projections rather than an operating portfolio with a track record (since OGX only held permits to construct at the time of its IPO).

This encouraging trend has recently included project bond debt. Select sponsors such as Odebrecht and Queiroz Galvão have accessed capital market debt for infrastructure projects on a limited recourse basis. These issuances have been limited to institutional investors such as pension funds and financial institutions.

Project bonds often include local debt instruments such as debentures or international bonds issued under Regulation 144-A or Regulation S of the Securities Exchange Act of the US (or their equivalent in other jurisdictions).

Amongst project bonds successfully issued by Brazilian companies in 2010 are:

- Rota das Bandeiras SA, a toll road concessionaire controlled by Odebrecht which raised Reais1.1bn through local debentures with a 14 year tenor at a IPCA + 9.57 per cent annual interest rate;
- Odebrecht Drilling Norbe VIII/IX Ltd., a special purpose entity controlled by Odebrecht Óleo e Gás which issued 144-A/Reg S bonds of US$1.5bn maturing in 2021 with a 6.375 per cent annual interest rate; and
- Lancer Finance Company, a special purpose entity controlled by Shahin which issued 144-A/Reg S bonds of US$270m maturing in 2016 at a 5.85 per cent annual interest rate.

Oil and Gas

The National Agency for Petroleum, Natural Gas and Biofuels (ANP) created in 1997 regulates natural gas and biofuel. The export of crude oil and liquefied natural gas is subject to obtaining prior authorization from ANP. Only companies incorporated in Brazil with their headquarters and management in Brazil may export crude oil and liquefied natural gas. One important objective of the National Energy Policy Council (CNPE) and ANP is to create a competitive environment for oil and natural gas exploitation. Amongst ANP's main responsibilities are the regulation of concession conditions for the development of the upstream industry and the granting of new concessions. Also in 1997, Petrobras's monopoly on the exploration and production of oil and gas (which began in 1953) was eliminated, giving way to private investment.

Following the major deep water pre-salt reserves discovery in Brazil, the legal framework was amended in 2010 through new laws that:

- Introduce production sharing contracts (PSCs), as opposed to the concession regime, for new pre-salt blocks and other strategic areas to be defined by the Federal Government;
- Create Pré-Sal Petróleo SA, another governmental controlled entity incorporated especially to represent the Federal Government in PSCs and commercialize its production share;

- Appoint Petrobras as sole and mandatory operator of all new pre-salt blocks; and
- Create the Social National Fund to accumulate and invest profits from PSCs.

Petrobras

In September 2010, Brazil's oil and gas giant Petroleo Brasileiro SA (Petrobras), one of the 10 largest companies in the world according to Forbes' April 2011 ranking, completed the largest capitalization in the history of the world, raising US$70 billion in equity (most of which is allocated to pre-salt exploration and production activities).

Petrobras' 2011–2015 business plan calls for total investment of almost US$225bn. Highlights of the plan include:

- New projects centred around Petrobras's exploration and production business, with the main projects related to the development of the pre-salt and transfer of rights;
- Attempting to double Petrobras' proven reserves; and
- Capital expenditures (financed mainly by operating cash flow and debt, without the need of equity issuances) of between US$7.2 billion and US$12bn per year.

Ninety seven per cent of the funds (US$213.5bn) will go to activities in Brazil and 5 per cent (US$11.2bn) to foreign operations, involving 688 projects in all, 57 per cent of which have already been authorized. The table below shows planned investments by business segment.

Table 34.1 Petrobras 2011–2015 business plan

Segment Investments	2011–2015 Business Plan	per cent
Exploration and Production	US$127.5bn	57 per cent
Refining, Transportation and Marketing	US$70.6bn	31 per cent
Gas & Power	US$13.2bn	6 per cent
Petrochemicals	US$3.8bn	2 per cent
Distribution	US$3.1bn	1 per cent
Biofuels	US$4.1bn	2 per cent

Investments in the Petrobras' refining, transportation and marketing business are estimated at US$70.6bn employing a strategy to expand refining capacity in Brazil. Approximately US$35.4bn will be allocated to expand refining capacity. Additional investments will continue to be made for operational improvements, fleet expansion and logistics (US$17.6bn). Investments in oil product quality (such as lower sulphur content oil), in order to comply with the local legislation, are budgeted at US$16.9bn.

In its petrochemical business, Petrobras expects to invest US$3.8bn and is maintaining a strategy of expanding petrochemical and biopolymer production through shareholdings in petrochemical companies including the implementation of the Suape petrochemical complex in the State of Pernambuco.

Petrobras' gas and power segment plans to invest a total of US$13.2bn. With its first phase gas transportation infrastructure now completed, new investment will be directed at optimizing the market for associated gas, especially from the pre-salt discoveries. Most investments in this segment (approximately US$9bn), are designed to meet the demand for natural gas, including the development of gas-fired thermal power plants and plants for the transformation of natural gas chemicals into fertilizers. The remainder is expected to be allocated primarily to the construction of liquid natural gas (LNG) regasification and natural gas liquefaction/processing terminals.

Table 34.2   Brazilian natural gas projected supply and demand (MMm3/d)

Sources	2011	2015	2020	Demand	2011	2015	2020
Domestic natural gas	55	78	102	Thermal plants: Petrobras + other companies	38	59	76
LNG terminals	21	41	41	Distribution companies	41	53	63
Bolivia	30	30	30	Petrobras: Refineries and fertilizer plants	17	39	61
Total	106	149	173	Total	96	151	200

Petrobras' distribution business will receive US$3.1bn, mainly focussed on logistics to keep up with domestic market growth and meet legal and/or regulatory requirements.

Petrobras' biofuels segment will invest US$4.1bn, of which US$2.8bn will be direct investments through the wholly-owned subsidiary Petrobras Biocombustível (PBIO) and US$1.3bn will be invested in distribution logistics. From the total direct investments, US$1.9bn will be directed to the ethanol production and bio-diesel.

Mining

The National Department of Mineral Production (DNPM) was established in 1934 to regulate minerals and mining.

Brazil's constitution makes all natural resources the property of the Brazilian state. States have title to natural resources related to the water and land unless such is already controlled by the Brazilian state by federal law.

Nevertheless, according to the Mining Code, the exploration and production of minerals in Brazil may be awarded under long-term mining concessions to private companies. Minerals extracted from soil through the awarded mining activities belong to the concessionaire, subject to the payment of royalties to the Federal Government and any required compensation to the owner of the surface property.

Electricity

Brazil is the largest electricity market in South America, with total power consumption more than double that of Argentina, Bolivia, Chile and Uruguay combined.

The Brazilian electricity network consists of one main interconnected power system, comprised of four sub-systems and several smaller, isolated systems in the North. Those four sub-systems (which together account for approximately 98.0 per cent of Brazil's electricity capacity) are interconnected by a network of high voltage transmission lines (the so-called Basic Grid).

Eletrobrás, a state owned company controlled by the Brazilian government, accounts for approximately 50–60 per cent of Brazil's installed capacity and over 60 per cent of transmission lines above 230 kilowatts. Privately controlled companies hold approximately 30 per cent, 29 per cent and 63 per cent of electricity generation, transmission and distribution, respectively, in terms of total capacity.

The Brazilian power industry is comprehensively regulated by the Federal Government, acting through the Ministério de Minas e Energia (Ministry of Mines and Energy or the MME) and the National Agency for Electrical Energy (ANEEL), which have exclusive authority over the industry. An exception to this exclusive authority is the Crisis Committee – CNPE, created in response to the electricity shortage in Brazil and granted extraordinary powers over the electricity sector.

The MME is in charge of developing policy and regulations to organize and regulate the electricity sector and is responsible for coordinating other related ministries as well.

ANEEL was established in 1996. ANEEL's responsibilities include, amongst others, (i) granting and supervising concessions for electricity generation, transmission and distribution, including the approval of the concessionaires' tariffs in case of transmission and distribution concessions, (ii) establishing regulations for the electricity sector, (iii) supervising and auditing the activities of electric power concessionaires, (iv) planning, coordinating and executing water resource studies, (v) implementing and regulating the use of electricity and the use of hydroelectric power, (vi) promoting the bidding process for new concessions, and (vii) determining the criteria for the establishment of the cost of electricity transmission.

ANEEL also has authority to impose penalties for noncompliance with certain legal, regulatory and contractual obligations introduced in 2004.

The Wholesale Energy Chamber (CCEE) was created in August 2004 as a private body subject to ANEEL regulation and supervision. The CCEE is responsible for (i) registering all CCEARs (discussed below), as well as the power and electricity volumes covered by contracts in the free contracting market, (ii) accounting for and organizing the sales of electricity in the spot market, etc., (iii) carrying out electric power auctions in the regulated contracting market, and (iv) imposing penalties for the lack of physical or contractual performance.

Generators are required to demonstrate physical backing in order to sell electricity through bilateral electricity purchase contracts, whether it is produced by them or by third parties. Physical backing is defined by the MME as the maximum electricity and power volume that a generator, including electricity importers, can sell to third parties. Failure to present physical backing (i.e. purchases in the spot market) subjects the generator to sanctions imposed by ANEEL.

In the regulated contracting market, distribution companies purchase power to meet their projected electricity needs for distribution to their captive consumers. Distribution companies can purchase electricity from generators in auctions coordinated by ANEEL and deployed by CCEE. Electricity purchases can only be carried out under two types of bilateral contracts: (1) electricity contracts, used by hydroelectric plants and (2) capacity contracts, used by thermoelectric plants.

Under electricity contracts, a generator agrees to provide a certain volume of electricity and assumes the risk of a possible impairment of supply due to hydrological conditions and low water levels, and other conditions that might discontinue or reduce the supply of electricity. If necessary, the generator agrees to purchase electricity from other parties to meet its supply commitments. Under capacity contracts, a generator agrees to provide a certain capacity to the regulated contracting market distribution companies. In this case, generator revenues are guaranteed by the amount of their stated commitments and possible exposure to financial short-term market risks assumed by distribution companies, thus ensuring supply to end consumers, notwithstanding the penalties to generators for the discontinuation of supply. Jointly, these contracts form CCEARs.

The MME is responsible for defining the volume of electricity to be purchased in the regulated contracting market, as well as a list of the generation projects authorized to participate in the auctions in each year.

In general, by August 1 of each year, all distribution, generation and marketing companies, and Free Consumers must report their demand or electricity generation estimates, as applicable, for the following five-year period to ANEEL. Each distribution company must report to ANEEL the volume of electricity that it intends to contract in an auction within 60 days after each electricity auction.

Electricity Auctions

Distribution companies must have contracts in force for all of their expected electricity demand for the following five years. To accomplish this, distribution companies must purchase electricity from existing or new generation projects in auctions regulated by ANEEL.

Electricity auctions for new generation projects in progress must be held five years prior to the initial delivery date (referred to as A-5 auctions), and three years prior to the initial delivery date (referred to as A-3 auctions). There are also auctions of electricity from existing generation hydroelectric plants carried out one year before the initial delivery date (referred to as A-1 auctions) and approximately four months before the initial delivery date (referred to as adjustment auctions). The auction notices are prepared by ANEEL pursuant to the guidelines set by the MME, including if the highest bid is considered the basis to determine the auction winner. The MME sets the auctions' maximum sales price.

Free Contracting Market

In the free contracting market, electricity sales are freely negotiated by generation companies, independent electricity producers, self-producers, electricity sellers, electricity importers and Free Consumers (discussed below).

Free Consumers

Free Consumers are those whose demand is equal to or above 3 megawatts, at a voltage level equal to or higher than 69 kilowatts. Free Consumers may choose to purchase electricity from the distribution companies to which they are physically connected at regulated tariffs or to purchase electricity directly from independent producers or self-producers with surplus electricity or sellers, at freely negotiated prices.

Power Project Finance

Given their large capital requirements, fairly predictable cash flows and generally well-established sponsors, power generation and transmission projects are usually good candidates for project financing. Whilst currently a net exporter of electricity, some projections indicate Brazil plans to add approximately 5,000MW of installed capacity per year through 2020.

Hydroelectric

Brazil has the largest capacity for water storage in the world and is highly dependent on hydroelectric generation.

Hydroelectric power dominates Brazil's 100,000 plus MW of installed capacity and provides approximately 80 per cent of Brazil's electric power resource.

Some hydroelectric plants under construction or in their final stages of technical studies are amongst the best illustrations of mega projects being developed in Brazil, such as the Belo Monte, Rio Madeira, Teles Pires and Tapajós projects.

Nuclear

Brazil has two nuclear power plants and Eletrobras operates both Angra 1 and Angra 2. In July 2009, Brazil's audit court approved the resumption of construction of the Angra 3 nuclear power plant. BNDES reports it is considering a loan for the project. Construction of Angra 3 is expected to cost approximately US$4bn. It will have a capacity of around 1,400MW and is reported to be completed in 2014.

Thermal

Natural gas-fired power plants are expected to gain a larger share in the Brazilian power generation portfolio, considering the anticipated development of the natural gas market associated with massive pre-salt gas discoveries and other initiatives such as liquified natural gas (LNG) projects.

Despite the preference for environmentally cleaner natural gas, coal-fired stations and fuel oil plants are also being developed. BNDES approved a 17-year loan worth US$585m to local utility MPX Energia for construction of the 350MW Itaqui, a coal-fired power station. Brazilian utility Energias do Brasil, a subsidiary of Energias de Portugal, announced that it had secured a loan of US$412m from BNDES. The loan is financing construction of the Pecern coal-fired power plant located in Ceara state in northeast Brazil.

Wind

Brazil's first wind-energy turbine was installed in Fernando de Noronha Archipelago in 1992. Ten years later, the government created the Programme for Incentive of Alternative Electric Energy Sources (Proinfa) to encourage the use of other renewable sources, such as wind power, biomass and Small Hydroelectric Power Stations (PCHs). Many wind power contracts have been awarded by ANEEL for more than 50 wind park projects in an attempt to bolster Brazil's commitment to renewable energy with awards going to such players as Iberdrola of Spain, Contour Global of the US and Enel of Italy. Many of these projects are seeking project financing.

Electric Transmission and Distribution

In addition to installation of generation capacity, over 40,000km of transmission lines are expected to be built in the near future in Brazil. There are more than 60 electricity distribution companies in Brazil. The country's constitution allocates to the Federal Government the power to carry on directly or delegate distribution of electricity to captive consumers in Brazil. However, many distribution companies were delegated to the federative states many decades ago. As of the early 1990s, many of these companies were being privatized (including Light, Electropaulo and CPFL etc.), although some remain controlled by the state and some appear to be on the slate for future privatization. ANEEL has a programme to auction transmission lines as concessions, many to state-owned power companies. These concessions by their terms will require capital investments.

The national transmission grid operator, Operador Nacional do Sistema Elétrico (ONS), operates the national transmission grid, which consists of two large grids (one in the north and the other in the southeast, interconnected to each other) and many small networks in isolated regions mostly in the North region of Brazil. ONS, created in 1998, is a private, non-profit organization comprised of representatives from customers and private and state-owned companies involved in the electricity generation, transmission and distribution.

ONS uses data provided by generators to order optimal system dispatch. Hydroelectric generators provide ONS with reservoir levels, rate of inflow and turbine-generator availability. The primary role of ONS is to coordinate operation of the interconnected system to (i) achieve appropriate levels of load supply that minimize operating costs, (ii) ensure and maintain adequate reliability levels, and (iii) ensure open access.

The isolated system is located mainly in the Amazon region owing to several geological and environmental reasons which increase the complexity of energy supply for the population in that part of the country. The system in terms of electric power supply is divided into two types: (i) those which supply the regional capitals, in general composed by hydroelectric and thermal power plants, and (ii) those which supply the hinterland, through thermal plants using diesel fuel. Energy production in the isolated system is mainly generated by thermoelectric plants connected directly to the local distribution grid.

The interconnected system comprises regions located in the south, southeast, westcentral and northeast of Brazil. The power rationing that occurred during 2001–2002 could have likely been avoided if transmission capacity between the south (excess supply) and the southeast (severe deficit) had been available. Brazil has an installed capacity in the interconnected power system of more than 134GW, approximately 67 per cent of which is hydroelectric. This installed capacity includes half of the installed capacity of Itaipu, which corresponds to a total of 14,000MW owned equally by Brazil and Paraguay. There are approximately 70,000km of transmission lines with voltages equal to or higher than 230 kilovolts in Brazil. Approximately 38 per cent of Brazil's installed generating capacity and 56 per cent of Brazil's high voltage transmission lines are operated by Eletrobras, a company owned by the Federal Government. Energy traded in the interconnected system is usually generated by (i) hydroelectric plants; (ii) small hydroelectric plants; (iii) thermoelectric plants; (iv) nuclear plants; (v) wind farms; (vi) biomass and cogeneration units; and (vii) solar plants.

Expansion of the Basic Grid is dictated by mandatory planning guidelines issued by the Expansion Committee – CCPE. ANEEL, as an independent regulator, is responsible for conducting the public bidding process for the construction and maintenance of newly added segments of the Basic Grid.

Transmission tariffs are calculated in accordance with a nodal method and tariffs are readjusted annually.

Bidding laws for instalment of and transmission on the Basic Grid, promoted by ANEEL, permit national and foreign companies and private equity owners to participate in the bidding.

Airports

The authority for Brazilian airports (created in 1973) is Empresa Brasileira de Infra Estrutura Aeroportuária (INFRAERO), a state controlled corporation reporting to the High Command of Aeronautics. Of Brazil's more than 3,500 airports some 67 airports are managed by INFRAERO, accounting for more than 90 per cent of air carriage activity in Brazil. In addition, INFRAERO manages some 81 air navigation stations and 32 cargo logistics terminals.

Brazil's PAC II programme envisages an investment of US$1.4bn for the upgrade and expansion of 20 airports. Massive investments, including expansion of the Guarulhos Airport, are paramount given the rapid growth of the air travel market over the last decade and in anticipation of the upcoming FIFA World Cup in 2014 and Olympic Games in 2016. Of this amount, US$470m will be financed by INFRAERO, which also plans to construct eight to 12 regional airports along the northeastern coastline to boost tourism in the region.

Camargo Correa and Andrade Gutierrez have also announced plans to sponsor a new airport in metropolitan São Paulo. Although experts believe there would be sufficient demand for that without putting a damper on the further expansion and renovation of the Congonhas, Guarulhos and Viracopos airports, it is still legally debatable whether a public airport could be delegated under a simple authorization to private parties, as opposed to a concession preceded by public bidding.

Brazil's Applied Economics Research Institute (IPEA) notes that a number of airports in the country are overloaded. The situation is critical at a number of the 2014 FIFA World Cup host cities' airports, many of which are already operating at capacity. The worst over-capacity appears to occur at Manaus International Airport, which reportedly operates at nearly 200 per cent of capacity on occasion. The IPEA report notes that demand for air travel is expected to triple in the next 20 years.

A second report, by consultancy company McKinsey – funded by BNDES – found that investment of US$14–19bn is needed to meet growing demand in the airport sector over the coming 20 years. The need for investment is clear given that air passenger travel is estimated to grow at the 20 largest airports from 111m in 2009 to 312m in 2030, with passenger terminals already saturated at 13 of these airports. In 2009, INFRAERO announced plans to invest Reais5.3bn in preparation for the 2014 FIFA World Cup.

In August 2010, the Brazilian Government completed the first concession of a public airport to a private investor. A consortium led by Engevix and including an Argentine operator was awarded a 25-year contract for the São Gonçalo do Amarante Airport (AGGA), in the State of Rio Grande do Norte, through a bidding procedure where Engevix consortium offered Reais170m as the winning bid. Technical and economic feasibility studies for the potential concession of three major international airports are in advanced stage. The concession model for each airport should be customized, but general terms and conditions should follow the AGGA model.

Roads

Most freight in Brazil is hauled over roads. In 2001, the National Agency for Overland Transport (ANTT) was formed to regulate the national highways and railways.

Although Brazil's transportation is dependent on highways and not railways or waterways, many believe Brazil's highways have received much less investment in recent decades than is necessary for proper maintenance and expansion.

As a result, highways controlled by the government are often poorly maintained and have not been upgraded to handle transportation demands. In contrast, roads have been privatized by the Federal Government, and states such as São Paulo, Rio de Janeiro, Minas Gerais, Rio Grande do Sul, Paraná and Bahia and many of these roads are adequate.

Private concessions have generally been structured as common concessions. Concessionaires earn their revenue solely through tariff (toll) collection, in some cases after having paid a lump-sum amount to the granting authority for the concession award. In 2006, MG-50 in the State of Minas Gerais was the first highway awarded under a PPP concession to a private party and its concessionaire is entitled to receive periodic governmental payments in addition to its tariff collection. The PPP regime is especially well-suited for projects that are not economically self-sustainable from their own toll receipts but which offer important 'externalities' to justify their receiving governmental subsidies.

It is reported that the country's transport infrastructure department, Departamento Nacional de Infraestrutura de Transportes (DNIT), has many investments planned for the near future.

Ports

Brazil has thousands of kilometres of ocean and inland coastlines. In 2001, the National Agency for Water Transportation (ANTAQ) was set up to oversee water transport and ports. There are more than 30 main public ports in Brazil and over 130 privately-operated terminals.

According to IPEA, only US$4.7bn has been invested in Brazil's 37 publicly owned ports in the past 10 years. In light of this, it is no surprise that the country's ports are said to be underdeveloped.

Brazil's port infrastructure is ranked 127 out of 133 countries in the World Economic Forum's '2010 Global Competitiveness Report'. ANTAQ is forecasting total throughput at the country's ports to reach 1.2bn tons a year by 2013. To meet growing demand, private sector investments will be required in addition to government spending. According to a report by IPEA, Brazil's ports are in need of US$23.4bn to upgrade capacity and meet significant long-term growth forecast for the sector to bring it up to standard, including upgrading existing facilities and new port projects. New ports, however, are not the main focus of investment needs, with the IPEA noting that just 9 per cent of the recommended amount should go to new projects. The remainder should be invested in upgrading infrastructure at existing ports.

Under the Ports Law passed in 1993 and supplemented by Law 10,233 of 2001, the same law that created ANTAQ, there are two main types of ports in Brazil: (i) public ports, managed by a port authority (under a concession from the Federal Government) and which may contain several terminals leased to private parties after a mandatory bidding procedure, and (ii) private terminals, developed by private investors under an authorization regime, which terminals are usually divided in private terminals for exclusive use (handling solely their own cargo) or for mixed use (handling their own cargo and providing services to third parties as well).

Until 2008, ANTAQ issued authorizations for mixed use private terminals without requiring minimum owned cargo volumes. Under this regime, key private terminals have been developed to address the growing demand for port capacity, including container terminals such as Portonave, Embraport and Itapoá.

However, ABRATEC, an association of private parties leasing public terminals in Brazil, filed in early 2008 a constitutional lawsuit against ANTAQ, arguing that it would be unconstitutional for ANTAQ to authorize private investors to handle substantial volumes of third party cargo in private terminals, especially those designed for containers, without complying with the legal regime adopted for public service concessions, including a mandatory prior bidding procedure.

Although ABRATEC's lawsuit is still pending decision on its merits by the Brazilian Supreme Court, Decree 6,620 of 2008 changed the criteria for granting new private terminal authorizations and it now requires that mixed use private terminals present major 'owned' cargo volumes, capable of justifying, by themselves, from both a technical and an economic perspective, the development and operation of the terminal. Accordingly, third party cargo may only be handled on an ancillary and sporadic basis.

Under the new regime, mixed use private terminals have been severely restricted, and no new private terminals for containers have been developed. The unresolved constitutional lawsuit adds uncertainty to the future of mixed use private terminals.

Nevertheless, Decree 6,620 has encouraged the concession of new public ports to private parties, as an alternative for the governmental controlled port authorities that manage most of the public terminals in Brazil (Codesp, Companhia Docas do Rio de Janeiro, Codeba, etc). However, to date, no concession has been accomplished as a result of the inherent difficulties experienced by the Federal Government in carrying out feasibility and modelling studies required to launch a concession bidding.

Therefore, better description of the role to be played by private investors in both private and public terminals will be crucial to creating a favourable environment for investments.

Rail

Brazil has fewer than 30,000km of railways, of which only around 1,600km are electrified. Despite on-going investment into the railways, some projects fell victim to the global downturn in 2009. Two projects that have been impacted are the US$1.5bn tenders for the concessions of the southern stretch of the 1,500km North-South railway and the 1,504km East-West railway. The Federal Government has postponed launching these tenders.

Also in jeopardy may be the proposed high-speed bullet train between São Paulo and Rio de Janeiro. Halcrow, the UK company contracted to carry out the feasibility study, noted to the Brazilian transport ministry that the project will cost at least US$15bn, and that in the worst case scenario costs could exceed US$20bn. The report noted that without the government's help, the project would likely not be feasible. Accordingly, the project was planned to be executed under a concession model, subject to the mandatory equity participation of a governmental controlled entity, which would contribute pro rata to the funding of the project. Additionally, the concessionaire could count upon a huge credit line from BNDES, which has committed to finance at least 60 per cent of the project's total cost, equal to (US$11.8bn). The loan would be repayable over a 30-year period, starting six months after the train becomes operational. However, in the latest tender round no bids were received, which has prompted the Federal Government to review its concession model. The Federal Government intends to review its concession model for railway services focussed on both cargo and passenger transportation. Instead of concentrating infrastructure construction, operation and transportation services within the same single concessionaire, the new model contemplates two separate concessions: one for construction and operation of the infrastructure itself and another solely for investment in rolling stock and provision of transportation services. The Federal Government believes the new model will be more attractive for investors because they will be able to focus on their particular areas of expertise and assume only the risks with which they are comfortable and prepared to assume, without being forced to become part of a consortium. It also is expected to offer more transparent and effective conditions for free access by different carriers to the same railway infrastructure.

Urban Infrastructure

The Cities Ministry of Brazil announced that the Government is prepared to invest US$ 2.4bn in over 100 sanitation projects. The projects, forming a part of PAC II, are to be carried out in 90 municipalities. Cities minister Maucio Fortes said US$1.6bn will be used to finance sewerage projects and US$800m will be spent on potable water projects with US$426.67m provided by state and city governments. The remaining US$1.97bn will be contributed by the country's federal unemployment insurance fund and the workers support fund.

A US$4.3bn tender for a gigantic urban renovation PPP in the old port area of Rio de Janeiro (Porto Maravilha) was awarded in October 2010 under a novel structure that combines a PPP with issuance of CEPACs (a negotiable instrument granting its holder the right to construct above the general limitations set forth by local urban laws). This represents an important step towards greater private procurement of public projects in the country. As Rio de Janeiro's first PPP and Brazil's largest PPP, the successful development of the project will help encourage further private sector involvement in public projects. In March 2011, the CEPACs were successfully auctioned and raised sufficient funds to secure project completion without requiring municipal expenditures or indebtedness.

Hotels

The 2014 World Cup will require massive expansion of hotel capacity in host cities. Marriott International has announced plans to increase its number of hotels in Brazil from four to more than 50. The company reports that it will develop 50 of its Fairfield brand hotels in the country in cooperation with Rio-based developer PDG Realty SA Empreendimentos & Participacoes.

Outbound Investment

In recent years, many large Brazilian companies have focussed aggressively on international expansion through acquisitions and by developing new projects. For instance, in 2007, mining giant Vale SA initially developed a coal mining capability through acquisition of Australian mining company AMCI Holdings. It has since expanded its capabilities through development of the Moatize coal mining project in Mozambique, which commenced operations in May 2011 and will constitute a 150 per cent increase in Vale SA's total worldwide coal production.

Whilst the Moatize coal project was not developed on a project-finance limited recourse basis, there is increasing interest by Vale SA and other Brazilian companies in developing international projects using limited recourse financing. For instance, the Camargo Corrêa conglomerate is pursuing development of the US$2bn Mphanda Nkuwa hydropower project in Mozambique on a limited recourse basis.

Brazil and the Tenets of Project Finance

Although Brazil's economic stability might not yet be free from local risks and thereby necessitate higher profit return expectations for international investors and financiers, Brazil's legal infrastructure can support even the most ambitious project financings.

Inbound Capital

There are no restrictions on capital flowing into Brazil in any sector although foreign exchange transactions must be conducted only through authorized Brazilian agents. Registration of inbound investments in any currency must be registered in the foreign loan registry system of the Central Bank (SISBACEN) in the case of loans or other debt transactions in excess of six months and the foreign registry of direct investment run by SISBACEN in the case of equity investments. (The Central Bank, however, will not register credit transactions providing for interest payments that are excessive compared to market practices). Foreign currency cannot be legally used for payments in Brazil and, therefore, must be converted into Reais. Brazilian entities are usually not allowed to hold local foreign currency accounts, but they are allowed to access the foreign exchange market to make investments abroad or to pay for imports.

As an exception to the general rule, companies engaged in the development of energy projects, such as electric power infrastructure (generation, transmission) and oil and gas exploration, production and transportation, are allowed to hold foreign currency denominated bank accounts in Brazil. The funds in deposit into such accounts must be used exclusively to service cross-border foreign currency financing incurred in connection with the construction or expansion of the project, although they may be invested offshore pending maturity of the indebtedness intended to be serviced.

Hedging

Hedging of commodity prices, currencies and interest rates are all permitted and liquid local markets generally exist for all these arrangements. Long-term foreign exchange hedgings tend to be very expensive, however.

Return and Repatriation of Capital

There are no restrictions on the return of debt or equity capital (and no taxes on dividends), which may be repatriated in foreign currency or Reais. Various withholding taxes apply as noted in the chart below although Brazil has tax treaties with Argentina, Austria, Belgium, Canada, Chile, China, Czech Republic, Denmark, Ecuador, Finland, France, Hungary, India, Israel, Italy, Japan, Korea, Luxembourg, Mexico, the Netherlands, Norway, the Philippines, Portugal, the Slovak Republic, South Africa, Spain, Sweden and Ukraine amongst others to reduce these taxes. Except for dividends, which are currently exempt from withholding income tax, most income paid by Brazilian sources to foreign creditors or investors (including capital gains) are subject to withholding income tax at rates that vary between 15 per cent and 25 per cent, depending on the type of income and on the jurisdiction where the payee is located.

Importing Equipment and Materials

An import licence must be obtained for certain types of goods as can be determined from the Internal Revenue Services system SISCOMEX. Various incentives and programmes exist for importation of equipment and materials regarding value added sales (the so-called ICMS, subject to the laws of each federative state) and import, excise tax 'IPI', PIS and Cofins contributions, as illustrated below.

Table 34.3   Importing equipment and materials

Type of Incentive	Nature of Incentive
Ex – tarifário	Reduction of Import Tax
Drawback	Suspension of all taxes
Repetro	Suspension/exemption of taxes on oil related equipment

Importing Services

Services are assessed a municipal value added tax (ISS) that may vary from 2 per cent to 5 per cent, as well as PIS and COFINS contributions. Payments are also subject to withholding income tax at a rate of 15 per cent or 25 per cent. Technical services are subject to a 15 per cent withholding income tax (to the extent that the service provider is not located in a low tax jurisdiction as defined under Brazilian laws), but an additional 10 per cent CIDE contribution is also applicable.

Visas for Skilled Workers

Visas are typically available for professionals and skilled workers on both a short and long term basis upon application to the Ministry of Labour and Employment. Expatriates living in Brazil are subject to a worldwide federal income taxation. However, taxes levied by a foreign jurisdiction on income produced in its territory are usually deductible as tax credits in Brazil so long as such other jurisdiction maintains a tax treaty with Brazil or extends reciprocal treatment to Brazilian expatriates.

Visas for Unskilled Workers

Visas for unskilled workers (especially in large numbers) may be more difficult to obtain than those for skilled workers. Generally, they only are granted on an exceptional basis and for relatively short duration. They are more likely to be granted in cases where a project sponsor or contractor requires its personnel to speak the language of its home country in order to be able to carry out proper procedures, standards or quality control to ensure safety and mechanical integrity. Sponsors are generally responsible for the welfare and exit from Brazil of visa holders.

Minimum Brazilian Content

Other than as may be mandated under a particular concession or contractual agreement (such as in the case of oil and gas exploration and production concessions, where local content requirements must be satisfied by the concessionaire), there are no requirements that products or services used or rendered in Brazil be sourced from Brazil.

Technology Transfer

Agreements involving transfer of technology into Brazil must be registered with the INPI (the Brazilian intellectual property agency) as a condition for the remittance of any payments abroad. In general, these contracts are restricted to a five-year term, under the assumption that this should allow sufficient time for the recipient of the technology to absorb it.

Intellectual Property

Intellectual property may be protected and licenced in, to, or from Brazil in a manner that generally protects its owner or originator.

Local Financing

Local financing (whilst generally expensive and of relatively short tenor) is not restricted in any way other than that it must be lent in Reais and repaid in Reais.

Taxation Depreciation of Capital Investments

Investments in fixed assets may be depreciated generally according to Table 34.4.

Table 34.4   Taxation depreciation

Asset Class	Depreciable Life/Treatment
Buildings and fixtures	25 years
Vehicles	5 years
Assets in general	10 years

Accounting

Publicly listed companies are required to keep audited books and state their financial condition according to International Financial Reporting Standards (IFRS).

Taxes

Real estate owners are subject to real estate taxes unless granted a specific federal or local governmental exemption. Individuals and companies are subject to federal income tax. Consortia and branches are not subject to income tax. All entities are subject to employment, social security, payroll and similar taxes as well as value added and sales taxes. Foreign investors may choose without restriction to conduct their business through any of the foregoing entities. There are no stamp taxes in Brazil.

Project Entities

Entities that own projects are most typically corporations given their governance and liability protections for investors but other forms can be employed as well.

Sanctity of Contractual Arrangements

Parties to contracts in Brazil are generally free to agree upon terms they desire irrespective of the place of incorporation or the domicile of the parties. Provisions typically called for in an international financing such as New York or English governing law, international arbitration and waiver of sovereign immunity are all enforceable other than in very limited situations. For contracts governed by Brazilian law, liquidated damages for delay or performance, warranty repair provisions, waivers of consequential damages, and indemnification coverage can all be expected to be respected by Brazilian courts if properly draughted. Step-in rights for lenders to take possession of property to operate it are typically seen (but not so typically used) in project finance and are not prohibited under Brazilian law. Nevertheless, certain 'self-help' remedies are illegal: for instance, a secured party is not allowed to keep and retain its collateral for itself, in payment of its credit, unless specifically agreed by the debtor at the time of the debtor's default. In general, secured parties are expected to sell their collateral through private or judicial auctions, applying the proceeds therefrom to the satisfaction of their loans and returning to the debtor any excess.

Arbitration and Brazilian Law

Brazil is not party to any bilateral or regional investment treaties, and is not a signatory to the 1966 Convention on the Settlement of Investment Disputes between States and Nationals of Other States (the ICSID Convention). Foreign investors, therefore, do not have the protection accorded by such international investment treaties and may not submit investment related disputes to arbitration before an ICSID arbitral tribunal.

Commercial disputes between private parties or between private parties and the State may be resolved through arbitration. Whilst there has been some controversy within the legal community regarding the use of arbitration to resolve disputes involving public contracts, recent court decisions by the Brazilian Superior Court of Justice (STJ) notably, CEEE v AES Uruguaiana Emp Ltd and TMC Terminal Multimodal de Coroa Grande v Ministry of Science and Technology have held that public bodies must comply with arbitration clauses.

Brazil is a member of the 1958 Convention on the Recognition and Enforcement of Foreign Arbitral Awards (the New York Convention) and of the 1975 Inter American Convention on International Commercial Arbitration (the Panama Convention). These treaties generally obligate Brazil to recognize and enforce foreign arbitration agreements and foreign arbitration awards, subject to certain limited exceptions.

In keeping with its international obligations, Brazilian courts typically will enforce foreign arbitral awards, provided they comply with the conditions set forth in the Brazilian Arbitration Law and they do not offend the Brazilian public order, sovereignty or morals. In addition, foreign arbitration awards must be homologated by the STJ, a process by which the court approves and confirms the award. Once the foreign arbitration award is confirmed by the STJ, the judgment creditor is entitled to enforce the award in Brazil through Brazilian courts. Generally speaking, Brazilian courts appear to have a good track record for enforcing arbitration awards. However, Brazil's current arbitration law is relatively new and Brazilian courts have not yet addressed a number of important issues affecting the interpretation of arbitration agreements and enforcement of arbitration awards.

Brazil has adopted a commonly held view that arbitration is an alternative form of dispute resolution and that parties may not be subjected or required to arbitrate without their consent. Nevertheless, once parties have agreed to resolve their dispute through arbitration, that agreement is considered binding and irrevocable.

Under Brazilian law, parties are free generally to choose the rules that will govern an arbitration and may use an international arbitral institution (e.g., the International Chamber of Commerce) as an administering body. The rules of arbitration may not violate Brazil's public policy, including its general principles of law, custom and usage and international commercial rules. In fact, STJ has suggested that it may refuse to enforce an award if that arbitral tribunal does not articulate the reasons for its decision in the award.

Outside the context of the commercial arbitration, Brazilian courts will uphold the choice of a foreign law and/or courts unless it contravenes Brazilian governmental or public policy interests or fails to meet the perfunctory requirements of Brazilian law.

Real Estate and Title Insurance

Title to real estate and related rights must be recorded to be valid. Title insurance for real estate rights is not available in Brazil.

Mortgages

Mortgages over real property and easements can be obtained by lenders upon compliance with registration procedures of the applicable real estate registry. Mortgages generally can be foreclosed upon in a public sale without undue delay if properly documented and registered (with the payment of filing fees based upon the amount secured).

Pledges

Financiers can obtain liens on their borrowers' personal and intangible property in a manner that should be acceptable to most project finance lenders without undue burden by means of executing a security agreement (and making proper filings with the registry of titles and deeds, real estate registry and/or corporate books of the borrower in the case of stock) to secure their priority. In addition to the pledge itself (penhor), recent Brazilian laws have permitted a broader use of fiduciary securities (alienação fiduciária or cessão fiduciária) for real estate assets and rights. These fiduciary securities offer a more favourable treatment for the secured party in case of bankruptcy, because, unlike the pledge, they are not subject to any mandatorily preferred obligations (nor is their collateral incorporated into the bankruptcy estate of the debtor).

Priority in Collateral

A lender's priority in its collateral is established by its time of filing in the case of mortgages and pledges or can be established by contractual arrangements agreed between the secured party and all the creditors who have a secured interest in the collateral. Priority is not difficult to determine by searching with the applicable real estate registry. The Real

Estate Registry and Registry of Title and Deeds with jurisdiction over the place where the property is located or where the owner thereof is headquartered (or both) are able to issue, upon request, certificates as to any liens on particular property after a search they perform.

Trustees

Trustees, as such, are not contemplated under Brazilian law. The convention of a "security trustee" which acts for secured parties in order to hold collateral had developed, but its powers have to be specifically delineated.

Bankruptcy

Once a court has ordered a bankruptcy proceeding, no party is able to continue any claim against the debtor outside of the bankruptcy case. Unfortunately, claims in foreign currency are converted into Reais at the exchange rate on the date the court orders the bankruptcy proceeding commenced. In the case of a reorganization (as opposed to a liquidation) once the court has approved a plan, it is binding on all creditors although the collateral of any secured party cannot be sold or affected without its approval.

Governmental entities are not covered under bankruptcy laws.

Insurance

Construction, liability and property insurance are all available in Brazil but must be purchased from local insurers unless they do not offer the coverage in question. 'Cut through' provisions for insureds directly to off-shore re-insurers' proceeds are usually not permitted.

Political Risk Insurance

There are no restrictions on the right for investors or lenders to obtain political risk insurance for their activities in Brazil.

Lender Liability

There are no known precedents of environmental liability being imposed on project finance lenders in Brazil, but there is a growing trend, already supported by decision of the SCJ, holding that project finance lenders may be held liable for environmental damages caused by the projects financed by them, especially if such lenders fail to carry out proper due diligence and to require environmental compliance by their borrowers. Aware of such trends, most Brazilian banks active in the project finance industry have adopted and apply the Equator Principles to their lending practices. Rules have been introduced by the National Environmental Policy which provide that governmental financing must condition their approval of projects on environmental licensing and fulfilment of the rules, criteria and standards of CONAMA (the Conselho Nacional de Meio Ambiente, Brazil's environmental agency).

Conclusion

Some still may claim that Brazil continues to be the country of the future and not today. However, given Brazil's staggering infrastructure need, the apparent availability of capital for prudently structured projects and the attractive returns which may need to be offered to bear what may be somewhat heightened economic risk compared to other jurisdictions, project finance may finally be the discipline that can refute that ominous placard and deliver Brazil across the threshold.

4 Case Studies

Top Ten Case Studies

Project finance is all about deals and how they are transacted and structured. Some project financings take years of painstaking contractual, legal and financial work to put together. Here is a selection of 10 leading project financings from around the world. All these case studies were first published in the pages of Thomson Reuters Project Finance International (PFI), the leading global source of project finance information.

CASE STUDY

Nord Stream – It's done!
PFI Global Energy Report 2010

*The €3.9bn debt for the €5.5bn phase one of the Nord Stream gas pipeline
project reached financial close in April after 18 months in the market.*

MARK KOLMAR

The debt financing was the last pre-construction stage of the project that took its current form in late 2006 as the culmination of ideas for a north-European scheme that has been mooted since the start of the century.

The principle of the project is provide an export route for Russian gas to the European Union that bypasses Eastern European transit countries. The pipe will run from Russia's Baltic coastline at Vyborg, through the Baltic sea to Germany at Greifswald. The Nord Stream project company is led by Gazprom, which holds 51 per cent, and also comprises BASF's Wintershall (20 per cent), E.ON Ruhrgas (20 per cent), and Gasunie (9 per cent). GDF Suez is in the process of acquiring a 9 per cent stake, bringing the two German firms' stakes down to 15.5 per cent each.

The entire two-phase project envisages 1,220km of two parallel pipes transporting a combined 55bcm of gas. The project has a total capex of €7.4bn, and a total project cost of nearly €9bn. It is scheduled to be completed in 2012.

Connections at each end are provided by Gazprom building a 917km onshore connection to the Russian transmission system, and Wintershall/Gazprom subsidiary WINGAS and E.ON Ruhrgas building two onshore connections in Germany totalling 850km. The first pipe carrying half the gas is scheduled to be completed in 2011, and is the portion financed by the 2010 loan package.

The €3.9bn of loans covering 70 per cent of the phase one total cost was split 80:20 between ECA-covered and uncovered commercial tranches. The ECA tranches, all for 16 years, were €1.6bn, 95 per cent covered by Hermes, priced at 160bp; €1bn, 90 per cent covered by UFK, priced at 180bp; and €500m, 100 per cent covered by Sace, priced at 165bp. Fees were 65bp–75bp on all tranches. The uncovered tranche was €800m for 10 years, priced at 275bp pre-completion, then at 430bp, rising to 450bp at seven years. Fees were 110bp. The sponsors are providing construction completion guarantees.

The commercial banks on the uncovered tranche were BBVA, Bank of Tokyo-Mitsubishi UFJ, BayernLB, BNP Paribas, Caja Madrid, Commerzbank (financial adviser and Hermes agent), Credit Agricole (documentation bank), Credit Suisse, Deutsche, Dexia, DZ Bank, Espirito Santo, Fortis, ING, Intesa Sanpaolo, KfW Ipex, Mediobanca, Natixis, Nordea, Raiffeisen Zentralbank Oesterreich, Royal Bank of Scotland (financial adviser), Société Générale (financial adviser, Sace and intercreditor bank), Standard Bank, SMBC (technical and environmental bank), UniCredit (UFK agent) and WestLB.

The sponsor company wanted a minimum 50 per cent of the €3.9bn deal swapped, and hoped for 80 per cent. Banks were asked to bid on the basis of a set spread, between 10bp and 15bp, and once this position was covered banks that bid higher were allowed to bid again at the established price. The full 80 per cent swap target was allocated. The swaps do not benefit from the export credit cover.

The project's revenues are set out in the gas transportation agreement with Gazprom export. Gazprom export has complete responsibility for putting the gas through the pipeline, with the project company required solely to make the pipe available. The project company is subject to no volume risk or price risk on the gas.

The availability payment comprises a debt service allocation, an operating cost allocation, and a fixed return. The debt service and operating cost allocations are recalculated annually. Coverage ratios for the loans are quite low at ×1.25– ×1.3, but are robust due to protection of revenues built into the gas transportation agreement's availability payments. This also avoided any suggestion of the sponsors guaranteeing the ratios themselves.

A critical issue throughout the financing process was the country risk, and whether an offshore account structure could be used to mitigate this. The potential for banks hitting Russian exposure limits was avoided by the ECAs covering 80 per cent of the debt, but when the deal was presented to banks many were still keen for an offshore structure to protect against the reliance on Gazprom.

Swiss-based project company Nord Stream has solely European accounts, but with the payments coming directly from Gazprom export this makes little difference from a lender protection perspective. A truly offshore structure would have seen buyers of the gas paying Gazprom export separate payments for the fuel itself and for transportation, with a percentage of proceeds hived off to a separate offshore entity to pay the project company. This proved difficult, however, with strict Russian restrictions against revenues from gas sales being channelled out of the country.

With the offshore structure ruled out, lenders had to content themselves with the protection offered by 80 per cent multilateral cover, and sought a higher pricing to account for the Gazprom risk that remained. Banks had first been approached with pricing in the 250bp–300bp range on the uncovered tranche, and 150bp–200bp on the ECA tranches.

Inevitably for a project put together in late 2008 and 2009, the credit crisis stamped its mark on the financing. Whilst an early 2008 deal for a project with strong revenues would probably have seen a handful of mandated lead arrangers and quick progress towards financial close, times of high liquidity were gone by the time the project was ready, meaning a huge club deal and accordingly slow-moving process.

Financial advisers Royal Bank of Scotland, Dresdner Kleinwort (pre-Commerzbank rebranding), and Société Générale started sounding banks in January 2009 on a 14-year deal. ECA involvement of some level was already expected, as ECAs had been approached much earlier. When feedback from banks came in in February, the long-term exposure to Gazprom was raised as an issue, with talk of an offshore account structure to avoid it allowing a bank group to be together by May.

As the middle of the year approached with no resolution, a July launch to market was targeted, with suggestions that the tenor could be as high as 17 years. Gazprom was keen to extend the tenor as much as possible, as a longer tenor would lower the amount of the availability payment Gazprom export would need to pay the project company.

The debt was launched to banks in August, with the final structure regarding ECA levels, tenor and onshore accounts emerging for the first time. The ECA-covered portion was set at 80 per cent to protect banks against Russian exposure limits and Gazprom risk, and these tranches had the tenor upped to 16 years to satisfy Gazprom, whilst allowing the 20 per cent of uncovered commercial loan to drop to 10 years to reassure lenders.

Banks were asked to bid on pricing and fees, and given a bid deadline of October 9. Bank meetings in September saw banks disappointed with the onshore account structure, but happy with an indicative model pricing of 175bp and 400bp–450bp on the sweet and sour portions respectively.

The adjusted tenor also compared favourably with other oil and gas mega projects that many desks were looking at at the same time – the Oil Search/ExxonMobil/Santos LNG project in Papua New Guinea that was looking for US$1bn–$3bn of 15-year commercial debt, and the Saudi Jubail refinery that was looking for US$1.4bn of 16-year commercial debt.

With the October 9 commitment date set, sponsors were looking to close by the end of November. Whilst most lenders considered this ambitious, the strong political will behind the project was expected to see the deal done by the end of the year.

The sheer number of banks involved delayed commitments slightly, with €6bn worth of bids coming in. A final term sheet with pricing details was sent to banks in early November, and within a fortnight a 26-strong bank group was in place with the sponsors still hoping for a 2009 close, setting December 15 as signing day.

Final documentation work did not progress sufficiently quickly, however, and the date for final documents to be sent out was revised once to December 23, and then again to mid-February, with an early March close hoped for. The deal eventually was signed in March, before swaps were placed and a full financial close the following month.

The €3.9bn total finances only the first phase of the project, with banks to be asked for a further €2.5bn for the second pipe. Phase two is cheaper, thanks to phase one encompassing both work preparing the route, including landfall in Germany and Russia, and laying of the first pipe, whereas the second phase is just laying the second pipe along the already prepared route.

With phase two an integral part of the project, rather than merely a potential add-on, the phase one financing is structured with the phase two financing in mind. Given that the sponsors are providing completion guarantees, and construction of the two pipes is staggered, Nord Stream needs to be able to source additional financing from lenders that will remain recourse to the sponsors as guarantees fall away on the phase on the financing.

Technical analysis puts the risk of phase two construction work interfering with phase one as minimal. Although parallel, the two pipes are a few hundred metres apart. The major contracts on the project have been let to Saipem (pipe-laying), Europipe (75 per cent of the pipes), OMK (25 per cent of the pipes) and Eupec (concrete weighting on the pipes).

CASE STUDY

YLNG Goes the Distance
PFI Global Energy Report 2008

Major energy projects take time to put together, and Yemen LNG has taken longer than most. To get to financial close, the scheme and its backers have had to overcome some very large hurdles. But the challenges have been met and Yemen has its deal.

ROD MORRISON

The Yemen LNG scheme's history goes well back into the early 1990s when the liquefied natural gas market was a niche business dominated by just a few buyers and producers. Even the Qataris had not started building their plants when Yemen LNG (YLNG) was first mooted.

Looking back into Project Finance International's files, one is reminded that Enron was selected as the government's first partner on the scheme in 1993 after a battle with Hunt Oil. This was during the time of a civil war between North and South Yemen. When the war ended and the two parts of the country were united, Total emerged between the two American companies in 1995 to become the government's partner.

Credit Suisse was appointed financial adviser in 1997, by which time Turkey's Botas had been signed up as the 50 per cent offtaker. Hunt and Exxon, which held rights over the Marib oil and gas Block 18, were signed up to take care of the upstream gas supply in the north whilst Total would be responsible for the downstream LNG terminal at Balhaf in the south.

But this scheme failed to progress. Asian buyers became less active in the LNG market and Botas, awash with gas, disappeared. It took another decade before the scheme seriously came back into the reckoning.

Perhaps the key to YLNG's return was the Korean Gas Company (Kogas) tender for a 2mtpa contract in late 2004. YLNG obviously decided to bid hard and easily beat Australia LNG, Sakhalin 2, NIOC LNG and Malaysia LNG. When YLNG won the deal, Kogas announced that the prices would be US$3.80 to US$4.20/mmbtu, some 35 per cent to 40 per cent cheaper than its existing contracts. In addition, there were various flexibilities built into the 20-year sales and purchase agreements (SPAs), such as assignment to other South Korean companies and a winter/summer buy split.

The Kogas bedrock contract was then combined with two deals with US buyers, linked to Henry Hub gas prices. Suez signed up for 2.55mtpa and Total took the rest of the 6.7mtpa scheme. The specification had been changed to allow for this Asian/US mix of buyers but the gas calorific value (GCV) wanted by Asian buyers is higher than that of US buyers.

The YLNG plant was therefore designed in the middle of the requirement of the two markets at 1,050btu/scf. This put the scheme in a good position when the Kogas deal came out to put the rest of the volumes to tender in the US. The Kogas and Suez deals are free on board (FOB) at Balhaf whilst the Total contract is ex-ship to specified ports in the US, including Sabine Pass.

Citigroup was appointed the financial adviser in early 2005. By that time, Exxon had left the scheme as another hurdle had emerged. Just as the YLNG scheme was coming together again, the Yemeni government fell out with Hunt and Exxon. In 2004, the Block 18 licence to the two US companies was extended for five years but very soon after the government took the field over.

The issue is still in the international courts, with Hunt and Exxon demanding US$2.9bn and the government demanding US$8bn from the two US companies. Despite the dispute, Hunt remains an important sponsor in scheme – although early last year there were rumours that it was selling out to China's CNOOC.

The issue over Block 18, however, had an important consequence for the scheme's project financing. It would be delayed. New upstream arrangements had to be put in place to ensure the gas would get from the Marib to Balhaf. These arrangements would have to satisfy non-recourse lenders but Total, as the lead sponsor, took a more flexible view and simply started building the project through an EPC with JGC, Technip and KBR.

The upstream side was put in the hands of Yemeni state-owned company Safer Exploration and Production Company. A three-part agreement was signed between Safer and YLNG that includes assistance from YLNG shareholders to Safer. The government, under the gas sales agreement (GSA) that was ratified by the Yemeni parliament, has committed to supply 9tcf to YLNG.

This could mean other gas has to be diverted, perhaps from gas injection needed on oil fields, to YLNG if the Marib field cannot produce the required amounts. Total has some potential gas at Block 69 in the Marib in joint venture with CNOOC which, in addition, could be utilized.

The LNG scheme has been controversial locally, with calls for the gas to be used for domestic use. However, YLNG could bring up to US$20bn into the country over the next 20 years. And 1tcf at Marib has been earmarked for local use.

Citi launched the deal to the project finance market at its Canary Wharf offices in March 2005, before the Hunt/Exxon issue arose. The US$3bn plan was fairly detailed apart from one ingredient. As PFI said at the time: "Where will the debt come from?" No banks had credit lines for Yemen. No international capital market deals had been done in the country. So YLNG, as an entré into the global capital markets for Yemen, was a big splash.

Political risk was perceived as high, particularly after incidents such as the USS Cole incident and tourist kidnappings. Citi said that the export credit agency (ECA) component would be capped at US$1.5bn within the US$1.8bn of debt needed in total under a 60/40 debt equity split. The question, therefore, was how much uncovered debt would be provided by the banks. At that time, maximizing the uncovered portion through a secured project financing was part of the adviser's role. Once the EPC contractor was identified, five ECAs were bought in – Coface, Opic, JBIC/Nexi, Kexim and Exim. Calyon was hired to advise the ECAs.

The scheme did not re-emerge in the lending market until summer 2007 – by which time new factors were rearing their heads, the EPC crunch and the credit crunch. The project was now costed at US$5bn with the EPC set to cost US$4bn. The cost increase was covered, however, by the YLNG sponsors. Total put a US$1.1bn shareholder loan into the package and the debt equity split on the scheme remained at 60/40.

The impact of the credit crunch was still not being fully felt when banks responded to the request for expressions of interest from Citi in June 2007 with pre-crunch style bids, but by the time the request for proposals (RFP), based on the EoI feedback, went out in January 2008, the credit crunch was starting to hit the loan market.

Seven mandated lead arrangers (MLAs) were attracted into underwriting the deal, plus one more on the Total loan. Syndication of the deal began in late March, by which time the full effects of the crunch were hitting home, post-Bear Stearns. As a result, the deal did not sell that well in syndication and had to be slightly reduced in size – by US$100m to US$648m on the uncovered tranche.

Total, however, stuck to its guns and kept most aspects of the deal it had put together. Pascal Breant, Total's corporate finance manager for the Middle East and chairman of the YLNG Finance Committee summed up the French company's attitude by saying: "Margins are acceptable in the context of a first in Yemen, and in these market conditions" and added "what helped a lot is that we did not want to push the envelope too far in terms of structuring, so it's a classic project financing typical of the Middle East and LNG business."

The discussion of the deal in the bank market has mainly focussed on pricing – 165bp to 210bp on the uncovered commercial loan with 115bp to 145bp fees. This says something for the project itself, particularly given its location. Under normal circumstances one would have expected a good deal of discussion about the word 'Yemen' – as there was at the initial Citi briefing in spring 2005.

However, by March 2008 many banks were simply focussing on the margins. Because the deal is in Yemen, banks wanted much higher margins in relation to the risk weightings and margins on other deals in less exotic countries. "They could have had a much more successful syndication but Total has always been mean on margins," said one French banker.

Perhaps some banks hid behind the margins as an excuse and really did not want a Yemeni deal. But Total is a good sponsor in a market now dominated by the need for good sponsors. It is interesting that fellow French sponsor Suez makes a point of having successful banking deals, even if it means putting extreme pressure on its banks.

Total, in the past, has not favoured using project finance and can hardly be described as a serial user of the technique. But Breant says that YLNG will be the first in a pipeline of deals. Royal Bank of Scotland has just been appointed to advise on the refinancing of the US$4bn Dolphin gas pipeline from Qatar to the Emirates. Total has one-third stake in the scheme, which is now built and operating. One could say Total has sent a clear message to the market – although banks that follow Total closely already had that message.

There is another important aspect to pricing questions – export credit agency tranche pricing. Pre-crunch, ECA tranche pricing was below 20bp, or even less. Post-crunch, the risk weighting on these tranches has not changed but the cost of funds of the banks funding them has altered dramatically. Even Double A banks have been struggling to raise funds below 70bp–80bp at times.

Therefore, ECA pricing has simply had to jump. On YLNG, the ECA margins reached 35bp to 40bp with 25bp fees, but even this was not really enough. On the latest ECA-linked LNG deal in the market, the US$800m Angola LNG ship deal, the ECA tranche margins have reached a more attractive 70bp.

And one final point on pricing – the Total guaranteed shareholder loan came in at around 40bp to 45bp. This was decent enough for a credit such as Total, but unfortunately not quite high enough. One MLA, Bank of Tokyo Mitsubishi, took a large allocation of this tranche – assuming that the French banks would join later. But they didn't. Interestingly, BOTM's actions can be contrasted with those of fellow Japanese bank Mizuho. It felt the need to join the deal in syndication to retain good relations with Total, but found few others had a similar view and only took a token amount.

In the final analysis, discussions concerning political risk on the deal did not feature that highly on their own, although some internal events during syndication did cause some nervousness. As said, the discussion was more along on the lines of "this is Yemen, therefore we need this margin."

The due diligence package for the lenders was extensive. Control Risks had produced a large political risk report and even Phil Fletcher paid a state visit to Sana'a. One might have thought that the 320km pipeline from Block 18 to the terminal might be most at risk but it is buried and in the event of a problem remedial action can be taken quickly.

On the commercial side of the deal, gas prices across the world are booming. The base case price for the deal is around US$5.50. The financing package was standard with no innovations and, of course, is backed by strong offtake contracts.

Total put a US$1.1bn shareholder loan into the structure for extra comfort. The ECAs are all committed to the project, apart from Opic/Exim, which pulled out last summer due to the Total/Iran issue – or perhaps even the Exxon/Yemen issue. The Yemeni government has committed to the scheme through its share of the sponsors' guarantees during what is left of the construction period.

Construction progress is said to be good, with some hiccups along the way. The banks are, however, covered by the sponsor construction guarantees. Commercial start-up was targeted for December 2008 but the commitment appears to have changed to 2008/09.

Many of the project variables were therefore dealt with. And to put the deal in a proper context, what price back in 1993 for a US$650m uncovered tranche in Yemen? Perhaps one question was why the sponsors pushed ahead with the deal. By arranging the financing before financial close, the ECAs could come on board and spread the political risk. In some ways, this is a throw-back to the old days of project financing – raising money for schemes in tough environments for a range of joint venture partners and bringing in the multilaterals to mitigate the political risk.

The specifics of the deal are as follows. The seven MLAs are Bank of Tokyo Mitsubishi, BNP Paribas, Calyon, Citigroup, ING, Royal Bank of Scotland, SG and SMBC. Calyon is an additional MLA on the Total tranche. The US$750m commercial loan was priced at 165bp rising to 180bp then 210bp with fees, 115bp for US$20m, 130bp for US$35m and 145bp for US$50m with a 40bp flex option. This was not exercised and instead the commercial loan was reduced to US$648m with the sponsors making up the difference. British Arab Commercial Bank, Dexia, Fortis, Lloyds TSB, Korea Development Bank and Mizuho joined the syndication.

The Total loan totalled US$1.1bn. The various multilateral tranches were split into a US$423m Coface-covered tranche, reduced from US$450m during syndication; US$400m from Kexim; and US$200m from JBIC/Nexi. The Kexim portion was split into a US$240m direct loan and a US$160m covered tranche, and the JBIC/Nexi portion was split into a US$120m direct loan and a US$80m covered tranche. Margins were 35bp to 40bp with fees of 25bp.

Mizuho joined the seven MLAs in the ECA tranches. The following roles were allocated to the banks on the deal – BOTM was the intercreditor agent, JBIC/Nexi and Total agent; RBS was the Coface agent; ING was the Kexim agent; SG was the facility agent; and SMBC had the docs. Citigroup was, of course, financial adviser. On the legal side, Milbank Tweed acted for the lenders and Sullivan & Cromwell for the sponsors.

The sponsor group on the scheme is Total with 39.62 per cent, Hunt Oil 17.22 per cent, Yemen Gas Company 16.73 per cent, SK Corp 9.55 per cent, Kogas 6 per cent, Hyundai 5.88 per cent, and General Authority for Social Security & Pension 5 per cent.

So what is next for the partners in YLNG? For Total's finance division more work is expected in the project finance stream. Looking forwards two monster financings are being planned by the French major to add to this year's YLNG and Total Gabon. RBS has been appointed to refinance the US$2.95bn bridge loans on the operational Dolphin gas pipeline from Qatar to UAE. Mubadala and Occidential are Total's partners on the scheme. And then there is the vast Shtokman gas field scheme in Russia with Gazprom and StatoilHydro. The competition for a financial adviser on the scheme has just begun. The technical challenge on this scheme is immense and the project could cost up to US$30bn.

Yemen has been struggling to get various other energy linked schemes off the ground. There have been proposals for refinery upgrades and independent power projects (IPPs) announced over the years. The Aden refinery is to be expanded. There are said to be bidders for the Ras Isa oil terminal and interest in the Marib refinery and petrochemical scheme. Hood Oil has delayed its refinery scheme at Rsa Isa. One promising prospect is the award of eleven offshore oil field blocks on July 31st. Twenty five international companies have applied.

CASE STUDY

Pueblo Viejo Mines Golden PF PFI Yearbook 2011

The project financing of the US$3bn Pueblo Viejo gold project was a significant deal this year.

MAX VAUGHAN, managing director Ogmore Capital, now chief financial officer, Gabriel Resources

High amongst many challenges overcome by the sponsors of one of the world's largest ever upstream mining projects was the August 2008 kick-off to the financing – one month before the collapse of Lehman and the downward spiral of the credit markets. The strength of the sponsors, a robust long-life asset, positive investor sentiment towards gold and a robust arranging club enabled the financing to close in challenging markets and in a challenging jurisdiction.

The project sponsors are Barrick Gold Corp (60 per cent) and Goldcorp Inc (40 per cent), both with significant experience of developing and operating gold mines. The sponsors' base case equity component was well above norms for this type of project at about US$1,965m (ca. 67 per cent), more than 50 per cent of which was invested prior to financial close. The US$1,035m limited-recourse project financing consisted of three tranches of senior debt: a 15-year US$400m direct loan by EDC, a 15-year US$375m direct loan by US Ex-Im and a 12-year US$260m bank facility (with PRI from EDC). The sponsors provided several pre-completion guarantees to the lenders subject to carve-out for political force majeure events.

The project is located in the central part of the Dominican Republic on the Caribbean island of Hispanola in the province of Sanchez Ramirez about 100km northwest of the national capital of Santo Domingo. The project involves the open pit mining and production of gold, silver, and copper by conventional processing methods. The project's ore reserves are about 23.7m ounces, resulting in a mine life of some 25 years. Over the first full five years of operations the project is forecast to produce an average in excess of 1m ounces per annum.

Mining activity within the project boundary dates back to 1505, although records indicate there was a roughly 400-year period of low activity. In 1979 the Dominican Central Bank purchased all foreign-held shares in the then Pueblo Viejo mine and ran the operation until the late 1990s. During this time, Pueblo Viejo produced 5.3m ounces of gold and 24.4m ounces of silver in 24 years of production. Barrick acquired Pueblo Viejo in 2006, at the time of the Placer Dome acquisition, and simultaneously sold a 40 per cent stake in the Pueblo Viejo asset to Goldcorp.

The extended historical activities at Pueblo Viejo were one of the main challenges facing the sponsors and lenders, as the environmental legacy issues were significant. However, the remediation benefits that the project is bringing to the local environment are also a key source of value to stakeholders. CAM acted as the independent technical and environmental consultant for the lenders and worked closely both with CIBC and the in-house social and environmental teams at EDC and US Ex-Im. The social and environmental due diligence was extensive and for long periods of the financing was the key focus of attention for all parties.

In addition to the above environmental benefits, as the single largest ever foreign direct investment the project will also bring significant economic benefits to the Dominican Republic. Pueblo Viejo will employ ca. 3,500 people at its peak and will potentially generate billions of dollars for the state over the life of the operation. These economic benefits are affected by the prevailing gold price and derived through the special lease agreement signed between the state and PVDC.

The special lease agreement sets out the framework that gives the sponsors exclusive rights to a broad range of rights over the licence area, including rights to explore, develop and mine. The special lease agreement also provides for stabilization of taxation and other payments to the government and certain other requirements customary for raising project finance.

Country risk mitigation was one of the key drivers for the sponsors in raising project finance, who place value in having agencies of the United States and Canadian governments along with the commercial banks directly associated with the in-country borrower. This manifested itself in the 15-year tenor of the financing from the agency lenders and the 12-year tenor of the commercial bank tranche, which was a significant increase for most of the lenders over precedent in other similar jurisdictions.

In addition to the special lease agreement and strong environmental and economic factors, the project financing incorporated the usual offshore account and reinsurance structures. The sponsors also established an offtake agreement to take the gold ore mine production for onward refining offshore. These features, combined with US dollar revenue generation and sponsor strength and experience in emerging markets, were the primary underlying political risk mitigants, although the risk was explicitly addressed for the commercial bank lenders through political risk insurance.

The mine plan for Pueblo Viejo results in potentially significant free cashflow generation during ramp-up/the early operational period. Lenders' customary requirement to not have the financing go non-recourse prior to completion testing at the long-term mine output resulted in a two-phase structure around completion, thus permitting possible flexibility to make restricted payments to the sponsors prior to final completion (including cash sharing to the lenders).

This approach incorporates an interim completion stage that is not a compulsory obligation upon the borrower. Whilst this flexibility is not customary in such financings, this is a feature considered to be in the interests of all parties. To otherwise fully restrict up-streaming of cash prior to final completion could have resulted in significant cash being trapped onshore in the early years of operations.

Over the course of the financing, given the global events that were giving rise to increases in cost of funds, there were ongoing discussions on pricing with the commercial bank lenders. This wasn't a particular issue in respect of the US Ex-Im direct loan, as its commercial interest reference rate is set at an institutional level by reference to the prevailing US Treasury bond rate plus 1 per cent.

Notwithstanding pricing pressure in general from the bank market, the gold price environment continued to be a favourable factor for the sponsors. Between August 2008 and April 2010, the spot gold price rose from ca. US$830/oz to ca. US$1,150/oz. Whilst the gold price that the lenders had agreed to use for the financial analysis had not changed, when the project was viewed in the context of the rising gold price it became more and more robust, especially given the low debt to equity ratio of about 33:67.

The final agreed pricing was: (i) for the US$400m EDC tranche, Libor +3.25 per cent pre-completion scaling gradually post-completion to Libor +5.1 per cent (inclusive of political risk insurance premia) for years 13–15; (ii) for the US$375m US Ex-Im tranche, 4.02 per cent fixed rate for the entire 15 years; and (iii) for the US$260m commercial bank tranche, Libor +3.25 per cent pre-completion, scaling gradually to Libor +4.85 per cent (inclusive of political risk insurance premia) for years 11–12.

The structure of the project financing provides for risk sharing amongst the sponsors and the lenders. Pre-completion, the sponsors, pursuant to the several pre-completion guarantees, assume all risks except for political force majeure. Post-completion, the lenders do not have recourse to the sponsors. The due diligence processes and final completion testing regime are the primary explicit means through which the lenders mitigate the ongoing operational risk. The experience and track record of the sponsors, supported by formal ongoing shareholder transfer restrictions, were also significant qualitative factors – between them the sponsors have about 34 operating mines.

Post-completion, the lenders also share in future gold price risk. A fundamental tenet of the financing for the sponsors was that it should not limit their upside exposure to gold prices. Sources of comfort for the lenders are the low operating cost base of the project and low gearing providing for robust gold price downside sensitivities. The financial resources of the sponsors, size of equity commitment and long mine life are additional mitigants. For any short-term borrower cashflow issues post-completion, the financing structure also incorporated a traditional offshore debt service reserve account.

The gold price following financial close has generally continued its upward trajectory, which will add significant additional cashflow over the lenders' base case following initial gold production (expected end-2011). As at the end of Q3 2010, overall project construction was nearly 40 per cent complete, with ca. 75 per cent of the capital committed and engineering and procurement about 95 per cent complete. The project financing is about 75 per cent utilized.

The financing took longer than either sponsor envisaged but given the jurisdiction of the project, the complexities of the environmental and social issues and the state of the credit markets, that the financing closed at all early in 2010 is testament to the strength of the sponsors and the determination of all parties.

The parties	
Sponsors	Barrick (60 per cent), Goldcorp (40 per cent)
Borrower	Pueblo Viejo Dominicana Corporation
Facility	US$1,035m
Agency Lenders	EDC (US$400m) US Ex-Im (US$375m)
Bank Lenders	Bank of Nova Scotia (Admin agent) CIBC (Technical agent) ING (Documentation agent) KfW Ipex-Bank Standard Chartered (Insurance agent)
Other Advisors	Rothschild (Sponsors' financial advisor) Shearman & Sterling (Sponsors' counsel) Milbank (Lenders' counsel) CAM (Independent technical consultant) Ogmore Capital/RBS (US Ex-Im advisor)

CASE STUDY

Innovative Emirates Steel PFI Middle East Report 2010

Financial adviser to both Emirates Steel Industries and its parent company explain the financing of Emirates Steel's US$2.5bn expansion project. General Holding Corporation

JEAN-MARC MANGIAVELLANO, IAN COGSWELL
and ANTOINE TRIEUX
Natixis

In August 2010, Emirates Steel closed the financing of its US$2.5bn expansion project, with US$1.6bn of senior debt facilities and US$600m of subordinated working capital facilities making this the single largest steel financing ever closed in the Middle East and one of the largest project financings closed in the region in that year. The debt was raised through a three-stage funding programme, which re-financed US$1.2bn of bridge loan facilities that were raised in 2008 at both the Emirates Steel and GHC level. The financing comprised of:

- A US$733m conventional project financing raised at the Emirates Steel level;
- A US$367m Sharia-compliant Islamic project financing raised at the Emirates Steel level;
- A US$500m SACE-covered term loan raised at the GHC level; and
- US$600m of subordinated working capital facilities arranged on a bilateral basis.

The financing structure incorporates a combination of tried and tested precedents, together with innovative variations, which were necessary to achieve a successful financing.

Background

Originally established in 2001 as Emirates Iron & Steel Factory (EISF), Emirates Steel is indirectly wholly-owned by the government of Abu Dhabi, through GHC, and is strategically located at the recently developed Industrial City of Abu Dhabi (ICAD). The company acts as the platform for the Government of Abu Dhabi's initiative to establish a leading local and regional integrated steel producer.

Emirates Steel is a key element in the development strategy of the Emirate, which involves the industrialization and diversification of its economy, with strong fundamentals underpinned by an access to abundant and low-cost energy resources.

The original factory was already the largest steel plant in the UAE, utilizing the latest rolling mill technology to produce reinforcing bars (rebars) for the construction industry. It remains the only significant domestic supplier of rebars and the original rolling mill had a design capacity of 600,000 metric tons per annum (tpa).

In 2006, Emirates Steel announced a significant expansion of its activities, to be undertaken in two phases. The Phase 1 Expansion comprised a 1.6m tpa direction reduction plant (DRP), a 1.4m tpa steel melt plant (SMP), a 0.62m tpa rebar rolling mill (RM2) and a 0.48m tpa wire rod and coil rolling mill (RM3), together with associated infrastructure and facilities, which was completed in December 2009.

The Phase 2 expansion will comprise a 1.6m tpa DRP, a 1.4m tpa SMP, a 1m tpa heavy sections rolling mill (RM4) and associated infrastructure and facilities. The DRP and the SMP of the Phase 1 and Phase 2 expansions programmes are sister plants and are scheduled to be completed by December 2012. Construction of both Phase 1 and Phase 2 (jointly, the expansion project) is being undertaken by Italian firm Danieli & C Officine Spa.

Whilst the expansion project is not yet fully completed, Emirates Steel is already now one of the leading steel producers in the Middle East. The output capacity currently stands at 2m tpa and should reach 3m tpa by 2011, moving the company closer to becoming the Middle East region's largest steel manufacturer.

The Financing

The financing needs of Emirates Steel (debt amount to be raised) were substantial, amounting to US$2.2bn including subordinated working capital facilities. This represents the largest ever steel industry financing in the Middle East region. In structuring the project financing there were a number of key considerations to be taken into account, which included:

- The financing structure needed to be developed immediately after the peak of the financial crisis, at a time when bank liquidity was extremely tight, especially for transactions in challenging sectors such as steel. Furthermore, the UAE was facing a economic downturn (especially the construction sector in Dubai);
- The nature of Emirates Steel's output results in an appreciable level of merchant risk. In addition, steel prices, which are inherently cyclical, experienced increased volatility following the global economic crisis;
- The global steel sector was restructured at the beginning of 2010 (the leading iron ore producers unilaterally changed the raw material pricing mechanism); and
- The expansion project was provisionally financed with bridge loan facilities, the maturity of which established a firm deadline by which this complex and multi-sourced project financing needed to be completed.

Maximizing the liquidity and minimizing the financing cost of the transaction in such a context was clearly the key challenge for the Emirates Steel financing team.

As described by James Finucane, project finance manager at Emirates Steel, the deal required a pragmatic approach.

"Throughout the financing process it was necessary to react to changing market conditions within the local and the international financial markets," said Finucane. "We had to work closely with our key relationship banks and also draw upon the support of our sponsor, GHC. By adopting a flexible approach married with the strength of our project, Emirates Steel was able to maximize liquidity and minimise the overall financing costs."

Project Economics

Beyond these hurdles, the underlying business of Emirates Steel benefits from a number of favourable economic factors, on the basis of which Emirates Steel built the structure of the financing:

- Emirates Steel benefits from strong government support, as an indirectly wholly-owned subsidiary of GHC, which is itself wholly-owned by the Government of Abu Dhabi;
- The expansion project will transform Emirates Steel into a vertically integrated steel producer, whereby it will complete its evolution from a simple and relatively low value-added processing operation into a sophisticated, highly productive and high value-added manufacturing business. On a UAE-delivered basis (delivery costs being added) it has been calculated that Emirates Steel will fall within the first (ie, lowest) percentile of the global cost curve;
- The highly competitive nature of the plant is further enhanced by the use of proven technologies and the substantial economies of scale and synergies associated with the combination of the Phase 1 and Phase 2 expansion projects, which will transform Emirates Steel's production facilities into a world-scale asset;
- The EPC contracts, comprising the Phase 1 and Phase 2 EPC contracts, have all been signed on a lump sum turnkey basis with Danieli, one of the largest and most reputable suppliers of equipment and plant to the global metals industry; and
- Emirates Steel has been successfully producing and selling steel for almost 10 years. It has gained considerable expertise through the use of state of the art technologies and the employment of highly qualified personnel. This mutually beneficial combination has resulted in the achievement of record production levels and the establishment of strong customer relationships with local and regional steel traders and end-users.

The Structure

Whilst capitalizing on the plant's robust intrinsic strengths, the Emirates Steel financing team, together with financial adviser Natixis and legal adviser Denton Wilde Sapte, has developed an innovative and ambitious financing structure combining highly diversified funding sources to ensure that the required debt amount was raised at the most competitive pricing achievable despite adverse economic conditions.

Total cost of the expansion project amounted to US$2.5bn. GHC and Emirates Steel sought financing on a 60:40 senior debt to equity ratio and successfully raised a total of US$1.6bn of senior facilities (and additional subordinated facilities).

Maximizing bank market liquidity for the transaction was achieved through the development of an advanced financing strategy, with four distinct facilities targeting separate investor groups:

At the Emirates Steel level:

- A US$733m conventional limited recourse senior project finance facility targeted at the local and regional bank market;
- A US$367m senior Sharia-compliant Islamic limited recourse project financing (Ijara) targeted at local and regional Islamic institutions; and
- A total of US$600m of subordinated working capital facilities raised on a bilateral basis with core local relationship banks;

At the GHC level:

- A US$500m ECA-covered facility (SACE) targeted at the international bank market.

The senior debt facilities have a seven-year door-to-door tenor, which was established as the optimum term following a preliminary market sounding. Furthermore, the repayment profile was sculpted with a back-ended profile in order to accommodate the ramp-up period and, in common with similar capital-intensive regional projects, the sponsor, GHC, provided a completion guarantee to be released upon the satisfaction of comprehensive technical and financial tests.

The US$733m conventional project financing was entirely subscribed by local and regional banks. Restricting the conventional loan to local and regional lenders that had developed strong relationships with both Emirates Steel and GHC enabled Emirates Steel to take advantage of favourable terms and conditions offered by close relationship banks. The final group of six MLAs included National Bank of Abu Dhabi, as global co-ordinating bank, together with Union National Bank, First Gulf Bank, Bank of Baroda, Arab Banking Corporation and Al Khaliji Bank.

The Islamic facility was structured as a standard forwards lease (Ijara). The Islamic institutions acquired the assets (already constructed in the case of the Emirates Steel financing) and leased them back to Emirates Steel.

Islamic finance is increasingly sought by borrowers in the UAE and the wider Middle East region. Emirates Steel and GHC were no exception and consequently chose to maximize the size of the Islamic tranche, which supported the national objective of promoting Sharia-compliant borrowing. The facility was fully subscribed by the local institutions and MLAs on the transaction, Abu Dhabi Islamic Bank and Al Hilal Bank.

The syndication of these two facilities proved to be extremely successful and the total project finance facilities of US$1.1bn were more than two times oversubscribed.

Supporting the project finance facilities was a US$500m SACE-covered facility at the GHC corporate level. This was offered to international lenders and was more than four times oversubscribed. Competition for this portion of debt was intense and bids were extremely competitive, with the result that GHC was able to obtain particularly attractive terms from HSBC, which was appointed sole MLA. The SACE facility pricing helped minimize the project's all-in financing cost.

Finally, a further US$600m of bilateral subordinated working capital facilities, sized upon the combination of the current trends in the steel industry and the scale and integrated nature of the expanded plant, were negotiated directly between Emirates Steel and its core local banks, to ensure that, despite the significant working capital requirement, the most competitive terms could be achieved.

Commenting on the deal Stephen Pope, CFO of Emirates Steel, said: "This is a real vote of confidence by the local, regional and international banks in Emirates Steel and in Abu Dhabi's wider 'Vision 2030' initiative. This successful financing represents a true coming of age for our company and it was achieved through strong support from GHC, excellent relationship with our banking group and a state of the art steel making facility based in Abu Dhabi."

Summary

Financing for the Emirates Steel expansion project was first launched in 2006 and the final funding structure is unrecognizable from that originally envisaged. However, the project clearly demonstrates the values of perseverance and flexibility. The sound underlying business rationale of Emirates Steel and its expansion project – to turn a simple low value-added rolling mill into a world-scale high value-added integrated steel complex – was widely acknowledged.

However, the announcement of a second phase expansion, the global financial crisis and the restructuring of the global steel industry, all of which occurred during the financing process, resulted in a delay in closing the financing and a more innovative and multi-sourced financing than originally expected.

The willingness of GHC to support Emirates Steel with guarantees for the bridge financing confirmed to lenders the strategic nature of the project and persuaded them to stay with the transaction over the course of almost four years.

In negotiating the financing terms, Emirates Steel acknowledged the need for a traditional project finance structure that would appeal to lenders in a more capital-constrained world and lenders responded with competitive pricing that acknowledged the strength of both the underlying business and of the multi-sourced finance structure.

The funding mix – conventional and Islamic project finance, SACE-covered corporate financing and bilateral working capital facilities – ensured sufficient liquidity for a financing of US$2.2bn in a notoriously cyclical sector and was key to the success of the transaction.

CASE STUDY

Innovative Mix for GNPower PFI Yearbook 2011

The GMCP IPP in the Philippines.

DUNG HO, Head of Power for Asia, Project and Export Finance
Standard Chartered Bank
MICHAEL R. CAHIGAS, Vice-President
BDO Capital & Investment Corp

The success of GNPower Mariveles Coal Plant Ltd Co (GMCP) provides an example of an innovative financing structure for power projects across several Asian countries where electricity is needed more than ever to drive and sustain economic growth. It also demonstrates the strong collaboration of international, local and Chinese banks in financing coal-fired power projects whilst upholding the goals of sustainable development in full compliance with the Equator Principles.

Prolonged blackouts in the middle of the day are not without precedent in the Philippines, particularly on Luzon Island, the centre of demand for electricity in the country. In fact, the demand for electricity in the Philippines, as forecast by the Philippine Department of Energy, is increasing by 4 per cent–5 per cent per annum. In Luzon alone, the supply and demand balance this year has already reached critical levels where capacity will not be able to meet the demand and statutory reserve margin requirement.

In the last 10 years, however, no large-scale power plants have been built. Most of the capacity expansion has come from the rehabilitation of existing plants. The supply of electricity, without any new capacity additions, has long lagged behind demand, necessitating extensive use of expensive and aged heavy fuel oil-fired power plants to satisfy demand and prevent the recurrence of the power shortages experienced during the early 1990s.

GMCP is the first large-scale greenfield IPP project to commence construction in more than a decade and is the only project expected to be on line in time to alleviate the severe power shortages in Luzon. Of the required additional capacity of 12.5GW in the next 20 years, only 600MW from GMCP is committed to be on line in 2013.

The Project

The project is a 600MW coal-fired power plant located in an industrial zone on the Bataan Peninsula of Luzon, the Philippines. It uses proven pulverized coal-fired technology and equipment from China and was specifically designed for low sulphur, low ash and low calorific value coal.

The project is being built by China National Electric Equipment Corporation, the EPC contractor, on a fixed price, lump-sum, date-certain, turnkey basis. Key equipment (e.g., the boiler, turbine and generator) are provided by world-class Chinese manufacturers.

Construction commenced in early 2010 following financial close on January 29 and will take approximately 36 months to complete. The project will source coal from Indonesia under a long-term coal supply contract with PT Arutmin Indonesia. As one of Luzon's critical base load providers, the project will contract nearly 90 per cent of its electricity output to approximately 15 distribution utilities and electricity co-operatives and large private sector end-users under mostly 15-year take-or-pay arrangements, with the balance to be sold in the spot market.

GMCP, when commissioned, will be one of the most modern and lowest cost coal-fired power plants in the Philippines. It is also the only coal-fired power plant in the Philippines that complies with the Equator Principles.

The Firsts and the Challenges

The project is the first IPP project in the Philippines and in the region that has adopted a non-traditional offtake structure. As of today, most power projects of this scale would have a single or an anchor offtaker, which is often a state-owned utility or power generation company with an acceptable international credit rating or with credit backstopped by sovereign support in various forms (e.g., support letter, undertaking under power purchase agreement or guarantee from the government).

The creditworthiness of the offtaker or the government backstop is critical as it dictates the credit profile of a power project and influences the appetite of lenders for the project.

The model adopted by the project, however, deviated from the traditional Asian IPP model in two fundamental respects; namely, the mix of contracted sales and merchant sales and the involvement of a large portfolio of offtakers without any Philippine sovereign support. Of its 600MW capacity, GMCP will sell up to 525MW (or 87 per cent) of its electrical output to approximately 15 distribution utilities and 10 large end-users under long-term power purchase agreements (PPAs). The balance will be sold in the spot market in Luzon.

The credit ratings of the commercial users and electricity distribution utilities are not comparable with those of the large state-owned power companies or corporations that typically are the primary offtakers in other IPP projects in Asia. None of the offtakers benefited from any sovereign support.

Adding to the above challenge was the source of the equipment and contractor chosen by the project. The sponsors, GNPower, Denham Capital and Sithe Global, chose Chinese equipment and a Chinese EPC contractor. Whilst Chinese equipment is becoming a significant part of some power projects in a few places in the world due to its cost advantage, it remains an untested alternative for coal-fired power plants in the Philippines as well as most countries in Asia.

In fact, prior to this transaction, Chinese equipment installed by a Chinese EPC contractor had not been readily accepted by international financial institutions. The project is the pioneer international project financing for a major IPP power project in the Philippines that has accepted a full range of Chinese equipment and a Chinese contractor.

The sponsors also had to meet a tight financing deadline required under the project's numerous contracts. Any failure to achieve a timely financial close would not only give rise to some unwanted unwinding of the project structure but also restrain the project from reaping the most profit by selling electricity right at the expected period of severe shortages of power supply in the system.

Due to the non-traditional offtake structure, the choice of Chinese equipment and EPC contractor, and the time constraints, there were very limited sources of debt available for the financing of the project. The situation was made even more precarious due to the continuing uncertainties in the debt markets following the global financial crisis. Raising sufficient funds for the project alone was already a great challenge, but achieving it with competitive pricing and within a short timeframe would make it even more exigent.

The Innovative Financing Solution

The total project cost is US$1,025m, composed of a base project cost of US$960m, US$40m committed contingent equity and a working capital requirement of US$25m. The base project cost was funded by 75 per cent debt (US$720m) and 25 per cent equity (US$240m).

As the project adopted a non-traditional offtake structure with approximately 25 distribution utilities and other large end-users having limited credit ratings, it presented a unique challenge for the project to attract sufficient lenders' appetite. This was partially addressed by maximizing the involvement of local banks. It was the local banks that had interacted with GNPower and these local offtakers on a regular basis and were therefore in a good position to understand and feel comfortable with the risk.

However, due to the large size of the project, the US dollar liquidity of the local banks was not sufficient, especially in light of the recent global financial crisis. This was in addition to the limited tenor (up to 12 years) inherent in local US dollar funding, which added another dimension of difficulty to the financing. Similar to other power projects, the project required debt with the longest possible tenor to ensure its long-run competitiveness.

Reliance only on local US dollar funding therefore did not fully resolve the problem and looking for other pockets of liquidity was unavoidable. This was where Chinese financing came into the picture, thanks to the involvement of Sinosure, which provided political and partial commercial insurance to Chinese financing sources. The participation of the Chinese equipment providers and EPC contractor in the project was the key reason behind the involvement of Sinosure and China Development Bank – the sole Chinese lender.

The financing structure successfully tapped both Chinese financing and the limited US dollar liquidity of local banks in the Philippines. The Chinese tranche was innovatively structured to maximize to the full extent possible both the long-term tenor (up to 15.5 years) and the back-ended amortization profile (having more than 50 per cent outstanding at the maturity of the local tranche) with the benefit of having political and partial commercial risks insurance from Sinosure. This unique feature of the Chinese tranche not only addressed the limited liquidity of US dollar local funding but also accommodated the tenor constraint of the local tranche, which, however, had no benefit from Sinosure insurance.

Standard Chartered Bank, as the global structuring financial adviser, and BDO Capital & Investment Corp, as the mandated lead arranger for the local tranche, were able to successfully raise the requisite financing for the project. China Development Bank committed US$493m (or 67 per cent of the project debt) and the remaining US$227m was funded by Banco de Oro Unibank (as lead local bank), Standard Chartered Bank and three other local banks (Bank of Philippine Islands, China Banking Corporation and Security Bank Corp).

Debt capacity was sized to accommodate an internationally acceptable debt service coverage ratio. A debt service reserve account was established to ensure the project would have sufficient cashflow to service debt during the transitory reduction of revenue inherent in the merchant power market.

A significant portion of the debt facilities was hedged against interest rate risk by the GMCP entering into an interest rate swap agreement with Standard Chartered Bank for the local tranche and arranging a fixed-rate swap on the China Development Bank debt. As additional comfort for the local banks, in view of the continuing uncertainties in the global financial markets, the floating interest rate tranche of the local loans included a mechanism tied to credit default swap pricing to compensate for sovereign risk and restricted liquidity in the interbank markets.

The Achievement and its Significant Market Impact

Most of all, the financial closing of GMCP will contribute to alleviating Philippine's power shortages that are expected to occur with increasing severity in 2012. The scheduled construction of GMCP will improve the everyday lives of millions of Filipino people in Metro Manila as well as Luzon.

The success of the project heralds a breakthrough in the Asian IPP market, which typically relies on large state-owned power companies as the primary offtakers or sovereign credit support. The application of the model adopted by the project – a diversified portfolio of offtakers without sovereign support – pioneers a pathway for future power projects in the Philippines and elsewhere in the region that can benefit countless end-users such as small utilities and co-operatives in remote areas.

This project is an achievement from an environmental and social perspective as well as by setting an example for the sustainable development of power projects in the Philippines. As the only international lender and the only Equator Principles bank in the project, Standard Chartered advocated the importance of sustainable power development in the Philippines and achieved the sponsors' commitment to comply with the Equator Principles (which mandated higher environmental and social standards for the project).

This achievement provides a valuable precedent that any other international or Equator Principles bank can cite to elevate environmental and social standards in financing power projects in the Philippines and across Asia.

By adopting an innovative financing structure, the sponsors achieved financial close within the time constraints they had. This not only helped the sponsors avoid unwanted unwinding of the project structure that might incur additional development costs but also positioned the project to start operation in a time when the project can reap the most profit by selling electricity right at the expected period of most power shortages in the Philippines.

Conclusion

GMCP is an important transaction in international power project financing, in the Philippines and across Asia, that broke barriers by financing a non-traditional offtake structure as well as using a full-range of Chinese equipment and a Chinese EPC contractor. The success of GMCP provides an unprecedented example of an innovative financing structure for power projects across several Asian countries where electricity is needed more than ever to drive and sustain economic growth. The project is also an exemplary environmental model demonstrating the strong collaboration of international, local and Chinese banks, as well as the sponsors, in supporting and safeguarding the environment through the adoption of the Equator Principles.

CASE STUDY

Jhajjar Power – Financing an IPP

PFI India Report 2010

S. JEYAKUMAR, General Manager
YASHPAL GUPTA, General Manager Structuring, Syndication and
Advisory
IDBI Bank

Until 1990, the responsibility and authority of power generation, transmission and distribution in India was mainly with the Government-owned agencies, with a few exceptions. As part of an economic reform process initiated in the 1990s, the Government facilitated private sector participation in various infrastructure sectors including power.

To begin with, the Electricity (Supply) Act of 1948 was amended in 1991 to promote the entry of Independent Power Producers. This was followed by restructuring of State Electricity Boards and the participation of the private sector in transmission and distribution of electricity. These reforms have encouraged private companies to make large investments in the Indian power sector. However, there is still a huge gap between demand and availability of power.

Haryana is one of the smaller states of India located in the northern part of the country, touching Delhi, Punjab, Rajasthan and Uttar Pradesh. It is rich in agricultural production and is economically better off than most of the other states. However, it faces a power deficiency of 12–15 per cent.

Haryana State Electricity Board (HSEB) was incorporated in 1967 as the nodal agency for power generation, transmission and distribution within the state. In August 1998, the State Government unbundled the erstwhile HSEB into two entities – Haryana Power Generation Corporation Limited (HPGCL) for generation and Haryana Vidyut Prasaran Nigam Limited (HVPNL) for transmission cum distribution.

Subsequently, in July 1999, the distribution businesses of HVPNL were carved out and vested into two discoms to cover the northern and southern parts of the state.

Jhajjar Thermal Power Project

During the last few years, the Government of Haryana has initiated several measures to increase the power generation capacity in the state. As part of this plan, it was decided to set up a project comprising the construction of a 1,320MW (2 × 660MW) supercritical coal-fired power plant in the village of Khanpur in the Jhajjar District (about 90km from Delhi) on a build, own and operate (BOO) basis.

After going through a tariff-based competitive bidding process as per the guidelines of the Electricity Act 2003, HPGCL in July 2008 awarded the project to CLP Power India Private Ltd (CLP PIPL). As per the guidelines of the Government of India, availability of land, water linkage, fuel linkage and environmental clearance is ensured to the bidders by the Haryana Government. CLP PIPL incorporated an SPV by the name of Jhajjar Power Ltd (JPL) to implement the project. JPL appointed IDBI as the sole arranger for tying up the entire debt requirement for the project.

Promoters

CPL PIPL belongs to China Light Power (CLP) group of Hong Kong, one of the leading power companies in the Asia-Pacific region. The CLP group owns a 655MW gas-fired combined cycle power plant in Gujarat through a company named Gujarat Paguthan Energy Company Ltd (GPEC). It has also set up a few wind power projects in India.

However, JPL's project would be the first thermal power project to be set up by the CLP group in India. The promoters are required to induct Rs20,661m (which would be inducted in US dollars and would therefore change depending on the prevailing exchange rate) as their contribution for part-financing the overall project cost of Rs59,681m.

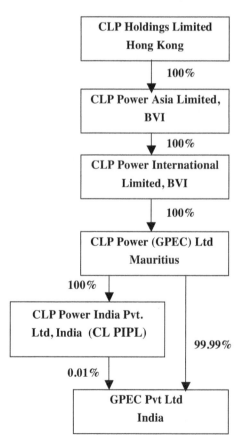

This contribution would be met through a combination of equity and compulsorily convertible preference shares (CCPS). CLP PIPL will contribute by way of equity to the extent of Rs200m, whereas the balance of equity would come from the GPEC/CLP group by way of subscription to CCPS. The CCPS (face value Rs10/share) would be issued in a phased manner during the construction period and would have a tenure that would at least match the tenure of the loan. GPEC/CLP would convert the same into equity shares (at a ratio to be decided at the time of conversion) at any time during the tenure of the CCPS. In addition to CLP PIPL and GPEC, one more overseas entity belonging to the CLP group would also be considered as a promoter, which would furnish the various promoters' related undertakings to the lenders to the proposed project. The structure of CLP Group in terms of companies incorporated in India is given in Figure CS1.

Figure CS1   CLP Group companies incorporated in India

Project Details

CLP PIPL was awarded the project, as it was the lowest bidder with a levellized tariff of Rs2.99/unit. A Power Purchase Agreement valid for 25 years has already been executed between JPL and Uttar Haryana Bijli Vitharan Nigam (UHBVNL) and Dakshin Haryana Bijli Vitharan Nigam (DHBVNL), the State Distribution Companies of the Haryana Government. These DISCOMs, as per the PPA, would purchase 90 per cent of the power produced by JPL whereas 10 per cent of the power would be sold by JPL on merchant basis. The company has already made arrangements for sale of this 10 per cent. The PPA has adequate payment security mechanism as well as a provision for third-party sales in case of default by the DISCOMS.

The project would require about 497 hectares of land, which has already been acquired by UHBVNL and DHBVNL and handed over to the company. JPL proposes to implement the project through an EPC contract route and has awarded the EPC contract to Shandong Electric Power Construction Corporation No. 3 (SEPCO III) group of companies as the EPC contractors considering their prior project execution experience with CLP Group.

SEPCO III would be sourcing boilers, turbines and generators from any one of the two leading original equipment manufacturers in China, i.e., Dong Fang Electric Corporation Ltd and Harbin Power Company Ltd. SEPCO III would finalize the sourcing strategy in consultation with the company. The contractual structure of the proposed power project is depicted in Figure CS2.

JPL proposes to carry out the O&M of the project in-house utilizing the technical support, training, scientific and research capability existing within the CLP Group. The O&M personnel would be provided with suitable training by the EPC contractors. The annual coal requirement for the proposed project has been estimated at 5.21m tonnes per annum (mtpa) at a PLF of 87.4 per cent. (GCV: 4,265 kcal/kg; Gross Station Heat Rate: 2181kcal/kWh).

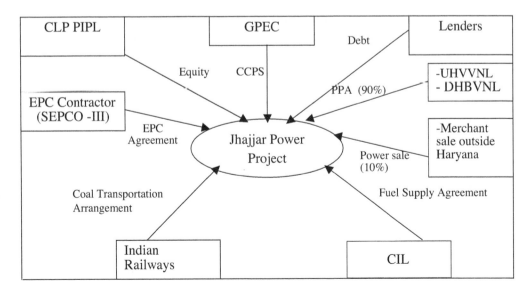

Figure CS2 Jhajjar project financing structure

The coal would be sourced from North Karanpura coalfield of Central Coalfields Limited (CCL), a subsidiary of Coal India Limited (CIL), located at a distance of about 1,000km from the plant site. The coal would be transported through Indian Railways. Light Diesel Oil (LDO) would be used as a secondary fuel, which would be sourced from nearby refineries. The DISCOMs are responsible for making the necessary evacuation arrangements.

Financing Arrangements

IDBI acted as the sole arranger for the entire debt requirement for the project. As per the appraisal carried out by IDBI's project team, the overall project cost was estimated at Rs59,681m, comprising a rupee portion of Rs24,974m and a foreign currency portion of US$771.25m (exchange rate of US$1 = Rs45).

The project was funded at debt equity ratio of 65:35. The total debt requirement of Rs3,902m comprising a rupee portion of Rs33,985m and foreign currency portion of US$112m was syndicated solely by IDBI. The company has been provided with an option to replace a part of the rupee debt to the extent of US$400m by way of ECBs/ECA/domestic bonds/multilateral agencies, within 12 months of the signing of the loan documents. JPL was permitted to cancel the equivalent amount of undrawn RTL.

The consortium consists of a total of 15 lenders comprising 10 banks and five financial institutions. The tenor of the loan is for a period of 15 years with an initial moratorium of four years, (including a construction period of 40 months and eight months moratorium post-COD from the date of notice to proceed). The entire financing exercise was completed within eight months of signing of the PPA by the company during the period when the entire world was facing financial crisis. There was an oversubscription of more than 30 per cent.

The members of the consortium are IDBI Bank Ltd, Indian Infrastructure Finance Company Ltd UK (for foreign currency loan), Power Finance Corporation, Rural Electrification Corporation, Infrastructure Development Finance Company Ltd, PTC Financial Services Ltd, Allahabad Bank, Bank of Baroda, Bank of India, Dena Bank, Oriental Bank of Commerce, State Bank of Mysore, State Bank of Patiala, State Bank of Travancore and United Bank of India.The debt is based on different interest rates for different sets of lenders. The interest rate structure for the project is styled in such a manner that the lenders and borrowers would have the benefit of changing market conditions during the period of the loan.

Key Features of the Transaction

- Long-term loan of 15 years door-to-door tenor was structured on a non-recourse basis for a PPP project.
- It is the one of first IPPs in Haryana and the coal needs to be transported over 1,000km by rail to the site.
- Structuring of promoter equity in a suitable form for foreign investors to invest in the project.
- Flexibility to refinance a portion of the debt through ECA/ECB without any penalty.

- Arranged foreign currency loan overcoming the global meltdown conditions that were prevailing during the mandate period.
- Arranged the funding by including five different financial institutions, which normally stipulate different covenants.

CASE STUDY

CHUM Opts for Bonds
PFI Global Infrastructure
Report 2011

The Montreal University Health Centre (CHUM) is the largest P3 transaction in Canadian history, financed in one large bond transaction following a long lead time.

ALISON HEALEY

CHUM was created in 1996 as a combination of hospitals including l'Hôtel Dieu, l'Hôpital Notre-Dame and Hôpital Saint-Luc. The CHUM P3 project includes a new hospital and research centre built in downtown Montreal on the St-Luc Hospital site. The new hospital itself will be 24 storeys high, in addition to five underground parking levels, and will contain 772 beds. The research centre, connecting to the existing office building, will have 11 storeys.

Approximately 345,000 outpatients, 22,000 inpatients and 65,000 emergency patients are seen at the CHUM every year. The CHUM is the largest university hospital centre in Quebec, not only in terms of care but also in terms of training and research.

The mammoth project involves the redevelopment of the three existing hospitals into one new facility. The new hospital will act as a tertiary referral centre for 1.7m people in Quebec. The government will pay 45 per cent of the cost of the new hospital upfront.

Construction of the project will be done in two phases. The main hospital building, the logistics building and ambulatory building will be all constructed during Phase 1, which represents approximately 80 per cent of the capital costs. Phase 1 also includes excavation and the construction of a new thermal power plant.

Phase 2 of the construction process involves decanting the old hospitals into the new, the demolition of the St-Luc Hospital and construction of the north wing of the ambulatory site, the parking office building and auditorium.

Phase 1 construction will start this month and will be followed by Phase 2 construction, and a 33.9-year service period beginning upon substantial completion of Phase 1 and ending in March 2050.

Total capital expenditure for both phases is approximately C$2bn spread over an 8.8-year construction period. The St-Luc Hospital will remain operational until construction of Phase 1 is complete.

Plans for the new CHUM began solidifying in 2008 following months of indecision after the hospital's former director was edged out of the process. In November 2008, the CHUM board of directors held a special meeting and unanimously approved a series of modifications that added significantly to the cost of the project.

The University of Montreal's Guy Breton was the CHUM's special consultant on the project and led the planning for the modifications, including a total of 39 operating rooms, an increase from the initial 30, a total of 772 beds, up from 700, plus an office for every doctor at the hospital. Also, instead of originally envisioned renovations to the 50 year-old St-Luc Hospital, the new plans called for demolishing the building to start the new health complex from scratch.

The credit crunch threatened to derail the project early on, causing Infrastructure Quebec to restructure parts of the transaction to appeal to a changing market. In the wake of the collapse of negotiations between Partnerships BC and the Macquarie-led preferred bidding group for the C$2.3bn Port Mann/Highway 1 project, the P3 hospital deals in Quebec were heavily scrutinized in the media. Some brought up concerns that raising debt for two such projects in the same sector might exceed the limits of available lenders in the current tight credit market.

But in April 2009, Infrastructure Quebec took a significant step to get the project back on track, hiring RBC Capital Markets to act as financial adviser on CHUM.

Two bidding teams were prequalified in 2007. Acces Sante CHUM found itself in need of a new equity partner after Babcock & Brown dropped out fairly early in the process. The consortium ultimately was led by Fiera-Axium. The second team, CHUM Collectif, was made up of Innisfree with 30 per cent, OHL and Laing O'Rourke with 25 per cent each, and Dalkia with 20 per cent.

Final bids came in by the end of January. CHUM Collectif was announced as the winner in February with the only bid below C$2.1bn. Health Montréal Collective Ltd Partnership will design, build, finance and maintain the new facility under a 38.8-year contract. Investec acted as the team's financial adviser. The other team, Acces Sante CHUM, exceeded the C$2.1bn limit.

AECOM, the project's structure and civil engineering master team, pointed out some of the major challenges involved in constructing 160,000m^2 of new buildings and rehabilitating 90,000m^2 of existing building. For example, the St-Luc Hospital's operations need to be maintained at all times and its emergency department has to be continuously accessible. Both old and new buildings will have to meet national building code requirements, which involve a major seismic retrofit, site decontamination, vibrations and water control and environment preservation.

In the early days of planning for CHUM to be done as a P3, lending capacity was thought to be an issue and stapled financing was considered as a means of financing multiple hospital projects. Later in the process bank/bond financing was thought to be the preferred route based on the success of the McGill hospital deal.

In terms of size, the CHUM deal trumped the combination bank/bond financing for the McGill University Health Centre in Montreal, which was the largest greenfield P3 hospital scheme in Canada. The 51-month construction period on McGill was also considered lengthy.

The C$1.157bn deal included a four-year C$393m short-term bank facility and a 34-year C$764m long-term bond tranche. The McGill financing was able to get better than expected terms, however, with the amortizing bonds, which mature in 2044, priced to yield 290bp over the benchmark, significantly tighter than originally expected. The bank loan portion of the financing was priced at 225bp over Libor.

Although bank/bond financing was considered, ultimately it was a single long bond issue that was selected for CHUM and RBC was tapped to lead the transaction.

Health Montreal Collective Ltd Partnership, the special-purpose entity contracted to design, build, finance and maintain the hospital under a long-term agreement, in early June 2011 raised C$1.37bn from an offering of long bonds. The amortizing bonds were priced at 315bp over the Government of Canada 5 per cent 2037 benchmark to yield 6.721 per cent. The pricing was higher than the rough early guidance of 300bp or even slightly lower.

The amortizing bonds carry a maturity date of September 2049, but because the bonds' principal is paid down with each interest payment, the average life of the bonds is expected to be 28.5 years.

The payment mechanism comprises a base service payment with indexing and non-indexing components. The payment mechanism is similar to those used for all Ontario AFP projects and all Quebec P3 projects.

CHUM will be legally responsible for all payments to the project company, and the Province of Quebec has confirmed a grant to cover the debt and equity-related portions of the monthly service payments, corresponding to approximately 69 per cent of payments to the project company.

Payments by the project company to the contractor are made one month in arrears. Therefore, the contractor will be paid on a monthly basis by submitting invoices for work completed.

The bonds were rated BBB by Moody's and BBB (high) by DBRS, lower than McGill and CRCHUM, a C$470m project done by Fiera-Axium Infrastructure/Meridiam and financed with a 30-year bond transaction.

The length of the construction period was highlighted as a concern for both rating agencies. The construction work has been contracted by the project company to the design-build joint venture consisting of Laing O'Rourke and OHL under a fixed-price, date-certain contract valued at C$1.988m.

In terms of credit positives, Moody's highlighted the CHUM's importance as a leading healthcare institution in Quebec and pointed out that the CHUM had a seasoned managerial team with an effective and prudent management style.

Ring-fencing is also a positive feature of the deal. The project's total construction cost is approximately C$2bn, with about C$1.6bn to be spent during Phase 1. With 90 per cent of the clinical facility completed in Phase 1, the project will be largely complete within the first five years. Once the project hits Phase 1 substantial completion, construction risk is materially less.

Moody's points out that senior debt proceeds are only used to fund construction of Phase 1 and the project agreement ring-fences Phase 1 from Phase 2 in terms of compensation on termination in that if the project gets terminated before the substantial completion date for Phase 2 but Phase 1 is not affected by the default, the compensation on termination will cover at least the senior debt amount.

The deal also features a letter of credit (LC) provided by HSBC Canada. For Phase 1 there is an LC in the amount of 17 per cent of construction costs, or C$270m; for Phase 2 it is in the amount of 25 per cent of construction costs, or C$101m.

A performance bond was provided by Zurich and Liberty. For Phase 1 the performance bond is in the amount of 12.5 per cent of construction costs, or C$198m; for Phase 2 it is also in the amount of 12.5 per cent of construction costs, or C$50m.

The parent company guarantee to the design-build joint venture is capped at 50 per cent of total capital expenditures, or C$994m for both phases. Delay-related liquidated damages are capped at about 11.39 per cent of Phase 1 construction costs, or approximately C$181m, and about 10.49 per cent of Phase 2 construction costs, or approximately C$42m.

Debt service coverage ratios are sculpted to achieve a minimum projected senior average of 1.25×, says Moody's. Leverage will be high at the end of the first full year of operations and debt-to-cash flow available for debt servicing will stand at approximately 10×, according to DBRS.

The bonds pay interest only during construction of both phases, with principal amortization beginning on September 30 2020, approximately six months after the March 27 2020 target substantial completion date.

CASE STUDY

Innovating on the Highways PFI India Report 2011

IDFC has recently achieved the financial closure of two innovative highway projects.

SANJAY GREWAL, Group Head, Project Finance
IDFC

The first scheme is the Bangalore-Mysore Infrastructure Corridor (BMIC). Conceptualized in the mid-1990s, this integrated PPP infrastructure project comprises a 54km access-controlled, grade-separated ring road (with links/interchanges with other important arterial roads) around the periphery of India's IT hub, an 111km expressway between Bangalore and the neighbouring city of Mysore and well-planned townships along the expressway and at the interchanges.

The Government of Karnataka (GoK), through a framework agreement and toll concession agreement signed in 1997, has granted the concession for this project to a group that is majority owned by the promoters of Bharat Forge, a diversified engineering group.

The concession period for the road components of the BMIC project is 40 years (including a construction period of 10 years). The investment in the project is recovered through a combination of the tolls and development rights in the townships. The following schematic describes the various entities involved in the project.

Considering the overall size of the BMIC project, Nandi Infrastructure Corridor Enterprise (NICE), the project development company, is adopting a stage-wise approach and has set up a separate SPV – Nandi Economic Corridor Enterprises Ltd (NECE) – for undertaking Stage 1 of the BMIC project. A tripartite agreement was executed by NICE, NECE and GoK assigning the rights for development of Stage 1 in favour of NECE.

In Stage 1 of the project, the entire ring road with links/interchanges, 13km of the expressway and about 1,800 hectares of modern townships will be developed. Whilst the ring road is largely complete and has been tolled since December 2008, the expressway and townships are now beginning to be developed. Land for the project is being acquired by GoK using acquisition procedures under the Karnataka Industrial Areas Development Board (KIADB) Act.

The total investment in Stage 1 will amount to about Rs24.5bn (approximately US$550m). IDFC was mandated by the sponsors to raise Rs16.5bn (US$365m) of project finance debt for the scheme. Whilst structuring the project financing for the project, which has a tenor of 14.5 years, IDFC had to take into account the changing road transportation and urban development patterns that would be triggered by this project, for which specialized studies were undertaken.

The loan structure is such that the exposure of the lenders to the real estate sector risk is low. In addition to servicing the debt, the project needs to generate internal accruals for investment in the remaining stages of the project. The loan has been structured in such a manner that a significant portion of the loan can be serviced through the toll revenues themselves. Any surplus will be used for an accelerated pay-down of the debt in a pre-defined manner before reinvesting in the subsequent phases. These provisions are operated using the escrow accounts through which all the cashflows of the project are to be routed.

The state government has established a dedicated authority to plan and regulate the development of the project. The project concession also envisages a mass transit system and other urban infrastructure such as water/waste-water and power infrastructure along the corridor at a later date. The well-planned townships will cater for industrial, commercial, corporate and residential uses and help decongest the city. This project gives Bangalore an opportunity to continue its growth in a well-planned and systematic manner.

This scheme is an example of a project conceptualized and driven entirely by the state government. States in India have been actively pursuing the PPP route for developing their highway networks. The states of Gujarat, Andhra Pradesh, Karnataka, Maharashtra and Madhya Pradesh have been the early entrants in this field. More recently, others such as Punjab, Haryana and Bihar have also started bidding out PPP projects.

National Highway No. 1A

The second project is the National Highway No. 1A between Jammu and Udhampur. The NH-1A is the lifeline of the state of Jammu & Kashmir (J&K). The highway traverses through the difficult terrain of the Himalayan mountain range. There was an urgent need to upgrade this landslide and accident-prone two-lane highway to a modern four-lane highway with divided carriageways that facilitate safe and speedy travel.

The Government of India took the decision to develop this stretch through a PPP. After following a competitive bidding process, one 65km stretch of the highway costing Rs24 bn (US$530m), between Jammu and Udhampur, was awarded by the National Highway Authority of India (NHAI) to Shapoorji Pallonji & Company Ltd (SPCL), a large Indian construction company, using an BOT (annuity) structure for a concession period of 20 years (including the construction period of three years). On the completion of construction, NHAI will pay an annuity of about US$45m semi-annually to SP Jammu Udhampur Highway Pvt Ltd (the SPV developing the project).

The project has many technical challenges, including building new tunnels totalling almost 3km, 59 major and minor bridges, 12 underpasses, 20km of new road alignments and 17km of service roads, all in mountainous terrain. SPCL has awarded a fixed-price, fixed-time EPC contract to Afcons Infrastructure Ltd, which has considerable experience in constructing bridges and tunnelling in mountainous regions and is handling a large construction contract for Indian Railways in J&K.

The key risk in such a project is that of construction delays. The support from the sponsors to fund cost overruns and an appropriate repayment moratorium of two years adequately address this risk for the lenders.

IDFC, and Standard Chartered Bank, as the joint mandated lead arrangers, have recently achieved financial close for a Rs21.6bn (about US$480m) project finance loan for the scheme. The debt is a combination of foreign currency (US$350m) and local currency (in rupees, equivalent to US$130m) loans. Standard Chartered Bank has underwritten the US$ component, whilst IDFC has underwritten the rupee portion.

The US dollar loan has a bullet repayment at the end of 6.5 years and this exposes the project to a potential refinance risk. However, this risk has been mitigated by using innovative financial structures and instruments. The refinance risk is also mitigated by a well-developed bond refinancing market in India, in which such projects, post-construction, attract many investors due to the strong credit rating of NHAI. The door-to-door tenor of the rupee project finance loan facility is 18 years.

Given that the project's construction costs and revenue would be rupees, whilst 73 per cent of the debt is in US dollars, there was also a foreign currency risk that had to be addressed. The risk during the construction period is from an appreciation of the rupee, whilst post-construction the risk is from a weakening of the rupee.

An additional uncertainty was that interest payments during the construction phase cannot be predicted accurately because construction and the drawdown of the loans can be affected by delays. These risks have been addressed through appropriate hedging.

Another benefit of having a large part of the loan in US dollars is that instruments are readily available for hedging the interest rate of US dollar Libor-linked loans, whereas presently in India rupee loans can be hedged only with considerable difficulty. Thus, the sponsors are able to reduce the interest rate risk on a majority of the debt

The lenders have a substitution right granted by NHAI under the concession agreement and a tripartite substitution agreement that can be used by the lenders to appoint a substitute in place of the concessionaire in the event of a default to the lenders. In addition, all cashflows of the project are escrowed and are utilized in a predefined sequence of priorities. In the event that NHAI seeks to terminate the concession, it is required to pay the termination payments into the escrow account.

Indian financial regulations prohibit foreign currency borrowings with maturities shorter than five years. At the same time, the pool of longer-tenor US dollar loans available to Indian companies for infrastructure projects is much more restricted. Hence, innovative structuring was required to balance these constraints. The combination of foreign currency and rupee debt helps the sponsors to lower the financing costs for the project, and enhances their returns from their investment. The structure innovatively addresses the cost over-run risk, refinance risk, foreign exchange risk and interest rate risk.

CASE STUDY

Barca Wins Trophy Deal

Two phases of the €2.5bn Barcelona Metro Line 9 PPP have reached financial close and two more are pending. The scheme is one of the biggest metro rail projects in Europe.

AZADEH SHARAFSHAHI

Banks have closed the debt financing for both stretches of the €2.5bn Barcelona Metro Line 9 PPP: the 26-year €770m commercial loan for Stretch I (Terminal-Amadeu Torner) and the 26-year €360m loan for the financing of Stretch IV (Gorg-Sagrera/Meridiana).

Seven commercial banks are providing the €770m loan, which consists of €750m in senior debt plus a €20m VAT facility. Lenders are La Caixa, Santander, BBVA and Caja Madrid – the four original lenders – plus Banesto, Dexia and ICO. La Caixa is taking the biggest stake, about half of the senior debt.

The €360m loan for the financing of Stretch IV is provided by La Caixa, Santander, BBVA and Caja Madrid. Again, La Caixa is taking the biggest stake, about half of the senior debt, whilst the other three commercial banks take roughly equal stakes. The €360m loan includes a €20m VAT facility.

In addition to the commercial loans, the European Investment Bank (EIB) is making two €200m contributions for the financing of Stretches I and IV. Commercial banks and the EIB rank pari passu.

Conditions are the same on both commercial loans. Margins start at 290bp in years one to four and step up to 315bp in years five and six, to 340bp in year seven, and finally to 365bp from year eight onwards. The loan is fully amortizing with a cash sweep profile (25 per cent at year four, depending on ratios). This is linked to the debt service cover ratio, which is 1.25×. About 80 per cent of project costs are covered by swaps. The debt/equity ratio is 90/10.

Cuatrecasas acted as legal adviser to the banks on both tranches. Barcelona-based partner Hector Bros led his team on the transactions. The regional government (Infraestructures Ferroviàries de Catalunya) was advised by Garrigues (Lluís Cases (partner), David Sanz (associate), and Mikel Tejada). Sponsors for Stretch I of the Barcelona Metro were advised by Uria Menendez, whilst Clifford Chance advised the sponsors on Stretch IV. Ineco acted as technical adviser. No financial advisers were mandated in either of the two tranches.

The lenders are receiving strong support from both the regional government and the EPC contractors of the Barcelona Metro project. Construction risk is covered through strong EPC agreements rather than sponsor guarantees.

First drawdown took place on July 19 this year, the date of financial close. It was used to repay the €1.16bn bridge loan, which expired at the end of June. The first drawdown covered most of the project cost because the bridge had already paid for a large part of completed works.

In December 2008, Santander, BBVA, Caja Madrid and La Caixa signed two one-year bridge facilities, totalling €1.16bn, for the €773m downpayment that FCC, OHL, Copisa; and Dragados, Acciona, Comsa and Acsa Sorigué had to collectively make for two 13-station tranches under 30-year DBFM concessions for Line 9 of the Barcelona metro. Margins were around 180bp.

Sponsors FCC (Stretch I) and Dragados/ACS (Stretch IV) had struggled to raise long-term financing and the bridges had been guaranteed by the Catalonian government, the concession grantor, in case the loans were not covered by the termination payments, should there be a default.

The PPP Contract

The Barcelona Metro PPP is characterized by three important features. It is not a typical greenfield concession, but replaced and incorporated an array of existing public works contracts between various EPC contractors and the Catalonian government. So in effect, the concessionaires stepped into the administration's shoes and inherited its existing agreements with the EPC contractors. The project is also marked by a strong concession agreement and by the limited support offered by the project sponsors.

The operation of the Barcelona Metro is outside the scope of the PPP and will be handled by Transport Metropolitans de Barcelona (TMB), the main public transit authority in Barcelona.

The concession agreement provides substantial coverage in the event of termination. The indemnities offered by the tendering authority to the private sponsor are very favourable. On the other hand, the collateral and guarantees provided by the sponsors are limited compared to standard project finance deals.

Instead, it is the EPC contractors that are providing the guarantees usually given by the sponsor of a project. So the lack of sponsor support is offset by both a favourable concession agreement and by strong EPC contracts.

Most of the construction works on Stretch IV (Gorg-Sagrera/Meridiana) are carried out by the EPC contractor that belongs to the same holding as the project sponsor. The EPC contractor is Dragados, which is part of the ACS group.

In the case of Stretch I (Terminal-Amadeu Torner), the majority of works are carried out by the sponsors themselves. So FCC, OHL and Copisa are also the EPC contractors on this tranche of the Barcelona Metro.

When the concession for the PPP was granted at the end of 2008 by GISA (the infrastructure management agency of the Catalan government), an important part of the works had already been completed. The fact that the infrastructure was already under construction constituted one of the main challenges to the structuring of the project as a PPP.

The concessionaires had to subjugate themselves within the existing contractor agreements between the government and EPC contractors. More than 30 per cent of the station construction works had already been carried out and these works were inherited by the project sponsors, who took full responsibility for completed works and inherited the government's contractual relationship with the EPC contractors. The PPP contract transferred to the private partner the majority of construction and availability risk.

However, after the concession had been granted, it had to be modified to adjust it to the financial parameters of the PPP project. This was possible because certain legal parameters that justified the readjustment of the concession agreement had been met.

When the concession for the project was granted, no due diligence had been carried out, because the public works contracts already existed. So throughout 2009, comprehensive due diligence was undertaken. The concession also had to be redraughted because parts of the projects had not been taken into account and some outstanding works on the stations had yet to be approved.

In parallel, negotiations were taking place between the banks and the government. The process was time-consuming because the terms of the adjustment of the concession had to be analysed whilst banks were negotiating the financing. The lenders had to structure their long-term financing to be compatible with the concession as it was being redraughted. Very important were the tariff and the payment in case of termination. The formal concession agreement was signed in July this year, simultaneously with the closing of the financing.

Whilst the Barcelona Metro PPP was not a greenfield project, it still carried substantial construction risk, particularly Stretch I, where none of the 13 stations had yet been completed. In the case of Stretch IV, on the other hand, 10 of the 13 stations had already been delivered.

The last station on Stretch IV connects with the high speed train station that links Barcelona with the French border, the Sagrera station. This high speed rail link will not be built as a PPP project but as a public works contract. It was saved in the latest wave of public works cuts and is currently under construction. It is due to be operational in 2014, one year after the Barcelona Metro.

Although Stretch I carries more construction risk than the more advanced Stretch IV, loan margins are the same on both tranches. The higher risk involved in the first tranche is tackled by the involvement of more lenders in the financing of the first tranche.

The government is also offering to the project sponsors the possibility to request a participative loan during the last years of the PPP, when bank financing terminates. The participative loan acts as mezzanine finance.

In an effort to promote PPPs, the Spanish government last year passed a law authorizing the government when draughting a concession agreement to provide funding through participative loans. These loans are subordinate debt and function like equity. The Barcelona Metro PPP was one of the first projects to use this form of financial aid. Now participative loans are used in most of the country's infrastructure PPPs.

The participative loan is subject to certain conditions. In the case of the Barcelona Metro PPP, the tariff will decrease after 2035. The participative loan can be used if the reduction of the tariff breaks the financial balance of the concessionaire. So it only applies for the last five years of the project. The gap of five years between the end of long-term debt and the termination of the concession exists to give the banks some room for risk protection.

The Barcelona Metro PPP is an availability based project. Payments are made by the government. The fees paid by the passengers are not collected by the concessionaire but by an entity within the regional Catalonian government, which differs from the project grantor.

To transfer construction and availability risk to the private party, the payment is deferred until the stations and other infrastructures within the scope of the Line 9 PPP have been delivered to Ifercat (Infraestructures Ferroviàries de Catalunya). Ifercat was commissioned in 2003 by the Catalonia regional government to oversee the execution of the Line 9 by GISA, and was consequently named Line 9 manager.

To transfer availability risk to the private partners, whilst TMB will operate the transport system, annual payments to the project sponsors will be subject to performance-based deductions and penalties.

Construction of Stretches I and IV is due to be completed in 2013. At that point, the project will carry little risk and is expected to become interesting to the syndication market. Syndication is expected to be launched towards the end of the construction period.

Next in Line

The Barcelona Line 9 was introduced in the Infrastructures Director Plan for the years 2001 to 2010, approved by the Metropolitan Transport Authority (ATM) in 2001. The metro line is divided into four stretches.

Bids for Stretch II of the Barcelona Metro PPP have been postponed to September 30. Offers had previously been due at the beginning of July.

Interested parties are said to include some of the same groups that had participated in the tender for Stretch IV. However, financing is proving to be a major hurdle for the project, which has a total investment volume of nearly €2bn. Some important Spanish banks are said to be hesitant to get involved in financing the project.

Whilst lenders have been approached by various companies interested in participating in the tender for Stretch II, it remains to be seen which consortia will gain the necessary financial backing to submit an offer. Some sources expect only one consortium, a group led by Iridium/ACS, to make an offer.

The possibility also remains that the concession will be postponed or that the project will be financed through a different scheme.

Banks are said to be concerned about the outcome of elections in Catalonia at the end of October. A change in government is considered likely, and whilst a new government would not stop the project, it would be more inclined than the incumbent to delay the project. The current government is eager to move on quickly with the project and aims to sign the concession within one month. But this is considered very unlikely.

Details of the final Stretch III of the Barcelona Metro have not yet been published and it is expected to be tendered at the earliest in 2011.

When completed, the Barcelona Metro Line 9 will be one of the longest in Europe, spanning 47.8km and carrying almost 100m passengers per year. It will connect the suburban cities of Badalona and Santa Coloma to the north of Barcelona with the airport and the Free Zone of the Barcelona Port in the south. Line 9 will interchange with every other rapid transit system in the Barcelona metropolitan area.

CASE STUDY

Rationalizing Thieno-Schio

UniCredit and Efibanca have entered as MLA and lenders a loan agreement with Summano Sanità SpA, the concessionaire of the Thiene-Schio hospital project, near Vicenza in north-eastern Italy.

ANGELO COLOMBO
UniCredit

The Thiene-Schio project follows a rationalization programme set up by the Ulss no. 4 Alto Vicentino (the local health unit and grantor) which will determine that the two existing outdated hospitals of Thiene and Schio (totalling 513 beds) will close down. The project consists of a 74.000m² building, with 460 beds (of which some 119 will be dedicated to day hospital and day surgery). Total project costs amount to €164m and VAT is partly covered by a €76m public grant.

The tenor of the concession, which will expire in March 2036, is 28.3 years, of which three years is for the construction phase. The concession was awarded in 2007 to a consortium led by Gemmo, Mantovani and CMB, three major contractors, equipment and service providers widely operating in the industry of healthcare project finance.

Equity provider Palladio Finanziaria completed the picture of the main parties of the consortium, with its subsidiary Palladio Corporate Finance delivering financial advisory services to the group. The consortium companies together account for 94 per cent of the share capital of the Newco that was subsequently incorporated as the concessionaire (Summano Sanità) entering the concession agreement on November 12 2007, two months after the award of the tender.

The concession is a rather straightforward DBFO and, with limited exceptions, is in line with other healthcare PPPs. It must be remembered that the framework law that rules PPPs in Italy is based on the concept of economic and financial equilibrium as measured in the business plan provided with the bid submission.

Such equilibrium is to be preserved from modifications of basic assumptions during the concession period set up by the grantor or determined by changes in law (usually excluding what relates to normal business and financial risk). In the Thiene-Schio case, if an agreement is not reached for the business plan review within 30 days from the occurrence of the event that has triggered it, the concessionaire has the right, recognized by law, to terminate the concession contract.

In any case of termination, however, the concessionaire is entitled to receive a termination payment based on the value of the works plus charges, net of depreciation and of grants received.

Events that can be invoked for the activation of the rebalancing procedure are variation orders, change in law, suspension orders, changes in the scope of services, extended event of force majeure, the grantor failing to complete the testing phase in due time, and others.

The payments scheme of the concession is based on availability and service fees. After completion, the grantor will pay a €4.2m availability fee, regardless of any failure to perform the services provided for the concession. During operation, the concessionaire will also provide facility management, global services and other non-medical services; in turn the grantor will pay the SPV a fee for each service (for a total €14.7m), which is proportionate to the quantity supplied. Volume risk is limited, however, since:

- Only few services are directly connected to the hospital's occupancy rate (catering for patients, cleaning of linen, etc.);
- The concession provides for a re-equilibrium process in the case that each service revenue decreases more than 30 per cent, with respect to the base case, and economic-financial stability of the SPV is jeopardized;
- All services are outsourced and pass-through schemes are set up vis-à-vis the service providers (shareholders) to transfer changes in service revenues.

The grantor will also pay a fee totalling €5.3m for the availability and maintenance of equipment (hardware, furniture and medical equipment). The service fee for medical equipment will be paid only for the first eight years, because at the end of this period it is foreseen that they will be fully depreciated and transferred for free to the grantor.

It must be noted that the equipment (totalling €16m) is not included in the construction costs acknowledged by the grantor, since it has just to be made available by the concessionaire; consequently, it is not likely to be included in any termination value.

In this context, sponsors initially decided to allocate the equipment investment outside the concessionaire (on sub-contractors' maintenance providers owned by some of the sponsors) with separate non-recourse financing but, due to a number of reasons including the high amount of expenditure required, this turned out to be anything but simple.

Leasing companies were not prepared to commit on such basis and, on the other hand, the MLAs were not available to give up the pledge on those assets since, at the end of the eight-year period, Summano is committed to hand over the equipment to the grantor, and therefore control over the assets could not be delivered to any third party outside the project finance perimeter.

The possible alternative to directly finance the sub-contractors was dropped by the MLAs because of its legal/security implications and contractual complexity. Eventually, sponsors decided to allocate on Summano the purchase of the equipment (with the exception of IT hardware) by using additional equity and a specific 10-year credit facility and then make it available to the grantor.

The revenue scheme of Summano is completed by commercial activities (car parking management, renting of commercial spaces, food service to visitors and hospital employees) provided by the SPV and for which the grantor doesn't recognize any fee. For the start-up of operation (the first six years), Ebitda generated by these services is partially secured by contingent equity provided by the sponsor (and backed by bank guarantees).

Although also these external revenues contribute to the borrower's cashflow, it is the grantor that secures debt service capacity: generally speaking more than 95 per cent of revenues and 90 per cent of margins are contractualized with the Ulls nr. 4 Alto Vicentino. In terms of counterparty risk, the grantor is the local health unit established as a public autonomous legal entity but under regional control and is not subject to bankruptcy;

funds are provided by the regional administration (Veneto, Aa2, one of the most active areas in the PPP industry), although this cannot be regarded as a sovereign guarantee securing the grantor's obligations.

To set up all this, besides the concession agreement, Summano entered a number of project contracts, most of them with its shareholders as sub-contractors: for the construction phase one EPC contract and three contracts for the supply/lease of the equipment; for the operation phase, 16 different service contracts (although most based on a common template).

Total expenditures foreseen for the project in the construction phase are in the region of €164m (including equipment, financial expenses and DSRA). Public grants are paid on a work in progress basis, covering some 46 per cent of the above amount. The balance is provided by the concessionaire with a mix of pure equity, subordinated shareholders' loan and senior debt, the latter mainly represented by the base facility (€52.5m) and the equipment loan (€15m), with the D/E ratio in the region of 78:22. Equity is injected upfront up to €15.5m whilst €4m related to the equipment is deferred and secured by bank guarantees.

The repayment profile of the base facility was set targeting an SADSCR of 1.25×, resulting in a 1.46x average LLCR. Based on that, the maximum tenor of the senior debt is 22 years door-to-door, providing an almost five-year tail before the concession maturity. The availability fee alone represents about 85 per cent of debt service related to the base facility.

On top of that, the lenders are also providing a €10m VAT facility and ancillary credit facilities. In fact, during the structuring phase the need emerged to provide the borrower with additional support that would satisfy all of its requirements during the project life. Some non-cash guarantee facilities were therefore inserted into the loan agreement, as well as two performance bonds in favour of the grantor (one for the construction phase and one for the operation period) plus a facility to guarantee the tax authorities for VAT refunds.

Eventually, debt raised for the financing of the project was €95.8m and, considering internal credit limits for interest rate derivatives (80 per cent of the base facility was hedged), the package exceeded €100m.

At a certain point in 2009, as the amount was soaring compared with initially expected requirements, the potential commitment of the two MLAs seemed not to fit any more with their underwriting capacity, as pointed to by the respective credit policies during the harsh months of the financial crisis. It was therefore considered to ask a third bank to join the group at signing but, after some time, the dust was settling and market conditions were easing enough to convince UniCredit to submit a credit application for a higher amount. UniCredit and Efibanca ended up with 66.7 per cent and 33.3 per cent respectively, on a take-and-hold basis.

The financing of the Thiene-Schio PPP transaction was the first to complete in Italy in the healthcare sector since the end of 2007, the year when a number of deals in the same sector were funded. Afterwards, certain issues, such as a reduced pipeline, a focus on previously closed deals (e.g., Niguarda and Vimercate Hospital transactions, which received increased financing to fund a wider scope of work) and, most of all, the financial crisis, cleared 2008 and 2009 from signing of new deals in healthcare project financing.

The time required to reach financial close from the award of the concession was about 31 months; on the date of signing, the works had already progressed by 27 per cent: from

November 2008, when the yard opened, the EPC contractor had to sustain financial costs caused by the SPV being able to pay only the portion of invoices covered by the public grant. The balance was accounted for as a receivable, bearing an interest rate to be paid after the financial close.

Such a long time to close the deal may sound bizarre and is certainly above average; but the average itself is extremely high in Italy: according to a survey conducted by Finlombarda on a sample of 11 projects in the healthcare sector that reached financial close between 2002 and 2007, the average structuring time was 22.4 months (with a peak of 33 and a low of 11).

This can be explained by the fact that, unlike PPP transactions in most countries, the award of a concession and entering the contract with the grantor doesn't mean that the concessionaire has previously secured financing, as well. In fact, tenders are launched based on a preliminary stage of design and incomplete authorization process from local authorities (two elements that may cause substantial increases in capex to emerge in the following phases).

In addition, easy and frequent recourse to the courts by the losing bidders encourage consortia to postpone the structuring of financing (and project contracts, sometimes) until the award is indisputable and when project costs are certain; in other words, they choose to run the risk to sustain design and initial construction costs without the comfort of a loan agreement in place nor with banks' commitments.

The Thiene-Schio Hospital Project made no exception to that and although Efibanca was advising the consortium already during the tender, the two MLAs (with UniCredit joining Efibanca) were actually mandated after the award, and so were the independent advisers (Marsh, the law firms GOGP and SL Lombardo, the engineer Aren srl) so that actual structuring of the deal started well into 2008.

The concession agreement, as tendered and then signed, although it can be judged as more "lender-friendly" than others, requested all the necessary attention: in Italy, although the framework law may serve as a reference basis, PPP documentation is not standardized at all and each project is different from any other: two PPPs in the same sector may be originated by different awarding entities and worked out by different consultants, with the obvious consequence that no previous transaction can be fully replicated as a sample for the next deal structure.

In addition, the complexity of the Thiene-Schio project affected not only financing but also the commercial side, as many of the negotiations between the concessionaire and its service providers (all actual or potential shareholders) took some time to finalize as well, so that all the elements to complete due diligences and approach arrangement phase were not on the table until the end of 2Q 2009. Some of the findings needed some time to fix and working out the medical equipment financing issue alone caused the structuring period to lengthen by at least a couple of months.

The constructive reciprocal co-operation of sponsors, advisers and lenders, though, was of paramount importance to get the deal done and add another case history to the list of new hospitals that will be erected and operated in the framework of a public-private partnership, the healthcare sector proving again to be the one where project finance is most successful and effective in Italy.

Index

Note: Page numbers in *italics* represents tables and figures.

For Product Safety Concerns and Information please contact our
EU representative GPSR@taylorandfrancis.com Taylor & Francis
Verlag GmbH, Kaufingerstraße 24, 80331 München, Germany